# 2

# Accounting and Reporting
## Taxation, Managerial, Governmental and Not-for-Profit Organizations

by    Vincent W. Lambers, MBA, CPA
Donald T. Hanson, MBA, CPA
Richard DelGaudio, MBA, CPA
Arthur Reed, MBA, MST, CPA

Published by

CPA REVIEW

**Chapter Subjects of Volume 2—ACCOUNTING AND REPORTING**

Chapter Fifteen
COST ACCOUNTING: ACTUAL COST, JOB ORDER AND PROCESS

Chapter Sixteen
COST ACCOUNTING: JOINT PRODUCTS AND STANDARD COSTS

Chapter Seventeen
MANAGERIAL ANALYSIS AND CONTROL

Chapter Eighteen
MANAGERIAL PLANNING AND CONTROL

Chapter Nineteen
GOVERNMENTAL ACCOUNTING

Chapter Twenty
NOT-FOR-PROFIT ACCOUNTING

**Chapter Subjects for FEDERAL INCOME TAXES:**

Introduction

Chapter One
FILING STATUS AND EXEMPTIONS, FILING REQUIREMENTS AND PENALTIES

Chapter Two
INCOME - INCLUSIONS AND EXCLUSIONS

Chapter Three
DEDUCTIONS FOR ADJUSTED GROSS INCOME

Chapter Four
DEDUCTIONS FROM ADJUSTED GROSS INCOME

Chapter Five
ACCOUNTING METHODS AND PERIODS, AND COMPUTATION OF TAX LIABILITY AND TAX CREDITS

Chapter Six
CAPITAL TRANSACTIONS

Chapter Seven
PARTNERSHIPS

Chapter Eight
C CORPORATIONS

Chapter Nine
CORPORATE DISTRIBUTIONS, S CORPORATIONS AND OTHER CORPORATE MATTERS

Chapter Ten
TAXATION OF GIFTS, ESTATES AND FIDUCIARIES, AND EXEMPT ORGANIZATIONS

Appendix
OTHER OBJECTIVE ANSWER FORMAT PROBLEMS FROM RECENT EXAMS

# CPA EXAM CONTENT SPECIFICATIONS

## Financial Accounting and Reporting
I. Concepts and standards for financial statements (20%)
II. Recognition, measurement, valuation, and presentation of typical items in financial statements in conformity with generally accepted accounting principles (40%)
III. Recognition, measurement, valuation, and presentation of specific types of transactions and events in financial statements in conformity with generally accepted accounting principles (40%).

## Accounting and Reporting -- taxation, managerial, and governmental and not-for-profit organizations
I. Federal taxation -- individuals (20%)
II. Federal taxation -- corporations (20%)
III. Federal taxation -- partnerships (10%)
IV. Federal taxation -- estates and trusts, exempt organizations, and preparers' responsibilities (10%)
V. Accounting for governmental and not-for-profit organizations (30%)
VI. Managerial accounting (10%)

## Auditing
I. Evaluate the prospective client and engagement, decide whether to accept or continue the client and the engagement, enter into an agreement with the client, and plan the engagement (40%)
II. Obtain and document information to form a basis for conclusions (35%)
III. Review the engagement to provide reasonable assurance that objectives are achieved and evaluate information obtained to reach and to document engagement conclusions (5%)
IV. Prepare communications to satisfy engagement objectives (20%)

## Business Law and Professional Responsibilities
I. Professional and legal responsibilities (15%)
II. Business organizations (20%)
III. Contracts (10%)
IV. Debtor-creditor relationships (10%)
V. Government regulation of business (15%)
VI. Uniform commercial code (20%)
VII. Property (10%)

# THE CPA EXAM – 2000

| SECTION | HOURS | DAY | TIME | FORMAT 4-Option Multiple-choice | FORMAT Other Objective Answer Formats | FORMAT Free Response |
|---|---|---|---|---|---|---|
| Business Law and Professional Responsibilities (LPR) | 3 | Wed. | 9:00 am - 12n | 50-60% | 20-30% | 20-30% |
| Auditing (AUDIT) | 4 1/2 | Wed. | 1:30 - 6:00 pm | 50-60% | 20-30% | 20-30% |
| Accounting and Reporting: Taxation, Managerial, Governmental & Not-for-Profit Organizations (ARE) | 3 1/2 | Thur. | 8:30 am - 12 n | 50-60% | 40-50% | —- |
| Financial Accounting & Reporting (FARE) | 4 ½ | Thur. | 1:30 - 6:00 pm | 50-60% | 20-30% | 20-30% |

## ACKNOWLEDGMENTS

It would be impossible to write a CPA examination preparation book of any kind without the assistance of the American Institute of Certified Public Accountants, and their various operating divisions, in grating permission to use various materials. We respectfully acknowledge and thank those persons in the American Institute who promptly answered our inquiries.

Those areas of the set for which we received permission to use copyrighted material from the American Institute are:

- *CPA Examination Questions, Problems and Solutions*
- *Opinions of the Accounting Principles Board and The Financial Accounting Standards Board*
- *Statements on Auditing Standards*
- *The Code of Professional Ethics and Interpretations Thereof*

We also wish to thank our editorial advisor, William A. Grubbs, CPA, of Greensboro, North Carolina.

Vincent W. Lambers, CPA
Donald T. Hanson, CPA
Richard DelGaudio, CPA
No. Andover, Massachusetts
November 1999

# 2

# Accounting and Reporting

## Managerial, Governmental and Not-for-Profit Organizations

### (Chapters 15-20)

by    Vincent W. Lambers, MBA, CPA
Donald T. Hanson, MBA, CPA
Richard Del Gaudio, MBA, CPA

Published by

CPA REVIEW

# Chapter Subjects of ACCOUNTING AND REPORTING

Chapter Fifteen
COST ACCOUNTING: ACTUAL COST, JOB ORDER AND PROCESS

Chapter Sixteen
COST ACCOUNTING: JOINT PRODUCTS AND STANDARD COSTS

Chapter Seventeen
MANAGERIAL ANALYSIS AND CONTROL

Chapter Eighteen
MANAGERIAL PLANNING AND CONTROL

Chapter Nineteen
GOVERNMENTAL ACCOUNTING

Chapter Twenty
NOT-FOR-PROFIT ACCOUNTING

# Chapter Fifteen
# Cost Accounting: Actual Cost, Job Order and Process

# Chapter Fifteen
# Cost Accounting: Actual Cost, Job Order and Process

## BASICS

For financial accounting, the purpose of cost accounting is to determine the cost of a product or service. There are two basic cost accounting systems:

1. **Job Order**—Costs are accumulated by specific job or lot.
2. **Process**—Costs are accumulated by department or productive process and allocated to the units processed based upon a cost flow assumption (generally weighted average or FIFO).

(Standard cost can be applied to either system.)

The cost system used by an enterprise will be determined by the type of operations performed. A job order costing system is appropriate when custom made or unique goods or services are produced, such that direct costs can be identified with the specific units of production. Job order costing is often used in industries such as printing, construction, auto repair, furniture and machinery manufacture, and professional services. A process costing system is appropriate when the operation continuously mass produces like units, one unit being indistinguishable from another. Process costing is often used in industries such as chemicals, food processing, petroleum, mining, and in the manufacturing of other standard products.

Basic cost elements of production:

**Direct (raw) materials:** Cost of materials that become part of the finished product and are directly traceable to the finished product. Examples: the cost of paper used in printing books and wood used in making desks.

**Direct labor:** Cost of labor which works directly on the product, converting raw materials to a finished product, and is directly traceable to the finished product. Examples: wages of a printing press operator, or worker who assembles desks.

**Overhead:** All other manufacturing costs. These costs are indirectly related to production of the finished product. Other terms that are synonymous with overhead include: manufacturing or factory overhead, burden, indirect costs, and applied manufacturing expense. Examples include indirect materials (oil for machines), indirect labor (supervisor's wages), utilities and property taxes on the manufacturing facility.

### Cost Classifications:

*Prime cost:* Direct material cost plus direct labor cost.

*Conversion cost:* Direct labor cost plus overhead cost.

*Product cost:* The sum of direct material, direct labor and overhead costs which comprise the inventoriable costs.

*Period cost:* Non-inventoriable cost which is expensed in the current period as incurred.

*Variable cost:* Costs which vary in total directly with changes in the level of activity. The cost per unit is constant at different levels of activity.

*Fixed costs:* Costs which remain constant in total, regardless of changes in the level of activity. Therefore, the per unit cost changes with changes in the level of operations.

*Relevant range:* The limits within which the level of activity may vary and the above variable and fixed cost-volume relationships will remain valid.

Basic cost accounting cost expiration computations:

Cost of Materials Used:

| | |
|---|---:|
| Beginning Inventory Material | $ 12,000 |
| Purchases | 280,000 |
| Total | $292,000 |
| Less: Ending Inventory Material | 15,000 |
| Cost of Materials Used | $277,000 |

Cost of Goods Manufactured:

| | |
|---|---:|
| Beginning Work-in-Process Inventory | $ 16,000 |
| Direct Material | 277,000 |
| Direct Labor | 204,000 |
| Overhead | 306,000 |
| Total | $803,000 |
| Less: Ending Work-in-Process Inventory | 23,000 |
| Cost of Goods Manufactured | $780,000 |

Cost of Goods Sold:

| | |
|---|---:|
| Beginning Finished Goods Inventory | $ 81,000 |
| Cost of Goods Manufactured | 780,000 |
| Goods Available for Sale | $861,000 |
| Less: Ending Finished Goods Inventory | 96,000 |
| Cost of Goods Sold | $765,000 |

## JOB ORDER COST

## Accumulation of Costs

a. Costs for each job or lot are accumulated on Job Cost sheets. Job cost sheets show cost of material and labor charged to the job based on actual cost. Overhead, however, cannot be charged to the job at actual—a predetermined rate must be used. A job cost sheet might appear as follows:

**Job 525**

| | |
|---|---:|
| Direct Material—18 lbs. @ $4.50 | $ 81.00 |
| Direct Labor—24 hrs. @ $4.25 | 102.00 |
| Mfg. Overhead—$3 per labor hour | 72.00 |
| Cost of job charged to work-in-process | $255.00 |

b. An upward accumulation of job and departmental costs is maintained in plant or factory ledgers.

c. Control accounts are maintained in the General Ledger.

## Activity Base Computation—Predetermined Rates

While actual direct material and direct labor costs can be readily obtained, the books must be closed to assign actual overhead costs to specific jobs. Jobs must be continually costed for billing and control purposes and such procedures could not be delayed until actual overhead is determined. Therefore, the predetermined overhead rate is used. The overhead rate chosen will vary with the type of manufacturing operation, but generally will be computed as follows:

$$\frac{\text{Budget Estimated Manufacturing Expense}}{\text{Budget Estimated Activity Base}}$$

The Activity Base ideally should be an activity or quantity that is closely related to changes in overhead cost. In this way an increase in the activity base will measure the resulting increase in overhead. Activity bases frequently used are:

1. Units
2. Material Cost
3. Labor Cost

4. Prime Cost (D.M. + D.L.)
5. Machine Hours
6. Labor Hours

**Illustrative Problem**—Computation of Predetermined Rate
The Jigsaw Company has three departments—Molding, Fabrication and Finishing. Budgeted costs and production data for the three departments are as follows:

| | BUDGETED | | | |
|---|---|---|---|---|
| Department | Material Cost | Labor Cost | Labor Hours | Manufacturing Expense |
| Molding | $12,000 | $6,000 | 1,200 | $18,000 |
| Fabrication | 6,000 | 4,000 | 800 | 8,000 |
| Finishing | 3,000 | 4,500 | 900 | 9,000 |

Compute overhead rates for each of the departments assuming management has selected overhead activity bases as follows:

(1) Molding—Material Cost
(2) Fabrication—Labor Cost
(3) Finishing—Labor Hours

(1) $\dfrac{\$18,000}{12,000} = 150\%$

(2) $\dfrac{\$8,000}{4,000} = 200\%$

(3) $\dfrac{\$9,000}{900} = \$10$

Assume that Job #120 accumulated costs and labor hour data as follows:

| | Material | Labor |
|---|---|---|
| Molding | $80 | 7 hrs. @ $5 |
| Fabrication | $30 | 3 hrs. @ $6 |
| Finishing | $25 | 2 hrs. @ $5.50 |

Determine the cost of Job #120 which is to be charged to Work in Process.

| | Molding | Fabrication | Finishing | Total |
|---|---|---|---|---|
| Material | $ 80 | $30 | $25 | $135 |
| Labor | 35 | 18 | 11 | 64 |
| Overhead | (1) 120 | (2) 36 | (3) 20 | 176 |
| Total | $235 | $84 | $56 | $375 |

(1) 150% × $80
(2) 200% × $18
(3) 2 × $10

In Job #120 we notice that work-in-process is charged with a total of $375 and upon completion finished goods will be charged likewise.

## Allocation of Service Department Costs

While Direct Material and Labor are at actual, the use of a predetermined rate for overhead will necessitate comparison with actual and, if done properly, can furnish management with some useful information, which we will consider later. Actual overhead costs are accumulated in the Manufacturing Expense Control Account to be compared with the overhead applied (predetermined rate) to the product. The accumulation of actual overhead costs is a relatively simple accounting matter in total; however, since these costs are indirect, they must be allocated to departments on some basis. Overhead costs that are directly attributable to a department or activity are, of course, assigned to that department or activity which is called a "cost center." Costs that are accumulated in service departments must ultimately be reallocated to the producing departments. The producing departments must ultimately bear all costs.

**Illustrative Problem** (Allocation of Service Department Costs)
The Edelweiss Co. has three producing departments, D, E and F. Costs are also accumulated in the Building Service, Power Plant, Maintenance and Personnel Departments. At the end of the period, overhead costs have been accumulated in these departments as follows:

|  | _Costs_ |
| --- | --- |
| Department D | $ 22,420 |
| Department E | 28,760 |
| Department F | 39,880 |
| Building Service | 13,000 |
| Power Plant | 16,000 |
| Maintenance | 19,000 |
| Personnel | 4,000 |
| Total Costs | $143,060 |

Other data is also given concerning these departments:

| | | | | | _Departments_ | | | |
| --- | --- | --- | --- | --- | --- | --- | --- | --- |
| | D | E | F | B/S | P/P | M | P | Total |
| Number of employees | 16 | 22 | 32 | 4 | 12 | 18 | 6 | 110 |
| Floor space | 1,200 | 1,800 | 3,000 | — | 1,600 | 1,400 | 1,000 | 10,000 |
| Power used—Kilowatt Hours | 12,000 | 16,000 | 18,000 | — | — | 4,000 | — | 50,000 |
| Machine Hours | 3,600 | 2,400 | 4,000 | — | — | — | — | 10,000 |

If we use the step method, we can close out the departments one by one. There are no rules except common sense in determining the basis of allocation. The above shows an obvious relationship. In some situations considerable judgment may be required and the allocation basis can be quite complex. When a service department's costs are allocated, no reallocation of costs is made to that department.

**Solution:**
1. Allocate building service costs to all departments. (Floor Space)
2. Allocate personnel costs to all other departments. (Number of Employees)
3. Allocate power plant costs to the producing departments and maintenance. (Power Used)
4. Allocate maintenance costs to the producing departments. (Machine Hours)

## Allocation of Costs

|  | Producing Departments | | | | | | |  |
|  | D | E | F | B/S | P/P | M | P | Total |
|---|---|---|---|---|---|---|---|---|
| | $22,420 | $28,760 | $39,880 | $13,000 | $16,000 | $19,000 | $4,000 | $143,060 |
| | 1,560 | 2,340 | 3,900 | ($13,000) | 2,080 | 1,820 | 1,300 | |
| | | | | | | | 5,300 | |
| | 848 | 1,166 | 1,696 | | 636 | 954 | ($5,300) | |
| | | | | | 18,716 | | | |
| | 4,490 | 5,990 | 6,736 | | ($18,716) | 1,500 | | |
| | | | | | | 23,274 | | |
| | 8,378 | 5,586 | 9,310 | | | ($23,274) | | |
| | $37,696 | $43,842 | $61,522 | | | | | $143,060 |

*Note*: This is not the only possible solution to the problem. As no basis of allocation was specified, any systematic and rational allocation can be used.

There are other methods of allocating departmental overhead costs such as the direct method, where costs of non-producing departments are allocated directly to producing departments. Another more complicated method can be used where service departments perform services for each other such as the above problem in that the Personnel and Building Service Departments perform services for each other. Solving this type of problem, giving recognition to this fact requires the use of simultaneous equations. While more accurate than the step method, it is not widely used in practice, because the difference in results is usually not significant.

## Application of Overhead to the Product—Overhead Over and Under Applied.

We have seen that Direct Costs, Material and Labor are applied to the product based on actual costs, but because costs must be assigned to the product before actual overhead can be determined and allocated, a predetermined rate is used for overhead. Later, when actual overhead is determined, the difference between actual and estimated results in an over or under application of overhead to the product, such as:

a. If actual overhead exceeds the overhead applied by means of a rate, this results in overhead being underapplied.

b. If actual overhead is less than the overhead applied to the product, this results in overhead being overapplied.

The over- or under-applied overhead, if material, should be allocated to work-in-process, finished goods, and cost of goods sold to adjust these balances to full cost in accordance with GAAP. If immaterial, the over- or under-applied overhead is usually treated as an adjustment to the cost of goods sold.

Actual overhead costs are accumulated in the Manufacturing Expense Control Account.

Journal entries typically leading up to this situation are as follows:

(1)

Stores                                                          Material is purchased for plant use.
   Accounts Payable

(2)

W in P—Direct Material                          Materials are requisitioned for use in the plant,
Mfg. Exp. Control                                   some as direct material. Material overhead costs
   Stores                                           are charged to Mfg. Exp. Control.

(3)

Payroll                                                        Wages are paid.
   Cash
   Sundry payroll tax credits

|  | (4) |  |
| --- | --- | --- |
| W in P—Direct Labor | | Wages are assigned to the product |
| Mfg. Exp. Control | | (direct) or charged to actual |
| Payroll | | overhead (indirect). |

|  | (5) |  |
| --- | --- | --- |
| Mfg. Exp. Control | | Overhead costs are charged to Mfg. Exp. |
| Sundry Credits | | Control such as rent, insurance, |
| Allowance for Depreciation | | taxes and depreciation. |

|  | (6) |  |
| --- | --- | --- |
| W in P Overhead Dept. 1 | | Overhead charged to product based on |
| W in P Overhead Dept. 2 | | the predetermined rate is recorded. |
| W in P Overhead Dept. 3 | | An alternate method would be to credit |
| Mfg. Overhead Applied Dept. 1 | | "Mfg. Exp." directly. If this is done |
| Mfg. Overhead Applied Dept. 2 | | entry 8 would be unnecessary. |
| Mfg. Overhead Applied Dept. 3 | | |

|  | (7) |  |
| --- | --- | --- |
| Mfg. Exp. Dept. 1 | | Mfg. Exp. Control is closed out to the |
| Mfg. Exp. Dept. 2 | | departments based on the company's method of |
| Mfg. Exp. Dept. 3 | | allocating actual costs to the |
| Mfg. Exp. Control | | producing departments. |

|  | (8) |  |
| --- | --- | --- |
| Mfg. Overhead Applied Dept. 1 | | Mfg. Overhead applied is closed out to |
| Mfg. Overhead Applied Dept. 2 | | Mfg. Expense. |
| Mfg. Overhead Applied Dept. 3 | | Differences result in |
| Mfg. Exp. Dept. 1 | | Mfg. Exp. Over/Under Applied. |
| Mfg. Exp. Dept. 2 | | |
| Mfg. Exp. Dept. 3 | | |

|  | (9) |  |
| --- | --- | --- |
| Mfg. Exp. Dept. 1 | | Difference between actual and applied |
| Mfg. Exp. Dept. 2 | | overhead as indicated by the results of |
| Mfg. Exp. Dept. 3 | | entry #8. |
| Mfg. Exp. Over/Under Applied | | |

## Flexible Budgets and Overhead Analysis

Flexible budgeting is a reporting system wherein the planned level of activity is adjusted to the actual level of activity before the budget to actual comparison report is prepared. It may appropriately be employed for any item which is affected by the level of activity.

Assume that F Co. has a flexible budget as follows:

| Percent of Normal | 80% | 90% | 100% | 110% |
| --- | --- | --- | --- | --- |
| Fixed Cost | $10,000 | $10,000 | $10,000 | $10,000 |
| Variable | 12,000 | 13,500 | 15,000 | 16,500 |
|  |  |  | $25,000 |  |
| Direct labor hours | 16,000 | 18,000 | 20,000 | 22,000 |

Predetermined Rate—$1.25 per labor hour @ 100% ($.50 FC + $.75 VC) or ($25,000 ÷ 20,000 D.L. hrs.)

During the period the plant operated at 92% of normal and incurred overhead costs of $23,960. For management information purposes the manufacturing expense over/under applied account can be analyzed and broken up into two variances—a budget variance and a volume or capacity variance.

## Overhead Analysis

|  |  | (Unfavorable) DR | (Favorable) CR |
|---|---|---|---|
| Actual Overhead |  | **$23,960** |  |

**Budget Variance**
Budget at actual direct labor hours
92% × 20,000 hrs. = 18,400 hrs.

| FC (20,000 × .50) | 10,000 |  |  |
| VC (18,400 × .75) | 13,800 |  |  |
|  |  | 23,800 | $160 |

**Volume or Capacity Variance**
Mfg. Overhead Applied

| FC 18,400 × .50 | 9,200 |  |  |
| VC 18,400 × .75 | 13,800 |  |  |
|  |  | 23,000 | *800 |
| Total Variance |  | $ 960 | $960 |

*Caused by volume falling short of normal by 1,600 hours at .50 per hour (FC rate).

# PROCESS COST

## Basics

In process cost a continuous flow of product is assumed and under ordinary conditions the cost per unit would not change significantly from period to period. Cost computations, admittedly oversimplified, can be expressed as follows:

$$\frac{\overset{4/1 \qquad\qquad 4/30}{\text{PERIOD COSTS M, L \& OH}}}{\text{UNITS PRODUCED}} = \text{UNIT COST}$$

Things get complicated, however, because of beginning and ending inventories of work-in-process and the assumptions under which costs are assigned. In process cost, we may compute costs using FIFO or weighted average. Where there is no beginning inventory, there is no difference in the two inventory methods. The basic steps in working process cost problems for both the FIFO and weighted average methods is shown in five steps. Note that step four is called a "cost of production report" which simply stated is the computation of inventory costs for finished product and the ending inventory of work-in-process. Step 5 is not usually a required step, but a check to determine if prior computations are correct. Treatment for spoiled units is covered after Process Cost Procedure.

## Process Cost Procedure
### 1. Account for all units (do not use equivalents)

Beginning Inventory
+ units started
− transferred out
− lost
− ending inventory
= zero

If one item is missing, for example, lost units, the number lost will be the number used to equal zero.

## 2. Compute equivalent finished units (EFU)

| FIFO | | Average |
|---|---|---|
| Finished Units | Finish Beginning Inventory[3] | Finished |
| +Ending Inventory[1] | + Units started and finished[4] | +Ending Inv.[1] |
| +Abnormal Spoilage[1]  OR | + Abnormal Spoilage[1] | +Abnormal Spoilage[1] |
| −Beginning Inventory[2] | + Ending Inventory[1] | |

[1]Units × % complete
[2]Units × % complete at beginning of period
[3]Units × % completed during the current period (100% − the % complete at beginning of period)
[4]Finished units − beginning inventory units (not equivalents)

Separate EFU's may have to be computed for material, labor, overhead and prior department costs.

## 3. Compute unit costs. Set up a schedule as follows:

**FIFO**

| | Period Cost | ÷ | EFU | = | Unit Cost |
|---|---|---|---|---|---|
| Material | xxxx | | xxx | | xx |
| Labor | xxxx | | xxx | | xx |
| Overhead | xxxx | | xxx | | xx |
| Departmental unit cost | | | | | xx |
| Prior dept. cost (if applicable) | xxxx | | xxxx | | xx |
| Total unit cost | | | | | xx |

**AVERAGE COST**

| | Beg. Inv. | + | Period | = | Total | ÷ | EFU | = Unit Cost |
|---|---|---|---|---|---|---|---|---|
| Material | xxxx | | xxxx | | xxxx | | xxx | xx |
| Labor | xxxx | | xxxx | | xxxx | | xxx | xx |
| Overhead | xxxx | | xxxx | | xxxx | | xxx | xx |
| Departmental Unit Cost | | | | | | | | xx |
| Prior Dept. Cost | xxxx | | xxxx | | xxxx | | xxxx | xx |
| Total Unit Cost | | | | | | | | xx |

## 4. Cost of Production Report—FIFO.
In FIFO, the cost flow assumption is that the beginning inventory cost flows through first. Therefore, the first step is to complete the beginning inventory.

| | | |
|---|---|---|
| Cost of units finished and transferred out | | |
|   Beginning inventory costs | xxx | (1) |
| + Cost to complete | | |
|   (units × % completed this period × unit cost) | xxx | (2) |
|   Total cost of beginning inventory units | xxx | |
| + Cost of units started and finished | | |
|   (finished − beginning inventory) × total unit cost | xxx | |
|   Cost of units finished and transferred out | xxx | |
| Cost of ending work-in-process inventory | | |
|   Units × % complete × unit cost | xxx | (3) |
| Cost of abnormal spoilage (loss) | | |
|   Units × % complete × unit cost | xxx | (3) |
| Total manufacturing costs accounted for | xxx | |

(1) Includes material, labor, overhead and, if applicable, prior department costs.

(2) Separate computations may be required for material, labor, and overhead costs. NOTE: Prior department costs would **not** be applied as they are already included in the beginning inventory if applicable.

(3) Separate computations may be required for material, labor, overhead and prior department costs.

**Cost of Production Report—Average.** In average, costs and units are not isolated for the period, but instead, beginning inventory costs and units are merged as can be seen in the unit cost computation in Step 3.

| | |
|---|---|
| Cost of units finished and transferred out | |
| Units × total unit cost | xxx |
| Cost of ending work-in-process inventory | |
| Units × % complete × unit cost | xxx (1) |
| Cost of abnormal spoilage (loss) | |
| Units × % complete × unit cost | <u>xxx</u> (1) |
| Total manufacturing costs accounted for | <u>xxx</u> |

(1) Separate computations may be required for material, labor, overhead and prior department costs.

**5. Costs to be accounted for:**

Dr. Beginning inventory  
    Period costs (M, L and OH)  
    Prior dept. costs

Cr. Finished transferred  
    Finished remaining  
    Ending inventory  
    Lost units (if computed separately)

## Treatment of Spoiled Units (Lost, Defective, Spoiled, etc.)

1. Abnormal spoilage should be computed as a separate cost and written off as a period loss.
2. Normal spoilage is included in production costs for the period as follows:
   a. Units lost during production are simply ignored in the computation of the EFU and their period costs will be absorbed by the units produced including both finished good units and ending inventory of work-in-process. **Note**: If the problem is silent as to when units are lost, assume loss at beginning of process.
   b. When units are transferred in from another department, it will be necessary to compute a new unit cost, such as:

   18,000 units transferred from B to C at a cost of $36,000; 2,000 units were lost at the beginning of the process. The new unit cost becomes $36,000 ÷ 16,000, or $2.25.

At times problems may ask for a lost unit adjustment computation. In the foregoing situation this would be computed as follows:

| | |
|---|---|
| Transferred-in Unit Cost | $2.00 |
| Lost unit adjustment | |
| 18,000 − 16,000 = 2,000 lost | |
| 2,000 × $2.00 = $4,000 ÷ 16,000 = | <u>.25</u> |
| New unit cost | <u>$2.25</u> |

**Note to Students**: Cost accounting textbooks vary in their treatment of units normally lost in production. Some advocate computing a cost on the lost units and adding such cost to the good units. Others recommend ignoring the lost units, thus having the effect of spreading the cost over both the finished and ending inventory work in process. If you are instructed in a problem to compute a cost on lost units, you must include the lost units in the EFU to the extent such lost units were completed.

## Exercises

1. 20,000 units were started in the department, 8,000 were in process one-half complete at the end of the month, 27,000 were completed and 4,000 were found defective. How many units were in process at the beginning of the month? _____

2. 26,000 units were transferred into the department. Units in process at the beginning of the month, one-third complete, 18,000. At the end of the month 12,000 units were in process, three-fourths complete. 1,000 units were lost and 31,000 were finished and transferred. Compute the EFU for FIFO assuming that:
   - a. Material is added as work in process    _____
   - b. Material is added at the beginning of processing    _____
   - c. Material is added at the end of the process    _____

   Compute the EFU for average costing purposes assuming that
   - d. Material is added when the process is one-half complete    _____
   - e. Material is added at the beginning of processing    _____

3. 15,000 units were transferred in from the mixing department to cooking at a cost of $28,000. Beginning units totaled 6,000 at a cost of $13,000. One-thousand units were lost. Compute the transferred-in costs per unit for FIFO costing purposes. _____

   Make the same computation for average costing purposes. _____

## Solutions to Exercises
1. 19,000; 2. (a) 34,000, (b) 25,000, (c) 31,000, (d) 43,000, (e) 43,000; 3. $2.00, $2.05.

## Process Cost Illustrative Problem
The Joy Manufacturing Co. manufactures a single product that passes through two departments: extruding and finishing-packing. The product is shipped at the end of the day that it is packed in the finishing-packing department. The production in the extruding and finishing-packing departments does not increase the number of units started.

The cost and production data for the finishing-packing department for the month of January are as follows:

| Cost Data | Finishing-Packing Dept. |
|---|---|
| Work in process, January 1: | |
| Cost from preceding department | $34,500 |
| Material | $14,750 |
| Labor | 15,800 |
| Overhead | 6,230 |
| | |
| Costs added during January: | |
| Cost from preceding department | 93,500 |
| Material | 41,250 |
| Labor | 48,800 |
| Overhead | 23,370 |
| | |
| Percentage of completion of work in process | |
| January 1: | |
| Material | 100% |
| Labor | 60% |
| Overhead | 50% |
| January 31: | |
| Material | 100% |
| Labor | 80% |
| Overhead | 70% |

January Production Statistics

| | |
|---|---|
| Units in process, January 1 | 5,000 |
| Units in process, January 31 | 4,000 |
| Units received from prior department | 13,000 |
| Units completed and transferred or shipped | 12,000 |

Required: Compute each of the following assuming the company uses A) FIFO and B) Weighted Average Process Cost:

1. Account for all units.
2. Compute the equivalent finished units for material, labor, overhead, and prior department costs.
3. Compute the unit cost.
4. Prepare a cost of production summary.
5. Show all the debits to the Work-in-Process account, all credits and reconcile the balance to the ending inventory of work-in-process computed in (4) above.

**Solution: A) FIFO**

**Step #1**

| | *Finishing-Packing* |
|---|---|
| In Process 1/1 | 5,000 |
| Started | 13,000 |
| Total units to account for | 18,000 |
| | |
| Completed | 12,000 |
| In Process 1/31 | 4,000 |
| Lost in Production | 2,000 |
| Total units accounted for | 18,000 |

**Step #2—EFU (FIFO)**

| | | Finishing-Packing | | | |
|---|---|---|---|---|---|
| | | *Material* | *Labor* | *Overhead* | *Prior Dept.* |
| Finished | | 12,000 | 12,000 | 12,000 | 12,000 |
| + Ending Inv. | 4000 × 100% | 4,000 | | | |
| | 4000 × 80% | | 3,200 | | |
| | 4000 × 70% | | | 2,800 | |
| | 4000 × 100% | | | | 4,000 |
| | | 16,000 | 15,200 | 14,800 | 16,000 |
| - Beginning Inv. | 5000 × 100% | (5,000) | | | |
| | 5000 × 60% | | (3,000) | | |
| | 5000 × 50% | | | (2,500) | |
| | 5000 × 100% | | | | (5,000) |
| EFU - FIFO | | 11,000 | 12,200 | 12,300 | 11,000 |

**Step #3—Unit Cost**

| | *Period Cost* | *EFU* | *Unit Cost* |
|---|---|---|---|
| M | $41,250 | 11,000 | $ 3.75 |
| L | 48,800 | 12,200 | 4.00 |
| OH | 23,370 | 12,300 | 1.90 |
| | | | $ 9.65 |
| Transferred in costs | $93,500 | 11,000 | 8.50 |
| | | | $18.15 |

**Step #4—Cost of Production Report**

**Cost of Finished Units**

| | | |
|---|---|---|
| Opening WIP Costs 1/1 (34,500 + 14,750 + 15,800 + 6,230) | $ 71,280 | |
| Cost to Complete | | |
|     Material 5,000 × 0% × $3.75 | — | |
|     Labor 5,000 × 40% × $4.00 | 8,000 | |
|     Overhead 5,000 × 50% × $1.90 | 4,750 | |
|     Prior Dept. 5,000 × 0% × 8.50 | — | |
| Cost of 5,000 complete units | $ 84,030 | |
| Add: Cost of units started and finished during January | | |
|   7,000 × $18.15 | 127,050 | |
| Cost of 12,000 finished units | | $211,080 |

**Cost of WIP 1/31**

| | | |
|---|---|---|
| Material 4,000 × 100% × $3.75 | $ 15,000 | |
| Labor 4,000 × 80% × $4.00 | 12,800 | |
| Overhead 4,000 × 70% × $1.90 | 5,320 | |
| Transferred in Costs 4,000 × 100% × $8.50 | $ 34,000 | |
| | | 67,120 |
| | | |
| Total manufacturing cost accounted for | | $278,200 |

**Step #5—Costs To Be Accounted For**

| Costs | Finishing-Packing |
|---|---|
| Beginning Inventory | $ 71,280 |
| Period Costs | 206,920 |
| | $278,200 |
| | |
| Transfers from WIP | $211,080 |
| Ending Inventory WIP | 67,120 |
| | $278,200 |

**Solution: B) Weighted Average**
**Step #1**

| | Finishing-Packing Department |
|---|---|
| Units in process, January 1 | 5,000 |
| Units received from preceding department | 13,000 |
| Total units to be accounted for | 18,000 |
| | |
| Units completed and transferred or shipped | 12,000 |
| Units in process, January 31 | 4,000 |
| Units lost during January | 2,000 |
| Total units accounted for | 18,000 |

**Step #2—EFU (Weighted Average)**

| | Material | *Finishing-Packing* Labor | Overhead | Prior Dept. |
|---|---|---|---|---|
| | *Material* | *Labor* | *Overhead* | *Prior Dept.* |
| Finished | 12,000 | 12,000 | 12,000 | 12,000 |
| +Ending Inventory | | | | |
| 4000 × 100% | 4,000 | | | |
| 4000 × 80% | | 3,200 | | |
| 4000 × 70% | | | 2,800 | |
| 4000 × 100% | | | | 4,000 |
| EFU Weighted Average | 16,000 | 15,200 | 14,800 | 16,000 |

**Step #3—Unit Cost**

| Finishing-Packing Dept. | *Beg. Inv.* | *Costs* *Period* | *Total* | *EFU* | *Unit Cost* |
|---|---|---|---|---|---|
| M | $14,750 | $41,250 | $56,000 | 16,000 | $3.50 |
| L | 15,800 | 48,800 | 64,600 | 15,200 | 4.25 |
| OH | 6,230 | 23,370 | 29,600 | 14,800 | 2.00 |
| Preceding Dept. | | | | | |
| Costs | $34,500 | $93,500 | 128,000 | 16,000 | 8.00 |
| Total manufacturing costs | | | $278,200 | | $17.75 |

**Step #4—Cost of Production Report**

**Cost of Finished Units**

| | | |
|---|---|---|
| 12,000 units × $17.75 | | $213,000 |

**Cost of WIP 1/31**

| | | | |
|---|---|---|---|
| Material | 4000 × 100% × $3.50 | $14,000 | |
| Labor | 4000 × 80% × $4.25 | 13,600 | |
| Overhead | 4000 × 70% × $2.00 | 5,600 | |
| Prior Dept. | 4000 × 100% × $8.00 | 32,000 | 65,200 |
| Total manufacturing costs accounted for | | | $278,200 |

## ACTIVITY BASED COSTING:

Activity Based Costing is a method of assigning costs to goods and services that assumes all costs are caused by the activities (cost drivers) used to produce those goods and services. ABC first relates costs to the activities that cause the costs (cost drivers), then assigns costs to products/services based upon their use of those activities (cost driver) in production. ABC results in the use of multiple predetermined rates for overhead costs as companies engage in many different activities that cause overhead cost (multiple cause/effect relationships exist within a company for overhead costs). As a result, ABC provides more detailed measures of cost than departmental or plantwide allocation methods.

Advantages of ABC include:
- Provide more insight into the causes of cost. Managers must know: 1) the activities that go into making the good/service and 2) the cost of those activities to employ ABC.
- Stresses cost control results from control of activities. ABC is based on the concept that the production of goods and services consumes activities, and activities consume economic resources (costs).
- Promotes improved quality/continuous improvement. Nonvalue-added activities (cost drivers), such as movement, storage, set up, inspection, defective rework are minimized or eliminated.

# Chapter Fifteen
# Cost Accounting Questions
# Actual Cost, Job Order and Process

**Items 1 through 4** are based on the following information:

| | Fabrication | Assembly | General Factory Administration | Factory Maintenance | Factory Cafeteria |
|---|---|---|---|---|---|
| Direct-labor costs | $1,950,000 | $2,050,000 | $90,000 | $82,100 | $87,000 |
| Direct-material costs | $3,130,000 | $950,000 | — | $65,000 | $91,000 |
| Manufacturing-overhead | $1,650,000 | $1,850,000 | $70,000 | $56,100 | $62,000 |
| Direct-labor hours | 562,500 | 437,500 | 31,000 | 27,000 | 42,000 |
| Number of employees | 280 | 200 | 12 | 8 | 20 |
| Square-footage occupied | 88,000 | 72,000 | 1,750 | 2,000 | 4,800 |

The Parker Manufacturing Company has two production departments (fabrication and assembly) and three service departments (general factory administration, factory maintenance, and factory cafeteria.) A summary of costs and other data for each department prior to allocation of service-department costs for the year ended June 30, 19X3, appears above.

The costs of the general-factory-administration department, factory-maintenance department, and factory cafeteria are allocated on the basis of direct-labor hours, square-footage occupied, and number of employees, respectively. There are no manufacturing-overhead variances. **Round all final calculations to the nearest dollar.**

1. Assuming that Parker elects to distribute service-department costs directly to production departments without interservice department cost allocation, the amount of factory-maintenance department costs which would be allocated to the fabrication department would be
a. $0.
b. $111,760.
c. $106,091.
d. $91,440.

2. Assuming the same method of allocation as in item 1, the amount of general-factory-administration department costs which would be allocated to the assembly department would be
a. $0.
b. $63,636.
c. $70,000.
d. $90,000.

3. Assuming that Parker elects to distribute service-department costs to other service departments (starting with the service department with the greatest total costs) as well as the production departments, the amount of factory-cafeteria department costs which would be allocated to the factory-maintenance department would be (**Note:** Once a service department's costs have been reallocated, no subsequent service-department costs are recirculated back to it.)
a. $0.
b. $96,000.
c. $3,840.
d. $6,124.

4. Assuming the same method of allocation as in item 3, the amount of factory-maintenance department costs which would be allocated to the factory cafeteria would be
a. $0.
b. $5,787.
c. $5,856.
d. $148,910.

_____

*M95*

5. Which measures would be useful in evaluating the performance of a manufacturing system?

I.   Throughput time.
II.  Total setup time for machines/Total production time.
III. Number of rework units/Total number of units completed.

a. I and II only.
b. II and III only.
c. I and III only.
d. I, II, and III.

6. Gram Co. develops computer programs to meet customers' special requirements. How should Gram categorize payments to employees who develop these programs?

|     | Direct costs | Value-adding costs |
| --- | --- | --- |
| a. | Yes | Yes |
| b. | Yes | No |
| c. | No | No |
| d. | No | Yes |

7. Spoilage occurring during a manufacturing process can be considered normal or abnormal. The proper accounting for each of these costs is

|     | Normal | Abnormal |
| --- | --- | --- |
| a. | Product | Period |
| b. | Product | Product |
| c. | Period | Product |
| d. | Period | Period |

8. In developing a predetermined factory overhead application rate for use in a process costing system, which of the following could be used in the numerator and denominator?

|     | Numerator | Denominator |
| --- | --- | --- |
| a. | Actual factory overhead. | Actual machine hours. |
| b. | Actual factory overhead. | Estimated machine hours. |
| c. | Estimated factory overhead. | Actual machine hours. |
| d. | Estimated factory overhead. | Estimated machine hours. |

9. Following are Mill Co.'s production costs for October:

| Direct materials | $100,000 |
| --- | --- |
| Direct labor | 90,000 |
| Factory overhead | 4,000 |

What amount of costs should be traced to specific products in the production process?
a. $194,000
b. $190,000
c. $100,000
d. $90,000

10. Direct labor cost is a

|     | Conversion cost | Prime cost |
| --- | --- | --- |
| a. | No | No |
| b. | No | Yes |
| c. | Yes | Yes |
| d. | Yes | No |

11. What is the normal effect on the numbers of cost pools and allocation bases when an activity-based cost (ABC) system replaces a traditional cost system?

|     | Cost pools | Allocation bases |
| --- | --- | --- |
| a. | No effect | No effect |
| b. | Increase | No effect |
| c. | No effect | Increase |
| d. | Increase | Increase |

12. Under the two-variance method for analyzing overhead, which of the following variances consists of both variable and fixed overhead elements?

|     | Controllable (budget) variance | Volume variance |
| --- | --- | --- |
| a. | Yes | Yes |
| b. | Yes | No |
| c. | No | No |
| d. | No | Yes |

13. The Forming Department is the first of a two-stage production process. Spoilage is identified when the units have completed the Forming process. Costs of spoiled units are assigned to units completed and transferred to the second department in the period spoilage is identified. The following information concerns Forming's conversion costs in May 1995:

|     | Units | Conversion Costs |
| --- | --- | --- |
| Beginning work-in-process (50% complete) | 2,000 | $10,000 |
| Units started during May | 8,000 | 75,500 |
| Spoilage -- normal | 500 | |
| Units completed & transferred | 7,000 | |
| Ending work-in-process (80% complete) | 2,500 | |

Using the weighted average method, what was Forming's conversion cost transferred to the second production department?
a. $59,850
b. $64,125
c. $67,500
d. $71,250

M95

14. In an activity-based costing system, what should be used to assign a department's manufacturing overhead costs to products produced in varying lot sizes?
a. A single cause and effect relationship.
b. Multiple cause and effect relationships.
c. Relative net sales values of the products.
d. A product's ability to bear cost allocations.

M92

15. During the month of March 1992, Nale Co. used $300,000 of direct materials. At March 31, 1992, Nale's direct materials inventory was $50,000 more than it was at March 1, 1992. Direct material purchases during the month of March 1992 amounted to
a. $0
b. $250,000
c. $300,000
d. $350,000

N91

16. A direct labor overtime premium should be charged to a specific job when the overtime is caused by the
a. Increased overall level of activity.
b. Customer's requirement for early completion of job.
c. Management's failure to include the job in the production schedule.
d. Management's requirement that the job be completed before the annual factory vacation closure.

N88

17. The fixed portion of the semivariable cost of electricity for a manufacturing plant is a

|  | Period cost | Product cost |
|---|---|---|
| a. | Yes | No |
| b. | Yes | Yes |
| c. | No | Yes |
| d. | No | No |

18. Baker Co., a manufacturer, had inventories at the beginning and end of its current year as follows:

|  | Beginning | End |
|---|---|---|
| Raw materials | $22,000 | $30,000 |
| Work in process | 40,000 | 48,000 |
| Finished goods | 25,000 | 18,000 |

During the year the following costs and expenses were incurred:

| | |
|---|---|
| Raw materials purchased | $300,000 |
| Direct-labor cost | 120,000 |
| Indirect factory labor | 60,000 |
| Taxes and depreciation on factory building | 20,000 |
| Taxes and depreciation on salesroom and office | 15,000 |
| Salesmen's salaries | 40,000 |
| Office salaries | 24,000 |
| Utilities (60% applicable to factory, 20% to salesroom, 20% to office) | 50,000 |

Baker's cost of goods sold for the year is
a. $514,000.
b. $521,000.
c. $522,000.
d. $539,000.

19. When should process-costing techniques be used in assigning costs to products?
a. If the product is manufactured on the basis of each order received.
b. When production is only partially completed during the accounting period.
c. If the product is composed of mass-produced homogeneous units.
d. In situations where standard costing techniques should not be used.

N92

20. Nile Co.'s cost allocation and product costing procedures follow activity-based costing principles. Activities have been identified and classified as being either value-adding or nonvalue-adding as to each product. Which of the following activities, used in Nile production process, is nonvalue-adding?
a. Design engineering activity.
b. Heat treatment activity.
c. Drill press activity.
d. Raw materials storage activity.

21. A job order cost system uses a predetermined factor overhead rate based on expected volume and expected fixed cost. At the end of the year, underapplied overhead might be explained by which of the following situations?

| | Actual volume | Actual fixed costs |
|---|---|---|
| a. | Greater than expected | Greater than expected |
| b. | Greater than expected | Less than expected |
| c. | Less than expected | Greater than expected |
| d. | Less than expected | Less than expected |

22. In order to compute equivalent units of production using the FIFO method of process costing, work for the period must be broken down to units
a. Completed during the period and units in ending inventory.
b. Completed from beginning inventory, started and completed during the month, and units in ending inventory.
c. Started during the period and units transferred out during the period.
d. Processed during the period and units completed during the period.

23. A process costing system was used for a department that began operations in January 1991. Approximately the same number of physical units, at the same degree of completion, were in work in process at the end of both January and February. Monthly conversion costs are allocated between ending work in process and units completed. Compared to the FIFO method, would the weighted average method use the same or a greater number of equivalent units to calculate the monthly allocations?

| | Equivalent units for weighted average compared to FIFO | |
|---|---|---|
| | January | February |
| a. | Same | Same |
| b. | Greater number | Greater number |
| c. | Greater number | Same |
| d. | Same | Greater number |

24. Walton, Incorporated, had 8,000 units of work in process in Department A on October 1, 19X8. These units were 60% complete as to conversion costs. Materials are added in the beginning of the process. During the month of October, 34,000 units were started and 36,000 units completed. Walton had 6,000 units of work in process on October 31, 19X8. These units were 80% complete as to conversion costs. By how much did the equivalent units for the month of October using the weighted-average method exceed the equivalent units for the month of October using the first-in, first-out method?

| | Materials | Conversion Costs |
|---|---|---|
| a. | 0 | 3,200 |
| b. | 0 | 4,800 |
| c. | 8,000 | 3,200 |
| d. | 8,000 | 4,800 |

25. Information for the month of May concerning Department A, the first stage of Wit Corporation's production cycle, is as follows:

| | Materials | Conversion Costs |
|---|---|---|
| Work in process, beginning | $ 4,000 | $ 3,000 |
| Current costs | 20,000 | 16,000 |
| Total costs | $24,000 | $19,000 |
| Equivalent units based on weighted-average method | 100,000 | 95,000 |
| Average unit costs | $ 0.24 | $0.20 |
| Goods completed | | 90,000 units |
| Work in process, end | | 10,000 units |

Material costs are added at the beginning of the process. The ending work in process is 50% complete as to conversion costs. How would the total costs accounted for be distributed, using the weighted-average method?

| | Goods Completed | Work in Process, End |
|---|---|---|
| a. | $39,600 | $3,400 |
| b. | $39,600 | $4,400 |
| c. | $43,000 | $0 |
| d. | $44,000 | $3,400 |

26. The Wiring Department is the second stage of Flem Company's production cycle. On May 1, the beginning work in process contained 25,000 units which were 60% complete as to conversion costs. During May, 100,000 units were transferred in from the first stage of Flem's production cycle. On May 31, the ending work in process contained 20,000 units which were 80% complete as to conversion costs. Material costs are

added at the end of the process. Using the weighted-average method, the equivalent units were

| | Transferred-in Costs | Materials | Conversion Costs |
|---|---|---|---|
| a. | 100,000 | 125,000 | 100,000 |
| b. | 125,000 | 105,000 | 105,000 |
| c. | 125,000 | 105,000 | 121,000 |
| d. | 125,000 | 125,000 | 121,000 |

27. The Cutting Department is the first stage of Mark Company's production cycle. Conversion costs for this department were 80% complete as to the beginning work-in-process and 50% complete as to the ending work-in-process. Information as to conversion costs in the Cutting Department for January is as follows:

| | Units | Conversion costs |
|---|---|---|
| Work-in-process at January 1 | 25,000 | $ 22,000 |
| Units started and costs incurred during January | 135,000 | $143,000 |
| Units completed and transferred to next department during January | 100,000 | |

Using the FIFO method, what was the conversion cost of the work-in-process in the Cutting Department at January 31?
a. $33,000.
b. $38,100.
c. $39,000.
d. $45,000.

28. Under Heller Company's job order cost system, estimated costs of defective work (considered normal in the manufacturing process) are included in the predetermined factory overhead rate. During March, Job No. 210 for 2,000 hand saws was completed at the following costs per unit:

| | |
|---|---|
| Direct materials | $ 5 |
| Direct labor | 4 |
| Factory overhead (applied at 150% of direct-labor cost) | 6 |
| | $15 |

Final inspection of Job No. 210 disclosed 100 defective saws which were reworked at a cost of $2 per unit for direct labor, plus overhead at the predetermined rate. The defective units on Job No. 210 fall within the normal range. What is the total rework cost and to what account should it be charged?

| | Rework cost | Account charged |
|---|---|---|
| a. | $200 | Work-in-process |
| b. | $200 | Factory overhead control |
| c. | $500 | Work-in-process |
| d. | $500 | Factory overhead control |

M95

29. In its April 1995 production, Hern Corp., which does not use a standard cost system, incurred total production costs of $900,000, of which Hern attributed $60,000 to normal spoilage and $30,000 to abnormal spoilage. Hern should account for this spoilage as
a. Period cost of $90,000.
b. Inventoriable cost of $90,000.
c. Period cost of $60,000 and inventoriable cost of $30,000.
d. Inventoriable cost of $60,000 and period cost of $30,000.

M87

Items 30 through 32 are based on the following data pertaining to Lam Co.'s manufacturing operations:

| Inventories | 4/1/87 | 4/30/87 |
|---|---|---|
| Direct materials | $18,000 | $15,000 |
| Work-in-process | 9,000 | 6,000 |
| Finished goods | 27,000 | 36,000 |

Additional information for the month of April 1987:

| | |
|---|---|
| Direct materials purchased | $42,000 |
| Direct labor payroll | 30,000 |
| Direct labor rate per hour | $ 7.50 |
| Factory overhead rate per direct labor hour | 10.00 |

30. For the month of April 1987, prime cost incurred was
a. $75,000
b. $69,000
c. $45,000
d. $39,000

31. For the month of April 1987, conversion cost incurred was
a. $30,000
b. $40,000
c. $70,000
d. $72,000

32. For the month of April 1987, cost of goods manufactured was
a. $118,000
b. $115,000
c. $112,000
d. $109,000

_____

33. Brooks Company uses the following flexible budget formula for the annual maintenance cost in department T:

   Total cost = $7,200 + $0.60 per machine hour

The July operating budget is based upon 20,000 hours of planned machine time. Maintenance cost included in this flexible budget is
a. $11,400
b. $12,000
c. $12,600
d. $19,200

34. Walden Company has a process cost system using the FIFO cost flow method. All materials are introduced at the beginning of the process in department One. The following information is available for the month of January:

|  | Units |
|---|---|
| Work-in-process, 1/1 (40% complete as to conversion costs) | 500 |
| Started in January | 2,000 |
| Transferred to department Two during January | 2,100 |
| Work-in-process, 1/31 (25% complete as to conversion costs) | 400 |

What are the equivalent units of production for the month of January?

|  | Materials | Conversion |
|---|---|---|
| a. | 2,500 | 2,200 |
| b. | 2,500 | 1,900 |
| c. | 2,000 | 2,200 |
| d. | 2,000 | 2,000 |

M90

35. The following information was taken from Cody Co.'s accounting records for the year ended December 31, 1989:

| | |
|---|---|
| Decrease in raw materials inventory | $ 15,000 |
| Increase in finished goods inventory | 35,000 |
| Raw materials purchased | 430,000 |
| Direct labor payroll | 200,000 |
| Factory overhead | 300,000 |
| Freight-out | 45,000 |

There was no work-in-process inventory at the beginning or end of the year. Cody's 1989 cost of goods sold is
a. $895,000
b. $910,000
c. $950,000
d. $955,000

36. Axe Co. has a job order cost system. The following debits (credits) appeared in the work-in-process account for the month of March 1989:

| March | Description | Amount |
|---|---|---|
| 1 | Balance | $ 2,000 |
| 31 | Direct materials | 12,000 |
| 31 | Direct labor | 8,000 |
| 31 | Factory overhead | 6,400 |
| 31 | To finished goods | (24,000) |

Axe applies overhead to production at a predetermined rate of 80% based on direct labor cost. Job No. 9, the only job still in process at the end of March 1989, has been charged with direct labor of $1,000. The amount of direct materials charged to Job No. 9 was
a. $12,000
b. $4,400
c. $2,600
d. $1,500

_____

Items 37 through 39 are based on the following information pertaining to Arp Co.'s manufacturing operations:

| Inventories | 3/1/89 | 3/31/89 |
|---|---|---|
| Direct materials | $36,000 | $30,000 |
| Work-in-process | 18,000 | 12,000 |
| Finished goods | 54,000 | 72,000 |

Additional information for the month of March 1989:

| | |
|---|---|
| Direct materials purchased | $84,000 |
| Direct labor payroll | 60,000 |
| Direct labor rate per hour | 7.50 |
| Factory overhead rate per direct labor hour | 10.00 |

37. For the month of March 1989, prime cost was
a. $90,000
b. $120,000
c. $144,000
d. $150,000

38. For the month of March 1989, conversion cost was
a. $90,000
b. $140,000
c. $144,000
d. $170,000

39. For the month of March 1989, cost of goods manufactured was
a. $218,000
b. $224,000
c. $230,000
d. $236,000

_____

40. Barkley Company adds materials at the beginning of the process in department M. Data concerning the materials used in March production are as follows:

|  | Units |
| --- | --- |
| Work-in-process at March 1 | 16,000 |
| Started during March | 34,000 |
| Completed and transferred to next department during March | 36,000 |
| Normal spoilage incurred | 4,000 |
| Work-in-process at March 31 | 10,000 |

Using the weighted-average method, the equivalent units for the materials unit cost calculation are
a. 30,000
b. 34,000
c. 40,000
d. 46,000

M92
41. Book Co. uses the activity-based costing approach for cost allocation and product costing purposes. Printing, cutting, and binding functions make up the manufacturing process. Machinery and equipment are arranged in operating cells that produce a complete product starting with raw materials. Which of the following are characteristics of Book's activity-based costing approach?

I.   Cost drivers are used as a basis for cost allocation.
II.  Costs are accumulated by department or function for purposes of product costing.
III. Activities that do not add value to the product are identified and reduced to the extent possible.

a.   I only.
b.   I and II.
c.   I and III.
d.   II and III.

M93
42. The benefits of a just-in-time system for raw materials usually include
a.   Elimination of nonvalue adding operations.
b.   Increase in the number of suppliers, thereby ensuring competitive bidding.
c.   Maximization of the standard delivery quantity, thereby lessening the paperwork for each delivery.

d.   Decrease in the number of deliveries required to maintain production.

M92
43. Fab Co. manufactures textiles. Among Fab's 1991 manufacturing costs were the following salaries and wages:

| Loom operators | $120,000 |
| --- | --- |
| Factory foremen | 45,000 |
| Machine mechanics | 30,000 |

What was the amount of Fab's 1991 direct labor?
a.   $195,000
b.   $165,000
c.   $150,000
d.   $120,000

M93
44. In a traditional job order cost system, the issue of indirect materials to a production department increases
a.   Stores control.
b.   Work in process control.
c.   Factory overhead control.
d.   Factory overhead applied.

45. Barnett Company adds materials at the beginning of the process in department M. Conversion costs were 75% complete as to the 8,000 units in work-in-process at May 1, and 50% complete as to the 6,000 units in work-in-process at May 31. During May 12,000 units were completed and transferred to the next department. An analysis of the costs relating to work-in-process at May 1 and to production activity for May is as follows:

|  | Costs | |
| --- | --- | --- |
|  | Materials | Conversion |
| Work-in-process, 5/1 | $ 9,600 | $ 4,800 |
| Costs added in May | 15,600 | 14,400 |

Using the weighted-average method, the total cost per equivalent unit for May was
a. $2.47
b. $2.50
c. $2.68
d. $3.16

N92
46. Ral Co.'s target gross margin is 60% of the selling price of a product that costs $5.00 per unit. The product's selling price per unit should be
a.   $17.50
b.   $12.50
c.   $8.33
d.   $7.50

47. Wages paid to factory machine operators of a manufacturing plant are an element of

| | Prime Cost | Conversion Cost |
|---|---|---|
| a. | No | No |
| b. | No | Yes |
| c. | Yes | No |
| d. | Yes | Yes |

48. Property taxes on a manufacturing plant are an element of

| | Conversion Cost | Period Cost |
|---|---|---|
| a. | Yes | No |
| b. | Yes | Yes |
| c. | No | Yes |
| d. | No | No |

49. In process 2, material G is added when a batch is 60 percent complete. Ending work-in-process units, which are 50 percent complete, would be included in the computation of equivalent units for

| | Conversion cost | Material G |
|---|---|---|
| a. | Yes | No |
| b. | No | Yes |
| c. | No | No |
| d. | Yes | Yes |

50. Assuming that there was no beginning work in process inventory, and the ending work in process inventory is 50% complete as to conversion costs, the number of equivalent units as to conversion costs would be

a. The same as the units placed in process.
b. The same as the units completed.
c. Less than the units placed in process.
d. Less than the units completed.

51. The fixed portion of the semivariable cost of electricity for a manufacturing plant is a

| | Conversion cost | Product cost |
|---|---|---|
| a. | No | No |
| b. | No | Yes |
| c. | Yes | Yes |
| d. | Yes | No |

52. A flexible budget is appropriate for a(an)

| | Administrative budget | Marketing budget |
|---|---|---|
| a. | Yes | Yes |
| b. | Yes | No |
| c. | No | No |
| d. | No | Yes |

53. Assuming that there was **no** beginning work in process inventory, and the ending work in process inventory is 100% complete as to material costs, the number of equivalent units as to material costs would be

a. The same as the units placed in process.
b. The same as the units completed.
c. Less than the units placed in process.
d. Less than the units completed.

54. Nonfinancial performance measures are important to engineering and operations managers in assessing the quality levels of their products. Which of the following indicators can be used to measure product quality?

I. Returns and allowances.
II. Number and types of customer complaints.
III. Production cycle time.

a. I and II only.
b. I and III only.
c. II and III only.
d. I, II, and III.

55. During March 1985 Bly Co.'s Department Y equivalent unit product costs, computed under the weighted-average method, were as follows:

| | |
|---|---|
| Materials | $1 |
| Conversion | 3 |
| Transferred-in | 5 |

Materials are introduced at the end of the process in Department Y. There were 4,000 units (40% complete as to conversion cost) in work-in-process at March 31, 1985. The total costs assigned to the March 31, 1985, work-in-process inventory should be

a. $36,000
b. $28,800
c. $27,200
d. $24,800

56. Birk Co. uses a job order cost system. The following debits (credit) appeared in Birk's work-in-process account for the month of April 1992:

| April | Description | Amount |
|---|---|---|
| 1 | Balance | $ 4,000 |
| 30 | Direct materials | 24,000 |
| 30 | Direct labor | 16,000 |
| 30 | Factory overhead | 12,800 |
| 30 | To finished goods | (48,000) |

Birk applies overhead to production at a predetermined rate of 80% of direct labor cost. Job No. 5, the only job still in process on April 30, 1992, has been charged with direct labor of $2,000. What was the amount of direct materials charged to Job No. 5?
a. $3,000
b. $5,200
c. $8,800
d. $24,000

57. The flexible budget for a producing department may include

| | Direct labor | Factory overhead |
|---|---|---|
| a. | No | Yes |
| b. | No | No |
| c. | Yes | No |
| d. | Yes | Yes |

58. In a job order cost system, the use of indirect materials previously purchased usually is recorded as a decrease in
a. Stores control.
b. Work-in-process control.
c. Factory overhead control.
d. Factory overhead applied.

59. The following data were available from Mith Co.'s records on December 31, 1988:

| | |
|---|---|
| Finished goods inventory, 1/1/88 | $120,000 |
| Finished goods inventory, 12/31/88 | 110,000 |
| Cost of goods manufactured | 520,000 |
| Lost on sale of plant equipment | 50,000 |

The cost of goods sold for 1988 was
a. $510,000
b. $520,000
c. $530,000
d. $580,000

60. Boa Corp. distributes service department overhead costs directly to producing departments without allocation to the other service department. Information for the month of June 1985 is as follows:

| | Service Departments | |
|---|---|---|
| | Maintenance | Utilities |
| Overhead costs incurred | $20,000 | $10,000 |
| Service provided to departments: | | |
| Maintenance | | 10% |
| Utilities | 20% | |
| Producing—A | 40% | 30% |
| Producing—B | 40% | 60% |
| Totals | 100% | 100% |

The amount of maintenance department costs distributed to Producing—A department for June 1985 was
a. $8,000
b. $8,800
c. $10,000
d. $11,000

61. In manufacturing its products for the month of March 1989, Elk Co. incurred normal spoilage of $5,000 and abnormal spoilage of $9,000. How much spoilage cost should Elk charge as a period cost for the month of March 1989?
a. $0
b. $5,000
c. $9,000
d. $14,000

62. In developing a factory overhead application rate for use in a process costing system, which of the following could be used in the numerator?
a. Actual direct labor hours.
b. Estimated direct labor hours.
c. Actual factory overhead costs.
d. Estimated factory overhead costs.

63. In a process cost system, the application of factory overhead usually would be recorded as an increase in
a. Cost of goods sold.
b. Work in process control.
c. Factory overhead control.
d. Finished goods control.

64. Parat College allocates support department costs to its individual schools using the step method. Information for May 1995 is as follows:

|  | Support departments | |
|---|---|---|
|  | *Maintenance* | *Power* |
| Costs incurred | $99,000 | $54,000 |

| Service percentages provided to: | | |
|---|---|---|
| Maintenance | -- | 10% |
| Power | 20% | -- |
| School of Education | 30% | 20% |
| School of Technology | 50% | 70% |
|  | 100% | 100% |

What is the amount of May 1995 support department costs allocated to the School of Education?

a.   $40,500
b.   $42,120
c.   $46,100
d.   $49,125

# Chapter Fifteen
# Cost Accounting Problems
# Actual Cost, Job Order and Process

## NUMBER 1

In the course of your examination of the financial statements of the Zeus Company for the year ended December 31, 19X1, you have ascertained the following concerning its manufacturing operations:

- Zeus has two production departments (fabricating and finishing) and a service department. In the fabricating department polyplast is prepared from miracle mix and bypro. In the finishing department each unit of polyplast is converted into six tetraplexes and three uniplexes. The service department provides services to both production departments.
- The fabricating and finishing departments use process cost accounting systems. Actual production costs, including overhead, are allocated monthly.
- Service department expenses are allocated to production departments as follows:

| Expense | Allocation Base |
|---|---|
| Building maintenance | Space occupied |
| Timekeeping and personnel | Number of employees |
| Other | 1/2 to fabricating, 1/2 to finishing |

- Raw materials inventory and work in process are priced on a FIFO basis.
- The following data were taken from the fabricating department's records for December 19X1.

Quantities (units of polyplast):

| | |
|---|---|
| In process, December 1 | 3,000 |
| Started in process during month | 25,000 |
| Total units to be accounted for | 28,000 |
| | |
| Transferred to finishing department | 19,000 |
| In process, December 31 | 6,000 |
| Lost in process | 3,000 |
| Total units accounted for | 28,000 |

Cost of work in process, December 1:

| | |
|---|---|
| Materials | $ 13,000 |
| Labor | 17,500 |
| Overhead | 21,500 |
| | $ 52,000 |
| | |
| Direct labor costs, December | $154,000 |
| | |
| Departmental overhead, December | $132,000 |

- Polyplast work in process at the beginning and end of the month was partially completed as follows:

| | Materials | Labor and Overhead |
|---|---|---|
| December 1 | 66 2/3% | 50% |
| December 31 | 100 % | 75% |

- The following data were taken from raw materials inventory records for December:

| | Miracle Mix | | Bypro | |
| --- | --- | --- | --- | --- |
| | Quantity | Amount | Quantity | Amount |
| Balance, December 1 | 62,000 | $62,000 | 265,000 | $18,550 |
| Purchases: | | | | |
| December 12 | 39,500 | 49,375 | | |
| December 20 | 28,500 | 34,200 | | |
| Fabricating department usage | 83,200 | | 50,000 | |

- Service department expenses for December (not included in departmental overhead above) were:

| | |
| --- | --- |
| Building maintenance | $ 45,000 |
| Timekeeping and personnel | 27,500 |
| Other | 39,000 |
| | $111,500 |

- Other information for December 19X1 is presented below:

| | Square Feet of Space Occupied | Number of Employees |
| --- | --- | --- |
| Fabricating | 75,000 | 180 |
| Finishing | 37,500 | 120 |
| | 112,500 | 300 |

**Required:**

a. Compute the equivalent number of units of polyplast, with separate calculations for materials and conversion cost (direct labor plus overhead), manufactured during December.

b. Compute the following items to be included in the fabricating department's production report for December 19X1, with separate calculations for materials, direct labor and overhead. Prepare supporting schedules.

   1. Total costs to be accounted for.

   2. Unit costs for equivalent units manufactured.

   3. Transfers to finishing department during December and work in process at December 31. Reconcile to your answer to part **b.** 1.

# NUMBER 2

Stein Company is going to use a predetermined annual factory overhead rate to charge factory overhead to products. In conjunction with this, Stein Company must decide whether to use direct labor hours or machine hours as the overhead rate base.

**Required:**

Discuss the objectives and criteria that Stein Company should use in selecting the base for its predetermined annual factory overhead rate.

# NUMBER 3

Presented below are four independent questions concerning a typical manufacturing company that uses a process-cost accounting system. Your response to each question should be complete, including simple examples or illustrations where appropriate.

**Required:**

a. What is the rationale supporting the use of process costing instead of job-order costing for product-costing purposes? Explain.

b. Define equivalent production (equivalent units produced). Explain the significance and use of equivalent production for product-costing purposes.

c. Define normal spoilage and abnormal spoilage. Explain how normal-spoilage costs and abnormal-spoilage costs should be reported for management purposes.

d. How does the first-in, first-out (FIFO) method of process costing differ from the weighted-average method of process costing? Explain.


# NUMBER 4

**Part a.** The Rebecca Corporation is a manufacturer which produces special machines made to customer specifications. All production costs are accumulated by means of a job-order costing system. The following information is available at the beginning of the month of October.

| | |
|---|---|
| • Direct materials inventory, October 1 | $16,200 |
| • Work-in-process, October 1 | 3,600 |

A review of the job-order cost sheets revealed the composition of the work-in-process inventory on October 1, as follows:

| | |
|---|---|
| Direct materials | $1,320 |
| Direct labor (300 hours) | 1,500 |
| Factory overhead applied | 780 |
| | $3,600 |

Activity during the month of October was as follows:

• Direct materials costing $20,000 were purchased.
• Direct labor for job orders totaled 3,300 hours at $5 per hour.
• Factory overhead was applied to production at the rate of $2.60 per direct labor hour.

On October 31, inventories consisted of the following components:

| | |
|---|---|
| Direct materials inventory | $17,000 |
| Work-in-process inventory: | |
| Direct materials | $4,320 |
| Direct labor (500 hours) | 2,500 |
| Factory overhead applied | 1,300 |
| | $8,120 |

**Required:**
Prepare in good form a detailed statement of the cost of goods manufactured for the month of October.


**Part b.** Lakeview Corporation is a manufacturer that uses the weighted-average process-cost method to account for costs of production. Lakeview manufactures a product that is produced in three separate departments: Molding, Assembling, and Finishing. The following information was obtained for the Assembling Department for the month of June.

Work-in-process, June 1—2,000 units composed of the following:

|  | Amount | Degree of Completion |
|---|---|---|
| Transferred in from the Molding Department | $32,000 | 100% |
| Costs added by the Assembling Department: |  |  |
| Direct materials | $20,000 | 100% |
| Direct labor | 7,200 | 60% |
| Factory overhead applied | 5,500 | 50% |
|  | 32,700 |  |
| Work-in-process, June 1 | $64,700 |  |

The following activity occurred during the month of June:

- 10,000 units were transferred in from the Molding Department at a cost of $160,000.
- 150,000 of costs were added by the Assembling Department:

| Direct materials | $96,000 |
|---|---|
| Direct labor | 36,000 |
| Factory overhead applied | 18,000 |
|  | $150,000 |

- 8,000 units were completed and transferred to the Finishing Department.

At June 30, 4,000 units were still in work-in-process. The degree of completion of work-in-process at June 30, was as follows:

| Direct materials | 90% |
|---|---|
| Direct labor | 70% |
| Factory overhead applied | 35% |

**Required:**
Prepare in good form a cost of production report for the Assembling Department for the month of June. Show supporting computations in good form. The report should include:
- Equivalent units of production;
- Total manufacturing costs;
- Cost per equivalent unit;
- Dollar amount of ending work-in-process;
- Dollar amount of inventory cost transferred out.


# NUMBER 5

Noble Manufacturing Company uses the weighted-average method of process costing when computing manufacturing cost per equivalent unit. The work in process inventory at the beginning of the period was complete as to materials, and one-third complete as to conversion costs. The work in process inventory at the end of the period was complete as to materials, and one-quarter complete as to conversion costs.

**Required:**
1. Describe how the cost of the beginning work in process inventory is handled using the weighted-average method of process costing when computing manufacturing cost per equivalent unit. Do not describe determination of equivalent units.
2. Identify the conditions under which the weighted-average method of process costing would be inappropriate.
3. Specify the advantages of the weighted-average method of process costing in contrast to the first-in, first-out method.
4. How would Noble compute the amount of the conversion cost portion of its ending work in process inventory using the weighted-average method?

# Chapter Fifteen
# Solutions to Cost Accounting Questions
# Actual Cost, Job Order and Process

1. (b)

| | Square Footage | Share of % of Total | Factory Maint. Costs |
|---|---|---|---|
| Fabrication | 88,000 | 55 | $111,760 |
| Assembly | 72,000 | 45 | 91,440 |
| Total | 160,000 | 100 | $203,200 |

Total factory maintenance costs = $82,100 + $65,000 + $56,100 = $203,200.

2. (c)

| | Direct Labor Hrs. | Share of Gen'l Factory % of Total | Administration Costs |
|---|---|---|---|
| Fabrication | 562,500 | 56.25 | $ 90,000 |
| Assembly | 437,500 | 43.75 | 70,000 |
| Total | 1,000,000 | 100.00 | $160,000 |

Total general-factory-administration costs = $90,000 + $70,000 = $160,000.

3. (c) Factory cafeteria will be allocated first because it has the greatest total costs.

| | No. of Employees | % of Total | Share of Cafeteria costs |
|---|---|---|---|
| Fabrication | 280 | 56.0 | $134,400 |
| Assembly | 200 | 40.0 | 96,000 |
| Gen.-Factory- Admin. | 12 | 2.4 | 5,760 |
| Factory Mtce. | 8 | 1.6 | 3,840 |
| Total | 500 | 100.0 | $240,000 |

Total factory cafeteria costs = $87,000 + $91,000 + $62,000 = $240,000.

4. (a) Factory cafeteria costs were allocated before factory maintenance costs. Once a service department's costs have been allocated, no subsequent service-department costs are recirculated back to it (per #3 above).

5. (d) All of these nonfinancial measures would be useful in evaluating a manufacturing system.
> Throughput time: Total production time required for a units production
> > measure of capacity and efficiency.
> Setup time to total production time: Nonvalue-added function as a % of total production time
> > measure of efficiency.
> Rework units as a % total units
> > measure of quality of production.

6. (a) Programmers for a computer programming company would be classified as direct labor which would be both a direct cost and a value-added cost of program development.

7. (a) The cost of normal spoilage is "absorbed" by the surviving units while abnormal spoilage is recognized immediately; that is, in the current period.

8. (d) Numerator: Estimated factory overhead; Denominator: Estimated machine hours.

$$\text{Predetermined overhead rate} = \frac{\text{Budget estimate of overhead cost}}{\text{Budget estimate of activity base}}$$

Only answer (d) has estimates for both overhead costs (the numerator) and an activity base (the denominator).

9. (b) Only direct manufacturing costs (direct materials and direct labor) should be traced to specific products. The other manufacturing costs, called indirect costs, should be allocated based upon activity cost drivers which only approximates the amount of cost incurred by the specific product.

10. (c) Direct labor is an element of both prime costs and conversion costs. Prime costs are direct material and direct labor. Conversion costs include direct labor and overhead costs.

11. (d) Activity based costing identifies the activities or transactions that cause costs to be incurred (cost drivers). Costs are accumulated (homogeneous cost pools) by activities and then assigned to products based upon the product's use of these activities in its production. Multiple cost drivers are usually employed in costing a single product as multiple activities are used in its production.

12. (b) Under the two variance method: The controllable (budget) variance is the difference between the actual overhead and the budgeted overhead. Both of these contain variable and fixed costs and either fixed or variable costs can vary from the budget.

The volume variance is due solely to fixed costs. It is the difference between the budgeted overhead and applied overhead based upon the same level of activity as the budget. Because the budget and applied activity bases are the same, budgeted variable overhead will equal applied variable overhead, and any volume variance is due solely to fixed costs.

*Note:* The answer is the same for both actual and standard costing. The difference between actual and standard, under the two variance method, is the activity base used for the budgeted overhead. Under actual costing, the activity base used would be the actual activity base achieved, while under standard costing, it would be the standard activity base for the production achieved.

13. (c) $67,500

Computation of Equivalent Finished Units (Conversion Costs)

| | |
|---|---:|
| Units finished and transferred out | 7,000 |
| + Normal spoilage -- finished | 500 |
| + Ending inventory    2500 x 80% | 2,000 |
| E.F.U. -- at average | 9,500 |

Conversion Cost Per E.F.U. (Wt. Aver.)

| | |
|---|---:|
| Beginning inventory conversion cost | $10,000 |
| Current period conversion cost | 75,500 |
| Total conversion cost | $85,500 |
| E.F.U. -- Conversion Cost | ÷ 9,500 |
| Conversion cost per E.F.U. | $   9.00 |

Conversion Costs transferred to Dept 2

| | |
|---|---:|
| Units finished and transferred out | 7,000 |
| Normal spoilage | 500 |
| | 7,500 |
| Conversion cost per unit | x  $9 |
| | $67,500 |

*Note:* Cost of spoiled units are assigned to units completed and transferred out; therefore, they are included in the E.F.U. computation.

14. (b) Activity based costing identifies the activities or transactions that cause costs to be incurred (cost drivers). Costs are then assigned to products based upon the product's use of these activities in its production. Multiple cost drivers are usually employed in costing a single product as multiple activities are used in its production.

15. (d) $350,000 direct material purchases.

| | |
|---|---|
| Direct materials used | $300,000 |
| Add: Increase in direct materials inventory | 50,000 |
| Purchases of direct materials | $350,000 |

16. (b) Generally, an overtime premium is charged to overhead, and allocated to all jobs, as the arbitrary scheduling of jobs should not affect the cost of jobs worked on during overtime. However, if an overtime premium is due to a specific job or customer's requirements, it is appropriately charged to that job, increasing its costs.

17. (c) The cost of electricity for a manufacturing plant (fixed and variable) would be classified as overhead, which is an element of conversion costs (direct material and direct labor) and a product cost. A period cost is a noninventoriable cost which is deducted as an expense in the current period.

18. (b) Computation of CGS Using Manufacturing Costs

| | | |
|---|---|---|
| Raw Material Beginning Inventory | | $ 22,000 |
| Purchases | | 300,000 |
| | | 322,000 |
| Less: Ending Inventory | | 30,000 |
| Cost of Materials Used | | $292,000 |
| | | |
| Work in Process Beginning Inventory | | 40,000 |
| Direct Material | | 292,000 |
| Direct Labor | | 120,000 |
| Overhead: | | |
| Indirect Labor | 60,000 | |
| Taxes & Depr. on Factory | 20,000 | |
| Utilities chgd. to Factory | | |
| 60% × 50,000 | 30,000 | 110,000 |
| | | 562,000 |
| Less: Ending Inv. of WIP | | 48,000 |
| Cost of Goods Manufactured | | $514,000 |
| | | |
| Finished Goods Beg. Inv. | | 25,000 |
| Add: Cost of Goods Mfg. | | 514,000 |
| | | 539,000 |
| Less: Fin. Goods End. Inv. | | 18,000 |
| Cost of Goods Sold | | $521,000 |

19. (c) Process-costing techniques should be used when the product is composed of mass-produced, homogeneous units. This does not preclude the use of standard costing (d). Answer (a) refers to job order costing.

20. (d) In the production process, storing raw materials until they are needed represents a non-value added step, whereas engineering, heat treatment or drilling represents improving the product. In addition, storage requires handling costs, cost of holding inventory, possible breakage or misappropriation, while inventory simply waits for use at a later time.

21. (c) Actual volume: Less than expected; Actual fixed cost: Greater than expected.

Overhead is applied to production with a predetermined overhead rate. The amount of overhead applied is equal to the predetermined rate times the actual or standard activity base for the volume of production achieved.

Underapplied overhead means that actual overhead costs were greater than the overhead applied to production (work-in-process). Therefore, either an increase in overhead costs or a decrease in the level of production (activity base) would result in underapplied overhead.

22. (b) This reflects the fact that the equivalent units include (1) those beginning inventory units that were completed, (2) the completed units all of whose costs were incurred in the current period, and (3) the partially completed units in ending inventory.

23. (d) The difference between FIFO and Weighted Average equivalent finished units (EFU) is the EFU of beginning inventory. Under the FIFO method, the EFU of beginning work-in-process inventory are excluded from the EFU computation for the period; however, under the Weighted Average method, these EFU are included in the EFU calculation.

For January, the EFU for Weighted Average and FIFO would be the same because there was no beginning inventory of work-in-process.

For February, the beginning inventory of work-in-process (January's ending inventory) would cause the Weighted Average EFU to be greater than the FIFO EFU for the month.

24. (d) 8,000 material; 4,800 conversion costs
Computation of equivalent units for material:

|  |  | FIFO | W/A |  |
|---|---|---|---|---|
| Finished |  | 36,000 | 36,000 |  |
| + Ending WIP | (1) | 6,000 | 6,000 |  |
|  |  | 42,000 | 42,000 |  |
| – Beginning WIP | (1) | 8,000 | — |  |
|  |  | 34,000 | 42,000 | + 8,000 |

(1) Material added at the beginning of the process

Computation of equivalent units for conversion costs:

|  | FIFO | W/A |  |
|---|---|---|---|
| Finished | 36,000 | 36,000 |  |
| + Ending WIP—6,000 × 80% | 4,800 | 4,800 |  |
|  | 40,800 | 40,800 |  |
| – Beginning WIP—8,000 × 60% | 4,800 | — |  |
|  | 36,000 | 40,800 | + 4,800 |

25. (a) $39,600 and $3,400

| Completed goods 90,000 × ($.24 + $.20) = | $39,600 |
|---|---|
| Goods in process | 3,400 |
| Total costs ($24,000 + $19,000) = | $43,000 |

The above is all that is needed for the answer, because the total costs are $43,000, the goods in process are $3,400. Computation of goods in process:

Material 10,000 × .24 (100%) = $2,400
Conversion Cost 10,000 × .20 ( 50%) = 1,000
$3,400

26. (c) 125,000; 105,000; 121,000.

|  | |
|---|---|
| B.I. WIP | 25,000 |
| + Transferred in | 100,000 |
| Total units | 125,000 (Also, E.U. – Transferred in)) |
| – E.I. WIP | 20,000 |
| Finished units | 105,000 |

Use finished units plus ending inventory of WIP to compute equivalent units.

|  | *M* | *C.C.* | *Transferred-in* |
|---|---|---|---|
| Finished | 105,000 | 105,000 | 105,000 |
| E.I. WIP 20,000 × 0% | — | | |
| 20,000 × 80% | | 16,000 | |
| 20,000 × 100% | | | 20,000 |
| | 105,000 | 121,000 | 125,000 |

27. (c) EFU Computation:

| | |
|---|---|
| Finished | 100,000 |
| EFU in ending inventory (60,000 × 50% complete) | 30,000 |
| Less: EFU in beginning inventory (25,000 × 80% complete) | (20,000) |
| | 110,000 |

| Unit cost computation: | Period Cost | ÷ | EFU | = | Unit Cost |
|---|---|---|---|---|---|
| | 143,000 | | 110,000 | | 1.30 |

Cost of ending WIP = $1.30 × 30,000 EFU = $39,000

Note ending inventory of 60,000 units = 25,000 B.I. + 135,000 started – 100,000 completed.

28. (d) Rework Cost:

| | |
|---|---|
| Labor Cost (100 units × $2) | $200 |
| Overhead ($200 D.L × 1.5) | 300 |
| | $500 |

The cost of rework should be charged to the factory overhead control account, as the predetermined rate used to apply overhead (cost jobs) during the period includes an estimate for such costs.

29. (d) The cost of normal spoilage ($60,000) is a product cost which should be absorbed by the good units produced and included in the recorded cost of both work-in-process and finished goods inventories.

The cost of abnormal spoilage ($30,000) is a period cost and should be expensed in the current period.

30. (a)

| | |
|---|---|
| Direct material purchased | $42,000 |
| Add: Decrease in direct material inventory | 3,000 |
| Direct materials used | $45,000 |
| Direct labor | 30,000 |
| Total prime cost | $75,000 |

31. (c)

| | |
|---|---|
| Direct labor | $30,000 |
| Overhead applied ($10 × 4,000 hours) | 40,000 |
| Total conversion costs | $70,000 |

Direct labor hours = $30,000 direct labor costs divided by $7.50 direct labor rate per hour = 4,000 hours.

32. (a)

| | |
|---|---:|
| Direct materials used | $ 45,000 |
| Direct labor | 30,000 |
| Overhead applied | 40,000 |
| Manufacturing costs of the period | $115,000 |
| Add: Decrease in work-in-process | 3,000 |
| Cost of goods manufactured | $118,000 |

33. (c)

| | |
|---|---:|
| Fixed maintenance cost per month ($7,200 ÷ 12) | $ 600 |
| Variable cost (20,000 hrs. × $.60) | 12,000 |
| Total maintenance cost budget for July | $12,600 |

34. (d)

| | Materials | Conversion |
|---|---:|---:|
| Finished Unit | 2,100 | 2,100 |
| Ending Inventory | | |
| 400 × 100% | 400 | |
| 400 × 25% | | 100 |
| Less: Beginning Inventory | | |
| 500 × 100% | (500) | |
| 500 × 40% | | (200) |
| E.F.U. (FIFO) | 2,000 | 2,000 |

35. (b)

| | |
|---|---:|
| Raw materials purchased | $430,000 |
| Decrease in raw materials inventory | 15,000 |
| Cost of raw materials used | $445,000 |
| Direct labor | 200,000 |
| Factory overhead | 300,000 |
| Cost of goods manufactured | $945,000 * |
| Increase in finished goods inventory | (35,000) |
| Cost of goods sold | $910,000 |

Freight-out is a selling expense (period cost) and therefore does not enter into the computations.

*There was no change in the work in process inventory to be included in the cost of goods manufactured computation. Beginning and ending work-in-process inventory was "0".

36. (c)

| | | |
|---|---|---:|
| Work-in-process March 1 | | $ 2,000 |
| Add: | Direct materials | 12,000 |
| | Direct labor | 8,000 |
| | Factory overhead | 6,400 |
| Less: | Transferred to finished goods | (24,000) |
| Work-in-process March 31 | | $ 4,400 |
| Less | Direct labor | ( 1,000) |
| | Factory overhead ($1,000 × 80%) | ( 800) |
| Direct materials, Job #9 | | $ 2,600 |

37. (d)

| | |
|---|---:|
| Direct material purchased | $ 84,000 |
| Add: decrease in direct materials inventory | 6,000 |
| Direct materials used | $ 90,000 |
| Direct labor | 60,000 |
| Total prime cost | $150,000 |

38. (b)

| | |
|---|---:|
| Direct labor costs | $ 60,000 |
| Overhead applied ($10 × 8,000 hrs) | 80,000 |
| Total conversion costs | $140,000 |
| Direct labor hours = $60,000 ÷ $7.50 = 8,000 | |

39. (d) 
| | |
|---|---:|
| Work in process 3/1/89 | $ 18,000 |
| Add: Direct materials (used) | 90,000 |
|     Direct labor | 60,000 |
|     Applied overhead | 80,000 |
| Total production costs | $248,000 |
| Less: Work in process 3/31/89 | (12,000) |
| Cost of goods manufactured | $236,000 |

40. (d) 
| | |
|---|---:|
| Finished units | 36,000 |
| Ending inventory (10,000 × 100%) | 10,000 |
| E.F.U. - Average | 46,000 |

**Note**: Materials are added at the beginning of the process in dept. M; therefore, the units in the ending inventory are 100% complete as to materials.

Normal spoilage is a cost of good production (product cost); therefore, units of normal spoilage (or loss) are excluded from the E.F.U. computation.

41. (c) Activity based costing assigns costs to products based upon the product's use of activities (cost drivers) which caused the costs to be incurred. Costs are accumulated (homogeneous cost pools) by activities (cost drivers) rather than by department or function as in more traditional costing systems. Nonvalue-added activities (cost drivers), such as movement of product, storage, set up, and inspection are minimized or eliminated without adversely affecting the product or service.

42. (a) Just-in-time strongly advocates the elimination of non-value added operations. In contrast with answers (b), (c) and (d), JIT recommends reducing the number of suppliers (for higher quality and consistency); minimizing the standard delivery quantity (less goods on hand to store and move); and increasing the number of deliveries (again decreasing inventory, and other non-value added steps).

43. (d) A loom operator's salary or wages would be classified as direct labor, as the loom operator works directly on the manufacture of the product. The salary or wages of factory foremen and machine mechanics are indirect labor costs and appropriately classified as overhead.

44. (c) When indirect materials were initially purchased, they would be charged to the stores control. However, when they are issued to a production department, they would be charged (increased) to the factory overhead control account.

45. (c) 
| *E.F.U. Computation* | *Materials* | *Conversion* |
|---|---:|---:|
| Finished units | 12,000 | 12,000 |
| Ending inventory | | |
|   6,000 units × 100% | 6,000 | |
|   6,000 units × 50% | | 3,000 |
| Wt. Avg. E.F.U. | 18,000 | 15,000 |

Unit Cost Computation:

| | *Beg. Inv. Cost* | + | *Period Cost* | = | *Total Cost ÷ EFU* | = | *Unit Cost* |
|---|---:|---|---:|---|---|---|---:|
| Materials | $9,600 | | $15,600 | | $25,200 ÷ 18,000 | = | $1.40 |
| Conversion | $4,800 | | $14,400 | | $19,200 ÷ 15,000 | = | 1.28 |
| Total Cost per E.F.U. | | | | | | | $2.68 |

46. (b) If the gross profit of the product is 60%, then its cost must be 40% (1.00 less 60%). Since the dollar cost of the product is $5.00 per unit, then that must equal 40% of the selling price. $5.00 divided by 40% = $12.50.

47. (d) Wages paid to factory machine operators are classified as direct labor. Direct labor is an element of prime costs (DM & DL) and an element of conversion costs (DL & OH).

48. (a) Property taxes on a manufacturing plant are classified as overhead which is an element of conversion costs (DL & OH). They would not be a period cost (which is an expense) as they are included as a product cost in overhead.

49. (a) Because Material G is added when a batch is 60% complete, the units in ending inventory, which are only 50% complete, would not have any Material G and would not be included in the computation of EFU for Material G. The ending inventory would be included in the computation of conversion costs (DL + overhead) EFU as they are 50% complete in process 2.

EFU computation:

|  | Finished units | # units |
| --- | --- | --- |
| + | Ending inventory EFU | # units × % complete |
|  | EFU average | |
| – | Beginning inventory EFU | # units × % complete |
|  | EFU  FIFO | |

50. (c) EFU Computations:

|  | Finished units | # |
| --- | --- | --- |
| + | Ending Inventory EFU | # × 50% complete |
|  | EFU average | |
| – | Beginning Inventory EFU | -0- |
|  | EFU FIFO | |

As there is no beginning inventory, average EFU are equal to FIFO EFU and the answer to this question is the same for both methods.

As there is no beginning inventory, and ending inventory is 50% complete:
1. EFU is less than units placed in process (all units started have not been completed) -Answer (c).
2. EFU are less than units started; therefore answer (a) is incorrect.
3. EFU are greater than units completed; therefore answers (b) and (d) are incorrect.

51. (c) The cost of electricity for a manufacturing plant (fixed and variable) would be classified as overhead which is an element of conversion costs (DL & OH) and is a product cost.
**Note**: This cost would not be a period cost which is an expense.

52. (a) Flexible budgeting is a reporting system wherein the planned level of activity is adjusted to the actual level of activity before the budget to actual comparison report is prepared. It may be appropriately employed for any item which is affected by the level of activity (such as production, administration, and marketing).

53. (a) EFU Computations:

|  | Finished units | # |
| --- | --- | --- |
| + | Ending Inventory EFU | # × 100% complete |
|  | EFU average | |
| – | Beginning Inventory EFU | -0- |
|  | EFU FIFO | |

As there is no beginning inventory, average EFU are equal to FIFO EFU and the answer to this question is the same for both methods.

As there is no beginning inventory and ending inventory is 100% complete:
1. EFU are equal to the units started (answer c) and therefore answer (c) is incorrect.
2. EFU are greater than units completed; therefore, answers (b) and (d) are incorrect.

54. (a) Product quality is best indicated by the returns and allowances made to customers, as well as their complaints about the product. The production cycle time refers only to the efficiency, not the quality.

55. (d)

| | Units | | % complete | | Unit cost | | Total cost |
|---|---|---|---|---|---|---|---|
| Materials | 4,000 | × | 0% | × | $1 | = | $ 0 |
| Conversion | 4,000 | × | 40% | × | $3 | = | 4,800 |
| Transferred in | 4,000 | × | 100% | × | $5 | = | 20,000 |
| | | | | | | | $24,800 |

56. (b) $5,200—Direct materials, Job #5.

| Work in process, April 1, 1992 | | $ 4,000 |
|---|---|---|
| Add: | Direct materials | 24,000 |
| | Direct labor | 16,000 |
| | Factory overhead | 12,800 |
| Less: | Transferred to finished goods | (48,000) |
| Work-in-process, April 30, 1992 | | $ 8,800 |
| Less: | Direct labor | (2,000) |
| | Overhead ($2,000 × 80%) | (1,600) |
| Direct materials, Job #5 | | $ 5,200 |

57. (d) Flexible budgeting is a reporting system wherein the planned level of activity is adjusted to the actual level of activity before the budget comparison report is prepared. It may appropriately be employed for any item which is affected by the level of activity (such as direct labor and overhead).

58. (a) When indirect materials are *purchased* they are charged to (increase) store supplies (an inventory account). When indirect materials are *used* they are charged to factory overhead control and credited against (decrease) store supplies.

59. (c)

| Beginning inventory, finished goods | $120,000 |
|---|---|
| Cost of goods manufactured | 520,000 |
| Cost of goods available for sale | $640,000 |
| Less ending inventory, finished goods | (110,000) |
| Cost of goods sold | $530,000 |

OR

| Cost of goods manufactured | $520,000 |
|---|---|
| Add: Decrease in finished goods inventory | |
| ($120,000 – $110,000) | 10,000 |
| | $530,000 |

60. (c)

| Producing Dept. | % Services Provided | Allocation % | Allocated Maintenance Cost |
|---|---|---|---|
| A | 40 | 50% | $10,000 |
| B | 40 | 50% | 10,000 |
| | 80 | | $20,000 |

As service department costs are allocated directly to producing departments, without allocation to other service departments, only the percentage of services provided to the producing departments A and B are relevant for the allocation.

61. (c) The cost of normal spoilage is a product cost which should be absorbed by the good units produced and included in the recorded cost of both work-in-process and finished goods inventories.
The cost of abnormal spoilage ($9,000) is a period cost and should be expensed in the current period.

62. (d)  Predetermined   =   Budget estimate overhead cost
          Rate               Budget estimate activity base

63. (b) Applied factory overhead is charged (debited) to work-in-process and credited to the factory overhead control account. This increases work-in-process inventory and decreases the control account. Factory overhead is **not** applied directly to finished goods or cost of goods sold, but is included in the cost of the units transferred to these accounts.

64. (c) $46,100

| | *Maintenance* | *Power* | *Education* | *Technology* |
|---|---|---|---|---|
| Costs incurred (to allocate) | 99,000 | 54,000 | | |
| | | | | |
| Allocation of Maintenance Costs: | | | | |
|     Power 20% x 99,000 | (19,800) | 19,800 | | |
|     Education 30% x 99,000 | (29,700) | | 29,700 | |
|     Technology 50% x 99,000 | (49,500) | | | 49,500 |
| | --0-- | 73,800 | | |
| | | | | |
| Allocation of Power Costs: | | | | |
|   * Maintenance | --0-- | | | |
|   ** Education 2/9 x 73,800 | | (16,400) | 16,400 | |
|      Technology 7/9 x 73,800 | | (57,400) | | 57,400 |
| | | --0-- | 46,100 | 106,900 |

\* Once a service department's cost is allocated, no reallocation to that department is made under the step method.

\*\* Maintenance department service percentage (10%) is not used as its cost has already been allocated.

Service percentage:  Education     20
                     Technology    70
                        Total      90
Education percentage = 2/9.

Under the step method, generally the service department with the greatest inter-service department percentage or cost is allocated first.

# Chapter Fifteen
# Solutions to Cost Accounting Problems
# Actual Cost, Job Order and Process

## NUMBER 1

a.

*Zeus Company*
**SUMMARY OF EQUIVALENT UNITS OF POLYPLAST MANUFACTURED**
*For the Month of December 19X1*

| | | Materials | | Labor and Overhead | |
| | Units | Per-centage | Equiv. Units | Per-centage | Equiv. Units |
|---|---|---|---|---|---|
| Units completed: | | | | | |
| From beginning inventory | 3,000 | 33 1/3% | 1,000 | 50% | 1,500 |
| From current production | | | | | |
| (19,000 – 3,000) | 16,000 | 100 | 16,000 | 100 | 16,000 |
| Units in process, Dec. 31 | 6,000 | 100 | 6,000 | 75 | 4,500 |
| | | | 23,000 | | 22,000 |

b. 1.

*Zeus Company*
*Fabricating Department*
**TOTAL COSTS TO BE ACCOUNTED FOR**
*For the Month of December 19X1*

| | |
|---|---|
| In process, December 1 | $ 52,000 |
| Added during month: | |
| Materials | 92,000 |
| Labor | 154,000 |
| Overhead | 198,000 |
| Total costs to be accounted for | $496,000 |

**Computation of Cost of Materials Added During December**

| | Units | Unit Cost | Amount |
|---|---|---|---|
| Miracle Mix: | | | |
| Beginning inventory | 62,000 | $1.00 | $62,000 |
| From December 12 purchase | 21,200 | 1.25 | 26,500 |
| | 83,200 | | 88,500 |
| Bypro—from beginning inventory | 50,000 | .07 | 3,500 |
| | | | $92,000 |

**Computation of Cost of Overhead Added During December**

| | | |
|---|---|---|
| Fabricating department overhead | | $132,000 |
| Allocation of service department overhead: | | |
| Building maintenance | | |
| (75,000 ÷ 112,500 × $45,000) | $30,000 | |
| Timekeeping and personnel | | |
| (180/300 × $27,500) | 16,500 | |
| Other (1/2 × $39,000) | 19,500 | 66,000 |
| | | $198,000 |

2.

*Zeus Company*
*Fabricating Department*
**UNIT COSTS FOR EQUIVALENT UNITS MANUFACTURED**
*For the Month of December 19X1*

| | |
|---|---|
| Materials ($92,000 ÷ 23,000) | $ 4 |
| Labor ($154,000 ÷ 22,000) | 7 |
| Overhead ($198,000 ÷ 22,000) | 9 |
| | $20 |

3.

*Zeus Company*
*Fabricating Department*
**TRANSFERS TO FINISHING DEPARTMENT AND ENDING WORK IN PROCESS**
*For the Month of December 19X1*

| | | |
|---|---|---|
| Transfers to finishing department: | | |
| Units started last month: | | |
| Costs last month | $52,000 | |
| Materials (1,000 × $4) | 4,000 | |
| Labor (1,500 × $7) | 10,500 | |
| Overhead (1,500 × $9) | 13,500 | $ 80,000 |
| Units started this month (16,000 × $20) | | 320,000 |
| | | 400,000 |
| Work in process, December 31: | | |
| Materials (6,000 × $4) | 24,000 | |
| Labor (4,500 × $7) | 31,500 | |
| Overhead (4,500 × $9) | 40,500 | 96,000 |
| Total costs accounted for | | $496,000 |

## NUMBER 2

An objective in selecting the base for Stein Company's predetermined annual factory overhead rate is to ensure the application of factory overhead in reasonable proportion to a beneficial or causal relationship to products. Ordinarily, the base selected should be closely related to functions represented by the applied overhead cost. If factory overhead costs are predominantly labor oriented, such as supervision and indirect labor, the proper base would probably be direct labor hours. If factory overhead costs are predominantly related to the costs incurred in the ownership and operation of the machinery, the proper base would probably be machine hours.

Another objective in selecting the base is to minimize clerical cost and effort relative to the benefits attained. When two or more bases provide approximately the same applied overhead cost to specific units of production, the simplest base should be used.

A predetermined annual factory overhead rate provides a feasible method of computing product costs promptly enough to serve management needs, such as identifying inefficiencies and minimizing month-to-month distortions in unit costs created by uneven expenditure patterns.

## NUMBER 3

**a.** The type of cost system used by a company will be determined by the type of manufacturing operations performed. A manufacturing company should use a process cost system for product costing purposes when it continuously mass produces like units; while the production of custom-made or unique goods would indicate a job-order cost system to be more appropriate.

Because there is continuous mass production of like units in a process cost system, the center of attention is the individual process (usually a department). The unit costs by cost category as well as total unit cost for each process (department) are necessary for product costing purposes.

Process costing is often used in industries such as chemicals, food processing, oil, mining, rubber and electrical appliances.

**b.** "Equivalent production" (equivalent units produced) is the term used to identify the number of completed units that would have been produced if all the work performed during the period had been applied to units that were begun and finished during the period. Thus, equivalent production represents the total number of units that could have been started and finished during the period, given the same effort, assuming no beginning or ending work-in-process inventories.

The work of each producing department must be expressed in terms of a common denominator; this denominator represents the total work of a department or process in terms of fully completed units. Units in process of production at the beginning and end of the period should not be counted the same as units started and completed during the period when determining the equivalent amount of production for a period. Each partially completed unit has received only part of the attention and effort that a finished unit has received and, therefore, each partially completed unit should be weighted accordingly.

The equivalent production figure computed represents the number of equivalent whole units for which materials, labor, and overhead were issued, used, or incurred during a period. The cost of each element of materials, labor, and overhead is divided by the appropriate equivalent production figure to determine the unit cost for each element. Should units be at a different stage of completion with respect to each type of cost element, then a separate equivalent production figure must be computed for that cost element.

**c.** Normal spoilage is the spoilage that arises under normal efficient operating conditions; i.e., it is inherent in the production process and is uncontrollable in the short run. Abnormal spoilage is the spoilage that is not expected to arise under normal efficient operating conditions; i.e., it is not inherent in the production process and is usually considered as avoidable, or controllable, by management. Thus, by definition, the critical factor in distinguishing between normal and abnormal spoilage is the degree of controllability of units spoiled. Any spoilage that occurs during a production process functioning within the expected usual range of performance is considered to be normal spoilage. Any spoilage occurring in amounts in excess of the defined usual range is considered abnormal (controllable) spoilage.

Conceptually, the cost of normal spoilage should be included in the cost of good units produced because of its association with normal production. Likewise, cost of abnormal spoilage should be accounted for as a loss because of its abnormal (unusual) nature. The cost of abnormal spoilage should be separately identified as a loss on reports for management.

For practical reasons, there may be no distinction made between normal and abnormal spoilage in reports for management. The primary reason for not distinguishing between types of spoilage is that it is sometimes very difficult (or impossible) to distinguish between normal and abnormal spoilage. The production process may be relatively new or the process may be altered often enough to make it impractical or too costly to distinguish between normal or abnormal spoilage. Whenever possible, though, the distinction between types of spoilage should be made and accounted for as discussed in the preceding paragraphs.

**d.** The primary difference between the FIFO method and the weighted-average method of process costing is in the treatment of the cost of the beginning work-in-process inventory. When applying the FIFO method the cost of the beginning work-in-process inventory is kept separate from the cost of production of the current period.

When determining the FIFO cost of units completed and transferred to the next department or to finished goods, the cost of the beginning work-in-process inventory plus the cost necessary to complete the beginning work-in-process units are added together. The sum of these two cost totals is the cost assigned to the units in the beginning work-in-process inventory that are transferred out. Units started and completed during the period are assigned costs on the basis of costs incurred during the period for the equivalent units produced during that period.

In applying the FIFO method, each department is regarded as a separate accounting unit. Thus, the application of the FIFO method in practice is modified to the extent that subsequent departments usually combine all transferred-in costs into one amount, even though they could identify and separately account for the costs relating to the preceding department's beginning inventory and the costs relating to the preceding department's units started and completed during the period.

The weighted-average method of process costing is simpler to apply than the FIFO method primarily because the beginning work-in-process inventory is considered to be part of current production. In applying the weighted-average method, the beginning work-in-process inventory costs are combined with current costs even though some of the production was begun prior to the current period. When equivalent units are determined, work done on the beginning inventory in a preceding period is regarded as if it were done in the current period.

The weighted-average method is applied by adding the beginning work-in-process inventory costs to the production costs incurred during the current period. Then unit costs are determined by dividing the sum of these costs by the equivalent units produced, including the units in the department's beginning work-in-process inventory. The cost of all units transferred out of a department (process) during the period is the product of the number of units completed multiplied by the average cost to produce a unit.

# NUMBER 4

**Part a.**

*The Rebecca Corporation*
**STATEMENT OF COSTS OF GOODS MANUFACTURED**
*For the Month Ended October 31*

| | |
|---|---:|
| Materials inventory, October 1 | $16,200 |
| Purchases | 20,000 |
| Materials available | 36,200 |
| Less: Materials inventory, October 31 | 17,000 |
| Materials used in production | 19,200 |
| Direct labor (3,300 hrs. × $5.00) | 16,500 |
| Factory overhead applied (3,300 hrs. × $2.60) | 8,580 |
| Total current manufacturing costs | 44,280 |
| Work-in-process inventory, October 1 | 3,600 |
| Total manufacturing costs | 47,880 |
| Less: Work-in-process inventory, October 31 | 8,120 |
| Cost of goods manufactured | $39,760 |

**Part b.**

*Lakeview Corporation Assembling Department*
**COSTS OF PRODUCTION REPORT**
*For the Month Ended June 30*

| Description | Total | Trans-<br>ferred in | Direct<br>Materials | Direct<br>Labor | Factory<br>Overhead |
|---|---|---|---|---|---|
| Physical units to be accounted for | | | | | |
| Beginning inventory | 2,000 | | | | |
| Transferred in | 10,000 | | | | |
| Units to be accounted for | 12,000 | | | | |
| | | | | | |
| Equivalent units of production | | | | | |
| Transferred out | 8,000 | 8,000 | 8,000 | 8,000 | 8,000 |
| Ending inventory* | 4,000 | 4,000 | 3,600 | 2,800 | 1,400 |
| Equivalent units | 12,000 | 12,000 | 11,600 | 10,800 | 9,400 |

*4,000 * percentage of completion.

| | | | | | |
|---|---|---|---|---|---|
| Manufacturing costs | | | | | |
| Beginning inventory | $ 64,700 | $ 32,000 | $ 20,000 | $ 7,200 | $ 5,500 |
| Current - June | 310,000 | 160,000 | 96,000 | 36,000 | 18,000 |
| Total manufacturing costs | $374,700 | $192,000 | $116,000 | $43,200 | $23,500 |
| | | | | | |
| Cost per equivalent unit* | $32.50 | $16.00 | $10.00 | $4.00 | $2.50 |

*Total manufacturing cost % equivalent units.

| | | | | | |
|---|---|---|---|---|---|
| Allocation of total costs | | | | | |
| Amount of ending | | | | | |
| work-in-process | $114,700 | $ 64,000 | $ 36,000 | $11,200 | $ 3,500 |
| Amount transferred out* | 260,000 | 128,000 | 80,000 | 32,000 | 20,000 |
| Total cost | $374,700 | $192,000 | $116,000 | $43,200 | $23,500 |

*8,000 * equivalent unit cost.

# NUMBER 5

1. The weighted-average method of process costing combines beginning work in process inventory costs with costs of the new period by adding the cost of the work in process inventory at the beginning of the period to the costs of the new period.

2. The weighted-average method of process costing would be inappropriate when beginning and ending inventories change radically from month to month and conversion costs per unit change radically from month to month.

3. The weighted-average method of process costing is generally easier to use than the first-in, first-out method primarily because the beginning work in process inventory is averaged in as part of current production. Furthermore, if several unit cost figures are used at the same time, extensive detail is required in the first-in, first-out method which can lead to complex procedures and even inaccuracy; and under such conditions the weighted-average method leads to more satisfactory cost computations.

The weighted-average method of process costing averages out uneven but expected cost incurrences over the entire period. This will reduce the fluctuations in unit costs and reflect operating experience for the period as a whole.

4. The units of the work in process inventory at the end of the period would be multiplied by one quarter (the portion complete as to conversion costs). The result would then be multiplied by the conversion cost per equivalent unit to arrive at the conversion cost portion of the ending work in process inventory.

# Chapter Sixteen
# Cost Accounting: Joint Products and Standard Costs

# Chapter Sixteen
# Cost Accounting: Joint Products and Standard Costs

## JOINT PRODUCTS

Joint products are two or more products of more than nominal value produced simultaneously in the same processing operation. Because the joint products are produced from the same operation, the cost of production must be allocated to the products on an estimated basis. The acceptable methods of allocation are:

### 1. The relative sales value method

Hilow and Hilee are produced simultaneously at a cost of $54,000 in the extracting operation. 15,000 gallons of Hilow and 22,500 gallons of Hilee sell for 1.50 and 2.00 per gallon, respectively. Allocate the cost of production.

| | | |
|---|---|---|
| Sales value Hilow | $15,000 \times \$1.50 =$ | $22,500 |
| Sales value Hilee | $22,500 \times \$2.00 =$ | 45,000 |
| Total Sales Value | | $67,500 |

Cost of producing Hilow
$$\frac{\$22,500}{\$67,500} \times \$54,000 = \$18,000$$

Cost of producing Hilee
$$\frac{\$45,000}{\$67,500} \times \$54,000 = \$36,000$$

Use of this method produces the same percentage of gross profit.

### 2. Unit of measurement

Joint costs are allocated based on units, pounds, tons or gallons, etc. Applying unit of measurement to Hilow and Hilee would result in the following cost allocation:

Hilow—15,000 gallons
Hilee—22,500 gallons
  Total 37,500

$$\text{Hilow } \frac{15,000}{37,500} \times \$54,000 = \$21,600$$

$$\text{Hilee } \frac{22,500}{37,500} \times \$54,000 = \$32,400$$

### 3. Assignment of weights

This method is quite arbitrary whereby consideration is given to such factors as volume, selling price, technical engineering and marketing processes.

### 4. Profit contribution method

Costs are allocated based on the profit margin or contribution remaining after deduction of all direct costs and expenses from the selling price.

## Joint Costs—Processing After Split-Off

Frequently, joint products must pass through one or more processes after split-off with other joint products. The relative sales value may be unknown at point of split-off or because of the extensive additional processing required to make the product salable, may be difficult to determine. It is recommended that costs incurred after joint processing be applied as reductions in revenue on a dollar-for-dollar basis and the remaining revenue used as a basis for assignment of cost.

**Case example**: Products X and Y are produced in Department 1. Product X is further processed in Department 2 and Y is further processed in Department 3. Cost data for the three departments are:

| | | Product | | |
|---|---|---|---|---|
| Department | X | | Y | Total Cost |
| 1 | Joint | | Joint | $36,000 |
| 2 | $ 8,000 | | | 8,000 |
| 3 | | | $19,000 | 19,000 |
| | | | | $63,000 |
| Sales Value | $36,000 | | $54,000 | |

**Solution**: Adjustment of Sales Value

| | X | Y |
|---|---|---|
| Sales Value | $36,000 | $54,000 |
| Less: Incremental Cost | 8,000 | 19,000 |
| Adjusted Relative Sales Value | $28,000 | $35,000 |

Assigned to X $\dfrac{\$28,000}{\$28,000 + \$35,000} = \dfrac{28}{63} = 4/9$

Assigned to Y $\dfrac{35}{63} = 5/9$

**Joint Dept. 1 costs assigned**

| | | |
|---|---|---|
| X - 4/9 × $36,000 = | $16,000 | |
| Y - 5/9 × $36,000 = | 20,000 | |
| Total joint costs | $36,000 | |

## By-Products

A by-product is an item of relatively small value produced incidental to the production or manufacture of one or more main products.

The recovery value of by-products may be treated as
1.  Other income
2.  Reduction of total production cost of the main product(s).
3.  Replacement cost method—only applicable to those situations where the by-product is used within the plant eliminating the need to purchase materials from suppliers. Production costs of the main product are reduced accordingly.

Bilow, a by-product, is produced by the Extracting Department along with Hilow and Hilee. In March $370 was received from Bilow sales. Journal Entries:

Method 1

| | | |
|---|---|---|
| Cash | $370 | |
| Other income | | $370 |

Method 2

| | | |
|---|---|---|
| Cash | $370 | |
| Work in Process, Extracting | | $370 |

Method 3, except that Bilow is used to replace material in the Foundry.

| | | |
|---|---|---|
| WIP, Foundry | $370 | |
| WIP, Extracting | | $370 |

# STANDARD COSTS

## Variance Analysis

Standard cost systems are used because it is relatively easy to assign uniform costs to the product and the use of standards gives management a yardstick by which performance can be evaluated. In most standard systems all charges to Work-in-Process are at standard. A typical cost card for one unit of product may be as follows:

*Cost Card-Standard*
*One Unit of Product G*

| | |
|---|---|
| Material 4 lbs. @ $1.50 | $ 6.00 |
| Labor 2 hrs. @ $4.00 | 8.00 |
| Overhead $2 per labor hour | 4.00 |
| Total | $18.00 |

Other Information:

| | |
|---|---|
| Actual Units Produced | 9,000 |
| Actual Materials Used | 38,000 lbs. |
| Actual Material Cost | $55,100 |
| Actual Labor Used | 18,500 hrs. @ $4.10 per hr. |
| Actual Overhead | $38,600 |

From this information we can compute material and labor variances.

### Material

| Units | | Price | | Variances Debit | Credit |
|---|---|---|---|---|---|
| Actual | × | Actual | | | |
| 38,000 | × | $1.45 | = $55,100 | | |
| **Price Variance** | | | | | (38,000 × .05) |
| Actual | × | Standard | | | |
| 38,000 | × | $1.50 | = $57,000 | | $1,900 |
| **Quantity/Usage Variance** | | | | (2,000 × 1.50) | |
| Standard | × | Standard | | | |
| (9,000 × 4) | | | | | |
| 36,000 | × | $1.50 | = $54,000 | $3,000 | |
| Net Variance | | | | $1,100 | |

### Labor

| Hours | | Rate | | | |
|---|---|---|---|---|---|
| Actual | × | Actual | | | |
| 18,500 | × | $4.10 | = $75,850 | | |
| **Rate/Wage Variance** | | | | (18,500 × .10) | |
| Actual | × | Standard | | | |
| 18,500 | × | $4 | = $74,000 | $1,850 | |
| **Efficiency Variance** | | | | (500 × $4) | |
| Standard | × | Standard | | | |
| 18,000 | × | $4 | = $72,000 | $2,000 | |
| Net Variance | | | | $3,850 | |

## Flexible Budgets

For analysis and control purposes, the Company set up a flexible budget for overhead (manufacturing expenses). This budget is used to determine the overhead rate ($2 per labor hour) which is based on normal or expected capacity.

| Manufacturing Expenses | 90% | 95% | 100% | 105% |
|---|---|---|---|---|
| Fixed | $20,000 | $20,000 | $20,000 | $20,000 |
| Variable | 18,000 | 19,000 | 20,000 | 21,000 |
| | 38,000 | 39,000 | 40,000 | 41,000 |
| Labor Hours | 18,000 | 19,000 | 20,000 | 21,000 |
| Overhead Rate | | | $2 | |

This means that management has selected an activity level of 20,000 labor hours on which to base the standard overhead rate. If the company based the rate on **normal capacity**, a moving average of production for several years is probably being used. If the rate is based on **expected capacity**, the rate is based on the amount which the company **expects** to produce during the period, taking into consideration inventory levels at the beginning of the year, sales estimates, and planned inventory levels at year end.

## Mixed Costs—Use of the High-Low Method

It may be necessary to determine whether a cost or group of costs contain both fixed and variable elements and if so, to what extent. There are many statistical methods used for this purpose such as the scattergraph method, least squares, but the simplest is the high and low points method.

This technique requires the use of two levels of cost and related activity. It is assumed that the change in cost from a lower level of activity to a higher level is variable. The variable cost change is translated into variable costs per unit of activity which can be used to compute the total variable cost at any level of activity and consequently the fixed cost. For example:

Machining costs for various parts show costs as follows:

| Activity Level | Costs |
|---|---|
| 3,000 Machine Hours | $10,500 |
| 5,000 Machine Hours | 13,500 |
| | |
| Change in Activity | 2,000 |
| Change in Costs | $3,000 |

Cost Per Machine Hour $\dfrac{\$3,000}{2,000}$ = 1.50 Variable Cost Per Machine Hour

Fixed cost computation:
3,000 level of activity = $10,500 - (3,000 × 1.50) = $6,000
5,000 level of activity = $13,500 - (5,000 × 1.50) = $6,000

Once the computation is made as above for the 3,000 machine hour level, it is not necessary to make the computation for the 5,000 hour or any other level because the result should be the same. The level used need not necessarily be the high and low points, but when using this method keep the following points in mind.

1. The costs used at the levels selected should represent normal conditions.
2. The levels selected should be within the "relevant range" of activity, i.e., the range of activity within which fixed costs are valid.
3. The computation assumes that variable costs are linear, i.e., changes in activity result in uniform changes in cost and graphically would represent a straight line.

## Manufacturing Overhead Variances

Total Variance—Basic Computation

| | |
|---|---|
| Actual Expenses | $38,600 |
| Standard 9,000 × 2 × 2 | 36,000 |
| Total Variance | $ 2,600  UNF |

Regardless of what analysis of overhead is made, the resulting variances must equal the total variance of $2,600.

### Two-Variance Method—Controllable and Volume Variance (see Appendix A)

These overhead variances have been the most frequently required in recent CPA examination problems. All variances are simply the difference between **actual** and **standard** cost, which is called the net variance, divided into two or more variances to furnish management information. In the two-variance method, the controllable variance is a measure of the control of spending and efficient use of resources in that actual costs are compared with the budget at standard hours instead of actual hours. Hence, the term controllable refers to the fact that the two items measured by this variance, efficiency and spending, are controllable within the plant. The volume variance, which is caused by producing more or less than the level at which the overhead rate was computed (normal or expected capacity) is normally beyond the control of the plant and is sometimes referred to as the noncontrollable variance.

_DR_ _CR_

| | |
|---|---|
| Actual | $38,600 |

$600 Controllable UNF

| | |
|---|---|
| Budget at Standard Hours | 38,000 |
| ($20,000 + 18,000 × $1) | |

*2,000 Volume UNF

| | |
|---|---|
| Standard 9,000 × 2 × $2 | 36,000 |

*May also be referred to as capacity or non-controllable variance.

### Three-Variance Method—Budget, Efficiency and Capacity Variance (see Appendix A)

The budget variance is computed at actual activity and for that reason is considered a measure of control of spending. To measure the spending effectiveness of **fixed** and variable elements individually, a breakdown of actual fixed and variable costs is needed, and converts the three variances into four variances. (See the four-variance method which follows.) Note also that a budget variance computed by using actual activity is a better measure of spending effectiveness since the activity base selected (labor hours, machine hours, etc.) is intended to be an indicator of changes in variable costs.

The efficiency variance is a function of either more or less than standard usage of the activity base. The capacity variance is attributable to the over- or under-application of **fixed** costs. For example:

An analysis of the capacity variance may be more clear by breaking down the overhead rate into the fixed and variable components.

| | Cost | Labor Hours | Rate |
|---|---|---|---|
| Fixed | $20,000 | 20,000 | $1.00 |
| Variable | 20,000 | 20,000 | 1.00 |
| | | | $2.00 |

Then compare the manufacturing overhead budget at standard with standard.

| | Hours | Standard Costs | Budget at Standard | Variance |
|---|---|---|---|---|
| Fixed | 18,000 × $1 = | $18,000 | $20,000 | $2,000 |
| Variable | 18,000 × $1 = | 18,000 | 18,000 | —0— |
| Variance | | | | $2,000 |

We can see that the Fixed Costs cause the variance in that the failure to produce at or above the level on which the overhead rate is fixed will produce an unfavorable capacity variance.

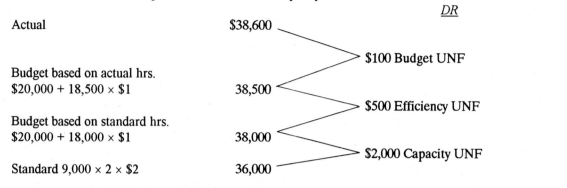

|  |  | *DR* | *CR* |
|---|---|---|---|
| Actual | $38,600 | | |
| | | $100 Budget UNF | |
| Budget based on actual hrs.<br>$20,000 + 18,500 × $1 | 38,500 | | |
| | | $500 Efficiency UNF | |
| Budget based on standard hrs.<br>$20,000 + 18,000 × $1 | 38,000 | | |
| | | $2,000 Capacity UNF | |
| Standard 9,000 × 2 × $2 | 36,000 | | |

Journal entries for the three variance method are as follows:

(1)  Manufacturing expense control (actual)  $38,600
        Indirect costs (material, labor, depreciation)  $38,600

(2)  Work-in-process (standard)  $36,000
        Overhead applied (an accumulation account)  $36,000
  WIP is charged at standard at the end of the period.

(3)  Overhead applied  $36,000
        Manufacturing expense control  $36,000
  To close out overhead applied to manufacturing expense control.

(4) Manufacturing expense control is closed to variance accounts. This entry shows unfavorable variances.
     Budget Variance  $ 100
     Efficiency Variance  500
     Capacity Variance  2,000
        Manufacturing Expense Control  $2,600

(5)  Inventories and cost of goods sold, cost of goods
     sold only or income summary  $2,600
        Budget Variance  $ 100
        Efficiency Variance  500
        Capacity Variance  2,000

If the variances are allocated to the inventories and cost of goods sold, these accounts are converted to actual. If the variances are closed to cost of goods sold only, the inventory accounts are not converted to actual and the current period bears all the effects of such variances. If the variances are charged to expense (income summary), the current period likewise bears the effects of the variances, but with no effect on gross profit. If the variances are material, they should be allocated to all inventories and cost of goods sold.

**Four-Variance Method for Overhead** (See Appendix A)
The four-variance method appeared in the CPA exam for the first time in November 1977. Even the three-variance method has appeared infrequently in the examination in recent years; therefore, it is unknown as to the extent the four-variance method will be tested in the future.

Assume the same facts used to compute the variances by the three-variance method and, in addition, the actual overhead of $38,600 consists of $20,500 of fixed costs and $18,100 of variable costs.

**Fixed Spending, Fixed Volume, Variable Spending and a Variable Efficiency Variance**

Fixed Cost Variances:

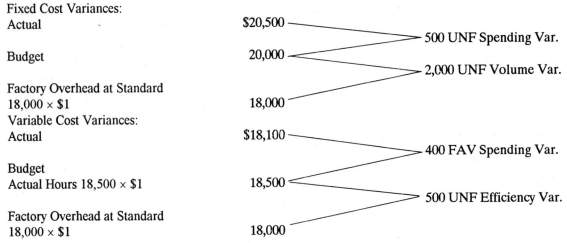

Actual     $20,500

                             500 UNF Spending Var.

Budget     20,000

                             2,000 UNF Volume Var.

Factory Overhead at Standard
$18,000 \times \$1$     18,000

Variable Cost Variances:

Actual     $18,100

                             400 FAV Spending Var.

Budget
Actual Hours $18,500 \times \$1$     18,500

                             500 UNF Efficiency Var.

Factory Overhead at Standard
$18,000 \times \$1$     18,000

The computation of these variances compares to the three-variance method as follows:

| *Three-Variance* | | | | *Four-Variance* | |
|---|---|---|---|---|---|
| | | | | Fixed | 500 UNF |
| Budget (Spending) | | 100 UNF | | | |
| | | | | Variable | 400 FAV |
| Efficiency | | 500 UNF | | Same | |
| Volume or Capacity | | 2,000 UNF | | Same | |

The volume variance is the same in the two, three and four-variance methods. In the four-variance method the Budget Variance is divided into its fixed and variable elements, thus creating two spending variances, whereas the efficiency and volume variances are the same.

## Favorable or Unfavorable Variances

In job order cost overhead was applied to product cost by means of a pre-determined rate. In standard cost systems all the elements of production cost are assigned to product based on a standard established before production begins. Even the most carefully established standards will differ from reality, and after all, the actual cost of the product must be controlling.

Since work-in-process, finished goods and cost of goods sold are assigned standard costs (and even raw materials in some cases) we might say that such accounts are on an estimated or tentative basis. When actual costs are determined, they are compared with standard. These comparisons result in variances. If we have applied to product costs an amount that is less than the actual cost, we must say that the particular cost element, material, labor or overhead is understated. Since these tentative costs flow through work-in-process to finished goods to cost of goods sold, an understatement of these accounts results in an additional debit or charge. We call this additional charge unfavorable since it results in an additional cost added to the product. For example:

| | |
|---|---|
| Cost of Material — Actual | $75,000 |
| Standard Material Cost | 74,000 |
| Unfavorable Variance | $ 1,000 |

Conversely, when costs at standard exceed actual, then product costs have been overstated and the resulting adjustment to actual is a credit and since costs are reduced by a credit, it is favorable. For example:

| | |
|---|---|
| Cost of Labor — Actual | $102,000 |
| Standard Labor Cost | 105,000 |
| Favorable Variance | $ 3,000 |

## Disposition of Variances

Variances enter into the determination of periodic net income by:

   a. closing the variances to the income summary; in effect, the variances are treated as income or expense items.
   b. close the variance to cost of goods sold
   c. allocate the variances to the inventory accounts and cost of goods sold.

Inventories cannot properly be carried at standard unless such standard cost approximates actual costs. Therefore, where the variances are material only, (c) above is a viable option.

## Another Method of Computing Material Price Variance

Because purchasing is a separate and distinct function from manufacturing, some companies compute the price variance on material at the time of purchase. This results in the Stores or Materials account being carried at standard cost and requires an additional computation to compute the usage variance.

**Illustration:**

Pertinent data for Product R

> Purchased—16,000 ft. of plastic @ $1.20
> Requisitioned from stock—12,500 ft.
> Standard price—$1.25 per foot
> Standard usage—5 ft. per unit
> Units produced—2,000—100% complete
>                       500— 80% complete

Compute variances for material.

| Solution: | | *Variance* |
|---|---|---|
| Actual Cost | | |
| 16,000 × $1.20 | $19,200 | |
| Price Variance | | (16,000 × $.05) |
| <u>16,000 × $1.25</u> | 20,000 | 800 FAV |
| | | |
| Actual Usage at Standard Cost | | |
| 12,500 × $1.25 | 15,625 | |
| Usage Variance (2,400 × 5) | | (500 × $1.25) |
| 12,000 × $1.25 | 15,000 | 625 UNF |

*Journal entries:*

| | | | |
|---|---|---|---|
| Material (Stores) | $20,000 | | |
| Price Variance | | $ 800 | |
| Accounts Payable | | 19,200 | |
| Work-in-Process | $15,000 | | |
| Usage Variance | 625 | | |
| Material | | $15,525 | |

**Example:** Convert the Materials and Work-in-Process Account to actual cost based on the above.

**Allocation of Variances**

*Quantity Balances:*

| | | |
|---|---|---|
| Material | 3,500 | × .05 = $175 |
| Work-in-Process | 12,500 | × .05 = 625 |
| Total Purchased | 16,000 | $800 FAV |

| | | |
|---|---|---|
| Material at Standard Price | 3,500 × $1.25 | $4,375 |
| Less: Price Variance Adjustment | | 175 |
| Actual Cost | | $4,200 |

| | |
|---|---|
| Proof: 3,500 units at $1.20 | $4,200 |

| | | |
|---|---|---|
| Work-in-Process at Standard | 12,000 × $1.25 | $15,000 |
| Less: Price Variance Adjustment | | (625) |
| Add: Usage Variance Adjustment | | 625 |
| Actual Cost | | $15,000 |

| | |
|---|---|
| Proof: 12,500 units at $1.20 | $15,000 |

**APPENDIX A**
**OVERHEAD VARIANCE ANALYSIS**

Facts: (1) Actual Overhead—$178,500 ($112,500 Fixed; 66,000 Variable)
(2) Budget—$110,000 plus $.50 per labor hour
(3) Total Overhead Application Rate—$1.50 per hour
(4) Standard labor hours—115,000
(5) Actual labor hours—121,000

(A) Budget based on Standard Hours
$110,000 + 115,000 × $.50 = $167,500
(B) Budget based on Actual Hours
$110,000 + 121,000 × $.50 = $170,500

Standard
115,000 × 1.50
$172,500

**2-Variance Method (Controllable and Noncontrollable)**

Actual Overhead $178,500 .......... $167,500 (A) .......... $172,500

CONTROLLABLE – 11,000 U          NON-CONTROLLABLE OR VOLUME 5,000 F

**3-Variance Method (Spending, Efficiency, Volume Variance)**

$167,500 .......... $172,500

$170,500 (B)          EFFICIENCY VAR. 3,000 U          VOLUME VARIANCE 5,000 F
($110,000 + 121,000 × $.50)

BUDGET (SPENDING) VAR. 8,000 U

**4-Variance Method (The spending variance is divided into a fixed and variable portion.)**

$170,500 .......... $172,500

SPENDING VARIANCES 8,000 U          SAME AS ABOVE

| | | |
|---|---|---|
| FIXED ACTUAL | $112,500 | |
| FIXED STD. | 110,000 | 2,500 U |
| VAR. ACTUAL | 66,000 | |
| VAR. STD. | 60,500 | 5,500 U |
| TOTAL SPENDING VAR. | | $8,000 U |

## APPENDIX B
## COST AND MANAGERIAL ACCOUNTING TERMS

**ABNORMAL SPOILAGE**: Spoilage that does not normally occur in a particular production process.

**ABSORPTION COSTING**: Both fixed and variable costs are assigned to product. Opposed to direct costing in which only variable costs are assigned to product and fixed costs are period costs.

**ACCOUNTING METHOD**: A Capital Budgeting term. Another name for the unadjusted rate of return method. Also called Book Value Method. The increase in future average annual net income from a project divided by the investment.

**BUDGET**: A financial plan for future activity.

**BUDGET VARIANCE**: The difference between actual and budgeted costs. As to overhead, comparison is made at actual production level.

**BY-PRODUCTS**: One or more products of relatively small value which are obtained during production of the main product.

**CAPITAL BUDGETING**: Financial evaluation procedure for proposed or planned capital outlays.

**CASH BUDGET**: A budget on a cash basis to determine projected cash position.

**CASH FLOW**: The excess of cash received over cash disbursed (or vice versa) over a period.

**CONTRIBUTION MARGIN**: Selling price less variable costs.

**CONTROLLABLE COST**: A cost which can be controlled at some level of management.

**CONVERSION COST**: Direct labor plus factory overhead.

**COST CENTER**: A unit of production or service activity for which costs are accumulated.

**DIFFERENTIAL COST**: Also called incremental or relevant cost. Two or more alternatives are compared by determining the change in costs under each alternative.

**DIRECT COSTING**: Fixed overhead becomes a period cost and is excluded as a cost element of inventory. See Absorption Costing.

**EFFICIENCY VARIANCE**: A variance applied to both direct labor and overhead. As to labor, the variance measures the difference between actual and standard labor hours times the standard overhead rate. As to overhead, the variance measures the difference between the actual usage of the activity base (e.g., labor hours or machine hours) and the standard usage times the variable overhead rate.

**EQUIVALENT FINISHED UNITS**: The number of units complete in terms of whole units. For example, 1500 units 2/3 complete are 1000 units in equivalents.

**EXPECTED ANNUAL ACTIVITY**: The activity which management anticipates for the year. Expected activity may not always be used to determine the overhead rate. See Normal Activity.

**EXPECTED VALUE**: In probability, the value of a particular act times its probability.

**EXPIRED COST**: A cost that becomes an expense of the current period because of the lack of future utility.

**FACTORY OVERHEAD**: Factory costs other than Direct Material and Direct Labor. Also called manufacturing expense, indirect expense, or burden.

**FIXED COST**: A cost which remains constant over a given period of activity. See Relevant Range.

**FLEXIBLE BUDGET**: A budget prepared for more than one level of production.

**IDEAL CAPACITY**: Absolute maximum production with no allowances for work stoppages. Also called Theoretical Capacity.

**IMPUTED COST**: Costs not computed under conventional accounting methods and are not expenditures, but involve a foregone opportunity. Similar to Opportunity Cost.

**INCREMENTAL COST**: Two or more alternatives are evaluated by considering only the change in cost factors. Same as Differential Costs.

**INDIRECT LABOR**: Labor costs not traceable to specific units of output.

**INVENTORIABLE COST**: Costs assigned to units for inventory purposes.

**JOB ORDER COSTING**: Cost system in which costs of production are assigned to specific jobs or lots.

**JOINT COST**: A cost applicable to more than one cost center or activity.

**JOINT PRODUCT COSTS**: Costs applicable to two or more products produced by a single process. Up to the point of split-off costs must be assigned on an estimated basis. See Relative Sales Value Method.

**MANAGEMENT BY EXCEPTION**: Concentrates on deviations from expected results.

**MARGINAL COSTING**: See Direct Costing.

**MARGINAL INCOME**: See Contribution Margin.

**MIXED COST**: A cost which contains both fixed and variable elements.

**NET PRESENT VALUE METHOD**: In Capital Budgeting, a project is evaluated by computing the net present value of expected cash flows based on a predetermined rate of return. If the result exceeds the investment, the project meets the basic investment criteria. An index can be constructed:

$$\frac{\text{Net Present Value}}{\text{Investment}}$$

**NORMAL ACTIVITY**: Production expected in a given year based on an average over a period of years which includes seasonal, cyclical and trend factors. An overhead rate based on normal activity may result in sizeable under- and overapplications of overhead over a period of years.

| **Budgeted Overhead** | = | Overhead Rate based |
|---|---|---|
| Average production for the past 5 years. | | on normal activity |
| **Budgeted Overhead** | = | Overhead rate based |
| Management's estimate of production for the year | | on expected activity |

Also see Practical Capacity.

**NORMAL SPOILAGE**: Anticipated spoilage under efficient operations.

**OPERATIONS RESEARCH**: Various mathematical and statistical models used in decision making.

**OPPORTUNITY COST**: Income that could have been derived from a resource had it been applied to an alternate use. For example, warehouse space used to store inventory has an opportunity cost equal to the rental value.

**OUT-OF-POCKET COSTS**: Current costs or outlays related to a particular activity.

**OVERAPPLIED OVERHEAD**: The excess of overhead cost applied to product over costs actually incurred. Can be broken down to a Budget and Capacity Variance in Job Order Cost.

**PAYBACK**: Period in which cash flow equals the investment in a project. Does not measure profitability.

**PAYBACK RECIPROCAL**: Method of approximating the true rate of return. Can be used only when the life of the project is twice the payback period and inflows are uniform.

| Investment | $100,000 | |
|---|---|---|
| Payback | 30,000 | per year for 10 years |

$$\text{Payback} \quad \frac{\$300,000}{100,000} = 3/1$$

Reciprocal 1/3 or 33 1/3% approximate true rate of return.

**PAYOFF TABLE**: Used to evaluate various alternatives under different probabilities of occurrence to determine the alternative which maximizes profits.

**PERFORMANCE REPORT**: Comparison of actual with budget.

**PERIOD COST**: A cost associated with a particular period which cannot be carried forward to the succeeding period as an asset. See Expired Cost.

**PERT**: A formal diagram of the timing relationships of a complex series of planned activities.

**PRACTICAL CAPACITY**: Maximum level of production that a plant or department can operate efficiently. Ideal capacity less allowance for unavoidable stoppages.

**PRICE VARIANCE**: A Direct Material Variance. The difference between the units acquired at actual and at standard. The price variance can also be computed based on the difference between the units used in production at actual and standard.

**PRIME COST**: Direct Material and Direct Labor.

**PROCESS COSTING**: A costing system in which unit costs are computed within a time frame, usually a month, by dividing the units produced into the costs during the period. Used with FIFO or Average. Used in production of similar type product over extended periods.

**PRO-FORMA STATEMENTS**: Forecasted statements or statements prepared to show what would result "as if" certain events had taken place.

**QUANTITY VARIANCE**: The difference between the actual quantity used and the standard allowed multiplied by the standard price. Also called the Usage Variance.

**RATE VARIANCE**: A Direct Labor Variance, similar to the Price Variance for Direct Material. The difference between the actual and standard wage rate multiplied by actual amount of Direct Labor used.

**REALLOCATION**: Allocation of service department costs to the various producing departments based on some criteria of allocation related to benefits derived.

**RELATIVE SALES VALUE METHOD**: Assignment of joint product costs based on the relative sales value of each joint product. Results in the same gross profit percentage for all joint products.

**RELEVANT RANGE**: A range of activity within which cost data is valid, particularly fixed costs. Takes recognition of the fact that if production increases or decreases enough, fixed costs will change.

**SALES MIX**: The combination of quantities of products that make up total sales. Also, combination of items and various gross profit percentages that make up total contribution.

**SERVICE DEPARTMENTS**: Departments that render specialized assistance to the producing departments. Costs must be ultimately borne by the producing departments.

**SPENDING VARIANCE**: An overhead price variance comparing actual variable overhead with budgeted variable overhead.

**SPLIT-OFF POINT**: Separation point for joint products.

**STANDARD COST**: Predetermined cost that should be attained.

**STANDARD HOURS ALLOWED**: Units produced times standard hours.

**STEP VARIABLE COSTS**: Describe the effect of variable costs which change abruptly, thereby appearing on a graph as steps.

**SUNK COST**: A cost which has been incurred and has no effect on contemplated action.

**TIME ADJUSTED RATE OF RETURN**: A capital budgeting term. The rate of interest at which the present value of future cash flows from a project is equal to the present value of the investment.

**TRANSFER PRICE**: Exchange price by segments of the same organization when goods or resources are transferred. Example, manufactured goods shipped to retail outlets of the same company.

**UNADJUSTED RATE OF RETURN**: The ratio of the future average annual net income to the initial investment. Also called the accounting method and the book value method.

**UNDERAPPLIED OVERHEAD**: Excess of overhead cost incurred over the amount of overhead cost applied.

**UNEXPIRED COST**: A cost which may be properly carried forward to future periods as an asset.

**USAGE VARIANCE**: See Quantity Variance.

**VARIABLE COST**: A cost which is constant per unit, but changes in total in proportion to changes in production activity.

**VARIANCE**: Difference between actual from expected or budgeted results.

**WORK-IN-PROCESS INVENTORY**: Cost of incomplete goods still in production stage.

# Chapter Sixteen
# Cost Accounting Questions
# Joint Products and Standard Costs

## JOINT AND BY-PRODUCTS

1. Each of the following is a method by which to allocate joint costs **except**
a. Relative sales value.
b. Relative profitability.
c. Relative weight, volume, or linear measure.
d. Average unit cost.

_____

**Items 2 and 3** are based on the following information:
 Forward, Inc., manufactures products P, Q, and R from a joint process. Additional information is as follows:

|  | Product | | | |
|  | _P_ | _Q_ | _R_ | _Total_ |
|---|---|---|---|---|
| Units produced | 4,000 | 2,000 | 1,000 | 7,000 |
| Joint cost | $36,000 | ? | ? | $60,000 |
| Sales value at split-off | ? | ? | $15,000 | $100,000 |
| Additional costs if processed further | $ 7,000 | $ 5,000 | $ 3,000 | $ 15,000 |
| Sales value if processed further | $70,000 | $30,000 | $20,000 | $120,000 |

2. Assuming that joint costs are allocated using the relative-sales-value-at-split-off approach, what were the joint costs allocated to products Q and R?
a. $12,000 for Q and $12,000 for R.
b. $14,400 for Q and $9,600 for R.
c. $15,000 for Q and $9,000 for R.
d. $16,000 for Q and $8,000 for R.

3. Assuming that joint costs are allocated using the relative-sales-value-at-split-off approach, what was the sales value at split-off for product P?
a. $58,333.
b. $59,500.
c. $60,000.
d. $63,000.

_____

4. Helen Corp. manufactures products W, X, Y, and Z from a joint process. Additional information is as follows:

| | | Sales | If Processed Further | |
| | Units | Value at | Additional | Sales |
| Product | Produced | Split-off | Costs | Value |
|---|---|---|---|---|
| W | 6,000 | $ 80,000 | $ 7,500 | $ 90,000 |
| X | 5,000 | 60,000 | 6,000 | 70,000 |
| Y | 4,000 | 40,000 | 4,000 | 50,000 |
| Z | 3,000 | 20,000 | 2,500 | 30,000 |
| | 18,000 | $200,000 | $20,000 | $240,000 |

Assuming that total joint costs of $160,000 were allocated using the relative-sales-value at split-off approach, what were the joint costs allocated to each product?

| | _W_ | _X_ | _Y_ | _Z_ |
|---|---|---|---|---|
| a. | $40,000 | $40,000 | $40,000 | $40,000 |
| b. | $53,333 | $44,444 | $35,556 | $26,667 |
| c. | $60,000 | $46,667 | $33,333 | $20,000 |
| d. | $64,000 | $48,000 | $32,000 | $16,000 |

*R96*

5. A processing department produces joint products Ajac and Bjac, each of which incurs separable production costs after split-off. Information concerning a batch produced at a $60,000 joint cost before split-off follows:

| Product | Separable costs | Sales value |
|---|---|---|
| Ajac | $ 8,000 | $ 80,000 |
| Bjac | 22,000 | 40,000 |
| Total | $30,000 | $120,000 |

What is the joint cost assigned to Ajac if costs are assigned using the relative net realizable value?
a. $16,000
b. $40,000
c. $48,000
d. $52,000

*M95*

6. Kode Co. manufactures a major product that gives rise to a by-product called May. May's only separable cost is a $1 selling cost when a unit is sold for $4. Kode accounts for May's sales by deducting the $3 net amount from the cost of goods sold of the major product. There are no inventories. If Kode were to change its method of accounting for May from a by-product to a joint product, what would be the effect on Kode's overall gross margin?

a. No effect.
b. Gross margin increases by $1 for each unit of May sold.
c. Gross margin increases by $3 for each unit of May sold.
d. Gross margin increases by $4 for each unit of May sold.

7. The method of accounting for joint-product costs that will produce the same gross-profit rate for all products is the
a. Relative sales-value method.
b. Physical-measure method.
c. Actual-costing method.
d. Services-received method.

8. Ohio Corporation manufactures liquid chemicals A and B from a joint process. Joint costs are allocated on the basis of relative-sales-value at split-off. It costs $4,560 to process 500 gallons of product A and 1,000 gallons of product B to the split-off point. The sales value at split-off is $10 per gallon for product A and $14 for product B. Product B requires an additional process beyond split-off at a cost of $1 per gallon before it can be sold. What is Ohio's cost to produce 1,000 gallons of product B?
a. $3,360.
b. $3,660.
c. $4,040.
d. $4,360.

9. Superior Company manufactures products A and B from a joint process which also yields a by-product, X. Superior accounts for the revenues from its by-product sales as a deduction from the cost of goods sold of its main products. Additional information is as follows:

| | | Products | | |
|---|---|---|---|---|
| | A | B | X | Total |
| Units produced | 15,000 | 9,000 | 6,000 | 30,000 |
| Joint costs | ? | ? | ? | $264,000 |
| Sales value at split-off | $290,000 | $150,000 | $10,000 | $450,000 |

Assuming that joint product costs are allocated using the relative-sales-value at split-off approach, what was the joint cost allocated to product B?
a. $79,200.
b. $88,000.
c. $90,000.
d. $99,000.

10. Which of the following statements best describes a by-product?
a. A product that is produced from material that would otherwise be scrap.

b. A product that has a lower unit selling price than the main product.
c. A product created along with the main product whose sales value does **not** cover its cost of production.
d. A product that usually produces a small amount of revenue when compared to the main product revenue.

11. At the split-off point, products may be salable or may require further processing in order to be salable. Which of the following have both of these characteristics?

| | By-products | Joint products |
|---|---|---|
| a. | No | No |
| b. | No | Yes |
| c. | Yes | No |
| d. | Yes | Yes |

12. Which of the following is (are) acceptable regarding the allocation of joint product cost to a by-product?

| | None allocated | Some portion allocated |
|---|---|---|
| a. | Acceptable | Not acceptable |
| b. | Acceptable | Acceptable |
| c. | Not acceptable | Acceptable |
| d. | Not acceptable | Not acceptable |

———————

**Items 13 and 14** are based on the following information:

Warfield Corporation manufactures products C, D and E from a joint process. Joint costs are allocated on the basis of relative-sales-value at split-off. Additional information is as follows:

| | | Product | | |
|---|---|---|---|---|
| | C | D | E | Total |
| Units produced | 6,000 | 4,000 | 2,000 | 12,000 |
| Joint costs | $72,000 | ? | ? | $120,000 |
| Sales value at split-off | ? | ? | $30,000 | $200,000 |
| Additional costs if processed further | $14,000 | $10,000 | $6,000 | $30,000 |
| Sales value if processed further | $140,000 | $60,000 | $40,000 | $240,000 |

13. How much of the joint costs should Warfield allocate to product D?
a. $24,000
b. $28,800
c. $30,000
d. $32,000

14. Assuming that the 2,000 units of product E were processed further and sold for $40,000, what was Warfield's gross profit on the sale?
a. $ 4,000
b. $14,000
c. $16,000
d. $22,000

---

N95

15. For purposes of allocating joint costs to joint products, the sales price at point of sale, reduced by cost to complete after split-off, is assumed to be equal to the
a.  Joint costs.
b.  Total costs.
c.  Net sales value at split-off.
d.  Sales price less a normal profit margin at point of sale.

M90

16. The diagram below represents the production and sales relationships of joint products P and Q. Joint costs are incurred until split-off, then separable costs are incurred in refining each product. Market values of P and Q at split-off are used to allocate joint costs.

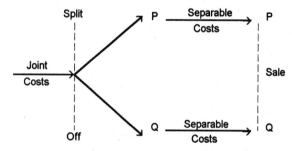

If the market value of P at split-off increases and all other costs and selling prices remain unchanged, then the gross margin of

|     | P         | Q         |
| --- | --------- | --------- |
| a.  | Increases | Decreases |
| b.  | Increases | Increases |
| c.  | Decreases | Decreases |
| d.  | Decreases | Increases |

M92

17. The following information pertains to a byproduct called Moy:

| Sales in 1991         | 5,000 units |
| --------------------- | ----------- |
| Selling price per unit | $6          |
| Selling costs per unit | 2           |
| Processing costs       | 0           |

Inventory of Moy was recorded at net realizable value when produced in 1990. No units of Moy were produced in 1991. What amount should be recognized as profit on Moy's 1991 sales?
a.   $0
b.   $10,000
c.   $20,000
d.   $30,000

N89

18. Actual sales values at split-off point for joint products Y and Z are not known. For purposes of allocating joint costs to products Y and Z, the relative sales value at split-off method is used. An increase in the costs beyond split-off occurs for product Z, while those of product Y remain constant. If the selling prices of finished products Y and Z remain constant, the percentage of the total joint costs allocated to Product Y and Product Z would
a.   Decrease for Product Y and increase for Product Z.
b.   Decrease for Product Y and Product Z.
c.   Increase for Product Y and decrease for Product Z.
d.   Increase for Product Y and Product Z.

## STANDARD COST AND VARIANCES

19. Which of the following is one of the purposes of standard costs?
a.   To simplify costing procedures and expedite cost reports.
b.   To replace budgets and budgeting.
c.   To use them as a basis for product costing for external-reporting purposes.
d.   To eliminate having to account for underapplied or overapplied factory overhead at the end of the period.

N90

20. When a manager is concerned with monitoring total cost, total revenue, and net profit conditioned upon the level of productivity, an accountant would normally recommend

|     | Flexible budgeting | Standard costing |
| --- | ------------------ | ---------------- |
| a.  | Yes                | Yes              |
| b.  | Yes                | No               |
| c.  | No                 | Yes              |
| d.  | No                 | No               |

21. Which of the following standard costing variances would be **least** controllable by a production supervisor?
a. Overhead volume.
b. Overhead efficiency.
c. Labor efficiency.
d. Material usage.

22. If a company follows a practice of isolating variances at the earliest point in time, what would be the appropriate time to isolate and recognize a direct material price variance?
a. When material is issued.
b. When material is purchased.
c. When material is used in production.
d. When purchase order is originated.

23. How should a usage variance that is significant in amount be treated at the end of an accounting period?
a. Reported as a deferred charge or credit.
b. Allocated among work-in-process inventory, finished goods inventory, and cost of goods sold.
c. Charged or credited to cost of goods manufactured.
d. Allocated among cost of goods manufactured, finished goods inventory, and cost of goods sold.

24. What is the normal year-end treatment of immaterial variances recognized in a cost accounting system utilizing standards?
a. Reclassified to deferred charges until all related production is sold.
b. Allocated among cost of goods manufactured and ending work-in-process inventory.
c. Closed to cost of goods sold in the period in which they arose.
d. Capitalized as a cost of ending finished goods inventory.

25. Palo Corp. manufactures one product with a standard direct labor cost of 2 hours at $6.00 per hour. During March, 500 units were produced using 1,050 hours at $6.10 per hour. The unfavorable direct labor efficiency variance is
a. $100
b. $105
c. $300
d. $305

26. A standard cost system may be used in
a. Neither process costing nor job order costing.
b. Process costing but **not** job order costing.
c. Either job order costing or process costing.
d. Job order costing but **not** process costing.

———————

**Items 27 through 31** are based on the following information:

Tolbert Manufacturing Company uses a standard-cost system in accounting for the cost of production of its only product, product A. The standards for the production of one unit of product A are as follows:
- Direct materials: 10 feet of item 1 at $.75 per foot and 3 feet of item 2 at $1.00 per foot.
- Direct labor: 4 hours at $3.50 per hour.
- Manufacturing overhead: applied at 150% of standard-direct-labor costs.

There was no inventory on hand at July 1, 19X2. Following is a summary of costs and related data for the production of product A during the year ended June 30, 19X3.
- 100,000 feet of item 1 were purchased at $.78 per foot.
- 30,000 feet of item 2 were purchased at $.90 per foot.
- 8,000 units of product A were produced which required 78,000 feet of item 1, 26,000 feet of item 2, and 31,000 hours of direct labor at $3.60 per hour.
- 6,000 units of product A were sold.

At June 30, 19X3, there are 22,000 feet of item 1, 4,000 feet of item 2, and 2,000 completed units of product A on hand. All purchases and transfers are "charged in" at standard.

27. For the year ended June 30, 19X3, the total debits to the raw-materials account for the purchase of item 1 would be
a. $75,000.
b. $78,000.
c. $58,500.
d. $60,000.

28. For the year ended June 30, 19X3, the total debits to the work-in-process account for direct labor would be
a. $111,600.
b. $108,500.
c. $112,000.
d. $115,100.

29. Before allocation of standard variances, the balance in the material-usage-variance account for item 2 was
a. $1,000 credit.
b. $2,600 debit.
c. $600 debit.
d. $2,000 debit.

30. If all standard variances are prorated to inventories and cost of goods sold, the amount of material-usage variance for item 2 to be prorated to raw-materials inventory would be
a. $0.
b. $333 credit.
c. $333 debit.
d. $500 debit.

31. If all standard variances are prorated to inventories and cost of goods sold, the amount of material-price variance for item 1 to be prorated to raw-materials inventory would be
a. $0.
b. $647 debit.
c. $600 debit.
d. $660 debit.

_____

N92
32. In connection with a standard cost system being developed by Flint Co., the following information is being considered with regard to standard hours allowed for output of one unit of product:

|  | Hours |
|---|---|
| Average historical performance for the past three years | 1.85 |
| Production level to satisfy average consumer demand over a seasonal time span | 1.60 |
| Engineering estimates based on attainable performance | 1.50 |
| Engineering estimates based on ideal performance | 1.25 |

To measure controllable production inefficiencies, what is the best basis for Flint to use in establishing standard hours allowed?
a.   1.25
b.   1.50
c.   1.60
d.   1.85

33. Which of the following is the most probable reason a company would experience an unfavorable labor rate variance and a favorable labor efficiency variance?
a.   The mix of workers assigned to the particular job was heavily weighted towards the use of higher paid experienced individuals.
b.   The mix of workers assigned to the particular job was heavily weighted towards the use of new relatively low paid unskilled workers.
c.   Because of the production schedule workers from other production areas were assigned to assist this particular process.
d.   Defective materials caused more labor to be used in order to produce a standard unit.

M92
34. The following were among Gage Co.'s 1991 costs:

| | |
|---|---|
| Normal spoilage | $ 5,000 |
| Freight out | 10,000 |
| Excess of actual manufacturing costs over standard costs | 20,000 |
| Standard manufacturing costs | 100,000 |
| Actual prime manufacturing costs | 80,000 |

Gage's 1991 actual manufacturing overhead was
a.   $40,000
b.   $45,000
c.   $55,000
d.   $120,000

35. What does a credit balance in a direct-labor efficiency variance account indicate?
a.   The average wage rate paid to direct labor employees was less than the standard rate.
b.   The standard hours allowed for the units produced were greater than actual direct-labor hours used.
c.   Actual total direct-labor costs incurred were less than standard direct-labor costs allowed for the units produced.
d.   The number of units produced was less than the number of units budgeted for the period.

36. Information on Material Company's direct-material costs is as follows:

| | |
|---|---|
| Actual units of direct materials used | 20,000 |
| Actual direct-material costs | $40,000 |
| Standard price per unit of direct materials | $2.10 |
| Direct-material efficiency variance-favorable | $ 3,000 |

What was Material's direct-material price variance?
a. $1,000 favorable.
b. $1,000 unfavorable.
c. $2,000 favorable.
d. $2,000 unfavorable.

37. What type of direct material variances for price and usage will arise if the actual number of pounds of materials used exceeds standard pounds allowed but actual cost was less than standard cost?

| | Usage | Price |
|---|---|---|
| a. | Unfavorable | Favorable |
| b. | Favorable | Favorable |
| c. | Favorable | Unfavorable |
| d. | Unfavorable | Unfavorable |

38. Information on Kennedy Company's direct-material costs is as follows:

| | |
|---|---|
| Standard unit price | $3.60 |
| Actual quantity purchased | 1,600 |
| Standard quantity allowed for actual production | 1,450 |
| Materials purchase price variance-favorable | $240 |

What was the actual purchase price per unit, rounded to the nearest penny?
a. $3.06.
b. $3.11.
c. $3.45.
d. $3.75.

39. Lab Corp. uses a standard cost system. Direct labor information for Product CER for the month of October is as follows:

| | |
|---|---|
| Standard rate | $6.00 per hour |
| Actual rate paid | $6.10 per hour |
| Standard hours allowed for actual production | 1,500 hours |
| Labor efficiency variance | $600 unfavorable |

What are the actual hours worked?
a. 1,400.
b. 1,402.
c. 1,598.
d. 1,600.

40. Air, Inc., uses a standard cost system. Overhead cost information for Product CO for the month of October is as follows:

| | |
|---|---|
| Total actual overhead incurred | $12,600 |
| Fixed overhead budgeted | $ 3,300 |
| Total standard overhead rate per direct labor hour | $4.00 |
| Variable overhead rate per direct labor hour | $3.00 |
| Standard hours allowed for actual production | 3,500 |

What is the overall (or net) overhead variance?
a. $1,200 favorable.
b. $1,200 unfavorable.
c. $1,400 favorable.
d. $1,400 unfavorable.

---

**Items 41 and 42** are based on the following information:

Data on Goodman Company's direct-labor costs is given below:

| | |
|---|---|
| Standard direct-labor hours | 30,000 |
| Actual direct-labor hours | 29,000 |
| Direct-labor usage (efficiency) variance--favorable | $4,000 |
| Direct-labor rate variance-- favorable | $5,800 |
| Total payroll | $110,200 |

41. What was Goodman's actual direct-labor rate?
a. $3.60.
b. $3.80.
c. $4.00.
d. $5.80.

42. What was Goodman's standard direct-labor rate?
a. $3.54.
b. $3.80.
c. $4.00.
d. $5.80.

43. During 1990, a department's three-variance overhead standard costing system reported unfavorable spending and volume variances. The activity level selected for allocating overhead to the product was based on 80% of practical capacity. If 100% of practical capacity had been selected instead, how would the reported unfavorable spending and volume variances be affected?

|    | Spending variance | Volume variance |
|----|-------------------|-----------------|
| a. | Increased         | Unchanged       |
| b. | Increased         | Increased       |
| c. | Unchanged         | Increased       |
| d. | Unchanged         | Unchanged       |

44. If over- or underapplied overhead is interpreted as an error in allocating actual costs against the production of the year, this suggests that the over- or underapplied overhead of this year should be
a. Carried forward in the overhead control account from year to year.
b. Eliminated by changing the predetermined overhead rate in subsequent years.
c. Apportioned among the work-in-process inventory, the finished goods inventory, and the cost of goods sold.
d. Treated as a special gain or loss occurring during the year.

45. Yola Co. manufactures one product with a standard direct labor cost of four hours at $12.00 per hour. During June, 1,000 units were produced using 4,100 hours at $12.20 per hour. The unfavorable direct labor efficiency variance was
a. $1,220
b. $1,200
c. $820
d. $400

46. Under the two-variance method for analyzing factory overhead, the factory overhead applied to production is used in the computation of the

|    | Controllable (budget) variance | Volume variance |
|----|-------------------------------|-----------------|
| a. | Yes                           | No              |
| b. | Yes                           | Yes             |
| c. | No                            | Yes             |
| d. | No                            | No              |

47. Carr Co. had an unfavorable materials usage variance of $900. What amounts of this variance should be charged to each department?

|    | Purchasing | Warehousing | Manufacturing |
|----|-----------|-------------|---------------|
| a. | $0        | $0          | $900          |
| b. | $0        | $900        | $0            |
| c. | $300      | $300        | $300          |
| d. | $900      | $0          | $0            |

48. The variable factory overhead rate under the normal-volume, practical-capacity, and expected activity levels would be the
a. Same except for normal volume.
b. Same except for practical capacity.
c. Same except for expected activity.
d. Same for all three activity levels.

49. Lanta Restaurant compares monthly operating results with a static budget. When actual sales are less than budget, would Lanta usually report favorable variances on variable food costs and fixed supervisory salaries?

|    | Variable food costs | Fixed supervisory salaries |
|----|---------------------|----------------------------|
| a. | Yes                 | Yes                        |
| b. | Yes                 | No                         |
| c. | No                  | Yes                        |
| d. | No                  | No                         |

Items 50 and 51 are based on the following information:

The following information relates to a given department of Herman Company for the fourth quarter 19X4:

| | |
|---|---|
| Actual total overhead (fixed plus variable) | $178,500 |
| Budget formula | $110,000 plus $0.50 per hr. |
| Total overhead application rate | $1.50 per hr. |
| Spending variance | $8,000 unfavorable |
| Volume variance | $5,000 favorable |

The total overhead variance is divided into three variances—spending, efficiency, and volume.

50. What were the actual hours worked in this department during the quarter?
a. 110,000.
b. 121,000.
c. 137,000.
d. 153,000.

51. What were the standard hours allowed for good output in this department during the quarter?
a. 105,000.
b. 106,667.
c. 110,000.
d. 115,000.

---

**Items 52 and 53** are based on the following information:

Beth Company's budgeted fixed factory overhead costs are $50,000 per month plus a variable factory overhead rate of $4 per direct labor hour. The standard direct labor hours allowed for October production were 18,000. An analysis of the factory overhead indicates that, in October, Beth had an unfavorable budget (controllable) variance of $1,000 and a favorable volume variance of $500. Beth uses a two-way analysis of overhead variances.

52. The actual factory overhead incurred in October is
a. $121,000.
b. $122,000.
c. $122,500.
d. $123,000.

53. The applied factory overhead in October is
a. $121,000.
b. $122,000.
c. $122,500.
d. $123,000.

---

54. The following information is available from the Tyro Company:

| | |
|---|---|
| Actual factory overhead | $15,000 |
| Fixed overhead expenses, actual | $ 7,200 |
| Fixed overhead expenses, budgeted | $ 7,000 |
| Actual hours | 3,500 |
| Standard hours | 3,800 |
| Variable overhead rate per direct labor hour | $2.50 |

Assuming that Tyro uses a three-way analysis of overhead variances, what is the spending variance?
a. $750 favorable.
b. $750 unfavorable.
c. $950 favorable.
d. $1,500 unfavorable.

55. Information on Fire Company's overhead costs is as follows:

| | |
|---|---|
| Actual variable overhead | $73,000 |
| Actual fixed overhead | $17,000 |
| Standard hours allowed for actual production | 32,000 |
| Standard variable overhead rate per direct-labor hour | $2.50 |
| Standard fixed overhead rate per direct-labor hour | $0.50 |

What is the total overhead variance?
a. $1,000 unfavorable.
b. $6,000 favorable.
c. $6,000 unfavorable.
d. $7,000 favorable.

**Items 56 and 57** are based on the following:
The diagram below depicts a factory overhead flexible budget line DB and standard overhead application line OA. Activity is expressed in machine hours with Point V indicating the standard hours required for the actual output in September 1990. Point S indicates the actual machine hours (inputs) and actual costs in September 1990.

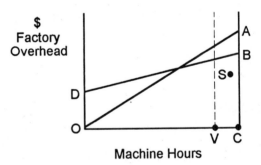

56. Are the following overhead variances favorable or unfavorable?

| | Volume (capacity) variance | Efficiency variance |
|---|---|---|
| a. | Favorable | Favorable |
| b. | Favorable | Unfavorable |
| c. | Unfavorable | Favorable |
| d. | Unfavorable | Unfavorable |

57. The budgeted total variable overhead cost for C machine hours is
a. AB
b. BC
c. AC minus DO
d. BC minus DO

N95

58. The standard direct material cost to produce a unit of Lem is 4 meters of material at $2.50 per meter. During May 1995, 4,200 meters of material costing $10,080 were purchased and used to produce 1,000 units of Lem. What was the material price variance for May 1995?
a. $400 favorable.
b. $420 favorable.
c. $80 unfavorable.
d. $480 unfavorable.

N95

59. Sender, Inc. estimates parcel mailing costs using data shown on the chart below.

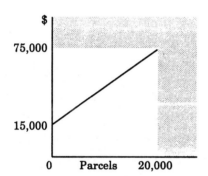

What is Sender's estimated cost for mailing 12,000 parcels?
a. $36,000
b. $45,000
c. $51,000
d. $60,000

M92

60. The following direct labor information pertains to the manufacture of product Glu:

| | |
|---|---|
| Time required to make one unit | 2 direct labor hours |
| Number of direct workers | 50 |
| Number of productive hours per week, per worker | 40 |
| Weekly wages per worker | $500 |
| Workers' benefits treated as direct labor costs | 20% of wages |

What is the standard direct labor cost per unit of product Glu?
a. $30
b. $24
c. $15
d. $12

M88

61. Under the two-variance method for analyzing factory overhead, the actual factory overhead is used in the computation of the

| | Controllable (budget) variance | Volume variance |
|---|---|---|
| a. | Yes | Yes |
| b. | Yes | No |
| c. | No | No |
| d. | No | Yes |

N89

62. Which of the following variances would be useful in calling attention to a possible short-term problem in the control of overhead costs?

| | Spending variance | Volume variance |
|---|---|---|
| a. | No | No |
| b. | No | Yes |
| c. | Yes | No |
| d. | Yes | Yes |

N92

63. The following information pertains to Roe Co.'s 1991 manufacturing operations:

| | |
|---|---|
| Standard direct labor hours per unit | 2 |
| Actual direct labor hours | 10,500 |
| Number of units produced | 5,000 |
| Standard variable overhead per standard direct labor hour | $3 |
| Actual variable overhead | $28,000 |

Roe's 1991 unfavorable variance overhead efficiency variance was
a. $0
b. $1,500
c. $2,000
d. $3,500

64. Information on Cox Company's direct-material costs for the month of January was as follows:

| | |
|---|---|
| Actual quantity purchased | 18,000 |
| Actual unit purchase price | $ 3.60 |
| Materials purchase price variance-- unfavorable (based on purchases) | $ 3,600 |
| Standard quantity allowed for actual production | 16,000 |
| Actual quantity used | 15,000 |

For January there was a favorable direct-material usage variance of
a. $3,360
b. $3,375
c. $3,400
d. $3,800

M95

65. Companies in what type of industry may use a standard cost system for cost control?

| | Mass production industry | Service industry |
|---|---|---|
| a. | Yes | Yes |
| b. | Yes | No |
| c. | No | No |
| d. | No | Yes |

M90

66. On the diagram below, the line OW represents the standard labor cost at any output volume expressed in direct labor hours. Point S indicates the actual output at standard cost, and Point A indicates the actual hours and actual cost required to produce S.

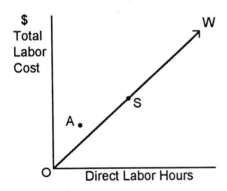

Which of the following variances are favorable or unfavorable?

| | Rate variance | Efficiency variance |
|---|---|---|
| a. | Favorable | Unfavorable |
| b. | Favorable | Favorable |
| c. | Unfavorable | Unfavorable |
| d. | Unfavorable | Favorable |

67. Under the three-variance method for analyzing factory overhead, which of the following is used in the computation of the spending variance?

| | Budget allowance based on actual hours | Budget allowance based on standard hours |
|---|---|---|
| a. | Yes | No |
| b. | Yes | Yes |
| c. | No | Yes |
| d. | No | No |

68. Under the two-variance method for analyzing factory overhead, the budget allowance based on standard hours allowed is used in the computation of the

| | Controllable (budget) variance | Volume variance |
|---|---|---|
| a. | Yes | Yes |
| b. | Yes | No |
| c. | No | No |
| d. | No | Yes |

N89

69. Dahl Co. uses a standard costing system in connection with the manufacture of a "one size fits all" article of clothing. Each unit of finished product contains 2 yards of direct material. However, a 20% direct material spoilage calculated on input quantities occurs during the manufacturing process. The cost of the direct material is $3 per yard. The standard direct material cost per unit of finished product is
a. $4.80
b. $6.00
c. $7.20
d. $7.50

_____

**Items 70 and 71** are based on the following data:

The following information pertains to Nell Company's production of one unit of its manufactured product during the month of June:

| | |
|---|---|
| Standard quantity of materials | 5 lbs. |
| Standard cost per lb. | $.20 |
| Standard direct labor hours | .4 |
| Standard wage rate per hour | $7.00 |
| Materials purchased | 100,000 lbs. |
| Cost of materials purchased | $.17 per lb. |
| Materials consumed for manu- facture of 10,000 units | 60,000 lbs. |
| Actual direct labor hours required for 10,000 units | 3,900 |
| Actual direct labor cost per hour | $7.20 |

The materials price variance is recognized when materials are purchased.

70. Nell's materials price variance for June was
a. $3,000 favorable.
b. $3,000 unfavorable.
c. $2,000 favorable.
d. $2,000 unfavorable.

71. Nell's labor efficiency variance for June was
a. $780 favorable.
b. $780 unfavorable.
c. $700 favorable.
d. $700 unfavorable.

_____

72. The following relationships pertain to a year's budgeted activity for the Smythe Company:

| | | |
|---|---|---|
| Direct-labor hours | 300,000 | 400,000 |
| Total costs | $129,000 | $154,000 |

What are the budgeted fixed costs for the year?
a. $25,000
b. $54,000
c. $75,000
d. $100,000

_____

**Items 73 and 74** are based on the following information:

Maintenance expenses of a company are to be analyzed for purposes of constructing a flexible budget. Examination of past records disclosed the following costs and volume measures:

| | Highest | Lowest |
|---|---|---|
| Cost per month | $39,200 | $32,000 |
| Machine hours | 24,000 | 15,000 |

73. Using the high-low-point method of analysis, the estimated variable cost per machine hour is
a. $1.25
b. $12.50
c. $0.80
d. $0.08

74. Using the high-low technique, the estimated annual fixed cost for maintenance expenditures is
a. $447,360
b. $240,000
c. $230,400
d. $384,000

_____

75. Under the two-variance method for analyzing overhead, which of the following variances consists of both variable and fixed overhead elements?

| | Controllable (budget) variance | Volume variance |
|---|---|---|
| a. | Yes | Yes |
| b. | Yes | No |
| c. | No | No |
| d. | No | Yes |

# Chapter Sixteen
# Cost Accounting Problems
# Joint Products and Standard Costs

## NUMBER 1

An important part of managerial accounting is the analysis of the types of costs that a business entity can incur. These types of costs are generally classified as variable, fixed, and semivariable.

**Required:**
**a.** Define and discuss the identifying characteristics of a
    1. Variable cost.
    2. Fixed cost.
**b.** With respect to a semivariable cost
    1. Define and discuss the identifying characteristics of a semivariable cost.
    2. Discuss the three basic methods employed to "break down" a semivariable cost into its component parts.

## NUMBER 2

Webb & Company is engaged in the preparation of income tax returns for individuals. Webb uses the weighted average method and actual costs for financial reporting purposes. However, for internal reporting, Webb uses a standard cost system. The standards, based on equivalent performance, have been established as follows:

| | |
|---|---|
| Labor per return | 5 hrs. @ $20 per hr. |
| Overhead per return | 5 hrs. @ $10 per hr. |

For March performance, budgeted overhead is $49,000 for the standard labor hours allowed. The following additional information pertains to the month of March:

| *Inventory data* | |
|---|---|
| Returns in process, March 1 (25% complete) | 200 |
| Returns started in March | 825 |
| Returns in process, March 31 (80% complete) | 125 |

| *Actual cost data* | |
|---|---|
| Returns in process March 1: | |
|     Labor | $ 6,000 |
|     Overhead | 2,500 |
| Labor, March 1 to 31 | |
|     4,000 hours | 89,000 |
| Overhead, March 1 to 31 | 45,000 |

**Required:**

**a.** Using the weighted average method, compute the following for each cost element:
> (1) Equivalent units of performance.
> (2) Actual cost per equivalent unit.

**b.** Compute the actual cost of returns in process at March 31.

**c.** Compute the standard cost per return.

**d.** Prepare a schedule for internal reporting analyzing March performance, using the following variances, and indicating whether these variances are favorable or unfavorable:
> (1) Total labor.
> (2) Labor rate.
> (3) Labor efficiency.
> (4) Total overhead.
> (5) Overhead volume.
> (6) Overhead budget.

# NUMBER 3

Armando Corporation manufactures a product with the following standard costs:

| | |
|---|---:|
| Direct materials—20 yards @ $1.35 per yard | $27 |
| Direct labor—4 hours @ $9.00 per hour | 36 |
| Factory overhead—applied at five-sixths of direct labor. | |
| Ratio of variable costs to fixed costs: 2 to 1 | 30 |
| Total standard cost per unit of output | $93 |

Standards are based on normal monthly production involving 2,400 direct labor hours (600 units of output).

The following information pertains to the month of July:

| | |
|---|---:|
| Direct materials purchased—18,000 yards @ $1.38 per yard | $24,840 |
| Direct materials used—9,500 yards | |
| Direct labor—2,100 hours @ $9.15 per hour | 19,215 |
| Actual factory overhead | 16,650 |

500 units of the product were actually produced in July.

**Required:**

**a.** Prepare the following schedules computing:
> 1. Variable factory overhead rate per direct labor hour.
> 2. Total fixed factory overhead based on normal activity.

**b.** Prepare the following schedules for the month of July, indicating whether each variance is favorable or unfavorable:
> 1. Materials price variance (based on purchases).
> 2. Materials usage variance.
> 3. Labor rate variance.
> 4. Labor efficiency variance.
> 5. Controllable factory overhead variance.
> 6. Capacity (volume) factory overhead variance.

# NUMBER 4

Meyer Company's cost accounting department has prepared a factory overhead variance analysis report using the two-variance method. The plant manager of Meyer Company is interested in understanding the managerial usefulness of this report.

**Required:**
1. What are the purposes of a factory overhead variance analysis report?
2. Identify and explain the underlying assumptions associated with the two-variance method. Discuss the significance of each variance.

# NUMBER 5

Lond Co. produces joint products Jana and Reta, together with byproduct Bynd. Jana is sold at split-off, whereas Reta and Bynd undergo additional processing. Production data pertaining to these products for the year ended December 31, 1989, were as follows:

| | Jana | Reta | Bynd | Total |
|---|---|---|---|---|
| Joint costs | | | | |
| Variable | | | | $ 88,000 |
| Fixed | | | | 148,000 |
| Separable costs | | | | |
| Variable | | $120,000 | $3,000 | 123,000 |
| Fixed | | 90,000 | 2,000 | 92,000 |
| Production in pounds | 50,000 | 40,000 | 10,000 | 100,000 |
| Sales price per pound | $4.00 | $7.50 | $1.10 | |

There were no beginning or ending inventories. No materials are spoiled in production. Variable costs change in direct proportion to production volume. Bynd's net realizable value is deducted from joint costs. Joint costs are allocated to joint products to achieve the same gross margin percentage for each joint product.

Although 1989 performance could be repeated for 1990, Lond is considering possible operation of the plant at full capacity of 120,000 pounds. The relative proportions of each product's output with respect to cost behavior and production increases would be unchanged. Market surveys indicate that prices of Jana and Bynd would have to be reduced to $3.40 and $0.90, respectively. Reta's expected price decline cannot be determined.

**Required:**
Prepare the following schedules for Lond Co. for the year ended December 31, 1989:
> 1. Total gross margin.
> 2. Allocation of joint costs to Jana and Reta.
> 3. Separate gross margins for Jana and Reta.

Tredoc Co. is engaged in the business of seasonal tree-spraying and uses chemicals in its operations to prevent disease and bug-infestation. Employees are guaranteed 165 hours of work per month at $8 per hour and receive a bonus equal to 75% of their net favorable direct labor efficiency variance. The efficiency variance represents the difference between actual time consumed in spraying a tree and the standard time allowed for the height of the tree (specified in feet), multiplied by the $8 standard hourly wage rate. For budgeting purposes, there is a standard allowance of one hour per customer for travel, setup, and clearup time. However, since several factors are uncontrollable by the employee, this one-hour budget allowance is excluded from the bonus calculation. Employees are responsible for keeping their own daily time-cards.

Chemical usage should vary directly with the tree-footage sprayed. Variable overhead includes costs that vary directly with the number of customers, as well as costs that vary according to tree-footage sprayed. Customers pay a service charge of $10 per visit and $1 per tree-foot sprayed.

The standard static budget and actual results for June are as follows:

|  |  |  | Static budget |  | Actual results |
|---|---|---|---|---|---|
| Service calls | (200 customers) |  | $ 2,000 | (210 customers) | $ 2,100 |
| Footage sprayed | (18,000 feet) |  | 18,000 | (21,000 feet) | 21,000 |
| Total revenues |  |  | 20,000 |  | 23,100 |
| Chemicals | (1,800 gallons) |  | 4,500 | (2,400 gallons) | 5,880 |
| Direct labor: |  |  |  |  |  |
| Travel, setup, and clearup | (200 hours) | $1,600 |  | (300 hours) $2,400 |  |
| Tree-spraying | (900 hours) | 7,200 |  | (910 hours) 7,280 |  |
| Total direct labor |  |  | 8,800 |  | 9,680 |
| Overhead: |  |  |  |  |  |
| Variable based on number of customers |  | 1,200 |  |  |  |
| Variable based on tree-footage |  | 1,800 |  |  |  |
| Fixed |  | 2,000 |  |  |  |
| Total overhead |  |  | 5,000 |  | 5,400 |
| Total costs |  |  | 18,300 |  | 20,960 |
| Gross profit before bonus |  |  | $ 1,700 |  | $ 2,140 |

July's demand is expected to be in excess of June's and may be met by either paying a 25% overtime premium to current employees or by hiring an additional employee. A new employee will cause fixed costs to increase by $100 per month. The potential increased demand may be estimated by considering the impact of increases of 20 and 30 customers, with probabilities of 70% and 30%, respectively.

**Required:**

a. Compute the following for June:
   1. Direct materials price variance.
   2. Direct materials usage (efficiency) variance.
   3. Direct labor travel, setup, and clearup variance.
   4. Direct labor bonus.
   5. Overhead spending (flexible budget) variance.

   Indicate whether each variance is favorable or unfavorable.

b. Assume that Tredoc accepts all orders for services in July. Should Tredoc hire an additional employee? Provide supporting computations based on standard costs.

**Items 1 through 5** are based on the following:

The diagram below depicts a manufacturing total cost flexible budget line KI and standard cost line OI. Line OJ is parallel to line KI, and revenues are represented by line OH.

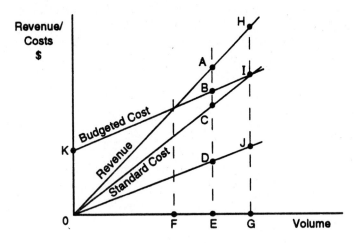

**Required:**

For Items 1 through 5, identify the line on the graph that represents each item.

**Items to be Answered:**

1. The budgeted fixed cost at volume OE.
2. The budgeted variable cost at volume OE.
3. The standard gross profit at volume OE.
4. The budgeted gross profit at volume OE, assuming **no** change between beginning and ending inventories.
5. The normal capacity, assuming standard costs are based on normal capacity.

Problem Number 8 consists of 5 items. Select the best answer for each item. **Answer all items.** Your grade will be based on the total number of correct answers.

_____

**Items A through E** are based on the following:

Bilco Inc. produces bricks and uses a standard costing system. On the diagram below, the line OP represents Bilco's standard material cost at any output volume expressed in direct material pounds to be used. Bilco had identical outputs in each of the first three months of 1992, with a standard cost of V in each month. Points Ja, Fe, and Ma represent the actual pounds used and actual costs incurred in January, February, and March, respectively.

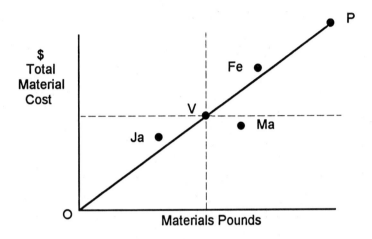

**Required:**
For Items A through E, determine whether each variance is favorable or unfavorable.

**Items to be answered:**
A.   January material price variance.
B.   January material usage variance.
C.   February material price variance.
D.   February material usage variance.
E.   March material net variance.

# Chapter Sixteen
## Solutions to Cost Accounting Questions
## Joint Products and Standard Costs

1. (b) Relative profitability is inappropriate because profitability itself is affected by the allocation method; that is, there is circularity of reasoning.

2. (c) $15,000 for Q and $9,000 for R

Joint cost allocated to R:

$$\frac{\text{Sales value R at split-off}}{\text{Sales value of P, Q and R at split-off}} \quad \frac{\$15,000}{\$100,000} \times \text{Joint Cost } \$60,000 = \$9,000$$

Joint cost allocated to Q:

| | |
|---|---|
| To P | $36,000 |
| To R | 9,000 |
| | $45,000 |
| Balance to Q | 15,000 |
| Total Joint Cost | $60,000 |

3. (c) $60,000

$$\frac{\text{P's Joint Cost}}{\text{Total Joint Cost}} \quad \frac{\$36,000}{\$60,000} = 60\%$$

60% × Total Sales Value at split-off – $100,000 = $60,000

4. (d) Allocation of joint costs

| Product | Sales Value at Split-Off | Percent | Cost to be Allocated | Allocated Cost |
|---|---|---|---|---|
| W | $ 80,000 | 40 | $160,000 | $ 64,000 |
| X | 60,000 | 30 | 160,000 | 48,000 |
| Y | 40,000 | 20 | 160,000 | 32,000 |
| Z | 20,000 | 10 | 160,000 | 16,000 |
| Totals | $200,000 | 100 | | $160,000 |

5. (c) $48,000.

| | Sales Value | - Separable Cost | = | N.R.V. | Relative NRV |
|---|---|---|---|---|---|
| Ajac | 80,000 | 8,000 | | 72,000 | 72/90 = 80% |
| Bjac | 40,000 | 22,000 | | 18,000 | 18/90 = 20% |
| | | | | 90,000 | |

Joint cost allocated to Ajac:

80% x $60,000 = $48,000

6. (b) $1 increase per unit sold

| | |
|---|---|
| Increase in sales revenue | $4 per unit |
| Increase in cost of goods sold* | 3 per unit |
| Increase in gross profit | 1 per unit |

* As unit would no longer be considered a by-product, cost of goods sold would not be reduced by the net realizable value of the units sold.

7. (a) The relative sales-value method under which joint-product costs are prorated to each product according to total sales value will result in a uniform gross-profit rate for all products.

| e.g.: | *Product A* | *Product B* | *Total* |
|---|---|---|---|
| Sales Value | $100 (1/3) | $200 (2/3) | $300 |
| Less: Joint Costs | 50 (1/3) | 100 (2/3) | 150 |
| Gross Profit | $ 50 (50%) | $100 (50%) | $150 (50%) |

8. (d) Sales value at split-off:

| | |
|---|---|
| A    500 gal. × $10 | $ 5,000 |
| B 1,000 gal. × $14 | 14,000 |
| Total | $19,000 |

| | |
|---|---|
| Joint cost allocated to B: | |
| $4,560 × 14,000/19,000 | $ 3,360 |
| Cost of subsequent processing | |
| 1,000 gal. × $1 | 1,000 |
| Total cost of 1,000 gal. of B | $ 4,360 |

9. (c) Joint cost allocated to B

Sales value B at split-off $\dfrac{150,000}{440,000}$ × joint cost $264,000 = $90,000
Sales value A + B at split-off

*Note*: The sales value at split-off of the by-product X is irrelevant as joint costs are not allocated to by-products in this problem.

10. (d) A by-product is a product of relatively small value which is obtained during production of the main product. Answer (d) would be the best description of this.

11. (d) The "split-off point" occurs when two or more products which are produced simultaneously can be specifically identified and separated as individual products. These products may or may not require subsequent processing in order to be salable. Classification of simultaneously produced products as "joint products" or "by-products" is determined by their relative sales values. Simultaneously produced products of more than nominal value are classified as joint products, while those of relatively small or insignificant sale value are classified as by-products.

12. (b) The cost of by-products **may** include an allocation of joint costs; however, this allocation is normally not made.

13. (c) Joint cost allocated to E

$$\frac{\text{E's Sales value at split off}}{\text{Total Sales value at split off}} \times \text{Joint Cost}$$

$$\frac{\$\,30{,}000}{\$200{,}000} \times \$120{,}000 = \$18{,}000$$

*Joint cost allocated to D*

| | |
|---|---:|
| Total Joint Cost | $120,000 |
| Less: Joint cost allocated to: | |
| C (given) | (72,000) |
| E (above) | (18,000) |
| Joint cost allocated to D | $ 30,000 |

14. (c)

| | | |
|---|---:|---:|
| Sales of E | | $40,000 |
| Less: Cost of E | | |
| Joint cost (above) | 18,000 | |
| Subsequent Costs | 6,000 | 24,000 |
| Gross Profit on E | | $16,000 |

**Note**: 2,000 units of E were originally produced and all 2,000 were processed further and sold; therefore, all joint costs and subsequent processing costs for E are included in cost of goods sold.

15. (c) The relative sales value of joint products may be unknown at the point of split-off or because of extensive subsequent processing required to make the product salable, may be difficult to determine. In such cases, it is recommended that the subsequent costs be applied as a reduction in revenue on a dollar-for-dollar basis and the remaining revenue used as the sales value at split-off for assignment of joint cost.

16. (d) Under the relative sales value at split-off method of allocating joint costs, an increase in the market value of P at split-off would increase the proportion and amount of joint costs allocated to P and decrease the joint costs allocated to Q. As all other costs and selling prices remain unchanged, the increase in joint costs allocated to P would result in a decrease in P's gross margin while the decrease in joint costs allocated to Q would result in an increase in Q's gross margin.

17. (a) $0 profit.
Net realizable value is an item's selling price less the costs to complete and dispose of the item. When a by-product (or an inventory item) is valued at its net realizable value, no profit or loss results from its sale.

| | |
|---|---:|
| 1991 sales of Moy ($5,000 × $6) | $30,000 |
| Less cost of goods sold ($5,000 × $4)* | (20,000) |
| Gross profit—Moy | $10,000 |
| Less selling costs ($5,000 × $2) | (10,000) |
| Net profit | —0— |

* Net realizable value = selling price – cost to complete and dispose = $6 – $2 = $4.

18. (c) When the actual sales value at the split-off point is not known, the final sales value is reduced by costs subsequent to the split-off point to determine the relative value at split-off. Therefore, if subsequent costs for product Z increase while those of Y remain constant, Z's relative value would decrease resulting in less joint costs being allocated to Z and more being allocated to Y.

19. (a) Self-explanatory.

20. (a) Flexible budgeting is a reporting system wherein the planned level of activity is adjusted to the actual level of activity before the budget to actual comparison report is prepared. It may be appropriately employed for any item which is affected by the level of activity.

In standard costing, product costs are predetermined and set up as a goal to be attained. Actual performance is compared to the standard. A primary objective of a standard costing system is to control costs.

21. (a) The amount being produced within a period (volume) is driven by the sales forecast, which is generally more controllable by the sales department rather than the production department. Production then, in turn, controls material, labor and overhead efficiency or usage.

22. (b) Since the material price variance relates to the difference between standard price and actual price and might be viewed as measuring the performance of the company's purchasing department, the variance should be determined on the basis of the units purchased and should therefore be computed when the purchase occurs.

23. (b) This method provides for allocation among all units that were handled during the period.

24. (c) Because the amounts are immaterial, allocation is not warranted; hence, they are treated as a determinant of the current period's earnings only.

25. (c)

| | |
|---|---:|
| Actual direct labor hours used | 1,050 |
| Standard direct labor hours allowed | |
| 500 units × 2 hours per unit | 1,000 |
| Excess hours | 50 |
| Standard direct labor rate | × $6 |
| Direct labor efficiency variance | $ 300 (UF) |

26. (c) Standard costs may be used in either job order costing or process costing. Standard costing is a cost estimation technique used for control purposes and to simplify costing procedures and expedite cost reports. The system of recording costs (job order or process) is independent of the costs to be recorded (standard or actual).

27. (a) All purchases are "charged in" at standard. Therefore, the debit to raw materials for the purchase of item 1 would be: 100,000 ft. × $.75 = $75,000.

28. (c) Debits to work-in-process for direct labor:    8,000 units × 4 hrs. × $3.50 = $112,000.

29. (d) Materials usage variance for item 2:

| Units | | Price | |
|---|---|---|---:|
| Actual | × | Standard | |
| 26,000 ft. | | $1.00 | $26,000 |
| Standard | × | Standard | |
| 24,000 ft.* | | $1.00 | 24,000 |
| Unfavorable variance (debit) | | | $ 2,000 |

\* 8,000 units × 3 ft. per unit.

30. (a) The materials-usage variance does not arise until the materials are placed into production. Therefore, no part of the variance will be prorated to raw-materials inventory.

31. (d)

| | |
|---|---:|
| Actual price paid per foot | $.78 |
| Less: Standard price per foot | .75 |
| Material-price variance per foot | $.03 (unfav.) |
| | |
| Ending raw materials inventory | 22,000 ft. |
| Price variance per foot | × $ .03 |
| Material price variance to be prorated to raw materials | $ 660 dr |

32. (b) The best basis upon which standards should be established is always the normal, or currently attainable performance. Setting them at the ideal or theoretical maximum capacity creates standards which may never be met, resulting in frustration amongst the workers and rendering the cost reports meaningless. By establishing performance standards too low, they may cause workers to reduce their output in order to hit the low standards, unknown to management.

33. (a) An unfavorable labor rate variance suggests that the labor cost was higher than anticipated, and a favorable labor efficiency variance implies that more productive work occurred than had been expected.

34. (a) $40,000 actual overhead.

| | |
|---|---:|
| Standard manufacturing costs | $100,000 |
| Add: Excess of actual manufacturing costs over standard costs | 20,000 |
| Total actual manufacturing costs | $120,000 |
| Less: Actual prime costs (direct materials and direct labor) | (80,000) |
| Actual manufacturing overhead costs | $ 40,000 |

35. (b) A credit balance indicates a favorable variance, with standard hours allowed being greater than actual hours used.

36. (c) 2,000 favorable.

Set-up information given:
$$20,000 \times \ ? \ = \$40,000$$
$$20,000 \times 2.10 = \ ?$$

Fill in the blanks:
$$20,000 \times \$2.00 = \$40,000$$
$$20,000 \times \$2.10 = \$42,000 \qquad \text{Fav. 2,000 CR}$$

or simply $20,000 \times (2.10 - 2.00) = \$2,000$ FAVORABLE

37. (a) Actual number of pounds in excess of standard is unfavorable; actual cost being less than standard cost is favorable.

38. (c)

| | |
|---|---:|
| Actual quantity 1,600 @ std. price $3.60 | = 5,760 |
| Less: Favorable price variance | (240) |
| Actual quantity 1,600 @ actual price | 5,520 |
| ÷ actual quantity | ÷ 1,600 |
| = actual price per unit | $3.45 |

39. (d) 1,600. Set up a variance computation schedule and work backwards.

| | | | | |
|---|---|---|---|---|
| Standard hours | × | Standard rate | | |
| 1,500 | × | $6.00 | = $9,000 | |
| Actual hours | × | Standard rate | | $600 U |
| (1) | × | $6.00 | = (2) | |

(2) = $9,000 + $600 unfavorable variance or $9,600
(1) = $9,600 ÷ $6.00 or $1,600

Also, since the efficiency variance is the difference between actual hours and standard hours times the standard rate, the variance can be divided by $6.00 ($600 ÷ 6.00 = 100 hours + 1,500 hours = 1,600)

**40. (c) $1,400 favorable**
The net overhead variance is the difference between actual overhead, $12,600, and overhead applied to product cost or standard.

| | |
|---|---|
| Actual overhead | $12,600 |
| Standard 3,500 hours allowed × total overhead rate per hour $4.00 | 14,000 |
| Favorable total variance | $ 1,400 |

**41. (b)**

$$\text{Actual hours} \times \text{actual rate} = \text{Total payroll}$$

$$\text{Actual rate} = \frac{\text{Total payroll}}{\text{Actual hours}}$$

$$= \frac{\$110,200}{29,000}$$

$$= \$3.80$$

**42. (c)**   Rate variance = Actual hours × the difference between the standard and actual rates (D)

$$\$5,800 = 29,000\ D$$
$$D = \$.20 \text{ per hour}$$

Because the rate variance is favorable, the standard rate must be $.20 more than the actual rate of $3.80, or $4.00.

**43. (c) Spending variance—unchanged; Volume variance—increased.**
   The overhead spending (budget) variance is the difference between actual overhead costs and budgeted overhead costs at the actual level of activity achieved. The activity level used to determine the predetermined rate for overhead allocation has no effect on this variance.
   The overhead volume variance is the difference between budgeted overhead costs at the standard level of activity for the production achieved and applied overhead costs. It is attributable to the over- or under-application of fixed costs, due to production at an activity level other than where the predetermined overhead rate was determined. If the activity level used to determine the predetermined overhead rate was increased (80% of practical capacity to 100%), the fixed overhead application rate would decrease and less fixed overhead would be applied per unit of activity achieved. This would result in an increase in an unfavorable (underapplied) or a decrease in a favorable (overapplied) volume variance.

**44. (c)** If over- or underapplied overhead is interpreted as an error in allocating actual costs, then this error should be corrected by prorating the variance to the components affected: cost of goods sold and ending inventories.
   (Note: Over- or underapplied overhead is the difference between actual overhead and overhead applied at a predetermined rate.)

**45. (b)** An unfavorable direct labor efficiency variance represents the number of actual hours required over the number of standard labor hours allowed for that level of output, multiplied by the standard labor rate. For making 1,000 we were allowed:

| | | |
|---|---|---|
| 1,000 units @ 4 hours per unit = | 4,000 | hours allowed |
| Actual hours | 4,100 | |
| Excess hours over standard | 100 | |
| Standard rate | $ 12 | |
| Variance | $1,200 | |

**46. (c)** Under the two variance method of overhead analysis:
**Controllable Variance** = actual overhead vs. budgeted overhead at standard activity base allowed for the production achieved (if using standard costs) or budgeted overhead at actual activity base used (if using actual costing techniques—not standard costing).
**Volume Variance** = budgeted overhead at standard activity base (or actual activity base if not using standard costing) vs. applied overhead.

47. (a) Material usage variances cannot occur until materials are placed into production. Production does not occur in purchasing and warehousing. Purchasing and warehousing may be charged the material purchase price variance.

48. (d) The variable overhead rate would be the same for all three activity levels. By definition, variable overhead would be the same per unit, machine hour, etc., within a relevant range of capacity.

49. (b) A static budget is not adjusted to the actual level of activity before the budget to actual comparison report is prepared. Therefore, a level of activity below the budget level would usually result in favorable variance for variable cost items (total cost changes with change in the level of activity). However, fixed cost items (total cost does not change with changes in the level of activity) would not usually show favorable (or unfavorable) variances as the cost would not differ from budget as a result of the decrease in activity.

50. (b)

| | |
|---|---|
| Actual Overhead | $178,500 |
| Less: Spending Variance | 8,000 Unf |
| Budget | 170,500 |
| Less: Fixed Costs | 110,000 |
| | $ 60,500  ÷ $.50 = 121,000 hours |

51. (d)

| | |
|---|---|
| Overhead Rate | $1.50 |
| Variable Portion | .50 |
| Fixed Portion | $1.00 |
| Fixed Cost | $110,000 |
| Normal Volume | 110,000 hours |
| Volume Variance | $5,000 ÷ $1 = 5,000 hours |
| Standard Hours | 110,000 + 5,000 = 115,000 |

*Total Variance Computation:*

| | | |
|---|---|---|
| Actual | 178,500 | |
| Budget | 170,500 | 8,000 UNF |
| 110,000 + 121,000 × .50 | | |
| Efficiency | 167,500 | 3,000 UNF |
| 110,000 + 115,000 × .50 | | |
| Volume | 172,500 | 5,000 FAV |
| 115,000 × 1.50 | | |

This answer is based on the use of standard hours in computing the efficiency variance. This is not the only way this variance can be computed, but the question does not allow for alternative answers.

52. (d) $123,000

| | |
|---|---|
| Budget $50,000 + 18,000 × $4 = | $122,000 |
| Add: Budget variances | |
| (unfavorable) | 1,000 |
| Actual Overhead | $123,000 |

53. (c) 122,500

 Actual Overhead

  (see previous solution)       $123,000

  Budget $50,000 + 18,000 × $4    122,000 Unf. $1,000 Budget Var.

  Applied Overhead        [1]122,500 Fav. $500 Volume Var.

[1]Add the volume variance to Budget $122,000 + $500 = $122,500

Note: For further practice compute the total overhead rate and normal activity:

    Total overhead rate = $122,500 ÷ 18,000 = $6.80 (rounded)

    Normal = $6.80 – $4.00 = $2.80 (fixed portion of rate)

    FC $50,000 ÷ 2.80 = 17,857 labor hours

54. (a) $750 favorable

  Actual overhead      $15,000

  Budget (actual hours)

  $7,000 + 3,500 × $2.50    $15,750  $750 spending var. (favorable)

  * Budget (standard hours)

  $7,000 + 3,800 × $2.50    $16,500  $750 efficiency var. (favorable)

* Not required. The volume variance cannot be determined with the facts given.

55. (b)

| | | |
|---|---|---|
| Actual overhead: variable | 73,000 | |
| Actual overhead: fixed | 17,000 | 90,000 |
| Applied overhead | | |
|  Variable  2.50 × 32,000 std. hrs. | 80,000 | |
|  Fixed     .50 × 32,000 std. hrs. | 16,000 | 96,000 |
| Favorable variance (overapplied) | | 6,000 |

56. (b) Volume variance—favorable; Efficiency variance—unfavorable.

  The overhead volume variance is the difference between budgeted overhead costs at the standard level of activity for the production achieved (line DB, overhead flexible budget line) and applied overhead costs (line OA, standard overhead application line). As line OA (applied overhead) is above line OB (budgeted overhead) at point V, the standard hours required for actual output, the volume variance is favorable (applied over head exceeds budget at standard).

  The overhead efficiency variance is the difference between budgeted overhead at the actual level of activity and budgeted overhead at the standard level of activity for the production achieved. As point S, the actual level of activity (machine hours) is greater than (is to the right of) point V, the standard hours required for actual output, the budget at actual activity exceeds the budget at standard activity and the overhead efficiency variance is unfavorable.

57. (d) BC minus DO.

Line BC = Total costs at C machine hours

Line DO = Fixed costs, total cost at zero machine hours

Variable cost  = Total cost – fixed costs

    = BC – DO

58. (b) $420 Favorable.

  Material Price Variance    =  Actual Quantity (Actual Price vs. Standard Price)

             =  $4200  ($2.40 - $2.50)

             =  $420

  Actual Price = $10,080 / 4200 meters = $2.40

  The Variance is favorable as the actual price is less than the standard price.

59. (c) $51,000

| Change in Cost | = | 75,000 - 15,000 | = | $60,000 | = | $3 Variable Cost |
| Change in Units | | 20,000 | | 20,000 | | per unit |

Total Cost of 12,000 Units:
|  |  |
|---|---|
| Variable Cost ($3 x 12,000) | $36,000 |
| Fixed Cost | 15,000 |
| Total Cost | $51,000 |

60. (a) $30 standard direct labor costs per unit.

|  |  |
|---|---|
| Weekly wages per worker | $500 |
| Add: Benefits treated as direct labor | 100 |
|  | $600 |
| # of productive hours per week, per worker | ÷ 40 |
| Standard direct labor costs per hour | $ 15 |
| # hours required per unit | × 2 |
| Standard direct labor costs per unit | $ 30 |

61. (b) Under the two variance method of overhead analysis:
Controllable variance = **actual overhead** vs. budgeted overhead at standard activity base allowed for the production achieved.
Volume variance = budgeted overhead at standard activity base allowed for the production achieved vs. applied overhead based upon standard activity base allowed for production achieved.

62. (c) The spending (budget) variance is considered a measure of the control of spending in that actual overhead costs are compared with budgeted overhead costs at the actual activity achieved.

The volume (capacity) variance does not relate to the control of overhead costs as it is attributable to the over- or under-application of fixed costs, due to production at an activity level other than where the predetermined overhead rate was originally determined.

63. (b) Overhead is generally applied based upon direct labor hours. The unfavorable overhead efficiency variance represents the number of actual hours required over the number of standard labor hours allowed for that level of output, multiplied by the standard variable overhead rate. For making 5,000 units we were allowed:

|  |  |  |
|---|---|---|
| 5,000 units @ 2 hours per unit = | 10,000 | hours allowed |
| Actual hours | 10,500 | |
| Excess hours over standard | 500 | |
| Standard rate | $ 3 | |
| Variance | $1,500 | |

64. (c)
|  |  |
|---|---|
| Actual unit price | $ 3.60 |
| Less unfavorable price variance per unit | |
| $3,600 ÷ 18,000 | ( .20) |
| Standard price per unit | 3.40 |
| Standard quantity allowed | 16,000 |
| Actual quantity used | 15,000 |
| Quantity difference (favorable) | 1,000 |
| Standard price per unit | × $3.40 |
| Favorable quantity variance | $ 3,400 |

65. (a)   A Standard cost system can be used for cost control by/for any company, product, process or service for which standard costs can be established.

66. (d) As point A is above line OW (standard), the actual rate exceeds the standard rate for the direct labor hours used, therefore, the rate variance is unfavorable.

As point A is to the left of point S, the actual direct labor hours used were less than the standard hours allowed for the actual output, therefore, the efficiency variance is favorable.

67. (a) Under the three (3) variance method, the spending variance is the difference between actual overhead and the budget for overhead at actual activity base.

68. (a) Under the two variance method of overhead analysis:

**Controllable variance**  =  actual overhead vs. budgeted overhead at standard activity base allowed for the production achieved.

**Volume variance**  =  Budgeted overhead at standard activity base allowed for the production achieved vs. applied overhead based upon standard activity base allowed.

69. (d)  Direct materials requirement per unit

| | |
|---|---|
| (2 yards per finished unit ÷ 80%*) | 2.5  yards |
| Cost per yard | × $3 |
| Standard direct materials cost per unit | $7.50 |

* If direct material spoilage is 20% of input quantities, output quantities are 80% of input (100% – 20%).

70. (a)  Actual quantity purchased @ actual cost = 100,000 lbs @ $.17 =     $17,000
Actual quantity purchased @ standard cost = 100,000 lbs. @ $.20 =     20,000
Favorable material price variance (on purchases)     $ 3,000

71. (c)  Actual hours @ standard rate = 3900 hrs. @ $7 =     $27,300
Standard hours @ standard rate = 4000 hrs. @ $7 =     28,000
Favorable labor efficiency variance     $  700

Standard hours = .4 hrs./unit × 10,000 units produced = 4000 standard hrs.

72. (b) High-low points method:

| | *High* | *Low* | *Change* |
|---|---|---|---|
| Direct-labor hours | 400,000 | 300,000 | 100,000 |
| Total costs | $154,000 | $129,000 | $25,000 |

The change between the high and low points isolates the variable costs which are $.25 per hour ($25,000 % 100,000 hours).

At the high point, total variable costs are $100,000 (400,000 hours × $.25). Therefore, total fixed costs budgeted are $54,000 ($154,000 – $100,000). Budgeted fixed costs can also be calculated using the low point.

(300,000 hrs. × $.25 = $75,000 total variable costs + $54,000 fixed costs = $129,000 total costs)

73. (c) Analysis of Fixed and Variable Costs Through the High-Low, Two-Point Method
The high-low method is used to isolate the fixed and variable portions of costs by analysis of the high and low points of activity.

| | *Cost* | *Machine Hours* |
|---|---|---|
| High | $39,200 | 24,000 |
| Low | 32,000 | 15,000 |
| Change | $ 7,200 | 9,000 |
| | | |
| Change per machine hour | | $7,200 = $.80 |
| | | 9,000 |

By definition of a variable cost (changes proportionately with changes in volume), the $.80 per machine hour change is the variable portion of the maintenance costs.

74. (b) Computation of Fixed Costs

|  | High | Low |
|---|---|---|
| Total Costs | $39,200 | $32,000 |
| Less:   Variable Costs from above: | | |
|    24,000 × $.80 | 19,200 | |
|    15,000 × $.80 | | 12,000 |
| Fixed costs per month | $20,000 | $20,000 |

**NOTE**: Only one computation is needed; however, both are shown to illustrate that the result is the same.
12 × $20,000 = $240,000 total annual fixed costs.

75. (b) Under the two variance method: The controllable (budget) variance is the difference between the actual overhead and the budgeted overhead. Both of these contain variable and fixed costs and either fixed or variable costs can vary from the budget.

The volume variance is due solely to fixed costs. It is the difference between the budgeted overhead and applied overhead based upon the same level of activity as the budget. Because the budget and applied activity bases are the same, budgeted variable overhead will equal applied variable overhead, and any volume variance is due solely to fixed costs.

*Note:* The answer is the same for both actual and standard costing. The difference between actual and standard, under the two variance method, is the activity base used for the budgeted overhead. Under actual costing, the activity base used would be the actual activity base achieved, while under standard costing, it would be the standard activity base for the production achieved.

# Chapter Sixteen
# Solutions to Cost Accounting Problems
# Joint Products and Standard Costs

## NUMBER 1

**a.**  1. A variable cost is a cost that increases in a linear manner (within a relevant range) with respect to an activity factor, such as units of production, direct labor hours, or machine hours. The variable cost may or may not increase in a one-to-one ratio with the activity factor. For example, each unit produced may incur more than one unit of labor (hour) or material (pound), but it is assumed that for each unit produced the same number of units of labor (hours) or materials (pounds) will be used. Another essential assumption of a true variable cost is that if a unit of activity does not occur, the cost is not incurred. In theory, if the variable cost per unit of activity is known and the total activity factor is known, the variable cost can be computed by multiplying the per-unit cost by the activity factor.

2. A fixed cost, as opposed to a true variable cost, does not react to activity in that the amount remains constant regardless of the level of activity within a relevant range. Fixed costs are often referred to as "step costs." For a given range of activity the amount of fixed costs is constant; however, if one additional unit of activity occurs, the next entire relevant range of cost may be incurred. When presented graphically, this situation appears to be an ascending series of steps, the breadth of each step being one relevant range. As an example, when the productive capacity of a plant is fully utilized, additional plant capacity will be needed to produce one additional unit of product. This additional capacity represents an entirely new fixed cost (rent or depreciation) with a new range of production. Fixed costs generally occur whether or not activity occurs; however, some fixed costs may be stair-stepped upward or downward as activity is increased or reduced, and fixed costs per unit of activity within a relevant range have an inverse relationship to activity. That is, the more units produced within a relevant range, the less fixed cost to be "absorbed" by each unit.

**b.**  1. A semivariable cost is a cost that reacts to a change in activity, but not with the direct relationship that a true variable cost exhibits. A semivariable cost is made up of two components: a variable cost and a fixed cost. Therefore (within a relevant range), there is an element of a semivariable cost that does respond in direct proportion to a change in the activity factor, but there is also an element of cost that remains unchanged in relation to the activity factor.

2. The managerial accountant analyzes a semivariable cost by separating the cost into its variable and fixed components. Three basic methods can be used to separate these components.

The first is the *"scattergraph" method*, by which a graph is drawn with semivariable cost amounts on the vertical *y* axis and activity on the horizontal *x* axis. The accountant then plots various values of the semivariable cost at different activity levels and attempts to draw a straight line through the points that will approximate the trend shown by the greatest number of plotted points. The point at which this line intersects the *y* axis is approximately the fixed-cost element of the semivariable cost. The variable component is determined by subtracting the fixed element from the total cost.

The second method is the *high-low method*, which analyzes the change in the semivariable cost at two different activity levels. Since the only change in the cost is brought about by the variable element of the cost, the difference in amounts of the cost divided by the change in activity level will give the variable cost per unit of change in the activity level. At any given activity level, the variable component of the cost is computed by multiplying the activity level by the variable cost per unit of activity. The fixed component is then computed by subtraction. It must be noted that because the high-low method uses only two data points, it may not yield answers that are as accurate as those derived when a larger number of points are considered as in the other two methods.

The third method of breaking out the variable and fixed components of a semivariable cost is called the *"least-squares" method* or *"simple regression" analysis*. This method analyzes the difference between the mean activity and mean amounts of the total cost as compared to the actual values for activity and amounts and mathematically computes a line drawn through a set of plotted points such that the sum of the squared deviations of each actual plotted point from the point directly above or below it on the regression line is at a minimum. The computation is as follows. For each known value of the total cost, the difference between the actual activity and average activity is squared; the results of this operation are then added together. Simultaneously, for each known value of the total cost, the difference between the actual cost and average cost for all known values is multiplied by the difference between actual activity level and average activity level at that cost; the results of this operation are then added together. Finally, the summed results of the squared activity differences are divided into the summed results of the differences for activity times difference from mean cost to yield the variable factor per unit of activity. The fixed-cost component can be computed by subtraction after computing total variable cost at a given activity level. The fixed-cost component can also be computed by substituting the variable cost factor and mean total cost and activity factors into the general equation for a straight line; $y = a + bx$. In this equation $y$ equals average total cost, $a$ equals the fixed-cost element, $b$ equals the variable cost factor, and $x$ equals the average activity level.

There must be a high level of correlation between the activity base and the cost for any of the three methods to be reliable. Correlation can be computed mathematically.

## NUMBER 2

**Webb & Company**
**March**

**a.**

| (1) *Equivalent Units* | *Labor* | *Overhead* |
|---|---|---|
| Returns completed (200 + 825 – 125) | 900 | 900 |
| Returns in process, 3/31 (125 × 80%) | 100 | 100 |
| Equivalent units | 1,000 | 1,000 |

| (2) *Actual Cost Per Equivalent Unit* | *Labor* | *Overhead* |
|---|---|---|
| Cost of returns in process, 3/1 | $ 6,000 | $ 2,500 |
| Add: March costs | 89,000 | 45,000 |
| Total costs | 95,000 | 47,500 |
| Divided by weighted average equivalent units | ÷ 1,000 | ÷ 1,000 |
| Actual cost per equivalent unit | $95.00 | $47.50 |

**b.** *Actual Cost of Returns in Process at 3/31*

| | |
|---|---|
| Labor (125 returns × 80% × $95.00) | $ 9,500 |
| Overhead (125 returns × 80% × $47.50) | 4,750 |
| Total | $14,250 |

**c.** *Standard Cost Per Return*

| | |
|---|---|
| Labor (5 hrs. @ $20) | $100 |
| Overhead (5 hrs. @ $10) | 50 |
| Total | $150 |

**d.** *Analysis of March Performance*

(1) Total labor variance (actual minus standard)
   $89,000 – (950* × $100) = $6,000 favorable
(2) Labor rate variance
   [($89,000 ÷ 4,000) - $20)] × 4,000 = $9,000 unfavorable
(3) Labor efficiency variance
   [4,000 – (950* × 5)] × $20 = $15,000 favorable
(4) Total overhead variance (actual minus standard)
   $45,000 – (950* × $50) = $2,500 favorable
(5) Overhead volume variance
   $49,000 – (950* × $50) = $1,500 unfavorable
(6) Overhead budget variance
   $45,000 – $49,000 = $4,000 favorable

|  | Labor | Overhead |
|---|---|---|
| *Equivalent units (weighted average method) | 1,000 | 1,000 |
| Less equivalent units beginning inventory | | |
| (25% × 200) | 50 | 50 |
| Equivalent units for current production | 950 | 950 |

# NUMBER 3

**a.**

*Armando Corporation*
## COMPUTATION OF VARIABLE AND FIXED FACTORY OVERHEAD PER UNIT

| Factory overhead per unit | | |
|---|---|---|
| Variable ($30 × 2/3) | $20.00 | |
| Fixed ($30 × 1/3) | 10.00 | |
| Total | $30.00 | |

*Schedule 1--Computation of Variable Factory Overhead Rate Per Direct Labor Hour*

| Variable factory overhead per unit | $20.00 | |
|---|---|---|
| Direct labor hours per unit | 4 | $ 5.00 |

*Schedule 2--Computation of Total Fixed Factory Overhead*

Direct labor hours (2,400) × Fixed factory overhead rate per direct
labor hour ($10.00 ÷ 4 hours) — $ 6,000

**b.**
## COMPUTATION OF VARIANCES
*Month Ended July 31*

*Schedule 1--Materials Price Variance Based on Purchases*

| Direct materials actually purchased (18,000 × $1.38) | $24,840 |
|---|---|
| Standard cost of above (18,000 × $1.35) | 24,300 |
| Materials price variance—unfavorable | $ 540 |

*Schedule 2--Materials Usage Variance*

| Actual quantity used at standard cost (9,500 × $1.35) | $12,825 |
|---|---|
| Standard quantity allowed (500 units × 20 yards) at | |
| standard cost (10,000 × $1.35) | 13,500 |
| Materials usage variance—favorable | $ 675 |

*Schedule 3--Labor Rate Variance*

| Actual hours at actual rate (2,100 × $9.15) | $19,215 |
|---|---|
| Actual hours at standard rate (2,100 × $9.00) | 18,900 |
| Labor rate variance—unfavorable | $ 315 |

*Schedule 4--Labor Efficiency Variance*

| Actual hours at standard rate (2,100 × $9.00) | $18,900 |
|---|---|
| Standard hours allowed—500 units × 4 at | |
| standard rate (2,000 × $9.00) | 18,000 |
| Labor efficiency variance—unfavorable | $ 900 |

*Schedule 5--Controllable Factory Overhead Variance*

| Actual total factory overhead | | $16,650 |
|---|---|---|
| Budgeted factory overhead at standard hours | | |
| Fixed | $ 6,000 | |
| Variable (500 units × 4 hours × $5.00) | 10,000 | 16,000 |
| Controllable factory overhead variance—unfavorable | | $ 650 |

_Schedule 6--Capacity (Volume) Factory Overhead Variance_

| | |
|---|---:|
| Budgeted factory overhead at standard hours | $16,000 |
| Applied total factory overhead | |
| Hours allowed—2,000 × $7.50 (5/6 × $9.00) | 15,000 |
| Capacity factory overhead variance—unfavorable | $ 1,000 |

# NUMBER 4

1. A factory overhead variance analysis report provides periodic identification of deviations from planned outcomes. It provides a basis for further analysis, investigation, and follow-up action. It is useful in developing budgets and standards for future operations. Variances can be used to identify changes in operations that need to be reflected in such activities as product pricing, compensation rates, maintenance levels, and so forth. The report can be helpful in identifying costs incurred that should be classified as losses rather than product costs.

2. The two-variance method breaks down the overall factory overhead variance--that is, the difference between the actual factory overhead and the factory overhead applied to production--into two components. They are *(a)* the controllable (budget) variance and *(b)* the volume (denominator) variance.

The controllable (budget) variance is the difference between the actual factory overhead and the budget allowance based on standard hours allowed. The department managers have the responsibility to exercise control over the costs to which the variances relate.

The volume (denominator) variance is the difference between the budget allowance based on standard hours allowed and the factory overhead applied to production. The variance indicates the cost of capacity available but not utilized or not utilized efficiently, and such variance is generally considered the responsibility of management.

# NUMBER 5

1.

*Lond Co.*
**TOTAL GROSS MARGIN**
*For the Year Ended December 31, 1989*

| | Jana | Reta | Total |
|---|---:|---:|---:|
| Sales | $200,000 | $300,000 | $500,000 |
| Cost of sales | | | |
|    Joint costs ($236,000 – $6,000) | | | 230,000 |
|    Separable costs | | 210,000 | 210,000 |
| Total costs | | | 440,000 |
| Total gross margin (12%) | | | $ 60,000 |

2.

*Lond Co.*
**ALLOCATION OF JOINT COSTS**
*For the Year Ended December 31, 1989*

| | Jana | Reta | Total |
|---|---:|---:|---:|
| Sales | $200,000 | $300,000 | $500,000 |
| Less gross margin (12%)* | 24,000 | 36,000 | 60,000 |
| Less separable costs | | 210,000 | 210,000 |
| Total deductions | 24,000 | 246,000 | 270,000 |
| Joint costs | $176,000 | $ 54,000 | $230,000 |

*Gross margin = $60,000 total gross margin ÷ $500,000 total sales (from part 1).

3.

*Lond Co.*
**PRODUCT GROSS MARGINS**
*For the Year Ended December 31, 1989*

|  | Jana | Reta | Total |
|---|---|---|---|
| Sales | $200,000 | $300,000 | $500,000 |
| Cost of sales |  |  |  |
|    Joint costs (from part 2) | 176,000 | 54,000 | 230,000 |
|    Separable costs |  | 210,000 | 210,000 |
|      Total costs | 176,000 | 264,000 | 440,000 |
| Gross margins | $ 24,000 | $ 36,000 | $ 60,000 |

# NUMBER 6

**a. 1.**          **DIRECT MATERIALS PRICE VARIANCE**

| | | |
|---|---|---|
| Actual cost | 2,400 gallons @ $2.45 per gallon | $5,880 |
| Standard cost | 2,400 gallons @ $2.50 per gallon | 6,000 |
| Price variance | | $ 120  Favorable |

**a. 2.**          **DIRECT MATERIALS USAGE VARIANCE**

Actual usage      2,400   gallons

Standard usage:

$\dfrac{1,800}{18,000} \times 21,000 \text{ feet} =$     2,100   gallons

Usage variance      300   gallons @ $2.50      $ 750  Unfavorable

**a. 3.**          **DIRECT LABOR TRAVEL, SETUP, AND CLEARUP VARIANCE**

| | | |
|---|---|---|
| Actual cost | 300 hours @ $8.00 per hour | $2,400 |
| Standard cost: | | |
|   210 customers | | |
|   × 1 hour each | 210 hours @ $8.00 per hour | 1,680 |
| Variance | | $ 720  Unfavorable |

**a. 4.**          **DIRECT LABOR BONUS**

Actual direct labor (tree-spraying)     910 hours @ $8.00 per hour     $7,280

Standard direct labor:

$\dfrac{900}{18,000} \times 21,000 \text{ feet} =$     1,050 hours @ $8.00 per hour     8,400

| | |
|---|---|
| Direct labor efficiency variance | $1,120  Favorable |
| Incentive | × .75 |
| Bonus | $ 840 |

**a. 5.**          **OVERHEAD SPENDING VARIANCE**

| | | |
|---|---|---|
| Actual overhead | | $5,400 |
| Standard overhead: | | |
|   Variable | | |
|     210 customers × ($1,200/200) | $1,260 | |
|     21,000 feet × ($1,800/18,000) | 2,100 | |
|   Fixed | 2,000 | 5,360 |
| Spending variance | | $ 40  Unfavorable |

**b.**

**ANALYSIS TO DETERMINE ADVISABILITY OF**
**HIRING AN ADDITIONAL EMPLOYEE**

*Direct labor costs of overtime for current employees*

Estimated increase in volume:

| | |
|---|---:|
| 20 additional customers with 70% probability | 14 |
| 30 additional customers with 30% probability | 9 |
| Weighted average number of new customers | 23 |

Travel, setup, and clearup
    1 hour for each of 23 new customers ....................................... 23.0

Tree-spraying
    4.5 hours for each of 23 new customers ................................. 103.5

            Total overtime hours ................................................. 126.5

Total direct labor overtime costs
    126.5 hours × \$8 per hour × 1.25 (for 25% overtime premium) ........ **\$1,265**

vs.

*Costs of hiring an additional employee*

| | |
|---|---:|
| Variable (165 hours at \$8 per hour) | \$1,320 |
| Fixed | 100 |
| Total costs of hiring an additional employee | **\$1,420** |

This analysis demonstrates that it would not be cost effective for Tredoc to hire an additional employee.

# NUMBER 7

The diagram presented depicts a manufacturing total cost flexible budget with lines for revenue (OH) and standard costs (OI) superimposed. It may also be viewed as a breakeven chart with a standard cost line added.

The manufacturing costs are represented as follows:

| Line | Description |
|---|---|
| OJ | Variable costs |
| KI | Total costs |
| KO | Fixed costs (total cost at zero volume) |

1.  Line BD
    Line KI is parallel to line OJ.
    Therefore, line BD (at E volume) equals line KO (at zero volume), the fixed costs.

2.  Line DE
    Line OJ represents variable costs.
    Therefore, line DE represents total variable costs at volume OE.

3.  Line AC
    Standard gross profit = Revenue -- Standard cost.
    At volume OE, line AC is the difference between Revenue (line OH) and standard cost (line OI).

4.  Line AB
    Budgeted gross profit = Revenue -- Budgeted cost.
    At volume OE, line AB is the difference between Revenue (line OH) and Budgeted cost (line KI).

5.  Line OG
    Standard cost equals budgeted cost at point I; therefore, the standard was based upon volume OG. Assuming standard costs are based on normal capacity, as stated, then volume OG equals normal capacity.

# NUMBER 8

A.  Unfavorable—January material price variance.
    As point Ja is above the standard material cost line (OP), the actual price exceeded the standard price for actual pounds used, therefore, January's material price variance is unfavorable.

B.  Favorable—January material usage variance.
    As point Ja lies to the left of point V (standard for actual production), actual pounds used were less than the standard pounds allowed for actual output, therefore, January's material usage variance is favorable.

C.  Unfavorable—February material price variance.
    As point Fe is above the standard cost line (OP), the actual price exceeded the standard price for actual pounds used, therefore, February's material price variance is unfavorable.

D.  Unfavorable—February material usage variance.
    As point Fe lies to the right of point V (standard for the actual production), actual pounds used exceeded the standard pounds allowed for actual output, therefore, February's material usage variance is unfavorable.

E.  Favorable—March material net variance.
    As point Ma is below point V (standard cost for the actual production), total actual material cost is less than the standard cost allowed, therefore, March's material net variance is favorable.

# Chapter Seventeen
# Managerial Analysis and Control

# Chapter Seventeen
# Managerial Analysis and Control

## DIRECT COSTING

### Defined

Direct Costing, also called marginal and variable costing, is an accounting concept in which **only variable manufacturing costs are assigned to the products** manufactured. All fixed costs are excluded from the cost of the product and expensed as period costs. The fixed costs are considered to be more closely related to the ability to produce than to the actual production of goods, and therefore are considered a cost of the period rather than the product.

### Comparison of Absorption Costing with Direct Costing

- Absorption Costing (conventional or full costing) requires that **all manufacturing costs be assigned to the products** manufactured either directly or indirectly by allocation; therefore, the inventories include the fixed portion of overhead costs which are excluded under direct costing. Compare the standard cost for a single product under absorption and direct costing.

| | | *Absorption* | *Direct* |
|---|---|---|---|
| Direct materials | 2 yards @ $1 | $ 2.00 | $ 2.00 |
| Direct labor | 2 hours @ $4 | 8.00 | 8.00 |
| Overhead | variable .50 per labor hr. | 1.00 | 1.00 |
| | fixed     .75 per labor hr. | 1.50 | —0— |
| Total Standard Cost Per Unit | | $12.50 | $11.00 |

- Direct and absorption costing yield the same net profit when sales and production are the same.
- Direct costing yields more net profit than absorption costing when sales exceed production. The beginning inventory used during the period includes fixed cost from the prior period under absorption accounting; therefore, the costs expensed during the period are greater under absorption costing.
- Direct costing yields less net profit than absorption costing when production exceeds sales. The ending inventory includes fixed costs of the current period which are transferred to the next period under absorption costing, thereby reducing the expense of the current period.
- Direct costing is **not** acceptable for financial reporting purposes because an element of inventory cost is excluded. This can easily be corrected by adjusting the inventories and cost of goods sold to include fixed costs.
- Direct costing is **not** acceptable for tax purposes or S.E.C. reporting.

**Illustrative Problem**: The following sales, cost and production data relate to the only product produced by Roy Manufacturing Company:

| | | |
|---|---|---|
| Sales price per unit | $ | 15 |
| Variable manufacturing costs per unit | | 2 |
| Variable selling costs per unit | | 1 |
| Fixed manufacturing cost | | 1,600,000 |
| Fixed selling costs | | 400,000 |
| Normal production capacity | | 200,000  units |

| Actual units in year | *1* | *2* | *3* |
|---|---|---|---|
| Production | 300,000 | 200,000 | 170,000 |
| Sales | 300,000 | 170,000 | 200,000 |

**Required:**

**a.** Prepare income statement for Roy Manufacturing Co. for years 1 through 3 using the Absorption Costing method.

**b.** Prepare income statements for Roy Manufacturing Co. for years 1 through 3 using the Direct Costing Method.


**Solution:**

**a.**

### Absorption Costing—(000 omitted)

|  | Year 1 | Year 2 | Year 3 |
|---|---|---|---|
| Sales (300,000 × $15) | $4,500 | | |
| (170,000 × $15) | | $2,550 | |
| (200,000 × $15) | | | $3,000 |
| | | | |
| *Cost of Goods Sold:* | | | |
| Beginning Inventory | —0— | —0— | |
| (30,000 × $10) | | | $ 300 |
| Cost of goods manufactured | | | |
| (300,000 × $10) | $3,000 | | |
| (200,000 × $10) | | $2,000 | |
| (170,000 × $10) | | | $1,700 |
| Capacity variance | | —0— | |
| (100,000 × $8) | (800) | | |
| ( 30,000 × $8) | | | 240 |
| Cost of goods available for sale | $2,200 | $2,000 | $2,240 |
| Less: Ending inventory | —0— | | —0— |
| (30,000 × $10) | | $ 300 | |
| Cost of goods sold | $2,200 | $1,700 | $2,240 |
| Gross Profit | $2,300 | $ 850 | $ 760 |
| | | | |
| *Selling Expenses:* | | | |
| Variable costs | | | |
| (300,000 × $1) | 300 | | |
| (170,000 × $1) | | 170 | |
| (200,000 × $1) | | | 200 |
| Fixed costs | 400 | 400 | 400 |
| Net Income before tax | $1,600 | $ 280 | $ 160 |

**b.**

## Direct Costing

|  | Year 1 | Year 2 | Year 3 |
|---|---|---|---|
| Sales (same as Absorption) | $4,500 | $2,550 | $3,000 |
| | | | |
| *Cost of Goods Sold:* | | | |
| Beginning inventory | —0— | —0— | |
|    (30,000 × $2) | | | $ 60 |
| Cost of goods manufactured | | | |
|    (300,000 × $2) | $ 600 | | |
|    (200,000 × $2) | | $ 400 | |
|    (170,000 × $2) | | | $ 340 |
| Cost of goods available for sale | $ 600 | $ 400 | $ 400 |
| Less: Ending inventory | —0— | | —0— |
|    (30,000 × $2) | | $ 60 | |
| Cost of goods sold | $ 600 | $ 340 | $ 400 |
| **Contribution margin—Mfg.** | $3,900 | $2,210 | $2,600 |
| Variable selling expenses | 300 | 170 | 200 |
| **Contribution margin—final** | $3,600 | $2,040 | $2,400 |
| Fixed Costs—manufacturing | 1,600 | 1,600 | 1,600 |
|         selling | 400 | 400 | 400 |
| Net income before taxes | $1,600 | $ 40 | $ 400 |

Note the following:

- When sales and production are equal (Year 1) the two methods provide the same net profit.
- When sales are less than production (Year 2) Absorption Costing produces higher net income than Direct Costing. This is due to the transfer of fixed cost from the current year to the next under Absorption Costing. In Year #2, $240,000 of fixed cost is transferred to Year #3 in the ending inventory. (30,000 units × $8 FC per unit)
- When sales are greater than production (Year 3) Direct Costing produces higher net income than Absorption Costing. Again, the difference is due to the transfer of fixed cost in Absorption Costing. $240,000 of fixed cost was transferred into Year #3 in the beginning inventory.
- In Direct Costing, net income follows sales. Note the increase in profit from Year 2 to Year 3 as sales increase.
- In Absorption Costing, net income may or may not follow sales. Note the decrease in net income from Year 2 to Year 3 as sales increase. This, again, is caused by the transfer of fixed costs. It may be analyzed as follows:

| | | |
|---|---|---|
| Increase in revenue | 30,000 units × $15 | $450,000 |
| Less: Increase in variable cost—mfg. | 30,000 units × $ 2 | 60,000 |
|     Increase variable cost—selling | 30,000 units × $ 1 | 30,000 |
| Increased contribution in Year 3 | | $360,000 |
| Difference in Fixed Cost from Year 2 to 3 | | |
|    Decrease in Year 2 FC | 240,000 | |
|    Increase in Year 3 FC | 240,000 | |
|    Total difference in FC | | $480,000 |
| Change in net income | | ($120,000) |

## Arguments for Using Direct Costing

- Reports are easier for management to interpret because the statements emphasize contribution margin which is the excess of selling price over variable costs.
- Direct costing emphasizes the cost-volume-profit relationships and facilitates its analysis.
- Other things remaining constant, profits move in the same direction as sales when direct costing is used, as profit is not affected by changes in the absorption of fixed costs resulting from increases or decreases in inventory. Under absorption costing, an increase in sales may result in an increase or decrease in profit as fixed costs are transferred from period to period. A decrease in sales may also result in an increase or decrease in profit under absorption costing.
- Permits a more uniform and direct evaluation of product lines, sales areas, classes of customers because of the absence of fixed cost allocation.
- The effect of fixed costs on income is emphasized by the inclusion of all such costs on the income statement.
- Because it is simpler, clerical costs are lower.

## Arguments Against Using Direct Costing

- Exclusion of fixed costs from inventory might adversely affect management decisions about pricing by emphasizing the short term aspects of the problem—(capacity, variable costs and contribution to fixed cost recovery).
- Direct costing is not acceptable for financial reporting, tax or S.E.C. purposes.
- Separation of costs into fixed and variable categories may be very difficult.


## COST-VOLUME-PROFIT RELATIONSHIPS (ANALYSIS)

Frequently referred to as break-even analysis. CVP analysis stresses the relationships between the factors which affect profit, and serves as a basis for profit planning by management.

## Break-even Analysis

- **Fixed Costs**—Costs which remain constant **in total** regardless of changes in the level of activity. Therefore, the per unit cost changes with changes in the level of operations.
- **Variable Costs**—Costs which vary in total directly with changes in the level of activity. The cost per unit is constant at different levels of activity.
- **Relevant Range**—The limits within which the level of activity may vary and the above cost-volume relationships will remain valid.
- **Contribution Margin**—Selling price less variable cost.
- **Break-even Point**—The level of operations at which there is no profit and no loss. Determined as follows:

$$\text{(a) B.E.P. (units)} = \frac{\text{Fixed Cost}}{\text{Contribution Margin}}$$

$$\text{(b) B.E.P. (\$)} = \frac{\text{Fixed Cost}}{1 - \text{VC/SP}} \quad \textbf{OR} \quad \frac{\text{Fixed Cost}}{\text{CM/SP}}$$

Fixed cost divided by the contribution margin ratio.

- **Margin of Safety**—The excess of actual or budgeted sales over sales at the break-even point. It reveals the amount by which sales could decrease before losses occur.

- **Break-even Chart**—Graphical representation of the C.V.P. relationships.

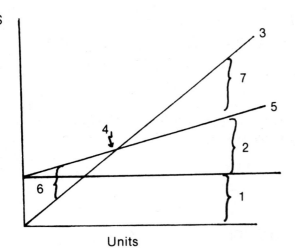 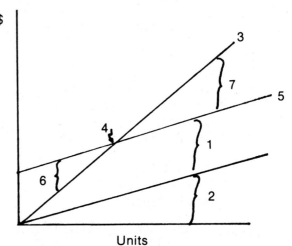

Key:  1. Fixed cost
      2. Variable cost
      3. Total revenue line
      4. Break-even point
      5. Total cost line
      6. Loss area (line 5 vs. line 3)
      7. Profit area (line 3 vs. line 5)

**Examples of Break-even Computations**—Assume the following:

| | |
|---|---|
| Selling price per unit | $2.00 |
| Variable cost per unit | $1.40 |
| Fixed Costs per year | $12,000 |
| Tax rate | 40% |

- B.E.P. (units) = $\dfrac{FC}{CM}$ = $\dfrac{\$12,000}{\$2.00 - 1.40} = \dfrac{\$12,000}{\$.60}$ = <u>20,000</u> units

- B.E.P. ($) = $\dfrac{FC}{CM\%}$ = $\dfrac{\$12,000}{\dfrac{.60}{2.00}}$ = $\dfrac{12,000}{.30}$ = <u>40,000</u> sales

Or 20,000 units × $2.00 = <u>$40,000</u>

Break-even analysis may be extended to determine the number of units or dollar sales required to earn or maintain certain profit before or after tax. Continuing the above example:

- Volume required to produce a net income of $9,000 before income taxes.

   # units = $\dfrac{FC + NIBT}{CM}$ = $\dfrac{\$12,000 + 9,000}{.60}$ = <u>35,000</u> units

   $ sales = $\dfrac{FC + NIBT}{CM\%}$ = $\dfrac{\$12,000 + 9,000}{.30}$ = <u>70,000</u>

   Margin of safety  $70,000 − $40,000 = <u>$30,000</u>

- Volume required to produce a net income of $9,000 after taxes.

$$\frac{FC + \dfrac{NIAT}{1-TR}}{CM} = \frac{\$12,000 + \dfrac{\$9,000}{1-.4}}{\$.60} = \frac{\$12,000 + \$15,000}{.60} = \underline{45,000 \text{ units}}$$

Margin of safety ($2 × 45,000) – $40,000 = $50,000

- Assume labor negotiations are underway that will increase variable costs by 20%. How many units will the company have to sell to maintain a net income of $9,000 before taxes?

| | |
|---|---|
| Selling Price | $2.00 |
| Variable cost ($1.40 × 1.20) | 1.68 |
| Contribution margin | $ .32 |

$$\# \text{ units} = \frac{FC + NIBT}{CM} = \frac{\$12,000 + \$9,000}{\$.32} = \underline{65,625} \text{ units}$$

Calculate the margin of safety. (Answer: $56,250)

## Incremental Analysis (Relevant Costing)

The concepts of C.V.P. Analysis (particularly contribution margin) may also be used to evaluate the effects of proposed changes or alternatives on profitability and the level of operations. In the application of C.V.P. concepts the candidate must be able to identify for analysis the relevant quantitative information, which varies depending on the nature of the problem. Historic amounts or amounts which do **not** change are irrelevant in decision making. The relevant amounts are the future, differential amounts (incremental analysis), the amounts which are different or change in the future depending on which alternative is selected.

**Illustrative Problem**

1. Able Company operates at 90% of plant capacity, producing 90,000 units of product. The total cost of manufacturing 90,000 units is $76,500 (VC = $49,500, FC = $27,000), resulting in a cost per unit of $.85. Recently, a large customer, who purchases 15,000 units per year, canceled his orders for the following year. Rather than operate at 75% of capacity, the company is seeking new customers. A potential customer, Buy-More Co. has offered to purchase 20,000 units at $.65 per unit. Should Abel Co. accept this special order?

| Solution: | | |
|---|---|---|
| | Selling Price | $.65 |
| | Variable Cost | .55 ($49,500 ÷ 90,000) |
| | C.M. | $.10 |

Yes. It makes a contribution to the recovery of F.C. and profit.

2. Referring to problem 1, if a second customer, Could-Be Co. is willing to buy 12,000 units at $.75 per unit, which order should be accepted?

**Answer:** "Could-Be" resulting in $400 additional contribution. (12,000 @ $.20 CM vs. 20,000 @ $.10 CM)

3. Zelta Co. manufactures a single product which it sells to other manufacturers for further processing and sale to ultimate consumers. The unit selling price and unit cost data for present production of 100,000 units per year are as follows:

| | | |
|---|---:|---:|
| Selling Price | | $7.00 |
| Direct Materials | $1.15 | |
| Direct Labor | 1.80 | |
| Variable OH | 1.15 | |
| Fixed OH | .80 | |
| Variable selling expense | .85 | |
| Fixed selling expense | .35 | 6.10 |
| Profit per unit B.T. | | $ .90 |

Zelta Co. is considering performing the required further processing itself and selling the product to the ultimate consumer. Additional processing requires no special facilities. The unit selling price and cost data of the further processing are estimated to be:

| | |
|---|---:|
| Selling price per unit | $8.50 |
| Direct labor per unit | .70 |
| Variable overhead per unit | .20 |
| Variable selling expense per unit | .10 |
| Fixed overhead per year | 15,000 |
| Fixed selling expense per year | 10,000 |

Should Zelta perform the further processing?

**Answer**: Yes, $50,000 added profit. The fixed overhead and selling expenses are not incremental costs but rather reallocations of existing costs. Note that no additional facilities were required for the additional processing. Incremental revenue is $1.50 ($8.50 - $7.00) and incremental costs are $1.00 ($.70 + $.20 + $.10). The incremental contribution margin is $.50 per unit or $50,000 total.

## Assumptions Which Underlie C.V.P. Analysis
1. Costs which can be classified as either fixed or variable.
2. Variable costs change at a linear rate.
3. Fixed costs remain unchanged over the relevant range.
4. Selling price does not change as the physical sales volume changes.
5. There is only a single product, or the sales mix remains constant.
6. Productive efficiency does not change.
7. Inventories are either kept constant or are zero.
8. Volume is the only relevant factor affecting cost.
9. There is a relevant range of validity for all of the underlying assumptions and concepts.

## PROBABILITY

Probability is the mathematical representation of the likelihood that a particular event will occur. It may be expressed in the form of a percentage, a fraction or a decimal. For example, the probability that heads will result on the flip of a fair coin is 50% (1/2 or .5). The probabilities of the various possible occurrences are collectively called the probability distribution, which totals 100% or 1.0.

Probability distributions may be either objective or subjective. Objective probability distributions are established by the application of statistical procedures to empirical evidence. Examples would include the probability distributions associated with the flip of a fair coin or the rolling of fair dice. Subjective probability distributions are those which cannot be established by the application of statistical procedures but rather are the result of subjective estimation by knowledgeable persons; for example, the probability distribution associated with the likelihood of Congress passing a specific bill.

It is important that a candidate be familiar with the terminology and basic application of probability theory. Specifically, the candidate should have a working knowlege of the following:

- Probability distribution
- Payoff tables
- Expected profit
- Value of perfect information
- Regret tables
- Expected loss

These points may best be explained and illustrated by use of an example.

Assume that a specialty food store stocks a perishable item which costs $3 per case and sells for $7 per case. If the item is not sold during the first day it is offered for sale, it must be destroyed. Analysis of the sales records for the past 80 days shows that there has been no trend in the sales for this item.

Sales of the item during this period were as follows:

| Cases sold per day | Number of days |
|:---:|:---:|
| 5 | 8 |
| 6 | 16 |
| 7 | 32 |
| 8 | 24 |

## Probability Distribution

The probability that a particular event will occur may be determined as the ratio of the number of times the event occurs in observations to the total observations. The probability distribution (objective) for the example is shown below.

| Sales | Observations | Probability |
|:---:|:---:|:---:|
| 5 | 8 | 8/80 = 10% = .1 |
| 6 | 16 | 16/80 = 20% = .2 |
| 7 | 32 | 32/80 = 40% = .4 |
| 8 | 24 | 24/80 = 30% = .3 |
| | 80 | 80/80 = 100% = 1.0 |

## Payoff Table (Conditional Profits Table)

The payoff table shows the profit from any possible combination of available alternative actions and potential event occurrences. Each value in the table is conditional on an action being taken and a particular event occurring. The payoff table for the example is as follows:

**Payoff Table**

Alternative Inventory Actions

| Possible Demand | 5 cases | 6 cases | 7 cases | 8 cases |
|:---|:---:|:---:|:---:|:---:|
| 5 cases | $20a | $17b | $14 | $11 |
| 6 cases | 20 | 24 | 21 | 18 |
| 7 cases | 20 | 24 | 28 | 25 |
| 8 cases | 20 | 24 | 28 | 32 |

(a) profit per case = $7 selling price – $3 cost = $4 profit for sales of 5 cases = 5 × $4 = $20

(b) loss per case unsold = $3 cost, profit from sale of 5 cases less loss for 1 case = $20 – 3 = $17

## Expected Profit

The expected profit for an alternative action is obtained by weighting the conditional profit of each possible outcome of the alternative by the probability of its occurrence and totaling the results. The expected daily profit resulting from stocking 8 cases in the example would be determined as follows:

**Expected Profit from Stocking 8 Cases**

| Demand | Conditional Profit | × | Probability of Demand | = | Expected Profit |
|--------|--------------------|----|-----------------------|----|-----------------|
| 5 | $11 | | .10 | | $ 1.10 |
| 6 | 18 | | .20 | | 3.60 |
| 7 | 25 | | .40 | | 10.00 |
| 8 | 32 | | .30 | | 9.60 |
| | | | 1.00 | | $24.30 |

The expected daily profits for the alternative stock action of the example are:

| Cases Stocked | Expected Profits |
|---------------|------------------|
| 5 | $20.00 |
| 6 | 23.30 |
| 7 | 25.20 |
| 8 | 24.30 |

The optimum inventory action would be for the store to stock 7 cases as this alternative yields the greatest expected profit.

## Value of Perfect Information

To determine the value of perfect information it is first necessary to compute the expected profit with perfect information. Obviously, if the outcome of an event were known prior to its occurrence, the alternative action which provided the greatest profit for that outcome would be selected as the course of action. The expected profit with perfect information for the example is computed below.

**Expected Profit with Perfect Information**

| Demand | Cases Stocked | Conditional Profit | × | Probability of Demand | = | Expected Profit |
|--------|---------------|--------------------|----|-----------------------|----|-----------------|
| 5 | 5 | $20 | | .1 | | $ 2.00 |
| 6 | 6 | 24 | | .2 | | 4.80 |
| 7 | 7 | 28 | | .4 | | 11.20 |
| 8 | 8 | 32 | | .3 | | 9.60 |
| | | | | 1.00 | | $27.60 |

The value of perfect information may now be determined as the difference between the expected profit with perfect information and the expected profit of the optimum action without perfect information. For the example, this would be $2.40 ($27.60 – $25.20). To pay more than this amount, the store would be losing the advantage to be gained with the perfect information.

## Regret Table (Conditional Loss Table)

The regret table shows the losses from any possible combination of available alternative actions and potential event occurrences. There are two types of losses which may occur: (a) Opportunity losses which are the losses of profit from inability to meet demand, and (b) obsolescence losses which are the losses from declining values of excess stock. Each value in the table is conditional on an action being taken and a particular event occurring. The regret table for the example appears below.

## Regret Table
## Alternative Inventory Actions

| Demand | 5 Cases | 6 Cases | 7 Cases | 8 Cases |
|--------|---------|---------|---------|---------|
| 5 | $0 | $3b | $6 | $9 |
| 6 | 4a | 0 | 3 | 6 |
| 7 | 8 | 4 | 0 | 3 |
| 8 | 12 | 8 | 4 | 0 |

(a) if 5 cases are stocked and demand is 6 cases, the profit on sales of 1 case or $4 has been lost (opportunity loss)

(b) If 6 cases are stocked and demand is 5 cases, the cost of 1 case or $3 will be lost as spoilage (obsolescence loss)

## Expected Loss

The expected loss for an alternative action is determined in the same manner as the expected profit. For the example, the expected daily loss from stocking 8 cases is computed below.

### Expected Loss from Stocking 8 Cases

| Demand | Conditional Loss | × | Probability of Demand | = | Expected Loss |
|--------|------------------|---|-----------------------|---|---------------|
| 5 | $9 | | .1 | | $ .90 |
| 6 | 6 | | .2 | | 1.20 |
| 7 | 3 | | .4 | | 1.20 |
| 8 | 0 | | .3 | | 0.00 |
| | | | 1.00 | | $3.30 |

The expected daily loss for the alternative stock actions are:

| Cases Stocked | Expected Loss |
|---------------|---------------|
| 5 | $7.60 |
| 6 | 4.30 |
| 7 | 2.40 |
| 8 | 3.30 |

The optimum inventory action is the one which minimizes the expected loss and is the same as when expected profits were used for the selection of the optimum inventory action.

Note that the expected loss plus the expected profit computed earlier is equal to the expected profit with perfect information, and that the expected loss of the optimum solution is equal to the value of the perfect information.

**Illustrative Problem**

Commercial Products Corp., an audit client, requests your assistance in determining the potential loss on a binding purchase contract which will be in effect at the end of the corporation's fiscal year. The corporation produces a chemical compound which deteriorates and must be discarded if it is not sold by the end of the month during which it is produced.

The total variable cost of the manufactured compound is $25 per unit and it is sold for $40 per unit. The compound can be purchased from a vertically integrated competitor at $40 per unit plus $5 freight per unit. It is estimated that failure to fill orders would result in the complete loss of 8 out of 10 customers placing orders for the compound.

The corporation has sold the compound for the past 30 months. Demand has been irregular and there is no sales trend. During this period, sales per month have been:

| Units Sold per Month | Number of Months* | |
|---|---|---|
| 4,000 | 6 | |
| 5,000 | 15 | *Occurred in random |
| 6,000 | 9 | sequence |

**Required**: For each of the following, prepare a schedule (with supporting computations in good form) of the

1. Probability of sales of 4,000, 5,000 or 6,000 units in any month.
2. Marginal income if sales of 4,000, 5,000 or 6,000 units are made in one month and 4,000, 5,000 or 6,000 units are manufactured for sale in the same month. Assume all sales orders are filled. (Such a schedule is sometimes called a "payoff table".)
3. Average monthly marginal income the corporation should expect over the long run if 5,000 units are manufactured every month and all sales orders are filled.

**Solution:**

1.

### Commercial Products Corp.
### Schedule Computing the Probability of Unit Sales per Month

| Unit Sales per Month | No. of Months | Probability |
|---|---|---|
| 4,000 | 6 | 6/30 = .2 |
| 5,000 | 15 | 15/30 = .5 |
| 6,000 | 9 | 9/30 = .3 |
| | 30 | 1.0 |

2.

### Schedule of Marginal Income
### For Various Combinations of Unit Sales and Units Manufactured

Units Manufactured (and Purchased)

| Unit Sales | 4,000 | 5,000 | 6,000 |
|---|---|---|---|
| 4,000 | $60,000 (1) | $35,000 (2) | $10,000 (2) |
| 5,000 | 55,000 (3) | 75,000 (1) | 50,000 (2) |
| 6,000 | 50,000 (3) | 70,000 (3) | 90,000 (1) |

**Notes:**
**Computation of Marginal Income**
(1) When all units manufactured are sold:
  $4,000 \times (\$40 - 25) = \$60,000$
  $5,000 \times (\$40 - 25) = 75,000$
  $6,000 \times (\$40 - 25) = 90,000$
(2) Reduction per 1,000 units when more units are manufactured than are sold:
  $1,000 \times \$25 = \$25,000$
(3) Reduction per 1,000 units when units must be purchased to fill sales orders:
  $1,000 \times (\$40 - [\$40 + \$5]) = \$5,000$

3.

**Schedule Computing Expected Marginal Income if 5,000 Units
are Manufactured and All Sales Orders are Filled**

| Unit Sales | Probability | Marginal Income | Expected Value |
|---|---|---|---|
| 4,000 | .2 | $35,000 | $ 7,000 |
| 5,000 | .5 | 75,000 | 37,500 |
| 6,000 | .3 | 70,000 | 21,000 |
| Expected average monthly MI | | | $65,500 |

# REGRESSION ANALYSIS

Regression analysis is a mathematical technique used to predict the value of one variable and its changes (the dependent variable) based upon the value of some other variable (the independent variable). When the independent variable is a function of time such as months, quarters, or years, then the term "time regression", "time trend", or "time series" analysis is sometimes used. Simple regression analysis involves the use of only one independent (explanatory) variable, while multiple regression analysis allows for more than one independent variable. Regression analysis may be used to predict future sales, revenues, profits, demands, costs, etc. or to separate a semi-variable item into its fixed and variable components.

Methods of Measuring Relationships Between Variables:

1. **High-Low Method**: Only two observations of the variables are used to measure the relationship between them. The values of the variables are measured at a high and low level of the independent variable, and the change in the dependent variable is divided by the change in the independent variable to determine its relationship to the independent variable. The fixed portion or minimum level of the dependent variable can be determined by deducting from its total value (at the high or low observation) its value determined in relation to the independent variable (at that same observation). The observations should be within the relevant range for the variables, and be representative of normal results at these levels.

The High-Low Method has the advantage of being easy and inexpensive to use; however, it has the disadvantage of being the least accurate of the methods as it uses only two observations and these may not be representative of the relationship between the variables.

**Example**:

| Observations | Direct Labor Hours | Cost of Utilities |
|---|---|---|
| High | 2800 | $1334 |
| Low | 1300 | 884 |
| Change | 1500 | $ 450 |

Relationship  $450 ÷ 1500 = $0.30 per direct labor hour

Determination of fixed portion:

| | High | Low |
|---|---|---|
| Total Utilities Cost | $1334 | $884 |
| Cost based on direct labor hours ($.30 per) | 840 | 390 |
| Fixed portion | $ 494 | $494 |

Predicted Utilities Cost at 2000 direct labor hours:
  $494 + ($.30 × 2000) = $494 + $600 = $1094

2. **Scattergraph Method**: Multiple observations of the two variables are plotted on a graph in order to visually determine their relationship. The values of the dependent variable are plotted on the Y axis (vertical axis) and those of the independent variable on the X axis (horizontal axis). Each point on the graph represents an observation of the variables (X and Y). A straight line (Trend Line) is then drawn through the plotted points so that there is an equal distance between the Trend Line and the plotted points above and below the line. The Trend Line is then used to describe the relationship between the variables and to predict the value of the dependent variable for given values of the independent variable. The point at which the trend line intersects the Y axis indicates the fixed portion or minimum value of the dependent variable. If the plotted points on the scattergraph follow a generally straight line, a linear relationship is assumed to exist, and the variables are said to be correlated with each other.

The Scattergraph Method has the advantage of being relatively simple to apply and understand; however, it is not objective as personal bias may distort the fitting of the trend line.

**Example**:

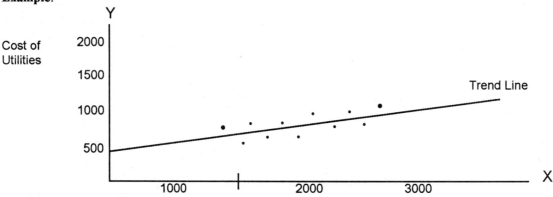

Fixed portion is $500 (intercept of the Y axis)
The variable relationship is indicated by the slope of the trend line.

3. **Regression (Least Squares) Analysis**: A Regression Line is a mathematically fitted line to the observations of the variables which were plotted in the scattergraph. The least squares method fits the line to the observations so that the sum of the squared variances of the observations above and below the line are minimized. The regression line is to the scattergraph as an average is to a list of values; it indicates the average value of the dependent variable (y) associated with a particular value of the independent variable (x). The method assumes a linear relationship and is based upon the formula for a straight line, $Y = a + bx$, where $Y =$ the independent variable; $a =$ the fixed portion or minimum value of the independent variable; $b =$ the slope of the line or the rate of variability in the dependent variable for changes in the independent variable; and $x =$ the value of the independent variable. The method has the advantage of being more objective and accurate; however, it is time-consuming if done manually.

Multiple regression analysis is a further expansion of the least squares method, allowing for the consideration of more than one independent variable. The formula could appear as $Y = a + bx + cz$, where c is the rate of variability for z, an additional independent variable.

**Correlation**: The statistical measure of the relationship of dependent and independent variables is the Coefficient of Correlation (r). If perfect correlation exists all points (observations) lie on the regression line, and the coefficient of correlation would be +1 or −1, depending upon whether they are directly (positively) or inversely (negatively) related. If no correlation exists the coefficient would be 0, indicating that there is no statistical relationship between the variables.

The Coefficient of Determination ($r^2$) is the statistical measure of the fit of the regression line to the observations of the variables, and is found by squaring the coefficient of correlation. A coefficient of determination of .94 would mean that 94% of the change in the dependent variable (x) is related to the change in the independent variable (y).

# Chapter Seventeen
# Managerial Analysis and Control Questions

## DIRECT COSTING, C.V.P. RELATIONSHIPS

**Items 1 through 5** are based on the following information:

The following data relate to a year's budgeted activity for Patsy Corporation, a single product company:

|  | Units |
|---|---|
| Beginning inventory | 30,000 |
| Production | 120,000 |
| Available | 150,000 |
| Sales | 110,000 |
| Ending inventory | 40,000 |

|  | Per Unit |
|---|---|
| Selling price | $5.00 |
| Variable manufacturing costs | 1.00 |
| Variable selling costs | 2.00 |
| Fixed manufacturing costs (based on 100,000 units) | .25 |
| Fixed selling costs (based on 100,000 units) | .65 |

Total fixed costs remain unchanged within the relevant range of 25,000 units to total capacity of 160,000 units.

1. The projected annual breakeven sales in units for Patsy Corporation is
a. 30,000.
b. 37,143.
c. 45,000.
d. 50,000.

2. The projected net income for Patsy Corporation for the year under direct (variable) costing is
a. $110,000.
b. $127,500.
c. $130,000.
d. $150,000.

3. If all the variances are charged to cost of goods sold, the projected net income for Patsy Corporation for the year under absorption costing is
a. $122,500.
b. $127,500.
c. $130,000.
d. $132,500.

4. A special order is received to purchase 10,000 units to be used in an unrelated market. Given the original data, what price per unit should be charged on this order to increase Patsy Corporation's net income by $5,000?
a. $3.50.
b. $4.40.
c. $5.00.
d. $6.50.

5. Concerning the data for Patsy Corporation, assume selling price increases by 20%; variable manufacturing costs increase by 10%; variable selling costs remain the same; and total fixed costs increase to $104,400. How many units must now be sold to generate a profit equal to 10% of the contribution margin?
a. 36,000.
b. 40,000.
c. 43,320.
d. 45,390.

_____

*N86*

6. Kent Co.'s 1985 operating percentages were as follows:

| | | |
|---|---|---|
| Sales | | 100% |
| Cost of sales | | |
| Variable | 50% | |
| Fixed | 10 | 60 |
| Gross profit | | 40 |
| Other operating expenses | | |
| Variable | 20 | |
| Fixed | 15 | 35 |
| Operating income | | 5% |

Kent's 1985 sales totaled $2,000,000. At what 1985 sales level would Kent break even?
a. $1,900,000
b. $1,666,667
c. $1,250,000
d. $833,333

*M95*

7. Jago Co. has 2 products that use the same manufacturing facilities and cannot be subcontracted. Each product has sufficient orders to utilize the entire manufacturing capacity. For short-run profit maximization, Jago should manufacture the product with the

a. Lower total manufacturing costs for the manufacturing capacity.
b. Lower total variable manufacturing costs for the manufacturing capacity.
c. Greater gross profit per hour of manufacturing capacity.
d. Greater contribution margin per hour of manufacturing capacity.

8. The following information pertains to Mete Co.:

| | |
|---|---|
| Sales | $400,000 |
| Variable costs | 80,000 |
| Fixed costs | 20,000 |

Mete's breakeven point in sales dollars is
a. $20,000
b. $25,000
c. $80,000
d. $100,000

9. In an income statement prepared as an internal report using the direct (variable) costing method, fixed selling and administrative expenses would
a. Be used in the computation of the contribution margin.
b. Be used in the computation of operating income but **not** in the computation of the contribution margin.
c. Be treated the same as variable selling and administrative expenses.
d. Not be used.

10. At the end of Killo Co.'s first year of operations, 1,000 units of inventory remained on hand. Variable and fixed manufacturing costs per unit were $90 and $20, respectively. If Killo uses absorption costing rather than direct (variable) costing, the result would be a higher pretax income of
a. $0
b. $20,000
c. $70,000
d. $90,000

11. Quo Co. rented a building to Hava Fast Food. Each month Quo receives a fixed rental amount plus a variable rental amount based on Hava's sales for that month. As sales increase so does the variable rental amount, but at a reduced rate. Which of the following curves reflects the monthly rentals under the agreement?

Quo's rental revenue — Hava's monthly sales

a. I
b. II
c. III
d. IV

12. A single-product company prepares income statements using both absorption and variable costing methods. Manufacturing overhead cost applied per unit produced in 1990 was the same as in 1989. The 1990 variable costing statement reported a profit whereas the 1990 absorption costing statement reported a loss. The difference in reported income could be explained by units produced in 1990 being
a. Less than units sold in 1990.
b. Less than the activity level used for allocating overhead to the product.
c. In excess of the activity level used for allocating overhead to the product.
d. In excess of units sold in 1990.

**Item 13** is based on the following:
The diagram below is a cost-volume-profit chart.

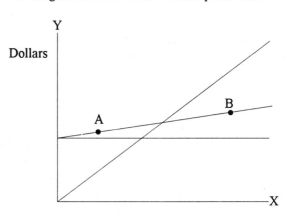

13. At point A compared to point B, as a percentage of sales revenues

| | Variable costs are | Fixed costs are |
|---|---|---|
| a. | Greater | Greater |
| b. | Greater | The same |
| c. | The same | The same |
| d. | The same | Greater |

14. The most likely strategy to reduce the breakeven point would be to
a. Increase both the fixed costs and the contribution margin.
b. Decrease both the fixed costs and the contribution margin.
c. Decrease the fixed costs and increase the contribution margin.
d. Increase the fixed costs and decrease the contribution margin.

15. Buff Co. is considering replacing an old machine with a new machine. Which of the following items is economically relevant to Buff's decision? (Ignore income tax considerations.)

| | Carrying amount of old machine | Disposal value of new machine |
|---|---|---|
| a. | Yes | No |
| b. | No | Yes |
| c. | No | No |
| d. | Yes | Yes |

16. The Lantern Corporation has 1,000 obsolete lanterns that are carried in inventory at a manufacturing cost of $20,000. If the lanterns are remachined for $5,000, they could be sold for $9,000. If the lanterns are scrapped, they could be sold for $1,000. What alternative is more desirable and what are the total relevant costs for that alternative?
a. Remachine and $5,000.
b. Remachine and $25,000.
c. Scrap and $20,000.
d. Neither, as there is an overall loss under either alternative.

17. Jarvis Co. has fixed costs of $200,000. It has two products that it can sell, Tetra and Min. Jarvis sells these products at a rate of 2 units of Tetra to 1 unit of Min. The contribution margin is $1 per unit for Tetra and $2 per unit for Min. How many units of Min would be sold at the breakeven point?
a. 44,444.
b. 50,000.
c. 88,888.
d. 100,000.

___

**Items 18 and 19** are based on the following information:

Taylor, Inc., produces only two products, Acdom and Belnom. These account for 60% and 40% of the total sales dollars of Taylor, respectively. Variable costs (as a percentage of sales dollars) are 60% for Acdom and 85% for Belnom. Total fixed costs are $150,000. There are no other costs.

18. What is Taylor's breakeven point in sales dollars?
a. $150,000.
b. $214,286.
c. $300,000.
d. $500,000.

19. Assuming that the total fixed costs of Taylor increase by 30%, what amount of sales dollars would be necessary to generate a net income of $9,000?
a. $204,000.
b. $464,000.
c. $659,000.
d. $680,000.

___

20. Thomas Company sells products X, Y, and Z. Thomas sells three units of X for each unit of Z, and two units of Y for each unit of X. The contribution margins are $1.00 per unit of X, $1.50 per unit of Y, and $3.00 per unit of Z. Fixed costs are $600,000. How many units of X would Thomas sell at the breakeven point?
a. 40,000.
b. 120,000.
c. 360,000.
d. 400,000.

21. In an income statement prepared using the variable costing method, fixed factory overhead would
a. Not be used.
b. Be used in the computation of the contribution margin.
c. Be used in the computation of operating income but **not** in the computation of the contribution margin.
d. Be treated the same as variable factory overhead.

22. Cuff Caterers quotes a price of $60 per person for a dinner party. This price includes the 6% sales tax and the 15% service charge. Sales tax is computed on the food plus the service charge. The service charge is computed on the food only. At what amount does Cuff price the food?
a. $56.40
b. $51.00
c. $49.22
d. $47.40

23. Cardinal Company needs 20,000 units of a certain part to use in its production cycle. The following information is available:

Cost to Cardinal to make the part:
| | |
|---|---|
| Direct materials | $ 4 |
| Direct labor | 16 |
| Variable overhead | 8 |
| Fixed overhead applied | 10 |
| | $38 |

| | |
|---|---|
| Cost to buy the part from the Oriole Company | $36 |

If Cardinal buys the part from Oriole instead of making it, Cardinal could not use the released facilities in another manufacturing activity. 60% of the fixed overhead applied will continue regardless of what decision is made.

In deciding whether to make or buy the part, the total relevant costs to make the part are
a. $560,000.
b. $640,000.
c. $720,000.
d. $760,000.

*N95*

24. Product Cott has sales of $200,000, a contribution margin of 20%, and a margin of safety of $80,000. What is Cott's fixed cost?
a. $16,000
b. $24,000
c. $80,000
d. $96,000

*N87*

25. In an income statement prepared as an internal report using the variable costing method, which of the following terms should appear?

| | Gross profit (margin) | Operating income |
|---|---|---|
| a. | Yes | Yes |
| b. | Yes | No |
| c. | No | No |
| d. | No | Yes |

*N89*

26. The following information pertains to Sisk Co.:

| | |
|---|---|
| Sales (25,000 units) | $500,000 |
| Direct materials and direct labor | 150,000 |
| Factory overhead: | |
| Variable | 20,000 |
| Fixed | 35,000 |
| Selling and general expenses: | |
| Variable | 5,000 |
| Fixed | 30,000 |

Sisk's breakeven point in number of units is
a. 4,924
b. 5,000
c. 6,250
d. 9,286

*M91*

27. In the profit-volume chart below, EF and GH represent the profit-volume graphs of a single-product company for 1989 and 1990, respectively.

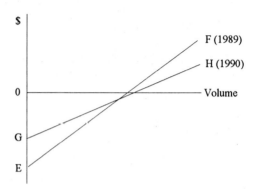

If 1989 and 1990 unit sales prices are identical, how did total fixed costs and unit variable costs of 1990 change compared to 1989?

| | 1990 total fixed costs | 1990 unit variable costs |
|---|---|---|
| a. | Decreased | Increased |
| b. | Decreased | Decreased |
| c. | Increased | Increased |
| d. | Increased | Decreased |

*M95*

28. Using the variable costing method, which of the following costs are assigned to inventory.?

| | Variable selling and administrative costs | Variable factory overhead costs |
|---|---|---|
| a. | Yes | Yes |
| b. | Yes | No |
| c. | No | No |
| d. | No | Yes |

29. Motor Company manufactures 10,000 units of Part M-1 for use in its production annually. The following costs are reported:

| | |
|---|---|
| Direct materials | $ 20,000 |
| Direct labor | 55,000 |
| Variable overhead | 45,000 |
| Fixed overhead | 70,000 |
| | $190,000 |

Valve Company has offered to sell Motor 10,000 units of Part M-1 for $18 per unit. If Motor accepts the offer, some of the facilities presently used to manufacture Part M-1 could be rented to a third party at an annual rental of $15,000. Additionally, $4 per unit of the fixed overhead applied to Part M-1 would be totally eliminated. Should Motor accept Valve's offer, and why?

a. No, because it would be $5,000 cheaper to make the part.
b. Yes, because it would be $10,000 cheaper to buy the part.
c. No, because it would be $15,000 cheaper to make the part.
d. Yes, because it would be $25,000 cheaper to buy the part.

M87

30. In an income statement prepared as an internal report using the absorption costing method, which of the following terms should appear?

|   | Contribution margin | Gross profit (margin) |
|---|---|---|
| a. | No | Yes |
| b. | No | No |
| c. | Yes | No |
| d. | Yes | Yes |

M92

31. The following information pertains to Clove Co. for the year ending December 31, 1992:

| Budgeted sales | $1,000,000 |
|---|---|
| Breakeven sales | 700,000 |
| Budgeted contribution margin | 600,000 |
| Cashflow breakeven | 200,000 |

Clove's margin of safety is

a. $300,000
b. $400,000
c. $500,000
d. $800,000

**Items 32 and 33** are based on the following information:

Selected information concerning the operations of Kern Company for the year ended December 31, 19X1, is available as follows:

| Units produced | 10,000 |
|---|---|
| Units sold | 9,000 |
| Direct materials used | $40,000 |
| Direct labor incurred | $20,000 |
| Fixed factory overhead | $25,000 |
| Variable factory overhead | $12,000 |

| Fixed selling and administrative expenses | $30,000 |
|---|---|
| Variable selling and administrative expenses | $ 4,500 |
| Finished goods inventory, Jan. 1, 19X1 | None |

There were no work-in-process inventories at the beginning and end of 19X1.

32. What would be Kern's finished goods inventory cost at December 31, 19X1, under the variable (direct) cost method?

a. $7,200.
b. $7,650.
c. $8,000.
d. $9,700.

33. Which costing method, absorption or variable costing, would show a higher operating income for 19X1 and by what amount?

|   | Costing method | Amount |
|---|---|---|
| a. | Absorption costing | $2,500 |
| b. | Variable costing | $2,500 |
| c. | Absorption costing | $5,500 |
| d. | Variable costing | $5,500 |

34. Jordan Company budgeted sales of 400,000 calculators at $40 per unit for 19X2. Variable manufacturing costs were budgeted at $16 per unit, and fixed manufacturing costs at $10 per unit. A special order offering to buy 40,000 calculators for $23 each was received by Jordan in March 19X2. Jordan has sufficient plant capacity to manufacture the additional quantity; however, the production would have to be done on an overtime basis at an estimated additional cost of $3 per calculator. Acceptance of the special order would not affect Jordan's normal sales and no selling expenses would be incurred. What would be the effect on operating profit if the special order were accepted?

a. $120,000 decrease.
b. $160,000 increase.
c. $240,000 decrease.
d. $280,000 increase.

M95

35. Del Co. has fixed costs of $100,000 and breakeven sales of $800,000. What is its projected profit at $1,200,000 sales?

a. $50,000
b. $150,000
c. $200,000
d. $400,000

36. Manor Company plans to discontinue a department with a contribution to overhead of $24,000 and allocated overhead of $48,000, of which $21,000 cannot be eliminated. The effect of this discontinuance on Manor's pretax profit would be a (an)
a. Decrease of $3,000.
b. Increase of $3,000.
c. Decrease of $24,000.
d. Increase of $24,000.

37. Gandy Company has 5,000 obsolete desk lamps that are carried in inventory at a manufacturing cost of $50,000. If the lamps are reworked for $20,000, they could be sold for $35,000. Alternatively, the lamps could be sold for $8,000 to a jobber located in a distant city. In a decision model analyzing these alternatives, the sunk cost would be
a. $ 8,000.
b. $15,000.
c. $20,000.
d. $50,000.

*M92*

38. On January 1, 1992, Lake Co. increased its direct labor wage rates. All other budgeted costs and revenues were unchanged. How did this increase affect Lake's budgeted break-even point and budgeted margin of safety?

|   | *Budgeted break-even point* | *Budgeted margin of safety* |
|---|---|---|
| a. | Increase | Increase |
| b. | Increase | Decrease |
| c. | Decrease | Decrease |
| d. | Decrease | Increase |

*M92*

39. When using a flexible budget, a decrease in production levels within a relevant range
a. Decreases variable cost per unit.
b. Decreases total costs.
c. Increases total fixed costs.
d. Increases variable cost per unit.

*N91*

40. When production levels are expected to decline within a relevant range, and a flexible budget is used, what effect would be anticipated with respect to each of the following?

|   | *Variable costs per unit* | *Fixed costs per unit* |
|---|---|---|
| a. | No change | No change |
| b. | Increase | No change |
| c. | No change | Increase |
| d. | Increase | Increase |

41. In an income statement prepared as an internal report, total fixed costs normally would be shown separately under

|   | *Absorption costing* | *Variable costing* |
|---|---|---|
| a. | No | No |
| b. | No | Yes |
| c. | Yes | Yes |
| d. | Yes | No |

42. Based on potential sales of 500 units per year, a new product has estimated traceable costs of $990,000. What is the target price to obtain a 15% profit margin on sales?
a. $2,329
b. $2,277
c. $1,980
d. $1,935

43. The following information pertains to Syl Co.:

| Sales | $800,000 |
|---|---|
| Variable costs | 160,000 |
| Fixed costs | 40,000 |

What is Syl's breakeven point in sales dollars?
a. $200,000
b. $160,000
c. $50,000
d. $40,000

**Items 44 and 45** are based on the following information:

Gordon Company began its operations on January 1, 19X2, and produces a single product that sells for $10 per unit. Gordon uses an actual (historical) cost system. In 19X2, 100,000 units were produced and 80,000 units were sold. There was no work-in-process inventory at December 31, 19X2. Manufacturing costs and selling and administrative expenses for 19X2 were as follows:

|  | *Fixed costs* | *Variable costs* |
|---|---|---|
| Raw materials | — | $2.00 per unit produced |
| Direct labor | — | 1.25 per unit produced |
| Factory overhead | $120,000 | .75 per unit produced |
| Selling and administrative | 70,000 | 1.00 per unit sold |

44. What would be Gordon's operating income for 19X2 under the variable (direct) costing method?
a. $114,000
b. $210,000
c. $234,000
d. $330,000

45. What would be Gordon's finished goods inventory at December 31, 19X2, under the absorption costing method?
a. $ 80,000
b. $104,000
c. $110,000
d. $124,000

_____

46. Cook Co.'s total costs of operating five sales offices last year were $500,000, of which $70,000 represented fixed costs. Cook has determined that total costs are significantly influenced by the number of sales offices operated. Last year's costs and number of sales offices can be used as the bases for predicting annual costs. What would be the budgeted costs for the coming year if Cook were to operate seven sales offices?
a. $700,000
b. $672,000
c. $614,000
d. $586,000

_____

**Items 47 and 48** are based on the following data:
The following information pertains to Rica Company:

| | |
|---|---|
| Sales (50,000 units) | $1,000,000 |
| Direct materials and direct labor | 300,000 |
| Factory overhead: | |
| Variable | 40,000 |
| Fixed | 70,000 |
| Selling and general expenses: | |
| Variable | 10,000 |
| Fixed | 60,000 |

47. How much was Rica's break-even point in number of units?
a. 9,848
b. 10,000
c. 18,571
d. 26,000

48. What was Rica's contribution margin ratio?
a. 66%
b. 65%
c. 59%
d. 35%

_____

49. Break-even analysis assumes that over the relevant range
a. Unit revenues are nonlinear.
b. Unit variable costs are unchanged.
c. Total costs are unchanged.
d. Total fixed costs are nonlinear.

50. At December 31, 1990, Zar Co. had a machine with an original cost of $84,000, accumulated depreciation of $60,000, and an estimated salvage value of zero. On December 31, 1990, Zar was considering the purchase of a new machine having a five-year life, costing $120,000, and having an estimated salvage value of $20,000 at the end of five years. In its decision concerning the possible purchase of the new machine, how much should Zar consider as sunk cost at December 31, 1990?
a. $120,000
b. $100,000
c. $24,000
d. $4,000

## Probability and Regression Analysis

**Items 51 through 53** are based on the following information:

As the accounting consultant for Leslie Company you have compiled data on the day-to-day demand rate from Leslie's customers for Product A and the lead time to receive Product A from its supplier. The data are summarized in the following probability tables:

| Demand for Product A | |
|---|---|
| Unit Demand per Day | Probability of Occurrence |
| 0 | .45 |
| 1 | .15 |
| 2 | .30 |
| 3 | .10 |
| | 1.00 |

| Lead Time for Product A | |
|---|---|
| Lead Time in Days | Probability of Occurrence |
| 1 | .40 |
| 2 | .35 |
| 3 | .25 |
| | 1.00 |

Leslie is able to deliver Product A to its customers the same day that Product A is received from its supplier. All units of Product A demanded but not available, due to a stock-out, are backordered and are filled immediately when a new shipment arrives.

51. The probability of the demand for Product A being nine units during a three-day lead time for delivery from the supplier is
a. .00025.
b. .10.
c. .025.
d. .25.

52. If Leslie reorders 10 units of Product A when its inventory level is 10 units, the number of days during a 360-day year that Leslie will experience a stock-out of Product A is
a. 0.75 days.
b. 36 days.
c. 10 days.
d. 0 days.

53. Leslie has developed an inventory model based on the probability tables and desires a solution for minimizing total annual inventory costs. Included in inventory costs are the costs of holding Product A, ordering and receiving Product A, and incurring stockouts of Product A. The solution would state:
a.  At what inventory level to reorder and how many units to reorder.
b.  Either at what inventory level to reorder or how many units to reorder.
c.  How many units to reorder but not at what inventory level to reorder.
d.  At what inventory level to reorder but not how many units to reorder.

---

54. A sales office of Helms, Inc., has developed the following probability distribution for daily sales of a perishable product.

| X (Units Sold) | P (Sales = X) |
|---|---|
| 100 | .2 |
| 150 | .5 |
| 200 | .2 |
| 250 | .1 |

The product is restocked at the start of each day. If the Company desires a 90% service level in satisfying sales demand, the initial stock balance for each day should be
a. 250.
b. 160.
c. 200.
d. 150.

55. Your client wants your advice on which of two alternatives he should choose. One alternative is to sell an investment now for $10,000. Another alternative is to hold the investment three days after which he can sell it for a certain selling price based on the following probabilities:

| Selling Price | Probability |
|---|---|
| $5,000 | .4 |
| $8,000 | .2 |
| $12,000 | .3 |
| $30,000 | .1 |

Using probability theory, which of the following is the most reasonable statement?
a.  Hold the investment three days because the expected value of holding exceeds the current selling price.
b.  Hold the investment three days because of the chance of getting $30,000 for it.
c.  Sell the investment now because the current selling price exceeds the expected value of holding.
d.  Sell the investment now because there is a 60% chance that the selling price will fall in three days.

*N92*

56. To assist in an investment decision, Gift Co. selected the most likely sales volume from several possible outcomes. Which of the following attributes would that selected sales volume reflect?
a.  The mid-point of the range.
b.  The median.
c.  The greatest probability.
d.  The expected value.

*M95*

57. Dough Distributors has decided to increase its daily muffin purchases by 100 boxes. A box of muffins costs $2 and sells for $3 through regular stores. Any boxes not sold through regular stores are sold through Dough's thrift store for $1. Dough assigns the following probabilities to selling additional boxes:

| Additional sales | Probability |
|---|---|
| 60 | .6 |
| 100 | .4 |

What is the expected value of Dough's decision to buy 100 additional boxes of muffins?
a.  $28
b.  $40
c.  $52
d.  $68

*M87*

58. Joe Neil, CPA, has among his clientele a charitable organization that has a legal permit to conduct games of chance for fund-raising purposes. Neil's client derives its profit from admission fees and the sale of refreshments, and therefore wants to "break even" on the games of chance. In one of these games, the player draws one card from a standard deck of 52 cards. A player drawing any one of four "queens" wins $5, and a player drawing any one of 13 "hearts" wins $2. Neil is asked to compute the price that should be charged per draw, so that the total amount paid out for winning

draws can be expected to equal the total amount received from all draws. Which one of the following equations should Neil use to compute the price (P)?

a. $5 - 2 = \dfrac{35}{52}P$

b. $\dfrac{4}{52}(5) + \dfrac{13}{52}(2) = \dfrac{35}{52}P$

c. $\dfrac{4}{52}(5 - P) + \dfrac{13}{52}(2 - P) = P$

d. $\dfrac{4}{52}(5) + \dfrac{13}{52}(2) = P$

59. Duguid Company is considering a proposal to introduce a new product, XPL. An outside marketing consultant prepared the following payoff probability distribution describing the relative likelihood of monthly sales volume levels and related income (loss) for XPL:

| Monthly sales volume | Probability | Income (loss) |
|---|---|---|
| 3,000 | 0.10 | $(35,000) |
| 6,000 | 0.20 | 5,000 |
| 9,000 | 0.40 | 30,000 |
| 12,000 | 0.20 | 50,000 |
| 15,000 | 0.10 | 70,000 |

If Duguid decides to market XPL, the expected value of the added monthly income will be
a. $24,000.
b. $26,500.
c. $30,000.
d. $120,000.

*N89*

60. The following information pertains to three shipping terminals operated by Krag Co.:

| Terminal | Percentage of cargo handled | Percentage of error |
|---|---|---|
| Land | 50 | 2 |
| Air | 40 | 4 |
| Sea | 10 | 14 |

Krag's internal auditor randomly selects one set of shipping documents, ascertaining that the set selected contains an error. The probability that the error occurred in the Land Terminal is
a. 2%
b. 10%
c. 25%
d. 50%

61. If the coefficient of correlation between two variables is zero, how might a scatter diagram of these variables appear?
a. Random points.
b. A least squares line that slopes up to the right.
c. A least squares line that slopes down to the right.
d. Under this condition, a scatter diagram could not be plotted on a graph.

*N90*

62. Which of the following may be used to estimate how inventory warehouse costs are affected by both the number of shipments and the weight of materials handled?
a. Economic order quantity analysis.
b. Probability analysis.
c. Correlation analysis.
d. Multiple regression analysis.

63. A quantitative technique used to make predictions or estimates of the value of a dependent variable from given values of an independent variable(s) is
a. Linear programming.
b. Regression analysis.
c. Trend analysis.
d. Queuing theory.

64. Your client, a retail store, is interested in the relationship between sales (independent variable) and theft losses (dependent variable). Using the proper formula, you compute the coefficient of correlation at .95. What can you definitely conclude about these factors (sales and theft losses)?
a. An increase in sales causes an increase in theft losses.
b. Movement of these factors is in opposite directions.
c. Movement of these factors is entirely unrelated.
d. Movement of these factors is in the same direction.

*N88*

65. Multiple regression analysis involves the use of

| | Dependent variables | Independent variables |
|---|---|---|
| a. | One | More than one |
| b. | More than one | More than one |
| c. | More than one | One |
| d. | One | One |

66. Under frost-free conditions, Cal Cultivators expects its strawberry crop to have a $60,000 market value. An unprotected crop subject to frost has an expected market value of $40,000. If Cal protects the strawberries against frost, then the market value of the crop is still expected to be $60,000 under frost-free conditions and $90,000 if there is a frost. What must be the probability of a frost for Cal to be indifferent to spending $10,000 for frost protection?

a. .167
b. .200
c. .250
d. .333

67. What is the appropriate range for the coefficient of correlation (r)?

a. $0 \setminus r \setminus 1$.
b. $-1 \setminus r \setminus 1$.
c. $-100 \setminus r \setminus 100$.
d. $-infinity \setminus r \setminus infinity$.

68. A scatter chart depicting the relationship between sales and salesmen's automobile expenses is set forth below:

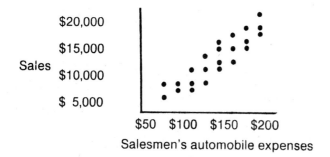

What can we deduce from the chart about the relationship between sales and salesmen's automobile expenses?

a. A high degree of linear correlation.
b. A high degree of nonlinear correlation.
c. No apparent correlation.
d. Both sales and salesmen's automobile expenses are independent variables.

69. Day Mail Order Co. applied the high-low method of cost estimation to customer order data for the first 4 months of 1995. What is the estimated variable order filling cost component per order?

| Month | Orders | Cost |
|---|---|---|
| January | 1,200 | $ 3,120 |
| February | 1,300 | 3,185 |
| March | 1,800 | 4,320 |
| April | 1,700 | 3,895 |
| | 6,000 | $14,520 |

a. $2.00
b. $2.42
c. $2.48
d. $2.50

70. Multiple regression analysis

a. Establishes a cause and effect relationship.
b. Is **not** a sampling technique.
c. Involves the use of independent variables only.
d. Produces measures of probable error.

71. Multiple regression differs from simple regression in that it

a. Provides an estimated constant term.
b. Has more dependent variables.
c. Allows the computation of the coefficient of determination.
d. Has more independent variables.

# Chapter Seventeen
# Managerial Analysis and Control Problems

## NUMBER 1

Management of Bicent Company uses the following unit costs for the one product it manufacturers:

|  | Projected Cost per Unit |
|---|---|
| Direct material (all variable) | $30.00 |
| Direct labor (all variable) | 19.00 |
| Manufacturing overhead: | |
| Variable cost | 6.00 |
| Fixed cost (based on 10,000 units per month) | 5.00 |
| Selling, general and administrative: | |
| Variable cost | 4.00 |
| Fixed cost (based on 10,000 units per month) | 2.80 |

The projected selling price is $80 per unit. The fixed costs remain fixed within the relevant range of 4,000 to 16,000 units of production.

Management has also projected the following data for the month of June 19X1:

|  | Units |
|---|---|
| Beginning inventory | 2,000 |
| Production | 9,000 |
| Available | 11,000 |
| Sales | 7,500 |
| Ending inventory | 3,500 |

**Required:**
Prepare projected income statements for June 19X1 for management purposes under **each** of the following product-costing methods:
      1. Absorption costing with all variances charged to cost of goods sold each month.
      2. Direct (variable) costing.

Supporting schedules calculating inventoriable production costs per unit should be presented in good form. **Ignore Income taxes.**

## NUMBER 2

A company is presently using breakeven analysis. The president has requested an explanation of this analytical tool.

**Required:**
1. What is the breakeven point and how is it computed?
2. What are the major uses of breakeven analysis?

# NUMBER 3

Grisp Company, a manufacturer with heavy investments in property, plant, and equipment, is presently using absorption costing for both its external and internal reporting. The management of Grisp Company is considering using the direct costing method for internal reporting only.

**Required:**
1. What would be the rationale for using the direct costing method for internal reporting?
2. Assuming that the quantity of ending inventory is higher than the quantity of beginning inventory, would operating income using direct costing be different from operating income using absorption costing? If so, specify if it would be higher or lower. Discuss the rationale for your answer.

# NUMBER 4                                                                                     *M88*

Seco Corp., a wholesale supply company, engages independent sales agents to market the company's lines. These agents currently receive a commission of 20% of sales, but they are demanding an increase to 25% of sales made during the year ending December 31, 1989. Seco had already prepared its 1989 budget before learning of the agents' demand for an increase in commissions. The following pro forma income statement is based on this budget:

Seco Corp.<br>PRO FORMA INCOME STATEMENT<br>For the Year Ending December 31, 1989

| | | |
|---|---:|---:|
| Sales | | $10,000,000 |
| Cost of sales | | 6,000,000 |
| Gross margin | | 4,000,000 |
| Selling and administrative costs | | |
|   Commissions | $2,000,000 | |
|   All other costs (fixed) | 100,000 | 2,100,000 |
| Income before income tax | | 1,900,000 |
| Income tax (30%) | | 570,000 |
| Net income | | $1,330,000 |

Seco is considering the possibility of employing its own salespersons. Three individuals would be required, at an estimated annual salary of $30,000 each, plus commissions of 5% of sales. In addition, a sales manager would be employed at a fixed annual salary of $160,000. All other fixed costs, as well as the variable cost percentages, would remain the same as the estimates in the 1989 pro forma income statement.

**Required:**
a. Compute Seco's estimated breakeven point in sales dollars for the year ending December 31, 1989, based on the pro forma income statement prepared by the company.
b. Compute Seco's estimated breakeven point in sales dollars for the year ending December 31, 1989, if the company employs its own salespersons.
c. Compute the estimated volume in sales dollars that would be required for the year ending December 31, 1989, to yield the same net income as projected in the pro forma income statement, if Seco continues to use the independent sales agents and agrees to their demand for a 25% sales commission.
d. Compute the estimated volume in sales dollars that would generate an identical net income for the year ending December 31, 1989, regardless of whether Seco employs its own salespersons or continues to use the independent sales agents and pays them a 25% commission.

# NUMBER 5

Daly Company has determined the number of units of Product Y that Daly would have to sell in order to break even. However, Daly would like to attain a 20 percent profit on sales of Product Y.

**Required:**

1. Explain how breakeven analysis can be used to determine the number of units of Product Y that Daly would have to sell to attain a 20 percent profit on sales.
2. If variable cost per unit increases as a percentage of the sales price, how would that affect the number of units of Product Y that Daly would have to sell in order to break even and why?
3. Identify the limitations of breakeven analysis in managerial decision making.

# NUMBER 6

Leif Company is faced with the necessity of making the following financial management decision involving its Sigma Division:

*Establishment of a selling price for a new product, called Kace, developed by Sigma.* Kace's variable cost is $3 per unit. The following probabilities of reaching annual sales levels for Kace have been estimated:

| Sales | If each unit is sold for | | |
|---|---|---|---|
| (in units) | $6 | $7 | $8 |
| 70,000 | 10% | 40% | 70% |
| 80,000 | 50% | 30% | 20% |
| 90,000 | 40% | 30% | 10% |

**Required:**

As a guide to Leif Company in determining a selling price for Kace, prepare a schedule of the expected annual contribution margin for each of the sales prices proposed for Kace.

Lond Co. produces joint products Jana and Reta, together with byproduct Bynd. Jana is sold at split-off, whereas Reta and Bynd undergo additional processing. Production data pertaining to these products for the year ended December 31, 1989, were as follows:

| | *Jana* | *Reta* | *Bynd* | *Total* |
|---|---|---|---|---|
| Joint costs | | | | |
| Variable | | | | $ 88,000 |
| Fixed | | | | 148,000 |
| Separable costs | | | | |
| Variable | | $120,000 | $3,000 | 123,000 |
| Fixed | | 90,000 | 2,000 | 92,000 |
| Production in pounds | 50,000 | 40,000 | 10,000 | 100,000 |
| Sales price per pound | $4.00 | $7.50 | $1.10 | |

There were no beginning or ending inventories. No materials are spoiled in production. Variable costs change in direct proportion to production volume. Bynd's net realizable value is deducted from joint costs. Joint costs are allocated to joint products to achieve the same gross margin percentage for each joint product.

Although 1989 performance could be repeated for 1990, Lond is considering possible operation of the plant at full capacity of 120,000 pounds. The relative proportions of each product's output with respect to cost behavior and production increases would be unchanged. Market surveys indicate that prices of Jana and Bynd would have to be reduced to $3.40 and $0.90, respectively. Reta's expected price decline cannot be determined.

**Required:**

a.  Compute Lond's breakeven point in pounds for the year ended December 31, 1989.
b.  Prepare the following schedules for Lond Co. for the year ending December 31, 1990:
   1.  Projected production in pounds for each product at full capacity.
   2.  Differential revenues (excluding Reta).
   3.  Differential costs.
   4.  Sales price required per pound of Reta in order for Lond to achieve the same gross margin as that for 1989.

The following information pertains to a product for a 10-week budget period:

- Sales price $11 per unit

  Materials $3 per unit
  Manufacturing conversion costs
      Fixed $210,000
      Variable $2 per unit
  Selling and administrative costs
      Fixed $45,000
      Variable $1 per unit
  Beginning accounts payable for materials $40,000

- Manufacturing and sales of 70,000 units are expected to occur evenly over the period.

- Materials are paid for in the week following use.

- There are no beginning inventories.

**Required:**
For **Items 1 through 5,** determine the correct amount using the above information. Any information contained in an item is unique to that item and is **not** to be incorporated in your calculations when answering other items.

1. What amount should be budgeted for cash payments to material suppliers during the period?

2. Using variable costing, what is the budgeted income for the period?

3. Using absorption costing, what is the budgeted income for the period?

4. Actual results are as budgeted, except that only 60,000 of the 70,000 units produced were sold. Using absorption costing, what is the difference between the reported income and the budgeted net income?

5. If a special order for 4,000 units would cause the loss of 1,000 regular sales, what minimum amount of revenue must be generated from the special order so that net income is not reduced? (All cost relationships are unchanged.)

# Chapter Seventeen
# Solutions to Managerial Analysis and Control Questions

1. (c)  
| | |
|---|---:|
| Selling price per unit | $5.00 |
| Less: Variable cost per unit | 3.00 |
| Contribution margin | $2.00 |
| Fixed Cost mfg. (.25 × 100,000 units) | $25,000 |
| Fixed cost selling (.65 × 100,000 units) | 65,000 |
| Total Fixed Costs | $90,000 |

$$\text{B.E.P.} = \frac{\text{Fixed Costs}}{\text{Contribution margin}} = \frac{\$90,000}{\$2} = \underline{45,000}\text{ units}$$

2. (c)  
| | |
|---|---:|
| Total Contribution Margin ($2 × 110,000 units) | $220,000 |
| Less: Total fixed costs | 90,000 |
| Net Income | $130,000 |

3. (d) If all variances are charged to cost of goods sold, the net income under absorption costing will differ from that under direct costing by the amount of fixed cost assigned to the increase or decrease in inventory. If inventory increases, fixed costs are transferred to the following period, thereby increasing net income under absorption costing. If inventory decreases, fixed costs from prior periods are expensed, thereby reducing net income.

Increase in inventory 10,000 units × $.25 fixed manufacturing costs per unit = $2,500 fixed cost transferred to the next period. Therefore, net income under absorption costing is $132,500—($130,000 + $2,500).

4. (a) (Selling price – $3 variable cost) × 10,000 units = $5,000 net income

$$
\begin{aligned}
10,000\ (X - 3) &= 5000 \\
10,000X - 30,000 &= 5000 \\
10,000X &= 35,000 \\
X &= 35,000 \div 10,000 = \underline{\$3.50}\text{ Selling Price}
\end{aligned}
$$

5. (b)  
| | |
|---|---:|
| Selling price ($5.00 × 1.20) | $6.00 |
| Less:   V.C. mfg. ($1.00 × 1.10) | (1.10) |
|          V.C. selling | (2.00) |
| Contribution Margin | $2.90 |
| Less: Profit per unit (.1 × $2.90) | .29 |
| Adjusted C.M. per unit | $2.61 |

# units = $104,400 ÷ 2.61 = $\underline{40,000}$ units

OR

$$\text{\# units} = \frac{\text{FC} + \text{Profit}}{\text{CM}}$$

$$X = \frac{\$140,400 + .29(X)}{2.90}$$

$$
\begin{aligned}
2.90X &= \$104,400 + .29X \\
2.90X - .29X &= \$104,400 \\
2.61X &= \$104,400 \\
X &= \$104,400 \div 2.61 = \underline{40,000}\text{ units}
\end{aligned}
$$

6. (b) BEP = Fixed Costs % Contribution Margin %

Fixed Cost:

|  |  |  |
|---|---|---|
| Cost of goods sold (10% × $2,000,000 sales) |  | $200,000 |
| Other expenses (15% × $2,000,000 sales) |  | 300,000 |
| Total fixed costs |  | $500,000 |

Contribution margin %

|  |  |  |
|---|---|---|
| Selling price |  | 100% |
| Less: Variable cost % |  |  |
| Cost of goods sold | 50% |  |
| Other expenses | 20% | 70% |
| Contribution margin % |  | 30% |

BEP = FC ÷ CM % = $500,000 ÷ 30% = $1,666,667

7. (d) As both products can utilize full capacity, the greatest profit will result from the greatest contribution margin (selling price - variable costs) for capacity. Fixed costs are irrelevant as they are not effected by the decision.

8. (b)     BEP in dollar sales = Fixed costs ÷ contribution margin %
                                 = $20,000 ÷ 80%*
                                 = $25,000

     * Contribution margin % = 1 – [variable cost ÷ sales]
                             = 1 – [$80,000 ÷ $400,000]
                             = 1 – .20
                             = 80%

9. (b) Under the direct or variable costing method, variable costs are deducted from revenue to determine contribution margin, and *all* fixed costs (manufacturing, selling, general and administrative) are then deducted to obtain net income or income from operations.
     The contribution margin is calculated in two steps:
     1. Revenue less variable cost of goods sold = Contribution margin: manufacturing
     2. Contribution margin: manufacturing less other variable costs (S, G & A) = Contribution margin: final

10. (b) $20,000.

|  |  |  |
|---|---|---|
| Increase in inventory |  | 1000 units |
| Fixed manufacturing costs per unit | × | $20 |
| Fixed manufacturing costs included in ending inventory |  | $20,000 |

If inventory increases (production exceeds sales), absorption costing results in greater net income than direct (variable) costing, due to the fixed manufacturing costs included in inventory.

11. (a) Generally when you plot activity on a graph, your vertical axis (Y) is your cost, while your horizontal axis (X) is your activity. Since there is a fixed rental cost, this would be plotted by a straight horizontal line originating part way up on the Y axis at the zero level of activity (X), thus indicating I or II as possible answers. The variable portion of the rent is based upon sales, which is added to the straight fixed line at increasingly smaller increments as sales (plotted on the X axis) are increased. Therefore, A or line I is your answer. Answer (b) is incorrect because it shows larger increments being added to the fixed costs.

12. (a) If inventory decreases (production is less than units sold) absorption costing results in less net income than direct (variable) costing due to the fixed manufacturing costs included in the beginning inventory under absorption costing.

13. (d) Breakeven (cost-volume-profit) analysis assumes sales revenue per unit and variable cost per unit are constant within the relevant range. Therefore, variable cost as a percentage of sales revenue would be **the same** at all levels of activity within the relevant range.

Breakeven (CVP) analysis assumes that total fixed costs remain constant within the relevant range. Therefore, fixed costs as a percentage of sales revenue would be **greater** at lower levels of activity (a) than at higher levels of activity (b).

For explanation of chart, refer to text page 17-5.

14. (c) Breakeven point represents your fixed costs divided by your contribution margin. Mathematically, by decreasing your numerator (fixed costs) or increasing your denominator (contribution margin), your breakeven point must decrease.

15. (b) The original cost and carrying value (cost less accumulated depreciation) of an old asset is a "sunk cost" for replacement decisions as the replacement would not affect these amounts. A sunk cost is a cost which has been incurred and will not be changed by any future decisions. It is, therefore, irrelevant to a decision and excluded in its analysis.

The disposal value (fair market value) of the *new* asset (or the *old* asset) is a cash flow that will only result if the replacement is made and the old asset is disposed of. Because it is dependent upon the replacement decision it is relevant to the decision.

16. (a) Remachine and $5,000.

|  | Alternatives | |
|---|---|---|
|  | *Remachine* | *Scrap* |
| Proceeds | $9,000 | $1,000 |
| Additional Cost | 5,000 | —0— |
| Net proceeds | $4,000 | $1,000 |

The inventory carrying value of $20,000 is not relevant to the decision since under either alternative the $20,000 is a cost (sunk cost).

17. (b) Fixed costs = $200,000
　　　　Contribution margin—Tetra = $1
　　　　Contribution margin—Min = $2

For every unit of Min sold, two units of Tetra are sold. Therefore, the combined contribution margin for each unit of Min sold would be: (1 unit × $2) + (2 units × $1) = $4.

　　　　Breakeven　= Fixed costs ÷ Contribution margin
　　　　　　　　　= $200,000 ÷ $4
　　　　　　　　　= 50,000 units (Min)

Proof: (50,000 Min × $2) + (100,000 Tetra × $1) = $200,000 (Fixed costs)

18. (d) $500,000.
Weighted average of variable costs to sales:

|  | *Percent of Sales* | *Percent of VC* | *Value* |
|---|---|---|---|
| A | 60 | 60 | 36% |
| B | 40 | 85 | 34% |
|  |  |  | 70% |

| Sales | 1.00 | (100%) |
|---|---|---|
| Variable cost | .70 | (70%) |
| Contribution | .30 | (30%) |

Breakeven = $\dfrac{\text{FC } \$150,000}{\text{Contribution } .30}$ = $500,000

19. (d) $680,000.

| | | |
|---|---|---|
| Fixed cost = $150,000 + 30% × 150,000 = | | $195,000 |
| Add: Net Income generated | | 9,000 |
| | | $204,000 |

Breakeven $\dfrac{\$204,000}{.30^1}$ = $680,000

[1] Computed in previous problem

Alternatively, the .30 composite contribution rate could be computed by subtracting the percent of variable cost from 100% and multiplying percent of sales by the result, e.g.:

A 60% × (100% – 60%) = 24%
B 40% × (100% – 85%) = 6%
30%

20. (b)

| | Ratio | CM | Total CM |
|---|---|---|---|
| X | 3 | $1.00 | $ 3.00 |
| Y | 6 | 1.50 | 9.00 |
| Z | 1 | 3.00 | 3.00 |
| | | | $15.00 |

$$BEP = \frac{FC}{CM} = \frac{600,000}{15} = 40,000 \text{ (of 3x, 6y, 1z)}$$

# of X at BEP = 40,000 × 3 = **120,000**.

21. (c) Under the direct or variable costing method, variable costs are deducted from sales revenue to determine contribution margin and **all** fixed costs (overhead, selling, general and administrative) are then deducted to obtain net income or income from operations. The contribution margin is calculated in two steps:
1. Sales revenue less (variable) cost of goods sold = Contribution margin: manufacturing
2. Contribution margin: manufacturing less other variable costs (S, G & A) = Contribution margin: final

22. (c) $49.22

| | | | | | | | |
|---|---|---|---|---|---|---|---|
| $60 | = | Food Cost | + | Service charge | + | Sales Tax | |
| | = | FC | + | 15% FC | + | .06 (FC + 15%FC) | |
| | = | FC | + | .15FC | + | .06 (1.15 FC) | |
| | = | | 1.15 FC | | + | .069 FC | |
| | = | | 1.219 FC | | | | |
| $\dfrac{60}{1.219}$ | = | FC | | | | | |
| $49.22 | = | Food Cost | | | | | |

23. (b) $640,000.

Relevant costs per unit:

| | |
|---|---|
| DM | $ 4 |
| DL | 16 |
| VOH | 8 |
| FOH @ 40% | 4 |
| | $32  × 20,000 = $640,000 |

The fixed overhead of $6 per unit will continue regardless; therefore, only the cost that will not be incurred if part is bought outside is considered.

24. (b) $24,000 B.E.P.

| | |
|---|---|
| Sales | 200,000 |
| Less: margin of safety | (80,000) |
| Sales at Break-even point | 120,000 |
| Contribution margin | x    .20 |
| Fixed Cost | 24,000 |

BEP in $ Sales = Fixed Costs ÷ Contribution Margin %
Therefore, Fixed Cost = BEP $ Sales x Contribution Margin %

25. (d) Gross profit (margin) is a term associated with absorption costing; however, it is not applicable to variable (or direct) costing. Under variable (direct) costing, the cost of goods sold includes only the variable costs associated with the inventory sold and sales less (variable) cost of goods sold is referred to as contribution margin—manufacturing. Operating income applies to both variable and absorption costing.

26. (b)

| | Total | *Per unit (25,000 units)* |
|---|---|---|
| Sales | $500,000 | $20.00 |
| Less: Variable costs: | | |
| Direct materials and labor | (150,000) | (6.00) |
| Overhead | ( 20,000) | ( .80) |
| Selling and general | ( 5,000) | ( .20) |
| Contribution margin | $325,000 | $13.00 |

$$\text{Breakeven point in units} = \text{Fixed costs} \div \text{contribution margin per unit}$$
$$= (\$35,000 + \$30,000) \div \$13$$
$$= 5,000$$

27. (a) 1990 total fixed costs—decreased; 1990 unit variable costs—increased.

*Decrease in fixed costs:* At zero volume, the lines 0G (zero G) and 0E (zero E) represent the fixed costs (loss at zero volume) for 1990 and 1989, respectively. The fixed costs for 1990 (line 0G), are less than the fixed costs for 1989 (line 0E). Therefore, fixed costs decreased from 1989 to 1990.

*Increase in variable costs:* The slop of the profit-volume line for 1990, line GH, is less than the slope of the 1989 profit-volume line EF; therefore, the contribution margin for 1990 is less than 1989. If selling price is unchanged, the decrease in contribution margin must be due to an increase in variable costs for 1990.

*Alternative:* The breakeven point is the point where the profit line intersects the zero dollar line. Despite the decrease in fixed costs for 1990, the breakeven point for 1990 is greater than for 1989; therefore, the contribution margin for 1990 must be less than 1989. If selling price is unchanged, the decrease in contribution margin is due to an increase in variable costs.

28. (d) Under direct or variable costing, product costs or inventoriable costs include only variable manufacturing costs (direct material, direct labor and variable overhead). Variable selling costs are used in the calculation of contribution margin; however, they are not a product cost (inventoriable).

29. (a)

| | |
|---|---|
| Direct materials | $ 20,000 |
| Direct labor | 55,000 |
| Variable overhead | 45,000 |
| Avoidable fixed overhead ($4 × 10,000) | 40,000 |
| Foregone rent | 15,000 |
| Cost to make | $175,000 |
| Cost to buy ($18 × 10,000) | 180,000 |
| Additional cost of buying | $   5,000 |

30. (a) Contribution margin is a term associated with variable (direct) costing; however, it is not applicable to absorption costing. Contribution margin is sales less all variable costs and it is from this amount that all fixed costs (manufacturing, selling and administrative) are deducted to determine operating income.

Under absorption costing, cost of goods sold includes both variable and fixed manufacturing costs and sales less cost of goods sold is referred to as gross profit or gross margin.

31. (a) $300,000 margin of safety.

Margin of safety is the excess of actual or budgeted sales ($1,000,000) over sales at the breakeven point ($700,000). It is the amount by which sales could decrease before a loss occurs.

32. (a)

| | |
|---|---:|
| Direct material ($40,000 ÷ 10,000) | $4.00 |
| Direct labor ($20,000 ÷ 10,000) | 2.00 |
| Variable overhead ($12,000 ÷ 10,000) | 1.20 |
| Per unit cost | $7.20 |
| Ending inventory units | × 1,000 |
| | $7,200 |

33. (a)

| | |
|---|---:|
| Fixed cost per unit ($25,000 ÷ 10,000 units) | $ 2.50 |
| Increase in inventory units | × 1,000 |
| Fixed costs assigned to inventory | $2,500 |

34. (b)

| | |
|---|---:|
| Selling price | $23 |
| Variable manufacturing cost | (16) |
| Incremental cost (overtime premium) | ( 3) |
| Contribution margin per unit | $ 4 |
| Units | × 40,000 |
| Total contribution from special order | $160,000 |

35. (a) $50,000.

| BEP $ Sales | = | FC/CM% |
|---|---|---|
| $800,000 | = | $100,000/CM% |
| 1/8 | = | CM% |

| | |
|---|---:|
| Sales | $1,200,000 |
| - Sales @ BEP | 800,000 |
| Sales over BEP | $ 400,000 |
| CM% | x     1/8 |
| Profit @ $1,200,000 Sales | $   50,000 |

36. (b)

| | |
|---|---:|
| Allocated overhead | $48,000 |
| Less: Non avoidable overhead | (21,000) |
| Decrease in overhead cost | 27,000 |
| Less decrease in contribution margin | (24,000) |
| Increase in income | $ 3,000 |

37. (d) Sunk costs are costs that will not change or be affected by the selection of available alternatives. In this situation, the prior manufacturing costs of $50,000 will be unaffected by subsequent processing or sale.

38. (b) Increase budgeted breakeven; Decrease margin of safety.

An increase in direct labor costs (a variable cost) would decrease the contribution margin (selling price – variable costs) and result in an increase in the breakeven point (FC/CM).

Margin of safety is the excess of actual or budgeted sales over sales at the breakeven point. It is the amount by which sales could decrease before a loss occurs. An increase in the breakeven point, resulting from an increase in direct labor costs, would cause a decrease in margin of safety.

39. (b) Within the relevant range, **total** fixed costs do not change and variable cost per unit does not change (total variable costs change proportionately with activity). Therefore, a decrease in the production level (within the relevant range) would result in an increase in fixed costs per unit as the total fixed costs are allocated to fewer units and a decrease in total variable costs as they change proportionally with activity or production.

40. (c) Within the relevant range, variable costs per unit do not change and *total* fixed costs do not change. Therefore, a decline in the production level (within the relevant range) would result in no change in variable costs per unit while fixed costs per unit would increase.

41. (b) Under the direct or variable costing method, variable costs are deducted from sales revenue to determine contribution margin and **all** fixed costs (overhead, selling, general and administrative) are then deducted to obtain net income or income from operations. The contribution margin is calculated in two steps:

       1. Sales revenue less (variable) cost of goods sold = Contribution margin: manufacturing
       2. Contribution margin: manufacturing less other variable costs (S, G & A) = Contribution margin: final

Under the absorption costing method, each cost classification (cost of goods sold, selling, general and administrative, etc.) includes both its fixed cost and variable cost components.

42. (a) $2,329 Target price

| | | |
|---|---|---|
| Sales revenue | = | Cost of goods / cost percentage |
| | = | $990,000 / .85 |
| | = | $1,164,706 |
| | | |
| Target price | = | Sales revenue / # units |
| | = | $1,164,706 / 500 |
| | = | $2,329 |

Cost percentage: If profit margin on sales is 15%, then the cost of goods sold percentage is 85% (100% - 15%).

43. (c) The breakeven point in sales dollars represents your fixed costs divided by your contribution margin percentage. Fixed costs are given, but the contribution margin must be determined.

| | | |
|---|---|---|
| Sales | $800,000 | 100% |
| Variable costs | 160,000 | 20% |
| Contribution margin | $640,000 | 80% |
| | | |
| Fixed costs | $ 40,000 | |
| Divided by contribution margin | 80% | |
| Breakeven sales | $ 50,000 | |

44. (b)

| | |
|---|---|
| Selling price | $ 10 |
| less: Variable costs | 5 |
| Contribution margin | 5 |
| # Units sold | × 80,000 |
| Total contribution | 400,000 |
| less: Fixed costs | $190,000 |
| Net Income | $210,000 |

45. (b) Absorption Cost Per Unit:

| | | |
|---|---|---:|
| Raw materials | | 2.00 |
| Direct labor | | 1.25 |
| Overhead | | .75 |
| Variable | | |
| Fixed ($120,000 ÷ 100,000 units) | | 1.20 |
| | | 5.20 |
| Ending Inventory (100,000 – 80,000) | | × 20,000 |
| | | $104,000 |

**Note**: Selling and administrative costs are not part of the product costs.

46. (b) This is a problem in the analysis of variable and fixed costs. Since costs are either variable or fixed, then of the $500,000 in total costs, $430,000 must be variable ($500,000 less $70,000 in fixed). It takes $430,000 in variable costs to run five sales offices, or $86,000 per office. If seven offices are being run, then:

| | |
|---|---:|
| 7 offices @ $86,000 = | $602,000 |
| Fixed costs | 70,000 |
| Total costs | $672,000 |

47. (b)

| | Total | Per unit (50,000 units) |
|---|---:|---:|
| Sales | $1,000,000 | $20.00 |
| Less variable costs | | |
| Direct materials & labor | (300,000) | (6.00) |
| Overhead | ( 40,000) | ( .80) |
| Selling, general admin. | ( 10,000) | ( .20) |
| Contribution margin | $ 650,000 | $13.00 |

$$\text{Breakeven point in units} = \frac{\text{Fixed cost}}{\text{Contribution margin per unit}}$$

$$= \frac{\$70,000 + \$60,000}{\$13}$$

$$= \underline{\$10,000}$$

48. (b)  $\dfrac{\text{Contribution margin}}{\text{Ratio}} = \dfrac{\text{Contribution margin}}{\text{Selling price}} = \dfrac{\$13}{\$20} = .65$

**Note:** Can also be calculated based on total contribution margin and sales ($650,000 ÷ $1,000,000 = .65).

49. (b) Within the relevant range, variable costs per unit do not change.

A basic assumption of break-even / C.V.P. analysis is linearity; therefore, answers (a) and (d) are incorrect. As variable cost per unit are unchanged, total variable cost changes proportionately with activity. Therefore, total cost change and answer (c) is incorrect.

50. (c) A "sunk cost" is a cost which has been incurred and will not be changed by any future decision; it is therefore irrelevant to a decision and excluded in its analysis. The original cost of an asset less its accumulated depreciation (book value) is a sunk cost for replacement decisions as the replacement would not affect these amounts.

51. (a) The probability of the lead time being 3 days is 25%, and the probability of demand being 3 units in a day is 10%. The probability of 3 days of demand being 3 units (3 × 3 = 9) coupled with a 3-day lead time is as follows:
$$.25 \times .1 \times .1 \times .1 = .00025$$

52. (d) Maximum possible lead time is 3 days, and the maximum possible demand on any day is 3 units. Therefore, the maximum possible demand during lead time is 9 units (3 days × 3 units per day). If 10 units are ordered when inventory is 10 units, there will be at least one unit in inventory when the shipment arrives.

53. (a) In order to control the cost of stock-outs as well as ordering and carrying costs, the model would have to state when to order (reorder point) as well as how many units to order (EOQ).

54. (c) The probability of demand being greater than 200 units is 10%; therefore, the probability that sales will be 200 units or less is 90% (100% – 10%). The 90% probability for sales of 200 or less units could also be determined by adding the individual probabilities for sale of 200 units or less (.2 + .5 + .2).

55. (a) Computation of expected selling price

| Selling Price | × | Probability of Selling Price | = | Expected Value |
|---|---|---|---|---|
| $ 5,000 | | .4 | | $ 2,000 |
| 8,000 | | .2 | | 1,600 |
| 12,000 | | .3 | | 3,600 |
| 30,000 | | .1 | | 3,000 |
| Expected Selling Price | | | | $10,200 |

This solution does not provide for an analysis or evaluation of the individual's aversion to risk.

56. (c) Most probability problems have you compute the expected value from a series of possible outcomes, each weighted with its own likelihood of occurrence. However, in this problem, the company only wants to select the *most likely* sales volume figure. That would be the one with the greatest probability of occurrence.

57. (c) $52.

| | | |
|---|---|---|
| Additional sales 60 boxes | | |
| #60 boxes  x  ($3 selling price  -  $2 cost) | $60 | |
| #40 boxes  x  ($1 selling price  -  $2 cost) | (40) | |
| Profit | $20 | |
| Probability | x .6 | |
| Expected value | | $12 |
| Additional sales 100 boxes | | |
| #100 boxes  x  ($3 selling price  -  $2 cost) | $100 | |
| -0- boxes  x  ($1 selling price) | -0- | |
| Profit | $100 | |
| Probability | x  .4 | |
| Expected Profit | | 40 |
| Expected profit (value) of decision | | $52 |

58. (d) Because the games of chance are to break even, the price charged (P) is to equal the expected payoff of the games.

The expected value of the payoffs are as follows:

Queens   $\frac{4}{52}$   ($5) The probability of drawing a queen from the deck of cards is 4/52.

Hearts   $\frac{13}{52}$   ($2) The probability of drawing a heart from the deck of cards is 13/52.

Therefore,   $P = \frac{4}{52}$ ($5) + $\frac{13}{52}$ ($2)

59. (b)

| Monthly Sales | Probability | Income (Loss) | Expected Profit |
|---|---|---|---|
| 3,000 | .10 | (35,000) | $(3,500) |
| 6,000 | .20 | 5,000 | 1,000 |
| 9,000 | .40 | 30,000 | 12,000 |
| 12,000 | .20 | 50,000 | 10,000 |
| 15,000 | .10 | 70,000 | 7,000 |
| Total expected profit | | | $26,500 |

60. (c)

| Terminal | % of Cargo | % of Error | Expected Error Occurrence Rate | Probability Error is from Terminal | |
|---|---|---|---|---|---|
| Land | 50% | 2% | 1.0% | 1.0÷4.0 = | 25% |
| Air | 40% | 4% | 1.6% | 1.6÷4.0 = | 40% |
| Sea | 10% | 14% | 1.4% | 1.4÷4.0 = | 35% |
| | | | 4.0% | | 100% |

61. (a) When a correlation analysis produces a coefficient of zero, the implication is that there is absolutely no causal connection between the two variables. Plotting the points would show them as random points forming no pattern or cluster whatever.

62. (d) Multiple regression analysis.
Regression analysis is a mathematical technique used to predict the value of one variable and its changes (the dependent variable) based upon the value of some other variable (the independent variable). Simple regression analysis involves the use of only one independent (explanatory) variable, while multiple regression analysis allows for more than one independent variable.

63. (b) Regression analysis develops a mathematical function or formula. A function yields dependent variable values from independent variable values.

64. (d) .95 as a coefficient of correlation is very high (the maximum is at 1.0), thus showing a definite cause-effect relationship. (b) and (c) are obviously incorrect. (a) is incorrect because it does not provide for the fact that a decrease in sales would be associated with a decrease in theft. (d) is correct because it covers both possibilities, or, in other words, it is more correct than (a).

65. (a) Regression analysis (simple or multiple) is a sampling technique which measures the relationship (does not establish) of a dependent variable to one or more independent variables. If one independent variable is used the method is referred to as simple regression. If more than one independent variable is used the method is referred to as multiple regression.

66. (b) 20% probability of frost.

| | | |
|---|---|---|
| Cost of Protection | = | Benefit of Protection |
| Cost of Protection | = | Prob (Protected benefit - Unprotected benefit) |
| $10,000 | = | Prob ($90,000 - $40,000) |
| $10,000 | = | Prob ($50,000) |
| 20% | = | Probability |

67. (b) Maximum correlation exists between +1 and –1.

68. (a) The grouping of plotted dots clearly shows a thrust from lower left to upper right. Such a pattern clearly invites the reader to read the dots as a broad line thereby implying the linear correlation. The regularity and density of the dots implies a high degree of such correlation.

69. (a) $2.00.

|  | Orders | Cost |
|---|---|---|
| High | 1800 | $4320 |
| Low | 1200 | 3120 |
| Change | 600 | $1200 |

| Change in Cost | $1200 | = | $2 per order |
|---|---|---|---|
| Change in Order | 600 | | |

70. (d) The coefficient of correlation and coefficient of determination are measures of probable error. Answers (a), (b) and (c) are incorrect as regression analysis (simple or multiple) is a sampling technique which measures the relationship (does not establish) of a dependent variable to one or more independent variables.

71. (d) Regression analysis is a sampling technique which measures the relationship of a dependent variable to one or more independent variables. If one independent variable is used, the method is referred to as simple regression. If more than one independent variable is used, the method is referred to as multiple regression.

# Chapter Seventeen
# Solutions to Managerial Analysis and Control Problems

## NUMBER 1

1.

*Bicent Company*
**PROJECTED INCOME STATEMENT**
*For the Month of June 19X1 (Absorption Costing)*

| | | |
|---|---:|---:|
| Sales (7,500 units × $80) | | $600,000 |
| Beginning inventory (2,000 units × $60) *(Schedule 1)* | $120,000 | |
| Production (9,000 units × $60) | 540,000 | |
| Available | 660,000 | |
| Ending inventory (3,500 units × $60) | 210,000 | |
| Cost of goods sold before adjustment | 450,000 | |
| Adjustment for volume variance (production projected as 10,000 units as "normal"; 1,000 units underapplied × $5 fixed manufacturing overhead) | 5,000 | |
| | | 455,000 |
| Gross margin | | 145,000 |
| Variable selling, general, and administrative (7,500 units × $4) | 30,000 | |
| Fixed selling, general, and administrative (10,000 units × $2.80) | 28,000 | 58,000 |
| Projected income | | $ 87,000 |

2.

*Bicent Company*
**PROJECTED INCOME STATEMENT**
*For the Month of June 19X1 (Direct Costing)*

| | | |
|---|---:|---:|
| Sales (7,500 units × $80) | | $600,000 |
| Beginning inventory (2,000 units × $55) *(Schedule 2)* | $110,000 | |
| Production (9,000 units × $55) | 495,000 | |
| Available | 605,000 | |
| Ending Inventory (3,500 units × $55) | 192,500 | |
| Variable cost of goods sold | 412,500 | |
| Variable selling, general, and administrative (7,500 units × $4) | 30,000 | |
| Total variable costs | | 442,500 |
| Contribution margin | | 157,500 |
| Fixed manufacturing overhead (10,000 units × $5) | 50,000 | |
| Fixed selling, general, and administrative (10,000 units × $2.80) | 28,000 | |
| Total fixed costs | | 78,000 |
| Projected income | | $ 79,500 |

**Note** *(Not Required)*: The difference in the two projected income figures ($87,000 − $79,500) equals $7,500. This is accounted for as the increase in inventory (3,500 − 2,000) times the fixed manufacturing overhead application rate (1,500 units × $5). The $7,500 of fixed manufacturing overhead is included in ending inventory under absorption costing, but it is expensed under direct (variable) costing.

### Schedule of Inventoriable Production Costs Per Unit
#### (Absorption Costing)

| | |
|---|---|
| Direct material | $30 |
| Direct labor | 19 |
| Manufacturing overhead (variable) | 6 |
| Manufacturing overhead (fixed) | 5 |
| Total unit cost | $60 |

*Schedule 2*

### Schedule of Inventoriable Production Costs Per Unit
#### (Direct Costing)

| | |
|---|---|
| Direct material | $30 |
| Direct labor | 19 |
| Manufacturing overhead (variable) | 6 |
| Total unit cost | $55 |

## NUMBER 2

1.  The breakeven point is that level of activity (sales) at which neither profit nor loss results. The factors used in determining the breakeven point are sales price, variable cost, and fixed cost.

    The breakeven point in units is computed by dividing the total fixed cost by the unit contribution margin (sales price less variable cost). The breakeven point in dollars is computed by dividing the total fixed cost by the contribution margin ratio (sales price divided into contribution margin).

2.  The major uses of breakeven analysis are these:
    - It assists management in achieving profit objectives by enabling management to analyze fixed versus variable cost characteristics and production volumes.
    - It assists management in formulating pricing and product mix decisions.

## NUMBER 3

1.  The direct costing method is useful for internal reporting because it focuses attention on the fixed-variable cost relationship and the contribution margin concept. It facilitates managerial decision-making, product pricing, and cost control. It allows certain calculations to be readily made, such as breakeven points and contribution margins. The focus on the contribution margin (sales revenues less variable costs) enables management to emphasize profitability in making short-run business decisions. Fixed costs are not easily controllable in the short run and hence may not be particularly relevant for short-run business decisions.

2.  Assuming that the quantity of ending inventory is higher than the quantity of beginning inventory, operating income using direct costing would be lower than operating income using absorption costing. Direct costing excludes fixed manufacturing overhead from inventories as it considers such costs to be period costs, which are expensed immediately; whereas, absorption costing includes fixed manufacturing overhead in inventories as it considers such costs to be product costs, which are expensed when the goods are sold. When the quantity of inventory increases during a period, direct costing produces a lower dollar increase in inventory than absorption costing. As a result, operating income would be lower.

# NUMBER 4

*Seco Corp.*
*Year Ending December 31, 1989*

**a.**

### Estimated Breakeven Point Based on Pro Forma Income Statement

| | | |
|---|---:|---:|
| Sales | | $10,000,000 |
| Variable costs | | |
|     Cost of sales | $6,000,000 | |
|     Commissions | 2,000,000 | 8,000,000 |
| Contribution margin | | $ 2,000,000 |
| | | |
| Contribution margin ratio ($2,000,000 ÷ $10,000,000) | | 20% |
| | | |
| Fixed costs | | $ 100,000 |
| Contribution margin ratio | | ÷ .20 |
| Estimated breakeven point | | $ 500,000 |

**b.**

### Estimated Breakeven Point With Company Employing Its Own Salespersons

| | |
|---|---:|
| Variable cost ratios | |
|     Cost of sales | 60% |
|     Commissions | 5% |
|     Total | 65% |
| | |
| Contribution margin ratio (100% − 65%) | 35% |
| | |
| Fixed costs | |
|     Sales manager | $ 160,000 |
|     3 salespersons @ $30,000 each | 90,000 |
|     Administrative | 100,000 |
|     Total | $ 350,000 |
| | |
| Fixed costs | $ 350,000 |
| Contribution margin ratio | ÷ 35% |
| Estimated breakeven point | $1,000,000 |

**c.**

### Estimated Sales Volume Yielding Net Income
### Projected in Pro Forma Income Statement
### With Independent Sales Agents Receiving 25% Commission

| | |
|---|---:|
| Target income before income tax | $ 1,900,000 |
| Fixed costs | 100,000 |
| Total | $ 2,000,000 |
| | |
| Variable cost ratios | |
|     Cost of sales | 60% |
|     Commissions | 25% |
|     Total | 85% |
| | |
| Contribution margin ratio (100% − 85%) | 15% |
| | |
| Target income + fixed costs | $ 2,000,000 |
| Contribution margin ratio | ÷ .15 |
| Estimated sales volume | $13,333,333 |

**d.**

**Estimated Sales Volume Yielding An Identical Net Income**
**Regardless of Whether the Company Employs its Own Salespersons**
**or**
**Continues With Independent Sales Agents and Pays Them 25% Commission**

Total costs with agents receiving 25% commission = Total costs with company's own sales force

$$X = \text{sales volume}$$

$$\frac{\$8,500,000}{\$10,000,000} X + \$100,000 = \frac{\$6,500,000}{\$10,000,000} X + \$350,000$$

$$.85X + \$100,000 = .65X + \$350,000$$

$$.20X = \$250,000$$

$$X = \underline{\$1,250,000}$$

# NUMBER 5

1. Daly would determine the number of units of Product Y that it would have to sell to attain a 20 percent profit on sales by dividing total fixed costs plus desired profit (20 percent of the sales price per unit multiplied by the units to attain a 20 percent profit) by unit contribution margin (sales price per unit less variable cost per unit).

2. If variable cost per unit increases as a percentage of the sales price, Daly would have to sell more units of Product Y to break even. Because the unit contribution margin (sales price per unit less variable cost per unit) would be lower, Daly would have to sell more units to cover the fixed costs.

3. The limitations of breakeven analysis in managerial decision-making are as follows:
   - The breakeven chart is fundamentally a static analysis, and, in most cases, changes can only be shown by drawing a new chart or series of charts.
   - The amount of fixed and variable cost, as well as the slope of the sales line, is meaningful in a defined range of activity and must be redefined for activity outside the relevant range.
   - It is difficult to determine the fixed and variable components of cost.
   - It is assumed that product mix will be unchanged.
   - It is assumed that product technology will be unchanged.
   - It is assumed that labor productivity will be unchanged.
   - It is assumed that selling prices and other market conditions will be unchanged.

# NUMBER 6

*Leif Company*
*Sigma Division*

**SCHEDULE OF EXPECTED ANNUAL CONTRIBUTION MARGIN**
**FOR KACE AT VARIOUS SALES PRICES**

| Sales price | Expected sales level (units) | Expected total sales | Expected variable costs at $3 | Expected contribution margin |
|---|---|---|---|---|
| $6 | 83,000 [1] | $498,000 | $249,000 | $249,000 |
| 7 | 79,000 [2] | 553,000 | 237,000 | 316,000 |
| 8 | 74,000 [3] | 592,000 | 222,000 | 370,000 |

| [1] | | [2] | | [3] | |
|---|---|---|---|---|---|
| 70,000 × 10% = | 7,000 | 70,000 × 40% = 28,000 | | 70,000 × 70% = 49,000 | |
| 80,000 × 50% = | 40,000 | 80,000 × 30% = 24,000 | | 80,000 × 20% = 16,000 | |
| 90,000 × 40% = | 36,000 | 90,000 × 30% = 27,000 | | 90,000 × 10% = 9,000 | |
| | 83,000 | 79,000 | | 74,000 | |

# NUMBER 7

**a.**

*Lond Co.*
## COMPUTATION OF BREAKEVEN POINT
## IN POUNDS
*For the Year Ended December 31, 1989*

Sales
| | | |
|---|---|---|
| Jana | $200,000 | |
| Reta | 300,000 | |
| Bynd | 11,000 | $511,000 |

Variable costs
| | | |
|---|---|---|
| Joint | $ 88,000 | |
| Reta | 120,000 | |
| Bynd | 3,000 | 211,000 |
| Contribution margin | | $300,000 |

Contribution margin per pound $\dfrac{\$300,000}{100,000} = \underline{\$3.00}$

Fixed costs
| | |
|---|---|
| Joint | $148,000 |
| Reta | 90,000 |
| Bynd | 2,000 |
| Total fixed costs | $240,000 |

Breakeven point in pounds $\dfrac{\$240,000}{\$3} = \underline{80,000}$

**b.** 1.

*Lond Co.*
## PROJECTED PRODUCTION IN POUNDS
## AT FULL CAPACITY
*For the Year Ending December 31, 1990*

| | Jana | Reta | Bynd | Total |
|---|---|---|---|---|
| Pounds of production for the year ended December 31, 1989 | 50,000 | 40,000 | 10,000 | 100,000 |
| Projected increases | | | | |
| Jana .5 × 20,000 | 10,000 | | | |
| Reta .4 × 20,000 | | 8,000 | | |
| Bynd .1 × 20,000 | | | 2,000 | |
| Total increase | | | | 20,000 |
| Projected pounds of production at full capacity | 60,000 | 48,000 | 12,000 | 120,000 |

**b. 2.**

*Lond Co.*
### DIFFERENTIAL REVENUES (EXCLUDING RETA)
*For the Year Ending December 31, 1990*

| | | |
|---|---:|---:|
| Increase in sales of Jana at full capacity | | |
|     Projected sales for 1990 (60,000 pounds @ $3.40) | $204,000 | |
|     Sales of Jana for 1989 (50,000 pounds @ $4.00) | 200,000 | $4,000 |
| Decrease in sales of Bynd at full capacity | | |
|     Projected sales for 1990 (12,000 pounds @ $0.90) | $ 10,800 | |
|     Sales of Bynd for 1989 (10,000 pounds @ $1.10) | 11,000 | 200 |
| Net increase in sales (excluding Reta) | | $3,800 |

**b. 3.**

*Lond Co.*
### DIFFERENTIAL COSTS
*For the Year Ending December 31, 1990*

| | |
|---|---:|
| Joint [(120,000 − 100,000) × ($88,000/100,000)]* | $17,600 |
| Reta [(48,000 − 40,000) × ($120,000/40,000)]* | 24,000 |
| Bynd [(12,000 − 10,000) × ($3,000/10,000)]* | 600 |
| Increase in differential costs | $42,200 |

*Increase in pounds produced × 1989 variable cost per pound produced.

**b. 4.**

*Lond Co.*
### SALES PRICE REQUIRED PER POUND OF RETA IN 1990
### TO ACHIEVE TOTAL 1989 GROSS MARGIN

| | |
|---|---:|
| Sales of Reta for 1989 | $300,000 |
| Projected 1990 net increase in differential costs | |
|   ($42,200 cost increase − $3,800 sales increase) | 38,400 |
| Recovery required from Reta | $338,400 |

Sales price required per pound of Reta
    $338,400/48,000 = $7.05

### PROOF
### (Not Required)

| | Jana | Reta | Joint | Total |
|---|---:|---:|---:|---:|
| Projected 1990 sales | $204,000 | $338,400 | | $542,400 |
| Fixed costs | | 90,000 | $148,000 | 238,000 |
| Variable costs | | | | |
|   (20% higher than in 1989) | | 144,000 | 105,600 | 249,600 |
| Less Bynd's net realizable value | | | | |
|   ($10,800 − 2,000 − 3,600) | | | | (5,200) |
| Total costs | | | | 482,400 |
| Gross margin (1990 and 1989) | | | | $ 60,000 |

# NUMBER 8

1. 
| | | |
|---|---:|---:|
| Beginning accounts payable - materials | | $40,000 |
| Purchases of materials required for production: | | |
|     Units produced | 70,000 | |
|     Materials cost per unit | x    $3 | |
| | $210,000 | |
|     Change in inventory | -0- | 210,000 |
| | | $250,000 |
| Less: one week usage * ($210,000 /10 weeks) | | -- 21,000 |
| Payments for materials | | $229,000 |

\* Manufacturing occurs evenly over the 10 week period and materials are paid for in the week following usage.

2.
| | | |
|---|---:|---:|
| Selling price per unit | | $    11 |
| Less Variable costs: | | |
|     Materials | $  3 | |
|     Conversion costs | 2 | |
|     Selling and administrative cost | 1 | 6 |
| Contribution margin per unit | | $ 5 |
| # units produced and sold | | x  70,000 |
| Total contribution margin | | $ 350,000 |
| Less fixed costs: | | |
|     Conversion | $210,000 | |
|     Selling and administration | 45,000 | 255,000 |
| Budgeted variable costing net income | | $ 95,000 |

3. If there is no change in inventory (production equals sales), net income using Absorption Costing will be the same as net income using Direct Costing (Variable Costing). Therefore, budgeted net income using Absorption Costing is $95,000.

4. Net income under Direct Costing:
| | | |
|---|---:|---:|
|     # units sold | | 60,000 |
|     Contribution margin (refer to #2) | | x    $5 / unit |
|     Total contribution margin | | $300,000 |
|     Less fixed cost (refer to #2) | | 255,000 |
|     Net income -- direct costing | | $ 45,000 |
| Add: Fixed costs included in inventory | | |
|     Increase in inventory | 10,000 units | |
|     F.C. / unit     ($255,000 / 70,000 units) | $3 | 30,000 |
| Net income under Absorption Costing | | $ 75,000 |
| Budgeted net income under Absorption Costing | | 95,000 |
| Difference | | $ 20,000 |

Net income under Absorption Costing will differ from that under Direct Costing by the amount of fixed costs assigned to the increase or decrease in inventory. If inventory increases, fixed costs are transferred to the following period, thereby increasing net income under Absorption Costing. If inventory decreases, fixed costs from prior periods are expensed, thereby reducing net income under Absorption Costing.

5.  To not reduce net income, revenue from the special order (#4000 units) must equal the variable costs of the special order plus the contribution margin from the loss of regular sales (#1000 units).

Variable costs of special order
        4000 units @ $6 (refer to #2)                    $24,000
Less contribution on regular sales
        1000 units @ $5 (refer to #2)                      5,000
Minimum revenue on special order                    $29,000

# Chapter Eighteen
# Managerial Planning and Control

# Chapter Eighteen
# Managerial Planning and Control

## COMPOUND INTEREST COMPUTATIONS

Computations involving compound interest may be necessary in any problem in which money is to be paid or received in different periods of time, such as with leases, bonds, pensions, investments, notes receivable and payable, contracts, and capital budgeting, to name only a few examples. For this reason, the candidate must have a thorough understanding of the concepts and the time value of money.

### Compound Value of a Single Sum (Future Value)

If $1.00 is invested today in a savings account that pays five percent interest compounded annually, what amount will be on deposit at the end of two years if all monies are left on deposit?

**Compound interest** is interest for the period computed on the original principal plus the interest accumulated to the beginning of the interest period.

The amount on deposit at the end of two years can be determined as follows:

| Period | Beginning Principal | + | Interest | = | Ending Balance |
|--------|---------------------|---|----------|---|----------------|
| 1 | $1.00 | + | ($1.00 × .05) | = | $1.05 |
| 2 | 1.05 | + | ($1.05 × .05) | = | 1.1025 |

To develop a general formula for the compound value of a single sum, the following terms will be used:

$P$ = Principal
$I$ = Interest
$i$ = Interest rate
$n$ = Number of periods
$FV$ = Future value

Using these terms, the solution to the above problem may be illustrated as follows:

| Today | | End Period #1 | | End Period #2 |
|-------|---|---------------|---|---------------|
| | Interest Period | | Interest Period | |
| $1.00 | | $1.05 | | $1.1025 |

$P_0 \longrightarrow$ $P_0 + I$
$P_0 + P_0 i$
$P_0 (1 + i)$
$P_1 \longrightarrow$ $P_1 + I$
$P_1 + P_1 i$
$P_1 (1 + i)$
$P_2$

Note that the $P_2$ is determined as follows:

$$P_2 = P_1 (1 + i) = P_0 (1 + i) (1 + i) = P_0 (1 + i)^2$$

Using the information from the original problem, the compound value at the end of the second year is calculated as follows:

$$P_2 = P_0 (1 + i)^2 = \$1 (1 + .05)^2 = \$1 (1.1025) = \textbf{\$1.1025}$$

If the amount on deposit at the end of the second year were left on deposit for one more year, what would be the value on deposit at the end of the third year? Another year's interest would be earned. Therefore, the value at the end of the third year ($P_3$) would be $(1 + i)$ times the value at the end of the second year ($P_2$).

$$P_3 = P_2 (1 + i) = P_1 (1 + i)(1 + i) = P_0 (1 + i)(1 + i)(1 + i) = P_0 (1 + i)^3$$

For the original problem, the value at the end of the third year is determined as follows:

$$P_3 = P_0 (1 + i)^3 = \$1 (1 + .05)^3 = \$1 (1.1576) = \mathbf{\$1.1576}$$

It should now be evident that the formula for the future value (compound value) of a single sum for n interest periods is:

$$\underline{\underline{FV_n = P_0 (1+i)^n}}$$

This is the **fundamental formula of compound interest**, upon which the other formulae in this section will be based. Therefore, it is important that you understand its derivation. To assist in the application of this formula, tables of the coupound value interest factor $(1 + i)^n$ have been constructed for various values of i and n (refer to Appendix A, Table 1—Compound Value of \$1). Using these factors, it is only necessary to multiply the principal ($P_0$) by the appropriate interest factor for the given i and n values, to determine the future value. The fundamental formula may now be written as:

$$FV = P_0 \ (IF)$$

**Example:** If \$1,000 is invested for 5 years at 6% interest compounded annually, what will its value be at the end of 5 years?

To determine the appropriate interest factor from Table 1, first locate the 6% column, then read down the values of the column to the n=5 row. This factor is 1.338. The future value is then determined as follows:

$$\begin{aligned} FV &= P(IF) \\ &= \$1,000(1.338) \\ &= \underline{\$1,338} \end{aligned}$$

## Present Value of a Single Sum

Money has a time value. A dollar received today has a greater value than a dollar to be received one year from today because of the interest which it can earn. The value today of a dollar to be received one year from today can be no greater than the amount which invested at an appropriate interest rate will have a future value equal to a dollar. Therefore, given an interest rate greater than zero, the value today of a dollar received in the future must be less than a dollar. Under present value concepts a dollar to be received at some future date is made comparable to a dollar today by discounting.

**Discounting** is the reverse of compounding—the inherent interest in a future value is removed to determine the original principal. The present value (discounting) formula is developed from the fundamental compound value formula.

$$FV = P_0 \ (1+i)^n$$

$$P_0 = \frac{FV}{(1+i)^n}$$

$$P_0 = FV \times \frac{1}{(1+i)^n}$$

The present value may be identified as PV or $P_0$ as the subscript zero in the term $P_0$ indicates the present.

**Example:** Previously we determined that the future value of $1 at 5% compounded annually for two years was $1.1025. Conversely, we can state that the present value of $1.1025 at 5% compounded annually for two years is $1. This is computed as follows:

$$PV = FV \times \frac{1}{(1 + i)^n}$$

$$PV = \$1.1025 \times \frac{1}{(1.05)^2}$$

$$PV = \$1.1025 \times \frac{1}{1.1025}$$

$$PV = \underline{\$1.00}$$

To assist in the application of the present value formula, tables of the present value interest factor $1/(1 + i)^n$ have been constructed for various values of i and n (refer to Appendix A, Table 2—Present Value of $1). Using these factors, it is only necessary to multiply the future value by the appropriate interest factor for the given i and n values, to determine the present value. The present value formula may now be written as:

$$PV = FV \text{ (IF)}$$

**Example:** What is the present value of $1,216 to be received four years from today at 5% compounded annually?

To determine the appropriate interest factor from Table 2, first locate the 5% column, then read down the values of the column to the n=4 row. This factor is .82270. The present value is now determined as follows:

$$PV = FV \text{ (IF)}$$
$$PV = \$1,216 \ (.8227)$$
$$PV = \underline{\$1,000.40}$$

**Proof:** $FV = P_0 \text{ (IF)}$      (FV interest factor)
$$FV = \$1,000.40 \ (1.216)$$
$$FV = \$1,216.48$$

(The difference is due to rounding in the construction of the tables.)


## Compound Value of an Annuity (Future Value)

An annuity is a **series** of **equal** payments for a specified number of periods. There are two types of annuities:
- **Ordinary Annuity**—payments are made at the end of the period. Also called deferred annuity or annuity in arrears.
- **Annuity Due**—payments are made at the beginning of the period.

The concepts and techniques of compound interest and future value at the same for an annuity as for a single sum. Refer to compound value of a single sum for their review.

**Ordinary Annuity:** If $1 is invested at the end of each year for three years in a savings account that pays 5% compounded annually, what amount will be on deposit at the end of the three years?

The amount on deposit at the end of the third year is equal to the sum of the future values of the three ordinary annuity payments. The answer is illustrated graphically as follows:

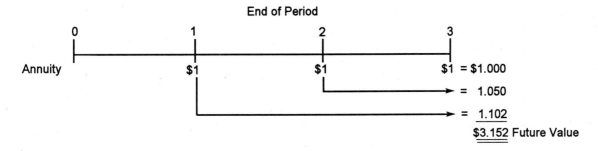

Computation of future value:

| Payment | Amount | Interest Periods | $FV =$ | $P(1+i)^n$ | |
|---------|--------|------------------|--------|-----------|---|
| 1. | $1.00 | 2 | $1(1.05)^2 =$ | $1(1.102) =$ | $1.102 |
| 2. | 1.00 | 1 | $1(1.05)^1 =$ | 1(1.050) = | 1.050 |
| 3. | 1.00 | 0 | $1(1.05)^0 =$ | 1(1.000) = | 1.000 |
| | | | | $1(3.152) = | $3.152 |

Note:
- For the third payment, $(1+i)^0 = 1$.
- The total of the interest factors $(1+i)^n$ times the annuity equals the future value ($1 × 3.152 = $3.152).

It is not necessary to compute each future value and sum them up. Rather, the total of the factors may be used to compute the future value of the annuity.

Expressed algebraically, the formula for the future value of an ordinary annuity is:

$$FV = A \sum_{m=1}^{n} (1+i)^{n-m}$$

(R, read sigma, means summation)

In the expression $\sum_{m=1}^{n} (1+1)^{n-m}$, m (a counter) begins at 1 because the first annuity payment earns interest for one less period than there are periods (n), and goes to n (shown above $\Sigma$) because the last payment earns no interest (n–m = 0).

To assist in the application of this formula, tables of the compound value interest factor $\sum_{m=1}^{n} (1+i)^n$ have been constructed for various values of i and n (refer to Appendix A, Table 3—Compound Value of an Annuity of $1). Using these factors, it is only necessary to multiply the Annuity (A) by the appropriate interest factor for the given i and n values to determine the future value of an ordinary annuity. The future value of an ordinary annuity formula may now be written as:

$$FV = A(IF)$$

**Example**: What is the future value of an ordinary annuity of $1,000 per year for 6 years at 7% compounded annually?

To determine the appropriate interest factor from table 3, first locate the 7% column, then read down the column of values to the n=6 row. This factor is 7.153. The future value of the ordinary annuity is determined as follows:

$$FV = A(IF)$$
$$= \$1,000(7.153)$$
$$= \underline{\$7,153}$$

**Annuity Due**: If $1 is invested at the beginning of each year for 3 years in a savings account that pays 5% compounded annually, what amount will be on deposit at the **end** of the third year?

The amount on deposit at the end of the third year is equal to the sum of the future value of the three annuity due payments. The answer is illustrated graphically as follows:

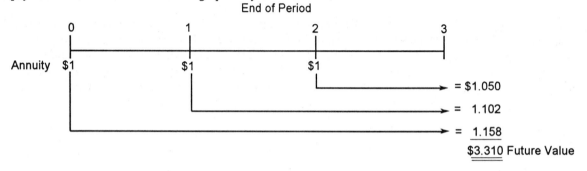

Computation of future value:

| Payment | Amount | Interest Periods | $FV =$ | $P(1+i)^n$ | |
|---------|--------|------------------|--------|-----------|---|
| 1. | $1.00 | 3 | $1(1.05)^3 =$ | $1(1.158) =$ | $1.158 |
| 2. | 1.00 | 2 | $1(1.05)^2 =$ | 1(1.102) = | 1.102 |
| 3. | 1.00 | 1 | $1(1.05)^1 =$ | $\underline{1(1.050) =}$ | $\underline{1.050}$ |
| | | | | $1(3.310) =$ | $\underline{\underline{\$3.310}}$ |

Note that the total of the interest factors $(1+i)^n$ times the annuity equals the future value ($1 × 3.310 = $3.31). As with the ordinary annuity it is not necessary to compute each future value and sum them up. The total of the factors may be used to compute the future value of the annuity.

Expressed algebraically, the formula for the future value of an ordinary annuity is:

$$FV = A \sum_{m=0}^{n-1} (1+i)^{n-m}$$

Here m begins at 0 because the first payment earns interest for each of the periods (n) and goes to n-1 because there is no payment at the end of the nth period.

Tables of the compound value interest factor for an annuity due $\left[ \sum_{m=0}^{n-1} (1+i)^{n-m} \right]$ are usually not available; however, the tables of the compound interest factor for an ordinary annuity can be adapted to show the interest factors of an annuity due. **This is accomplished by taking the factor for the period one greater than the actual period of the annuity (n+1) and subtracting 1 from this interest factor. The reasons for this are:**

- Each annuity due payment earns interest for one more period than an ordinary annuity payment, and
- There is no annuity due payment at the end of the last period such as there is in an ordinary annuity — $(1 + i)^0 = 1$

**Example**: What is the future value of an annuity due of $1,000 for 4 years at 7% compounded annually?

To determine the appropriate interest factor from Table 3, first locate the 7% column, then read down the column of figures to the n=5 row (4 years + 1). The factor is 5.751. The future value of the annuity due is determined as follows:

$$
\begin{aligned}
FV &= A \ (IF) \\
&= \$1,000 \ (5.751 - 1) \\
&= \$1,000 \ (4.751) \\
&= \$4,751
\end{aligned}
$$

To determine if an annuity table of compound value interest factors is for an ordinary annuity or an annuity due, you must **analyze the factor for the first period**. An annuity for one period is the same as a single sum. If the factor is 1.000 it shows that no interest has been earned at the end of the period; therefore, the amount must have been paid at the end of the period and is an ordinary annuity. If the factor is greater than 1.000, it shows that interest has been earned by the end of the period; therefore, the amount must have been paid at the beginning of the period and the annuity is an annuity due.

## Present Value of an Annuity

The concepts and techniques of discounting are the same for an annuity as for a single sum. Refer to present value of a single sum for their review.

**Ordinary Annuity**: What is the present value of a three year ordinary annuity of $1 per year discounted at 5% compounded annually?

The present value is equal to the sum of the present values of the individual annuity payments. The answer is illustrated graphically below:

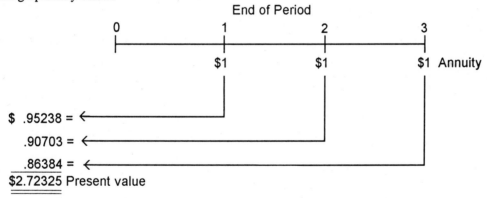

Computations of present value:

| Payment | Amount | Discount Periods | | PV $= FV \times \dfrac{1}{(1+i)^n}$ | |
|---|---|---|---|---|---|
| 1. | $1 | 1 | $1 × $\dfrac{1}{(1.05)^1}$ | = $1( .95238) | = .95238 |
| 2. | $1 | 2 | $1 × $\dfrac{1}{(1.05)^2}$ | = 1( .90703) | = .90703 |
| 3. | $1 | 3 | $1 × $\dfrac{1}{(1.05)^3}$ | = 1( .86384) | = .86384 |
| | | | | 1(2.72325) | = 2.72325 |

18-6

Note that the total of the interest factors $1 \div (1+i)^n$ times the annuity equals the present value of the annuity ($\$1 \times 2.72325 = \$2.72325$). As with the compound value of an annuity, it is not necessary to compute the value of each annuity payment and sum them up. The total of the interest factors may be used to compute the present value.

The formula for the present value of an ordinary annuity is:

$$PV = A \times \sum_{m=0}^{n-1} \frac{1}{(1+i)^{n-m}}$$

This formula is basically the reciprocal of the compound value of an annuity formula. However, m begins at 0 because the last payment is discounted for n periods and goes through n–1 because there is no payment at the beginning of the first period (n–m = 0).

To assist in the application of this formula, tables of the present value interest factor for an ordinary annuity have been constructed for various values of i and n (refer to Appendix A, Table 4—Present Value of an Annuity of $1). Using these factors, it is only necessary to multiply the annuity (A) by the appropriate interest factor for the given i and n values to determine the present value of ordinary annuity. The present value formula of an ordinary annuity now becomes:

$$PV = A(IF)$$

**Example**: What is the present value of an ordinary annuity of $1,000 per year for 6 years at 7% compounded annually?

To determine the appropriate interest factor from Table 4, first locate the 7% column; then read down the values of the column to the n = 6 row. The factor is 4.7665. The present value is now determined as follows:

$$
\begin{aligned}
PV &= A(IF) \\
&= \$1{,}000(4.7665) \\
&= \underline{\$4{,}766.50}
\end{aligned}
$$

**Annuity Due:** What is the present value of a three year annuity due of $1 discounted at 5% compounded annually?

The present value is equal to the sum of the present values of the individual payments. The answer is illustrated graphically below.

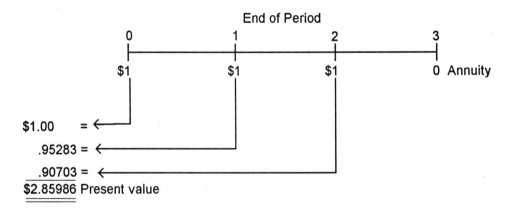

Computations of present value:

| Payment | Amount | Discount Periods | $PV = FV \times \dfrac{1}{(1+i)^n}$ | | |
|---|---|---|---|---|---|
| 1. | $1 | 0 | $1 \times \dfrac{1}{(1.05)^0}$ = | $1 \times 1.000 | = $1.00 |
| 2. | $1 | 1 | $1 \times \dfrac{1}{(1.05)^1}$ = | $1 \times .95283 | = .95283 |
| 3. | $1 | 1 | $1 \times \dfrac{1}{(1.05)^2}$ = | $\underline{\$1 \times .90703}$  $\underline{\$1 \times 2.85986}$ | = \underline{.90703}  = \underline{$2.85986} |

Note that the total of the interest factors times the annuity equals the future value ($1 × 2.85986 = $2.85986). As with the ordinary annuity it is not necessary to compute the present value of each annuity payment and sum them up. The total of the interest factors may be used to compute the present value.

The formula for the present value of an annuity due is:

$$PV = A \times \sum_{m=1}^{n} \frac{1}{(1+i)^{n-m}}$$

Here m begins at 1 because the last payment is discounted for n–1 periods and goes through n because the first payment is at the beginning of the first period (n–m = o).

Tables of the present value interest factor for an annuity due are usually not available; however, the tables of the present value factors for an ordinary annuity can be adapted to show the interest factors of an annuity due. **This is accomplished by taking the factor for the period one less than the actual period of the annuity (n–1) and adding 1 to this interest factor.** The reasons for this are:

- Each annuity due payment is discounted for one less period than an ordinary annuity payment and
- There is an annuity due payment at the beginning of the first period [1 ÷ (1 + i)$^0$ = 1] which does not exist in an ordinary annuity.

**Example**: What is the present value of an annuity due of $1,000 per year for 4 years at 7% compounded annually?

To determine the appropriate interest factor from table 4, first locate the 7% column; then read down the column values to the n = 3 row (4 years–1). The factor is 2.6243. The present value is now determined as follows:

PV = A (IF)
 = $1,000 (2.6243 + 1)
 = $1,000 (3.6243)
 = $3,624.30

To determine if an annuity table of present value interest factors is for an ordinary annuity or an annuity due, you must **analyze the first period factor**. If the factor is smaller than 1.000, it shows that interest has been removed; therefore, the amount must have been paid at the end of the period and it is an ordinary annuity. If the factor is 1.000, it shows that no interest was removed; therefore, the amount must have been paid at the beginning of the first period and it is an annuity due.

**Exercises** (Ignore the effects of income taxes in the following exercises.)

1. Approximately how long will it take for an investment to double given a growth rate of: a) 5%, b) 7%, and c) 12%?
2. A client has just won $5,000 from the Massachusetts State Lottery. If he invests this money now at 10% compounded annually, how much will he have at the end of 10 years?
3. You have determined that $10,000 will be needed in four years for the acquisition of new office machinery. How much money must you invest today at 9% compounded annually to provide this amount in four years?
4. Your client invested in a stock 10 years ago which cost $5 per share. This stock is now selling for $12.97 a share. The client would like to know at what rate of interest his investment has grown.
5. The Ryder Company is establishing a sinking fund to retire a mortgage that matures on December 31, 19X9. The first payment will be made on December 31, 19X0, and the last payment will be made on December 31, 19X9. Each payment will amount to $30,000 and the company anticipates that the sinking fund will earn 8% compounded annually. After the last payment is made, what will be the balance of the fund?
6. On January 2, 19X1, your client issued 5 year, 5% bonds payable with a face value of $1,000,000. These bonds pay interest semiannually on June 30 and December 31 of each year. What were the proceeds from this issuance if the bonds were sold to yield 8% compounded semi-annually?
7. On January 2, 19X2, your client entered into a lease for machinery which was in substance a purchase. The lease provided for four annual rental payments of $4,000 each. The first payment was due January 2, 19X2. At what amount should the machinery be recorded on the client's books if the lease is capitalized, and 10% is an appropriate rate of interest for such transactions?
8. Your client has recently deposited $20,000 in a savings account which pays 8% interest compounded annually. He plans to withdraw a constant amount each year for 10 years, so that at the end of the 10th year the balance will be zero. How much may he withdraw at the end of each year?
9. You plan to invest $500 of your salary, at the beginning of each year, for the next 10 years. If your investment will earn 10% compounded annually, what amount **will you have at the end of the 15th year**?

**Solutions to Exercises:**

1. (a) 14+, (b) 10+, (c) 6+, Table 1, Compound value factor of 2.00.

2. $FV = P \times FVF = \$5,000 \times 2.594 = \underline{\$12,970}$ (Table 1)

3. $PV = FV \times PVF = \$10,000 \times .70843 = \underline{\$7,084.30}$ (Table 2)

4. $PV = FV \times PVF \quad \$5 = 12.97 \times PVF \quad PVF = \$5 \div 12.97 = .385505 =$ Factor for <u>10%</u> and 10N Table 2
   or
   $FV = PV \times FVF \quad 12.97 = 5 \times FVF \quad FVF = 12.97 \div 5 = 2.594 =$ Factor for <u>10%</u> and 10N Table 1

5. $FV = A \times FVF = \$30,000 \times 14.487 = \underline{\$434,610}$   Table 3, Ordinary Annuity

6. 
| | | |
|---|---|---|
| $PV = FV \times PVF = \$ 25,000 \times 8.1109 =$ | $202,772.50 | Table 4 |
| $+ \underline{PV = \quad A \times PVF} = \$1,000,000 \times .67556 =$ | $\underline{\$675,560.00}$ | Table 2 |
| PV of Bond | $\underline{\$878,332.50}$ | |

   **Note**: Both maturity value and semi-annual interest payments are discounted at the yield rate 8% compounded semi-annually (4%, 10N).

7. $PV = A \times PVF = \$4,000 \times 3.4868 = \underline{\$13,947.20}$  Table 4

   Adjusted for annuity due (N–1, + 1.00)

8. $PV = A \times PVF$     $\$20,000 = A \times 6.7101$     $A = \$20,000 \div 6.7101 = \$2,980.58$

9. $FV = A \times FVF = \$500 \times 17.531 = \$8,765.50$ @ EOY#10,
   Table 3 adjusted for annuity due (N + 1, - 1.00)
   $FV = PV \times FVF = \$8,765.50 \times 1.611 = \underline{\$14,121.22}$ EOY #15

# CAPITAL BUDGETING

Capital budgeting is the process of planning capital expenditures—expenditures the benefits of which will be realized over a period longer than a year rather than in the current year (revenue expenditures).

Capital budgeting involves the:
1. generation of investment proposals
2. determination of investment benefits (profits and cash flow)
3. evaluation of investment benefits
4. ranking of investment proposals for decision purposes, based on their evaluation

The technique employed in the evaluation is of primary importance because the different techniques do not always result in the same ranking of investment alternatives. The ranking of investment proposals is necessary because firms usually have more potential capital expenditure proposals than they are capable of or willing to finance.

## Capital Budgeting Techniques
1. Payback Method
2. Unadjusted Rate of Return Method (Accounting Method)
3. Discounted Cash Flow Methods
    a. Internal Rate of Return
    b. Net Present Value

## Payback Method
Investments are ranked according to the length of time required to generate cash flows equal to their cost. The payback period is computed as:

$$\text{Payback Period} = \frac{\text{Cost of Investment}}{\text{Annual Cash Flows}}$$

The payback method is frequently used in practice because:
- it is easy to understand and apply.
- when estimates of profitability are not crucial because of a weak cash or credit position, the enterprise must look to a rapid return of its funds.

The payback method is theoretically unacceptable because:
- it ignores the time value of money
- it ignores profitability of the project
- it ignores cash flows beyond the payback period
- it is a measurement of liquidity, not profitability.

**Example**: Compute the payback period for an investment of $100,000 which generates an annual cash flow of $25,000.

**Solution**:

$$\text{Payback period} = \frac{\text{Investment cost}}{\text{Annual cash flow}} = \frac{\$100,000}{25,000} = \underline{4} \text{ years}$$

## Unadjusted Rate of Return Method

Investments are ranked according to the ratio of the expected average net income to either the original investment or the average investment of the project. The unadjusted rate of return is computed as:

$$\text{Unadjusted Rate of Return} = \frac{\text{Average Annual Net Income}}{\text{Investment or Average Investment}}$$

The attributes of this method are:
- it is easy to apply
- it is easily understood by persons familiar with ratio analysis
- it considers the profitability of the project over its entire life.

This method is theoretically unacceptable because **it ignores the time value of money**.

**Example**: Compute the accounting rate of return for an investment of $70,000 which generates gross annual cash flows of $22,000, and is expected to have a useful life of 10 years. The tax rate is 40%.

**Solution**:
(a) Determination of annual net income from project

| | |
|---|---|
| Annual cash flow | $22,000 |
| Less depreciation | 7,000 |
| Annual income before taxes | $15,000 |
| Taxes (40%) | 6,000 |
| Annual net income | $ 9,000 |

(b) $\text{Accounting Rate of Return} = \dfrac{\text{Average Annual Net Income}}{\text{Investment}} = \dfrac{\$9,000}{\$70,000} = \underline{12.9\%}$

**Note**: If average cost of the project were used, the computation would be $9,000 ÷ $35,000 ($70,000 × 1/2) or 25.8%. If all projects are computed in the same manner, i.e., either using the original investment or average investment, their relative ranking will be the same.

## Discounted Cash Flow Methods

The discounted cash flow methods of capital budgeting are the theoretically correct methods of capital budgeting as they explicitly consider the time value of money. In the determination of time value of money and the application of these methods, there are two important elements. **First** is the cash flow to be paid or received in a given period of time. For capital expenditure proposals, there are two distinct cash flows: the investment and the investment's benefits. Discounted cash flow methods of capital budgeting require reliable estimates of the investment's cash flows, for the results of these methods can be no more reliable than the data upon which they are based. The emphasis is upon cash flow rather than profit because money is the resource which is invested and reinvested to yield return to the enterprise. **Second** is the cost of capital for the enterprise. The cost of capital is the minimum rate of return which the firm must earn in order to fulfill the expectations of those who provide the firm's capital (creditors and owners) and maintain its present valuation. The cost of capital used in the discounted cash flow techniques is the marginal cost of capital (a weighted average cost of the last dollar of capital raised).

## Internal Rate of Return Method

Investments are ranked according to their projected rate of return. Projects with an internal rate of return less than the desired rate of return (usually the cost of capital) should normally be rejected. The internal rate of return of an investment is that **discount rate which equates the present value of the benefits to be received (cash flows) from the investment with the cost of the investment (initial cash outlay)**. The internal rate of return is found by trial and error or interpolation.

**Example**: Compute the internal rate of return for an investment of $100,000 which generates net annual cash flows of $20,000 and is expected to have a useful life of 10 years.

**Solution:**

$$\text{P.V. Investment} = \text{P.V. Benefits}$$

$$\$100,000 = \$20,000 \text{ (IF)}$$

$$\frac{\$100,000}{20,000} = \text{IF}$$

$$5 = \text{IF}$$

Referring to Appendix A, Table 4 (Present Value of an Annuity of $1), reading the values of the n = 10 row we find:

P.V. of $1 for ten periods at 15% = 5.0188
P.V. of $1 for ten periods at 16% = 4.8332

Therefore, the internal rate of return is approximately 15%.

## Net Present Value

Investments are ranked according to their net present value which is defined as the present value of the cash flows of an investment, **discounted at the cost of capital**, less the cost of the investment (initial cash outlay). Investments with a net present value equal to or greater than zero should be accepted because they are earning a rate of return equal to (NPV = 0) or greater than (NPV > 0) the minimum required rate of return (the cost of capital).

**Example**: Compute the net present value of the investment in the previous example assuming the cost of capital is 10%.

**Solution:**

| | |
|---|---:|
| Present value of benefits = A (IF) = $20,000 × 6.1446 = | $122,892 |
| Less: Present value of investment | 100,000 |
| Net Present Value | $ 22,892 |

## Profitability Index

Investments are ranked according to the ratio of the present value of the benefits (discounted at the cost of capital) to the investment. Investments with a profitability index equal to or greater than 1 should normally be accepted as they are earning a rate of return equal to (PI = 1) or greater than (PI > 1) the cost of capital.

**Example**: Compute the profitability index for the previous example.

**Solution:**

$$\text{Profitability index} = \frac{\text{Present Value of Benefits}}{\text{Investment}} = \frac{\$122,892}{100,000} = \underline{1.23}$$

**Illustrative Problem**

Investalot Corporation is considering the purchase of a new machine which will cost $106,111. Freight charges and installation costs are anticipated to be $5,000. Management estimates that variable costs will be reduced by $16,000 per year and that additional revenues of $14,000 per year will be generated if this machine is purchased. The machine has an estimated useful life of 10 years and will have a $15,000 salvage value. Investalot Corporation computes depreciation on the straight line basis, has an effective tax rate of 40% and a 15% cost of capital. If Investalot Corporation purchases this new machine it will trade in an old, idle machine, receiving a trade-in allowance equal to its book and fair value of $11,111. Should the company buy this machine?

**Solution**:
- Investment—initial cash outlay

| | |
|---|---|
| Purchase price | $106,111 |
| Add: Freight and installation | 5,000 |
| Depreciable cost | $111,111 |
| Less trade-in allowance | – 11,111 |
| Initial cash outlay | $100,000 |

- Benefits—Annual Cash Flows

  a. For years 1 through 10

| | |
|---|---|
| Additional revenues | $14,000 |
| Reduction in variable costs | 16,000 |
| | $30,000 |
| Less depreciation | |
| ($111,111 – 15,000 = 96,111 × 10%) | 9,611 |
| Increase in net income before taxes | $20,389 |
| Less: Taxes @ 40% | 8,156 |
| Increase in net income after taxes | $12,233 |
| Add: depreciation | 9,611 |
| Additional annual cash flows | $21,844 |

  b. For the 10th year

  In addition to the annual cash flows

| | |
|---|---|
| Investalot will receive the salvage value | $15,000 |

- Assuming use of the Net Present Value Method

| | |
|---|---|
| Present value of annuity—10 years @ 15% | $21,844 × 5.0188 = $109,631 |
| Present value of a single sum—10th year @ 15% | $15,000 × .2472 = 3,708 |
| Present value of benefits | $113,339 |
| Less: Present value of investment | 100,000 |
| Net present value | $ 13,339 |

Investalot Corporation should purchase the new machine as the net present value is equal to or greater than zero.

- Assuming use of the Internal Rate of Return Method

  To use interpolation the present value is needed at two rates such that one is above and the other below the present value of the investment. The present value at 20% is computed as follows:

| | |
|---|---|
| Present value of annuity | $21,844 × 4.1925 = $91,581 |
| Present value of single sum | $15,000 × .1615 = 2,423 |
| Present value of benefits @ 20% | $94,004 |

| Discount Rate | | Present Value | |
|---|---|---|---|
| 15% | = | $113,339 | |
| IRR | = | 100,000 | (Investment Cost) |
| 20% | = | 94,004 | |

Interpolation may now be used to determine the internal rate of return. A 5 percent change in the discount rate (15% to 20%) resulted in a change of $19,335 in the present value ($113,339 to $94,004). What is needed is some percentage change from 15 percent such that the change in present value will be $13,339 ($113,339 – $100,000). This percentage change is computed as follows:

$$\frac{.05}{\$19,335} = \frac{X}{\$13,339}$$

(5% is to $19,335 as X is to $13,339)

$$\$19,335\ X = \$666.95$$
$$X = \frac{666.95}{\$19,335}$$
$$X = .034$$

The internal rate of return is approximately 18.4% (15% + 3.4%).


## BUDGETING

A budget may be defined as a **plan for future operations expressed in dollars or units or both.** Its purpose is to show the results of future operations given the goals, policies, forecasts and standards of operations. Budgeting may also be referred to as **a managerial tool for profit planning and control,** as actual results of operation may be compared with budgeted results of operations to identify problem areas. The budgeting process is of the utmost importance in the successful management of complex business enterprises and necessarily embodies the consensus of top management concerning the future direction of the enterprise.

The budgeting process requires decisions which result in commitments critical to the financial success of the enterprise such as:
1. Expected sales levels (short and long run)
2. Individual product sales
3. Inventory levels by product
4. Production schedules to meet inventory levels
5. Purchasing of materials and supplies
6. Personnel to carry out planned activity level
7. Capital expenditures required to meet production
8. Cash balances required to carry out planned activities

### Sales Budget
The first step in the budgeting process (given the goals and policies of operation) is to forecast the level of sales for the budget period. Consideration must be given to general economic conditions, the company's pricing policy, expected sales effort, past sales levels, the company's relative market position, the trend of acceptance for the company's products, etc. The sales budget should be broken down by geographic locations, product lines and sales entities to facilitate the control function of budgeting.

### Inventory Budget
After the sales budget has been prepared, the inventory levels needed to meet sales and conform to company policy may be determined. This budget would be broken down by storage areas and product lines to facilitate control.

**Example**: Assume sales levels by month as follows:

| | |
|---|---|
| January | $ 900,000 |
| February | 1,200,000 |
| March | 1,000,000 |
| April | 1,500,000 |

Company policy is to maintain inventory levels at 30% of the cost of goods sold of the **following** month. All products are sold at a mark-up of 25% of cost. Compute the inventory levels at the end of January, February and March.

**Solution:**

Step 1. Compute the cost of goods sold for February, March and April.

| | |
|---|---|
| Cost | 100% |
| Mark-up | 25% |
| Selling price | 125% |

Cost as a percent of selling price = 100 ÷ 125 = 80%

Cost of goods sold for:

| | |
|---|---|
| February | $1,200,000 × 80% = $ 960,000 |
| March | $1,000,000 × 80% = $ 800,000 |
| April | $1,500,000 × 80% = $1,200,000 |

Step 2. Compute the ending inventory for January, February and March.

| | |
|---|---|
| January | $ 960,000 × 30% = $288,000 |
| February | 800,000 × 30% = $240,000 |
| March | 1,200,000 × 30% = $360,000 |

## Production Budget

After the required inventory levels have been determined, the production necessary to meet required inventory levels and forecast sales may be scheduled. This budget would be broken down by production facilities and product line for control purposes.

**Example:** Referring to the previous example, prepare a production budget for February and March, assuming that each unit costs $10 to produce.

**Solution:**

Computation of February production

| | Cost | Units |
|---|---|---|
| Beginning inventory | $288,000 | 28,800 |
| Production | ? | ? |
| Goods available for sale | $ ? | ? |
| Less: ending inventory | 240,000 | 24,000 |
| Cost of goods sold | $960,000 | 96,000 |

It is evident that we can back into the production required of $912,000 or 91,200 units as follows:

96,000 + 24,000 = 120,000 – 28,800 = 91,200

Production budget for February and March:

| | February Cost | Units | March Cost | Units |
|---|---|---|---|---|
| Production required to meet sales budget | $ 960,000 | 96,000 | $ 800,000 | 80,000 |
| Add: desired ending inventory | 240,000 | 24,000 | 360,000 | 36,000 |
| Total production required | $1,200,000 | 120,000 | $1,160,000 | 116,000 |
| Less: estimated beginning inventory | 288,000 | 28,800 | 240,000 | 24,000 |
| Budgeted production | $ 912,000 | 91,200 | $ 920,000 | 92,000 |

## Raw Materials Budget

After the production budget has been prepared, the inventory levels and purchase requirements for raw materials may be determined. This budget indicates the cost (usually standard) and quantities of raw materials needed to meet production requirements and conform with company policies.

**Example**: Referring to the previous example, assume that each unit produced requires 2 pounds of material X and 1 yard of material Y. Management desires that these raw materials be on hand in sufficient quantities to insure uninterrupted production. Planned inventory levels of material X, which can be obtained on short notice, are 10% of the next month's production. Material Y, however, must be ordered with considerable lead time and deliveries are erratic. Therefore, it has been decided that the inventory level of material Y be maintained at 40% of the next month's production. Compute the inventory levels of raw materials X and Y at the end of January and February.

**Solution**:

February production = 91,200 units
March production = 92,000 units

January 31 inventory requirements:

Material X          $91,200 \times 2 = 182,400 \times 10\% = \underline{18,240}$ pounds

Material Y          $91,200 \times 1 = 91,200 \times 40\% = \underline{36,480}$ yards

February 28 inventory requirements:

Material X          $92,000 \times 2 = 184,000 \times 10\% = \underline{18,400}$ pounds

Material Y          $92,000 \times 1 = 92,000 \times 40\% = \underline{36,800}$ yards

## Cash Budget

After all other budgets have been prepared (covering all aspects of the enterprise's operation), their effects on cash flows are summarized in the cash budget. The cash budget is usually broken down into monthly periods (or shorter for the very near future) showing the itemized cash receipts and disbursements during the budget period, including the financing activities and the beginning and ending cash balances.

The cash budget is usually set up as follows:

|  | *January* | *February* | *March* |
|---|---|---|---|
| Beginning cash balance | $15,000 | $ 30,000 | $ 25,000 |
| Add: cash receipts[1] | 60,000 | 75,000 | 100,000 |
|  | $75,000 | $105,000 | $125,000 |
| Less: cash disbursements[1] | 45,000 | 80,000 | 105,000 |
| Ending cash balance | $30,000 | $ 25,000 | $ 20,000 |

[1](These amounts would be itemized as to source or use)

The cash budget is a useful tool in the planning process for it provides management with information concerning the:

     1. expected sources and uses of funds
     2. availability of funds for investment purposes
     3. need for external financing
     4. availability of funds for the repayment of debt
     5. availability of funds for distribution to owners

## Pro-Forma Financial Statements

Once the budgeting process is completed through the cash budget, financial statements may be drawn up on a pro-forma basis. These statements will show the results of operation if the plans, as set forth in the budgets, are achieved. These statements will be analyzed by top management to determine if the results of planned future operations are consistent with the enterprise's objectives and goals. When conflicts are identified, the planning process begins anew.

## Illustrative Problem

Modern Products Corporation, a manufacturer of molded plastic containers, determined in October 19X7 that it needed cash to continue operations. The Corporation began negotiating for a one-month bank loan of $100,000 which would be discounted at 6 percent per annum on November 1. In considering the loan the bank requested a projected income statement and a cash budget for the month of November.

The following information is available:

1. Sales were budgeted at 120,000 units per month in October 19X7, December 19X7, and January 19X8, and at 90,000 units in November 19X7. The selling price is $2 per unit. Sales are billed on the 15th and last day of each month on terms of 2/10 net 30. Past experience indicates sales are even throughout the month and 50 percent of the customers pay the billed amount within the discount period. The remainder pay at the end of 30 days, except for bad debts which average 1/2 percent of gross sales. On its income statement the Corporation deducts from sales the estimated amounts for cash discounts on sales and losses on bad debts.
2. The inventory of finished goods on October 1 was 24,000 units. The finished goods inventory at the end of each month is to be maintained at 20 percent of sales anticipated for the following month. There is no work in process.
3. The inventory of raw materials on October 1 was 22,800 pounds. At the end of each month the raw materials inventory is to be maintained at not less than 40 percent of production requirements for the following month. Materials are purchased as needed in minimum quantities of 25,000 pounds per shipment. Raw material purchases of each month are paid in the next succeeding month on terms of net 30 days.
4. All salaries and wages are paid on the 15th and last day of each month for the period ending on the date of payment.
5. All manufacturing overhead and selling and administrative expenses are paid on the 10th of the month following the month in which incurred. Selling expenses are 10 percent of gross sales. Administrative expenses, which include depreciation of $500 per month on office furniture and fixtures, total $33,000 per month.
6. The standard cost of a molded plastic container, based on "normal" production of 100,000 units per month, is as follows:

| | |
|---|---|
| Materials—1/2 pound | $ .50 |
| Labor | .40 |
| Variable overhead | .20 |
| Fixed overhead | .10 |
| Total | $1.20 |

Fixed overhead includes depreciation on factory equipment of $4,000 per month. Over- or under- absorbed overhead is included in cost of sales.

7. The cash balance on November 1 is expected to be $10,000.

## Required:

Prepare the following for Modern Products Corporation assuming the bank loan is granted. (Do not consider income taxes.)

a. Schedules computing inventory budgets by months for
    1. Finished goods production in units for October, November and December.
    2. Raw material purchases in pounds for October and November.
b. A projected income statement for the month of November.
c. A cash forecast for the month of November showing the opening balance, receipts (itemized by dates of collection), disbursements and balance at end of month.

Solution (see page 18-21).

# INVENTORY PLANNING AND CONTROL

## Reasons for Inventory Control

The management of inventories to achieve the needs of the business at the lowest possible cost is of the utmost importance. Inventories are generally a relatively large balance sheet item and mismanagement of inventories, ranging from raw materials to finished goods, can cause a variety of serious problems. Among these are: disruptions of production, loss of customer goodwill, loss of contribution margin or lost sales. However, businesses that "never run out of anything" may be incurring needless high costs of carrying inventory that may prevent the realization of adequate profits. We can show the pros and cons of this in balanced form as follows:

| **Costs that may be incurred in carrying inventory** | **Costs that may be incurred by not carrying enough inventory** |
|---|---|
| 1. Management costs | 1. Discounts not realized |
| 2. Insurance | 2. Disruptions of production |
| 3. State and local taxes | 3. Additional purchasing cost |
| 4. Interest | 4. Additional transportation cost |
| 5. Space | 5. Customer relations |
| 6. Obsolescence | 6. Additional high cost of rush orders and/or production |
| 7. Handling | 7. Lost profit on sales not made |

## Costs Relevant to Inventory Control

It is apparent that many of these factors are not in the accounting records and must be determined by analysis. In some cases the cost may be insignificant or zero depending on the circumstances. Care must be used in determining whether a particular cost is relevant. For example, if the space is available (whether or not owned) and cannot be used for other profitable purposes, the cost of space is not relevant. However, if additional space must be obtained or inventory storage prevents the use of the space for other profitable activities, the cost is relevant. Interest cost of carrying inventory should be considered regardless of whether or not funds were borrowed to purchase inventory, since funds not used for such purpose could be profitably put to an alternate use. The rate of interest depends on the facts in each case, such as: the cost of borrowing, the average cost of capital (including debt and equity capital) or the rate that could be earned by an alternate use of the capital.

## Economic Order Quantity (Standard Order)

The economic order quantity is the amount of inventory that should be purchased at any one time in order to minimize to total costs associated with inventory (carrying costs and ordering costs). The economic order quantity may be computed by trial and error or by formula as follows:

**Symbols**
Q = Economic order quantity
S = Total units sold during the period
O = Ordering cost per order
C = Carrying cost per unit

**Formula**

$$Q = \sqrt{\frac{2SO}{C}}$$

**Example**: A manufacturer purchases bicycle frames at a cost of $5 per unit. The total annual needs are 50,000 units at an average rate of 200 frames per workday. Maximum daily usage is 250 frames. Delivery of an order normally takes 4 days.

Other information:

Cost of borrowing (or return that could be earned by
alternate use of funds) 8% × $5.00         $ .40

Rent per unit per year         .18

Taxes per unit per year         .06

Insurance         .06

Total carrying cost per year         $ .70

Cost per purchase order         $14.00

**Solution:**

(a) Formula:

$$Q = \sqrt{\frac{2SO}{C}}$$

$$Q = \sqrt{\frac{2(50,000)(\$14)}{.70}}$$

$$Q = \sqrt{2,000,000}$$

$$Q = \underline{\underline{1,415}}$$

(b) Trial and Error:

| | | | |
|---|---|---|---|
| Order size (Q) | 1,000 | 1,500 | 2,000 |
| Average Inventory (Q/2) | 500 | 750 | 1,000 |
| No. of orders (S/Q) | 50 | 33  1/3 | 25 |
| | | | |
| Annual storage cost (C × Q/2) | $ 350 | $525 | $ 700 |
| Purchase order cost (O × S/Q) | $ 700 | $467 | $ 350 |
| | $1,050 | $992 | $1,050 |

We can see that 1,500 units per order results in the lowest cost. If we try 1,400 or 1,600 we would know in which direction the cost trend is moving as follows:

| | | | |
|---|---|---|---|
| Order size | 1,400 | 1,600 | 1,415 |
| Average inventory | 700 | 800 | 708 |
| No. of orders | 35  5/7 | 62  1/2 | 35  1/3 |
| | | | |
| Annual storage cost | $490 | $560.00 | $496.00 |
| Purchase order cost | $500 | $437.50 | $493.50 |
| | $990 | $997.50 | $989.50 |

## Lead Time and Safety Stock

When we have determined the economic order quantity of the size of an order that minimizes annual cost, we must determine when to order. To do this we must know:

1. Lead time—interval between the placing of an order and delivery, in this case 4 days.
2. Economic order quantity—in this example, 1415.
3. Demand during Lead Time—4 × 200 = 800.

The order point is determined as the safety stock plus average usage during lead time. The safety stock must be sufficient to provide for maximum usage of stock during lead time. For example:

| | |
|---|---|
| Maximum daily usage | 250 |
| Average daily usage | 200 |
| Excess | 50 |
| Lead time | × 4 |
| Safety Stock | 200 |
| Average usage during lead time | 800 |
| Order Point | 1,000 units |

Or we could simplify this by saying that the order point should be:

Maximum usage × lead time or 250 × 4 = 1,000 units

Graphically, this can be shown as:

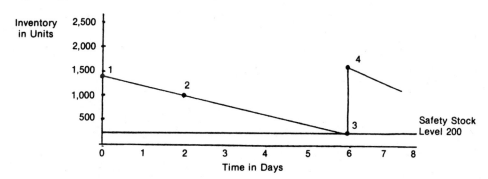

(1) Start—1415 units
(2) Order point—1,000 units
(3) Order received
(4) Inventory increases to 1,615

*Note*: If inventory level was zero, caused by maximum usage during lead time, the inventory level would go to only 1,415 when the order was received.

## JUST-IN-TIME INVENTORY PHILOSOPHY:

Under JIT inventory methods raw materials are obtained "just-in-time" for use in production, finished goods are produced "just-in-time" for delivery, and other inventory items are provided just when needed. A JIT system minimizes or potentially eliminates inventory and its related carrying costs. Implementation of a JIT system requires a backlog of orders and reliable suppliers so that the production process is not interrupted. The benefits of JIT would be lost if a company had to shut down its operation for long periods while waiting for new orders or materials/supplies.

Advantages of a JIT system include:
- Release of funds invested in inventory.
- Frees space.
- Reduces production time (throughput time).

- Reduces/eliminates nonvalue-add activities such as movement of inventory, storage, setup time.
- Improves quality as defective inventory must be corrected immediately; there are no inventory pools to hold defective units.
- As goods are produced to order not for inventory, better control is required over lost or spoiled goods.
- Simplifies accounting by charging costs directly to cost of goods sold (no inventory). If inventory exists, the inventory is "backed out" of the cost of goods sold account. Backing inventory amounts out of cost of goods sold is referred to as **backflush** accounting.

**Solution to Cash Budget Illustrative Problem**

a. 1.

**Modern Products Corporation**
## SCHEDULE COMPUTING FINISHED GOODS PRODUCTION BUDGET (UNITS)
### FOR OCTOBER, NOVEMBER AND DECEMBER 19X7

|  | October | November | December |
|---|---|---|---|
| Budgeted sales—units | 120,000 | 90,000 | 120,000 |
| Inventory required at end of month | 18,000 | 24,000 | 24,000 |
| Total to be accounted for | 138,000 | 114,000 | 144,000 |
| Less inventory on hand at beginning of month | 24,000 | 18,000 | 24,000 |
| Budgeted production—units | 114,000 | 96,000 | 120,000 |

a. 2.

## SCHEDULE COMPUTING RAW MATERIALS INVENTORY
### PURCHASE BUDGET (POUNDS)
### FOR OCTOBER AND NOVEMBER 19X7

|  | October | November |
|---|---|---|
| Budgeted production—pounds (1/2 lb. per unit) | 57,000 | 48,000 |
| Inventory required at end of month | 19,200 | 24,000 |
| Total to be accounted for | 76,200 | 72,000 |
| Less inventory on hand at beginning of month | 22,800 | 40,800 |
| Balance required by purchase | 53,400 | 31,200 |
| Budgeted purchases—pounds (based on minimum shipments of 25,000 lbs. each) | 75,000 | 50,000 |

b.

## PROJECTED INCOME STATEMENT
### FOR THE MONTH OF NOVEMBER

| | | |
|---|---|---|
| Sales (90,000 units at $2) | | $180,000 |
| Less: Cash discounts on sales | $ 1,800 | |
| Estimated bad debts (1/2% of gross sales) | 900 | 2,700 |
| Net sales | | 177,300 |
| Cost of sales: | | |
| Standard (90,000 units at $1.20) | 108,000 | |
| Add under-absorbed overhead (standard production of 100,000 units less budgeted production of 96,000 units equals 4,000 units times $.10) | 400 | 108,400 |
| Gross profit on sales | | 68,900 |
| Expenses: | | |
| Selling (10% of gross sales) | 18,000 | |
| Administrative ($33,000 per month) | 33,000 | |
| Interest expense | 500 | 51,500 |
| Net income | | $ 17,400 |

**c.**

## CASH FORECAST FOR THE MONTH OF NOVEMBER

| | | |
|---|---:|---:|
| Cash balance, beginning of month | | $ 10,000 |
| Receipts: | | |
| Bank loan | $ 99,500 | |
| Collections of receivables: | | |
| November 10—98% of $60,000 billed October 31 | 58,800 | |
| November 15—$60,000 billed October 15 | | |
| less ½% + $120,000 | 59,400 | |
| November 25—98% of $45,000 billed November 15 | 44,100 | |
| November 30—$60,000 billed October 31 | | |
| less ½% + $120,000 | 59,400 | 321,200 |
| Total | | $331,200 |
| Disbursements: | | |
| Accounts payable to suppliers for materials | | |
| purchased in October | $ 75,000 | |
| November labor (96,000 units × .40) | 38,400 | |
| October manufacturing overhead—variable | | |
| (114,000 units × .20) | 22,800 | |
| October manufacturing overhead—fixed portion | | |
| ($10,000 – $4,000 depreciation) | 6,000 | |
| October selling expenses (10% × $240,000) | 24,000 | |
| October administrative expenses | | |
| ($33,000 – $500 depreciation) | 32,500 | |
| Total disbursements | | 198,700 |
| Cash balance, end of month | | $132,500 |

# APPENDIX A
## Table 1 -- Compound Value of $1

| N | 1% | 2% | 3% | 4% | 5% | 6% | 7% | 8% | 9% | 10% | 12% | 14% |
|---|----|----|----|----|----|----|----|----|----|-----|-----|-----|
| 01 | 1.010 | 1.020 | 1.030 | 1.040 | 1.050 | 1.060 | 1.070 | 1.080 | 1.090 | 1.100 | 1.120 | 1.140 |
| 02 | 1.020 | 1.040 | 1.061 | 1.082 | 1.102 | 1.124 | 1.145 | 1.166 | 1.188 | 1.210 | 1.254 | 1.300 |
| 03 | 1.030 | 1.061 | 1.093 | 1.125 | 1.158 | 1.291 | 1.225 | 1.250 | 1.295 | 1.331 | 1.405 | 1.482 |
| 04 | 1.041 | 1.082 | 1.126 | 1.170 | 1.216 | 1.262 | 1.311 | 1.360 | 1.412 | 1.464 | 1.574 | 1.689 |
| 05 | 1.051 | 1.104 | 1.159 | 1.217 | 1.276 | 1.338 | 1.403 | 1.469 | 1.539 | 1.611 | 1.762 | 1.925 |
| 06 | 1.061 | 1.126 | 1.194 | 1.265 | 1.340 | 1.419 | 1.501 | 1.587 | 1.677 | 1.772 | 1.974 | 2.195 |
| 07 | 1.072 | 1.149 | 1.230 | 1.316 | 1.407 | 1.504 | 1.606 | 1.714 | 1.828 | 1.949 | 2.211 | 2.502 |
| 08 | 1.083 | 1.172 | 1.367 | 1.469 | 1.477 | 1.594 | 1.718 | 1.851 | 1.993 | 2.144 | 2.476 | 2.853 |
| 09 | 1.094 | 1.195 | 1.405 | 1.423 | 1.551 | 1.689 | 1.838 | 1.999 | 2.172 | 2.358 | 2.773 | 3.252 |
| 10 | 1.105 | 1.219 | 1.344 | 1.480 | 1.629 | 1.791 | 1.967 | 2.159 | 2.367 | 2.594 | 3.106 | 3.707 |
| 11 | 1.116 | 1.243 | 1.384 | 1.549 | 1.710 | 1.898 | 2.105 | 2.332 | 2.580 | 2.853 | 3.479 | 4.226 |
| 12 | 1.127 | 1.268 | 1.426 | 1.601 | 1.796 | 2.012 | 2.252 | 2.518 | 2.813 | 3.138 | 3.896 | 4.818 |
| 13 | 1.138 | 1.294 | 1.469 | 1.665 | 1.886 | 2.133 | 2.410 | 2.720 | 3.066 | 3.452 | 4.363 | 5.492 |
| 14 | 1.149 | 1.319 | 1.513 | 1.732 | 1.980 | 2.261 | 2.579 | 2.937 | 3.342 | 3.798 | 4.887 | 6.261 |
| 15 | 1.161 | 1.346 | 1.558 | 1.801 | 2.079 | 2.397 | 2.759 | 3.172 | 3.642 | 4.177 | 5.474 | 7.138 |

## Table 2 -- Present Value of $1

| N | 1% | 2% | 3% | 4% | 5% | 6% | 7% | 8% | 9% | 10% | 15% | 16% | 17% | 18% | 19% | 20% |
|---|----|----|----|----|----|----|----|----|----|-----|-----|-----|-----|-----|-----|-----|
| 01 | .99010 | .98039 | .97087 | .96154 | .95238 | .94340 | .93458 | .92593 | .91743 | .90909 | .86957 | .86207 | .85470 | .84746 | .84034 | .83333 |
| 02 | .98030 | .96117 | .94260 | .92456 | .90703 | .89000 | .87344 | .85734 | .84168 | .82645 | .75614 | .74316 | .73051 | .71818 | .70616 | .69444 |
| 03 | .97059 | .94232 | .91514 | .88900 | .86384 | .83962 | .81630 | .79383 | .77218 | .75131 | .65752 | .64066 | .62437 | .60363 | .59342 | .57870 |
| 04 | .96098 | .92385 | .88849 | .85480 | .82270 | .79209 | .76290 | .73503 | .70843 | .68301 | .57175 | .55229 | .53365 | .51579 | .49867 | .48225 |
| 05 | .95147 | .90573 | .86261 | .82193 | .78353 | .74726 | .71299 | .68058 | .64993 | .62092 | .49718 | .47611 | .45611 | .43711 | .41905 | .40188 |
| 06 | .94204 | .88797 | .83748 | .79031 | .74622 | .70496 | .66634 | .63017 | .59627 | .56447 | .43233 | .41044 | .38984 | .37043 | .35214 | .33490 |
| 07 | .93272 | .87056 | .81309 | .75992 | .71068 | .66506 | .62275 | .58349 | .54703 | .51316 | .37594 | .35383 | .33320 | .31392 | .29592 | .27908 |
| 08 | .92348 | .85349 | .78941 | .73069 | .67684 | .62741 | .58201 | .54027 | .50187 | .46651 | .32690 | .30503 | .28478 | .26604 | .24867 | .23257 |
| 09 | .91434 | .83675 | .76642 | .70259 | .64461 | .59190 | .54393 | .50025 | .46043 | .42410 | .28426 | .26295 | .24340 | .22546 | .20897 | .19381 |
| 10 | .90529 | .82035 | .74409 | .67556 | .61391 | .55839 | .50835 | .46319 | .42241 | .38554 | .24718 | .22668 | .20804 | .19106 | .17560 | .16151 |
| 11 | .89632 | .80426 | .72242 | .64958 | .58468 | .52679 | .47509 | .42888 | .38753 | .35049 | .21494 | .19542 | .17781 | .16192 | .14756 | .13459 |
| 12 | .88745 | .78849 | .70138 | .62460 | .55684 | .49697 | .44401 | .39711 | .35553 | .31863 | .18691 | .16846 | .15197 | .13722 | .12400 | .11216 |
| 13 | .87866 | .77303 | .68095 | .60057 | .53032 | .46884 | .41496 | .36770 | .32618 | .28966 | .16253 | .14523 | .12989 | .11629 | .10420 | .09346 |
| 14 | .86996 | .75787 | .66112 | .57747 | .50507 | .44230 | .38782 | .34046 | .29925 | .26333 | .14133 | .12520 | .11102 | .09855 | .08757 | .07789 |
| 15 | .86135 | .74301 | .64186 | .55526 | .48102 | .41726 | .36245 | .31524 | .27454 | .23939 | .12289 | .10793 | .09489 | .03352 | .07359 | .06491 |

## Table 3 -- Compound Value of an Annuity of $1

| N | 1% | 2% | 3% | 4% | 5% | 6% | 7% | 8% | 9% | 10% | 12% | 14% |
|---|----|----|----|----|----|----|----|----|----|-----|-----|-----|
| 01 | 1.000 | 1.000 | 1.000 | 1.000 | 1.000 | 1.000 | 1.000 | 1.000 | 1.000 | 1.000 | 1.000 | 1.000 |
| 02 | 2.010 | 2.020 | 2.030 | 2.040 | 2.050 | 2.060 | 2.070 | 2.080 | 2.090 | 2.100 | 2.120 | 2.140 |
| 03 | 3.030 | 3.060 | 3.091 | 3.122 | 3.153 | 3.184 | 3.215 | 3.246 | 3.278 | 3.310 | 3.374 | 3.440 |
| 04 | 4.060 | 4.122 | 4.184 | 4.246 | 4.310 | 4.375 | 4.440 | 4.506 | 4.573 | 4.641 | 4.779 | 4.921 |
| 05 | 5.101 | 5.204 | 5.309 | 5.416 | 5.526 | 5.637 | 5.751 | 5.867 | 5.985 | 6.105 | 6.353 | 6.610 |
| 06 | 6.152 | 6.308 | 6.468 | 6.633 | 6.802 | 6.975 | 7.153 | 7.336 | 7.523 | 7.716 | 8.115 | 8.536 |
| 07 | 7.214 | 7.434 | 7.662 | 7.898 | 8.142 | 8.394 | 8.654 | 8.923 | 9.200 | 9.487 | 10.089 | 10.731 |
| 08 | 8.286 | 8.583 | 8.892 | 9.214 | 9.549 | 9.897 | 10.250 | 10.637 | 11.029 | 11.436 | 12.300 | 13.233 |
| 09 | 9.369 | 9.755 | 10.159 | 10.583 | 11.027 | 11.491 | 11.978 | 12.488 | 13.021 | 13.580 | 14.776 | 16.085 |
| 10 | 10.462 | 10.950 | 11.464 | 12.006 | 12.578 | 13.181 | 13.816 | 14.487 | 15.193 | 15.937 | 17.549 | 19.337 |
| 11 | 11.567 | 12.169 | 12.808 | 13.486 | 14.207 | 14.972 | 15.784 | 16.646 | 17.560 | 18.531 | 20.655 | 23.045 |
| 12 | 12.683 | 13.412 | 14.192 | 15.026 | 15.917 | 16.870 | 17.889 | 18.977 | 20.141 | 21.384 | 24.133 | 27.271 |
| 13 | 13.819 | 14.680 | 15.618 | 16.628 | 16.613 | 18.882 | 20.141 | 21.495 | 22.953 | 24.523 | 28.029 | 32.089 |
| 14 | 14.957 | 15.974 | 17.086 | 18.292 | 19.599 | 21.015 | 22.551 | 24.215 | 26.019 | 27.975 | 32.393 | 37.581 |
| 15 | 16.106 | 17.293 | 18.599 | 20.029 | 21.579 | 23.276 | 25.129 | 27.152 | 29.361 | 31.773 | 37.280 | 43.842 |

## Table 4 -- Present Value of an Annuity of $1

| N | 1% | 2% | 3% | 4% | 5% | 6% | 7% | 8% | 9% | 10% | 15% | 16% | 17% | 18% | 19% | 20% |
|---|----|----|----|----|----|----|----|----|----|-----|-----|-----|-----|-----|-----|-----|
| 01 | .9901 | .9804 | .9709 | .9615 | .9524 | .9434 | .9346 | .9259 | .9174 | .9091 | .8696 | .8621 | .8547 | .8475 | .8403 | .8333 |
| 02 | 1.9704 | 1.9416 | 1.9135 | 1.8861 | 1.8594 | 1.8334 | 1.8080 | 1.7833 | 1.7591 | 1.7355 | 1.6257 | 1.6052 | 1.5852 | 1.5656 | 1.5465 | 1.5278 |
| 03 | 2.9410 | 2.8839 | 2.8286 | 2.7751 | 2.7232 | 2.6730 | 2.6243 | 2.5771 | 2.5313 | 2.4868 | 2.2832 | 2.2459 | 2.2096 | 2.1743 | 2.1399 | 2.1065 |
| 04 | 3.9020 | 3.8077 | 3.7171 | 3.6299 | 3.5459 | 3.4651 | 3.3872 | 3.3121 | 3.2397 | 3.1699 | 2.8550 | 2.7982 | 2.7432 | 2.6901 | 2.6386 | 2.5887 |
| 05 | 4.8535 | 4.7134 | 4.5797 | 4.4518 | 4.3295 | 4.2123 | 4.1002 | 3.9927 | 3.8896 | 3.7908 | 3.3522 | 3.2743 | 3.1993 | 3.1272 | 3.0576 | 2.9906 |
| 06 | 5.7955 | 5.6014 | 5.4172 | 5.2421 | 5.0757 | 4.9173 | 4.7665 | 4.6229 | 4.4859 | 4.3553 | 3.7845 | 3.6847 | 3.5692 | 3.4976 | 3.4098 | 3.3255 |
| 07 | 6.7282 | 6.4720 | 6.2302 | 6.0020 | 5.7863 | 5.5824 | 5.3893 | 5.2064 | 5.0329 | 4.8684 | 4.1604 | 4.0386 | 3.9224 | 3.8115 | 3.7057 | 3.6046 |
| 08 | 7.6517 | 7.3254 | 7.0196 | 6.7327 | 6.4632 | 6.2098 | 5.9713 | 5.7466 | 5.5348 | 5.3349 | 4.4873 | 4.3436 | 4.2072 | 4.0776 | 3.9544 | 3.8372 |
| 09 | 8.5661 | 8.1622 | 7.7861 | 7.4353 | 7.1078 | 6.8017 | 6.5152 | 6.2469 | 5.9952 | 5.7590 | 4.7716 | 4.6065 | 4.4506 | 4.3030 | 4.1633 | 4.0310 |
| 10 | 9.4714 | 8.9825 | 8.5302 | 8.1109 | 7.7217 | 7.3601 | 7.0236 | 6.7101 | 6.4176 | 6.1446 | 5.0188 | 4.8332 | 4.6586 | 4.4941 | 4.3389 | 4.1925 |
| 11 | 10.3677 | 9.7868 | 9.2526 | 8.7604 | 8.3064 | 7.8868 | 7.4987 | 7.1389 | 6.8052 | 6.4951 | 5.2337 | 5.0286 | 4.8364 | 4.6560 | 4.4865 | 4.3271 |
| 12 | 11.2552 | 10.5753 | 9.9539 | 9.3850 | 8.8632 | 8.3838 | 7.9427 | 7.5361 | 7.1607 | 6.8137 | 5.4206 | 5.1971 | 4.9884 | 4.7932 | 4.6105 | 4.4392 |
| 13 | 12.1338 | 11.3483 | 10.6349 | 9.9856 | 9.3935 | 8.8527 | 8.3576 | 7.9038 | 7.4869 | 7.1034 | 5.5831 | 5.3423 | 5.1183 | 4.9095 | 4.7147 | 4.5327 |
| 14 | 13.0038 | 12.1062 | 11.2960 | 10.5631 | 9.8986 | 9.2950 | 8.7454 | 8.2442 | 7.7861 | 7.3667 | 5.7245 | 5.4675 | 5.2293 | 5.0081 | 4.8023 | 4.6106 |
| 15 | 13.8651 | 12.8492 | 11.9379 | 11.1183 | 10.3796 | 9.7122 | 9.1079 | 8.5595 | 8.0607 | 7.6061 | 5.8474 | 5.5755 | 5.3242 | 5.0916 | 4.8759 | 4.6755 |

# Chapter Eighteen
# Managerial Planning and Control Questions

## COMPOUND INTEREST

1. Which of the following tables should be used to calculate the amount of the equal periodic payments which would be equivalent to an outlay of $3,000 at the time of the last payment?
a. Amount of 1.
b. Amount of an annuity of 1.
c. Present value of an annuity of 1.
d. Present value of 1.

2. Which of the following tables would show the largest value for an interest rate of 5% for six periods?
a. Amount of 1 at Compound Interest.
b. Present Value of 1 at Compound Interest.
c. Amount of Annuity of 1 per Period.
d. Present Value of Annuity of 1 per Period.

_____

**Items 3 through 6** apply to the appropriate use of present-value tables. Given below are the present-value factors for $1.00 discounted at 8% for one to five periods. Each of the following items is based on 8% interest compounded annually from day of deposit to day of withdrawal.

| Periods | Present value of $1 discounted at 8% per period |
|---------|--------------------------------------------------|
| 1 | 0.926 |
| 2 | 0.857 |
| 3 | 0.794 |
| 4 | 0.735 |
| 5 | 0.681 |

3. What amount should be deposited in a bank today to grow to $1,000 three years from today?
a. $\dfrac{\$1,000}{0.794}$
b. $1,000 × 0.926 × 3.
c. ($1,000 × 0.926) + ($1,000 × 0.857) + $1,000 × 0.794).
d. $1,000 × 0.794.

4. What amount should an individual have in his bank account today before withdrawal if he needs $2,000 each year for four years with the first withdrawal to be made today and each subsequent withdrawal at one-year intervals? (He is to have exactly a zero balance in his bank account after the fourth withdrawal.)
a. $2,000 + ($2,000 × 0.926) + ($2,000 × 0.857) + ($2,000 × 0.794).
b. $\dfrac{\$2,000}{0.735} × 4.$
c. ($2,000 × 0.926) + ($2,000 × 0.857) + ($2,000 × 0.794) + ($2,000 × 0.735).
d. $\dfrac{\$2,000}{0.926} × 4.$

5. If an individual put $3,000 in a savings account today, what amount of cash would be available two years from today?
a. $3,000 × 0.857.
b. $3,000 × 0.857 × 2.
c. $\dfrac{\$3,000}{0.857}$
d. $\dfrac{\$3,000}{0.926} × 2$

6. What is the present value today of $4,000 to be received six years from today?
a. $4,000 × 0.926 × 6.
b. $4,000 × 0.794 × 2.
c. $4,000 × 0.681 × 0.926.
d. Cannot be determined from the information given.

7. Jarvis wants to invest equal semi-annual payments in order to have $10,000 at the end of 20 years. Assuming that Jarvis will earn interest at an annual rate of 6% compounded semiannually, how would the periodic payment be calculated?
a. $10,000 divided by the future amount of an ordinary annuity of 40 payments of $1 each at an interest rate of 3% per period.
b. $10,000 divided by the present value of an ordinary annuity of 40 payments of $1 each at an interest rate of 3% per period.
c. The future amount of an ordinary annuity of 20 payments of $1 each at an interest rate of 6% per period divided into $10,000.
d. The present value of an ordinary annuity of 40 payments of $1 each at an interest rate of 3% per period divided by $10,000.

8. For the next 2 years, a lease is estimated to have an operating net cash inflow of $7,500 per annum, before adjusting for $5,000 per annum tax basis lease amortization, and a 40% tax rate. The present value of an ordinary annuity of $1 per year at 10% for 2 years is $1.74. What is the lease's after-tax present value using a 10% discount factor?
a.   $2,610
b.   $4,350
c.   $9,570
d.   $11,310

9. On January 1, 1987, Beal Corporation adopted a plan to accumulate funds for a new plant building to be erected beginning July 1, 1992, at an estimated cost of $1,200,000. Beal intends to make five equal annual deposits in a fund that will earn interest at 8% compounded annually. The first deposit is made on July 1, 1987. Present value and future amount factors are as follows:

Present value of 1 at 8%
   for 5 periods                                          0.68
Present value of 1 at 8%
   for 6 periods                                          0.63
Future amount of ordinary annuity
   of 1 at 8% for 5 periods                               5.87
Future amount of annuity in
   advance of 1 at 8%
   for 5 periods                                          6.34

Beal should make five annual deposits (rounded) of
a. $151,200
b. $163,200
c. $189,300
d. $204,400

10. Cooper plans to invest $2,000 at the end of each of the next ten years. Assume that Cooper will earn interest at an annual rate of 6% compounded annually. The future amount of an ordinary annuity of $1 for ten periods at 6% is 13.181. The present value of $1 for ten periods at 6% is 0.558. The present value of an ordinary annuity of $1 for ten periods at 6% is 7.360. The investment after the end of ten years would be
a. $14,720.
b. $21,200.
c. $26,362.
d. $27,478.

11. Cause Company is planning to invest in a machine with a useful life of five years and no salvage value. The machine is expected to produce cash flow from operations, net of income taxes, of $20,000 in each of the five years. Cause's expected rate of return is 10%. Information on present value and future amount factors is as follows:

|  | Period | | | | |
|---|---|---|---|---|---|
|  | 1 | 2 | 3 | 4 | 5 |
| Present value of $1 at 10% | .909 | .826 | .751 | .683 | .621 |
| Present value of annuity of $1 at 10% | .909 | 1.736 | 2.487 | 3.170 | 3.791 |
| Future amount of $1 at 10% | 1.100 | 1.210 | 1.331 | 1.464 | 1.611 |
| Future amount of annuity of $1 at 10% | 1.000 | 2.100 | 3.310 | 4.641 | 6.105 |

How much will the machine cost?
a. $32,220.
b. $62,100.
c. $75,820.
d. $122,100.

12. On May 1, 19X9, a company sold some machinery to another company. The two companies entered into an installment sales contract at a predetermined interest rate. The contract required five equal annual payments with the first payment due on May 1, 19X9. What present value concept is appropriate for this situation?
a.   Present value of an annuity due of $1 for five periods.
b.   Present value of an ordinary annuity of $1 for five periods.
c.   Future amount of an annuity of $1 for five periods.
d.   Future amount of $1 for five periods.

13. On January 1, 19X0, Liberty Company sold a machine to Bell Corporation in an "arms length" transaction. Bell signed a noninterest bearing note requiring payment of $20,000 annually for ten years. The first payment was made on January 1, 19X0. The prevailing rate of interest for this type of note at date of issuance was 12%. Information on present value factors is as follows:

| Period | Present value of $1 at 12% | Present value of ordinary annuity of $1 at 12% |
|---|---|---|
| 9 | 0.361 | 5.328 |
| 10 | 0.322 | 5.650 |

Liberty should record the above sale in January 19X0 at
a. $64,400.
b. $84,980.
c. $113,000.
d. $126,560.

14. Scott, Inc., is planning to invest $120,000 in a ten-year project. Scott estimates that the annual cash inflow, net of income taxes, from this project will be $20,000. Scott's desired rate of return on investments of this type is 10%. Information on present value factors is as follows:

|  | At 10% | At 12% |
|---|---|---|
| Present value of $1 for ten periods | 0.386 | 0.322 |
| Present value of an annuity of $1 for ten periods | 6.145 | 5.650 |

Scott's expected rate of return on this investment is
a. Less than 10%, but more than 0%.
b. 10%.
c. Less than 12%, but more than 10%.
d. 12%.

N91

15. On March 15, 1990, Ashe Corp. adopted a plan to accumulate $1,000,000 by September 1, 1994. Ashe plans to make four equal annual deposits to a fund that will earn interest at 10% compounded annually. Ashe made the first deposit on September 1, 1990. Future value and future amount factors are as follows:

| | |
|---|---|
| Future value of 1 at 10% for 4 periods | 1.46 |
| Future amount of ordinary annuity of 1 at 10% for 4 periods | 4.64 |
| Future amount of annuity in advance of 1 at 10% for 4 periods | 5.11 |

Ashe should make four annual deposits (rounded) of

a. $250,000
b. $215,500
c. $195,700
d. $146,000

## CAPITAL BUDGETING

**Items 16 through 19** are based on the following information:

The Apex Company is evaluating a capital-budgeting proposal for the current year. The relevant data follow:

| Year | Present Value of an Annuity in Arrears of $1 at 15% |
|---|---|
| 1 | $ .870 |
| 2 | 1.626 |
| 3 | 2.284 |
| 4 | 2.856 |
| 5 | 3.353 |
| 6 | 3.785 |

The initial investment would be $30,000. It would be depreciated on a straight-line basis over six years with no salvage. The before-tax annual cash inflow due to this investment is $10,000, and the income tax rate is 40% paid the same year as incurred. The desired rate of return is 15%. All cash flows occur at year end.

16. What is the after-tax accounting rate of return on Apex's capital-budgeting proposal?
a. 10%.
b. 16-2/3%.
c. 26-2/3%.
d. 33-1/3%.

17. What is the after-tax payback reciprocal for Apex's capital-budgeting proposal?
a. 20%.
b. 26-2/3%.
c. 33-1/3%.
d. 50%.

18. What is the net present value of Apex's capital-budgeting proposal?
a. $(7,290).
b. $280.
c. $7,850.
d. $11,760.

19. How much would Apex have had to invest five years ago at 15% compounded annually to have $30,000 now?
a. $12,960.
b. $14,910.
c. $17,160.
d. Cannot be determined from the information given.

_____

N95

20. The following selected data pertain to the Darwin Division of Beagle Co. for 1994:

| | |
|---|---|
| Sales | $400,000 |
| Operating income | 40,000 |
| Capital turnover | 4 |
| Imputed interest rate | 10% |

What was Darwin's 1994 residual income?
a. $0
b. $4,000
c. $10,000
d. $30,000

M90

21. Polo Co. requires higher rates of return for projects with a life span greater than five years. Projects extending beyond five years must earn a higher specified rate of return. Which of the following capital

budgeting techniques can readily accommodate this requirement?

|     | Internal rate of return | Net present value |
| --- | --- | --- |
| a. | Yes | No |
| b. | No | Yes |
| c. | No | No |
| d. | Yes | Yes |

*M89*

22. Residual income is income
a. To which an imputed interest charge for invested capital is added.
b. From which an imputed interest charge for invested capital is deducted.
c. From which dividends are deducted.
d. To which dividends are added.

———

*M92*

**Items 23 through 26** are based on the following:

Tam Co. is negotiating for the purchase of equipment that would cost $100,000, with the expectation that $20,000 per year could be saved in after-tax cash costs if the equipment were acquired. The equipment's estimated useful life is 10 years, with no residual value, and would be depreciated by the straight-line method. Tam's predetermined minimum desired rate of return is 12%. Present value of an annuity of 1 at 12% for 10 periods is 5.65. Present value of 1 due in 10 periods at 12% is .322.

23. Net present value is
a. $5,760
b. $6,440
c. $12,200
d. $13,000

24. Payback period is
a. 4.0 years.
b. 4.4 years.
c. 4.5 years.
d. 5.0 years.

25. Accrual accounting rate of return based on initial investment is
a. 30%
b. 20%
c. 12%
d. 10%

26. In estimating the internal rate of return, the factors in the table of present values of an annuity should be taken from the columns closest to

a. 0.65
b. 1.30
c. 5.00
d. 5.65

———

**Items 27 and 28** are based on the following information:

The Gravina Company is planning to spend $6,000 for a machine which it will depreciate on a straight-line basis over a ten-year period. The machine will generate additional cash revenues of $1,200 a year. Gravina will incur no additional costs except for depreciation. The income tax rate is 50%.

27. What is the payback period?
a. 3.3 years.
b. 4.0 years.
c. 5.0 years.
d. 6.7 years.

28. What is the accounting (book-value) rate of return on the initial increase in required investment?
a. 5%.
b. 10%.
c. 15%.
d. 20%.

———

*N91*

29. How are the following used in the calculation of the internal rate of return of a proposed project? Ignore income tax considerations.

|     | Residual sales value of project | Depreciation expense |
| --- | --- | --- |
| a. | Exclude | Include |
| b. | Include | Include |
| c. | Exclude | Exclude |
| d. | Include | Exclude |

———

**Items 30 and 31** are based on the following information:

Flemming, Inc., is planning to acquire a new machine at a total cost of $36,000. The estimated life of the machine is six years with no salvage value. The straight-line method of depreciation will be used. Flemming estimates that the annual cash flow from operations, before income taxes, from using this machine will be $9,000. Assume that Flemming's cost of capital is 8% and the income tax rate is 40%. The present value of $1 at 8% for six years is .630. The present value of an annuity of $1 in arrears at 8% for six years is 4.623.

30. What would the payback period be?
a. 4.0 years.
b. 4.6 years.
c. 5.7 years.
d. 6.7 years.

31. What would the net present value be?
a. $59.
b. $5,607.
c. $10,800.
d. $13,140.

---

32. Sant Company is planning to invest $40,000 in a machine with a useful life of five years and no salvage value. The straight-line method of depreciation will be used. Sant estimates that the annual cash inflow from operations, net of income taxes, from using this machine will be $10,000. Sant's desired rate of return on investments of this type is 10%. The present value of an ordinary annuity of $1 for five periods at 10% is 3.791. The present value of $1 for five periods at 10% is 0.621. Using the net present-value method, Sant's true rate of return on this investment is
a. 0%.
b. Less than 10%, but more than 0%.
c. 10%.
d. More than 10%.

*N90*

33. Which of the following capital budgeting techniques implicitly assumes that the cash flows are reinvested at the company's minimum required rate of return?

|    | Net present value | Internal rate of return |
|----|-------------------|-------------------------|
| a. | Yes               | Yes                     |
| b. | Yes               | No                      |
| c. | No                | Yes                     |
| d. | No                | No                      |

*M95*

34. Pole Co. is investing in a machine with a 3 year life. The machine is expected to reduce annual cash operating costs by $30,000 in each of the first 2 years and by $20,000 in year 3. Present values of an annuity of $1 at 14% are:

| Period 1 | 0.88 |
|----------|------|
| 2        | 1.65 |
| 3        | 2.32 |

Using a 14% cost of capital, what is the present value of these future savings?
a. $59,600
b. $60,800

c. $62,900
d. $69,500

35. The Polar Company is planning to purchase a new machine for $30,000. The payback period is expected to be five years. The new machine is expected to produce cash flow from operations, net of income taxes, of $7,000 a year in each of the next three years and $5,500 in the fourth year. Depreciation of $5,000 a year will be charged to income for each of the five years of the payback period. What is the amount of cash flow from operations, net of taxes, that the new machine is expected to produce in the last (fifth) year of the payback period?
a. $1,000.
b. $3,500.
c. $5,000.
d. $8,500.

*M92*

36. Following is information relating to Kew Co.'s Value Division for 1991:

| Sales                   | $500,000 |
|-------------------------|----------|
| Variable costs          | 300,000  |
| Traceable fixed costs   | 50,000   |
| Average invested capital| 100,000  |
| Imputed interest rate   | 6%       |

Vale's residual income was
a. $144,000
b. $150,000
c. $156,000
d. $200,000

37. Roberts, Inc., purchased a machine for $240,000. The machine has a useful life of six years and no salvage value. Straight-line depreciation is to be used. The machine is expected to generate cash flow from operations, net of income taxes, of $70,000 in each of the six years. Roberts' expected rate of return is 12%. Information on present value factors is as follows:

| Period | Present value of $1 at 12% | Present value of ordinary annuity of $1 at 12% |
|--------|----------------------------|------------------------------------------------|
| 1      | .893                       | .893                                           |
| 2      | .797                       | 1.690                                          |
| 3      | .712                       | 2.402                                          |
| 4      | .636                       | 3.037                                          |
| 5      | .567                       | 3.605                                          |
| 6      | .507                       | 4.111                                          |

What would be the net present value?
a. $35,490.
b. $47,770.
c. $121,680.
d. $123,330.

38. Under the internal rate of return capital budgeting technique, it is assumed that cash flows are reinvested at the
a. Cost of capital.
b. Hurdle rate of return.
c. Rate earned by the investment.
d. Payback rate.

*N92*
39. Lin Co. is buying machinery it expects will increase average annual operating income by $40,000. The initial increase in the required investment is $60,000, and the average increase in required investment is $30,000. To compute the accrual accounting rate of return, what amount should be used as the numerator in the ratio?
a.    $20,000
b.    $30,000
c.    $40,000
d.    $60,000

*N89*
40. Doro Co. is considering the purchase of a $100,000 machine that is expected to result in a decrease of $25,000 per year in cash expenses after taxes. This machine, which has no residual value, has an estimated useful life of 10 years and will be depreciated on a straight-line basis. For this machine, the accounting rate of return based on initial investment would be
a. 10%
b. 15%
c. 25%
d. 35%

*M91*
41. The discount rate (hurdle rate of return) must be determined in advance for the
a. Payback period method.
b. Time adjusted rate of return method.
c. Net present value method.
d. Internal rate of return method.

*N89*
**Items 42 and 43** are based on the following information pertaining to Yola Co.'s East Division for 1988:

| | |
|---|---|
| Sales | $620,000 |
| Variable costs | 500,000 |
| Traceable fixed costs | 100,000 |
| Average invested capital | 50,000 |
| Imputed interest rate | 18% |

42. The return on investment was
a. 40.00%
b. 29.00%
c. 18.00%
d. 8.33%

43. The residual income was
a. $3,600
b. $9,000
c. $11,000
d. $20,000

-----------

*N92*
44. Major Corp. is considering the purchase of a new machine for $5,000 that will have an estimated useful life of five years and no salvage value. The machine will increase Major's after-tax cash flow by $2,000 annually for five years. Major uses the straight-line method of depreciation and has an incremental borrowing rate of 10%. The present value factors for 10% are as follows:

| | |
|---|---|
| Ordinary annuity with five payments | 3.79 |
| Annuity due for five payments | 4.17 |

Using the payback method, how many years will it take to pay back Major's initial investment in the machine?
a.    2.50
b.    5.00
c.    7.58
d.    8.34

*N90*
45. Division A is considering a project that will earn a rate of return which is greater than the imputed interest charge for invested capital, but less than the division's historical return on invested capital. Division B is considering a project that will earn a rate of return which is greater than the division's historical return on invested capital, but less than the imputed interest charge for invested capital. If the objective is to maximize residual income, should these divisions accept or reject their projects?

| | *A* | *B* |
|---|---|---|
| a. | Accept | Accept |
| b. | Reject | Accept |
| c. | Reject | Reject |
| d. | Accept | Reject |

# BUDGETING

46. Neu Co. is considering the purchase of an investment that has a positive net present value based on Neu's 12% hurdle rate. The internal rate of return would be
a. 0.
b. 12%.
c. >12%.
d. <12%.

___

**Items 47, 48, 49** are based on the following information:

The January 31, 19XX, balance sheet of Shelpat Corporation follows:

| | |
|---|---|
| Cash | $8,000 |
| Accounts receivable (net of allowance for uncollectible accounts of $2,000) | 38,000 |
| Inventory | 16,000 |
| Property, plant and equipment (net of allowance for accumulated depreciation of $60,000) | 40,000 |
| | $102,000 |
| | |
| Accounts payable | $ 82,500 |
| Common stock | 50,000 |
| Retained earnings (deficit) | (30,500) |
| | $102,000 |

- Sales are budgeted as follows:
  February $110,000
  March $120,000
- Collections are expected to be 60% in the month of sale, 38% the next month, and 2% uncollectible.
- The gross margin is 25% of sales. Purchases each month are 75% of the next month's projected sales. The purchases are paid in full the following month.
- Other expenses for each month, paid in cash, are expected to be $16,500. Depreciation each month is $5,000.

47. What are the budgeted cash collections for February 19XX?
a. $63,800.
b. $66,000.
c. $101,800.
d. $104,000.

48. What is the pro forma income (loss) before income taxes for February 19XX?
a. ($3,700).
b. ($1,500).
c. $3,800.
d. $6,000.

49. What is the projected balance in accounts payable on February 29, 19XX?
a. $82,500.
b. $86,250.
c. $90,000.
d. $106,500.

___

50. A 1995 cash budget is being prepared for the purchase of Toyi, a merchandise item. Budgeted data are:

| | |
|---|---|
| Cost of goods sold for 1995 | $300,000 |
| Accounts payable 1/1/95 | 20,000 |
| Inventory - 1/1/95 | 30,000 |
| 12/31/95 | 42,000 |

Purchases will be made in 12 equal monthly amounts and paid for in the following month. What is the 1995 budgeted cash payment for purchases of 'Toyi?
a. $295,000
b. $300,000
c. $306,000
d. $312,000

51. Varsity Co. is preparing its cash budget for the month of May. The following information on accounts receivable collections is available from Varsity's past collection experience:

| | |
|---|---|
| Current month's sales | 12% |
| Prior month's sales | 75% |
| Sales 2 months prior to current mo. | 6% |
| Sales 3 months prior to current mo. | 4% |
| Cash discounts taken | 2% |
| Doubtful accounts | 1% |

Credit sales are as follows:
| | |
|---|---|
| May—estimated | $100,000 |
| April | 90,000 |
| March | 80,000 |
| February | 95,000 |

What are the estimated accounts receivable collections for May?
a. $85,100.
b. $87,100.
c. $88,100.
d. $90,100.

52. Lon Co.'s budget committee is preparing its master budget on the basis of the following projections:

| | |
|---|---|
| Sales | $2,800,000 |
| Decrease in inventories | 70,000 |
| Decrease in accounts payable | 150,000 |
| Gross margin | 40% |

What are Lon's estimated cash disbursements for inventories?
a. $1,040,000
b. $1,200,000
c. $1,600,000
d. $1,760,000

53. The purpose of a flexible budget is to
a. Allow management some latitude in meeting goals.
b. Eliminate cyclical fluctuations in production reports by ignoring variable costs.
c. Compare actual and budgeted results at virtually any level of production.
d. Reduce the total time in preparing the annual budget.

54. Serven Corporation has estimated its activity for June 19X9. Selected data from these estimated amounts are as follows:

- Sales $700,000
  Gross profit (based on sales) 30%
  Increase in trade
  accounts receivable
  during month $ 20,000
  Change in accounts payable
  during month $ 0
  Increase in inventory during
  month $ 10,000

- Variable selling, general and administrative expenses (S, G & A) includes a charge for uncollectible accounts of 1% of sales.
- Total S, G & A is $71,000 per month plus 15% of sales.
- Depreciation expense of $40,000 per month is included in fixed S, G & A.

On the basis of the above data, what are the estimated cash disbursements from operations for June?
a. $619,000.
b. $626,000.
c. $629,000.
d. $636,000.

55. The basic difference between a master budget and a flexible budget is that a master budget is
a. Only used before and during the budget period and a flexible budget is only used after the budget period.
b. For an entire production facility and a flexible budget is applicable to single departments only.
c. Based on one specific level of production and a flexible budget can be prepared for any production level within a relevant range.
d. Based on a fixed standard and a flexible budget allows management latitude in meeting goals.

56. The Fresh Company is preparing its cash budget for the month of May. The following information is available concerning its accounts receivable:

| | |
|---|---|
| Estimated credit sales for May | $200,000 |
| Actual credit sales for April | $150,000 |
| Estimated collections in May for credit sales in May | 20% |
| Estimated collections in May for credit sales in April | 70% |
| Estimated collections in May for credit sales prior to April | $ 12,000 |
| Estimated write-offs in May for uncollectible credit sales | $8,000 |
| Estimated provision for bad debts in May for credit sales in May | $7,000 |

What are the estimated cash receipts from accounts receivable collections in May?
a. $142,000.
b. $149,000.
c. $150,000.
d. $157,000.

57. Glo Co., a manufacturer of combs, budgeted sales of 125,000 units for the month of April 1987. The following additional information is provided:

| | Number of units |
|---|---|
| Actual inventory at April 1 | |
| Work-in-process | None |
| Finished goods | 37,500 |
| Budgeted inventory at April 30 | |
| Work-in-process (75% processed) | 8,000 |
| Finished goods | 30,000 |

How many equivalent units of production did Glo budget for April 1987?
a. 126,500
b. 125,500
c. 123,500
d. 117,500

N95

58. Mien Co. is budgeting sales of 53,000 units of product for Nous for October 1995. The manufacture of one unit of Nous requires 4 kilos of chemical Loire. During October 1995, Mien plans to reduce the inventory of Loire by 50,000 kilos and increase the finished goods inventory of Nous by 6,000 units. There is no Nous work-in-process inventory. How many kilos of Loire is Mien budgeting to purchase in October 1995?
a.   138,000
b.   162,000
c.   186,000
d.   238,000

N89

59. In preparing its cash budget for May 1989, Ben Co. made the following projections:

| | |
|---|---|
| Sales | $3,000,000 |
| Gross margin (based on sales) | 25% |
| Decrease in inventories | $ 140,000 |
| Decrease in accounts payable for inventories | $ 240,000 |

For May 1989 the estimated cash disbursements for inventories were
a. $2,350,000
b. $2,110,000
c. $2,100,000
d. $1,870,000

60. Lawton Company produces canned tomato soup and is budgeting sales of 250,000 units for the month of January 1983. Actual inventory units at January 1 and budgeted inventory units at January 31 are as follows:

| Actual inventory at January 1: | Units |
|---|---|
| Work-in-process | None |
| Finished goods | 75,000 |
| Budgeted inventory at January 31: | |
| Work-in-process (75% processed) | 16,000 |
| Finished goods | 60,000 |

How many equivalent units of production is Lawton budgeting for January 1983?
a. 235,000
b. 247,000
c. 251,000
d. 253,000

## INVENTORY

N95

61. The economic order quantity formula assumes that
a.   Periodic demand for the good is known.
b.   Carrying costs per unit vary with quantity ordered.
c.   Costs of placing an order vary with quantity ordered.
d.   Purchase costs per unit differ due to quantity discounts.

62. For inventory management, ignoring safety stocks, which of the following is a valid computation of the reorder point?
a.   The economic order quantity.
b.   The economic order quantity multiplied by the anticipated demand during the lead time.
c.   The anticipated demand during the lead time.
d.   The square root of the anticipated demand during the lead time.

M91

63. The economic order quantity formula assumes that
a.   Purchase costs per unit differ due to quantity discounts.
b.   Costs of placing an order vary with quantity ordered.
c.   Periodic demand for the good is known.
d.   Erratic usage rates are cushioned by safety stocks.

_____

**Items 64 and 65** are based on the following information:

Expected annual usage of a particular raw material is 2,000,000 units, and the standard order size is 10,000 units. The invoice cost of each unit is $500, and the cost to place one purchase order is $80.

64. The average inventory is
a. 1,000,000 units.
b. 5,000 units.
c. 10,000 units.
d. 7,500 units.

65. The estimated annual order cost is
a. $16,000.
b. $100,000.
c. $32,000.
d. $50,000.

_____

66. What effect, if any, will a last-in, first-out or first-in, first-out inventory method have on an Economic Order Quantity?
a. No effect.
b. LIFO will increase the order quantity in times of rising prices.
c. LIFO will reduce the order quantity in times of rising prices.
d. FIFO will increase the order quantity in times of rising prices.

_____

**Items 67 and 68** are based on the following information:
Brady Sporting Goods Incorporated buys baseballs at $20 per dozen from its wholesaler. Brady will sell 36,000 dozen baseballs evenly throughout the year. Brady desires a 10% return on its inventory investment. In addition, rent, insurance, taxes, etc., for each dozen baseballs in inventory is $0.40. The administrative cost involved in handling each purchase order is $10.

67. What is the economic order quantity?
a. Approximately 448.
b. Approximately 500.
c. Approximately 548.
d. Approximately 600.

68. Assuming that Brady ordered in order sizes of 800 dozen evenly throughout the year, what would be the total annual inventory expenses to sell 36,000 dozen baseballs?
a. $1,315.
b. $1,320.
c. $1,338.
d. $1,410.

_____
*M95*

69. Which changes in costs are most conducive to switching from a traditional inventory ordering system to a just-in-time ordering system?

| | Cost per purchase order | Inventory unit carrying costs |
|---|---|---|
| a. | Increasing | Increasing |
| b. | Decreasing | Increasing |
| c. | Decreasing | Decreasing |
| d. | Increasing | Decreasing |

70. The Aron Company requires 40,000 units of Product Q for the year. The units will be required evenly throughout the year. It costs $60 to place an order. It costs $10 to carry a unit in inventory for the year. What is the economic order quantity?

a. 400.
b. 490.
c. 600.
d. 693.

71. Politan Company manufactures bookcases. Set up costs are $2.00. Politan manufactures 4,000 bookcases evenly throughout the year. Using the economic-order-quantity approach, the optimal production run would be 200 when the cost of carrying one bookcase in inventory for one year is
a. $0.05.
b. $0.10.
c. $0.20.
d. $0.40.

72. The following information relates to Eagle Company's material A:

| | |
|---|---|
| Annual usage in units | 7,200 |
| Working days per year | 240 |
| Normal lead time in working days | 20 |
| Maximum lead time in working days | 45 |

Assuming that the units of material A will be required evenly throughout the year, the safety stock and order point would be

| | Safety Stock | Order Point |
|---|---|---|
| a. | 600 | 750 |
| b. | 600 | 1,350 |
| c. | 750 | 600 |
| d. | 750 | 1,350 |

73. The following information is available for Trencher Company's material B:

| | |
|---|---|
| Annual usage in units | 10,000 |
| Working days per year | 250 |
| Safety stock in units | 400 |
| Normal lead time in working days | 30 |

Assuming that the units of material B will be required evenly throughout the year, the order point would be
a. 400
b. 800
c. 1,200
d. 1,600

74. The economic order quantity formula can be used to determine the optimum size of a

|  | Production run | Purchase order |
|---|---|---|
| a. | Yes | No |
| b. | Yes | Yes |
| c. | No | Yes |
| d. | No | No |

N95

75. Key Co. changed from a traditional manufacturing operation with a job order costing system to a just-in-time operation with a back-flush costing system. What is(are) the expected effects(s) of these changes on Key's inspection costs and recording detail of costs tracked to jobs in process?

|  | Inspection costs | Detail of costs tracked to jobs |
|---|---|---|
| a. | Decrease | Decrease |
| b. | Decrease | Increase |
| c. | Increase | Decrease |
| d. | Increase | Increase |

# Chapter Eighteen
# Managerial Planning and Control Problems

## NUMBER 1

The Scarborough Corporation manufactures and sells two products, Thingone and Thingtwo. In July 19X7, Scarborough's budget department gathered the following data in order to project sales and budget requirements for 19X8.

19X8 Projected Sales:

| Product | Units | Price |
|---|---|---|
| Thingone | 60,000 | $ 70 |
| Thingtwo | 40,000 | $100 |

19X8 Inventories - in units:

| Product | Expected Jan. 1, 19X8 | Desired Dec. 31, 19X8 |
|---|---|---|
| Thingone | 20,000 | 25,000 |
| Thingtwo | 8,000 | 9,000 |

In order to produce one unit of Thingone and Thingtwo, the following raw materials are used:

| Raw Material | Unit | Amount used per unit Thingone | Thingtwo |
|---|---|---|---|
| A | lbs. | 4 | 5 |
| B | lbs. | 2 | 3 |
| C | each | | 1 |

Projected data for 19X8 with respect to raw materials is as follows:

| Raw Material | Anticipated Purchase Price | Expected Inventories January 1, 19X8 | Desired Inventories December 31, 19X8 |
|---|---|---|---|
| A | $8 | 32,000 lbs. | 36,000 lbs. |
| B | $5 | 29,000 lbs. | 32,000 lbs. |
| C | $3 | 6,000 each | 7,000 each |

Projected direct labor requirements for 19X8 and rates are as follows:

| Product | Hours per unit | Rate per hour |
|---|---|---|
| Thingone | 2 | $3 |
| Thingtwo | 3 | $4 |

Overhead is applied at the rate of $2 per direct labor hour.

**Required:**

Based upon the above projections and budget requirements for 19X8 for Thingone and Thingtwo, prepare the following budgets for 19X8:

1. Sales budget (in dollars)
2. Production budget (in units)
3. Raw materials purchase budget (in quantities)
4. Raw materials purchase budget (in dollars)
5. Direct labor budget (in dollars)
6. Budgeted finished goods inventory at December 31, 19X8 (in dollars)

# NUMBER 2

A company is presently using the payback method for evaluating capital budgeting projects and is considering using other more sophisticated capital budgeting techniques. The president has requested an explanation of the advantages and disadvantages of the payback method.

**Required:**
1. State the advantages and disadvantages of the payback method.
2. What other capital budgeting techniques could be used?

# NUMBER 3

The following information was available from Montero Corporation's books:

| 1982 | Purchases | Sales |
|------|-----------|-------|
| Jan. | $42,000 | $72,000 |
| Feb. | 48,000 | 66,000 |
| Mar. | 36,000 | 60,000 |
| Apr. | 54,000 | 78,000 |

Collections from customers are normally 70% in the month of sale, 20% in the month following the sale, and 9% in the second month following the sale. The balance is expected to be uncollectible. Montero takes full advantage of the 2% discount allowed on purchases paid for by the tenth of the following month. Purchases for May are budgeted at $60,000, while sales for May are forecasted at $66,000. Cash disbursements for expenses are expected to be $14,400 for the month of May. Montero's cash balance at May 1 was $22,000.

**Required:**
Prepare the following schedules:
1. Expected cash collections during May.
2. Expected cash disbursements during May.
3. Expected cash balance at May 31.

# NUMBER 4

The net present value method and the internal rate of return method are both sophisticated capital budgeting techniques.

**Required:**
1. State the advantages that both the net present value method and the internal rate of return method have over the payback method.
2. State the limitations of the net present value method.
3. State the limitations of the internal rate of return method.
4. How does each method (net present value and internal rate of return) handle depreciation? Discuss the rationale for your answer. Ignore income tax considerations in your answer.

# NUMBER 5

Spara Corp. is considering the various benefits that may result from the shortening of its product cycle by changing from the company's present manual system to a computer-aided design/computer-aided manufacturing (CAD/CAM) system. The proposed system can provide productive time equivalency close to the 20,000 hours currently available with the manual system. The incremental annual out-of-pocket costs of maintaining the manual system are $20 per hour.

The incremental annual out-of-pocket costs of maintaining the CAD/CAM system are estimated to be $200,000, with an initial investment of $480,000 in the proposed system. The estimated useful life of this system is six years. For tax purposes, assume a level accelerated cost recovery with a full year allowable in each year. The tax rate is expected to remain constant at 30% over the life of the project. Spara requires a minimum after-tax return of 20% on projects of this type. Full capacity will be utilized.

**Required:**
**a.** Compute the relevant annual after-tax cash flows related to the CAD/CAM project.
**b.** Based on the computation in **a.** above, compute the following on an after-tax basis:
    1. Payback period for recovery of investment.
    2. Internal rate of return (use the appropriate table below).
    3. Net present value (use the appropriate table below).
    4. Excess present value index (profitability index).

## TABLE 1

Compound Amount of $1.00 (The Future Value of $1.00)
$S = P(1 + r)^n$. In this table $P = \$1.00$.

| PERIODS | 4% | 6% | 8% | 10% | 12% | 14% | 16% | 18% | 20% | 22% | 24% | 26% |
|---|---|---|---|---|---|---|---|---|---|---|---|---|
| 1 | 1.040 | 1.060 | 1.080 | 1.100 | 1.120 | 1.140 | 1.160 | 1.180 | 1.200 | 1.220 | 1.240 | 1.260 |
| 2 | 1.082 | 1.124 | 1.166 | 1.210 | 1.254 | 1.300 | 1.346 | 1.392 | 1.440 | 1.488 | 1.538 | 1.588 |
| 3 | 1.125 | 1.191 | 1.260 | 1.331 | 1.405 | 1.482 | 1.561 | 1.643 | 1.728 | 1.816 | 1.907 | 2.000 |
| 4 | 1.170 | 1.262 | 1.360 | 1.464 | 1.574 | 1.689 | 1.811 | 1.939 | 2.074 | 2.215 | 2.364 | 2.520 |
| 5 | 1.217 | 1.338 | 1.469 | 1.611 | 1.762 | 1.925 | 2.100 | 2.288 | 2.488 | 2.703 | 2.932 | 3.176 |
| 6 | 1.265 | 1.419 | 1.587 | 1.772 | 1.974 | 2.195 | 2.436 | 2.700 | 2.986 | 3.297 | 3.635 | 4.002 |

## TABLE 2

Present value of $1.00

$$P = \frac{S}{(1+r)^n}. \text{ In this table } S = \$1.00.$$

| PERIODS | 4% | 6% | 8% | 10% | 12% | 14% | 16% | 18% | 20% | 22% | 24% | 26% |
|---|---|---|---|---|---|---|---|---|---|---|---|---|
| 1 | 0.962 | 0.943 | 0.926 | 0.909 | 0.893 | 0.877 | 0.862 | 0.847 | 0.833 | 0.820 | 0.806 | 0.794 |
| 2 | 0.925 | 0.890 | 0.857 | 0.826 | 0.797 | 0.769 | 0.743 | 0.718 | 0.694 | 0.672 | 0.650 | 0.630 |
| 3 | 0.889 | 0.840 | 0.794 | 0.751 | 0.712 | 0.675 | 0.641 | 0.609 | 0.579 | 0.551 | 0.524 | 0.500 |
| 4 | 0.855 | 0.792 | 0.735 | 0.683 | 0.636 | 0.592 | 0.552 | 0.516 | 0.482 | 0.451 | 0.423 | 0.397 |
| 5 | 0.822 | 0.747 | 0.681 | 0.621 | 0.567 | 0.519 | 0.476 | 0.437 | 0.402 | 0.370 | 0.341 | 0.315 |
| 6 | 0.790 | 0.705 | 0.630 | 0.564 | 0.507 | 0.456 | 0.410 | 0.370 | 0.335 | 0.303 | 0.275 | 0.250 |

**NUMBER 5 (cont.)**

## TABLE 3

Compound Amount of Annuity of $1.00 in Arrears* (Future Value of Annuity)

$$S_n = \frac{(1+r)^n - 1}{r}$$

| PERIODS | 4% | 6% | 8% | 10% | 12% | 14% | 16% | 18% | 20% | 22% | 24% | 26% |
|---|---|---|---|---|---|---|---|---|---|---|---|---|
| 1 | 1.000 | 1.000 | 1.000 | 1.000 | 1.000 | 1.000 | 1.000 | 1.000 | 1.000 | 1.000 | 1.000 | 1.000 |
| 2 | 2.040 | 2.060 | 2.080 | 2.100 | 2.120 | 2.140 | 2.160 | 2.180 | 2.200 | 2.220 | 2.240 | 2.260 |
| 3 | 3.122 | 3.184 | 3.246 | 3.310 | 3.374 | 3.440 | 3.506 | 3.572 | 3.640 | 3.708 | 3.778 | 3.848 |
| 4 | 4.246 | 4.375 | 4.506 | 4.641 | 4.779 | 4.921 | 5.066 | 5.215 | 5.368 | 5.524 | 5.684 | 5.848 |
| 5 | 5.416 | 5.637 | 5.867 | 6.105 | 6.353 | 6.610 | 6.877 | 7.154 | 7.442 | 7.740 | 8.048 | 8.368 |
| 6 | 6.633 | 6.975 | 7.336 | 7.716 | 8.115 | 8.536 | 8.977 | 9.442 | 9.930 | 10.442 | 10.980 | 11.544 |

## TABLE 4

Present value of Annuity of $1.00 in Arrears*          *Payments (or receipts) at the end of each period.

$$P_n = \frac{1}{r}\left| 1 \frac{1}{(1+r)^n} \right|$$

| PERIODS | 4% | 6% | 8% | 10% | 12% | 14% | 16% | 18% | 20% | 22% | 24% | 26% |
|---|---|---|---|---|---|---|---|---|---|---|---|---|
| 1 | 0.962 | 0.943 | 0.926 | 0.909 | 0.893 | 0.877 | 0.862 | 0.847 | 0.833 | 0.820 | 0.806 | 0.794 |
| 2 | 1.886 | 1.833 | 1.783 | 1.736 | 1.690 | 1.647 | 1.605 | 1.566 | 1.528 | 1.492 | 1.457 | 1.424 |
| 3 | 2.775 | 2.673 | 2.577 | 2.487 | 2.402 | 2.322 | 2.246 | 2.174 | 2.106 | 2.042 | 1.981 | 1.923 |
| 4 | 3.630 | 3.465 | 3.312 | 3.170 | 3.037 | 2.914 | 2.798 | 2.690 | 2.589 | 2.494 | 2.404 | 2.320 |
| 5 | 4.452 | 4.212 | 3.993 | 3.791 | 3.605 | 3.433 | 3.274 | 3.127 | 2.991 | 2.864 | 2.745 | 2.635 |
| 6 | 5.242 | 4.917 | 4.623 | 4.355 | 4.111 | 3.889 | 3.685 | 3.498 | 3.326 | 3.167 | 3.020 | 2.885 |

**Items 1 through 4** are based on the following:

A company has two mutually exclusive projects, A and B, which have the same initial investment requirements and lives. Project B has a decrease in estimated net cash inflows each year, and project A has an increase in estimated net cash inflows each year. Project A has a greater total net cash inflow. Diagram I below depicts the net cash inflows of each project by year. Diagram II depicts the net present value (NPV) of each project assuming various discount rates.

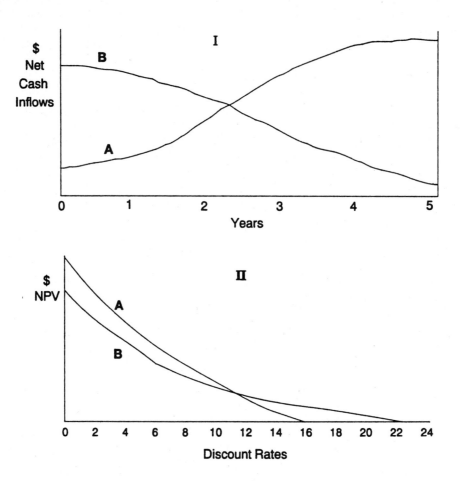

**Required:**
For items 1 through 4, select your answer from the following list.

A. Project A.
B. Project B.
C. Both projects equal.

1. Which project would be likely to have the shorter payback period?
2. Which project would have the greater average accounting rate of return?
3. Which project would have the greater internal rate of return?
4. Assume, due to innovation, the projects were to terminate at the end of year 4 with cash flows remaining as projected for the first 4 years and no cash flows in year 5. Which project would have the greater internal rate of return?

Lane College is developing schedules for its overall budget projection for the 1990-91 academic year. Relevant 1989-90 data include:

|  | *Undergraduates* | *Graduates* |
|---|---|---|
| Enrollment | 4,200 | 1,300 |
| Average number of credit hours carried each year per student | 30 | 24 |
| Average number of students per class | 25 | 14 |
| Average faculty teaching load in credit hours per year (number of classes taught multiplied by 3 credit hours per class) | (8 × 3) 24 | (6 × 3) 18 |
| Average faculty salary and benefits | $50,000 | $60,000 |
| Tuition per credit hour (no other fees required) | $ 200 | $ 300 |

Changes projected for 1990-91 and additional information:

1. Enrollments are expected to increase by 5 percent for both undergraduate and graduate programs.
2. Average faculty salary and benefits are expected to increase by 3 percent.
3. Lane has not previously used graduate students for teaching undergraduates, but will do so for 1990-91. All of the projected increased undergraduate enrollment will be taught by graduate students. Lane will recruit these graduate teaching assistants (TA's) in addition to the 5 percent student increase indicated. Each TA will carry half an average graduate student load and half an average faculty teaching load. TA's will receive a full remission of tuition fees and $10,000 in salary and benefits. For budgeting purposes, the tuition remission is considered both a tuition revenue and a tuition scholarship.
4. Non-faculty costs (excluding scholarships) for 1990-91 are to be budgeted by fixed and variable elements derived from estimates of cost at the following two levels of registration:

| Total student credit hours (both schools) | 140,000 | 180,000 |
|---|---|---|
| Total estimated non-faculty costs | $21,960,000 | $22,320,000 |

**Required:**

**a.** Prepare the following 1990-91 budget schedules for each program:
  1. Projected enrollment.
  2. Projected student credit hours.
  3. Projected number of full-time faculty and TA's.
  4. Projected salaries and benefits for full-time faculty and TA's.
  5. Projected tuition revenue.

**b.**  1. Calculate the fixed and variable elements in the non-faculty costs.
  2. Calculate the budgeted non-faculty costs, including scholarships, for the 1990-91 academic year.

# Chapter Eighteen
# Solutions to Managerial Planning and Control Questions

1. (b) The equal periodic payments are an annuity and the $3,000 is the future value of the annuity; therefore, the appropriate table of interest factors is the compound value (future value) of an annuity of $1.

2. (c) Compound value factors are larger than present value factors as they include principal plus interest for a given period. Annuity factors are larger than single sum factors as they represent a series of payments for a period.

3. (d)    PV = FV × PV Factor
          PV = 1000 × .794

4. (a) The present value of an annuity is equal to the sum of the present values of the individual amounts. The first annuity payment was to be made at the beginning of the first year; therefore, its present value was equal to the amount of the payment ($2,000).

5. (c)           PV =  FV × PV Factor
          $3,000 =  FV × .857
             FV =  $3,000 ÷ .857

6. (c) An amount may be compounded or discounted at a given rate of interest to determine its equivalent at another point in time given that rate of interest. This new amount may again be compounded or discounted at the same rate of interest to yield yet another value at another point in time which is equivalent to the original amount given that interest rate used in compounding or discounting.

   The $4,000 is first discounted for 5 years to determine its equivalent at the end of the first year. This amount is then discounted for one year to determine its equivalent at the beginning of the first year. Note that any combination which totaled 6 years could have been used.

7. (a)    1) Payments are to be semi-annual for 20 years. Therefore, there will be 40 payments.
          2) Because the annual interest rate is 6%, the semi-annual rate equals 3%.
          3) Because we are dealing with compounding, we are interested in future values.

Answer (a) is the only choice which reflects 1-3 listed above. If (a) is reduced to a formula, it can be more readily seen that it results in the appropriate answer:

$$\text{Period payment needed} = \frac{\$10,000 \text{ at the end of 20 years}}{40 \text{ payments at 3\%}}$$

8. (d) $11,310

| | |
|---|---|
| Net cash inflow before tax | $ 7500 |
| - Lease amortization | (5000) |
| | $ 2500 |
| - Tax    (2500 x 40%) | (1000) |
| | $ 1500 |
| + Lease amortization | 5000 |
| Net cash inflow after taxes | $ 6500 |
| Present value factor | x  1.74 |
| | $11,310 |

9. (c) A 5-year annuity starting 7/1/87 will have its last payment on 7/1/91. Because the future value of $1,200,000 is on 7/1/92, the annuity is an annuity due or annuity in advance (payment being made at the beginning of the period).

F.V. = Annuity × F.V. factor
Annuity = F.V. ÷ F.V. factor
Annuity = $1,200,000 ÷ 6.34 = <u>$189,274</u>

Note that answer (d) is for an ordinary annuity using 5.87 as the F.V. factor.

10. (c) $26,362
Use the future amount of an ordinary annuity of $1 for ten periods at 6%, or 13.181.
$2,000 × 13.181 = $26,362

11. (c) $20,000 cash flow × 3.791 PVF = $75,820
Cost of machine would be its present value. Therefore, the P.V. annuity factor for 5N is the appropriate factor.

12. (a) The first payment is to be made at the beginning of the first year. Therefore, the appropriate factor is the present value of an annuity due for 5N.

13. (d)  Payment 1/1/X0                                                    $20,000
         Present value of 9 future payments
             $20,000 × 5.328                                              <u>106,560</u>
                                                                          <u>$126,560</u>

             or
         $20,000 × (5.328 + 1.000)                                       <u>$126,560</u>

For present value of annuity due (beginning of year) the factor is the ordinary annuity factor for N-1 plus 1.0000 for the first payment.

14. (c) The true rate of return is that rate which equates the present value of the future returns with the cost of the investment.

PV   = FV × PVIF

120,000   = 20,000 × PVIF

$\frac{120,000}{20,000}$   = PVIF

6.000   = PVIF

As the factor is between the factors for 10% and 12% the rate of return is less than 12% and more than 10%.

15. (c) $195,700.

Future Value =   Annuity × Future Value Factor
$1,000,000 =   Annuity × 5.11
$1,000,000/5.11 =   Annuity
$195,700 =   Annuity

The annuity is an annuity due (in advance) as the payments are made at the beginning of the year (interest period). The last payment would be made on September 1, 1993, the beginning of the last period which ends September 1, 1994. An ordinary annuity would have the last payment at the end of the last period (September 1, 1994).

16. (a)  Before tax annual cash inflow                                       $10,000
         Less: depreciation ($30,000 ÷ 6 yrs.)                                  5,000
         Increase in income before tax                                         5,000
         Less: tax @ 40%                                                        2,000
         Increase in net income after tax                                    $ 3,000

$$\text{Accounting Rate of Return} = \frac{\text{Net Income}}{\text{Investment*}}$$

$$= \frac{3,000}{30,000}$$

$$= \underline{10\%}$$

\* Investment or average investment may be used. Note that the 20% rate of return based on average investment is not provided as an answer. When two or more methods may be used, the exam customarily provides only enough information for one method or only one method's answer.

17. (b)  Increase in net income                                              $3,000
         Add: depreciation expense                                            5,000
         Annual cash flow after tax                                          $8,000

$$\text{Payback period} = \frac{\text{Cost of investment}}{\text{Annual Cash Flow}} = \frac{30,000}{8,000}$$

$$\text{Reciprocal of payback} = \frac{8,000}{30,000} = \underline{.2666}$$

Note: Where the cash flows are uniform and the economic life of the project is at least twice the payback period (not true in this case), the payback reciprocal approximates the rate of return.

18. (b)  Present value of Benefits (Annual Cash Flow)
             8,000 × 3.785 =                                                  $30,280
         Less: Present value of investment                                     30,000
         Net Present Value                                                   $    280

19. (b) The present value factor for an annuity of n years is equal to the sum of the individual, single sum, present value factors for each of the n years. Therefore, the difference between the present value annuity factors for n and n − 1 years is equal to the present value factor of a single sum to be received at the end of the nth year.

         PV annuity factor for 5 years @ 15% =                               3.353
         - PV annuity factor for 4 years @ 15% =                             2.856
         PV factor for a single sum 5 years, 15%                              .497

The present value of 30,000 to be received 5 years from now given an interest rate of 15% compounded annually is determined as follows:

         PV =    FV × PV factor
         PV =    $30,000 × .497
         PV =    $14,910

20. (d) $30,000 Residual income

Residual income is income from which an imputed interest charge for invested capital is deducted.

| | |
|---|---|
| Darwin Division income | $40,000 |
| Less imputed interest on investment | |
| 10% x $100,000 | 10,000 |
| Residual income | $30,000 |

Invested Capital:

| | | | | |
|---|---|---|---|---|
| Capital turnover | = | Sales / Capital | = | 4 |
| 4 | = | $400,000 / Capital | | |
| Capital | = | $400,000 / 4 | = | $100,000 |

21. (d) The internal rate of return method determines an investment's rate of return which is compared with a "specified rate of return" to determine acceptability. The IRR of an investment is that discount rate which equates the present value of the benefits to be received (cash flows) from the investment with the cost of the investment (initial cash outlay).

The net present value of an investment is the present value of the cash flows of an investment, discounted at a "specified rate of return,*" less the cost of the investment (initial cash outlay). Investments with NPV equal to or greater than zero are earning a rate of return equal to (NPV=0) or greater than (NPV>0) the discount rate used.

* The specified rate of return used is normally the cost of capital; however, other rates may be used.

22. (b) An investment's residual income is the accounting income from the investment less an allowance for a return **on** investment (invested capital).

23. (d) $13,000 net present value.

| | |
|---|---|
| Present value of benefit* | |
| $20,000 × 5.65 | $113,000 |
| – Investment (present value) | 100,000 |
| Net present value | $ 13,000 |

* The accounting rate of return may also be based on average investment (Investment/2).

24. (d) 5.0 year payback period.

$$\text{Payback period} = \frac{\text{Investment cost}}{\text{Annual cash flows}}$$

$$= \frac{\$100,000}{\$ 20,000} = 5.0 \text{ years}$$

25. (d) 10% accounting rate of return

$$\text{Accounting rate of return} = \frac{\text{Average net income per year}}{\text{Investment*}}$$

$$= \frac{\$ 10,000}{\$100,000}$$

$$= 10\%$$

Average annual net income:

| | |
|---|---|
| After tax annual cash savings | $20,000 |
| Less: depreciation expense | |
| $100,000 ÷ 10 years | (10,000) |
| Annual net income after tax | $10,000 |

* The accounting rate of return may also be based on average investment (Investment/2).

26. (c) 5.0 internal rate of return factor.
The internal rate of return (time adjusted rate of return) is that discount rate at which the present value of the benefits equals the cost of the investment.

$$\text{Present value of benefit} = \text{Investment}$$
$$\$20,000 \text{ benefit} \times \text{PV factor} = \$100,000$$
$$\text{PV factor} = \$100,000/\$20,000 = \underline{5.0}$$

27. (d) The payback period is the time needed to receive cash flow equal to the investment.
Investment = $6,000

Cash Flow =

| | |
|---|---:|
| Additional revenue per year | $1,200 |
| Less: Depreciation ($6,000 ÷ 10) | 600 |
| Additional income | 600 |
| Tax at 50% | 300 |
| Additional net income | 300 |
| Add: Depreciation (non-cash) | 600 |
| Cash flow per year | $ 900 |

$$\text{Payback} = \frac{\text{Investment}}{\text{Cash Flow}} = \frac{\$6,000}{900} = 6.7 \text{ years.}$$

28. (a)

$$\text{Accounting (unadjusted) rate of return} = \frac{\text{Average net income per year}}{\text{Investment}}$$
$$= \frac{\$300}{\$6,000}$$
$$= 5\%$$

29. (d) The internal rate of return of an investment is that discount rate which equates the present value of the benefits to be received (cash flows) from the investment with the cost of the investment (initial cash outlay). Residual sales value of a profit (salvage value) is an estimated cash flow in the last year of a project's expected economic life, and as such would be included in the project's benefits. Depreciation expense is not a cash flow item, therefore, it would be excluded in the calculation of the internal rate of return.

30. (b) 4.6 years.

| | |
|---|---:|
| Cash flow | $9,000 |
| Less: Depreciation 36,000 ÷ 6 | 6,000 |
| Taxable portion | $3,000 |
| Income tax @ 40% | 1,200 |
| Net cash flow $9,000 – $1,200 | 7,800 |

Payback: Investment $36,000 ÷ 7,800 = 4.6 years.

31. (a) $59.
P.V. of annuity of $1 in arrears at 8% for 6 years—4.623
Net cash flow $9,000 – $1,200 = $7,800

| | |
|---|---:|
| P.V. of cash flow | $7,800 × 4.623 = $36,059 |
| Investment | 36,000 |
| Net present value | $    59 |

32. (b) Less than 10%, but more than 0%.
The present value of a cash flow of $10,000 per year for 5 years at 10% is $10,000 × 3.791 or $37,910. The present value must equal or exceed $40,000, the amount of the investment to equal a return of 10% or more.

33. (b) Both the internal rate of return method and the net present value method of capital budgeting employ compound interest computations and tables, and these tables explicitly assume reinvestment at the interest rate used (refer to construction of compound interest tables in text). The net present value method uses the cost of capital as the discount rate and therefore assumes reinvestment at this rate which is the minimum rate of return allowable from investments. The internal rate of return provides for a discount rate equal to the rate of return earned by the project, which may be equal to, greater than, or less than the minimum rate of return allowable from investment. Therefore, the internal rate of return allows for reinvestment at a rate which may be greater or less than the minimum rate assured on investments.

34. (c) $62,900.

| Period | Annuity | | P.V. Factor | | Present Value |
|--------|---------|---|-------------|---|---------------|
| 1-3 | $20,000 | x | 2.32 | = | $46,400 |
| 1-2 | 10,000 | x | 1.65 | = | 16,500 |
| | | | | | $62,900 |

or

| Period | Annuity | | P.V. Factor | | Present Value |
|--------|---------|---|-------------|---|---------------|
| 1-2 | $30,000 | x | 1.65 | = | $49,500 |
| 3 | 20,000 | x | .67* | = | 13,400 |
| | | | | | $62,900 |

* 3rd period factor = 2.32 (3 period annuity factor)
- 1.65 (2 period annuity factor)
.67 (3 period single sum factor)

35. (b)

| Cost of machine | | $30,000 |
|-----------------|---|---------|
| Less: Cash flow | | |
| First 3 years $7,000 × 3 | $21,000 | |
| 4th year | 5,500 | 26,500 |
| Required cash flow Year 5 | | $ 3,500 |

36. (a) $144,000 residual income.
Residual income is income from which an imputed interest charge for invested capital is deducted.

| Sales | | | $500,000 |
|-------|---|---|----------|
| Less: | Variable costs | $300,000 | |
| | Traceable fixed costs | 50,000 | 350,000 |
| Division income | | | $150,000 |
| Less: | Imputed interest on investment | | |
| | $100,000 av. investment × 6% | | 6,000 |
| Residual income | | | $144,000 |

37. (b)

| Present value of benefits: | |
|----------------------------|---|
| $70,000 × 4.111 | $287,770 |
| Less: Cost of investment | 240,000 |
| Net present value | $ 47,770 |

38. (c) The internal rate of return method provides for a discount rate equal to the rate of return earned by the investment or project. Compound interest computations and tables employed by the internal rate of return method explicitly assume reinvestment at the interest rate used (refer to construction of compound interest tables in text).

39. (c) The ratio to determine the accounting rate of return is the annual operating income from the investment divided by either the initial increase or average investment. The numerator in this problem is $40,000.

40. (b)   Net cash flow after taxes                        $25,000
          Less depreciation expense ($100,000 ÷ 10)         10,000
          Net income after taxes                           $15,000

          Accounting Rate of Return =   Net income ÷ initial investment
          (based on initial investment)

                                      =   $15,000 ÷ $100,000
                                      =   15%

41. (c) The Net Present Value method discounts future cash flow benefits using the cost of capital as the discount rate. Answer (a) is incorrect as the payback method does not employ a discount rate. Answers (b) and (d) are incorrect as they are the same method and it solves for the discount rate which equates the investment cost and the future cash benefits.

42. (a)        Rate of return on investment =   ___Net income___
                                                 Average investment

                                             =   $20,000 ÷ $50,000

                                             =   40%

          Sales                      $620,000
          Less:    Variable costs    (500,000)
                   Traceable fixed cost  (100,000)
          Net income                 $ 20,000

43. (c)   Net income (refer above)                          $20,000
          Less: Allowance for return on investment
                   (18% × $50,000)                            9,000
          Residual income                                   $11,000

44. (a) The payback method is the original investment divided by cash flow after taxes, or $5,000 divided by $2,000 for a payback of 2.5 years. Payback does **not** utilize discounted cash flows, so the information regarding the time value of money is not needed to solve the problem.

45. (d) A, Accept; B, Reject.
Residual income is income from which an imputed interest charge for invested capital is deducted. Division A's project will earn a rate of return greater than the imputed interest charge for invested capital; therefore, it will have a positive residual income. Division B's project will have a negative residual income as the project's rate of return is less than the imputed interest charge for invested capital. If the objective is to maximize residual income, Division A's project should be accepted and Division B's project rejected.

46. (c) The net present value method discounts future cash inflows by a predetermined percentage (12%) and compares that amount to the cash outlay to acquire the investment. If there is a positive NPV, it means the rate of return is greater than the state hurdle rate.

47. (d) Computation of February cash collections:
          Accounts receivable from January sales            $ 38,000
          Collections on February sales (60% × $110,000)      66,000
          Budgeted cash collections for February            $104,000

48. (c) Computation of February Net Income:

| | | |
|---|---:|---:|
| Sales | | $110,000 |
| Less: Cost of goods sold ($110,000 × 75%) | | 82,500 |
| Gross profit | | $ 27,500 |
| Less: Other expenses | $16,500 | |
| Depreciation | 5,000 | |
| Bad debts ($110,000 × 2%) | 2,200 | 23,700 |
| Net income | | $ 3,800 |

49. (c) Purchases are 75% of the following months' sales and are paid for in the following month.

75% × $120,000 March sales = $90,000

Purchases in February and accounts payable at Feb. 29

50. (c) $306,000.

| | | |
|---|---:|---:|
| Cost of goods sold | | $300,000 |
| + Increase in inventory ($30,000 vs. $42,000) | | 12,000 |
| Purchases | | $312,000 |
| - Increase in accounts payable: | | |
| Beginning balance | $20,000 | |
| Ending balance (312,000 ÷ 12) | 26,000 | (6,000) |
| Cash Payments for purchases | | $306,000 |

51. (c) $88,100

| | | |
|---|---|---:|
| May cash collected | 12% × $100,000 | $12,000 |
| April collections | 75% × 90,000 | 67,500 |
| March collections | 6% × 80,000 | 4,800 |
| February collections | 4% × 95,000 | 3,800 |
| | | $88,100 |

52. (d) To determine cash disbursements, we need to look at costs or expenses. The gross margin is 40%, which means the cost of goods sold is 60% (1.00 less 40%). To that we add or subtract cash payments needed to change asset or liability accounts.

| | |
|---|---:|
| Sales | $2,800,000 |
| Cost of goods sold % | 60% |
| Cost of goods sold | $1,680,000 |
| Less: cost of inventory on hand used | (70,000) |
| Add: cash paid to reduce accounts payable | 150,000 |
| | $1,760,000 |

53. (c) By definition.

54. (c) $629,000

Cash requirements for merchandise:

| | | |
|---|---:|---:|
| Sales | $700,000 | |
| Gross profit @ 30% | 210,000 | |
| Cost of sales | $490,000 | |
| Increase in inventory | 10,000 | $500,000 |
| Total SG&A expense: | | |
| $71,000 + (15% × $700,000) = | $176,000 | |
| Less: Charge for uncollectibles: | | |
| 1% × 700,000 | (7,000) | |
| Depreciation | (40,000) | 129,000 |
| Total cash requirements | | $629,000 |

The increase in accounts receivable does not require a cash outlay beyond that included in the cost of sales.

55. (c) The master budget is the budget plan for a planned level of operation.
Flexible budgeting is a reporting system wherein the planned level of activity is adjusted to the actual level of activity before the budget to actual comparison report is prepared.

56. (d) Collection on credit sales of

| | |
|---|---:|
| May 20% × $200,000 | $ 40,000 |
| April 70% × $150,000 | 105,000 |
| Prior to April | 12,000 |
| | $157,000 |

57. (c)

| | | |
|---|---:|---|
| Sales | 125,000 | units |
| Less: Decrease in finished goods inventory | (7,500) | units |
| Required production | 117,500 | units |
| Add: Increase in work-in-process | | |
| (8,000 × 75%) | 6,000 | E.F.U. |
| Production required | 123,500 | E.F.U. |

(E.F.U. = Equivalent Finished Units)

58. (c) 186,000 Kilos

| | | |
|---|---:|---|
| Budgeted sales - Oct. | 53,000 | units |
| + Budgeted increase in finished goods inventory | 6,000 | |
| Budgeted production - Oct. | 59,000 | |
| Kilos per Loire per unit | x 4 | |
| Budget Loire required in production | 236,000 | Kilos |
| - Budgeted decrease in Loire inventory | (50,000) | |
| Budgeted purchases of Loire - Oct. | 186,000 | Kilos |

59. (a) Estimated May cash disbursements for inventory: Cost of goods sold

| | |
|---|---:|
| $3,000,000 sale × 75%* | $2,250,000 |
| Less decrease in inventory | (140,000) |
| Purchases of inventory | $2,110,000 |
| Add decrease in accounts payable | 240,000 |
| Total May disbursements for inventory | $2,350,000 |

* If the gross profit is 25% of sales, cost of goods sold is 75% of sales (100% – 25%).

60. (b)

| | | |
|---|---|---|
| Sales | 250,000 | units |
| +Ending inventory—finished goods | 60,000 | " |
| –Beginning inventory—finished goods | (75,000) | " |
| Required production | 235,000 | " |
| +Ending inventory—work in process (16,000 × 75%) | 12,000 | EFU |
| -Beginning inventory—work in process | —0— | |
| Production required | 247,000 | EFU |

61. (a) The E.O.Q. formula is:  $EOQ = \sqrt{\dfrac{2SO}{C}}$ , where

$S$ = Total units sold / Demand during the period
$O$ = Ordering costs per order
$C$ = Carrying cost per unit

Periodic demand (S) for the goods is assumed to be known. Carrying costs and ordering costs are assumed to be constant. Therefore, answers (b) and (c) and incorrect. Purchase cost per unit is not part of the EOQ model; therefore, answer (d) is incorrect.

62. (c) Perfection, ignoring safety stocks, is to replenish supplies as they reach zero level.

63. (c) The economic order quantity is based upon demand (usage or sales), ordering cost per order (assumed constant) and carrying cost per unit of inventory (assumed constant).

$$EOQ = \sqrt{\dfrac{2SO}{C}} \text{ , where}$$

$S$ = units sold or manufactured
$O$ = cost per order (set-up cost)
$C$ = cost of carrying one unit in inventory

64. (b) 10,000 units ordered ÷ 2 = 5,000 units average inventory.

65. (a) Number of orders =  $\dfrac{\text{Total Usage}}{\text{Units per order}} = \dfrac{2,000,000 \text{ units}}{10,000 \text{ units}} = 200 \text{ orders}$ 

Ordering costs = # orders × cost per order = 200 × $80 = $16,000

66. (a) A LIFO or FIFO inventory method will have no effect on the EOQ, because EOQ does not deal with pricing of inventory. It merely indicates the amount of inventory which should be purchased at one time in order to minimize carrying and ordering costs.

67. (c)

$Q$ = Annual quantity in units
$P$ = Cost of placing an order
$S$ = Annual cost of storage for one unit

$$EOQ = \sqrt{\dfrac{2QP}{S}}$$

$$= \sqrt{\dfrac{2 \times 36,000 \times \$10}{\$.40 + (10\% \times \$20)}}$$

$$= \sqrt{300,000}$$

$$= \text{approximately 548}$$

*Note that the annual cost of storage includes rent, taxes, insurance, etc., plus the cost of borrowing or the return that could be earned by an alternate investment of funds.*

68. (d) Total annual inventory expenses:
    1) Order costs:

|  |  |  |
|---|---|---|
| Number of orders (36,000 ÷ 800) = | 45 |  |
| Cost per order | × $10 | $ 450 |

    2) Inventory costs:

|  |  |  |
|---|---|---|
| Average inventory (800 × 2) = | 400 units |  |
| Cost of storage for one unit | × $2.40 | 960 |
|  |  | $1,410 |

69. (b) JIT inventory system results in more frequent, small orders and ideally eliminates inventory. A decrease in purchase order costs and/or an increase in inventory carry costs would make JIT more attractive.

70. (d) 693.

$$EOQ = \sqrt{\frac{2SO}{C}} = \sqrt{\frac{2(40,000)(\$60)}{\$10}}$$

$$EOQ = \sqrt{\frac{4,800,000}{10}} = \sqrt{480,000} = 693$$

The above may also be accomplished by trial and error as follows:

| *Cost of ordering:* | *Cost of carrying:* |
|---|---|
| (a) 40,000 ÷ 400 = 100 orders × $60 = $6,000 | 400 ÷ 2 = 200 × $10 = $2,000 |
| (b) 40,000 ÷ 490 = 86 orders × $60 = $4,898 | 490 ÷ 2 = 245 × $10 = $2,450 |
| (c) 40,000 ÷ 600 = 67 orders × $60 = $4,000 | 600 ÷ 2 = 300 × $10 = $3,000 |
| (d) 40,000 ÷ 693 = 57 orders × $60 = $3,420 | 693 ÷ 2 = 347 × $10 = $3,470 |

71. (d)

$$EOQ = \sqrt{\frac{2 \cdot S \cdot O}{C}}$$

$$200 = \sqrt{\frac{2 \cdot 4000 \cdot 2}{C}}$$

$$40,000 = \frac{16,000}{C}$$

$$C = \underline{\$.40}$$

72. (d) 7,200 annual usage ÷ 240 days = 30 units per day
Reorder point equals maximum usage during lead time

|  |  |
|---|---|
| 30 units per day × 45 days = | 1350 |

Safety stock equals the difference between maximum and normal usage during lead time.

|  |  |
|---|---|
| Maximum usage | 1350 |
| Normal usage 30 × 20 days | 600 |
|  | 750 |

73. (d)

|  |  |
|---|---|
| Annual usage | 10,000 |
| Work days per year | ÷ 250 |
| Average usage per day | 40 |
| Lead time (days) | × 30 |
| Average usage during lead time | 1,200 |
| Plus safety stock | 400 |
| Reorder point | 1,600 |

74. (b) The economic order quantity formula can be used to determine the optimum size of either a production run or purchase order. For production runs, the costs associated with setting up a production run are used in the numerator as "O". For purchase orders, the costs associated with placing an order are used in the numerator as "O".

75. (a) A just-in-time operation generally improves quality as defective inventory must be corrected immediately; there are no inventory pools to hold defective units. Therefore, inspection costs should decrease with a J.I.T. operation.

J.I.T. operations simplify accounting by charging costs directly to cost of goods sold (no inventory). If inventory exists, the inventory is "backed out" of the cost of goods sold account. Backing the inventory amount out of cost of goods sold is referred to as **backflush** accounting. This process decreases the detail of costs tracked to jobs.

# Chapter Eighteen
# Solutions to Managerial Planning and Control Problems

## NUMBER 1

1. *Sales Budget—19X8*

| | Units | Price | Total |
|---|---|---|---|
| Thingone | 60,000 | $70 | $4,200,000 |
| Thingtwo | 40,000 | $100 | 4,000,000 |
| Projected sales | | | $8,200,000 |

2. *Production Budget (in units)—19X8*

| | Thingone | Thingtwo |
|---|---|---|
| Projected sales | 60,000 | 40,000 |
| Desired inventories December 31, 19X8 | 25,000 | 9,000 |
| | 85,000 | 49,000 |
| Less expected inventories, January 1, 19X8 | 20,000 | 8,000 |
| Production required (units) | 65,000 | 41,000 |

3. *Raw materials budget (in quantities)—19X8*

| | Raw Material | | |
|---|---|---|---|
| | *A* | *B* | *C* |
| Thingone (65,000 units projected to be produced) | 260,000 | 130,000 | — |
| Thingtwo (41,000 units projected to be produced) | 205,000 | 123,000 | 41,000 |
| Production requirements | 465,000 | 253,000 | 41,000 |
| Add desired inventories, December 31, 19X8 | 36,000 | 32,000 | 7,000 |
| Total requirements | 501,000 | 285,000 | 48,000 |
| Less expected inventories, January 1, 19X8 | 32,000 | 29,000 | 6,000 |
| Purchase requirements (units) | 469,000 | 256,000 | 42,000 |

4. *Raw Materials Purchase Budget—19X8*

| Raw material required (units) | Anticipated purchase price | Total |
|---|---|---|
| A—469,000 | $8 | $3,752,000 |
| B—256,000 | $5 | $1,280,000 |
| C— 42,000 | $3 | $ 126,000 |

5. *Direct Labor Budget—19X8*

| | Projected production (units) | Hours per unit | Total | Rate | Total |
|---|---|---|---|---|---|
| Thingone | 65,000 | 2 | 130,000 | $3 | $390,000 |
| Thingtwo | 41,000 | 3 | 123,000 | $4 | $492,000 |
| | | | | | $882,000 |

6. _Budgeted Finished Goods Inventory—December 31, 19X8_

_Thingone_

| | | | |
|---|---|---|---|
| Raw materials | | | |
| A—4 pounds @ $8 | $32 | | |
| B—2 pounds @ $5 | $10 | $42 | |
| Direct labor—2 hours @ $3 | | 6 | |
| Overhead—2 hours @ $2 per | | | |
| direct labor hour | | 4 | |
| | | $52 | |
| $52 × 25,000 units = | | | $1,300,000 |

_Thingtwo_

| | | | |
|---|---|---|---|
| Raw materials | | | |
| A—5 pounds @ $8 | $40 | | |
| B—3 pounds @ $5 | $15 | | |
| C—1 each @ $3 | $ 3 | $58 | |
| Direct labor—3 hours @ $4 | | 12 | |
| Overhead—3 hours @ $2 per | | | |
| direct labor hour | | 6 | |
| | | $76 | |
| $76 × 9,000 units = | | | 684,000 |
| Budgeted finished goods inventory, December 31, 19X8 | | | $1,984,000 |

# NUMBER 2

1.  The advantages of the payback method are these:
    - It is simple to compute.
    - It is easy to understand.
    - It may be used to select those investments yielding a quick return of cash.
    - It permits a company to determine the length of time required to recapture its original investment.
    - The reciprocal of the payback period may be used under certain conditions as a rough approximation of the rate of return calculated by the internal rate-of-return method. The approximation is valid when the project's life is long, approximately double or more that of the payback period, and when the annual savings and/or cash inflow are relatively uniform in amount.

    The disadvantages of the payback method are these:
    - It ignores the time value of money.
    - It ignores cash flow, including salvage value, which may be produced beyond the payback period.

2.  Other capital budgeting techniques that could be used are the accounting rate-of-return (average annual return on investment) method, and the two discounted cash flow methods—net present value and internal rate of return.

# NUMBER 3

1.

*Montero Corporation*
**EXPECTED CASH COLLECTIONS**
*May 1982*

| Month | Sales | Percent | Expected collections |
|-------|-------|---------|----------------------|
| March | $60,000 | 9 | $ 5,400 |
| April | 78,000 | 20 | 15,600 |
| May | 66,000 | 70 | 46,200 |
| Total | | | $67,200 |

2.

*Montero Corporation*
**EXPECTED CASH DISBURSEMENTS**
*May 1982*

| | |
|---|---|
| April purchases to be paid in May | $54,000 |
| Less: 2% cash discount | 1,080 |
| Net | $52,920 |
| Cash disbursements for expenses | 14,400 |
| Total | $67,320 |

3.

*Montero Corporation*
**EXPECTED CASH BALANCE**
*May 31, 1982*

| | | |
|---|---|---|
| Balance, May 1 | | $22,000 |
| Expected collections | $67,200 | |
| Expected disbursements | 67,320 | (120) |
| Expected balance | | $21,880 |

# NUMBER 4

1.  Both the net present value method and the internal rate-of-return method have the following advantages over the payback method:
    - Consider the time value of money.
    - Consider cash flow over the entire life of the project.

2.  The limitations of the net present value method are as follows:
    - It is more difficult to use than other less sophisticated capital budgeting techniques.
    - The discount rate (hurdle rate of return) must be determined in advance.
    - Certainty about cash flow is assumed.
    - Cash flows are reinvested at the discount rate (hurdle rate of return).

3.  The limitations of the internal rate-of-return method are as follows:
    - It is more difficult to use than other less sophisticated capital budgeting techniques.
    - Cash flows are reinvested at the rate earned by the investment.
    - Certainty about cash flow is assumed.

4.  Depreciation is excluded from the calculations for both the net present value method and the internal rate-of-return method. Deduction of depreciation would constitute a double-counting of a cost that has already been considered as a lump-sum outflow (the initial cost of the asset). Both the net present value method and the internal rate-of-return method focus on cash flow, while depreciation is an allocation of past cost and is not a cash flow.

# NUMBER 5

**a.**

*Spara Corp.*
**RELEVANT ANNUAL AFTER-TAX CASH FLOWS**
**CAD/CAM PROJECT**

| | | |
|---|---:|---:|
| Savings on elimination of current manual system (20,000 hrs. @ $20) | | $400,000 |
| Operating costs of CAD/CAM system | $200,000 | |
| Depreciation of CAD/CAM system ($480,000/6) | 80,000 | 280,000 |
| Pre-tax savings | | 120,000 |
| Less income taxes ($120,000 × 30%) | | 36,000 |
| Increase in reported income | | 84,000 |
| Add depreciation | | 80,000 |
| Increase in annual net cash flows | | $164,000 |

**b.1.**

**PAYBACK PERIOD**

Cost, $480,000/Increase in annual net cash flows, $164,000 — 2.93 years

**b.2.**

**INTERNAL RATE OF RETURN**

| Rate | Annual cash flows | Factor | Present value | Investment | Difference |
|---|---|---|---|---|---|
| 24% | $164,000 | 3.020 | $495,280 | $480,000 | $15,280 |
| 26% | 164,000 | 2.885 | 473,140 | | |
| 2% | | | $ 22,140 | | |

Interpolation:

$$\frac{15,280}{22,140} \times .02 = .0138$$

Internal rate of return (.24 + .0138) = 25.38%

**b.3.**

**NET PRESENT VALUE**

| | |
|---|---:|
| Present value of annual net cash flows ($164,000 × 3.326) | $545,464 |
| Less investment | 480,000 |
| Net present value | $ 65,464 |

**b.4.**

**EXCESS PRESENT VALUE INDEX**

| | | | |
|---|---:|---|---:|
| Present value of annual net cash flows | $545,464 | = | 114% |
| Investment | $480,000 | | |

# NUMBER 6

1.  B. The payback period is the time needed to receive net cash inflows from an investment equal to the initial cash outflow for the investment. Projects A and B have the same initial investment requirements and lives. Diagram I shows Project B produces most of its net cash inflows in the first three years and that this amount is substantially greater than that of Project A during this time. Although Project A provides the greater total net cash inflows, most of it is produced during the last two years. Therefore, it is most likely that Project B has the shorter payback period.

2.  A. The Average Accounting Rate of Return is equal to the average annual net income divided by the average investment. As Projects A and B have the same initial investment requirements and lives, they will have the same depreciation expense and average investment. As Project A has the greater total net cash inflow, it will have the greater average annual income and greater Average Accounting Rate of Return.

3.  B. The Internal Rate of Return is the discount rate which produces a zero net present value for an investment. Diagram II shows Project A has a zero N.P.V. at approximately 16% and Project B has a zero N.P.V. at approximately 22%. Project B has the greater internal rate of return.

4.  B. If the projects were to terminate at the end of four years, Project A would lose its greatest cash flows while Project B would lose its smallest cash flows. When discounted, Project A would have the greatest loss in present value; therefore, Project B would still have the greater present value and internal rate of return.


# NUMBER 7

**a.** 1.

*Lane College*
## PROJECTED ENROLLMENT
*For the Academic Year 1990-91*

|  | *Undergraduate* | *Graduate* | *Total* |
|---|---|---|---|
| Enrollment for 1989-90 | 4,200 | 1,300 | 5,500 |
| Projected increase for 1990-91—5% | 210 | 65 | 275 |
| TA enrollment for 1990-91 | | | |
|   Average number of undergraduate | | | |
|     students per class — 25 | | | |
|   Average faculty teaching load | | | |
|     in credit hours — × 24 | | | |
|   Product — 600 | | | |
|   One-half — 300 | | | |
|   Projected increase in undergraduate | | | |
|     enrollment for 1990-91 — 210 | | | |
|   Average number of credit hours carried | | | |
|     by each undergraduate student — × 30 | | | |
|   Product — 6,300 | | | |
| TA enrollment (6,300/300) | | 21 | 21 |
| Total expected enrollment | 4,410 | 1,386 | 5,796 |

**a. 2.**

*Lane College*
## PROJECTED STUDENT CREDIT HOURS
*For the Academic Year 1990-91*

|  | *Undergraduate* | *Graduate* | *Total* |
|---|---|---|---|
| Expected enrollment, excluding TA's | 4,410 | 1,365 | 5,775 |
| Average number of credit hours carried by each student | × 30 | × 24 | |
| Credit hours, excluding TA's | 132,300 | 32,760 | 165,060 |
| TA credit hours [21 × (½ of 24)] | | 252 | 252 |
| Total student credit hours | 132,300 | 33,012 | 165,312 |

**a. 3.**

*Lane College*
## PROJECTED NUMBER OF FULL-TIME FACULTY AND TA'S
*For the Academic Year 1990-91*

|  |  | *Full-time* | *TA's* |
|---|---|---|---|
| *For undergraduate program* | | | |
| Enrollment for 1989-90 | 4,200 | | |
| Average number of credit hours carried by each student | × 30 | | |
| Total undergraduate credit hours | 126,000 | | |
| | | | |
| Average number of undergraduate students per class | 25 | | |
| Average faculty teaching load in credit hours | × 24 | | |
| Total credit hours taught by faculty | 600 | | |
| | | | |
| Required full-time faculty (126,000/600) | | 210 | |
| TA's for projected increase in undergraduate enrollment for 1990-91: | | | |
|     Projected enrollment increase | 210 | | |
|     Average number of credit hours carried by each student | × 30 | | |
|     Increased number of credit hours | 6,300 | | |
|     Average faculty teaching load | 600 | | |
|     One-half carried by TA's | × .5 | | |
|     TA teaching load | 300 | | |
| | | | |
| Required number of TA's (6,300/300) | | | 21 |
| | | | |
| *For graduate program* | | | |
| Enrollment for 1990-91 (excluding TA's) | 1,365 | | |
| Average number of credit hours carried by each student | × 24 | | |
| Graduate credit hours (excluding TA's) | 32,760 | | |
| TA credit hours [21 × (½ of 24)] | 252 | | |
| Total graduate credit hours | 33,012 | | |
| | | | |
| Average number of students per class | 14 | | |
| Average faculty teaching load | × 18 | | |
| Total credit hours taught by faculty | 252 | | |
| | | | |
| Required full-time faculty (33,012/252) | | 131 | |
| Total required full-time faculty and TA's | | 341 | 21 |

**a. 4.**

*Lane College*
**PROJECTED SALARIES AND BENEFITS
FOR FULL-TIME FACULTY AND TA'S**
*For the Academic Year 1990-91*

|  | *Faculty* | | |
|  | *Undergraduate* | *Graduate* | *Total* |
|---|---|---|---|
| Full-time 210 × ($50,000 × 1.03) | $10,815,000 |  | $10,815,000 |
| TA's 21 × $10,000 | 210,000 |  | 210,000 |
| Full-time 131 × ($60,000 × 1.03) |  | $8,095,800 | 8,095,800 |
| Total salaries and benefits | $11,025,000 | $8,095,800 | $19,120,800 |

**a. 5.**

*Lane College*
**PROJECTED TUITION REVENUE**
*For the Academic Year 1990-91*

*Undergraduate*
132,300 student credit hours × $200 per credit hour $26,460,000
*Graduate*
33,012 student credit hours × $300 per credit hour 9,903,600
Total projected tuition revenue $36,363,600

**b. 1.**

*Lane College*
**FIXED AND VARIABLE ELEMENTS
IN NON-FACULTY COSTS**
*For the Academic Year 1990-91*

| Estimated non-faculty costs at level of | 180,000 | credit hours | $22,320,000 |
|---|---|---|---|
| Estimated non-faculty costs at level of | 140,000 | credit hours | 21,960,000 |
| Difference between two levels | 40,000 |  | $ 360,000 |

Variable costs per credit hour = 360,000/40,000 = $9
Fixed costs = $22,320,000 – $9 (180,000) = $20,700,000
or
$21,960,000 – $9 (140,000) = $20,700,000

**b. 2.**

*Lane College*
**BUDGETED NON-FACULTY COSTS**
*For the Academic Year 1990-91*

| Fixed costs | $20,700,000 |
|---|---|
| Variable costs (165,312 credit hours × $9) | 1,487,808 |
| Scholarships (21 TA's × 12 credits × $300 per credit) | 75,600 |
| Total budgeted non-faculty costs | $22,263,408 |

# Chapter Nineteen
# Governmental Accounting

# Chapter Nineteen
# Governmental Accounting

## OVERVIEW
Governmental Accounting is the accounting for state and local governments. Its generally accepted accounting principles are established by the Governmental Accounting Standards Board (GASB) which is the public sector equivalent of the FASB. The Accounting procedures are established based on the perceived needs of the financial statement **users** as well as the underlying nature of the reporting units.

## Primary Users of Governmental Financial Statements
GASB Concepts Statement #1 lists the following three groups as primary users of financial statements:

1. **Citizenry** – Want to evaluate the likelihood of tax or service fee increases, to forecast revenues in order to influence spending decisions, to ensure that resources were used in accordance with appropriations, to assess financial condition, and to compare budgeted to actual results.

2. **Legislative and oversite bodies** – Want to assess the overall financial condition when developing budgets and program recommendations, to monitor operating results to assure compliance with mandates, to determine the reasonableness of fees and the need for tax changes, and to ascertain the ability to finance new programs and financial needs.

3. **Investors and creditors** – Want to know the amount of available and likely future financial resources, to measure the debt position and the ability to service that debt, and to review operating results and cash flow data.

## Goals of Governmental Reporting
- The goal of making the government accountable to the public is the one goal that has been constant over the years. This goal should assist users in making economic, social and political decisions.

- **Interperiod equity** is an important component of accountability that is fundamental to public administration (Balance Budget Concept).

  Financial resources received by a government during a period should suffice to pay for the services provided during that period. Moreover, debt should be repaid during the probable period of usefulness of the assets acquired. Thus, financial reporting should help taxpayers assess whether future taxpayers will have to assume burdens for services already provided.

## Primary Accounting Emphasis
The primary accounting emphasis has traditionally been directed toward answering the following three basic questions:

1. Where did the financial resources come from?
2. Where did the financial resources go?
3. What amount of financial resources is presently held?

## FUND ACCOUNTING
One of the most unique aspects of governmental accounting is the use of fund accounting. Each fund is a **separate accounting entity** and all the funds taken together make up the government's financial reporting system. The GASB defines a fund as an independent fiscal and accounting entity with a self-balancing set of accounts recording cash and other financial resources together with all related liabilities and residual equities or balances and changes therein which are segregated for the purpose of carrying on specific activities or attaining certain objectives in accordance with special regulations, restrictions, or limitations.

# TYPES OF FUNDS

Three major categories of funds and one category of account groups should be used in accounting for governmental financial operations:

| **Governmental Funds** | **Proprietary Funds** | **Fiduciary Funds** |
|---|---|---|
| (Expendable) | (Non Expendable) | |

### Governmental Funds (Expendable)

1. **General Fund**

2. **Special Revenues**

3. **Capital Projects Fund**

4. **Debt Service Fund**

### Proprietary Funds (Non Expendable)

1. **Enterprise Fund**

   (Activities which benefit the population and are supported by user fees)

2. **Internal Service**

   (Provides services of facilities to other departments within the government)

### Fiduciary Funds

1. **Trust Funds**

   A. *Expendable*
   Use modified accrual

   Accounting is like a governmental fund

   B. *Non-Expendable*
   Use accrual basis

   Accounting is like a proprietary fund

   C. **Pension Funds**

   Accounts for contributions and payments for employee retirement plan

2. **Agency Fund**

   Only assets and liabilities; no equity, revenue, or expenditure accounts

## *Characteristics of Funds:*

A. All use Modified Accrual since they are expendable.
B. Records Budget – EXCEPT Debt Service Fund.
C. Encumbrance System – Funds are committed (ear-marked) EXCEPT Debt Service.
D. No fixed assets exist.
E. No Long term debt exists.

## *Accounting*

A. Accrual
B. Like a corporation
C. Equity includes RE and contributed capital

## *Self Balancing Group of Accounts*
(Not funds)

1. Fixed Assets Group
2. Long Term Debt Group

1. **GOVERNMENTAL FUNDS**—often called "expendable"—are those through which most governmental functions typically are financed. The acquisition, use and balances of the government's expendable financial resources and the related current liabilities—except those accounted for in proprietary funds—are accounted for through governmental funds (General, Special Revenue, Capital Projects, and Debt Service Funds).

Governmental funds are, in essence, accounting segregations of financial resources. Expendable assets are assigned to the various governmental funds according to the purposes for which they may or must be used; current liabilities are assigned to the fund from which they are paid; and the difference between assets and liabilities is the fund equity, referred to as "Fund Balance."

The governmental fund measurement focus is based upon determination of **financial position and changes in financial position** (sources, uses, and balances of financial resources), rather than upon net income determination. **The statement of revenues, expenditures, and changes in fund balance is the primary governmental fund operating statement.** It may be supported or supplemented by more detailed schedules of revenues, expenditures, transfers, and other changes in fund balance.

> **GENERAL FUND**—to account for all financial activities and resources not required to be accounted for in another fund. All accounts are "current".
>
> **SPECIAL REVENUE FUNDS**—to account for the proceeds of specific revenue sources (other than special assessments, expendable trusts, or for major capital projects) that are legally restricted to expenditure for specified purposes (roads, bridges).
>
> **DEBT SERVICE FUNDS**—to account for the accumulation of resources for, and the payment of, general long-term debt principal and interest.
>
> **CAPITAL PROJECTS FUNDS**—to account for financial resources to be used for the acquisition or construction of major capital facilities other than those financed by proprietary funds and trust funds.

2. **PROPRIETARY FUNDS**—sometimes referred to as "nonexpendable"—are used to account for a government's ongoing organizations and activities which are similar to those often found in the private sector (Enterprise and Internal Service Funds). All assets, liabilities, equities, revenues, expenses, and transfers relating to the government's business and quasi-business activities—where **net income and capital maintenance are measured**—are accounted for through proprietary funds. The generally accepted accounting principles here are those applicable to similar business in the private sector; and the measurement focus is upon determination of **net income, financial position, and changes in financial position**.

> **ENTERPRISE FUNDS**—to account for operations (a) that are financed and operated in a manner similar to private enterprises—where the intent of the governing body is that the costs (expenses, including depreciation) of providing goods or services to the general public on a continuing basis be financed or recovered primarily through user charges; or (b) where the governing body has decided that periodic determination of revenues earned, expenses incurred; and /or net income is appropriate for capital maintenance, public policy, management control, accountability, or other purposes.
>
> **INTERNAL SERVICE FUNDS**—to account for the financing of goods or services provided by one department or agency to other departments or agencies of the government unit, or to other governmental units, on a cost-reimbursement basis.

3. **FIDUCIARY FUNDS**—Trust Funds and Agency—are used to account for assets held by a governmental unit in a trustee capacity or as an agent for individuals, private organization and other funds. Each Trust Fund is classified as either a governmental fund or a proprietary fund. Expendable Trust Funds are accounted for as governmental funds. Nonexpendable Trust Funds and Pension Trust Funds are accounted for as proprietary funds. Agency Funds are purely custodial (assets equal liabilities) and thus do not involve measurement of results of operations.

## ACCOUNT GROUPS

Two additional account groups are used by a "governmental unit" : **the General Fixed Asset Account Group (GFAAG) and the General Long-Term Debt Account Group (GLTDAG).** These groups **are NOT funds.** They are a self-balancing group of accounts, the purpose of which is to keep an inventory of the fixed assets and the long term liabilities for the governmental funds.

The GFAAG is necessary because the governmental funds record fixed assets purchases as expenditures, which are current accounts closed at year end. As a result, there would not be a record of the fixed assets purchased if the GFAAG did not exist.

The GLTDAG accounts for all obligations of the governmental funds. The GLTDAG keeps a record of the general obligations (an inventory of debts) which will be repaid by the debt service fund.

*Example:* Financial Statements of the General Fund

## GUIL COUNTY
General Fund
Statement of Revenues, Expenditures, and
Changes in Fund Balance (Condensed)
Year Ended June 30, 19X9

| | | |
|---|---|---|
| Revenues | | $600,000 |
| Expenditures | | (533,000) |
| Excess of revenues over expenditures | | $ 67,000 |
| Other financing sources (uses): | | |
| Bond proceeds – Capital debt | $200,000 | |
| Operating transfers in | 100,000 | |
| Operating transfers out | (200,000) | |
| Total other financing sources (uses) | | 100,000 |
| Excess of revenues and other financing sources over expenditures and other financing uses | | $167,000 |
| Unreserved fund balance, July 1, 1998 | | 175,000 |
| Residual equity transfers out | | (85,000) |
| Less: Increase in reserve for encumbrances | | (20,000) |
| Unreserved fund balance, June 30, 1999 | | $237,000 |

## GUIL COUNTY
General Fund
Balance Sheet (Condensed)
June 30, 19X9

**Assets**

| | |
|---|---|
| Cash | $ 61,900 |
| Investments | 105,000 |
| Receivables (net of allowances): | |
| Taxes | 184,000 |
| Accounts | 48,850 |
| Due from other funds | 26,000 |
| Total assets | $425,750 |

**Liabilities**

| | |
|---|---|
| Vouchers payable | $125,930 |
| Contracts payable | 16,720 |
| Due to other funds | 26,100 |
| Total liabilities | $168,750 |

**Equity**

| | |
|---|---|
| Fund balances: | |
| Reserved for encumbrances | $ 20,000 |
| Unreserved, undesignated | 237,000 |
| Total fund balances | 257,000 |
| Total liabilities and equity | $425,750 |

## MODIFIED ACCRUAL BASIS (Part Cash and Part Accrual)

Modified accrual is used by the five expendable funds: the four governmental funds (general, special revenue, capital projects and debt service) and the expendable trust fund.

## Revenues

Revenues are recognized by the expendable funds when they are both "measurable and available."

*Examples:*
1. Property tax revenues are recognized on the accrual basis when the taxes are levied, assuming that all taxes are collected during the year or within 60 days from the end of the year. Any taxes expected to be collected after the 60 day period would be considered deferred revenue in the current period and revenue in the following period.

2. Income taxes and sales taxes are recognized when they become susceptible to accrual.

3. Miscellaneous revenues such as parking fees, traffic court fines, building permits and business licenses are recognized on a cash basis.

## Expenditures

Expenditures are generally recognized on the accrual basis. The exceptions are interest and long-term debt. Interest and long-term debt payments are not accrued but are recognized when due.

Inventory of supplies and prepaid insurance may be recognized on either the cash basis (purchase method) or the accrual basis (consumption method).

## SUMMARY OF MODIFIED ACCRUAL CONCEPTS

| Revenues/Expenditures | Accounting Treatment |
|---|---|
| Revenues (Concept) | Recognize when available and measurable |
| Property Tax Revenues | Usually accrual |
| Income Taxes and Sales Taxes Revenues | Recognize when susceptible to accrual |
| Miscellaneous Revenues (parking fees, traffic court fines, building permits, and business license) | Recognize when cash is received |
| Expenditures in General | Accrual basis |
| Interest and payments on long-term debt | Recognize when due |
| Expenditures for Supplies Inventory or Prepaid Insurance | Accrual (Consumption Method) / Cash (Purchase Method) |

# Governmental Funds

## GENERAL FUND

The General Fund accounts for all revenues and expenditures of a governmental unit which are not accounted for in other funds. It is usually the primary and most important fund for state and local governments, and it is used to account for most routine operations. Revenue received should be classified by source. The primary sources are taxes, fines, and licenses. All other resources that are **not** accounted for in other governmental funds are included in the general fund.

Typical Journal Entries of the General Fund:

1. To record the budget for the year (Budgets are recorded by the general, special revenue, capital projects and expendable trust funds).

   Budgetary accounts are a part of the double entry accounting system in fund accounting where appropriations and estimated revenues are subject to approval by a legislative body. This is necessary because of the need to **control expenditures** and to levy taxes sufficient to cover estimated expenditures.

   At the beginning of the year

   | | | |
   |---|---|---|
   | Estimated Revenue Control | $400,000 | |
   |     Appropriations Control | | $398,000 |
   |     Budgetary Fund Balance | | 2,000 |

2. To record the property tax levy.

   | | | |
   |---|---|---|
   | Property Tax Receivable – Current | $280,000 | |
   |     Allowance for uncollectible | | |
   |         Taxes – Current | | $ 20,000 |
   |     Revenues Control | | 260,000 |

   Notice that the revenues control is credited for the expected collections. Governmental funds do not use a bad debt expenditure account because it does not have any budgetary implications.

3. Revenues from fines, licenses, and permits amount to $30,000.

   | | | |
   |---|---|---|
   | Cash | $ 30,000 | |
   |     Revenues Control | | $ 30,000 |

   Note that miscellaneous revenues are recognized on a cash basis.

4. Received a letter from the state indicating the city's share of sales taxes amounted to $25,000.

   | | | |
   |---|---|---|
   | State Sales Tax Receivable | $ 25,000 | |
   |     Revenue Control | | $ 25,000 |

   Based on the letter from the state, the sales tax revenue is **susceptible** to accrual.

5. **Encumbrances.** Encumbrances are recorded obligations for unperformed contracts for goods or services. Because authorizations to spend are limited to appropriations, it is necessary to demonstrate compliance with legal requirements. This is done to prevent overspending of appropriations. For example, equipment is ordered with delivery expected in 60 days, at an estimated cost of $6,000 on July 1, 19X9.

July 1, 19X9       To Record the Encumbrance

| | | |
|---|---|---|
| Encumbrances Control | $6,000 | |
|     Budgetary Fund Balance | | |
|         Reserve for Encumbrances | | $6,000 |

August 30, 19X9   Equipment is received costing $6,200. The encumbrances entry is reversed.

| | | |
|---|---|---|
| Budgetary Fund Balance | | |
|     Reserve for Encumbrances | $6,000 | |
|         Encumbrances Control | | $6,000 |

August 30, 19X9   The actual expenditure is recorded.

| | | |
|---|---|---|
| Expenditures Control | $6,200 | |
|     Vouchers Payable | | $6,200 |

NOTE: When the entry for the expenditure in the general fund is made on August 30, 19X9, a second entry is made in the FIXED ASSET ACCOUNT GROUP to debit the Equipment for $6,200 and credit the Investment in Fixed Assets – General Fund for $6,200.

6. Expenditures for Supplies Inventory and Prepaid Insurance

Accounting for supplies inventory or prepaid insurance may be done using either the consumption method (accrual) or the purchase method (cash basis).

**THE KEY POINT IS THAT UNDER THE CONSUMPTION METHOD THE AMOUNT CHARGED TO EXPENDITURES IS THE <u>AMOUNT CONSUMED</u> AND THE AMOUNT CHARGED TO EXPENDITURES UNDER THE PURCHASE METHOD IS THE <u>AMOUNT PURCHASED</u>.**

The following example compares the accounting for supplies inventory under both methods.

## Comparison of Accounting for Inventories – Purchase versus Consumption Method

| Item | Purchase Method of Accounting | | Consumption Method of Accounting | |
|---|---|---|---|---|
| **November 1, 19X1:** | | | | |
| Record acquisition of $2,000 of inventory | Expenditures<br>    Vouchers Payable | 2,000<br>    2,000 | Expenditures<br>    Vouchers Payable | 2,000<br>    2,000 |
| | | | | |
| **December 31, 19X1:** | | | | |
| Recognize ending inventory of 600 | Inventory of Supplies<br>    Fund Balance Reserved<br>       for Inventories | 600<br><br>    600 | Inventory of Supplies<br>    Expenditures | 600<br>    600 |
| | | | Unreserved Fund Balance<br>    Fund Balance Reserved<br>       for Inventories | 600<br><br>    600 |
| **December 31, 19X2:** | | | | |
| Record use of remaining inventory in 19X2 | Fund Balance Reserved<br>    for Inventories<br>    Inventory of Supplies | <br>600<br>    600 | Expenditures<br>    Inventories of Supplies | 600<br>    600 |
| | | | Fund Balance Reserved<br>    for Inventories<br>    Unreserved Fund Balance | <br>600<br>    600 |

7.  *Interfund transactions* are used within most government units as a means of directing sufficient resources to all activities and functions; *monetary transfers* made from the *General Fund* are quite prevalent since many government *revenues* are originally accumulated in this fund.

   A.  *Operating transfers* are often made to provide financing for the broad range of government activities.

      •   The asset *outflow* is recorded as an *other financing use* by the fund making the transfer while the receipt is labeled as an *other financing source.*

      •   The other financing sources and the other financing uses accounts are reported as a part of the Statement of Revenues and Expenditures.

      *For example:*
      The general fund transfers $20,000 of operating funds to subsidize the swimming pool enterprise fund.

      | | | |
      |---|---|---|
      | Other Financing Uses – operating transfers out | $20,000 | |
      |     Cash | | $20,000 |

   B.  *Residual equity transfers* are *nonrecurring or nonroutine* transfers of equity between funds.

      •   A *residual equity transfer* is treated as a direct increase or decrease in the fund balance in both the paying and receiving funds.

      •   They are made to create *permanent financing* for an *Enterprise Fund* or an *Internal Service Fund.*

      •   The *transfer-out* is recorded as a *residual equity transfer* while the *transfer-in* is shown as *contributed capital.*

*For example:*
The general fund transfers $80,000 to an internal service fund to establish a centralized motor pool.

| | | |
|---|---|---|
| Residual Equity Transfer | $80,000 | |
| Cash | | 80,000 |

C. *Quasi-external transactions* are payments for work done within the government and are recorded as *normal revenues and expenditures.*

*For example:*
The city-owned water utility bills the general fund for water used in the city hall.

| | | |
|---|---|---|
| Expenditures Control | $5,000 | |
| Cash | | 5,000 |

## Illustrative Problem and Year-end reclassification and closing entries.

General Fund Transactions for the fiscal year ending June 30, 19X1:

1. A budget was approved for FY 19X1 showing estimated revenue of $1,896,000 and appropriations of $1,875,000 including estimated other financing uses of $20,000. The revenue estimate includes a real estate tax levy of $1,805,000 after allowing for estimated uncollectible taxes of 5%.

2. Supplies totaling $8,000 and two fire trucks costing $22,000 each were ordered.

3. An advance of $30,000 was made to establish an internal service fund (ISF) to acquire and maintain city owned vehicles. The $30,000 is expected to be repaid.

4. An annual payment of $20,000 was made to provide for redemption of serial bonds which begin to mature in ten years.

5. Wages of city departments totaled $678,000 during the year of which $11,200 was unpaid at June 30, 19X1. Included in wages was $62,000 in payments to the city pension fund which have not been paid.

6. The supplies inventory is $2,000 at year-end. It is the city's policy to show the supplies inventory in the balance sheet, but a city ordinance requires all supplies purchased to be charged to expenditures.

7. A total of $1,121,000 was transferred to the general fund of the town's school district which fund is operated independently of the city's general fund.

8. The supplies and one fire truck arrived costing $7,800 and $21,650 respectively. The other fire truck will be received in July.

9. Vouchers for the supplies and fire equipment were approved and paid.

10. Taxes previously written off in the amount of $850 were collected.

11. Miscellaneous tax receipts totaled $94,500. Real estate taxes of $1,802,000 were collected.

## REQUIRED:
a.   Journal entries for FY 19X1 transactions.

b.   Year-end reclassification and closing entries.

**Solution to Illustrative Problem:**

1.  

| | | | |
|---|---|---|---|
| Estimated Revenues Control | | $1,896,000 | |
| Appropriations Control | | | $1,855,000 |
| Estimated Other Financing | | | |
| Uses Control – Operating Transfers Out | | | 20,000 |
| Budgetary Fund Balance | | | 21,000 |
| Taxes Receivable—Current | | $1,900,000 | |
| Estimated Uncollectible Taxes | | | $   95,000 |
| Revenue Control | | | 1,805,000 |

$$X = \$1,805,000 + .05\, X$$
$$X = \$1,900,000$$

2.  

| | | |
|---|---|---|
| Encumbrances Control | $52,000 | |
| Budgetary Fund Balance | | |
| Reserve for Encumbrances | | $52,000 |

3.  

| | | |
|---|---|---|
| Due from Internal Service Fund | $30,000 | |
| Cash | | $30,000 |

4.  

| | | |
|---|---|---|
| Other Financing – Operating Transfers Out | $20,000 | |
| Cash | | $20,000 |

This transaction will result in entries in the Debt Service Fund and General Long-Term Debt Group of Accounts.

5.  

| | | |
|---|---|---|
| Expenditures Control—Wages | $678,000 | |
| Wages Payable | | $ 11,200 |
| Due Trust Fund—Pensions | | 62,000 |
| Cash | | 604,800 |

The Trust Fund for city pensions is affected by this entry.

6.  

| | | |
|---|---|---|
| Inventory of Supplies | $2,000 | |
| Fund Balance Reserved | | |
| for inventory of supplies | | $2,000 |

7.  

| | | |
|---|---|---|
| Expenditures Control—Schools | $1,121,000 | |
| Cash | | $1,121,000 |

8.  

| | | |
|---|---|---|
| Budgetary Fund Balance | | |
| Reserve for Encumbrances | $30,000 | |
| Encumbrances Control | | $30,000 |

Encumbrances for $8,000 in supplies and $22,000 for one fire truck are reversed. A $22,000 encumbrance remains open.

| | | |
|---|---|---|
| Expenditures Control | $29,450 | |
| Vouchers Payable | | $29,450 |
| ($7,800 supplies; $21,650 fire truck) | | |

Note: Another journal entry would be made in the Fixed Asset Group of Accounts: Debit Fire Truck and Credit Investment in Fixed Assets for $21,650.

| 9. | Vouchers Payable | $29,450 | |
| | Cash | | $29,450 |

| 10. | Cash | $850 | |
| | Revenue Control | | $850 |

| 11. | Cash | $94,500 | |
| | Revenue Control | | $94,500 |
| | Cash | $1,802,000 | |
| | Taxes Receivable—Current | | $1,802,000 |

Reclassification Journal Entry:

At the end of the accounting period, any uncollected taxes should be reclassified from current to delinquent along with the related estimated uncollectible taxes.

| 12. | Taxes Receivable – Delinquent | $98,000 | |
| | Estimated Uncollectible Taxes – Current | 95,000 | |
| | Taxes Receivable – Current | | 98,000 |
| | Estimated Uncollectible Taxes – Delinquent | | 95,000 |

## Closing Entries

13.     Step One:  Close the budgetary accounts.

| Budgetary Fund Balance | $21,000 | |
| Estimated Other Financing Uses – Operating Transfers Out | 20,000 | |
| Appropriations Control | 1,855,000 | |
| Estimated Revenues Control | | 1,896,000 |

14.     Step Two:  Close Revenue, Expenditures, and Other Financing accounts to Unreserved Fund Balance.

| Revenue Control | $1,900,350 | |
| Expenditure Control | | $1,828,450 |
| Other Financing Uses Control | | 20,000 |
| Unreserved Fund Balance | | 51,900 |

15.     Step Three:  Close Encumbrance Accounts

| Budgetary Fund Balance Reserve for Encumbrances | $22,000 | |
| Encumbrances Control | | $22,000 |

16.     Step Four:  Restrict Balance Sheet Fund Balance for outstanding Encumbrances

| Unreserved Fund Balance | $22,000 | |
| Fund Balance Reserved for Encumbrances | | $22,000 |

**Analysis of Changes in Fund Balance**
**For the Fiscal Year Ended June 30, 19X1**

| | | |
|---|---:|---:|
| Unreserved Fund Balance July 1, 19X0 | | $ 6,000 |
| Excess of Revenues Over Expenditures | | |
|     Revenues | $1,900,350 | |
|     Expenditures | 1,848,450 | 51,900 |
| Less: Fund Balance Reserved | | |
|   for Encumbrances | | (22,000) |
| Unreserved Fund Balance June 30, 19X1 | | $35,900 |

**General Fund**
**Balance Sheet**
**June 30, 19X1**

**ASSETS**

| | | |
|---|---:|---:|
| Cash | | $ 98,100 |
| Taxes Receivable—Current | $98,000 | |
| Less: Estimated Uncollectibles | 95,000 | 3,000 |
| Advance to Internal Service Fund | | 30,000 |
| Inventory of Supplies | | 2,000 |
|     TOTAL ASSETS | | $133,100 |

**LIABILITIES AND FUND EQUITY**

| | |
|---|---:|
| Wages Payable | $ 11,200 |
| Due Trust Fund—Pensions | 62,000 |
|     TOTAL LIABILITIES | 73,200 |
| Reserve for Inventory of Supplies | 2,000 |
| Unreserved Fund Balance | 35,900 |
| Fund Balance Reserved | |
|   for Encumbrances | 22,000 |
|     TOTAL LIABILITIES AND | |
|     FUND EQUITY | $133,100 |

## SPECIAL REVENUE FUNDS

Special Revenue Funds are used to account for revenues derived from specific taxes or other earmarked revenue sources. They are usually required by statute, charter provision, or local ordinance to finance particular functions or activities of government. Examples of such funds are those established for the benefit of facilities such as parks, schools, and museums and for particular functions or activities such as highway construction, street maintenance, law enforcement, and the licensing and regulation of professions and businesses. A Special Revenue Fund may be required for financing either current operating expenditures or capital outlays, or both.

The amount and nature of the revenue sources which finance a particular facility or program have a controlling influence on whether such a program should be accounted for as a Special Revenue Fund or as an Enterprise Fund. As a general rule, the distinguishing characteristic of a Special Revenue Fund is that most of the revenue involved in the operation comes from tax and non-tax sources not directly related to services rendered rather than from direct charges to users of the services.

The accounting principles applicable to the General Fund apply generally to all Special Revenue Funds, and in the absence of legal requirements to the contrary, the same basis of accounting should be used for the Special Revenue Funds of a governmental unit as is used for its General Fund.

As in the General Fund:
1. Depreciation is not taken on the assets acquired by Special Revenue Funds.
2. The fixed assets are not accounted for in the Special Revenue Fund but in the General Fixed Asset Group of Accounts.
3. Long-term debt incurred for Special Revenue Fund purposes is usually not carried in the Special Revenue Fund.
4. Debt service is normally not accounted for in this fund.

## CAPITAL PROJECTS FUND

Accounts for the purchase or construction of major capital facilities. Debt incurred in connection with such projects is recorded in the general long-term debt group of accounts. The payment of debt is **not** the responsibility of the Capital Projects Fund.

The Capital Projects Fund has a limited life. It continues to operate until all of the proceeds derived from the sale of the bonds are expended. When the fund finances the construction of improvements, proceeds are expended gradually as construction proceeds. At the end of the fiscal period, the opening entry of encumbrances control and the fund balance reserved for encumbrances are reversed. The portion of year-end fund balance segregated for expenditure upon contractor performance is set up by:

> DR—Unreserved Fund Balance.
> > CR—Fund Balance Reserved for Encumbrances.

Expenditures are closed at the end of each fiscal period. If the project is not completed, the amount closed out should be reflected as work in progress in the General Fixed Assets Group of Accounts.

To pay for the capital projects, various sources of financing are used:

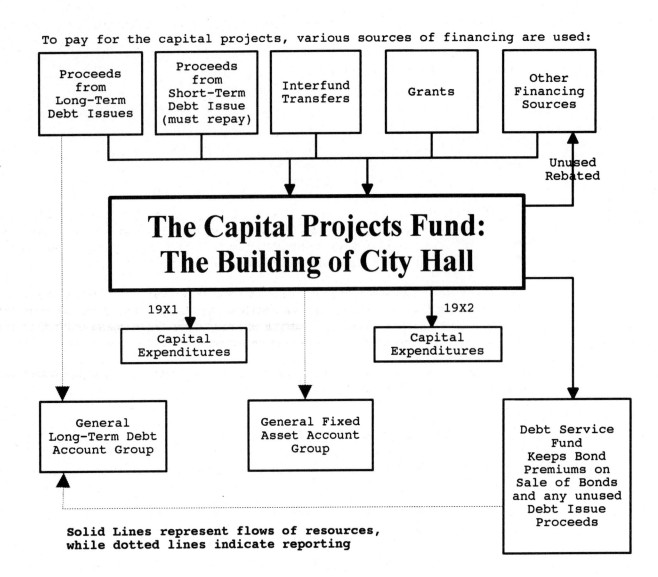

| Proceeds from Long-Term Debt Issues | Proceeds from Short-Term Debt Issue (must repay) | Interfund Transfers | Grants | Other Financing Sources |

Unused
Rebated

**The Capital Projects Fund:
The Building of City Hall**

19X1   Capital Expenditures        19X2   Capital Expenditures

General Long-Term Debt Account Group

General Fixed Asset Account Group

Debt Service Fund Keeps Bond Premiums on Sale of Bonds and any unused Debt Issue Proceeds

**Solid Lines represent flows of resources,
while dotted lines indicate reporting**

**Illustrative Problem:**
1. Hilltop City proposed the construction of a new $490,000 municipal building and authorized the issuance of $300,000 of bonds on April 1 with $200,000 to be financed equally by State and Federal matching funds.
2. The bonds are sold for $308,000, including a premium of $8,000.
3. A $300,000 contract is entered into with Paul Construction Co. for the main building to be completed in 4 months. The city is to purchase some material and furnish some labor for the project.
4. Wages up to the end of the fiscal year were $18,000 and were paid.
5. Purchase orders for $17,000 of materials were placed on May 15.
6. A bill for $150,000 was received from Paul Construction Co. on June 20 for construction to date.
7. On June 15 a bill for $15,000 for all of the materials ordered on May 15 was received.
8. On June 30 the city paid the bill due Paul Construction Co. but retained 10%.
9. On June 30 $6,000 of materials was ordered.

**Prepare**: Journal entries to record all transactions.

**Illustrative Solution:**

1.  Estimated Revenue Control ............................ $200,000
    Estimated Other Financing Source Control .... 300,000
        Appropriations Control .................................................. $490,000
        Budgetary Fund Balance ............................................... 10,000

1a. Due from State ............................................... $100,000
    Due from Federal Government ................... 100,000
        Revenues Control ...................................................... $200,000

2.  Cash ........................................................... $308,000
        Other Financing Sources Control ................................ $308,000
        (Proceeds of Gen'l Obligation Bonds)
    Other Financing Sources Control ............... $8,000
    (Operating Transfer Out)
        Cash ......................................................................... $8,000
    (to record transfer of premium to Debt Service Fund)

3.  Encumbrances Control ................................. $300,000
        Budgetary Fund Balance
         Reserve for Encumbrances ....................................... $300,000

4.  Expenditures Control .................................. $18,000
        Cash ......................................................................... $18,000

5.  Encumbrances Control ................................. $17,000
        Budgetary Fund Balance
         Reserve for Encumbrances ......................................... $17,000

6.  Expenditures Control .................................. $150,000
        Contracts Payable ..................................................... $150,000
    Budgetary Fund Balance
      Reserve for Encumbrances ....................... $150,000
        Encumbrances Control ................................................ $150,000

7.  Budgetary Fund Balance
      Reserve for Encumbrances ....................... $17,000
        Encumbrances Control ................................................ $17,000
    Expenditures Control .................................. $15,000
        Vouchers Payable ....................................................... $15,000

8.  Contracts Payable ....................................... $150,000
        Cash ....................................................................... $135,000
        Contracts Payable—Retained Percentage .................... 15,000

9.  Encumbrances Control ................................. $6,000
        Budgetary Fund Balance
         Reserve for Encumbrances ......................................... $6,000

**Closing Entries**

10.  Step One:  Close the budgetary accounts.

| | | |
|---|---:|---:|
| Appropriations Control | $490,000 | |
| Budgetary Fund Balance | 10,000 | |
|     Estimated Revenues Control | | $200,000 |
|     Estimated Other Financing Sources Control | | 300,000 |

11.  Step Two:  Close Revenue, Expenditures, and Other Financing accounts to Unreserved Fund Balance.

| | | |
|---|---:|---:|
| Revenues Control | $200,000 | |
| Other Financing Sources Control | 308,000 | |
|     Expenditures Control | | $183,000 |
|     Unreserved Fund Balance | | 317,000 |
|     Other Financing Sources Control | | 8,000 |

12.  Step Three:  Close Encumbrance Accounts

| | | |
|---|---:|---:|
| Budgetary Fund Balance | | |
|   Reserve for Encumbrances | $156,000 | |
|     Encumbrances Control | | $156,000 |

13.  Step Four:  Restrict Balance Sheet Fund Balance for outstanding Encumbrances

| | | |
|---|---:|---:|
| Unreserved Fund Balance | $156,000 | |
|     Fund Balance Reserved for Encumbrances | | $156,000 |

# DEBT SERVICE FUNDS

The function of this fund is to accumulate resources for the payment of principal and interest on general obligation long-term debt.

The debt service fund does not account for the debt itself (the debt is maintained by the GLTDAG), and does not use encumbrances.  The *"when due"* non accrual approach is normally used.  However, the GASB Codification *permits* the accrual of both principal and interest of debt **if** resources are available and accrual is done consistently each year.

Bonds, notes, and other long-term liabilities directly related to, and expected to be paid from, proprietary funds and trust funds should be included in the accounts of such funds. These are specific liabilities, even though the full faith and credit of the governmental unit may be pledged as further assurance that the liabilities will be paid.

Long-term debt service is of three types:
        1. Term or sinking fund bonds
        2. Serial bonds, and
        3. Notes having a maturity of more than one year.

Debt Service funds for term bonds require annual additions to a fund balance which, along with the earnings of the accumulated funds, will be sufficient to pay the debt principal at maturity.

A term-bond accumulation schedule is shown in the illustrative problem.

Debt Service fund requirements may be financed by one or more sources of revenue such as a general property, sales, gasoline or cigarette tax, etc. When revenues are earmarked for retirement of debt by levy of a special limited tax and operational activities are involved, a special revenue fund should be set up. The sequence of activities and funds involved is as follows:

## 1) SPECIAL REVENUE

If a special tax is levied and operational responsibility is involved, the funds should flow through a special revenue fund. For example, a school district or hospital to be operated by a special levy which includes capital construction for which bonds are sold.

## 2) CAPITAL PROJECTS

Bonds are sold and the capital construction carried out.

## 3) DEBT SERVICE

Required additions for debt payments may be received from the special revenue fund, or taxes levied for debt retirement exclusively will be levied and collected by the debt service fund. Funds for retirement of debt may also be received from the general fund, payable from general revenues. The Debt Service Fund **should not** record interest on general obligation bonds which may have accrued from the last interest payment date to the end of the fiscal year. For example, if an annual interest payment is made on April 1 and October 1 by a unit having a January 1-December 31 fiscal year, there should be no recording of interest cost for the period October 1 to December 31.

## 4) GENERAL LONG-TERM DEBT GROUP OF ACCTS.

The sale of bonds by the Capital Projects Fund results in the recording of the liability in this account.

> Dr. Amount to be provided for Payment of Bonds
> > Cr. Bonds Payable

Funds accumulated in the Debt Service Fund result in the following entry:

> Dr. Amount Available for Payment of Bonds
> > Cr. Amount to be Provided for Payment of Term Bonds

When the bonds mature, the bonds become a liability of the Debt Service Fund and the following entry would be made in the general long term debt group of accounts:

> Dr. Bonds Payable
> > Cr. Amount Available for Payment of Bonds

**Illustrative Problem:**

The City of William prepared a schedule of debt service requirements to retire a $500,000 issue of 6% term bonds by the Capital Projects Fund, when the bonds mature in 10 years. It is estimated that fund income will be 5% per year. The transactions shown are for year 2 and all the fund requirements of year 1 were collected and invested.

| Year | Required Annual Contribution | Estimated (Rounded) Required Fund Income | Amount Required to be Accumulated in Fund |
|---|---|---|---|
| 1 | $ 39,755 | $ —0— | $ 39,755 |
| 2 | 39,755 | 1,985 | 41,740 |
| 3 | 39,755 | 4,070 | 43,825 |
| 4 | 39,755 | 6,260 | 46,015 |
| 5 | 39,755 | 8,560 | 48,315 |
| 6 | 39,755 | 10,980 | 50,735 |
| 7 | 39,755 | 13,520 | 53,275 |
| 8 | 39,755 | 16,180 | 55,935 |
| 9 | 39,755 | 18,980 | 58,735 |
| 10 | 39,755 | 21,920 | 61,665 |
| | $397,550 | $102,455 | $500,000 |

1. Current tax levy is assessed for $40,000 of which $245 is estimated to be uncollectible.
2. $39,000 of taxes are collected.
3. Securities are purchased for $35,000.
4. Interest on purchased securities accrued in the amount of $2,000.
5. The first six months' interest on bonds is paid on August 1—$15,000.

**Illustrative Solution:**

| | | | |
|---|---|---|---|
| 1. | Taxes Receivable—Current | $40,000 | |
| | Estimated Uncollectible Current Taxes | | $ 245 |
| | Revenues Control | | 39,755 |
| | | | |
| 2. | Cash | $39,000 | |
| | Taxes Receivable—Current | | $39,000 |
| | | | |
| 3. | Investments | $35,000 | |
| | Cash | | $35,000 |
| | | | |
| 4. | Interest Receivable on Investments | $2,000 | |
| | Revenues Control | | $2,000 |
| | | | |
| 5. | Expenditures Control | $15,000 | |
| | Cash | | $15,000 |

**Closing Entry:**

| | | | |
|---|---|---|---|
| 6. | Revenues Control | $41,755 | |
| | Fund Balance Reserved for Debt Service | | $26,755 |
| | Expenditures Control | | 15,000 |

# Accounting for Bond Principal and Interest Paid to Fiscal Agents

Principal and interest on general obligation long-term debt need not be recognized as expenditures until due. If resources have been accumulated in Debt Service Funds for payments due within one year, expenditures and related fund liabilities may be recorded there. Year end fund balances of Debt Service Funds are reported as "amounts available" in the General Long-Term Debt Account Group. Entries to record debt service expenditures and related cash disbursements are as follows:

| | | |
|---|---|---|
| Cash with Fiscal Agents | $75,000 | |
|     Cash | | $75,000 |

To record transmittal of cash to fiscal agent for payment of bond principal and interest

| | | |
|---|---|---|
| Expenditures Control | $75,000 | |
|     Matured Bonds Payable | | $50,000 |
|     Matured Interest Payable | | 25,000 |

To record annual expenditures for bond principal and interest

| | | |
|---|---|---|
| Matured Bonds Payable | $50,000 | |
| Matured Interest Payable | 25,000 | |
|     Cash with Fiscal Agents | | $75,000 |

To record payment of bond principal and interest by fiscal agent

**Year End Closing Entry.** The following entry illustrates the Debt Service Fund year end closing process assuming revenues of $81,000.

| | | |
|---|---|---|
| Revenues Control | $81,000 | |
|     Expenditures Control | | $75,000 |
|     Fund Balance Reserved for Debt Service | | 6,000 |

To close revenues and expenditures into fund balance

---

**City of Passville**
**Debt Service Fund**
**Balance Sheet**
December 31, 19XX

<u>Assets</u>

Cash
Cash with fiscal agents
Taxes receivable - net of delinquent
Interest and penalties receivable on taxes
Tax liens receivable (net)
Investments
Unamortized premiums
      Less: unamortized discounts
          Total investments
Interest receivable on investments
      Total assets

<u>Liabilities and Fund Balances</u>

Bonds payable
Interest payable
Fund Balance - Reserved for debt service
      Total liabilities and fund balance

---

# Special Assessments

Special Assessment Funds were used to account for compulsory levies made against certain properties to defray part of all costs of specific capital improvements or services deemed to benefit primarily those properties.
GASB No. 6 eliminates the Special Assessment fund for financial reporting purposes and requires that these special assessments are accounted for in the Capital Project fund.

### Summary of "Governmental Accounting Standards Board Statement No. 6"

1) The "Special Assessment Fund" is eliminated for financial reporting purposes.

2) Transactions of a "service type" special assessment should be reported in the fund type that best reflects the nature of the transactions; usually the general fund, a special revenue fund, or an enterprise fund.
    a. "Service-type" special assessment revenues should be treated like "user fees."
    b. Assessment revenues and expenditures for which the assessments were levied should be recognized on the same basis of accounting as that normally used for that fund type.

3) If the government is obligated in some manner to assume payments on special assessment debt on "capital type" special assessments, in the event of default by the property owners, all transactions related to capital improvements financed by special assessments should be reported in the same fund types and on the same basis as any other capital improvement and financing transactions.
    a. The fixed assets constructed or acquired should be reported in the general fixed assets account group or in an enterprise fund, as appropriate.


# Account Groups

## GENERAL FIXED ASSETS GROUP OF ACCOUNTS

To be classified as a general fixed asset, an asset must be:
    1. tangible
    2. have a life extending beyond the current fiscal year, and
    3. have a significant value.

General fixed assets may be acquired by purchase, lease-purchase, eminent domain, tax foreclosure, and gift. The recommended classes of accounting for fixed assets including ancillary costs are (1) land, (2) buildings, (3) improvements other than buildings, (4) equipment, and (5) construction in progress. Property accounted for is debited to these accounts. Investment in General Fixed Assets is credited categorized by source such as:

    Capital Projects Funds:
        General Obligation Bonds
        Federal Grants
        State Grants
        Local Grants
    General Fund Revenues
    Special Revenue Fund Revenues
    Special Assessments
    Private Gifts

Fixed assets should be accounted for at cost or, if the cost is not practicably determinable, at estimated cost. **Donated fixed assets** should be recorded at their estimated fair value at the time received.

General fixed assets acquired via lease-purchase agreement are capitalized in the GFA Account Group at the inception of the agreement in the amount of the **discounted present value** of total stipulated payments.

**Illustrative Entries:**

| | | |
|---|---|---|
| Equipment | $21,450 | |
|      Investment in General Fixed Assets— | | |
|         General Fund Revenues | | $21,450 |
| To record purchase of equipment by general fund. | | |

Entry 6 in the Capital Projects Fund:

| | | |
|---|---|---|
| Construction in Progress | $150,000 | |
|      Investment in General Fixed Assets— | | |
|         Capital Projects Fund | | $150,000 |
| To record construction in progress of municipal building. | | |

When the project is completed, entries will be made recording the cost (debit) of land and building in separate accounts and construction in progress will be closed out.

When a fixed asset is **retired or disposed of**, the entry which was made to record the acquisition is reversed such as:

| | | |
|---|---|---|
| Investment in General Fixed Assets (Source) | xxxx | |
|     Land, Buildings, etc. | | xxxx |

---

**City of Passville**
**Statement of General Fixed Assets**
December 31, 19XX

**General Fixed Assets**

    Land
    Buildings
    Improvements other than buildings
    Equipment
    Construction work in progress
        Total General Fixed Assets

**Investment in General Fixed Assets From:**

    Capital project funds:
        General obligation bonds
        Federal grants
        State grants
        County grants
    General fund revenues
    Special revenue fund revenues
    Gifts
    Special Assessments
        Total investment in General fixed assets

# GENERAL LONG-TERM DEBT GROUP OF ACCOUNTS

The objective of this group of accounts is to show the governmental unit's long-term liability at any time from date of issuance until date of retirement. Contingent liabilities not requiring accrual should be disclosed in the notes to the financial statements. This includes situations where the governmental unit is contingently liable for Proprietary Fund or Trust Fund indebtedness.

The general long-term debt group essentially has only three accounts which function as follows:

a.  $500,000 of term bonds were sold by the Capital Projects Fund.

| | | |
|---|---|---|
| Amount to be provided for Payment of Term Bonds | $500,000 | |
| Bonds Payable | | $500,000 |

b.  A sinking fund payment of $39,755 was made by the General Fund to the Debt Service Fund for eventual retirement of the bonds.

| | | |
|---|---|---|
| Amount available in Debt Service Fund | $39,755 | |
| Amount to be provided for Retirement of Term Bonds | | $39,755 |

Note that this transaction affects three funds: the General Fund, the Debt Service Fund and General Long-Term Debt.

c.  When the bonds mature, the entry in the Debt Service Fund will be:

| | | |
|---|---|---|
| Fund Balance—Debt Service Fund | $500,000 | |
| Matured Bonds Payable | | $500,000 |

The General Long-Term Debt entry will be:

| | | |
|---|---|---|
| Bonds Payable | $500,000 | |
| Amount Available in Debt Service Fund | | $500,000 |

Long term liability includes noncurrent liabilities on lease-purchase agreements and other commitments that are not current liabilities properly recorded in governmental funds, while the entries are basically the same, terminology is changed as follows:

Assume a five-year lease entered into by the general fund for the purchase of computers. The present value of the lease payments is $250,000 with principal payments of $50,000 per year (plus interest) to be made from the general fund.

General fund entry when payments are made:

| | | |
|---|---|---|
| [1]Expenditures control | $50,000 | |
| Cash | | $50,000 |

[1]A similar entry would also be made for interest.

General long-term debt group account entries at the time the lease is executed.

| | | |
|---|---|---|
| Amount to be provided for lease payments | $250,000 | |
| Capital lease payable | | $250,000 |
| Lease entered into for lease-purchase of computers. | | |

| | | |
|---|---|---|
| Capital lease payable | $50,000 | |
| Amount to be provided for lease payments | | $50,000 |
| To record first of five annual lease principal payments. | | |

**City of Passville**
**Statement of General Long Term Debt**
Amount available and to be provided
for the payment of General Long Term Debt

Term Bonds:
      Amount available in debt service funds
      Amount to be provided
            Total term bonds

Serial Bonds:
      Amount available in debt service funds
      Amount to be provided
            Total serial bonds
Total available and to be provided

**General Long-Term Debt Payable**

Term bonds payable
Serial bonds payable

Total general long-term debt payable

Note 1: The city of X has a contingent liability of $XXX,000 to bondholders of special assessment bonds.

**Accounting Equations**

**The Governmental Funds:** (General, Special Revenue, Debt Service, Capital Projects)
Current Assets - Current Liabilities = Fund Balance

**The General Fixed Asset Account Group:**
General Fixed Assets = Investment in General Fixed Assets

**The General Long-Term Debt Group:**
Amount available in Debt Service Fund + Amount to be provided in Future Years = General Long-Term Debt

# Proprietary Funds

There are two proprietary funds, that use the accrual basis of accounting. These funds are like profit seeking business organizations where the intent is to have all costs and expenses of providing the services to be financed by the users of such services. They are : The Enterprise Fund and The Internal Service Fund.

## ENTERPRISE FUND

The Enterprise Fund is used to account for financing of self-supporting enterprises which render public service. Examples of enterprise funds are water, electricity, gas, steam, etc. Accounting for the enterprise fund is the same as that for privately owned utilities and no budgetary entries are necessary. Fixed assets and bonds are, therefore, included in the accounts of an enterprise fund. Enterprise activities are frequently administered by departments of general-purpose governments, such as a municipal water department or a state parks department. In other cases these activities are the exclusive function of a local special district—water district, power authority, port authority, etc. Regardless of the pattern of governmental organization, however, the significant attribute of such enterprise activities is that they are financed primarily by charges to consumers and that the accounting for them must make it possible to show whether they are operated at a profit or loss similar to private enterprises.

**City Of Passville**
**Enterprise Fund Type**
**Balance Sheet**
December 31, 19XX

**Current Assets:**
Cash
Accounts receivable - Customers
       Less: estimated uncollectible AR
Due from General Fund
Inventory of Materials and supplies
     Total current assets
**Restricted Assets:**
Revenue Bond reserves
     Cash
     Investments
**Customer Deposits:**
Investments
Interest Receivable on investments
     Total restricted Assets
**Utility plant in service:**
Land
Building
Less: Allowance for depreciation
     Construction in progress
        Total plant in service
          Total assets

**Liabilities, Reserves, Contributions, and Retained Earnings**
Current liabilities (payable from current assets)
Vouchers payable
Accrued wages payable
Advance from municipal general obligation Bonds
Current liabilities (Payable from restricted assets)
Construction contracts payable
Customer deposits
Other liabilities : Advance from municipal general obligation bonds
     Total liabilities
Reserves - for revenue bonds
Contributions from municipality
Contributions from customers
     Total contributions
Retained earnings
     Total

# INTERNAL SERVICE FUND

Internal Service Funds, are established to finance and account for services and commodities furnished by a designated agency of a governmental unit to other departments of the same governmental unit. Typical examples of Internal Service Funds are those established for central garages and motor pools, central printing and duplicating services, and central purchasing and stores departments.

Resources for the establishment of Internal Service Funds are derived from one or more of the following three sources: (1) contributions from another operating fund, such as the General Fund or an Enterprise Fund; (2) the sale of general obligations bonds, and (3) by long-term advances from other funds which are to be repaid over a specified period of time from the earnings of this fund. Once the fund's capital has been acquired from one or more of these sources, cash is expended for materials, parts and supplies which are used in the same form as purchased or are manufactured into other products and issued to the various using departments. These departments are charged with the cost of such materials, parts, and supplies plus labor and overhead. The Service Fund is then reimbursed by interdepartmental cash transfers from the budgeted appropriations of the departments served. Throughout the entire cycle of these operations, the financial objective of the fund is to recover the complete costs of operations, including overhead, without producing any significant amount of profit in the long run.

Since each department served by an Internal Service Fund will include among its estimated expenditures an amount sufficient to cover the estimated cost of services and commodities to be secured from the Service Fund, the latter fund does not have the same status or budgetary requirements in the annual budget as other operating funds. The accounting for all Service Funds should be on the accrual basis, with all charges to departments being billed at the time services are rendered and expenditures being recorded when incurred. With the exception of buildings financed from Capital Projects Funds, depreciation must be recorded on fixed assets to secure an accurate computation of costs and to prevent depletion of the fund's capital.

When a Service Fund is created, the entry to be made will depend upon the source of fund capital. If the fund's capital is acquired as a contribution from the General Fund, the entry would be a debit to **Cash** and a credit to **Contribution from General Fund**. If the fund is created by the proceeds of a general obligation bond issue—a less frequent procedure—the entry to be made in the Service Fund upon receipt of cash from the Capital Projects Fund is a debit to **Cash** and a credit to **Contribution from General Obligation Bonds**. Where fund capital is in the form of a long-term loan from another fund of the same governmental unit, the credit in this opening entry would be to **Advance from General (or other) Fund**. It is important that the latter account title be used to differentiate the resulting liability from the **Due to Other Funds** account which refers only to short-term liabilities.

Bonds, notes, and other long-term liabilities (e.g., for capital leases, pensions, judgements, and similar commitments) directly related to and expected to be paid from entity funds, should be included in the accounts. These are *specific fund* liabilities, even though the full faith and credit of the governmental unit may be pledged as further assurance that the liabilities will be paid. Too, such liabilities may constitute a mortgage or lien on specific fund properties or receivables.

At the time charges are billed, the exact amounts of overhead expenses are usually not known. Moreover, even if they were known, it is desirable to charge overhead expenses at a uniform rate throughout the year to prevent jobs worked on during a month when large indirect expenses were incurred from being charged more than identical jobs performed during another month when overhead expenses happened to be low. Therefore, departments are billed with direct costs plus a uniform rate per mile, per hour, or other applicable unit of measurement for their portion of the estimated total overhead charges for the fiscal year. The entry to record such billings is a debit to **Due from (name of) Fund** and a credit to **Operating Revenues Control**.

Accounting for the Internal Service Fund is the same as industrial accounting, and the balance sheet and the income statement follow GAAP. No budget is necessary. The excess of assets over liabilities consists of the source of funds to start the activity such as "Contribution from General Fund" and "Retained Earnings," which would ordinarily be small.

**Illustrative Journal Entries for Central Garage Fund**

1.     Inventory of Material and Supplies
           Vouchers Payable
    To record purchases of material and supplies.

2.     Operating Expenses Control
           Inventory of Material and Supplies
    To record usage of material and supplies.

3.     Operating Expenses Control
           Vouchers Payable
    To record liability of expenses incurred for salaries, wages, shop supplies and utilities.

4.     Building
    Equipment
           Vouchers Payable
    To record cost of addition to building and cost of equipment installed.

5.     Operating Expenses Control
           Accumulated Depreciation—Building
           Accumulated Depreciation—Equipment
    To record depreciation charges.

6.     Due from Special Revenue Fund—Schools
    Due from General Fund
           Operating Revenues Control
    To record billings for services rendered.

7.    Operating Revenues Control
           Operating Expenses Control
           Unreserved Retained Earnings
      To close out revenue and expense accounts and arrive at the excess of net charges
      over costs (net income) for the year.

# Fiduciary Funds

## TRUST FUNDS AND AGENCY

These funds are set up to account for money and property received from non-enterprise fund sources and held by a governmental unit as trustee, custodian or agent.

The distinction between a trust and agency fund is a matter of complexity, duration and purpose.

**Agency funds** are primarily clearing accounts for cash and other resources which are held for brief periods and disbursed to authorized recipients including:
1. Tax collections which more than one governmental unit share and remitting each unit's share less administrative charges.
2. Employee benefit funds such as hospital-surgical insurance or any situation under which funds are collected from employees to be disbursed for their benefit (payroll savings, etc.).
3. A clearance fund used to accumulate a variety of revenues from different sources apportioning them to various operating funds as required.

**Trust funds** operate to carry out the specific terms of the indenture, statute, ordinance or other regulations which created them. The most common types of trust funds are **pension** and **retirement systems**, endowment funds, loan funds, and performance deposit funds. The trust funds can be
- Expendable
- Non-expendable

**Expendable trust funds** are those whose principal and income may be expended for the designated purpose. The expendable funds are accounted for as the governmental funds. **Non-expendable funds** are those which must maintain principal intact and in some cases such as a loan fund must maintain both principal and interest intact. The non-expendable funds are accounted for as the proprietary funds.

Trust funds are also classified as **public** or **private**. **Public trust funds** are those whose principal or income or both must be used for some public purpose such as public employees' retirement funds. **Private trust funds** are those which will revert to private individuals and organizations or will be used for private persons.

**Illustrative Journal Entries—Trust Funds**
**Performance Deposit Fund** (Expendable)
           Cash
                 Fund Balance Reserved for Performance
           Deposits are received.

           Investments
                 Cash
           Deposit funds are invested.

           Fund Balance Reserved for Performance
                 Cash
           Deposit funds are returned.

**Loan Fund** (Non-expendable, Principal and Earnings)

    Cash
        Fund Balance Reserved for Loans
    Cash is received and fund is established.

    Loan Receivable
        Cash
    Funds are loaned according to fund requirements.

    Cash
        Loans Receivable
        Earnings
    Loan is repaid with interest.

    Earnings
        Fund Balance Reserved for Loans
    Earnings are closed to fund balance.

**Endowment Fund** (Non-expendable, principal only)

    Cash
        Fund Balance Reserved for Endowments
    Cash is received to establish the fund balance.

    Investments
        Cash
    Investments are made.

    Interest Receivable on Investments
        Operating Revenues Control
    Interest income is accrued.

    Cash
        Interest Receivable
    Interest income is received.

    Payment is made according to the purpose of the endowment.
    Gains and losses on sale of fund property increase or reduce the fund principal and do not affect fund earnings.

### Illustrative Journal Entries—Agency Funds

Agency fund operations typically involve a quick turnover of funds for some purpose such as collection of taxes for other governmental units, purchase of hospitalization insurance for employees, etc. Funds are received and disbursed, usually within a short period of time. The most complex operation of an agency fund is the collection of taxes for other governmental units, called a Tax Agency Fund. Assume an agency fund which is to collect $700,000 in taxes for other units.

| | | |
|---|---|---|
| Taxes Receivable for Other Units | $700,000 | |
|     Taxes Fund Balance | | $700,000 |

Taxes Receivable for other units:

| | | |
|---|---|---|
| City of Hope | $450,000 | |
| School District #1 | 150,000 | |
| Park District | 100,000 | |
| | $700,000 | |

| | | |
|---|---|---|
| Cash | $500,000 | |
| Taxes Receivable for Other Units | | $480,000 |
| Taxes Fund Balance | | 20,000 |

Taxes Receivable and Interest and Penalties are collected.

| | | |
|---|---|---|
| Taxes Fund Balance | $500,000 | |
| Cash | | $490,000 |
| Due to General Fund | | 10,000 |

Government Units are paid their respective taxes collected less a 2% collection fee which is due the General Fund, being a part of general revenues.

## Accounting Equations

**The Proprietary Funds:**

Current Assets + Fixed Assets = Current Liabilities + Contributed Capital + Retained Earnings

**The Fiduciary Funds:**

Assets = Liabilities + Fund Balance

Agency = Assets = Liabilities

---

### GAAP Hierarchy

| | GASB | AICPA | Other |
|---|---|---|---|
| Level 1 | Statements and Interpretations | | |
| Level 2 | Technical Bulletins | Audit and Accounting Guides/SOPs (Specific to Government and Cleared by GASB) | |
| Level 3 | Emerging Issues Task Force Consensus Positions | AcSEC Practice Bulletins (Specific to Government and Cleared by GASB) | |
| Level 4 | Implementation Guides | Audit and Accounting Guides/SOPs/AcSEC Practice Bulletins (Specific to Government but *Not* Cleared by GASB) | Widely Recognized and Prevalent Practice (e.g., 94 *GAAFR*) |
| Other Sources | Concepts Statements | | *GAAFR Review*/ Textbooks/ Articles/FASB Pronouncements |

---

EXHIBIT A
SUMMARY OF FUNDS AND GROUPS OF ACCOUNTS

| TYPE OF FUND OR ACCOUNT GROUP | FUND OR ACCOUNT GROUP | PURPOSE OF FUND | BASIS OF ACCOUNTING | BUDGETARY ACCOUNTS | USES ENCUMBRANCE SYSTEM | CARRIES FIXED ASSETS | CARRIES DEBT |
|---|---|---|---|---|---|---|---|
| A. Governmental (Expendable) | General | Accounts for all revenues and expenditures which are not accounted for in other funds. | Modified Accrual | YES | YES | NO | NO |
| | Special Revenue | Similar to the general fund except the fund accounts for revenue from specific taxes for special purposes. | Modified Accrual | YES | YES | NO | NO |
| | Capital Projects | Receives the proceeds of capital project bonds issues and other matching funds, if applicable; lets contracts and constructs capital project. | Modified Accrual | YES | YES | NO | NO |
| | Debt Service | Accounts for funds to be used for payment of principal and interest on long-term and general obligation debt for governmental funds. | Modified Accrual | Not Usually | NO | NO | NO |
| B. Account Group | General Fixed Asset Account Group | Accounts for all fixed assets for governmental funds. | Modified Accrual | NO | NO | YES, function | NO |
| | General Long-Term Debt Account Groups | Accounts for all long-term debt (maturity one year or more) for governmental funds. | Modified Accrual | NO | NO | NO | YES, function |
| C. Proprietary (Nonexpendable) | Internal Service Funds | Performs services to other government departments on a user-charge basis. | Accrual | Not Usually | NO | YES | YES |
| | Enterprise Uses GAAP | Accounts for self-supporting activities which render service on a user-charge basis to general public. | Accrual | NO | NO | YES | YES |
| D. Fiduciary | Trust -- Expendable | Used to account for assets held by a governmental unit in a trustee capacity or as an agent for individuals, private organizations, other governmental units, and/or funds. Expendable trust funds are accounted for in essentially the same manner as governmental funds. | Modified Accrual | NO | NO | NO | NO |
| | Trust -- Non-Expendable, Pension Trust | Focus is on determination of net income and capital maintenance. Accounting is essentially the same as a proprietary fund. | Accrual | NO | NO | YES | Only debt related to investments |
| | Agency | Mission is custodial in nature. Has the characteristic of a revolving account. | Modified Accrual | NO | NO | NO | NO |

# Chapter Nineteen
# Governmental Accounting Questions

## GASB

1. The primary authoritative body for determining the measurement focus and basis of accounting standards for governmental fund operating statements is the
a. Governmental Accounting Standards Board (GASB).
b. National Council on Governmental Accounting (NCGA).
c. Government Accounting and Auditing Committee of the AICPA (GAAC).
d. Financial Accounting Standards Board (FASB).

## Concepts, Objectives, and Emphasis

2. The primary emphasis in accounting and reporting for governmental funds is on
a. Flow of financial resources.
b. Income determination.
c. Capital maintenance.
d. Transfers relating to proprietary activities.

3. For governmental fund types, which item is considered the primary measurement focus?
a. Income determination.
b. Flows and balances of financial resources.
c. Capital maintenance.
d. Cash flows and balances.

4. Which event(s) is(are) supportive of interperiod equity as a financial reporting objective of a governmental unit?

I. A balanced budget is adopted.
II. Residual equity transfers out equal residual equity transfers in.

a. I only.
b. II only.
c. Both I and II.
d. Neither I nor II.

5. Interperiod equity is an objective of financial reporting for governmental entities. According to the Governmental Accounting Standards Board, is interperiod equity fundamental to public administration and is it a component of accountability?

| | Fundamental to public administration | Component of accountability |
|---|---|---|
| a. | Yes | No |
| b. | No | No |
| c. | No | Yes |
| d. | Yes | Yes |

6. Governmental financial reporting should provide information to assist users in which situation(s)?

I. Making social and political decisions.
II. Assessing whether current-year citizens received services but shifted part of the payment burden to future-year citizens.

a. I only.
b. II only.
c. Both I and II.
d. Neither I nor II.

7. The operating statements of governmental units should embody the
a. All-inclusive approach.
b. Current performance approach.
c. Prospective approach.
d. Retroactive approach.

## Type of Fund or Account Group

8. The special revenue fund of a governmental unit is an example of what type of fund?
a. Governmental.
b. Proprietary.
c. Internal service.
d. Fiduciary.

9. Which of the following funds of a governmental unit uses the modified accrual basis of accounting?
a. Internal service.
b. Enterprise.
c. Nonexpendable trust.
d. Debt service.

10. Which of the following funds of a governmental unit integrates budgetary accounts into the accounting system?
a. Enterprise.
b. Special revenue.
c. Internal service.
d. Nonexpendable trust.

11. A capital projects fund of a municipality is an example of what type of fund?
a. Internal service.
b. Proprietary.
c. Fiduciary.
d. Governmental.

12. Fixed assets should be accounted for in the general fixed assets account group for the

|  | Capital projects fund | Internal service fund |
|---|---|---|
| a. | Yes | Yes |
| b. | Yes | No |
| c. | No | No |
| d. | No | Yes |

13. Which type of fund can be either expendable or nonexpendable?
a. Debt service.
b. Enterprise.
c. Special revenue.
d. Trust.

14. The general fixed assets group of accounts would be used for the fixed assets of the
a. General fund.
b. Enterprise fund.
c. Trust fund.
d. Internal service fund.

15. Which of the following funds of a governmental unit would include contributed capital in its balance sheet?
a. Expendable pension trust.
b. Special revenue.
c. Capital projects.
d. Internal service.

16. The basis of accounting for a capital projects fund is the
a. Cash basis.
b. Accrual basis.

c. Modified cash basis.
d. Modified accrual basis.

17. Which of the following funds of a governmental unit would include retained earnings in its balance sheet?
a. Expendable pension trust.
b. Internal service.
c. Special revenue.
d. Capital projects.

18. A debt service fund of a municipality is an example of which of the following types of fund?
a. Fiduciary.
b. Governmental.
c. Proprietary.
d. Internal service.

19. Taxes collected and held by Eldorado Country for a school district would be accounted for in which of the following funds?
a. Trust.
b. Agency.
c. Special revenue.
d. Internal service.

20. The activities of a municipal employees' retirement and pension system should be recorded in a
a. General fund.
b. Capital projects fund.
c. Internal service fund.
d. Trust fund.

## Modified Accrual

21. The modified accrual basis of accounting should be used for which of the following funds?
a. Capital projects fund.
b. Enterprise fund.
c. Pension trust fund.
d. Proprietary fund.

22. Under the modified accrual basis of accounting for a governmental unit, revenues should be recognized in the accounting period in which they
a. Are earned and become measurable.
b. Are collected.
c. Become available and earned.
d. Become available and measurable.

23. Under which basis of accounting for a governmental unit should revenues be recognized in the accounting period in which they become available and measurable?

| | Accrual basis | Modified accrual basis |
|---|---|---|
| a. | Yes | No |
| b. | Yes | Yes |
| c. | No | Yes |
| d. | No | No |

24. Which of the following funds of a governmental unit recognized revenues in the accounting period in which they become available and measurable?

| | General fund | Enterprise fund |
|---|---|---|
| a. | Yes | No |
| b. | No | Yes |
| c. | Yes | Yes |
| d. | No | No |

25. Under which basis of accounting for a governmental unit should revenues be recognized in the accounting period in which they are earned and become measurable?

| | Accrual basis | Modified accrual basis |
|---|---|---|
| a. | No | No |
| b. | No | Yes |
| c. | Yes | Yes |
| d. | Yes | No |

26. Which of the following bases of accounting should a government use for its proprietary funds in measuring financial position and operating results?

| | Modified accrual basis | Accrual basis |
|---|---|---|
| a. | No | Yes |
| b. | No | No |
| c. | Yes | Yes |
| d. | Yes | No |

## Budget

**Items 27 through 29** are based on the following data:

The Board of Commissioners of Vane City adopted its budget for the year ending July 31, 19X5, comprising estimated revenues of $30,000,000 and appropriations of $29,000,000. Vane formally integrates its budget into the accounting records.

27. What entry should be made for budgeted revenues?
a. Memorandum entry only.
b. Debit estimated revenues receivable control, $30,000,000.
c. Debit estimated revenues control, $30,000,000.
d. Credit estimated revenues control, $30,000,000.

28. What entry should be made for budgeted appropriations?
a. Memorandum entry only.
b. Credit estimated expenditures payable control, $29,000,000.
c. Credit appropriations control, $29,000,000.
d. Debit estimated expenditures control, $29,000,000.

29. What entry should be made for the budgeted excess of revenues over appropriations?
a. Memorandum entry only.
b. Credit budgetary fund balance, $1,000,000.
c. Debit estimated excess revenues control, $1,000,000.
d. Debit excess revenues receivable control, $1,000,000.

---

30. The Board of Commissioners of the City of Rockton adopted its budget for the year ending July 31, 19X2, which indicated revenues of $1,000,000 and appropriations of $900,000. If the budget is formally integrated into the accounting records, what is the required journal entry?

| | | Dr. | Cr. |
|---|---|---|---|
| a. | Memorandum entry only | | |
| b. | Appropriations | $ 900,000 | |
| | General fund | 100,000 | |
| | Estimated revenues | | $1,000,000 |
| c. | Estimated revenues | $1,000,000 | |
| | Appropriations | | $ 900,000 |
| | Budgetary fund balance | | 100,000 |
| d. | Revenues receivable | $1,000,000 | |
| | Expenditures payable | | $ 900,000 |
| | General fund balance | | 100,000 |

31. The estimated revenues control account of a governmental unit is debited when
a. The budget is closed at the end of the year.
b. The budget is recorded.
c. Actual revenues are recorded.
d. Actual revenues are collected.

32. Which of the following accounts of a governmental unit is credited when the budget is recorded?
a. Encumbrances.
b. Reserve for encumbrances.
c. Estimated revenues.
d. Appropriations.

33. Authority granted by a legislative body to make expenditures and to incur obligations during a fiscal year is the definition of an
a. Appropriation.
b. Authorization.
c. Encumbrance.
d. Expenditure.

## Tax Levy

34. The revenues control account of a governmental unit is increased when
a. The budget is recorded.
b. Property taxes are recorded.
c. Appropriations are recorded.
d. The budgetary accounts are closed.

35. Which of the following accounts of a governmental unit is credited when taxpayers are billed for property taxes?
a. Appropriations.
b. Taxes receivable - current.
c. Estimated revenues.
d. Revenues.

36. The following information pertains to property taxes levied by Oak City for the calendar year 19X2:

| | |
|---|---|
| Collections during 19X2 | $500,000 |
| Expected collections during the first 60 days of 19X3 | 100,000 |
| Expected collections during the balance of 19X3 | 60,000 |
| Expected collections during January 19X4 | 30,000 |
| Estimated to be uncollectible | 10,000 |
| Total levy | $700,000 |

What amount should Oak report for 19X2 net property tax revenues?
a. $700,000.
b. $690,000.
c. $600,000.
d. $500,000.

37. Which of the following types of revenue would generally be recorded directly in the general fund of a governmental unit?
a. Receipts from a city-owned parking structure.
b. Interest earned on investments held for retirement of employees.
c. Revenues from internal service funds.
d. Property taxes.

## Encumbrances

38. The following related entries were recorded in sequence in the general fund of a municipality:

| | | |
|---|---|---|
| 1. Encumbrances Control | $12,000 | |
| Fund balance reserved for encumbrances | | $12,000 |
| 2. Fund balance reserved for encumbrances | $12,000 | |
| Encumbrances Control | | $12,000 |
| 3. Expenditures Control | $12,350 | |
| Vouchers payable | | $12,350 |

The sequence of entries indicates that
a. An adverse event was foreseen and a reserve of $12,000 was created; later the reserve was cancelled and a liability for the item was acknowledged.
b. An order was placed for goods or services estimated to cost $12,000; the actual cost was $12,350 for which a liability was acknowledged upon receipt.
c. Encumbrances were anticipated but later failed to materialize and were reversed. A liability of $12,350 was incurred.
d. The first entry was erroneous and was reversed; a liability of $12,350 was acknowledged.

39. The budgetary fund balance reserved for encumbrances account of a governmental fund type is increased when
a. A purchase order is approved.
b. Supplies previously ordered are received.
c. Appropriations are recorded.
d. The budget is recorded.

40. Elm City issued a purchase order for supplies with an estimated cost of $5,000. When the supplies were received, the accompanying invoice indicated an actual price of $4,950. What amount should Elm debit (credit) to the reserve for encumbrances after the supplies and invoice were received?
a. ($50).
b. $50.
c. $4,950.
d. $5,000.

41. Which of the following accounts of a governmental unit is credited when a purchase order is approved?
a. Reserve for encumbrances.
b. Encumbrances.
c. Vouchers payable.
d. Appropriations.

42. Repairs that have been made for a governmental unit, and for which a bill has been received, should be recorded in the general fund as a debit to an
a. Expenditure.
b. Encumbrance.
c. Expense.
d. Appropriation.

43. Which of the following amounts are included in a general fund's encumbrance account?

I. Outstanding vouchers payable amounts.
II. Outstanding purchase order amounts.
III. Excess of the amount of a purchase order over the actual expenditure for that order.

a. I only.
b. I and III.
c. II only
d. II and III.

44. The following balances are included in the subsidiary records of Burwood Village's Parks and Recreation Department at March 31, 19X2:

| | |
|---|---|
| Appropriations -- supplies | $7,500 |
| Expenditures -- supplies | 4,500 |
| Encumbrances -- supply orders | 750 |

How much does the Department have available for additional purchases of supplies?
a. $0.
b. $2,250.

c. $3,000.
d. $6,750.

## Closing Entries

45. When Rolan County adopted its budget for the year ending June 30, 19X0, $20,000,000 was recorded for estimated revenues control. Actual revenues for the year ended June 30, 19X0, amounted to $17,000,000. In closing the budgetary accounts at June 30, 19X0,
a. Revenues control should be debited for $3,000,000.
b. Estimated revenues control should be debited for $3,000,000.
c. Revenues control should be credited for $20,000,000.
d. Estimated revenues control should be credited for $20,000,000.

46. Which of the following accounts should Moon City close at the end of its fiscal year?
a. Vouchers payable.
b. Expenditures.
c. Fund balance.
d. Fund balance — reserved for encumbrances.

47. Which of the following accounts of a governmental unit is (are) closed out at the end of the fiscal year?

| | Estimated revenues | Fund balance |
|---|---|---|
| a. | No | No |
| b. | No | Yes |
| c. | Yes | Yes |
| d. | Yes | No |

48. Harbor City's appropriations control account at December 31, 19X9, had a balance of $7,000,000. When the budgetary accounts were closed at year-end, this $7,000,000 appropriations control balance should have
a. Been debited.
b. Been credited.
c. Remained open.
d. Appeared as a contra account.

49. Oro County's expenditures control account at December 31, 19X9, had a balance of $9,000,000. When Oro's books were closed, this $9,000,000 expenditures control balance should have
a. Been debited.
b. Been credited.
c. Remained open.
d. Appeared as a contra account.

50. The estimated revenues control account balance of a governmental fund type is eliminated when
a. The budget is recorded.
b. The budgetary accounts are closed.
c. Appropriations are closed.
d. Property taxes are recorded.

51. For state and local governmental units, generally accepted accounting principles require that encumbrances outstanding at year-end be reported as
a. Expenditures.
b. Reservations of fund balance.
c. Deferred liabilities.
d. Current liabilities.

## Special Revenue Fund

52. Revenues that are legally restricted to expenditures for specified purposes should be accounted for in special revenue funds, including
a. Accumulation of resources for payment of general long-term debt principal and interest.
b. Pension trust fund revenues.
c. Gasoline taxes to finance road repairs.
d. Proprietary fund revenues.

53. Revenues of a special revenue fund of a governmental unit should be recognized in the period in which the
a. Revenues become available and measurable.
b. Revenues become available for appropriation.
c. Revenues are billable.
d. Cash is received.

54. The following proceeds received by Grove City in 19X7 are legally restricted to expenditure for specified purposes:

Donation by a benefactor mandated
  to an expendable trust fund to
  provide meals for the needy          $300,000
Sales taxes to finance the
  maintenance of tourist facilities
  in the shopping district              900,000

What amount should be accounted for in Grove's special revenue funds?
a. $0
b. $300,000
c. $900,000
d. $1,200,000

## Capital Projects Fund

**Items 55 and 56** are based on the following information:

On December 31, 19X1, Madrid Township paid a contractor $2,000,000 for the total cost of a new firehouse built in 19X1 on Township-owned land. Financing was by means of a $1,500,000 general obligation bond issue sold at face amount on December 31, 19X1, with the remaining $500,000 transferred from the general fund.

55. What should be reported on Madrid's 19X1 financial statements for the capital project fund?
a. Revenues, $1,500,000;
   Expenditures, $1,500,000.
b. Revenues, $1,500,000; Other financing sources, $500,000; Expenditures, $2,000,000.
c. Revenues, $2,000,000;
   Expenditures, $2,000,000.
d. Other financing sources, $2,000,000; Expenditures, $2,000,000.

56. What should be reported on Madrid's .19X1 financial statements for the general fund?
a. Expenditures, $500,000.
b. Other financing uses, $500,000.
c. Revenues, $1,500,000;
   Expenditures, $2,000,000.
d. Revenues, $1,500,000; Other financing uses, $2,000,000.

_____

57. In 19X6, Menton City received $5,000,000 of bond proceeds to be used for capital projects. Of this amount, $1,000,000 was expended in 19X6. Expenditures for the $4,000,000 balance were expected to be incurred in 19X7. These bond proceeds should be recorded in capital projects funds for
a. $5,000,000 in 19X6.
b. $5,000,000 in 19X7.
c. $1,000,000 in 19X6 and $4,000,000 in 19X7.
d. $1,000,000 in 19X6 and in the general fund for $4,000,000 in 19X6.

58. Financing for the renovation of Fir City's municipal park, begun and completed during 19X2, came from the following sources:

| | |
|---|---|
| Grant from state government | 400,000 |
| Proceeds from general obligation | |
| bond issue | 500,000 |
| Transfer from Fir's general fund | 100,000 |

In its 19X2 capital projects fund operating statement, Fir should report these amounts as

| | Revenues | Other financing sources |
|---|---|---|
| a. | $1,000,000 | $0 |
| b. | $900,000 | $100,000 |
| c. | $400,000 | $600,000 |
| d. | $0 | $1,000,000 |

59. Lisa County issued $5,000,000 of general obligation bonds at 101 to finance a capital project. The $50,000 premium was to be used for payment of principal and interest. This transaction should be accounted for in the
a. Capital projects funds, debt service funds, and the general long-term debt account group.
b. Capital projects funds and debt service funds only.
c. Debt service funds and the general long-term debt account group only.
d. Debt service funds only.

## Debt Service Fund

60. In connection with Albury Township's long-term debt, the following cash accumulations are available to cover payment of principal and interest on

| | |
|---|---|
| Bonds for financing of water | |
| treatment plant construction | $1,000,000 |
| General long-term obligations | 400,000 |

The amount of these cash accumulations that should be accounted for in Albury's debt service funds is
a. $0
b. $400,000
c. $1,000,000
d. $1,400,000

61. Tott City's serial bonds are serviced through a debt service fund with cash provided by the general fund. In a debt service fund's statements, how are cash receipts and cash payments reported?

| | Cash receipts | Cash payments |
|---|---|---|
| a. | Revenues | Expenditures |
| b. | Revenues | Operating transfers |
| c. | Operating transfers | Expenditures |
| d. | Operating transfers | Operating transfers |

62. Wood City, which is legally obligated to maintain a debt service fund, issued the following general obligation bonds on July 1, 19X2:

| | |
|---|---|
| Term of bonds | 10 years |
| Face amount | $1,000,000 |
| Issue price | 101 |
| Stated interest rate | 6% |

Interest is payable January 1 and July 1. What amount of bond premium should be amortized in Wood's debt service fund for the year ended December 31, 19X2?
a. $1,000.
b. $500.
c. $250.
d. $0.

_____

**Items 63 and 64** are based on the following information:

The following events relating to the City of Albury's debt service funds occurred during the year ended December 31, 19X1:

| | |
|---|---|
| Debt principal matured | $2,000,000 |
| Unmatured (accrued) interest on | |
| outstanding debt at Jan. 1, 19X1 | 50,000 |
| Interest on matured debt | 900,000 |
| Unmatured (accrued) interest on | |
| outstanding debt at Dec. 31, 19X1 | 100,000 |
| Interest revenue from investments | 600,000 |
| Cash transferred from general fund | |
| for retirement of debt principal | 1,000,000 |
| Cash transferred from general fund | |
| for payment of matured interest | 900,000 |

All principal and interest due in 19X1 were paid on time.

63. What is the total amount of expenditures that Albury's debt service funds should record for the year ended December 31, 19X1?
a. $900,000.
b. $950,000.
c. $2,900,000.
d. $2,950,000.

64. How much revenue should Albury's debt service funds record for the year ended December 31, 19X1?
a. $600,000.
b. $1,600,000.
c. $1,900,000.
d. $2,500,000.

## Fixed Asset Account Group

65. Fixed assets should be accounted for in the general fixed asset account group for the

| | Enterprise fund | Special revenue fund |
|---|---|---|
| a. | Yes | No |
| b. | Yes | Yes |
| c. | No | Yes |
| d. | No | No |

66. Fixed assets should be accounted for in the general fixed assets account group for

| | Governmental funds | Proprietary funds |
|---|---|---|
| a. | No | Yes |
| b. | No | No |
| c. | Yes | No |
| d. | Yes | Yes |

67. Fixed assets used by a governmental unit should be accounted for in the

| | Capital projects fund | General fund |
|---|---|---|
| a. | No | Yes |
| b. | No | No |
| c. | Yes | No |
| d. | Yes | Yes |

68. Dodd Village received a gift of a new fire engine from a local civic group. The fair value of this fire engine was $400,000. The entry to be made in the general fixed assets account group for this gift is

| | | Debit | Credit |
|---|---|---|---|
| a. | Memorandum entry only | --- | --- |
| b. | General fund assets | $400,000 | |
| | Private gifts | | $400,000 |
| c. | Investment in general fixed assets | $400,000 | |
| | Gift revenue | | $400,000 |
| d. | Machinery & equipment | $400,000 | |
| | Investment in general fixed assets from private gifts | | $400,000 |

69. The recording of accumulated depreciation in the general fixed assets account group is
a. Never allowed.
b. Dependent on materiality.
c. Optional.
d. Mandatory.

70. The following assets are among those owned by the City of Foster:

| | |
|---|---|
| Apartment building (part of the principal of a nonexpendable trust fund) | $ 200,000 |
| City Hall | 800,000 |
| Three fire stations | 1,000,000 |
| City streets and sidewalks | 5,000,000 |

How much should be included in Foster's general fixed assets account group?
a. $1,800,000 or $6,800,000.
b. $2,000,000 or $7,000,000.
c. $6,800,000, without election of $1,800,000.
d. $7,000,000, without election of $2,000,000.

71. The general fixed assets group of accounts for a municipality can best be described as
a. A fiscal entity.
b. An accounting entity.
c. An integral part of the general fund.
d. The only fund in which to properly account for fixed assets.

## Long-Term Debt Group

72. The total assets of the general long-term debt account group of a governmental unit consist of the
a. Amount available in debt service funds account plus the amount to be provided for retirement of general long-term debt account.
b. Amount available in debt service funds account minus the amount to be provided for retirement of general long-term debt account.
c. Amount available in debt service funds account only.
d. Amount to be provided for retirement of general long-term debt account only.

73. Which of the following accounts would be included in the combined balance sheet for the long-term debt account group?
a. Amount to be provided for retirement of general long-term debt.
b. Unreserved fund balance.
c. Reserve for encumbrances.
d. Cash.

74. The amount available in debt service funds is an account of a governmental unit that would be included in the
a. Liability section of the general long-term debt account group.
b. Liability section of the debt service fund.
c. Asset section of the general long-term debt account group.
d. Asset section of the debt service fund.

75. Maple Township issued the following bonds during the year ended June 30, 19X0:

Bonds issued for the garbage
  collection enterprise fund
  that will service the debt     $500,000
Revenue bonds to be repaid from
  admission fees collected by the
  Township zoo enterprise fund     350,000

What amount of these bonds should be accounted for in Maple's general long-term debt account group?
a. $0
b. $350,000
c. $500,000
d. $850,000

## Proprietary Funds

76. The following funds are among those maintained by Arlon City:

| | |
|---|---|
| Enterprise funds | $2,000,000 |
| Internal service funds | 800,000 |

Arlon's proprietary funds amount to
a. $0
b. $800,000
c. $2,000,000
d. $2,800,000

77. The town of Hill operates municipal electric and water utilities. In which of the following funds should the operations of the utilities be accounted for?
a. Enterprise fund.
b. Internal service fund.
c. Agency fund.
d. Special revenue fund.

78. Which of the following is an appropriate basis of accounting for a proprietary fund of a governmental unit?

| | Cash basis | Modified accrual basis |
|---|---|---|
| a. | Yes | Yes |
| b. | Yes | No |
| c. | No | No |
| d. | No | Yes |

## Enterprise Fund

79. An enterprise fund would be used when the governing body requires that

I. Accounting for the financing of an agency's services to other government departments be on a cost-reimbursement basis.
II. User charges cover the costs of general public services.
III. Net income information be provided for an activity.

a. I only.
b. II only.
c. I and III.
d. II and III.

80. During 19X9, Spruce City reported the following receipts from self-sustaining activities paid for by users of the services rendered:

| | |
|---|---|
| Operation of water supply plant | $5,000,000 |
| Operation of bus system | 900,000 |

What amount should be accounted for in Spruce's enterprise funds?
a. $0
b. $900,000
c. $5,000,000
d. $5,900,000

81. Fixed assets of an enterprise fund should be accounted for in the
a. General fixed asset account group but **no** depreciation on the fixed assets should be recorded.
b. General fixed asset account group and depreciation on the fixed assets should be recorded.
c. Enterprise fund but **no** depreciation on the fixed assets should be recorded.
d. Enterprise fund and depreciation on the fixed assets should be recorded.

82. Which of the following accounts could be included in the balance sheet of an enterprise fund?

| | Reserve for encumbrances | Revenue bonds payable | Retained earnings |
|---|---|---|---|
| a. | No | No | Yes |
| b. | No | Yes | Yes |
| c. | Yes | Yes | No |
| d. | No | No | No |

83. Which of the following fund types or account group should account for fixed assets in a manner similar to a "for profit" organization?
a. Special revenue fund.
b. Capital projects fund.
c. General fixed assets account group.
d. Enterprise fund.

84. How would customers' security deposits which can **not** be spent for normal operation purposes be classified in the balance sheet of the enterprise fund of a governmental unit?

| | Restricted asset | Liability | Fund equity |
|---|---|---|---|
| a. | Yes | No | Yes |
| b. | Yes | Yes | No |
| c. | Yes | Yes | Yes |
| d. | No | Yes | No |

85. Long-term liabilities of an enterprise fund should be accounted for in the

| | Enterprise fund | Long-term debt account group |
|---|---|---|
| a. | No | No |
| b. | No | Yes |
| c. | Yes | Yes |
| d. | Yes | No |

## Internal Service Fund

86. The billings for transportation services provided to other governmental units are recorded by the internal service fund as
a. Interfund exchanges.
b. Intergovernmental transfers.
c. Transportation appropriations.
d. Operating revenues.

87. Lake City operates a centralized data processing center through an internal service fund, to provide data processing services to Lake's other governmental units. In 19X6, this internal service fund billed Lake's water and sewer fund $100,000 for data processing services. How should the internal service fund record this billing?

| | Debit | Credit |
|---|---|---|
| a. Memorandum entry only | -- | -- |
| b. Due from water and sewer fund | $100,000 | |
|     Data processing department expenses | | $100,000 |
| c. Intergovernmental transfers | $100,000 | |
|     Interfund exchanges | | $100,000 |
| d. Due from water and sewer fund | $100,000 | |
|     Operating revenues control | $100,000 | |

88. Gem City's internal service fund received a residual equity transfer of $50,000 cash from the general fund. This $50,000 transfer should be reported in Gem's internal service fund as a credit to
a. Revenues.
b. Other financing sources.
c. Accounts payable.
d Contributed capital.

89. Which of the following does **not** affect an internal service fund's net income?
a. Depreciation expense on its fixed assets.
b. Operating transfers in.
c. Operating transfers out.
d. Residual equity transfers.

## Trust and Agency Funds

90. Arlen City's fiduciary funds contained the following cash balances at December 31, 19X2:

Under the Forfeiture Act - cash
  confiscated from illegal activities;
  disbursements can be used only for
  law enforcement activities      $300,000
Sales taxes collected by Arlen to be
  distributed to other governmental
  units      500,000

What amount of cash should Arlen report in its expendable trust funds at December 31, 19X2?
a. $0.
b. $300,000.
c. $500,000.
d. $800,000.

91. The debt service transactions of a special assessment bond issue for which the government is **not** obligated in any manner should be reported in the
a. Agency fund.
b. Enterprise fund.
c. Special revenue fund.
d. Long-term debt account group.

92. Which of the following funds of a governmental unit uses the same basis of accounting as the enterprise fund?
a. Nonexpendable trust funds.
b. Expendable trust funds.
c. Special revenue funds.
d. Capital projects funds.

93. Stone Corp. donated investments to Pine City and stipulated that the income from the investments be used to acquire art for the city's museum. Which of the following funds should be used to account for the investments?
a. Endowment fund.
b. Special revenue fund.
c. Expendable trust fund.
d. Nonexpendable trust fund.

94. Maple City's public employee retirement system (PERS) reported the following account balances at June 30, 19X1:

Reserve for employer's contributions    $5,000,000
Actuarial deficiency in reserve for
  employer's contributions      300,000
Reserve for employees' contributions    9,000,000

Maple's PERS fund balance at June 30, 19X1, should be
a. $5,000,000
b. $5,300,000
c. $14,000,000
d. $14,300,000

95. Taxes collected and held by Franklin County for a separate school district would be accounted for in which fund?
a. Special revenue.
b. Internal service.
c. Trust.
d. Agency.

## Comprehensive Annual Financial Report (CAFR)

96. The comprehensive annual financial report (CAFR) of a governmental unit should contain a combined balance sheet for

|   | Governmental funds | Proprietary funds | Account groups |
|---|---|---|---|
| a. | Yes | Yes | No |
| b. | Yes | Yes | Yes |
| c. | Yes | No | Yes |
| d. | No | Yes | No |

97. In a government's comprehensive annual financial report (CAFR), account groups are included in which of the following combined financial statements?

|   | Balance sheet | Statement of revenues, expenditures, and changes in fund balances |
|---|---|---|
| a. | Yes | No |
| b. | No | Yes |
| c. | Yes | Yes |
| d. | No | No |

98. The comprehensive annual financial report (CAFR) of a city should contain a combined statement of revenues, expenditures, and changes in fund balances for

|    | Account groups | Proprietary funds |
|----|----------------|-------------------|
| a. | Yes | Yes |
| b. | Yes | No |
| c. | No | Yes |
| d. | No | No |

99. The comprehensive annual financial report (CAFR) of a governmental unit should contain a combined statement of revenues, expenses, and changes in retained earnings for

|    | Account groups | Governmental funds |
|----|----------------|--------------------|
| a. | Yes | Yes |
| b. | Yes | No |
| c. | No | No |
| d. | No | Yes |

100. In a government's comprehensive annual financial report (CAFR), proprietary fund types are included in which of the following combined financial statements?

|    | Statement of revenues expenditures, and changes in fund balances | Balance sheet |
|----|------------------------------------------------------------------|---------------|
| a. | Yes | Yes |
| b. | No | No |
| c. | No | Yes |
| d. | Yes | No |

101. Eureka City should issue a statement of cash flows for which of the following funds?

|    | Eureka City Hall capital projects fund | Eureka Water Enterprise fund |
|----|----------------------------------------|------------------------------|
| a. | No | Yes |
| b. | No | No |
| c. | Yes | No |
| d. | Yes | Yes |

102. The following transactions were among those reported by Cliff County's water and sewer enterprise fund for 19X1:

| | |
|---|---|
| Proceeds from sale of revenue bonds | $5,000,000 |
| Cash received from customer households | 3,000,000 |
| Capital contributed by subdividers | 1,000,000 |

In the water and sewer enterprise fund's statement of cash flows for the year ended December 31, 19X1, what amount should be reported as cash flows from capital and related financing activities?
a. $9,000,000
b. $8,000,000
c. $6,000,000
d. $5,000,000

## Review Questions

103. In which of the following fund types of a city government are revenues and expenditures recognized on the same basis of accounting?
a. Nonexpendable trust.
b. Internal service.
c. Enterprise.
d. Debt service.

104. A state governmental unit should use which basis of accounting for each of the following types of funds?

|    | Governmental | Proprietary |
|----|--------------|-------------|
| a. | Cash | Modified accrual |
| b. | Modified accrual | Modified accrual |
| c. | Modified accrual | Accrual |
| d. | Accrual | Accrual |

105. When the budget of a governmental unit, for which the estimated revenues exceed the appropriations, is adopted and recorded in the general ledger at the beginning of the year, the budgetary fund balance account is
a. Credited at the beginning of the year and **no** entry made at the end of the year.
b. Credited at the beginning of the year and debited at the end of the year.
c. Debited at the beginning of the year and **no** entry made at the end of the year.
d. Debited at the beginning of the year and credited at the end of the year.

106. Cal City maintains several major fund types. The following were among Cal's cash receipts during 19X3:

| | |
|---|---|
| Unrestricted state grant | $1,000,000 |
| Interest on bank accounts held for employees' pension plan | 200,000 |

What amount of these cash receipts should be accounted for in Cal's general fund?
a. $1,200,000.
b. $1,000,000.
c. $200,000.
d. $0.

107. The modified accrual basis of accounting is appropriate for which of the following fund categories of a county government?

| | *Governmental* | *Proprietary* |
|---|---|---|
| a. | No | No |
| b. | No | Yes |
| c. | Yes | Yes |
| d. | Yes | No |

108. For the budgetary year ending December 31, 19X3, Maple City's general fund expects the following inflows of resources:

| | |
|---|---|
| Property taxes, licenses, and fines | $9,000,000 |
| Proceeds of debt issue | 5,000,000 |
| Interfund transfers for debt service | 1,000,000 |

In the budgetary entry, what amount should Maple record for estimated revenues?
a. $9,000,000.
b. $10,000,000.
c. $14,000,000.
d. $15,000,000.

---

**Items 109 and 110 are based on the following:**
Ridge Township's governing body adopted its general fund budget for the year ended July 31, 19X4, comprised of estimated revenues of $100,000 and appropriations of $80,000. Ridge formally integrates its budget into the accounting records.

109. To record the appropriations of $80,000, Ridge should
a. Credit appropriations control.
b. Debit appropriations control.
c. Credit estimated expenditures control.
d. Debit estimated expenditures control.

110. To record the $20,000 budgeted excess of estimated revenues over appropriations, Ridge should
a. Credit estimated excess revenues control.
b. Debit estimated excess revenues control.
c. Credit budgetary fund balance.
d. Debit budgetary fund balance.

---

111. The revenues control account of a governmental unit is debited when
a. The budget is recorded at the beginning of the year.
b. The account is closed out at the end of the year.
c. Property taxes are recorded.
d. Property taxes are collected.

112. For which of the following governmental entities that use proprietary fund accounting should a statement of cash flows be presented ?

| | *Public benefit corporations* | *Governmental utilities* |
|---|---|---|
| a. | No | No |
| b. | No | Yes |
| c. | Yes | Yes |
| d. | Yes | No |

113. Wells Township issued the following long-term obligations:

| | |
|---|---|
| Revenue bonds to be repaid from admission fees collected by the township swimming pool | $500,000 |
| General obligation bonds issued for the township water and sewer fund which will service the debt | 900,000 |

Although the above-mentioned bonds are expected to be paid from enterprise funds, the full faith and credit of Wells Township has been pledged as further assurance that the liabilities will be paid. What amount of these bonds should be accounted for in the general long-term debt account group?
a. $1,400,000
b. $900,000
c. $500,000
d. $0

114. The appropriations control account of a governmental unit is debited when
a. Supplies are purchased.
b. Expenditures are recorded.
c. The budgetary accounts are closed.
d. The budget is recorded.

115. During 19X7, Pine City recorded the following receipts from self-sustaining activities paid for by users of the services rendered:

| | |
|---|---|
| Municipal bus system | $1,000,000 |
| Operation of water supply and sewerage plant | 1,800,000 |

What amount should be accounted for in Pine's enterprise funds?
a. $2,800,000
b. $1,800,000
c. $1,000,000
d. $0

116. Customers' security deposits that cannot be spent for normal operating purposes were collected by a governmental unit and accounted for in the enterprise fund. A portion of the amount collected was invested in marketable securities. How would the portion in cash and the portion in marketable securities be classified in the balance sheet of the enterprise fund?

| | Portion in cash | Portion in marketable securities |
|---|---|---|
| a. | Restricted asset | Restricted asset |
| b. | Restricted asset | Unrestricted asset |
| c. | Unrestricted asset | Unrestricted asset |
| d. | Unrestricted asset | Restricted asset |

117. Lake City incurred $300,000 of salaries and wages expense in its general fund for the month ended May 31, 19X9. For this $300,000 expense, Lake should debit
a. Fund balance -- unreserved, undesignated.
b. Encumbrances control.
c. Appropriations control.
d. Expenditures control.

118. The following revenues were among those reported by Ariba Township in 19X9:

| | |
|---|---|
| Net rental revenue (after depreciation) from a parking garage owned by Ariba | $ 40,000 |
| Interest earned on investments held for employees' retirement benefits | 100,000 |
| Property taxes | 6,000,000 |

What amount of the foregoing revenues should be accounted for in Ariba's governmental-type funds?
a. $6,140,000
b. $6,100,000
c. $6,040,000
d. $6,000,000

119. Pine City's year end is June 30. Pine levies property taxes in January of each year for the calendar year. One-half of the levy is due in May and one-half is due in October. Property tax revenue is budgeted for the period in which payment is due. The following information pertains to Pine's property taxes for the period from July 1, 19X0, to June 30, 19X1:

| | Calendar year | |
|---|---|---|
| | 19X0 | 19X1 |
| Levy | $2,000,000 | $2,400,000 |
| Collected in: | | |
| May | 950,000 | 1,100,000 |
| July | 50,000 | 60,000 |
| October | 920,000 | |
| December | 80,000 | |

The $40,000 balance due for the May 19X1 installments was expected to be collected in August 19X1. What amount should Pine recognize for property tax revenue for the year ended June 30, 19X1?
a. $2,160,000
b. $2,200,000
c. $2,360,000
d. $2,400,000

120. For governmental units, depreciation expense on assets acquired with capital grants externally restricted for capital acquisitions should be reported in which type of fund?

| | Governmental fund | Proprietary fund |
|---|---|---|
| a. | Yes | No |
| b. | Yes | Yes |
| c. | No | No |
| d. | No | Yes |

121. The general purpose financial statements of a state government
a. May **not** be issued separately from the comprehensive annual financial report.
b. Are comprised of the combined financial statements and related notes.
c. Are synonymous with the comprehensive annual financial report.
e. Contain more detailed information regarding the state government's finances than is contained in the comprehensive annual financial report.

122. The following equity balances are among those maintained by Cole City:

| | |
|---|---|
| Enterprise funds | $1,000,000 |
| Internal service funds | 400,000 |

Cole's proprietary equity balances amount to
a. $1,400,000.
b. $1,000,000.
c. $400,000.
d. $0.

---

**Items 123 and 124** are based on the following:
On December 31, 19X7, Vane City paid a contractor $3,000,000 for the total cost of a new municipal annex built in 19X7 on city-owned land. Financing was provided by a $2,000,000 general obligation bond issue sold at face amount on December 31, 19X7, with the remaining $1,000,000 transferred from the general fund.

123. What account and amount should be reported in Vane's 19X7 financial statements for the general fund?
a. Other financing uses control, $1,000,000.
b. Other financing sources control, $2,000,000.
c. Expenditure control, $3,000,000.
d. Other financing sources control, $3,000,000.

124. What accounts and amounts should be reported in Vane's 19X7 financial statements for the capital projects fund?
a. Other financing source control, $2,000,000; General long-term debt, $2,000,000.
b. Revenues control, $2,000,000; Expenditures control, $2,000,000.
c. Other financing sources control, $3,000,000; Expenditures control, $3,000,000.
d. Revenues control, $3,000,000; Expenditures control, $3,000,000.

---

125. Kew City received a $15,000,000 federal grant to finance the construction of a center for rehabilitation of drug addicts. The proceeds of this grant should be accounted for in the
a. Special revenue funds.
b. General fund.
c. Capital projects funds.
d. Trust funds.

126. The following information pertains to Pine City's general fund for 19X9:

| | |
|---|---|
| Appropriations | $6,500,000 |
| Expenditures | 5,000,000 |
| Other financing sources | 1,500,000 |
| Other financing uses | 2,000,000 |
| Revenues | 8,000,000 |

After Pine's general fund accounts were closed at the end of 19X9, the fund balance increased by
a. $3,000,000
b. $2,500,000
c. $1,500,000
d. $1,000,000

127. Through an internal service fund, Wood County operates a centralized data processing center to provide services to Wood's other governmental units. In 19X9, this internal service fund billed Wood's parks and recreation fund $75,000 for data processing services. What account should Wood's internal service fund credit to record this $75,000 billing to the parks and recreation fund?
a. Operating revenues control.
b. Interfund exchanges.
c. Intergovernmental transfers.
d. Data processing department expenses.

128. The appropriations control account of a governmental unit is credited when
a. Supplies are purchased.
b. Expenditures are recorded.
c. The budget is recorded.
d. The budgetary accounts are closed.

129. The estimated revenues control account balance of a governmental fund type is eliminated when
a. The budgetary accounts are closed.
b. The budget is recorded.
c. Property taxes are recorded.
d. Appropriations are closed.

130. At December 31, 19X1, the following balances were due from the state government to Clare City's various funds:

| | |
|---|---|
| Capital projects | $300,000 |
| Trust and agency | 100,000 |
| Enterprise | 80,000 |

In Clare's December 31, 19X1, combined balance sheet for all fund types and account groups, what amount should be classified under governmental funds?
a. $100,000
b. $180,000
c. $300,000
d. $480,000

131. The Amount Available in Debt Service Funds is an account of a governmental unit that would be included in the
a. Liability section of the debt service fund.
b. Liability section of the general long-term debt account group.
c. Asset section of the debt service fund.
d. Asset section of the general long-term debt account group.

132. Fixed assets donated to a governmental unit should be recorded
a. As a memorandum entry only.
b. At the donor's carrying amount.
c. At estimated fair value when received.
d. At the lower of donor's carrying amount or estimated fair value when received.

133. Which of the following funds of a governmental unit could use the general fixed asset account group to account for fixed assets?
a. Internal service.
b. Enterprise.
c. Special revenue.
d. Trust.

134. Which of the following funds of a governmental unit uses the modified accrual basis of accounting?
a. Enterprise funds.
b. Internal service funds.
c. Nonexpendable trust funds.
d. Special revenue funds.

135. In 19X9, a state government collected income taxes of $8,000,000 for the benefit of one of its cities that imposes an income tax on its residents. The state remitted these collections periodically to the city. The state should account for the $8,000,000 in the
a. General fund.
b. Agency funds.
c. Internal service funds.
d. Special assessment funds.

136. Which of the following funds of a governmental unit uses the same basis of accounting as an enterprise fund?
a. Special revenue.
b. Expendable trust.
c. Capital projects.
d. Internal service.

137. In 19X3, Palm City acquired, through forfeiture as a result of nonpayment of property taxes, a parcel of land that the city intends to use as a parking lot for general governmental purposes. The total amount of taxes, liens, and other costs incurred by Palm incidental to acquiring ownership and perfecting title was $20,000. The land's fair market value at the forfeiture date was $60,000. What amount should be capitalized in the general fixed assets account group for this land?
a. $0.
b. $20,000.
c. $60,000.
d. $80,000.

138. If a city legally adopts its annual general fund budget on the modified accrual basis of accounting, its estimated revenues should be
a. Reported on the modified accrual basis of accounting in the general fund statement of revenues, expenditures, and changes in fund balance - budget and actual.
b. Converted to the cash basis of accounting and reported in the general fund statement of revenues, expenditures, and other changes in fund balance - budget and actual.
c. Reported as current assets in the general fund balance sheet.
d. Reported as noncurrent assets in the general fund balance sheet.

139. Which of the following accounts would be included in the fund equity section of the combined balance sheet of a governmental unit for the general fixed asset account group?

|    | Investment in general fixed assets | Fund balance reserved for encumbrances |
|----|-----|-----|
| a. | Yes | Yes |
| b. | Yes | No  |
| c. | No  | No  |
| d. | No  | Yes |

140. Customers' security deposits that cannot be spent for normal operating purposes were collected by a governmental unit and accounted for in the enterprise fund. A portion of the amount collected was invested in marketable debt securities and a portion in marketable equity securities. How would each portion be classified in the balance sheet?

|    | Portion in marketable debt securities | Portion in marketable equity securities |
|----|-----|-----|
| a. | Unrestricted asset | Restricted asset |
| b. | Unrestricted asset | Unrestricted asset |
| c. | Restricted asset | Unrestricted asset |
| d. | Restricted asset | Restricted asset |

141. Which of the following statements is correct concerning a governmental entity's combined statement of cash flows?
a. Cash flows from capital financing activities are reported separately from cash flows from noncapital financing activities.
b. The statement format is the same as that of a business enterprise's statement of cash flows.
c. Cash flows from operating activities may **not** be reported using the indirect method.
d. The statement format includes columns for the general, governmental, and proprietary fund types.

142. Fixed assets used by a governmental unit should be accounted for in the

|    | Capital projects fund | General fund |
|----|-----|-----|
| a. | Yes | Yes |
| b. | Yes | No  |
| c. | No  | No  |
| d. | No  | Yes |

143. Through an internal service fund, New County operates a centralized data processing center to provide services to New's other governmental units. In 19X2, this internal service fund billed New's parks and recreation fund $150,000 for data processing services. What account should New's internal service fund credit to record this $150,000 billing to the parks and recreation fund?
a. Data processing department expenses.
b. Intergovernmental transfers.
c. Interfund exchanges.
d. Operating revenues control.

144. When fixed assets purchased from general fund revenues were received, the appropriate journal entry was made in the general fixed asset account group. What account, if any, should have been debited in the general fund?
a. No journal entry should have been made in the general fund.
b. Fixed assets.
c. Expenditures.
d. Due from general fixed asset account group.

145. Which of the following accounts of a governmental unit is debited when a purchase order is approved?
a. Appropriations control.
b. Vouchers payable.
c. Fund balance reserved for encumbrances.
d. Encumbrances control.

146. During its fiscal year ended June 30, 19X3, Cliff City issued purchase orders totaling $5,000,000, which were properly charged to encumbrances at that time. Cliff received goods and related invoices at the encumbered amounts totaling $4,500,000 before year end. The remaining goods of $500,000 were not received until after year end. Cliff paid $4,200,000 of the invoices received during the year.

What amount of Cliff's encumbrances were outstanding at June 30, 19X3?
a. $0.
b. $300,000.
c. $500,000.
d. $800,000.

147. A budgetary fund balance reserved for encumbrances in excess of a balance of encumbrances indicates
a. An excess of vouchers payable over encumbrances.
b. An excess of purchase orders over invoices received.
c. An excess of appropriations over encumbrances.
d. A recording error.

148. Gold County received goods that had been approved for purchase but for which payment had not yet been made. Should the accounts listed below be increased?

|    | Encumbrances | Expenditures |
|----|--------------|--------------|
| a. | No           | No           |
| b. | No           | Yes          |
| c. | Yes          | No           |
| d. | Yes          | Yes          |

149. During its fiscal year ended June 30, 19X8, Lake County financed the following projects by special assessments:

| Capital improvements | $2,000,000 |
|----------------------|------------|
| Service-type projects | 800,000 |

For financial reporting purposes, what amount should appear in special assessment funds?
a. $2,800,000
b. $2,000,000
c. $800,000
d. $0

150. Which of the following funds of a governmental unit uses the modified accrual basis of accounting?
a. Internal service funds.
b. Enterprise funds.
c. Special revenue funds.
d. Nonexpendable trust funds.

151. The encumbrance account of a governmental unit is debited when
a. The budget is recorded.
b. A purchase order is approved.
c. Goods are received.
d. A voucher payable is recorded.

152. Grove County collects property taxes levied within its boundaries and receives a 1% fee for administering these collections on behalf of the municipalities located in the county. In 19X7, Grove collected $1,000,000 for its municipalities and remitted $990,000 to them after deducting fees of $10,000. In the initial recording of the 1% fee, Grove's agency fund should credit
a. Fund balance -- agency fund, $10,000.
b. Fees earned -- agency fund, $10,000.
c. Due to Grove County general fund, $10,000.
d. Revenues control, $10,000.

153. In the comprehensive annual financial report (CAFR) of a governmental unit, the account groups are included in
a. Both the combined balance sheet and the combined statement of revenues, expenditures, and changes in fund balances.
b. The combined statement of revenues, expenditures, and changes in fund balances, but **not** the combined balance sheet.
c. The combined balance sheet but **not** the combined statement of revenues, expenditures, and changes in fund balances.
d. Neither the combined balance sheet nor the combined statement of revenues, expenditures, and changes in fund balances.

154. Lake County received the following proceeds that are legally restricted to expenditure for specified purposes:

| Levies on affected property owners to install sidewalks | $500,000 |
|----------------------------------------------------------|----------|
| Gasoline taxes to finance road repairs | 900,000 |

What amount should be accounted for in Lake's special revenue fund?
a. $1,400,000
b. $900,000
c. $500,000
d. $0

155. Kingsford City incurred $100,000 of salaries and wages for the month ended March 31, 19X2. How should this be recorded at that date?

|   |   | Dr. | Cr. |
|---|---|---|---|
| a. | Expenditures -- salaries and wages | $100,000 | |
| | Vouchers payable | | $100,000 |
| b. | Salaries and wages expense | $100,000 | |
| | Vouchers payable | | $100,000 |
| c. | Encumbrances -- salaries and wages | $100,000 | |
| | Vouchers payable | | $100,000 |
| d. | Fund balance | $100,000 | |
| | Vouchers payable | | $100,000 |

156. Central County received proceeds from various towns and cities for capital projects financed by Central's long-term debt. A special tax was assessed by each local government, and a portion of the tax was restricted to repay the long-term debt of Central's capital projects. Central should account for the restricted portion of the special tax in which of the following funds?
a. Internal service fund.
b. Enterprise fund.
c. Capital projects fund.
d. Debt service fund.

157. One feature of state and local government accounting and financial reporting is that fixed assets used for general government activities
a. Often are **not** expected to contribute to the generation of revenues.
b. Do **not** depreciate as a result of such use.
c. Are acquired only when direct contribution to revenues is expected.
d. Should **not** be maintained at the same level as those of businesses so that current financial resources can be used for other government services.

158. The budgetary fund balance reserved for encumbrances account of a governmental-type fund is increased when
a. The budget is recorded.
b. Appropriations are recorded.
c. Supplies previously ordered are received.
d. A purchase order is approved.

159. The debt service fund of a governmental unit is used to account for the accumulation of resources to pay, and the payment of, general long-term debt

|   | Principal | Interest |
|---|---|---|
| a. | Yes | Yes |
| b. | Yes | No |
| c. | No | No |
| d. | No | Yes |

160. The following items were among Kew Township's expenditures from the general fund during the year ended July 31, 19X1:

| | |
|---|---|
| Minicomputer for tax collector's office | $22,000 |
| Furniture for Township Hall | 40,000 |

How much should be classified as fixed assets in Kew's general fund balance sheet at July 31, 19X1?
a. $0.
b. $22,000.
c. $40,000.
d. $62,000.

161. Fred Bosin donated a building to Palma City in 19X3. Bosin's original cost of the property was $100,000. Accumulated depreciation at the date of the gift amounted to $60,000. Fair market value at the date of the gift was $300,000. In the general fixed assets account group, at what amount should Palma record this donated fixed asset?
a. $300,000.
b. $100,000.
c. $ 40,000.
d. $0.

———————

**Items 162 and 163** are based on the following:
Elm City contributes to and administers a single-employer defined benefit pension plan on behalf of its covered employees. The plan is accounted for in a pension trust fund. Actuarially determined employer contribution requirements and contributions actually made for the past three years, along with the percentage of annual covered payroll, were as follows:

| | Contribution made | | Actuarial requirements | |
|---|---|---|---|---|
| | Amount | Percent | Amount | Percent |
| 19X9 | $11,000 | 26 | $11,000 | 26 |
| 19X8 | 5,000 | 12 | 10,000 | 24 |
| 19X7 | None | None | 8,000 | 20 |

162. What account should be credited in the pension trust fund to record the 19X9 employer contribution of $11,000?
a. Revenues control.
b. Other financing sources control.
c. Due from special revenue fund.
d. Pension benefit obligation.

163. To record the 19X9 pension contribution of $11,000, what debit is required in the governmental-type fund used in connection with employer pension contributions?
a. Other financing uses control.
b. Expenditures control.
c. Expenses control.
d. Due to pension trust fund.

_____

164. The following information pertains to Wood Township's long-term debt:

Cash accumulations to cover payment of principal and interest on
| | |
|---|---|
| General long-term obligations | $350,000 |
| Proprietary fund obligations | 100,000 |

How much of these cash accumulations should be accounted for in Wood's debt service funds?
a. $0
b. $100,000
c. $350,000
d. $450,000

165. The following information pertains to certain monies held by Blair County at December 31, 19X2, that are legally restricted to expenditures for specified purposes:

| | |
|---|---|
| Proceeds of short-term notes to be used for advances to expendable trust funds | $8,000 |
| Proceeds of long-term debt to be used for a major capital project | 90,000 |

What amount of these restricted monies should Blair account for in special revenue funds?
a. $0.
b. $8,000.
c. $90,000.
d. $98,000.

166. Albee Township's fiscal year ends on June 30. Albee uses encumbrance accounting. On April 5,

19X4, an approved $1,000 purchase order was issued for supplies. Albee received these supplies on May 2, 19X4, and the $1,000 invoice was approved for payment. What journal entry should Albee make on April 5, 19X4, to record the approved purchase order?

| | Debit | Credit |
|---|---|---|
| a. Memorandum entry only | - | -- |
| b. Encumbrances control | $1,000 | |
|    Fund balance reserved for encumbrances | | $1,000 |
| c. Supplies | 1,000 | |
|    Vouchers payable | | 1,000 |
| d. Encumbrances control | 1,000 | |
|    Appropriations control | | 1,000 |

167. Which of the following accounts of a governmental unit is credited when supplies previously ordered are received?
a. Fund balance reserved for encumbrances.
b. Encumbrances control.
c. Expenditures control.
d. Appropriations control.

168. The fund balance reserved for encumbrances account of a governmental unit is decreased when
a. Supplies previously ordered are received.
b. A purchase order is approved.
c. The vouchers are paid.
d. Appropriations are recorded.

169. Which of the following accounts of a governmental unit is debited when supplies previously ordered are received?
a. Appropriations control.
b. Encumbrances control.
c. Fund balance reserved for encumbrances.
d. Vouchers payable.

170. On December 31, 19X8, Park Township paid a contractor $4,000,000 for the total cost of a new police building built in 19X8. Financing was by means of a $3,000,000 general obligation bond issue sold at face amount on December 31, 19X8, with the remaining $1,000,000 transferred from the general fund. What amount should Park record as revenues in the capital projects fund in connection with the bond issue proceeds and the transfer?
a. $0
b. $1,000,000
c. $3,000,000
d. $4,000,000

171. In what fund type should the proceeds from special assessment bonds issued to finance construction of sidewalks in a new subdivision be reported?
a. Agency fund.
b. Special fund.
c. Enterprise fund.
d. Capital projects fund.

172. In 19X8, Beech City issued $400,000 of bonds, the proceeds of which were restricted to the financing of a capital project. The bonds will be paid wholly from special assessments against benefited property owners. However, Beech is obligated to provide a secondary source of funds for repayment of the bonds in the event of default by the assessed property owners. In Beech's general purpose financial statements, this $400,000 special assessment debt should
a. Not be reported.
b. Be reported in the special assessment fund.
c. Be reported in the general long-term debt account group.
d. Be reported in an agency fund.

173. The budget of a governmental unit, for which the appropriations exceed the estimated revenues, was adopted and recorded in the general ledger at the beginning of the year. During the year, expenditures and encumbrances were less than appropriations; whereas revenues equaled estimated revenues. The budgetary fund balance account is
a. Credited at the beginning of the year and debited at the end of the year.
b. Credited at the beginning of the year and **not** changed at the end of the year.
c. Debited at the beginning of the year and credited at the end of the year.
d. Debited at the beginning of the year and **not** changed at the end of the year.

174. The following are Boa City's fixed assets:

| | |
|---|---|
| Fixed assets used in proprietary fund activities | $1,000,000 |
| Fixed assets used in governmental-type trust funds | 1,800,000 |
| All other fixed assets | 9,000,000 |

What aggregate amount should Boa account for in the general fixed assets account group?
a. $9,000,000
b. $10,000,000

c. $10,800,000
d. $11,800,000

175. Lori Township received a gift of an ambulance having a market value of $180,000. What account in the general fixed assets account group should be debited for this $180,000 gift?
a. None (memorandum entry only).
b. Investment in general fixed assets from gifts.
c. Machinery and equipment.
d. General fund assets.

176. Fixed assets donated to a governmental unit should be recorded
a. At estimated fair value when received.
b. At the lower of donor's carrying amount or estimated fair value when received.
c. At the donor's carrying amount.
d. As a memorandum entry only.

177. Encumbrances outstanding at year-end in a state's general fund should be reported as a
a. Liability in the general fund.
b. Fund balance reserve in the general fund.
c. Liability in the general long-term debt account group.
d. Fund balance designation in the general fund.

178. Customers' meter deposits which cannot be spent for normal operating purposes would be classified as restricted cash in the balance sheet of which fund?
a. Internal service.
b. Trust.
c. Agency.
d. Enterprise.

179. On December 31, 19X9, Elm Village paid a contractor $4,500,000 for the total cost of a new Village Hall built in 19X9 on Village-owned land. Financing for the capital project was provided by a $3,000,000 general obligation bond issue sold at face amount on December 31, 19X9, with the remaining $1,500,000 transferred from the general fund. What account and amount should be reported in Elm's 19X9 financial statements for the general fund?
a. Other financing sources control    $4,500,000
b. Expenditures control    $4,500,000
c. Other financing sources control    $3,000,000
d. Other financing uses control    $1,500,000

180. A public school district should recognize revenue from property taxes levied for its debt service fund when
a. Bonds to be retired by the levy are due and payable.
b. Assessed valuations of property subject to the levy are known.
c. Funds from the levy are measurable and available to the district.
d. Proceeds from collection of the levy are deposited in the district's bank account.

181. Bay Creek's municipal motor pool maintains all city-owned vehicles and charges the various departments for the cost of rendering those services. In which of the following funds should Bay account for the cost of such maintenance?
a. General fund.
b. Internal service fund.
c. Special revenue fund.
d. Special assessment fund.

182. Shared revenues received by an enterprise fund of a local government for operating purposes should be recorded as
a. Operating revenues.
b. Nonoperating revenues.
c. Other financing sources.
d. Interfund transfers.

183. Ariel Village issued the following bonds during the year ended June 30, 19X1:

| | |
|---|---|
| Revenue bonds to be repaid from admission fees collected by the Ariel Zoo enterprise fund | $200,000 |
| General obligation bonds issued for the Ariel water and sewer enterprise fund which will service the debt | 300,000 |

How much of these bonds should be accounted for in Ariel's general long-term debt account group?
a. $0.
b. $200,000.
c. $300,000.
d. $500,000.

184. The following information for the year ended June 30, 19X8 pertains to a proprietary fund established by Burwood Village in connection with Burwood's public parking facilities:

| | |
|---|---|
| Receipts from users of parking facilities | $400,000 |
| Expenditures | |
| Parking meters | 210,000 |
| Salaries and other cash expenses | 90,000 |
| Depreciation of parking meters | 70,000 |

For the year ended June 30, 19X8, this proprietary fund should report net income of
a. $ 0
b. $ 30,000
c. $100,000
d. $240,000

185. Dodd Village received a gift of a new fire engine from a local resident. The fair market value of this fire engine was $200,000. The entry to be made in the general fixed assets account group for this gift is

| | Debit | Credit |
|---|---|---|
| a. Machinery and equipment | $200,000 | |
| Investment in general fixed assets from private gifts | | $200,000 |
| b. Investment in general fixed assets | $200,000 | |
| Gift revenue | | $200,000 |
| c. General fund assets | $200,000 | |
| Private gifts | | $200,000 |
| d. Memorandum entry only | -- | -- |

186. The following information pertains to Grove City's interfund receivables and payables at December 31, 19X2:

| | |
|---|---|
| Due to special revenue from general fund | $10,000 |
| Due to agency fund from revenue fund | 4,000 |

In Grove's special revenue fund balance sheet at December 31, 19X2, how should these interfund amounts be reported?
a. As an asset of $6,000.
b. As a liability of $6,000.
c. As an asset of $4,000 and a liability of $10,000.
d. As an asset of $10,000 and a liability of $4,000.

187. Hill City's water utility fund held the following investments in U.S. Treasury securities at June 30, 19X3:

| Investment | Date purchased | Maturity date | Carrying amount |
|---|---|---|---|
| 3-month T-bill | 5/31/93 | 7/31/93 | $30,000 |
| 3-year T-note | 6/15/93 | 8/31/93 | 50,000 |
| 5-year T-note | 10/1/89 | 9/30/94 | 100,000 |

In the fund's balance sheet, what amount of these investments should be reported as cash and cash equivalents at June 30, 19X3?
a. $0.
b. $30,000.
c. $80,000.
d. $180,000.

188. The following information pertains to Park Township's general fund at December 31, 19X2:

| | |
|---|---|
| Total assets, including $200,000 of cash | $1,000,000 |
| Total liabilities | 600,000 |
| Reserved for encumbrances | 100,000 |

Appropriations do not lapse at year-end. At December 31, 19X2, what amount should Park report as unreserved fund balance in its general fund balance?
a. $200,000.
b. $300,000.
c. $400,000.
d. $500,000.

189. With regard to the statement of cash flows for a governmental unit's enterprise fund, items generally presented as cash equivalents are

| | 2-month treasury bills | 3-month certificates of deposit |
|---|---|---|
| a. | No | No |
| b. | No | Yes |
| c. | Yes | Yes |
| d. | Yes | No |

190. Flac City recorded a 20-year building rental agreement as a capital lease. The building lease asset was reported in the general fixed asset account group. Where should the lease liability be reported in Flac's combined balance sheet?
a. General long-term debt account group.
b. Debt service fund.
c. General fund.
d. A lease liability should **not** be reported.

# Chapter Nineteen
# Governmental Accounting Problems

## NUMBER 1

**Number 1** consists of 40 items. Select the **best** answer for each item.

The Wayne City Council approved and adopted its budget for 1993. The budget contained the following amounts:

| | |
|---|---|
| Estimated revenues | $700,000 |
| Appropriations | 660,000 |
| Authorized operating transfer to the Library debt service fund | 30,000 |

During 1993, various transactions and events occurred which affected the general fund.

**Required:**
**For items 1 through 40,** select whether the item should be debited, should be credited, or is not affected.

**Items 1 through 5** involve recording the adopted budget in the general fund.

1. Estimated revenues
2. Budgetary fund balance
3. Appropriations
4. Appropriations - Operating transfers out
5. Expenditures

**Items 6 through 10** involve recording the 1993 property tax levy in the general fund. It was estimated that $5,000 would be uncollectible.

6. Property tax receivable.
7. Bad debt expense.
8. Allowance for uncollectibles - current.
9. Revenues.
10. Estimated revenues.

**Items 11 through 15** involve recording, in the general fund, encumbrances at the time purchase orders are issued.

11. Encumbrances.
12. Budgetary fund balance reserved for encumbrances.
13. Expenditures.
14. Vouchers payable.
15. Purchases.

**Items 16 through 20** involve recording, in the general fund, expenditures which had been previously encumbered in the current year.

16. Encumbrances.
17. Budgetary fund balance reserved for encumbrances.
18. Expenditures.
19. Vouchers payable.
20. Purchases.

**Items 21 through 25** involve recording, in the general fund, the operating transfer of $30,000 made to the Library debt service fund. (No previous entries were made regarding this transaction.)

21. Residual equity transfer out.
22. Due from Library debt service fund.
23. Cash.
24. Other financial uses - operating transfers out.
25. Encumbrances.

**Items 26 through 36** involve recording, in the general fund, the closing entries (other than encumbrances) for 1993.

26. Estimated revenues.
27. Budgetary fund balance.
28. Appropriations.
29. Appropriations - Operating transfers out.
30. Expenditures.
31. Revenues.
32. Other financial uses - Operating transfers out.
33. Allowance for uncollectibles - current.
34. Bad debt expense.
35. Depreciation expense.
36. Residual equity transfer out.

**Items 37 through 40** involve recording, in the general fund, the closing entry relating to the $12,000 of outstanding encumbrances at the end of 1993 and an adjusting entry to reflect the intent to honor these commitments in 1994.

37. Encumbrances.
38. Budgetary fund balance reserved for encumbrances.
39. Unreserved fund balance.
40. Fund balance reserved for encumbrances.


## NUMBER 2

This problem consists of 20 items relating to a municipal government. Answer all items.

Items 1 through 10, in the left-hand column, represent various transactions pertaining to a municipality that uses encumbrance accounting. To the right of these items is a listing of possible ways to record the transactions. Items 11 through 20, also listed in the left-hand column, represent the funds, accounts, and account groups used by the municipality. To the right of these items is a list of possible accounting and reporting methods.

**Required:**
a. For each of the municipality's transactions (items 1 through 10), select the appropriate recording of the transaction. A method of recording the transactions may be selected once, more than once, or not at all.

b. For each of the municipality's funds, accounts, and account groups (items 11 through 20), select the appropriate method of accounting and reporting. An accounting and reporting method may be selected once, more than once, or not at all.

**Items to be answered:**

**a.**          Transactions                     Recording of Transactions

1. General obligation bonds were issued at par.

2. Approved purchase orders were issued for supplies.

3. The above-mentioned supplies were received and the related invoices were approved.

4. General fund salaries and wages were incurred.

5. The internal service fund had interfund billings.

6. Revenues were earned from a previously awarded grant.

7. Property taxes were collected in advance.

8. Appropriations were recorded on adoption of budget.

9. Short-term financing was received from a bank, secured by the city's taxing power.

10. There was an excess of estimated inflows over estimated outflows.

A. Credit appropriations control.

B. Credit budgetary fund balance - unreserved.

C. Credit expenditures control.

D. Credit deferred revenues.

E. Credit interfund revenues.

F. Credit tax anticipation notes payable.

G. Credit other financing sources.

H. Credit other financing uses.

I. Debit appropriations control.

J. Debit deferred revenues.

K. Debit encumbrances control.

L. Debit expenditures control.

**b.** Funds, Accounts, and Account Groups       Accounting and Reporting by Funds & Account Groups

11. Enterprise fund fixed assets.

12. Capital projects fund.

13. General fixed assets.

14. Infrastructure fixed assets.

15. Enterprise fund cash.

16. General fund.

17. Agency fund cash.

18. General long-term debt.

19. Special revenue fund.

20. Debt services fund.

A. Accounted for in a fiduciary fund.

B. Accounted for in a proprietary fund.

C. Accounted for in a quasi-endowment fund.

D. Accounted for in a self-balancing account group.

E. Accounted for in a special assessment fund.

F. Accounts for major construction activities.

G. Accounts for property tax revenues.

H. Accounts for payment of interest and principal on tax supported debt.

I. Accounts for revenues from earmarked sources to finance designated activities.

J. Reporting is optional.

# NUMBER 3

The following transactions represent practical situations frequently encountered in accounting for municipal governments. Each transaction is independent of the others.

1. The city council of Bernardville adopted a budget for the general operations of the government during the new fiscal year. Revenues were estimated at $695,000. Legal authorizations for budgeted expenditures were $650,000.
2. Taxes of $160,000 were levied for the special revenue fund for Millstown. One percent was estimated to be uncollectible.
3. a. On July 25, 1981, office supplies estimated to cost $2,390 were ordered for the city manager's office of Bullersville. Bullersville, which operates on the calendar year, does not maintain an inventory of such supplies.
   b. The supplies ordered July 25 were received on August 9, 1981, accompanied by an invoice for $2,500.
4. On October 10, 1981, the general fund of Washingtonville repaid to the utility fund a loan of $1,000 plus $40 interest. The loan had been made earlier in the fiscal year.
5. A prominent citizen died and left ten acres of undeveloped land to Harper City for a future school site. The donor's cost of the land was $55,000. The fair value of the land was $85,000.
6. a. On March 6, 1981, Dahlstrom City issued 4% special assessment bonds payable March 6, 1991, at face value of $90,000. Interest is payable annually. Dahlstrom City, which operates on the calendar year, will use the proceeds to finance a curbing project.
   b. On October 29, 1981, the full $84,000 cost of the completed curbing project was accrued. Also, appropriate closing entries were made with regard to the project.
7. a. Conrad Thamm, a citizen of Basking Knoll, donated common stock valued at $22,000 to the city under a trust agreement. Under the terms of the agreement, the principal amount is to be kept intact; use of revenue from the stock is restricted to financing academic college scholarships for needy students.
   b. On December 14, 1981, dividends of $1,100 were received on the stock donated by Mr. Thamm.
8. a. On February 23, 1981, the town of Lincoln, which operates on the calendar year, issued 4% general obligation bonds with a face value of $300,000 payable February 23, 1991, to finance the construction of an addition to the city hall. Total proceeds were $308,000.
   b. On December 31, 1981, the addition to the city hall was officially approved, the full cost of $297,000 was paid to the contractor, and appropriate closing entries were made with regard to the project. (Assume that no entries have been made with regard to the project since February 23, 1981).

**Required:**

For each transaction, prepare the necessary journal entries for **all** of the funds and groups of accounts involved. **No explanation of the journal entries is required.** Use the following headings for your workpaper:

| Transaction Number | Journal Entries | Dr. | Cr. | Fund or Group of Accounts |
|---|---|---|---|---|

In the far right column, indicate in which funds or group of accounts each entry is to be made, using the coding below:

Funds:

| | |
|---|---|
| General | G |
| Special revenue | SR |
| Capital projects | CP |
| Debt service | DS |
| Enterprise | E |
| Internal service | IS |
| Trust and agency | TA |

Groups of accounts:

| | |
|---|---|
| General fixed assets | GFA |
| General long-term debt | LTD |

# NUMBER 4

This question consists of 5 items. Select the **best** answer for each item.

Dease City is a governmental organization that has governmental-type funds and account groups.

**Required:**

**Items 1 through 5** represent transactions by governmental-type funds and account groups based on the following selected information taken from Dease City's 1996 financial records:

### *General fund*

| | |
|---|---|
| Fund balance at beginning of 1996 | $   700,000 |
| 1996 estimated revenues | 10,000,000 |
| 1996 actual revenues | 10,500,000 |
| 1996 appropriations | 9,000,000 |
| 1996 expenditures | 8,200,000 |
| Encumbrances at end of 1996 | 500,000 |
| Vouchers payable at end of 1996 | 300,000 |
| 1996 operating transfers in | 100,000 |
| 1996 property tax levy | 9,500,000 |
| 1996 property taxes estimated to be uncollectible when property tax levy for 1996 recorded | 100,000 |
| 1996 property taxes delinquent at end of 1996 | 150,000 |

### *Capital projects fund*

| | |
|---|---|
| 1996 operating transfers in | $   100,000 |
| Construction of new library wing started and completed in 1996 | |
| • Proceeds from bonds issued at 100 in 1996 | 2,000,000 |
| • Expenditures for 1996 | 2,100,000 |

For **items 1 through 5,** determine the amounts based solely on the above information.

1. What was the net amount credited to the budgetary fund balance when the budget was approved?

2. What was the amount of property taxes collected on the property tax levy for 1996?

3. What amount for the new library wing was included in the capital projects fund balance at the end of 1996?

4. What amount for the new library wing was charged to the general fixed assets account group at the end of 1996?

5. What amount for the new library wing bonds was included in the general long-term debt account group at the end of 1996?


# NUMBER 5

**Number 5** consists of 19 items. Select the **best** answer for each item.

The following selected information is taken from Shar City's general fund statement of revenues, expenditures, and changes in fund balance for the year ended December 31, 1995:

| | |
|---|---|
| Revenues | |
| Property taxes – 1995 | $825,000 |

| | |
|---|---|
| Expenditures | |
| Current services | |
| Public safety | 428,000 |
| Capital outlay (police vehicles) | 100,000 |
| Debt service | 74,000 |

| | |
|---|---|
| Expenditures -- 1995 | $1,349,000 |
| Expenditures -- 1994 | 56,000 |
| Expenditures | $1,405,000 |
| | |
| Excess of revenues over expenditures | $  153,000 |
| Other financing uses | (125,000) |
| | |
| Excess of revenues over expenditures and other financing uses | $    28,000 |
| Decrease in reserve for encumbrances during 1995 | 15,000 |
| Residual equity transfers out | (190,000) |
| | |
| Decrease in unreserved fund balance during 1995 | $ (147,000) |
| Unreserved fund balance January 1, 1995 | 304,000 |
| | |
| Unreserved fund balance December 31, 1995 | $  157,000 |

The following selected information is taken from Shar's December 31, 1995, general fund balance sheet:

Property taxes receivable --
    delinquent – 1995                                                                   $34,000
        Less: Allowance for estimated uncollectible taxes – delinquent          20,000

Vouchers payable                                                                        $89,000

Fund balance –
    reserved for encumbrances – 1995                                             $43,000
    reserved for supplies inventory                                                    38,000
    unreserved                                                                             157,000

Additional Information:

• Debt service was for bonds used to finance a library building and included interest of $22,000.

• $8,000 of 1995 property taxes receivable was written-off; otherwise the allowance for uncollectible taxes balance is unchanged from the initial entry at the time of the original tax levy at the beginning of the year.

• Shar reported supplies inventory of $21,000 at December 31, 1994.

**Required:**
a.  For **Items 1 through 3,** indicate the type of classification used by Shar:

    (A)    Character.
    (B)    Function.
    (C)    Object.

1.  Expenditures – current services.
2.  Expenditures – capital outlay.
3.  Expenditures – health.

b.  For **Items 4 through 6,** select the best answer to the question.

4.  What recording method did Shar use for its general fund supplies inventory?
    A.  Consumption.
    B.  Purchase.
    C.  Perpetual inventory.

5.  How should fund equity be reported in Shar's electric utility enterprise fund?
    A.  A single amount described as fund balance.
    B.  Separately for capital and retained income.
    C.  Separately for amount due to general fund and retained income.

6.  Shar's electric utility enterprise fund borrowed $1,000,000 subject to Shar's general guarantee. Where should the liability be reported?
    A.  The electric utility enterprise fund.
    B.  The general long-term debt account group.
    C.  Both the electric utility enterprise fund and the general long-term debt account group.

c. For **Items 7 through 13**, indicate the part of Shar's general fund statement of revenues, expenditures, and changes in fund balance affected by the transaction.

    (A)     Revenues.
    (B)     Expenditures.
    (C)     Other financing sources and uses.
    (D)     Residual equity transfers.
    (E)     Statement of revenues, expenditures, and changes in fund balance is **not** affected.

7. An unrestricted state grant is received.

8. The general fund paid pension fund contributions that were recoverable from an internal service fund.

9. The general fund paid $60,000 for electricity supplied by Shar's electric utility enterprise fund.

10. General fund resources were used to subsidize Shar's swimming pool enterprise fund.

11. $90,000 of general fund resources were loaned to an internal service fund.

12. A motor pool internal service fund was established by a transfer of $80,000 from the general fund. This amount will not be repaid unless the motor pool is disbanded.

13. General fund resources were used to pay amounts due on an operating lease.

d. **Items 14 through 19** require numeric responses. For each item, calculate the numeric amount.

14. What was the unreserved fund balance of the 1994 general fund?

15. What amount was collected from 1995 tax assessments?

16. What amount is Shar's liability to general fund vendors and contractors at December 31, 1995?

17. What amount should be included n the general fixed assets account group for the cost of assets acquired in 1995 through the general fund?

18. What amount arising from 1995 transactions decreased liabilities reported in the general long-term debt account group?

19. What amount of total actual expenditures should Shar report in its 1995 general fund statement of revenues, expenditures, and changes in fund balance–budget and actual?

# NUMBER 6

The following information pertains to Eden Township's construction and financing of a new administration center.

Estimated total cost of project

|  |  |
|---|---|
|  | $9,000,000 |
| Project financing: |  |
| State entitlement grant | 3,000,000 |
| General obligation bonds: |  |
| Face amount | 6,000,000 |
| Stated interest rate | 6% |
| Issue date | December 1, 1990 |
| Maturity date | November 30, 2000 |

During Eden's year ended June 30, 1991, the following events occurred that affect the capital projects fund established to account for this project:

- July 1, 1990 - The capital projects fund borrowed $300,000 from the general fund for preliminary expenses.
- July 9, 1990 - Engineering and planning costs of $200,000, for which no encumbrance had been recorded, were paid to Napp Associates.
- December 1, 1990 - The bonds were sold at 101. Total proceeds were retained by the capital projects fund.
- December 1, 1990 - The entitlement grant was formally approved by the state.
- April 30, 1991 - A $7,000,000 contract was executed with Caro Construction Corp., the general contractors, for the major portion of the project. The contract provides that Eden will withhold 4% of all billings pending satisfactory completion of the project.
- May 9, 1991 - $1,000,000 of the state grant was received.
- June 10, 1991 - The $300,000 borrowed from the general fund was repaid.
- June 30, 1991 - Progress billing of $1,200,000 was received from Caro.
- Eden uses encumbrance accounting for budgetary control. Unencumbered appropriations lapse at the end of the year.

**Required:**
**a.** Prepare journal entries in the administration center capital projects fund to record the foregoing transactions.
**b.** Prepare the June 30, 1991, closing entries for the administration center capital projects fund.
**c.** Prepare the administration center capital projects fund balance sheet at June 30, 1991.

# NUMBER 7

**Number 7** consists of 12 items. Select the best answer for each item.

The following events affected the financial statements of Jey City during 1995:

Budgetary activities:

- Total general fund estimated revenues      $8,000,000

- Total general fund budgeted expenditures      7,500,000

- Planned construction of a courthouse improvement expected to cost $1,500,000, and to be financed in the following manner: $250,000 from the general fund, $450,000 from state entitlements, and $800,000 from the proceeds of 20-year, 8% bonds dated and expected to be issued at par on June 30, 1995. Interest on the bonds is payable annually on July 1, together with one-twentieth of the bond principal from general fund revenues of the payment period.

- A budgeted general fund payment of $180,000 to subsidize operations of a solid waste landfill enterprise fund.

Actual results included the following:

- Jey recorded property tax revenues of $5,000,000 and a related allowance for uncollectibles-current of $60,000. On December 31, 1995, the remaining $56,000 balance of the allowance for uncollectibles-current was closed, and an adjusted allowance for uncollectibles-delinquent was recorded equal to the property tax receivables balance of 38,000.

- A police car with an original cost of $25,000 was sold for $7,000.

- Office equipment to be used by the city's fire department was acquired through a capital lease. The lease required 10 equal annual payments of $10,000, beginning with the July 1, 1995, acquisition date. Using a 6% discount rate, the 10 payments had a present value of $78,000 at the acquisition date.

- The courthouse was improved and financed as budgeted except for a $27,000 cost overrun that was paid for by the general fund. Jey plans to transfer cash to the debt service fund during 1996 to service the interest and principal payments called for in the bonds.

- Information related to the solid waste landfill at December 31, 1995:

| | |
|---|---|
| Capacity | 1,000,000 cubic yards |
| Usage prior to 1995 | 500,000 cubic yards |
| Usage in 1995 | 40,000 cubic yards |
| Estimated total life | 20 years |
| Closure costs incurred to date | $ 300,000 |
| Estimated future costs of closure and postclosure care | 1,700,000 |
| Expense for closure and postclosure care recognized prior to 1995 | 973,000 |

Jey does not record depreciation for nonproprietary fund-type assets.

**Required:**
For **Items 1 through 10,** determine the amounts based solely on the above information.

1. What was the net effect of the budgetary activities on the general fund balance at January 1, 1995?

2. What was the total amount of operating transfers out included in the general fund's budgetary accounts at January 1, 1995?

3. What amount of interest payable related to the 20-year bonds should be reported by the general fund at December 31, 1995?

4. What lease payment amount should be included in 1995 general fund expenditures?

5. What amount was collected from 1995 property taxes in 1995?

6. What was the total amount of the capital project fund's 1995 revenues?

7. What amount should be reported as liabilities in the general long-term debt account group at December 31, 1995?

8.	What net increase in assets should be reported in the general fixed assets account group at December 31, 1995?

9.	What 1995 closure and postclosure care expenses should be reported in the solid waste landfill enterprise fund?

10.	What should be the December 31, 1995, closure and postclosure care liability reported in the solid waste landfill enterprise fund?

For **Items 11 and 12,** indicate the measurement focus of the Jey fund mentioned.

(A)	Subsidy restrictions.
(B)	Bond restrictions.
(C)	Expenditures.
(D)	Financial resources.
(E)	Capital maintenance/intergenerational equity.

11.	Capital project fund.

12.	Solid waste landfill enterprise fund.

# NUMBER 8

Albury City was incorporated as a municipality and began operations on January 1, 1990. The budget approved by the City Council was recorded, but the cash basis was used in Albury's books for all 1990 transactions. Albury has decided to use encumbrance accounting. Albury's cash basis general fund trial balance at December 31, 1990, is presented below and in the worksheet that follows.

|  | |
|---|---|
| *Debits* | |
| Cash | $477,800 |
| Expenditures | 145,000 |
| Estimated revenues | 228,200 |
| Total | $851,000 |

|  | |
|---|---|
| *Credits* | |
| Appropriations | $204,000 |
| Revenues | 216,800 |
| Bonds payable | 400,000 |
| Premium on bonds payable | 6,000 |
| Fund balance | 24,200 |
| Total | $851,000 |

*Additional information:*

| | Budgeted | Actual |
|---|---|---|
| *Revenues* | | |
| Property taxes | $205,200 | $192,000 |
| Licenses | 14,800 | 15,800 |
| Fines | 8,200 | 9,000 |
| Totals | $228,200 | $216,800 |
| | | |
| *Appropriations* | | |
| Services | $ 90,000 | $ 77,000 |
| Supplies | 38,000 | 22,000 |
| Equipment | 76,000 | 46,000 |
| Totals | $204,000 | $145,000 |

It was estimated that 5% of the property taxes would not be collected. Accordingly, property taxes were levied to yield the budgeted amount of $205,200. Taxes of $192,000 had been collected by December 31, 1990, and it was expected that all remaining collectible taxes would be received by February 28, 1991.

Supplies of $8,000 and equipment of $20,000 were received, but the vouchers were unpaid at December 31, 1990. Purchase orders were still outstanding for supplies and equipment not yet received, in the amounts of $2,400 and $7,600, respectively.

It was decided to record the $3,400 physical inventory of supplies on hand at December 31, 1990. In conformity with a city ordinance, expenditures are based on purchases rather than usage.

On November 1, 1990, Albury issued 4% general obligation term bonds of $400,000 at 101½. Interest is payable each May 1 and November 1 until the maturity date of November 1, 2009. Cash from the bond premium is to be set aside and restricted for eventual retirement of bond principal. The bonds were issued to finance the construction of a firehouse, but no contracts had been executed by December 31, 1990.

**Required:**
Detach the worksheet that follows, and complete this worksheet showing adjustments and distributions to the proper funds or account groups, before closing entries, in conformity with generally accepted accounting principles applicable to governmental entities. Formal adjusting entries are **not** required.

### Albury City
# WORKSHEET TO CORRECT TRIAL BALANCE
*December 31, 1990*

| | Trial balance | Adjustments | | General fund | Debt service fund | Capital projects fund | Account groups | |
|---|---|---|---|---|---|---|---|---|
| | | Debit | Credit | | | | General fixed assets | General long-term debt |
| *Debits:* | | | | | | | | |
| Cash | $477,800 | | | | | | | |
| Expenditures | 145,000 | | | | | | | |
| Estimated revenues | 228,200 | | | | | | | |
| | | | | | | | | |
| | | | | | | | | |
| | | | | | | | | |
| | | | | | | | | |
| | | | | | | | | |
| | | | | | | | | |
| Totals | $851,000 | | | | | | | |
| *Credits:* | | | | | | | | |
| Appropriations | $204,000 | | | | | | | |
| Revenues and other financing sources | 216,800 | | | | | | | |
| Bonds payable | 400,000 | | | | | | | |
| Premium on bonds payable | 6,000 | | | | | | | |
| Fund balance | 24,200 | | | | | | | |
| | | | | | | | | |
| | | | | | | | | |
| | | | | | | | | |
| | | | | | | | | |
| | | | | | | | | |
| Totals | $851,000 | | | | | | | |

# NUMBER 9

**Number 9** consists of 24 items. Select the **best** answer for each item.

The following information relates to Bel City, whose first fiscal year ended December 31, 1994. Assume Bel has only the long-term debt specified in the information and only the funds necessitated by the information.

## I. General fund:

- The following selected information is taken from Bel's 1994 general fund financial records:

|  | Budget | Actual |
|---|---|---|
| Property taxes | $5,000,000 | $4,700,000 |
| Other revenues | 1,000,000 | 1,050,000 |
| Total revenues | $6,000,000 | $5,750,000 |
| Total expenditures | $5,600,000 | $5,700,000 |
| | | |
| Property taxes receivable – delinquent | | $ 420,000 |
| Less: Allowance for estimated uncollectible taxes – delinquent | | 50,000 |
| | | $ 370,000 |

- There were no amendments to the budget as originally adopted.

- No property taxes receivable have been written off, and the allowance for uncollectibles balance is unchanged from the initial entry at the time of the original tax levy.

- There were no encumbrances outstanding at December 31, 1994.


## 2. Capital project fund:
- Finances for Bel's new civic center were provided by a combination of general fund transfers, a state grant, and an issue of general obligation bonds. Any bond premium on issuance is to be used for the repayment of the bonds at their $1,200,000 par value. At December 31, 1994, the capital project fund for the civic center had the following closing entries:

| | | |
|---|---|---|
| Revenues | $ 800,000 | |
| Other financing sources -- bond proceeds | 1,230,000 | |
| Other financing sources -- operating transfers in | 500,000 | |
| Expenditures | | $1,080,000 |
| Other financing uses -- operating transfers out | | 30,000 |
| Unreserved fund balance | | 1,420,000 |

- Also, at December 31, 1994, capital project fund entries reflected Bel's intention to honor the $1,300,000 purchase orders and commitments outstanding for the center.

- During 1994, total capital project fund encumbrances exceeded the corresponding expenditures by $42,000. All expenditures were previously encumbered.

- During 1995, the capital project fund received no revenues and no other financing sources. The civic center building was completed in early 1995 and the capital project fund was closed by a transfer of $27,000 to the general fund.

3. *Water utility enterprise fund:*
- Bel issued $4,000,000 revenue bonds at par. These bonds, together with a $700,000 transfer from the general fund, were used to acquire a water utility. Water utility revenues are to be the sole source of funds to retire these bonds beginning in year 1999.

**Required:**

For **Items 1 through 16,** indicate if the answer to each item is (Y) yes, or (N) no.

**Items 1 through 8** relate to Bel's general fund.

1. Did recording budgetary accounts at the beginning of 1994 increase the fund balance by $50,000?

2. Should the budgetary accounts for 1994 include an entry for the expected transfer of funds from the general fund to the capital projects fund?

3. Should the $700,000 payment from the general fund, which was used to help to establish the water utility fund, be reported as an "other financing use—operating transfers out"?

4. Did the general fund receive the $30,000 bond premium from the capital projects fund?

5. Should a payment from the general fund for water received for normal civic center operations be reported as an "other financing use—operating transfers out"?

6. Not selected.

7. Would closing budgetary accounts cause the fund balance to increase by $400,000?

8. Would the interaction between budgetary and actual amounts cause the fund balance to decrease by $350,000?

**Items 9 through 16** relate to Bel's account groups and funds other than the general fund.

9. In the general fixed assets account group, should a credit amount be recorded for 1994 in "Investment in general fixed assets—capital projects fund"?

10. In the general fixed assets account group, could Bel elect to record depreciation in 1995 on the civic center?

11. In the general fixed assets account group, could Bel elect to record depreciation on water utility equipment?

12. Should the capital project fund be included in Bel's combined statement of revenues, expenditures, and changes in fund balances?

13. Should the water utility enterprise fund be included in Bel's combined balance sheet?

In which fund should Bel report capital and related financing activities in its 1994 statement of cash flows?

14. Debt service fund.

15. Capital project fund.

16. Water utility enterprise fund.

For **Items 17 through 24,** determine the amount.

**Items 17 and 18** relate to Bel's general fund.

17. What was the amount recorded in the opening entry for appreciations?

18. What was the total amount debited to property taxes receivable?

**Items 19 through 24** relate to Bel's account groups and funds other than the general fund.

19. In the general long-term debt account group, what amount should be reported for bonds payable at December 31, 1994?

20. In the general fixed assets account group, what amount should be recorded for "Investment in general fixed assets—capital project fund" at December 31, 1994?

21. What was the completed cost of the civic center?

22. How much was the state capital grant for the civic center?

23. In the capital project fund, what was the amount of the total encumbrances recorded during 1994?

24. In the capital project fund, what was the unreserved fund balance reported at December 31, 1994?

# Chapter Nineteen
# Solutions to Governmental Accounting Questions

1. (a) The primary authoritative body for determining governmental accounting standards is the GASB (Rule 203 AICPA Code of Conduct).

2. (a) GASB Concepts Statements and GASB Statement 11 emphasize that the measurement focus of governmental funds **is on the flow of financial resources.** Choice (b) is incorrect because governments do not operate for profit and income determination. Choice (c) is incorrect because capital maintenance (fixed assets) is not the primary emphasis. In fact, fixed assets are not even recorded in the funds, but in the general fixed assets group.

3. (b) The primary measurement focus of governmental fund types is the inflows, outflows, and balances of financial resources.

4. (a) Interperiod equity assumes that the revenues of a period will at least equal the expenditures of the period. This financial objective assumes that a balance budget will be adopted. Residual equity is not related to interperiod equity.

5. (d) GASB believes that Interperiod equity is a significant part of accountability and is fundamental to public administration.

6. (c) Governmental financial reporting should provide information to assist users in making social and political decisions and in assisting users in assessing whether current-year citizens receive services whose payment is shifted to future years.

7. (a) GASB 220.109 describes that **Operating statements embody the all-inclusive approach.** It means that all governmental fund types, revenues, expenditures, and similar trust funds are combined to determine the changes in fund balance.

8. (a) Governmental. The special revenue fund is a governmental fund by definition.

9. (d) Debt service. The modified accrual basis is recommended for all governmental funds which include debt service. The accrual basis is recommended for proprietary and nonexpendable trust funds.

10. (b) Special revenue. In that Governmental fund, budgetary accounts are used. Not so in proprietary and fiduciary funds.

11. (d) Governmental. Governmental funds include general, special revenue, debt service and capital projects.

12. (b) Yes, No. Capital project assets are accounted for in the general fixed assets account group. Internal service fund assets are accounted for within that fund because depreciation is computed on fixed assets so that costs can be properly allocated to users.

13. (d) Trust.
Trust (fiduciary) funds, other than pension trust funds, can be classified as either expendable or nonexpendable. Expendable trust funds, used where principal may be expended, follow the modified accrual basis of accounting. Examples are accounts maintained for contributions, grants or awards for specific expendable purposes such as student loans. Nonexpendable trust funds are used to account for endowments, gifts or awards that must be preserved (invested) while the income is made available for the intended purpose. Nonexpendable funds follow the accrual basis of accounting.

14. (a) General fund.
General fixed assets account group is used to account for fixed assets of the governmental funds which includes the general, special revenue, capital projects and debt service funds.

15. (d) Internal service. An internal service fund receives such capital to provide the services necessary to carry out its mission. The other funds have no such account.

16. (d) Modified accrual basis.
A capital projects fund is a governmental fund for which the modified accrual basis is recommended.

17. (b) Internal Service is a proprietary fund. The accounting and reporting for such funds is similar to that of for-profit entities (GAAP).

18. (b) Governmental. Governmental funds include general, special revenue, capital projects and debt service.

19. (b) Assets that are held for disbursement to a different entity are recorded in the agency fund. Eldorado County is an intermediary that has custody of these funds.

20. (d) Trust fund.
A trust fund is used to account for money or property received from non-enterprise fund sources to be held in the capacity of a trustee, custodian or agent. In a retirement system trust fund the focus is on determination of net income and capital maintenance.

21. (a) All governmental fund types use the modified accrual basis of accounting. The capital projects fund is a governmental fund. The other use full accrual.

22. (d) Become available and measurable.
The modified accrual basis of accounting, by definition, recognizes revenue when it is available and measurable. The term "available" means collectible in the current period or soon enough thereafter to be used to pay liabilities that are owed at the balance sheet date. Measurable refers to the ability to quantify in monetary terms the amount of the revenue and receivable.

23. (c) Accrual basis, no; Modified accrual basis, yes. Available and measurable is the definition of the modified method. Accrual basis differs in that "Other Revenues" are recorded as revenue when earned and become measurable (Proprietary funds).

24. (a) The general fund is a governmental fund, and recognizes revenue when they become available and measurable.

25. (d) "Earned and measurable" are attributes of the accrual method.

26. (a) The modified accrual basis of accounting is used by the governmental type funds. The full accrual basis is used by the proprietary type funds.

27. (c) Debit estimated revenues control, $30,000,000 - The entry to record the budget is as follows:

        DR   Estimated Revenue Control
               CR   Appropriations Control
               CR   Budgetary Fund

The above assumes that estimated revenues exceed estimated appropriations. This entry is reversed as a closing entry at the end of the period.

28. (c) Credit appropriations control, $29,000,000 - See previous answer.

29. (b) Credit budgetary fund balance, $1,000,000 - See above answer in series.

30. (c)   Estimated revenues                        $1,000,000
                  Appropriations                                      $900,000
                  Budgetary fund balance                              100,000

31. (b) The budget is recorded.
The recording of the budgetary opening entry is:
         Estimated revenue control                   xxx
                  Appropriation control                              xxx
                  Budgetary fund balance                             xxx

32. (d) Appropriations—The entry to record the budget:
         Estimated revenue control                   xxx
                  Appropriation control                              xxx
                  Budgetary fund balance                             xxx

This entry assumes that Estimated revenue exceeds appropriations, which is the normal condition.

33. (a) Definition: appropriation.

34. (b) Property taxes are recorded.
Revenue is increased when property taxes are recorded under both the accrual and modified accrual methods of accounting. Choices (a), (c) and (d) are incorrect as they involve budgetary accounts. Revenue control is not a budgetary account.

35. (d)          Property taxes receivable                   100
                  Allowance for uncollectible account                 10
                  Revenues                                            90

36. (c) Property taxes are recognized as a receivable when they are levied, however recognition must happen when they are both measurable and available.

         Collections during the year 19X2            $500,000
         Expected collections during first 60 days of 19X3   100,000
         Total net property tax revenue              $600,000

The other expected collections of 90,000 (60,000+30,000) would be recorded as a deferred revenue. The $10,000 estimated to be uncollectible would not be considered, because revenues are recorded net.

37. (d) Property taxes. Property taxes, unless otherwise designated would be general fund revenue and is the best answer. (a) is a possible answer, but would usually be enterprise fund revenue, (b) is clearly trust fund revenue, and (c) is internal service fund revenue.

38. (b) The sequence of entries is explained by the answer choice. Choices (a), (c) and (d) are foreign to fund accounting. An encumbrance is the recording of an obligation to incur an expenditure. When this obligation becomes a liability, it is reversed and the expenditure/liability is recorded.

39. (a) A purchase order is approved.
When a purchase order is approved the following entry is made:

> Encumbrances control
> > Budgetary fund balance reserved for encumbrances

A credit balance is the normal balance for this account, hence it is increased when a purchase order is approved. When supplies orders are received, the above entry is reversed, decreasing the balance. The account's function is to measure obligations outstanding **not** recorded as liabilities.

40. (d) Elm should debit the reserve for encumbrances account for the same $5,000 estimated amount when the account credited and the purchase order is issued.

| | | |
|---|---|---|
| Encumbrances control | 5,000 | |
|     Fund balance reserved for encumbrances | | 5,000 |

When supplies and invoices are received:

| | | |
|---|---|---|
| Fund balance reserved for encumbrances | **5,000** | |
|     Encumbrances control | | 5,000 |
| | | |
| Expenditure control | 4,950 | |
|     Vouchers payable | | 4,950 |

41. (a) Reserve for encumbrances. When a governmental unit approves (goods, equipment, etc.) orders the following entry is made:

| | | |
|---|---|---|
| Encumbrance control | xxx | |
|     Fund balance reserved for encumbrances | | xxx |

42. (a) Expenditure. Expenditures include current operating expenses which require the current or future use of net current assets, debt service, and capital outlays.

43. (c) Only the outstanding purchase order amounts.

44. (b) $2,250

| | |
|---|---|
| Appropriations | $7,500 |
| Expenditures | (4,500) |
| Encumbrances | ( 750) |
| Unobligated balance | $2,250 |

45. (d) Estimated revenue control should be credited for $20,000,000. Estimated revenues control is a budgetary account and it is debited when the budget is initially recorded. When closed at year-end the estimated revenue control account is credited.

46. (b) Expenditures.
Expenditures is a temporary account (operating and revenue) that must be closed at year end. The other choices are balance sheet accounts.

47. (d) Yes, No. Estimated revenues are closed by reversal of the opening budgetary entry. Fund balance cannot be closed because it is a balance sheet account representing the difference between fund assets and liabilities.

48. (a) When the budget is initially recorded appropriations control is credited. At year end the budget entry is reversed, thus the appropriations control account would be debited to close it out.

49. (b) The normal balance of the expenditures control account is a debit. Thus, to close the account at year end it is credited.

50. (b) The estimated revenue control is eliminated when the budgetary accounts are closed.

51. (b) Reservations of fund balance.
Encumbrances represent neither expenditures nor liabilities. In many governments, encumbrances outstanding at the end of a period are carried forward as a reservation of fund balance with a corresponding reduction in unreserved fund balance. Procedure:
1. Reverse outstanding encumbrances at year end.
2. DR Fund Balance; CR Fund balance reserved for encumbrances.
3. Reverse entry #2 in the next FY.
4. Record encumbrance outstanding at the beginning of the year.

52. (c) Gasoline taxes to finance road repairs. Special revenue funds are used to account for revenues derived from specific taxes or other earmarked revenue sources.

53. (a) Revenues become available and measurable—Per NCGA Statement 1.

54 (c) $900,000. The $300,000 amount is not special revenue, but an expendable trust fund. The $900,000 is a special revenue fund item used to account for specific revenue sources that are legally restricted to expenditure for specific purposes.

55. (d) Other financing sources $2,000,000; expenditures $2,000,000. NCGA #1 states that "Proceeds of long-term debt not recorded as fund liabilities—e.g. ... Capital Projects or Debt Service Funds -- normally should be reflected as 'Other Financing Sources' in the operating statement of the recipient fund. Such proceeds should be reported in captions such as 'Bond Issue Proceeds' . . . " With respect to the $500,000 transfer from the general fund, operating transfers are legally authorized transfers from a fund receiving revenue (GF) to the fund through which resources are to be expended (Capital Projects Fund). Operating transfers should be reported as "Other Financing Sources (Uses)".

56. (b) Other financing uses, $500,000. The $500,000 transfer from the general fund is considered an operating transfer and is to be reported as "Other Financing Uses".

57. (a) $5,000,000 in 19X6.
Bond proceeds are recorded in capital projects when received—not when used. DR Cash, CR Bond Proceeds. General long-term debt account group would also record the transaction: DR Amount to be provided, CR Bonds payable.

58. (c) The **$400,000** grant from state government is recorded as revenue. The other **$600,000** ($500,000 bond proceeds and $100,000 transfer from general fund) are recorded as other financing sources, not revenues.

59. (a) The $50,000 premium is initially recorded in the capital projects fund. An entry is made, however, to transfer the premium to the debt service fund. As cash is received in the debt service fund the general long-term debt account group records the status of funds available to pay long-term debt.

60. (b) $400,000. Bonds for the water treatment plant construction are accounted for in an enterprise fund which handles its own debt. Funds accumulated to pay the general obligation bonds would be accumulated in the debt service fund.

61. (c) The cash received from the general fund is recorded as an operating transfer. The payments for interest are operating activities of the fund and are recorded as expenditures.

62. (d) **$0.** Government entities are non-profit entities, they are not concerned with income determination. The debt service fund does not record or amortize a liability for the bond premium. General obligation bonds are recorded in the General LT Debt Account Group.

63. (c) $2,900,000

| | |
|---|---|
| Debt principal matured | $2,000,000 |
| Interest on matured debt | 900,000 |
| Expenditures (Modified accrual basis) | $2,900,000 |

NCGA #1 states that "Financial resources usually are appropriated in other funds for transfer to a Debt Service Fund in the period in which maturing debt principal and interest must be paid. Such amounts thus are not current liabilities of the Debt Service Fund as their settlement will not require expenditure of existing fund assets." The nonrecognition of accrued interest is a major distinction between the accrual and modified accrual basis.

64. (a) $600,000. Only the interest revenue from investments is recorded as revenue by debt service. NCGA #1 states, "Interfund transfers should be distinguished from revenues, expenses, or expenditures in financial statements." . . . "Operating transfers should be reported in the `Other Financing Sources (Uses)' section in the statement of revenues,— —" Operating transfers are legally authorized transfers from a fund receiving revenue to the fund through which the resources are to be expended. Therefore, the cash transferred from the general fund ($1,000,000 + $900,000) would not be recorded as revenue.

65. (c) No, yes.
Enterprise funds are proprietary funds and as such carry their own fixed assets. Special revenue funds are governmental funds in which fixed assets are recorded in the general fixed assets account group.

66. (c) Governmental: *Yes*—Proprietary: *No*
The general fixed asset group accounts for the fixed assets of Governmental funds only.

67. (b) Capital projects fund, *no;* General fund, *no.*
Fixed assets acquired by these funds are accounted for in the general fixed assets account. For the subject accounts the acquisition of these assets is an expenditure.

68. (d) Donated fixed assets are recorded in the general fixed asset account group at their estimated fair value at the time received. The entry to record the donated fixed asset is:

| | | |
|---|---|---|
| Machinery & equipment | 400,000 | |
| Investment in general fixed asset | | 400,000 |

69. (c) Accumulated depreciation may be recorded in the general fixed assets account group **if** the governmental entity chooses to do so.

70. (a) $1,800,000 or $6,800,000. The apartment is excluded, as trust fund assets are never included in the general fixed assets group of accounts. NCGA #1 (National Council on Governmental Accounting) states that "Reporting public domain or `infrastructure' fixed assets—roads, bridges, curbs and gutters, streets and sidewalks, drainage systems, lighting systems, and similar assets that are immovable and of value only to the governmental unit—is **optional**." Hence, the city streets and sidewalks are optional. The City Hall and fire stations are not optional.

71. (b) Each fund or group of accounts in governmental accounting is a self-balancing set of accounts which can be considered an accounting entity.

72. (a) Amount available in debt service funds account plus the amount to be provided for retirement of general long-term debt account.

The GLTDAG consists of the above assets and one liability account, i.e., bonds payable. The two asset accounts—"Amount available..." (represents the amount held for debt principal payment(s) in debt service) and "Amount to be provided..." (represents what it describes), the amount yet to be provided for the payment of the bond(s) in question.

73. (a) Amount to be provided for retirement of general long-term debt. The long-term debt account group has only three accounts, all of which are balance sheet accounts. In addition to the above are "Amount available for retirement of general long-term debt" and "bonds payable". Answers (b), (c) and (d) are common to the general fund and many others, but not general long-term debt.

74. (c) Asset section of the general long-term debt account group.

The asset section consists of only two accounts:
| | |
|---|---|
| Amount available | xxxx |
| Amount to be provided | xxxx |

The liability section consists of only one account:
| | |
|---|---|
| Bonds payable (properly described) | xxxx |

75. (a) $0. Only bonds of the governmental-type funds would be accounted for in the general long-term debt account group.

76. (d) $2,800,000. Proprietary funds, sometimes referred to as "income determination", "non-expendable", or commercial-type funds include both enterprise and internal service funds.

77. (a) Enterprise funds are used to account for those activities in which income determination is desired. Utilities are usually self supporting entities that should measure income.

78. (c) Cash basis, *no;* Modified accrual, *no.*
The accrual basis is required for proprietary funds.

79. (d) An enterprise fund is used for a self-supporting activity that charges the public for services, and measurement of income is important. Services provided to other departments on a cost reimbursement basis are accounted for by the internal service fund.

80. (d) $5,900,000. Self-sustaining activities are operated by governmental units as enterprise funds.

81. (d) Enterprise fund and depreciation on the fixed assets should be recorded.
Enterprise funds (proprietary) carry their own assets, record depreciation, follow GAAP and match costs and revenue as much as possible.

82. (b) No, Yes, Yes. Enterprise funds carry their own bonds, have a retained earnings account, but do not use budgetary accounts.

83. (d) Enterprise funds are "business type" funds and as such use the full accrual basis of accounting. The accounting for enterprise funds is similar to "for profit" enterprises and thus fixed assets and depreciation are accounted for as if the entity uses a "for profit" organization.

84. (b) Restricted asset, *yes;* liability, *yes;* Fund equity, *no.*
A restricted asset would be appropriately classified in the balance sheet with the credit side shown as a liability. Since the deposit must at some point be returned or applied to a customer's account, it could not properly be part of fund equity.

85. (d) Enterprise: *Yes*—Long-term debt: *No*
Enterprise funds carry their own long-term debt.

86. (d) Operating revenues.
Billings for services provided by the internal service fund to other funds of the same governmental entity, are reported as revenues.

87. (d)      Due from water and sewer fund                     $100,000
                        Operating revenues control                           $100,000

As a proprietary fund, the entry resembles that of a commercial enterprise—debit of a receivable and a credit to a proper revenue account.

88. (d) Residual equity transfers to proprietary funds should be reported as additions to contributed capital.

89. (d) **Residual equity transfers** are adjustments to fund balance, and does not affect an internal service fund's net income.

90. (b) The amount of cash confiscated by illegal activities to be reported in its expendable trust fund is **$300,000,** which specified and restrict disbursement purpose. The $500,000 sales tax collected are accounted for in an agency fund.

91. (a) An agency acts as an agent for a third party for whom the government has no direct responsibility.

92. (a) Nonexpendable trust funds.
The accrual basis of accounting is recommended for proprietary, nonexpendable trust funds and pension trust funds. Enterprise funds are proprietary funds. Special revenue and capital projects funds are governmental funds for which the modified accrual basis of accounting is recommended. Expendable trust funds are accounted for in a manner similar to governmental funds.

93. (d) Nonexpendable trust funds are used to account for the principal that must be held intact in order to produce income. In this case, the investment must be held in the nonexpendable fund in order to produce income. Only the income can be used by the museum.

94. (d) $14,300,000. The fund balance of Maple city's is composed of:
Reserve for employer's contributions                $5,000,000
Actuarial deficiency for contributions                    300,000
Reserve for employees' contributions                  9,000,000

95. (d) Agency funds are primarily clearing accounts for cash and other resources which are held for a brief period and disbursed to authorized recipients. Choice (a) is incorrect because the special revenue fund accounts are for revenues that are legally restricted to expenditures for specified purposes (roads, bridges). Choice (b) is incorrect because the internal service fund is established to finance and account for services and commodities furnished by a governmental entity to another unit or department such as central garages and central printing. Choice (c) is incorrect because a trust fund accounts for assets held in a trustee capacity for others.

96. (b) Yes, Yes, Yes. The CAFR requires a balance sheet for all fund types and account groups.

97. (a) The account groups are included in the balance sheet of the comprehensive report. The groups are not related to revenues, expenditures, or changes in fund balances.

98. (d) No, no.
Account groups do not have revenue and therefore would be included only in the combined balance sheet. Proprietary funds do not have "fund balances," but would be included in the CAFR combining revenue, expenses and changes in retained earnings.

99. (c) Account groups, *no;* Governmental funds, *no.*
Account groups and governmental funds do not have retained earnings as they do not measure periodic net income. Neither have expenses, account groups do not have revenues; however, governmental funds measure revenue using the modified accrual basis of accounting.

100. (c) CAFR is based on modified accrual basis, while the proprietary funds are reported on a full accrual basis. The balance sheets include all funds.

101. (a) A statement of cash flows is required for all proprietary funds but not for governmental funds. Capital projects fund is a governmental fund while the enterprise fund is a proprietary fund.

102. (c) $6,000,000. The amount to be reported as cash flows from capital and related financing activities would
include proceeds from sale of bonds     $5,000,000
capital contributed by subsidiaries     $1,000,000.

The $3,000,000 of cash received from customer households would be included in the operating activities.

103. (d) Governmental type funds use the modified accrual basis of accounting. All the other funds listed use full accrual.

104. (c) Modified accrual, Accrual. Per NCGA Statement 1, Governmental funds use the modified accrual and Proprietary funds use the accrual method.

105. (b) Credited at the beginning of the year and debited at the end of the year.
Beginning of the year opening entry:

| | | |
|---|---|---|
| Estimated revenue control | $1,000,000 | |
|     Appropriations | | $950,000 |
|     Budgetary fund balance | | 50,000 |
| End of year—reverse the above, as is | | |

106. (b) The **$1,000,000** unrestricted state grant would be recorded in the general fund. The $200,000 interest bank accounts held for employees pension plan would be recorded in the pension plan (trust fund).

107. (d) Yes, no.
The modified accrual basis of accounting is recommended for all governmental fund entities. The "accrual" basis of accounting is recommended for proprietary funds.

108. (a) Only the property taxes, licenses, and fines of **$9,000,000** would be classified as estimated revenue. Proceeds of debt issue of $500,000 and interfund transfers for debt service of $1,000,000 are both other financial sources and are not part of the estimated revenue.

109. (a)  Appropriation would be credited for $80,000.
          The entry to record the budget would be:

| | | |
|---|---|---|
| Estimated Revenue | 100,000 | |
| Appropriations | | **80,000** |
| Budgetary fund balance | | 20,000 |

110. (c) If estimated revenue exceeds appropriations, budgetary fund balance would be credited for **$20,000**.

111. (b) The account is closed out at the end of the year. At year end revenues control is debited in the amount of its credit balance. Likewise, expenditures are credited in the amount of its debit balance. Any difference becomes part of fund balance.

112. (c) GASB Code 2450.101 establishes standards for reporting cash flows of proprietary and nonexpendable trust funds & governmental entities that use proprietary fund accounting, including public benefit corporations authorities, governmental utilities, governmental hospitals.

113. (d) $0.
Bonds, notes, and other long-term liabilities directly related to, and expected to be paid from, proprietary funds and trust funds should be included in the accounts of such funds. These are specific liabilities, even though the full faith and credit of the governmental unit may be pledged as further assurance that the liabilities will be paid.

114. (c) The entry to record the budget is a debit to Estimated Revenues and a credit to Appropriations with the balance to Fund Balance (either a dr. or cr.). When the budgetary accounts are closed, this entry is reversed.

115. (a) $2,800,000.
The activities described classify these entities as enterprise funds.

116. (a) Cash: restricted asset; Marketable securities: restricted asset.
If the funds cannot be spent for normal operating purposes, the funds are restricted regardless of whether cash, marketable securities or something else.

117. (d) Expenditures control.
Salaries and wages and other similar type recurring items are not ordinarily subject to being recorded as encumbrances such as equipment or supplies. Item (d) is the only non-budgetary account listed.

118. (d) The $40,000 would be recorded in an enterprise fund. The $100,000 would be recorded in a trust fund. The $6,000,000 would be recorded in the general fund, a governmental type fund.

119. (b) In accordance with the modified accrual basis, Pine should recognize $2,200,000 of property taxes for the year ended June 30, 19X1.

| year | levy | | payment due 6-30-91 |
|---|---|---|---|
| 19X0 | $2,000,000 | 50% | $1,000,000 |
| 19X1 | $2,400,000 | 50% | $1,200,000 |

120. (d) Depreciation expenses on assets are not recorded for governmental funds but are recorded for all depreciable assets in the proprietary funds.

121. (b) GASB 1900 describes that the general purpose financial statements **include the basic financial statements and notes to the financial statements that are essential to fair prevention.**

122. (a) The proprietary funds include both :

| | |
|---|---|
| Enterprise funds | $1,000,000 |
| Internal service funds | 400,000 |
| Total proprietary balance | **$1,400,000** |

123. (a) Other financing uses control, $1,000,000.
The general fund is affected only by the $1,000,000 transfer to finance the cost of the annex. The proceeds of the $2,000,000 bond issue would be recorded in the capital projects fund and the bond liability would be recorded in general long-term debt.

124. (c) Other financing sources control, $3,000,000; Expenditures control, $3,000,000.
Capital projects records both the $1,000,000 transfer from the general fund and $2,000,000 proceeds of the bond issue as "other financing sources". Upon payment the disbursement is recorded as an "expenditure". Answer (d) is incorrect since the receipt of these funds is **not** recorded as "revenue," but as "other financing sources".

125. (c) Monies received for the construction of governmental-owned assets is recorded in the capital projects fund.

126. (b) The closing entry made at the end of 19X9 would be:

| | | |
|---|---|---|
| Other financing sources | $1,500,000 | |
| Revenues | 8,000,000 | |
| Expenditures | | $5,000,000 |
| Other financing uses | | 2,000,000 |
| Fund balance | | 2,500,000 |

Appropriations is part of the budget which is reversed at year end and does not affect fund balance.

127. (a) The internal service fund recognizes revenue in the same manner as "regular" business entities. Thus operating revenues is credited when sales are made.

128. (c) The budget is recorded.
Appropriations are credited when the budget is recorded.

129. (a) The budgetary accounts are closed.
The budgetary accounts are set up as opening entries as follows:

| | |
|---|---|
| Estimated revenues control | |
| Appropriations control | |
| Budgetary fund balance | |

At the end of the accounting period the above entry is reversed.

130. (c) $300,000. The amount to be classified under governmental fund would include only the amount related to the capital projects fund.

131. (d) Asset section of the general long-term debt account group.
General long-term debt account group has only three accounts, one being the above asset account, the other two being "bonds payable" and "amount to be provided...". Bonds payable is the only account having a normal credit balance.

132. (c) At estimated fair value when received.
Donated fixed assets should be recorded at their estimated fair value at the time received.

133. (c) Special revenue.
General fixed assets account group is used to account for fixed assets of the governmental funds which includes the general, special revenue, capital projects and debt service funds.

134. (d) Special revenue.
Two funds, (a) and (b), are proprietary funds which use the accrual basis. Nonexpendable trust funds also use the accrual method. Special revenue is a governmental fund which uses the modified method.

135. (b) Funds collected by one governmental unit for the benefit of another governmental unit are recorded in agency funds.

136. (d) Internal service.
Proprietary funds use the accrual basis of accounting. Internal service and enterprise are proprietary funds. Answers (a), (b) and (c) are governmental funds and use the modified accrual method.

137. (b) Donations are accounted for at fair market value, but forfeiture due to nonpayment is not a donation. The amount to be capitalized in the general fixed asset account group is **$20,000**.

138. (a) It should be reported on the general fund statement of revenues, expenditures, and changes in fund balance - budget and actual.

139. (b) Investment in GFA, *yes;* Fund balance, *no*.
The GFAAG does not have the need to record encumbrances for any reason. The account "investment in general fixed assets" represents the credit balance of all fixed assets (debits) recorded in the account.

140. (d) Restricted asset, restricted asset.
Since the customer deposits are not available to be spent for normal operating purposes, the investments cannot be accounted for as an unrestricted asset. The key factor here is the fact that the funds are restricted and are not available for current use.

141. (a) The statement formats are different from that of a business which combines non-capital financing activities with capital financing activities.

142. (c) No, no.
Fixed assets are accounted for in the general fixed assets group of accounts. Capital projects fund and general fund fixed assets are accounted for in that account group.

143. (d) When the Internal Service Fund bills other entities the journal entry is:

| | | |
|---|---|---|
| Due from park and recreation fund | 150,000 | |
| (Billings) **Operating revenue control** | | 150,000 |

144. (c) Expenditures. This term is used to denote spending of all types from the general fund. Cost expirations (expenses) and capital expenditures are treated alike in this regard, since the objective of Fund accounting is to control expenditures, not measure periodic net income.

145. (d) Encumbrances control.
When a purchase order is approved, the entry is:

| | | |
|---|---|---|
| Encumbrances control | xxx | |
| Fund balance reserved for encumbrances | | xxx |

When the order is received, this entry is reversed.

146. (c) When previously encumbered goods are received reserve for encumbrances is debited and encumbrances is credited for the amount of $5,000,000 originally charged. Of the original encumbrances $4,500,000 has been received. Only **$500,000** of the remaining goods ordered but not yet received at the year end is the remaining balance.

147. (d)            When a purchase order is approved -
                        Encumbrances                        100
                            Reserve for Encumbrances                        100

            When the order arrives the entry is reversed.-
                    Reserve for Encumbrances                100
                            Encumbrances                                100

        Only an error would cause a difference in balance.

148. (b) Encumbrances are established when the purchase order is written. When the goods arrive, the encumbrance is reduced, and the actual expenditure and liability recorded for the amount of the invoice. Thus the encumbrances decrease and the expenditures increase.

149. (d) $0. Special assessment funds are no longer used in general purpose financial statements to report the construction of capital improvements or the provision of services financed by special assessments.

150. (c) **Special revenue funds** of a government unit uses the modified accrual basis of accounting.

151. (b)            When purchase order is approved -
                        Encumbrances
                            Reserve for Encumbrances

152. (c) Due to Grove County general fund $10,000.
As an agency fund, no revenue is recorded, only an amount due to the general fund. Revenue will be recorded by the general fund, however.

153. (c) The combined balance sheet but **not** the combined statement of revenues, expenditures, and changes in fund balances.

Account groups (GFAAG and GLTDAG) do not have revenues, expenditures and fund balances; however, the balance sheet items do (fixed assets, for example, in the case of general fixed assets and bonds payable for general long-term debt group).

154. (b) $900,000. The amount to be accounted for in the special revenue fund would include only the gasoline taxes to finance road repairs. The special assessments levied on property owners to install sidewalks would be accounted for in the capital project fund.

155. (a) Expenditures:
        Salaries and wages                        $100,000
                Vouchers payable                                $100,000
(b) is not correct since cost expirations (expenses) are not measured by governmental funds. (c) Salaries, wages and other periodic type payments are not subject to the encumbrance system. Further (c) is not correct encumbrance entry. In (d) an expenditure cannot be recorded by reducing fund balance directly.

156. (d) The debt service fund is used to account for the accumulation of resources for the payment of debt interest and principal.

157. (a) Fixed assets are recorded in the general fixed assets account group as a record of items on hand for the governmental funds, because they are not expected to contribute to the generation of revenues. Furthermore, all the accounts in the governmental funds are "current", and are closed at year end.

158. (d) When a purchase is approved, a portion of fund balance is reversed with a debit to Encumbrances and a credit to Reserve for Encumbrance.

159. (a) Principal, *yes;* Interest, *yes.*
The function of the general long-term debt account group is to account for principal only. Funds may be accumulated, however, in debt service to pay both principal and interest of such debt.

160. (a) $0. General fixed assets are included in the general fixed assets group of accounts—not as part of the general fund balance sheet. Such items are recorded in the general fund as expenditures in the year of purchase.

161. (a) $300,000 - Fair market value is the basis for recording donated assets. Donor's cost or carrying value is not relevant to valuing recording value by the donee.

162. (a) Revenues control.
Employer contributions, employee contributions (if any) and investment income are recorded as revenue in a pension trust fund.

163. (b) Expenditures control.
A governmental fund employer contribution to a pension trust fund is an expenditure similar to wages.

164. (c) $350,000.
Proprietary funds maintain their own cash accumulations for payment of debt. General long-term obligations, however, would be paid from cash accumulated in a debt service fund.

165. (a) $0. Proceeds of long-term debt to be used for a major capital project should be recorded in a capital project fund. The short-term notes for the expendable trust should be accounted for in the trust fund.

166. (b) When a governmental unit approves orders (obligates expenditures) for goods or equipment, the entry in answer (b) is entered. Answer choices (a), (c), and (d) have no merit in fund accounting.

167. (b) Encumbrances control.
The subject account, debited when supplies are ordered, is reversed when supplies are received, consequently credited.

168. (a) Supplies previously ordered are received.
The receipt of supplies results in a reversal of the encumbrances entry made when supplies were ordered. The reversal decreases the fund balance reserved for encumbrances. This credit balance account **increases when supplies are ordered** and **decreases when supplies are received**.

169. (c) Fund balance reserved for encumbrances.
This account is credited when supplies are ordered or a purchase order is approved. When supplies are received the original entry is reversed.

170. (a) $0. Amounts received through bond issue, operating transfers-out and material proceeds of fixed asset dispositions, other sources for the purpose of capital projects are credited to revenue (a previous practice). The applicable credit is to **"Other financing sources control."**

171. (d) The special assessment proceeds are to be reported in the capital project fund.

172. (c) Be reported in the general long-term debt account group.

Bond issues resulting from special assessment activities are recorded in the general long-term debt account group similar to that of other governmental fund debt. Special assessment fund types are not used in general purpose financial statements to report the construction of public improvements or the provision of services financed by special assessments.

173. (c) The budgetary fund balance account is debited at the beginning since appropriations exceeded estimated revenues. *At year end the fund balance is credited.* (When possible, jot down journal entries with made up numbers to solve theory questions.)

| | | | |
|---|---|---|---|
| At beginning | Estimated Revenues | 10 | |
| | Budgetary Fund Balance | 5 | |
| | Appropriations | | 15 |

174. (a) $9,000,000. The amount to be included in the GFAAG should include all other fixed assets. Proprietary and Fiduciary funds carry their own assets.

175. (c) The entry to be made in the general fund asset account group would be:

| | | |
|---|---|---|
| Machinery and equipment | $180,000 | |
| Investment in general fixed assets from gifts | | $180,000 |

176. (a) This is a situation where not-for-profit accounting follows similar rules to for profit accounting. Donated fixed assets should be recorded at their estimated fair value at the time of acquisition.

177. (b) Encumbrances represent amounts set aside that are not available for expenditures.

178. (d) Enterprise. Because meter deposits imply a utility operation commonly an enterprise fund.

179. (d) The bond issue proceeds would be recorded in the capital projects fund. The general fund would make an entry to transfer $1,500,000 of cost to the capital projects fund as follows:

| | | |
|---|---|---|
| Other financing uses control | $1,500,000 | |
| Cash | | $1,500,000 |

180. (c) A public school district uses the same accounting model as a governmental fund, and therefore, recognizes revenues when they become available and measurable.

181. (b) Internal service funds are used to account for the financing of goods or services provided by one department or agency to the other departments or other agencies on a cost reimbursement basis.

182. (b) GASB 60.116 states that shared revenues received for proprietary fund operating purposes should be recognized as **nonoperating revenues** in the accounting period in which they are earned and become measurable.

183. (a) $0. NCGA Statement #1 states that "General long-term debt is the unmatured principal of bonds, warrants, notes, or other forms of noncurrent or long-term indebtedness that is not a specific liability of any proprietary fund, Special Assessment Fund or Trust Fund". The bonds in question being proprietary fund debt are not included in the GLTD group.

184. (d) $240,000. A careful reading of the facts reveals that the $210,000 for parking meters is a capital expenditure. Because this is an enterprise fund, this amount is capitalized and depreciation is recorded. GAAP is followed. $400,000 - $90,000 - $70,000 = $240,000 net income.

185. (a)  Machinery and equipment                               $200,000
                  Investment in GFA, private gifts                           $200,000

General fixed assets is an account group. Revenue is not recorded in this account. Assets under control of other funds are recorded, with the offsetting credit to "Investment in general fixed assets" (source).

186. (d) The amount due to special revenue fund from general fund **$10,000**, is an asset, because it is a receivable in the special revenue fund, and a liability in the general fund. The amount due to an agency from special revenue **$4,000**, is an asset to an agency and a liability to the special revenue fund.

187. (c) Cash equivalents are defined in GASB 9 as short-term, highly liquid investments that are both readily convertible to cash, and so near to their maturity that they present insignificant risk of changes in interest rates. Investments with maturities of 3 months or less qualify as cash equivalents. Both 3-month T-bills and 3-year T-notes mature in 3 months or less from the date purchased for a total cash equivalent of **$80,000.**

188. (b) Total fund balance would be $400,000 of which $100,000 would be reserved for encumbrances, and **$300,000** would be reported as unreserved fund balance in the general fund balance sheet.

|  |  |
|---|---|
| Total assets | $1,000,000 |
| Less: total liabilities | (600,000) |
| Fund balance | 400,000 |
| Less: reserved for encumbrances | (100,000) |
| Unreserved fund balance | **$300,000** |

189. (c) Cash equivalents are short-term highly liquid investments that are readily convertible into **known** amounts of cash and are near maturity so that the changes in rates represent insignificant risks (three months or less).

190. (a) The general long-term debt account group reports the liability in the same amount that the general fixed asset account group reports the amount.

# Chapter Nineteen
# Solutions to Governmental Accounting Problems

## NUMBER 1

|  | DR | CR |
|---|---|---|
| Estimated revenues | 700,000 | |
| Appropriations | | 600,000 |
| Appropriations - Operating transfers out | | 30,000 |
| Budgetary fund balance | | 10,000 |

1. Estimated revenues - dr.
2. Budgetary fund balance - cr.
3. Appropriations - cr.
4. Appropriations - Operating transfers out - cr.
5. Expenditures - Not affected

|  | DR | CR |
|---|---|---|
| Property tax receivable | XX | |
| Allowance for uncollectibles - current | | 5,000 |
| Revenues | | XX |

The property tax revenues are recorded when levied net of the allowance for uncollectible.

6. Property tax receivable - dr.
7. Bad debt expense - not affected
8. Allowance for uncollectibles - current cr.
9. Revenues - cr.
10. Estimated revenues - not affected

|  | DR | CR |
|---|---|---|
| Encumbrances | XX | |
| Budgetary fund balance reserved for encumbrances | | XX |

11. Encumbrances - dr.
12. Budgetary balance reserved for encumbrances - cr.
13. Expenditures - not affected
14. Vouchers payable - not affected
15. Purchases - not affected

|  | DR | CR |
|---|---|---|
| (1) Budgetary fund balance reserved for encumbrance | XX | |
| Encumbrances | | XX |
| (2) Expenditures | XX | |
| Vouchers payable | | XX |

The reversal of the reserve and the encumbrances is for the estimated purchase order amount. However the expenditures and vouchers payable is for the actual invoice amount.

16. Encumbrances - cr.
17. Budgetary fund balance reserved or encumbrances - dr.
18. Expenditures - dr.
19. Vouchers payable - cr.
20. Purchases - Not affected

|  | DR | CR |
|---|---|---|
| Other financial uses/Operating transfers out. | 30,000 | |
| Cash | | 30,000 |

The transfer of cash out of the general fund to the Library debt service fund is not a transfer in, so there is no "due from" the Library service fund.

21. Residual equity transfer out - not affected. This is an operating transfer.
22. Due from Library debt service fund - not affected
23. Cash - cr.
24. Other financial uses - operating transfers out - dr.
25. Encumbrances - not affected

|  | DR | CR |
|---|---|---|
| Appropriations | 550,000 | |
| Appropriations - operating transfers out | 30,000 | |
| Budgetary fund balance | 10,000 | |
| Estimated revenues | | 700,000 |
| | | |
| Revenues | XX | |
| Expenditures | | XX |
| Other financial uses - operating transfers out | | XX |
| Unserved fund balance (PLUG) | | XX |

The first closing entry reverses the budgetary entry recorded at the beginning of the year. The second entry closes out the actual revenues, expenditures and transfers accounts to unreserved fund balance.

26. Estimated revenues - cr.
27. Budgetary fund balance - dr.
28. Appropriations - dr.
29. Appropriations - dr.
30. Expenditures - cr.
31. Revenues - dr.
32. Other financial uses - operating transfers out - cr.
33. Allowance for uncollectibles - current - not affected
34. Bad debt expense - not affected
35. Depreciation expense - not affected
36. Residual equity transfer out - not affected

The allowance account is not closed out since it is a contra account to the property tax receivable account. Neither bad debt expense nor depreciation expense are recorded in the general fund so they would not be affected.

|  | DR | CR |
|---|---|---|
| (1) Budgetary fund balance reserved for encumbrances | 12,000 | |
| Encumbrances | | 12,000 |
| | | |
| (2) Unserved fund balance | 12,000 | |
| Fund Balance reserved for encumbrances | | 12,000 |

The first entry reverses the encumbrances entry made at the time the outstanding purchase orders were issued. The second entry establishes the reserve of fund balance for encumbrances.

37. Encumbrances - cr.
38. Budgetary fund balance reserved for encumbrances - dr.
39. Unreserved fund balance - dr.
40. Fund balance for encumbrances - cr.

## NUMBER 2

| 1. | G | The entry is to debit cash and credit other financing sources. |
|---|---|---|
| 2. | K | Debit encumbrances credit reserve for encumbrances. |
| 3. | L | Two journal entries are needed. The first is to debit reserve for encumbrance and credit encumbrances. The second is to debit expenditure control and credit to vouchers payable. |
| 4. | L | Debit expenditures control and credit vouchers payable. |
| 5. | E | Debit due from other funds, and credit billings. |
| 6. | J | If the award was accrued, debit deferred revenues, and credit revenues. |
| 7. | D | Debit cash and credit deferred revenues. |
| 8. | A | Debit estimated revenues, credit appropriations and plug fund balance (either a debit or a credit). |
| 9. | F | Debit cash and credit tax anticipation notes payable. |
| 10. | B | See #8. If inflows (Revenues) exceed outflows (Appropriations) credit Budgetary Fund Balance. |
| 11. | B | All proprietary fund assets are accounted for in the fund. |
| 12. | F | Capital projects fund are used to account for major construction activities or acquisitions. |
| 13. | D | Fixed assets acquired by the governmental funds are accounted for in the General fixed assets account group. |
| 14. | J | Accounting for infrastructures in the GFAAG is optional. |
| 15. | B | See #11. |

16.  G  Property tax revenues that are not specifically restricted are accounted for as a General fund revenues.

17.  A  Agency funds are fiduciary funds. They are accounted in the same manner as governmental fund.

18.  D  The General long term debt account group accounts for the obligation.

19.  I  The purpose for the special revenue fund is to account for revenues specifically marked.

20.  H  The purpose for the debt service fund is to account for the principal and interest payments on general obligations.


## NUMBER 3

| Transaction Number | Journal Entries | Dr. | Cr. | Fund or Group of Accounts |
|---|---|---|---|---|
| 1. | Estimated revenues control | $695,000 | | G |
| | Appropriations control | | $650,000 | |
| | Budgetary fund balance | | 45,000 | |
| | To record adoption of the budget. | | | |
| 2. | Taxes receivable—current | 160,000 | | SR |
| | Estimated uncollectible current taxes | | 1,600 | |
| | Revenues control | | 158,400 | |
| | To record levy of taxes in special revenue fund. | | | |
| 3.a. | Encumbrances control | 2,390 | | G |
| | Fund balance reserved for encumbrances | | 2,390 | |
| | To record encumbrances for purchase orders. | | | |
| b. | Fund balance reserved for encumbrances | 2,390 | | G |
| | Encumbrances control | | 2,390 | |
| | To record cancellation of encumbrances upon receipt of supplies. | | | |
| | Expenditures control | 2,500 | | G |
| | Vouchers payable | | 2,500 | |
| | To record actual expenditures on supplies encumbered for $2,390. | | | |
| 4. | Due to utility fund | 1,000 | | G |
| | Expenditures control | 40 | | |
| | Cash | | 1,040 | |
| | To record disbursement to liquidate a loan from the utility fund. | | | |
| | Cash | 1,040 | | E |
| | Interest income | | 40 | |
| | Due from general fund | | 1,000 | |
| | To record receipt to liquidate a loan to the general fund. | | | |
| 5. | Land | 85,000 | | GFA |
| | Investment in general fixed assets—donations | | 85,000 | |
| | To record land donated to city. | | | |

| | | | | |
|---|---|---|---|---|
| 6.a. | Cash | 90,000 | | CP |
| | Other financing sources control | | 90,000 | |
| | To record issuance of bonds for curbing project. | | | |
| | | | | |
| | Amount to be provided for in payment of bonds | 90,000 | | |
| | Bonds payable | | 90,000 | LTD |
| b. | Expenditures control | 84,000 | | CP |
| | Vouchers payable | | 84,000 | |
| | To record expenditures on curbing project. | | | |
| | Other financing sources control | 90,000 | | CP |
| | Unreserved fund balance | | $ 6,000 | |
| | Expenditures control | | 84,000 | |
| | To close expenditures. | | | |
| | | | | |
| | Improvements other than buildings—curbing | 84,000 | | GFA |
| | Investment in general fixed assets—capital projects | | 84,000 | |
| | To record cost of curbing. | | | |
| 7.a. | Investments | 22,000 | | TA |
| | Fund balance reserved for endowments | | 22,000 | |
| | To record the value of stock donated in trust. | | | |
| b. | Cash | 1,100 | | TA |
| | Revenues control | | 1,100 | |
| | To record dividend revenue in endowment revenues fund. | | | |
| 8.a. | Cash | 308,000 | | CP |
| | Other Financing Sources Control | | 308,000 | |
| | To record issuance of bonds to finance construction of a city hall addition. | | | |
| | | | | |
| | Amount to be provided for payment of term bonds | 300,000 | | LTD |
| | Term bonds payable | | 300,000 | |
| | To record the issuance of bonds to finance construction of a city hall addition. | | | |
| | | | | |
| | Other Financing Sources Control | 8,000 | | CP |
| | Cash | | 8,000 | |
| | To record transfer of bond premium to debt service fund. | | | |
| | | | | |
| | Cash | 8,000 | | DS |
| | Other Financing Sources Control | | 8,000 | |
| | To record transfer of bond premium from capital projects fund. | | | |
| | | | | |
| | Amount available in debt service fund—term bonds | 8,000 | | LTD |
| | Amount to be provided for payment of term bonds | | 8,000 | |
| | To record increases in assets available in debt service fund. | | | |

b.   Expenditures control                                 297,000                                            CP

|  | Debit | Credit | Fund |
|---|---|---|---|
| b.  Expenditures control | 297,000 | | CP |
|     Cash | | 297,000 | |

To record expenditures for construction of city hall addition.

| Other Financing Uses – Operating Transfers Out | 3,000 | | CP |
|---|---|---|---|
|     Cash | | 3,000 | |

To record transfer of remaining cash to debt service fund.

| Other Financing Sources Control | 300,000 | | CP |
|---|---|---|---|
|     Expenditures Control | | 297,000 | |
|     Other Financing Uses – Operating Transfers Out | | 3,000 | |

To close the revenues, expenditures and operating transfers accounts to fund balance.

| Buildings | 297,000 | | GFA |
|---|---|---|---|
|     Investment in fixed assets—capital project fund—general obligation bonds | | 297,000 | |

To record city hall addition.

| Cash | 3,000 | | DS |
|---|---|---|---|
|     Other Financing Sources Control | | 3,000 | |

To record transfer from capital projects fund.

| Amount available in debt service fund—term bonds | 3,000 | | LTD |
|---|---|---|---|
|     Amount to be provided for payment of term bonds | | 3,000 | |

To record increase in assets available in debt service fund.


# NUMBER 4

1.  $1,000,000.  The entries to approve the budget are:

| Estimated Revenue Control | 10,000,000 | |
|---|---|---|
| Other Financing Sources Control – Operating Transfers In | 100,000 | |
|     Appropriation Control | | 9,100,000 |
|     Budgetary Fund Balance | | 1,000,000 |

2.  $9,350,000.  The entries for property taxes in 1996 are as follows:

| Property Taxes Receivable – Current | 9,500,000 | |
|---|---|---|
|     Allowance For Uncollectible Taxes – Current | | 100,000 |
|     Revenues Control | | 9,400,000 |

| Cash | 9,350,000 | |
|---|---|---|

| Property Taxes – Delinquent | 150,000 | |
|---|---|---|
|     Property Taxes – Current | | 9,500,000 |

3.  $-0-. There is no balance in the fund balance account as shown by the following entries:

| | | |
|---|---|---|
| Cash | 2,100,000 | |
|     Other Financing Sources – Proceeds of Bonds | | 2,000,000 |
|     Other Financing Sources – Transfers In | | 100,000 |
| Expenditures | 2,100,000 | |
|     Construction Contracts Payable | | 2,100,000 |
|     Other Financing Sources – Transfers In | | 100,000 |
| Other Financing Sources – Proceeds of Bonds | 2,000,000 | |
| Other Financing Sources – Transfers In | 100,000 | |
|     Expenditures | | 2,100,000 |

Because the expenditures equals financing sources, the fund balance is zero.

4.  $2,100,000.  At the end of each year, expenditures accumulated on capital projects are recorded in the GFA Account Group. Since the project was completed during the year, the account debited is Building, not Construction in progress.

5.  $2,000,000.  Debt issued to finance capital projects is included in the GLTD Account Group.

## NUMBER 5

1.  A

Expenditures of governmental funds are classified by fund, function (or program), organization unit, activity, character, and object class. Classification by character is on the basis of the fiscal period presumed to be benefited. Expenditures – current services is therefore a character classification because it indicates that the expenditures benefit the current period.

2.  A

Expenditures of governmental funds are classified by fund, function (or program), organization unit, activity, character, and object class. Classification by character is on the basis of the fiscal period presumed to be benefited. Expenditures – capital outlay is a classification by character indicating that the expenditure is expected to benefit the current and future periods.

3.  B

Classification of governmental fund expenditures by function or program provides information on overall purposes or objectives. A function is a group of activities intended to perform a major service or meet a regulatory responsibility. The item expenditures-health is classified by function.

4.  B

A governmental fund recognizes inventories using either the purchase or the consumption method. Under the purchase method, a general fund supplies inventory is considered an expenditure when it is purchased. However, a significant amount of inventory remaining at year-end should be reported on the balance sheet. Recognition of inventory requires a segregation of fund equity similar to the reserve for encumbrances. Thus, the purchase method entry is to debit supplies inventory and credit unreserved fund balance and then to debit unreserved fund balance and credit a reserve for supplies inventory. Under the consumption method, supplies are charged to inventory only when used. Accordingly, the entry to record the ending inventory under this method debits inventory and unreserved fund balance and credits expenditures and reserve for supplies inventory. The effect is to reduce expenditures to the cost of the amount actually used. Shar City must have used the purchase method. The fund balance at January 1,

1995 was $383,000 ($304,000 unreserved + $79,000 reserved as calculated in question 14). The fund balance at December 31, 1995 was $238,000 ($43,000 + $38,000 + $157,000). Although residual equity transfers out totaled $190,000, the fund balance decreased by only $145,000 ($383,000 - $238,000). Other factors must therefore have increased fund balance by $45,000 ($190,000 - $145,000). These factors were the $28,000 excess of revenues over expenditures and other financing uses and the $17,000 increase in supplies inventory ($38,000 - $21,000). Under the consumption method, the $17,000 increase in inventory would have been treated as a decrease in expenditures, not as an increase in fund balance. Accordingly, the use of the purchase method requires that the statement of changes in revenue, expenditures, and fund balance include the inventory increase as an other financing source or a fund balance increase. The purpose is to reconcile the beginning and ending fund balance amounts.

5.   B
An enterprise fund is a proprietary fund. A proprietary fund's measurement focus is on determination of net income, financial position, and cash flows. Thus, an enterprise fund's accounting system is similar to that for private sector businesses. Its presentation of fund equity should distinguish between contributed equity and retained earnings from operations.

6.   A
General long-term debt is accounted for in the general long-term debt account group. However, long-term liabilities of proprietary funds and trust funds, such as an enterprise fund, are accounted for through those funds.

7.   A
Grants recorded in governmental funds, such as the general fund, should be recognized in revenue in the accounting period when they become susceptible to accrual, that is, when they are measurable and available.

8.   E
Reimbursements are made for expenditures or expenses of one fund that are applicable to another fund. They are recorded as an expenditure or expense of the reimbursing fund and as a reduction in the expenditure or expense of the reimbursed fund. Thus, after reimbursement, the expense for pension contributions is ultimately reflected only in the internal service fund, not in the general fund.

9.   B
Quasi-external transactions are interfund transactions that do not constitute transfers and are not revenues, expenditures, or expenses of the governmental unit, but they are nevertheless accounted for as revenues, expenditures, or expenses of the funds involved. The reason is that they are of a kind that would be treated as revenues, expenditures, or expenses of the governmental unit if they involved external entities. Examples are payments in lieu of taxes by an enterprise fund to the general fund, internal service fund billings to departments, routine employer contributions to a pension trust fund, and routine service charges for utilities. Accordingly, the payment of utility charges to the enterprise fund is a quasi-external transaction that should be recorded as an expenditure of the general fund.

10.   C
The subsidy to an enterprise fund is an interfund transaction that is not a loan, a quasi-external transaction, or a reimbursement. Thus, it is a transfer. All transfers that are not residual equity transfers are classified as operating transfers. Examples are legally authorized transfers from a fund receiving revenue to the expending fund, operating subsidy transfers from a general fund to an enterprise fund, transfers of tax revenue from a special revenue fund to a debt service fund, and transfers from a general fund to a special revenue or a capital projects fund. Operating transfers are not reported as revenues, expenditures, or expenses. They are reported as other financing sources (uses) in a governmental fund's statement of revenues, expenditures, and changes in fund balance and as operating transfers in a proprietary fund's statement of revenues, expenses, and changes in retained earnings (or equity).

## 11. E

The interfund loan does not meet the criteria for recognition as a revenue, expenditure, or transfer. The receivable recognized by the general fund and the payable recognized by the internal service fund are reported in the combined balance sheet, not in the statement of revenues, expenditures, and changes in fund balances.

## 12. D

Residual equity transfers are defined as nonrecurring or nonroutine transfers of equity between funds, for example, a contribution of enterprise fund capital by the general fund or a return of such capital. They are recorded as additions to or deductions from the beginning fund balance of a governmental fund. They do not result in recognition of other financing sources or revenues or of other financing uses or expenditures.

## 13. B

Payment of an amount due under an operating lease (one not meeting the capitalization criteria of SFAS 13) is reported as an expenditure of the period by the general fund (the user fund). For a capital lease, the asset is recorded in the GFAAG and the liability in the GLTDAG. Moreover, at the inception of the lease, an expenditure and an other financing source would also be recorded (usually in a capital projects fund). The debt service fund would record the periodic payments on the capital lease.

## 14. $79,000

The ending reserve for encumbrances was $43,000 after a decrease of $15,000. Furthermore, beginning supplies inventory was $21,000, an amount that should have been reserved. Thus, the reserved fund balance at the end of 1994 was $79,000 ($43,000 + $15,000 + $21,000).

## 15. $811,000

The entry to record the tax assessment is to debit a receivable, credit an allowance for uncollectible taxes, and credit revenues. Revenues are given as $825,000. The original credit to the allowance account must have been $28,000 ($20,000 ending balance + $8,000 of writeoffs). Hence, the assessed amount was $853,000 ($825,000 + $28,000). Given that $34,000 was transferred to the delinquent taxes account, the amount collected must have been $811,000 ($853,000 - $34,000 - $8,000 written off).

## 16. $89,000

An expenditure is recorded by a debit to expenditures and a credit to a liability (vouchers payable). Payment of the liability results in a debit. Accordingly, the year-end credit balance of $89,000 in vouchers payable represents amounts due to vendors and contractors.

## 17. $100,000

Fixed assets other than those accounted for in the proprietary or trust funds are general fixed assets of the governmental entity. Hence, the capital outlay of $100,000 for police vehicles by the general fund constitutes an acquisition of general fixed assets. They are accounted for in the GFAAG.

## 18. $52,000

The GLTDAG is a self-balancing entity that accounts for all unmatured general long-term debt of a governmental unit that is not a specific liability of a proprietary fund or a nonexpendable trust fund. The GLTDAG is concerned with transactions involving the payment of principal only, not with those concerning interest on the debt. Consequently, general fund expenditures for debt service pertain to liabilities recorded in the GLTDAG, not in the general fund. Given that debt service included $22,000 of interest, the reduction of liabilities reported in the GLTDAG from 1995 transactions equals $52,000 ($74,000 of debt service expenditures -- $22,000 of interest.)

## 19. $1,392,000

The actual amounts given in the statement of revenues, expenditures, and changes in fund balance – budget and actual – general and special revenue fund types will differ from those in the statement of revenues, expenditures, and changes in fund balance – all governmental fund types when the legally prescribed budgetary basis is materially different from GAAP. In the case of Shar City's general fund, the budgetary basis includes encumbrances. Accordingly, the budgetary data are not comparable with GAAP-based actual data. To achieve better comparability, the actual expenditures reported in the budgetary comparison statement for 1996 will include encumbrances remaining at year-end because they relate to the 1995 appropriation authority reflected in the budgetary amounts. However, the expenditures based on 1994 expenditure authority that were recognized in 1995 are excluded. These amounts are not reflected in the budget for 1995. Thus, total actual expenditures reported in the budgetary comparison statement equal $1,392,000 ($1,349,000 expenditures based on 1995 expenditure authority + $43,000 reserve for encumbrances at the end of 1995).

## NUMBER 6

**a**. Journal entries in the Capital Projects fund:

| 7-1-90 | Cash | $300,000 | |
| |     Due to General Fund | | $300,000 |

| 7-9-90 | Construction Expenditures | $200,000 | |
| |     Cash | | $200,000 |

| 12-1-90 | Cash | $6,060,000 | |
| |     Proceeds from Bonds | | $6,060,000 |

| 12-1-90 | A/R from State | $3,000,000 | |
| |     Revenues | | $3,000,000 |

| 4-30-91 | Encumbrances | $7,000,000 | |
| |     Reserve for Encumbrances | | $7,000,000 |

| 5-9-91 | Cash | $1,000,000 | |
| |     A/R form State | | $1,000,000 |

| 6-10-91 | Due to General Fund | $300,000 | |
| |     Cash | | $300,000 |

| 6-30-91 | Reserve for Encumbrances | $1,200,000 | |
| |     Encumbrances | | $1,200,000 |

| | Construction Expenditures | $1,200,000 | |
| |     Contracts Payable | | $1,200,000 |

**b**.  Closing entries:

| | | |
|---|---|---|
| Proceeds of bonds | $6,060,000 | |
| Revenues | $3,000,000 | |
|       Construction Expenditures | | $1,400,000 |
|       Encumbrances | | $5,800,000 |
|       Fund Balance | | $1,860,000 |

**c.**

Eden Township
Capital Project Fund
(Administration Center)
Balance Sheet
June 30, 1991

| | |
|---|---|
| Assets: | |
| Cash | $6,860,000 |
| Account Receivable from State | $2,000,000 |
| | |
| Total Assets | $8,860,000 |
| | |
| Liabilities: | |
| Contract Payable | $1,200,000 |
| | |
| Fund Balance: | |
| Reserve for Encumbrances | $5,800,000 |
| Unreserved | 1,860,000 |
| Total | $7,660,000 |
| | |
| Total Liabilities and Fund Balance | $8,860,000 |

## NUMBER 7

1. $70,000. The entry to record the budget is

| | | |
|---|---|---|
| Estimated Revenue Control | $8,000,000 | |
| Appropriation Control | | 7,500,000 |
| Estimated Other Financing Uses Control | | 430,000* |
| Budgetary Fund Balance | | 70,000 |

*($250,000 + 180,000)

2. $430,000. The general fund support of the new courthouse and the subsidy of $180,000 for the landfill operations are both budgeted transfers out at 1/1/95.

3. $0. No liability for interest exists at 12/31/95 because under the modified accrual basis used in governmental funds only interest that is to be paid with resources in the current period is a liability (Due to Debt Service Fund) of the general fund.

4. $10,000. Under the modified accrual basis of accounting used by the general fund, expenditures would include the reduction of the principal obligation on July 1, 1995. The entry is

| | | |
|---|---|---|
| Expenditures – Principal | $10,000 | |
| Cash | | 10,000 |

Since 7/1/95 was the inception date, there will be no expenditures for interest in 1995.

5. $5,018,000. The information given indicates that Jey recorded property tax revenues of $5,000,000. Because revenue is recorded by governmental entities net of the related allowance account, the allowance must be added to revenue to obtain the amount recorded as a receivable. The entry to record property taxes for 1995 is as follows:

| | | |
|---|---|---|
| Property Taxes Receivable – Current | 5,060,000 | |
| Allowance for Uncollectible Taxes – Current | | 60,000 |
| Revenues Control | | 5,000,000 |

The cash collected on property taxes can be derived using a T-account as follows:

Property Taxes Rec. – Current

| | | |
|---|---|---|
| 5,060,000 | 5,018,000 | Collected |
| Bal. 38,000 | | |
| | 4,000 | W/O (60,000 – 56,000) |

The amount recorded comes from the journal entry. All other amounts were given. With regard to the $38,000 ending balance in the receivable account, the information says the related allowance of $38,000 was recorded equal to the amount of the receivables. The write-offs are the difference between the $60,000 initial allowance provided and the $56,000 balance at 12/31/95.

6. $450,000. Only the state entitlement would represent revenue to be recorded in the capital projects fund.

7. $868,000. Liabilities in the GLTD Account Group would include $800,000 of bonds payable and the $68,000 capital lease obligation. The capital lease obligation of $78,000 was reduced by the initial payment of $10,000 on the inception date of the lease. No interest was included in the first payment (i.e., annuity due or annuity in advance). The $250,000 from the general fund is reported as Other Financing Sources – General Fund.

8. $1,580,000. The net increase in the GFA Account Group would be as follows:

| | |
|---|---|
| Courthouse improvement | $1,527,000 |
| Leased equipment | 78,000 |
| Police car sold | (25,000) |
| | $1,580,000 |

9. $107,000. 1995 closure and postclosure landfill expense is calculated as follows:

| *Cumulative usage to 12/31/95* | x | *Estimated total current cost* | - | *Expense recognized previously* | = | *1995 expense* |
|---|---|---|---|---|---|---|
| $\dfrac{500,000 + 40,000 \text{ cubic yds.}}{1,000,000 \text{ cubic yds.}}$ | x | $300,000 actual + 1,700,000 estimated costs) | - | $973,000 | = | 1995 expense |
| 54% | x | $2,000,000 total costs | - | $973,000 | = | $107,000 |

Since ones, tens, and hundreds do not appear on the answer sheet, the answer should be rounded off to $107,000.

10. $780,000. The liability can be determined by setting up a T-account as follows:

Closure and Postclosure Liability

| | | | |
|---|---|---|---|
| Incurred to date | 300,000 | 973,000 | Exp. rec. prior to 1995 |
| | | 107,000 | 1995 Expenses |
| | | 780,000 | Balance |

11. (D) The measurement focus of governmental-type funds such as the capital projects fund is financial resources.

12. (E) The measurement focus of enterprise funds is capital maintenance/intergenerational equity.

## NUMBER 8

*Albury City*
**WORKSHEET TO CORRECT TRIAL BALANCE**
*December 31, 1990*

| | Trial balance | Adjustments Debit | Adjustments Credit | General fund | Debt service fund | Capital projects fund | Account groups General fixed assets | Account groups General long-term debt |
|---|---|---|---|---|---|---|---|---|
| *Debits:* | | | | | | | | |
| Cash | $477,800 | | | $ 71,800 | $6,000 | $400,000 | | |
| Expenditures | 145,000 | $ 28,000 [b] | | 173,000 | | | | |
| Estimated revenues | 228,200 | | | 228,200 | | | | |
| Equipment | | 66,000 [c] | | | | | $66,000 | |
| Encumbrances | | 10,000 [d] | | 10,000 | | | | |
| Supplies inventory | | 3,400 [e] | | 3,400 | | | | |
| Taxes receivable — current | | 24,000 [a] | | 24,000 | | | | |
| Amount to be provided for retirement of term bonds | | 394,000 [g] | | | | | | $394,000 |
| Amounts available in debt service fund — term bonds | | 6,000 [g] | | | | | | 6,000 |
| Totals | $851,000 | | | $510,400 | $6,000 | $400,000 | $66,000 | $400,000 |
| | | | | | | | | |
| *Credits:* | | | | | | | | |
| Appropriations | $204,000 | | | $204,000 | | | | |
| Revenues and other financing sources | 216,800 | | $ 13,200 [a] 406,000 [f] | 230,000 | $6,000 | $400,000 | | |
| Bonds payable | 400,000 | 400,000 [f] | 400,000 [g] | | | | | $400,000 |
| Premium on bonds payable | 6,000 | 6,000 [f] | | | | | | |
| Fund balance | 24,200 | | | 24,200 | | | | |
| Vouchers payable | | | 28,000 [b] | 28,000 | | | | |
| Investment in general fixed assets — general fund revenue | | | 66,000 [c] | | | | $66,000 | |
| Reserved for encumbrances | | | 10,000 [d] | 10,000 | | | | |
| Reserved for supplies inventory | | | 3,400 [e] | 3,400 | | | | |
| Estimated uncollectible current taxes | | | 10,800 [a] | 10,800 | | | | |
| Totals | $851,000 | $937,400 | $937,400 | $510,400 | $6,000 | $400,000 | $66,000 | $400,000 |

# NUMBER 8 (cont.)

*Albury City*
**WORKSHEET ADJUSTMENTS**
*December 31, 1990*
(Not Required)

|  | Debit | Credit |
|---|---|---|
| [a] Taxes receivable—current | $ 24,000 | |
|     Estimated uncollectible current taxes | | $ 10,800 |
|     Revenues | | 13,200 |

To record current taxes receivable and amount estimated as
uncollectible, computed as follows:

| Total tax levy | $205,200 | = $216,000 |
|---|---|---|
| Divided by % collectible | .95 | |

Taxes receivable = $216,000 – $192,000      = $ 24,000

Estimated uncollectible
    taxes = 5% × $216,000      = $ 10,800

|  | Debit | Credit |
|---|---|---|
| [b] Expenditures | 28,000 | |
|     Vouchers payable | | 28,000 |
|     To record liabilities unrecorded at year-end. | | |
| [c] Equipment | 66,000 | |
|     Investment in general fixed assets—general fund revenue | | 66,000 |
|     To record purchase of equipment from general fund revenue. | | |
| [d] Encumbrances | 10,000 | |
|     Reserved for encumbrances | | 10,000 |
|     To record purchase orders outstanding at year-end. | | |
| [e] Supplies inventory | 3,400 | |
|     Reserved for supplies inventory | | 3,400 |
|     To record inventory of supplies on hand at year-end. | | |
| [f] Bonds payable | 400,000 | |
|     Premium on bonds payable | 6,000 | |
|         Other financing sources | | 406,000 |
|     To reclassify bond proceeds. | | |
| [g] Amount to be provided for retirement of term bonds | 394,000 | |
|     Amounts available in debt service fund—term bonds | 6,000 | |
|         Bonds payable | | 400,000 |
|     To record bond issue and amount restricted for bond retirement. | | |

# NUMBER 9

1. (N) The recording of budgetary accounts at the beginning of 1994 has no effect on fund balance. The recording of budgetary accounts would increase budgetary fund balance at the beginning of 1994. "Actual" fund balance will not change until revenues are recognized and expenditures incurred.

2. (Y) Budgetary accounts are incorporated into the governmental accounting system to provide legislative control over revenues and other resource inflows and expenditures and other resource outflows. Accordingly, budgetary accounts should include estimated revenues, appropriations, estimated other financing sources, estimated other financing uses, and budgetary fund balance.

3. (N) Nonroutine transfers of equity by a fund should be accounted for as a residual equity transfer. The GASB *Codification* specifically cites the following examples: contributions of capital to proprietary funds; the subsequent return to the general fund of capital contributed to proprietary funds; and, transfers of residual balances of discontinued funds to the general fund or a debt service fund.

4. (N) The general fund did not receive an operating transfer of $30,000. In this problem, as is generally true (i.e., required per the bond indenture), the premium was probably transferred to the debt service fund for future debt service payments.

5. (N) The receipt of water by the general fund (from the water utility fund) represents a quasi-external transaction. These are transactions that would be accounted for as revenues or expenditures/expenses if they involved an external party. The proper accounting is to treat them as revenues in the fund providing the goods or services and as expenditures/expense in the fund receiving the goods or services.

6. (Y or N) The AICPA accepted both answers in this situation. The net property taxes receivable of $370,000 may include amounts expected to be collected after March 15, 1995. Property taxes, which are expected to be collected after 60 days from the end of the fiscal year, are reported as deferred revenue. This problem does not state when the taxes were levied, and it is not possible to determine from the information given if deferred revenue was recorded.

7. (N) The closing of budgetary accounts has no effect on "actual" fund balance. The journal entry to close budgetary accounts at year end is simply a reverse of the adoption entry:

| | | |
|---|---|---|
| Dr. Appropriations control | 5,600,000 | |
| Dr. Budgetary fund balance | 400,000 | |
| Cr. Estimated revenues control | | 6,000,000 |

8. (N) The recording of budgeted amounts into budgetary accounts has no effect on actual amounts or "actual" fund balance. As a result of actual amounts recorded in the general fund in 1994, fund balance will increase by $50,000.

9. (Y) The entry in the General Fixed Asset account group is debit Construction-in-Progress and credit Investment in General Fixed Assets -- Capital Projects Fund.

10. (Y) It is optional to record accumulated depreciation in the general fixed assets account group, but it is seldom done. Even when accumulated depreciation is recorded in the general fixed assets account group, depreciation expense is not recorded in the accounts of governmental funds, nor in the general fixed asset account group.

11. (N) The Water Utility Fund is an enterprise fund, and accordingly, uses the accrual basis of accounting. Depreciation must be recognized on equipment used by an enterprise fund.

12. (Y) Per NCGAS 1, para 147, the combined statement of revenues, expenditures, and changes in fund balances should include all governmental fund types and expendable trust funds.

13. (Y) The combined balance sheet should include all fund types, account groups, and discretely presented component units.

14. (N) Per GASB 9, para 5, proprietary funds, nonexpendable trust funds and governmental entities that use proprietary fund accounting should present a statement of cash flows. Public Employee Retirement Systems and pension trust funds are exempt from this requirement, but are not precluded from preparing a statement of cash flows. Governmental fund types and expendable trust funds should not present a statement of cash flows.

15. (N) See #14 above.

16. (Y) See #14 above.

17. $5,600,000. Appropriations is the budgetary account established at the beginning of the year to provide control over expenditures. The answer is provided in General fund selected information under total expenditures for the budgeted information. Thus, Appropriations is $5,600,000.

18. $4,750,000. The journal entry to record the property taxes receivable is:

| | | |
|---|---|---|
| Property taxes receivable | 4,750,000 | |
| Allowance for estimated uncollectible taxes | | 50,000 |
| Revenues control | | 4,700,000 |

Thus, the actual property tax revenue recorded, which is net of uncollectible taxes, is added to the estimated uncollectible taxes to arrive at the amount debited to property taxes receivable.

19. $1,200,000. Only the par value of the general obligation bonds is recorded in the GLTDAG since this account group records transactions involving debt principal, not interest. The premium is transferred to the Debt Service Fund. Thus, the GLTDAG records the par value of $1,200,000 for the general obligation bonds.

20. $1,080,000. The General Fixed Assets Account Group (GFAAG) records fixed assets and uncompleted assets at cost which includes expenditures, not encumbrances. At year-end, the total expenditures for the capital project fund is $1,080,000 as shown in the closing entry. Thus, the GFAAG records the $1,080,000 for the uncompleted civic center.

21. $2,473,000. The completed cost of the civic center can be calculated by adding the expenditures ($1,080,000) occurred in 1994 and the unreserved fund balance ($1,420,000) and subtracting the transfer ($27,000) at the end of the project to the General Fund. The unreserved fund balance at 1994 year-end is the amount of funds available to be spent on the civic center. The transfer of $27,000 to the General Fund represents the residual amount not spent on the capital project. Thus, when considering the interaction between these accounts, the total completed cost is $2,473,000 ($1,080,000 + 1,420,000 − 27,000).

22. $800,000. As stated in the problem's information, the civic center's finances were provided by the general fund transfers, a state grant, and an issue of the general obligation bonds. By analyzing the closing entry for 1994 in the capital project fund, the $800,000 state grant is recognized as revenues, while the bonds and the transfer from the general fund are classified as other financing sources.

23. $2,422,000. Encumbrances for 1994 consist of the encumbrances recorded for expenditures (1,080,000) which, as explained in the instructions, exceeded the expenditures by $42,000 and also $1,300,000 recorded for the purchase orders and commitments outstanding for 1994. Thus, the total amount of encumbrances for the capital project fund is $2,422,000 ($1,080,000 + $42,000 + $1,300,000).

24. $120,000. Per NCGAS 1, par 118, the unreserved fund balance is the difference between the assets and liabilities including the encumbrances outstanding at year end. The unreserved fund balance in the closing entry is $1,420,000, but does not account for the encumbrances of $1,300,000 for purchase orders and commitments outstanding because the encumbrances account is not included in the closing entry. Thus, the unreserved fund balance at year end is $120,000 ($1,420,000 - $1,300,000).

# Chapter Twenty
# Not-for-Profit Accounting

# Chapter Twenty
# Not-for-Profit Accounting

## STANDARDS APPLICABLE TO ACCOUNTING FOR NOT-FOR-PROFIT ENTITIES

For hospitals, colleges, voluntary health and welfare organizations, and other not-for-profit entities, there are two sets of GAAP's.

Governmental (Public) sector not-for-profits must apply the following as G.A.A.P.

| | | |
|---|---|---|
| 1. | Hospitals | Audits of Providers of Health Care Services - AICPA 1994 |
| 2. | Colleges | Audits of Colleges and Universities - AICPA 1973 |
| 3. | Voluntary Health and Welfare Organizations | Audits of Voluntary Health and Welfare Organizations - AICPA 1974 |
| 4. | Other Not-for-Profit Organizations | Statement of Position 78-10 - AICPA 1978 |

Nongovernmental (Private) sector not-for-profits must apply as GAAP.

Statement of Financial Accounting Standards #116 (SFAS No. 116)
Statement of Financial Accounting Standards #117 (SFAS No. 117)

## SECTION I: ACCOUNTING FOR PUBLIC SECTOR NOT-FOR-PROFITS

## HOSPITAL ACCOUNTING

Governmental hospitals use the accrual basis of accounting. They do not record budgetary accounts, encumbrance, or expenditures. They have two categories of funds:

1.) General Unrestricted Fund
Includes all current assets and related liabilities that are not restricted for use.
Fixed assets less accumulated depreciation, long term liabilities, internally restricted funds
(restricted imposed by bond indenture covenants or other conditions).
Board designated funds, which are unrestricted, and designation is subject to change.
Externally earmarked resources are reported with a description of "limited use".

2.) Restricted Funds
Included assets and liabilities that are donor or grantor restricted to expenditure for specific purposes. There are three restricted funds:
(1) Specific Purpose Fund is used to record the principal and income of expendable resources that are to be used for restricted operating purposes specified by the donors and grantors (i.e. education and research). It is similar to the municipal Special Revenue Fund or the Expendable Trust Fund. Internally restricted funds should not be accounted for by this fund but should be included in the Unrestricted Fund with disclosure as to the restriction. The proceeds of special purpose activities that are part of the hospital's operations are recorded as "Other Operating Revenue" in the Unrestricted Fund.

(2) The Endowment Fund, like the non-expendable trust fund, is used to account for the principal (corpus) of gifts donated to the hospital to provide a continuous source of income for restricted or unrestricted purposes, similar to the non-expendable trust of a municipality. Corpus and earnings records must be maintained separately. Board-created endowment funds may also be maintained.

(3) Plant Replacement and Expansion Fund is similar to capital projects funds. It Includes plant replacement and expansion resources contributed for additions to Property, Plant, and Equipment. This fund balance includes amounts that are required to be used for property additions as specified in agreements with third-party payors. Donated fixed assets are reported here until placed in services. Resources are transferred to the general fund when spent.

## Revenue Classifications

Hospital accounting has unique features in the determination of revenues. Patient Service Revenues are recorded at **gross value of the service rendered** based on established standard rates within revenue producing centers rendering inpatient and outpatient services. Gross revenues are reduced by

Deductions:
  a. Charity service rendered.
  b. Contractual adjustments arising from third party agreements.
  c. Policy discounts extended to members of the medical profession.
  d. Administrative adjustments.
  e. Discount extended to doctors and nurses.

Other Operating Revenue:
  a. Donated medicines, linens, office supplies and other materials.
  b. Cafeteria, vending machine, parking, gift shops, etc.
  c. Medical transcript fees.
  d. Proceeds from specific-purpose fund.

Non-Restricted Grants and Gifts Operating Revenue:
  a. Contributions and gifts
  b. Endowment or board-designated funds
  c. Investment earnings
  d. Donated services

---

**Intensive Hospital for CPA Candidates**

| | |
|---|---|
| 1) Revenues from Patients (at gross) | Your money - when you check into the hospital because you are sick of studying |
| 2) Ancillary Revenues (sub-set of Patient Revenues) | From radiology: to cat scan your fried brain<br>From Pharmacy: for Valium to calm you |
| 3) Other Operating Revenues (Donations of Medicines) | Parking lot, Gift shop, Cafeteria<br>Specific Research Grant<br>(i.e. to study why you are always so tired and your brain does not want to cooperate) |
| 4) Nonoperating Revenues | Unrestricted gifts from your friends<br>Donation of Services you would pay for,<br>from spouse, significant others, parents<br>and children |

---

## Expense Classifications

1. Patient Service expenses (grouped by cost centers)
2. Other Service expenses (grouped by cost centers)

Donated goods that would be normally purchased by a hospital (medicines, supplies, etc.) are recorded at Fair Market Value, and credited directly to **other operating** revenues:

        Inventory Pharmacy - medicines
            **Other** operating revenues

Donated services provided by volunteers that the hospital would normally pay to obtain are accounted for as **Non**operating revenues if three conditions exist:
1) The services are an integral part of the hospital's effort.
2) The hospital exercises control in an employer-employees relationship.
3) The fair market value of the services are clearly measurable.

> Operating expenses
>> Nonoperating revenues-nursing services

## Investments

Investments should be accounted for by specific fund; principal and income transactions should be differentiated; and pooling of investments of various funds is common. Results from pooled investments are allocated based on the market value at date of pooling.

Marketable equity securities should be carried at the lower of its aggregate cost and market value at the balance sheet date.

Transfers between funds occur frequently. When funds are moved from restricted to restricted funds, the Fund Balance of the receiving fund is increased (credited) and the Fund Balance of the giving fund decreased (debited). When resources are moved between restricted fund and general unrestricted fund, "Transfer to/from, and Due to/from" accounts are often used.

## Interfund Transactions

1. The Unrestricted Fund received income from Endowment Fund investments of $10,000. Income from Endowment Fund investments is designated for use by the Unrestricted Fund.

Endowment Fund receives income:

| | | |
|---|---|---|
| Cash | $10,000 | |
| Fund Balance | | $10,000 |

Cash is transferred to Unrestricted General Fund:

| | | |
|---|---|---|
| Fund Balance | $10,000 | |
| Cash | | $10,000 |

Unrestricted General Fund receives income:

| | | |
|---|---|---|
| Cash | $10,000 | |
| Revenue from Endowment Fund | | $10,000 |

2. New equipment was purchased at a cost of $45,000.

Plant Replacement and Expansion Fund entry:

| | | |
|---|---|---|
| Fund Balance | $45,000 | |
| Cash | | $45,000 |

To record purchase of new equipment

Unrestricted General Fund entry:

| | | |
|---|---|---|
| Equipment | $45,000 | |
| Fund Balance—Transfer from Plant Replacement and Expansion Fund | | $45,000 |

3. Investment Income of the Plant Replacement and Expansion Fund of $12,000 was recorded.
Plant Replacement and Expansion Fund entry:

| | | |
|---|---|---|
| Interest Receivable | $12,000 | |
|     Fund Balance | | $12,000 |

4. To record unrestricted investment earnings that are initially recorded in various restricted funds.

Endowment Fund entry:

| | | |
|---|---|---|
| Cash | $5,000 | |
|     Due to General Fund | | $5,000 |

## Intra-fund entries—Unrestricted Fund

1. Patient Service Revenue of $560,000 at standard rates was recorded.

| | | |
|---|---|---|
| Accounts Receivable | $560,000 | |
|     Patient Service Revenue | | $560,000 |

2. Doubtful Accounts of $12,000 and Charity Service of $16,000 were recorded.

| | | |
|---|---|---|
| Provision for Doubtful Accounts | $12,000 | |
| Charity Service Allowances | 16,000 | |
|     Allowances and Doubtful Accounts | | $28,000 |

3. Mortgage Bonds Payable of $30,000 were paid.

| | | |
|---|---|---|
| Mortgage Bonds Payable | $30,000 | |
|     Cash | | $30,000 |

4. Unrestricted donations of $4,000 were received.

| | | |
|---|---|---|
| Cash | $4,000 | |
|     Unrestricted Donations and Bequests Revenue | | $4,000 |

5. Diagnostic equipment with a carrying value of $6,000, originally costing $15,000, was sold for $4,000.

| | | |
|---|---|---|
| Cash | $4,000 | |
| Accumulated Depr.—Equipment | 9,000 | |
| Loss on Disposal of Plant Assets | 2,000 | |
|     Equipment | | $15,000 |

6. Expenses for various hospital functional areas were recorded.

| | | |
|---|---|---|
| Laboratory supplies | $12,000 | |
| Nursing services | 27,000 | |
| Administrative services | 16,000 | |
| Operating room expense | 8,000 | |
|     Vouchers payable | | $63,000 |

7. Collection of Patient Service Revenue was $505,000

| | | |
|---|---|---|
| Cash | $505,000 | |
|     Accounts Receivable | | $505,000 |

8. Uncollectible accounts totaling $7,000 were written off.

| | | |
|---|---|---|
| Allowances and Doubtful Accounts | $7,000 | |
|     Accounts Receivable | | $7,000 |

9. Depreciation of $28,000 on buildings and $18,000 on equipment was recorded.

| Depreciation Expense | $46,000 | |
| A/D—Buildings | | $28,000 |
| A/D—Equipment | | 18,000 |

## Financial Statements

| *Operated* *as a Governmental Unit* | *Operated* *Privately* |
| --- | --- |
| Balance Sheet | Statement of Financial |
| Statement of Revenues and Expenses | Position |
| Statement of Changes in Fund Balances | Statement of Activity |
| Statement of Cash Flows | Statement of Cash Flows |

## COLLEGE AND UNIVERSITY ACCOUNTING

GAAP applicable to colleges and universities has been set forth by the National Association of College and University Business Officers (NABUCO), the AICPA, and the GASB. SFAS No. 116 sets forth requirements to account for contributions. See a complete discussion of SFAS 116 later in this chapter.

**Accrual accounting is used by all universities,** including those affiliated with governmental units; however the fund balance, accountability, budgetary accounts, encumbrances, transfers, interfunds, and other comparable fund accounting concepts are similar to that of governments and hospitals.

Depreciation is not recorded. SFAS 93 determined that depreciation should be taken by all not-for-profit organizations, including universities. Subsequently, GASB # 8 stated that Universities should not, so the FASB followed up with SFAS # 99 postponing implementation of SFAS #93 for Universities.

There are six major types of funds:

| Lambers University Funds | |
| --- | --- |
| **Major Funds** | **Major Subdivisions** |
| Current Funds | 1. Unrestricted Current Funds<br>2. Restricted Current Funds |
| Loan Funds | |
| Endowment and Similar Funds | 1. Endowment Funds<br>2. Term Endowment Funds<br>3. Quasi-Endowment Funds |
| Annuity and Life Income funds | 1. Annuity Funds<br>2. Life Income Funds |
| Plant Funds | 1. Unexpended Plant Funds<br>2. Renewals and Replacements Funds<br>3. Retirement and Indebtedness Funds<br>4. Investment in Plant |
| Agency | |

**Current Funds** is divided into unrestricted and restricted.

- The Unrestricted funds account for the resources and related current liabilities, of the institution that are available to use.
- The Restricted funds account for resources that have been earmarked by donors or grantors for specific purposes. Funds designated by the governing board are considered unrestricted (same as for hospitals) because they don't have externally imposed restrictions. Revenues are always equal to expenditures. When a grant or similar restricted amount is received, Fund Balance is credited. When expenditures are made, revenue is recognized to the extent of such expenditures.

**Loan Funds**
1. Established to account for resources available for loans to students, faculty or staff.
2. No revenue or expenditure accounts are used. The transactions are recorded directly in Fund Balance.
The loan funds does not account for loans, notes, or bond payable. Provision for uncollectible receivables and interest on balances, are handled through the fund balance.

**Endowment Funds**
1. Two types
    a. **Regular or pure endowment** - principal must remain intact and only income may be expended for specific purposes.
    b. **Term endowment** - principal and interest may be spent.
**2. Quasi-endowment** - board-designated or created - may be restricted or unrestricted depending upon nature of funds the board uses to create or designate the fund.
3. Income and/or principal is recorded by transferring the amount to the specific fund established in the endowment.

**Annuity and Life Income Funds**
1. Account for resources received by the university that have a stipulation of periodic payments being made to an individual for a specified period of time. The remainder becomes an asset of the entity.
2. The liability to the designated recipient is recorded at the discounted present value of the anticipated payment

- Annuity funds: make annuity payments of a fixed amount for a fixed period of time. It does guarantee a fixed amount.
- Life Income funds: pay the income earned by the invested assets to a specific recipient for a fixed period of time. It does not guarantee a fixed amount; only whatever income is earned.

**Plant funds** is used to account for all fixed assets and long term debts. The plant funds has four subdivisions:
1. **Unexpended Plant Fund** - amount designated for future addition to physical plant.
2. **Renewal and replacements** - amounts designated for major repairs or refurbishing.
3. **Retirement of indebtedness** - amounts designated for principal and interest payment on long-term debt.
4. **Investment in plant** - carries fixed assets and related debts, and the difference is referred to as "net investment in plant."

**Agency**
Resources which belong to others are held in agency with a liability equal to the asset collected.

# ILLUSTRATIVE COLLEGE ENTRIES

## UNRESTRICTED FUND

1. Tuition bills are mailed totaling $2,500,000. Of this amount $50,000 is estimated to be uncollectible.

| | | |
|---|---|---|
| Accounts receivable | $2,500,000 | |
|     Revenues | | $2,500,000 |

| | | |
|---|---|---|
| Expenditures/instruction | $50,000 | |
|     Allowance for uncollectible accounts | | $50,000 |

2. Unrestricted grants of $75,000 are received from a local corporation.

| | | |
|---|---|---|
| Cash | $75,000 | |
|     Revenues - Grants income | | $75,000 |

3. Unrestricted endowment income of $60,000 is received by the unrestricted current fund.

| | | |
|---|---|---|
| Cash | $60,000 | |
|     Revenue - Endowment Fund | | $60,000 |

4. $25,000 is received by the unrestricted fund for the rental of facilities to Lambers CPA Review and to the NFL for the Super Bowl.

| | | |
|---|---|---|
| Cash | $25,000 | |
|     Revenues - auxiliary enterprises | | $25,000 |

5. The following expenses are paid: Instructional $1,100,000; Research $75,000; Student Services $25,000; Maintenance $15,000.

| | | |
|---|---|---|
| *Expenditures:* | | |
|     Instructional | $1,100,000 | |
|     Research | 75,000 | |
|     Student Services | 25,000 | |
|     Maintenance | 15,000 | |
|         Cash | | $1,215,000 |

6. A mandatory transfer is made to the plant fund - retirement of indebtedness of $50,000.

| | | |
|---|---|---|
| Mandatory transfers for principal payment | $50,000 | |
|     Cash | | $50,000 |

Note the following entry is made in the plant fund - retirement of indebtedness

| | | |
|---|---|---|
| Cash | $50,000 | |
|     Fund Balance | | $50,000 |

7. Closing entries at year end

| | |
|---|---|
| *Revenues:* | |
|     Student Tuition | $2,500,000 |
|     Grant Income | 75,000 |
|     Endowment Fund | 60,000 |
|     Auxiliary Enterprises | 25,000 |

*Expenditures:*

| | |
|---|---|
| Instructional | $1,150,000 |
| Research | 75,000 |
| Student Services | 25,000 |
| Maintenance | 15,000 |
| Mandatory transfers for | |
|   principal payment | 50,000 |
| Fund balance - unrestricted | $1,345,000 |

## RESTRICTED CURRENT FUND

1. A $1,000,000 grant was received to conduct research into the reasons for the appearance of the "Loch-Ness Monster".

| | | |
|---|---|---|
| Cash | $1,000,000 | |
|     Fund balance - restricted | | $1,000,000 |

2. Expenditures in connection with the above grant were as follows:
    Salaries, $750,000; Materials, 25,000; Supplies, 25,000

Expenditures:

| | | |
|---|---|---|
|   - Supplies | $ 25,000 | |
|   - Materials | 25,000 | |
|   - Salaries | 750,000 | |
|     Cash | | $800,000 |
| | | |
| Fund Balance | $800,000 | |
|     Revenues | | $800,000 |

3. Closing Entries

| | | |
|---|---|---|
| Revenues | $800,000 | |
|     Expenditures: | | |
|     - Supplies | | 25,000 |
|     - Materials | | 25,000 |
|     - Salaries | | 750,000 |

Note:    Revenues are deferred until expended for the restricted purpose.
              Revenues are recognized to the extent of expenditures in the restricted fund.

## PLANT FUND

1. Bonds with a market value of $1,500,000 are donated to finance a new wing for the business school.

Entry in the Unexpended Plant Fund

| | | |
|---|---|---|
|   Investments | $1,500,000 | |
|     Fund Balance - restricted | | $1,500,000 |

2. Cash of $20,000 is transferred from the unrestricted current fund for the retirement of indebtedness.

Entry in the Retirement of Indebtedness Plant Fund

| | | |
|---|---|---|
|   Cash | $20,000 | |
|     Fund Balance - unrestricted | | $20,000 |

3. Payment of $1,000,000 is made on a mortgage related to a completed addition to a student union building

Entries in:
a) Retirement of indebtedness Plant Fund

| | | |
|---|---|---|
| Fund Balance–unrestricted | $1,000,000 | |
| Cash | | $1,000,000 |

b) Investment in Plant–Plant fund

| | | |
|---|---|---|
| Mortgage Payable | $1,000,000 | |
| Investment in Plant | | 1,000,000 |

4. A collection of Lambers CPA Review materials is donated to the college. The collection is valued at $15,000.
Entry in the Investment Plant—Plant Fund

| | | |
|---|---|---|
| Library Books | $15,000 | |
| Investment in Plant | | $15,000 |

5. During the year the addition to the Business School is completed at a cost of $2,000,000. The addition was financed with the donation received in entry 1 and the balance with a mortgage of $500,000.

Entries:
(a) Unexpended Plant Fund to record expenditure

| | | |
|---|---|---|
| Building | $2,000,000 | |
| Cash | | $1,500,000 |
| Mortgage payable | | 500,000 |

(b) Unexpended Plant Fund to transfer the addition to the investment in plant

| | | |
|---|---|---|
| Mortgage payable | $ 500,000 | |
| Fund balance—restricted | 1,500,000 | |
| Building | | $2,000,000 |

(c) Investment in Plant - to record the building and mortgage

| | | |
|---|---|---|
| Building | $2,000,000 | |
| Mortgage payable | | $ 500,000 |
| Investment in Plant | | 1,500,000 |

6. Repairs totaling $75,000 are paid

Entry—renewals and replacements

| | | |
|---|---|---|
| Fund Balance | $75,000 | |
| Cash | | $75,000 |

## Financial Statements

| Operated as a Governmental Unit | Operated Privately |
|---|---|
| Balance Sheet | Statement of Financial Position |
| Statement of Current Fund Revenue expenditures, and other changes | Statement of Activity |
| Statement of Changes in Fund Balances | Statement of Cash Flows |

## VOLUNTARY HEALTH AND WELFARE ORGANIZATIONS AND OTHER NONPROFIT ORGANIZATIONS

Voluntary Health and Welfare Organizations, and Other Nonprofit Organizations, are entities which provide services to the public made possible by the generosity of the public contributions. These organizations are accountable to the community for their administration and policies. Included in this category are United Way,

YMCA, religious, research and scientific organizations, public broadcasting stations, private and community foundations, museums and other cultural institutions, performing arts, libraries, zoological and botanical societies, political parties, cemetery, civic, fraternal, labor unions, professional and trade associations, private elementary schools, and social and country clubs.

SOP 78-10, *Accounting Principles and Reporting Practices for Certain Nonprofit Organizations,* recommends financial principles and reporting practices for nonprofit organizations for which there are no audit guides. This SOP does not apply to organizations that are primarily commercial businesses operated to benefit their members or stockholders, such as farm cooperatives, employee benefit and pension plans, trusts, mutual banks, and mutual insurance companies.

# SECTION II: ACCOUNTING FOR PRIVATE SECTOR NOT-FOR-PROFITS

## STATEMENT OF FINANCIAL ACCOUNTING STANDARDS NO. 116

### Applies to all Nongovernmental Nonprofits
### Contributions of Cash or Other Assets
SFAS 116 establishes standards of accounting and reporting for contributions. It applies to all organizations that receive or make contributions, therefore it affects hospitals, universities, businesses, individuals, and any other entities which make or receive contributions. SFAS 116 defines a contribution as "an unconditional transfer of cash or other assets to an entity or settlement or cancellation of its liabilities in a voluntary **non reciprocal transfer** by another entity acting other than as an owner."

This is consistent with earlier definitions, however SFAS 116 continues, "Other assets include [...] **unconditional promises to give** those items in the future." Thus SFAS 116 introduces the requirement that contributions be recognized as revenue (support) at fair market value on the date the unconditional promise to give occurs.

The definition of a promise to give is, "a written or oral agreement to contribute cash or other assets to another entity; however to be recognized in financial statements there must be sufficient evidence in the form of verifiable documentation that a promise was made and received." Therefore, if an unconditional promise to give is received in public with witnesses or in writing, the organization is required to record the support and an amount receivable for the promise. Prior to SFAS 116, these promises were not recorded in the financial statements because they are not legally enforceable.

An allowance for uncollectable support is appropriate and advisable. With the advent of SFAS 116, not-for-profits will now report on a full accrual basis.

### Contributed Services
Under SFAS 116, contributed services are "recognized if the services received
- create or enhance nonfinancial assets or
- require specialized skills, are provided by individuals possessing those skills, and would typically need to be purchased if not provided by donation."

No other contributed services can be recognized.

### Contributed Works of Art, etc.
Contributed collections of works of art, historical treasures, or similar assets may be recognized if they meet all of the following conditions:
- Are held for public exhibition, education, or research in furtherance of public service rather than financial gain
- Are protected, kept unencumbered, cared for, and preserved

- Are subject to an organizational policy that requires the proceeds from sales of collection items to be used to acquire other items for collections.

## Support

SFAS 116 makes a distinction between three types of support based solely upon the **donor's** instructions. Promises to give fall into three categories:
- unrestricted
- temporarily restricted
- permanently restricted

Unrestricted support is available for the organization to use immediately and for any purpose. Temporarily restricted support is restricted by the **donor** in such a way that availability of the support is dependent upon the happening of some event, the performance of a task, or the passage of time. Such support is available to the organization when the event occurs, the task is performed, or the time restraint passes. At that time, the support is reclassified from temporarily restricted to unrestricted and the support is available for use. Permanently restricted funds are those which the **donor** restricts in such a way that the organization will never be able to use the support itself. The organization may be able to use the income from the gift, but never the gift itself.

## STATEMENT OF FINANCIAL ACCOUNTING STANDARDS NO. 117

### Applies to all Nongovernmental Nonprofits

SFAS 117 establishes standards for not-for-profit organizations **general-purpose external statements** and designates **the statement of financial position, the statement of activities, the statement of cash flows** and the accompanying notes as a complete set of financial statements. The Statement of Financial Position is required to show total assets, total liabilities, and net assets. Following the lead of SFAS 116, SFAS 117 requires reporting of unrestricted net assets, temporarily restricted net assets, and permanently restricted net assets. The standard also requires that the statement of activities report the changes in net assets for each of the three categories of support separately. The Statement of Cash Flows can be reported under the direct or indirect method, with the change in net assets being the equivalent of net income. Aggregation and order of presentation should, generally, be similar to those of a business enterprise.

Not-for-profit organizations must present in the financial statements all information required by GAAP (unless specifically exempted) and all information required by specialized principles. This information includes display and disclosure provisions of:
- Accounting changes
- Financial instruments
- Extraordinary, unusual and infrequent events
- Loss contingencies

For the Statement of Cash Flows, the Statement of Activities takes the place of the Income Statement in a business enterprise and change in net assets takes the place of net income. Restricted resources that are used for long-term purposes because of donor stipulation are classified as financing activities.

### Revenue, Support and Capital

The primary sources and amounts of revenue, support, and capital funds should be disclosed in **the statement of activity**. Capital additions restricted for plant assets should be shown as deferred capital support in the balance sheet until they are used.

Current restricted funds should be reported as revenue and support to the extent that expenses conforming to the grantor's restrictions have been incurred. Any remaining funds should be reported as deferred revenue or support in the balance sheet until the restrictions are met and the expenses incurred. Unrestricted funds are reported in the unrestricted fund. Legally enforceable pledges should be reported as assets at the estimated realizable value and should be recognized as support when so designated by the donor. If that designation occurs after the balance sheet date, these pledges would be shown as deferred support in the balance sheet. If no designation is made, pledges should be reported when they are expected to be received. Revenue from the sale of goods or services is recognized when goods are sold or services are performed. Revenue from membership dues should be allocated over the dues period.

## Donated Material and Services
The method used to value, record, and report donated services should be disclosed in the financial statements. Furthermore, recorded services should be distinguished from unrecorded services.

## Expenses
Expenses should be identified by function unless another basis would be useful to the users of the financial statement. Expenses for specific program services and for supporting services such as management and general costs and fund-raising costs should be presented **separately** for each significant program or activity such as fund-raising, membership development, and unallocated management and general expenses.

Classification of expenditure by type may be presented also. Costs which are attributable to more than one function should be allocated on a reasonable basis.

An expense and a liability should be reported when grant recipients are entitled to receive the grant. Grants to be made over several years should be reported in the year the grant is first made, unless the grantor retains the right to revoke the grant or unless grants are subject to periodic renewal.

## Depreciation
Depreciation should be recognized. SFAS 93 also requires the disclosure of depreciation expense, balances of the major classes of depreciable assets, accumulated depreciation at the balance sheet date, and a description of the depreciation method used.

## Tax Allocation
Interperiod tax allocations should be made when temporary differences occur with respect to federal or state income taxes or federal excise taxes.

## Fund Accounting
Although fund accounting has not been required by the AICPA guides on not-for-profit organizations, it is used by many such organizations in preparing their annual financial statements. Often accounts are grouped into funds through calculations outside of the accounting system.

While SFAS No. 117 does not prohibit using fund accounting, it does require providing information about the three classes of net assets mentioned above:
- unrestricted
- temporarily unrestricted
- permanently restricted

(Internal restrictions of net assets, such as board designations, may be disclosed; however, they are considered to be unrestricted.)

Fund accounting may not accomplish the goal of informing the reader about donor restrictions. As an example, some of the net assets of a fund established to account for property and equipment may be unrestricted, either because they were acquired with unrestricted support or because the donor restriction was satisfied when specified equipment was purchased. Therefore, merely accounting for property and equipment in a separate fund would not satisfy the disclosure requirements about donor restrictions.

## Financially Interrelated Organizations

A combined financial statement should be used when one organization **controls** another and any of the following exist:

- An organization solicits funds for the reporting organization and the donor intends or requires the funds to be transferred or used by the reporting organization.
- An organization receives resources from the reporting organization to be used for the reporting organization.
- An organization, funded by nonpublic contributions, is assigned responsibilities by the reporting organization.

Disclosure of the basis for the combination is required. The combined financial statement should include all resources of the related organization. Organizations which are affiliated, but do not meet the requirements for combination, should be disclosed.

## Statement of Financial Position

According to paragraph 11 of SFAS No. 117, a statement of financial position should provide information about liquidity, financial flexibility, and the interrelationship of assets and liabilities. **Liquidity is the nearness to cash of an asset or liability, and financial flexibility is the ability to take effective actions to alter amounts and timing of cash flows to respond to unexpected needs and opportunities.** SFAS No. 117 requires using one or more of the following methods of presenting information about liquidity. They also might be used to provide information about financial flexibility:

- Sequencing assets according to their nearness to conversion to cash and sequencing liabilities according to the nearness of their maturity and resulting use of cash.
- Classifying assets and liabilities as current and noncurrent following the requirements of ARB No. 43.
- Disclosing in the notes to the financial statements relevant information about liquidity, including restrictions on the use of particular assets.

Sequencing assets and liabilities may require separating some items. The listing of assets may start with unrestricted cash, but cash that is restricted to current operating needs and cash that is restricted to the payment of long-term notes may be farther down the list. Promises to give may appear two or more times depending on whether the proceeds from some of them are restricted by the donors.

Presenting a classified statement of financial position for a not-for-profit organization requires some considerations that normally are not required for nonpublic commercial entities. Cash and promises to give that the donor has restricted to the payment of a long-term note are excluded from current assets. Similarly, all of the principal outstanding under a long-term note is classified as noncurrent if noncurrent assets will be used to liquidate it.

Information about restricted assets may be provided through financial statement captions, such as **cash restricted to operations** and **cash restricted to payment of long-term notes**, or through discussions in the notes to the financial statement.

## Lambers Social Club
## Statements of Financial Position
## June 30, 19X1 and 19X0
## (in thousands)

|  | 19X1 | 19X0 |
|---|---|---|
| Assets: |  |  |
| Cash and cash equivalents | $ 75 | $ 460 |
| Accounts and interest receivable | 2, 130 | 1,670 |
| Inventories and prepaid expenses | 610 | 1,000 |
| Contributions receivable | 3,025 | 2,700 |
| Short-term investments | 1,400 | 1,000 |
| **Assets restricted** to investment |  |  |
| in land, buildings, and equipment | 5,210 | 4,560 |
| Land, buildings, and equipment | 61,700 | 63,590 |
| Long-term investments | 218,070 | 203,500 |
| Total Assets | $ 292,220 | $ 278,480 |
|  |  |  |
| Liabilities and net assets: |  |  |
| Accounts payable | $ 2,570 | $ 1,050 |
| Refundable advance |  | 650 |
| Grants payable | 875 | 1,300 |
| Notes payable |  | 1,140 |
| Annuity obligations | 1,685 | 1,700 |
| Long-term debt | 5,500 | 6,500 |
| Total Liabilities | 10,630 | 12,340 |
|  |  |  |
| Net assets: |  |  |
| Unrestricted | 115,228 | 103,670 |
| Temporarily restricted (Note B) | 24,342 | 25,470 |
| Permanently restricted (Note C) | 142,020 | 137,000 |
| Total net assets | 281,590 | 266,140 |
| Total liabilities and net assets | $ 292,220 | $ 278,480 |

## Statement of Activity

The statement of activity is designed to provide information **about changes in the organization's net assets**. Paragraph 18 of SFAS No. 117 requires using a caption such as *change in net assets* or *change in equity* to designate the change. While the total net assets at the beginning and end of the period must be shown, there is no requirement for the statement to present a net change amount for each category of assets.

Information about the changes in the three categories of net assets--unrestricted, temporarily restricted, and permanently restricted--may be provided using a multi-column format or a layered format. Comparative presentations are more easily accommodated by a layered approach.

The order in which items are presented in the statement of activity is flexible. The most common format will be one that presents two groupings, increases in net assets and decreases in them, which is similar to the single-step approach to the income statement used by commercial enterprises. Multiple-step approaches also are acceptable and may be more appropriate when revenue-producing activities are significant to the organization's results of operations.

Netting Expenses and Support. Many not-for-profit organizations hold special events as a fund-raising technique. Practice currently nets expenses of those events against the proceeds, with the net amount reported as support. Under SFAS No. 117, that practice no longer will be acceptable; instead, gross amounts must be reported. Netting is permitted only for incidental transactions, such as a gain on the sale of equipment.

Statement of Functional Expenses. Voluntary health and welfare organizations are required to continue providing a statement of functional expenses which shows how the natural expense classifications are allocated to the significant program and supporting services. While other not-for-profit organizations are encouraged to present information about natural expense classifications, they only are required to present information about expenses by their functional classifications.

SFAS No. 117 suggests providing information about support by functional classifications as well. This information would be useful because readers of the financial statements can assess the financial effect of adding or deleting program services. While a variety of ways can be used to present the information, a useful technique is to disclose support restricted for individual programs, either on the face of the statement of activity or in a related note. An internal allocation of unrestricted support to the programs normally is not necessary unless the organization believes the program affects it.

SFAS 117 offers multiple formats for the Statement of Activities. We present here two of them. Format 1 is a layered presentation which would be necessary to report multiple periods and allow comparative statements. Format 2 is a columnar format which is easy to read and would be easily understood by most readers. Either format is acceptable, as are others. Note in both presentations that expenses are reported by program with managerial and fund raising expenses disclosed separately.

**Format 1**

## Lambers Social Club
## Statement of Activities
## Year Ended June 30, 19X1
## (in thousands)

Changes in unrestricted net assets:
  Revenues and gains:

| | |
|---|---:|
|     Contributions | $ 8,640 |
|     Fees | 5,400 |
|     Income on long-term investments (Note E) | 5,600 |
|     Other investment income (Note E) | 850 |
|     Net unrealized and realized gains on long-term investments (Note E) | 8,228 |
|     Other | 150 |
|       Total unrestricted revenues and gains | 28,868 |
| Net assets released from restrictions (Note D): | |
|   Satisfaction of program restrictions | 11,990 |
|   Satisfaction of equipment acquisition restrictions | 1,500 |
|   Expiration of time restrictions | 1,250 |
|     Total net assets released from restrictions | 14,740 |
|       Total unrestricted revenues, gains, and other support | 43,608 |
| | |
|   Expenses and losses: | |
|     Program A | 13,100 |
|     Program B | 8,540 |
|     Program C | 5,760 |
|     Management and general | 2,420 |
|     Fund raising | 2,150 |
|       Total expenses (Note F) | 31,970 |
|     Fire loss | 8O |
|       Total expenses and losses | 32,050 |
|         Increase in unrestricted net assets | 11,558 |
| | |
| Changes in temporarily restricted net assets: | |
|   Contributions | 8,110 |
|   Income on long-term investments (Note E) | 2,580 |
|   Net unrealized and realized gains on long-term investments (Note E) | 2,952 |
|   Actuarial loss on annuity obligations | (30) |
|   Net assets released from restrictions (Note D) | (14,740) |
|     Decrease in temporarily restricted net assets | (1,128) |
| Changes in permanently restricted net assets: | |
|   Contributions | 280 |
|   Income on long-term investments (Note E) | 120 |
|   Net unrealized and realized gains on long-term investments (Note E) | 4,620 |
|     Increase in permanently restricted net assets | 5,020 |
| Increase in net assets | 15,450 |
| Net assets at beginning of year | 266,140 |
| Net assets at end of year | $ 281,590 |

**Format 2**

**Lambers Social Club**
**Statement of Activities**
**Year Ended June 30, 19X1**
**(in thousands)**

| | Unrestricted | Temporarily Restricted | Permanently Restricted | Total |
|---|---|---|---|---|
| **Revenues, gains, and other support:** | | | | |
| Contributions | $ 8,640 | $ 8,110 | $ 280 | $ 17,030 |
| Fees | 5,400 | | | 5,400 |
| Income on long-term investments (Note E) | 5,600 | 2,580 | 120 | 8,300 |
| Other investment income (Note E) | 85O | | | 850 |
| Net unrealized and realized gains on long-term investments (Note E) | 8,228 | 2,952 | 4,620 | 15,800 |
| Other | 150 | | | 150 |
| **Net assets released from restrictions (Note D):** | | | | |
| Satisfaction of program restrictions | 11,990 | (11,990) | | |
| Satisfaction of equipment acquisition restrictions | 1,500 | (1,500) | | |
| Expiration of time restrictions | 1,250 | (1,250) | | |
| Total revenues, gains, and other support | 43,608 | (1,098) | 5,020 | 47,530 |
| **Expenses and losses:** | | | | |
| Program A | 13,100 | | | 13,100 |
| Program B | 8,540 | | | 8,540 |
| Program C | 5,760 | | | 5,760 |
| Management and general | 2,420 | | | 2,420 |
| Fund raising | 2,150 | | | 2,150 |
| Total expenses (Note F) | 31,970 | | | 31,970 |
| Fire loss | 80 | | | 80 |
| Actuarial loss on annuity obligations | | 30 | | 30 |
| Total expenses and losses | 32,050 | 30 | | 32,080 |
| Change in net assets | 11,558 | (1,128) | 5,020 | 15,450 |
| Net assets at beginning of year | 103,670 | 25,470 | 137,000 | 266,140 |
| Net assets at end of year | $ 115,228 | $ 24,342 | $ 142,020 | $281,590 |

(This space intentionally left blank)

## Statement of Cash Flows

A statement of cash flows, prepared following the requirements of SFAS No. 95, is a part of the basic financial statements once SFAS No. 117 is adopted. In general, SFAS No. 117 modifies SFAS No. 95 only to extend its requirements to financial statements of not-for-profit organizations and to address whether some transactions are operating, investing, or financing activities.

Although the statement of financial position is required to disclose the three categories of net assets and the statement of activity is required to disclose the changes in them, no distinction is required to be made in the statement of cash flows.

When the indirect method is used to present cash flows from operating activities, the statement begins with the change in total net assets for the reporting period. Adjustments of that to derive the cash effect remove noncash items, such as changes in unconditional promises to give; items that are to be presented as investing or financing activities. such as receipts from contributions for constructing a building; and items that are to be disclosed as noncash investing and financing activities, such as in-kind contributions.

# Chapter Twenty
# Not-for-Profit Accounting
# Questions

## Questions – Public Sector – Not-for-Profits (1 through 121)

1. Revenue from educational programs of a hospital normally would be included in
a. Ancillary service revenue.
b. Patient service revenue.
c. Other nonoperating revenue.
d. Other operating revenue.

2. Cliff Hospital, a voluntary institution, has a pure endowment fund, the income from which is required to be used for library acquisitions. State law and the donor are silent on the accounting treatment for investment gains and losses. In 19X9, Cliff sold 1,000 shares of stock from the endowment fund's investment portfolio. The carrying amount of these securities was $50,000. Net proceeds from the sale amounted to $120,000. This transaction should be recorded in the endowment fund as a debit to cash for $120,000 and as credits to
a. Endowment fund principal, $50,000 and endowment fund revenue, $70,000.
b. Endowment fund principal, $50,000 and due to general fund, $70,000.
c. Investments, $50,000 and endowment fund balance, $70,000.
d. Investments, $50,000 and endowment fund revenue, $70,000.

3. Glenmore Hospital's property, plant, and equipment (net of depreciation) consists of the following:

| | |
|---|---|
| Land | $ 500,000 |
| Buildings | 10,000,000 |
| Movable equipment | 2,000,000 |

What amount should be included in the restricted fund grouping?
a. $0.
b. $ 2,000,000.
c. $10,500,000.
d. $12,500,000.

4. During the year ended December 31, 19X1, Melford Hospital received the following donations stated at their respective fair values:

| | |
|---|---|
| Employee services from members of a religious group | $100,000 |
| Medical supplies from an association of physicians. These supplies were restricted for indigent care, and were used for such purpose in 19X1 | 30,000 |

How much revenue (both operating and non-operating) from donations should Melford report in its 19X1 statement of revenues and expenses?
a. $0.
b. $30,000.
c. $100,000.
d. $130,000.

5. On July 1, 19X1, Lilydale Hospital's Board of Trustees designated $200,000 for expansion of outpatient facilities. The $200,000 is expected to be expended in the fiscal year ending June 30, 19X4. In Lilydale's balance sheet at June 30, 19X2, this cash should be classified as a $200,000
a. Restricted current asset.
b. Restricted noncurrent asset.
c. Unrestricted current asset.
d. Unrestricted noncurrent asset.

6. Donated medicines which normally would be purchased by a hospital should be recorded at fair market value and should be credited directly to
a. Other operating revenue.
b. Other nonoperating revenue.
c. Fund balance.
d. Deferred revenue.

7. A gift to a voluntary not-for-profit hospital that is not restricted by the donor should be credited directly to
a. Fund balance.
b. Deferred revenue.
c. Operating revenue.
d. Nonoperating revenue.

**Items 8 through 10** are based on the following data: Under Abbey Hospital's established rate structure, the hospital would have earned patient service revenue of $6,000,000 for the year ended December 31, 19X3. However, Abbey did not expect to collect this amount because of charity allowances of $1,000,000 and discounts of $500,000 to third-party payors. In May 19X3, Abbey purchased bandages from Lee Supply Co. at a cost of $1,000. However, Lee notified Abbey that the invoice was being canceled and that the bandages were being donated to Abbey. At December 31, 19X3, Abbey had board-designated assets consisting of cash $40,000, and investments $700,000.

8. For the year ended December 31, 19X3, how much should Abbey record as patient service revenue?
a. $6,000,000
b. $5,500,000
c. $5,000,000
d. $4,500,000

9. For the year ended December 31, 19X3, Abbey should record the donation of bandages as
a. A $1,000 reduction in operating expenses.
b. Nonoperating revenue of $1,000.
c. Other operating revenue of $1,000.
d. A memorandum entry only.

10. How much of Abbey's board-designated assets should be included in the unrestricted fund grouping?
a. $0
b. $40,000
c. $700,000
d. $740,000

_____

11. On May 1, 19X4, Lila Lee established a $50,000 endowment fund, the income from which is to be paid to Waller Hospital for general operating purposes. Waller does not control the fund's principal. Anders National Bank was appointed by Lee as trustee of this fund. What journal entry is required on Waller's books?

| | Debit | Credit |
|---|---|---|
| a. Memorandum entry only | -- | -- |
| b. Nonexpendable | | |
| endowment fund | $50,000 | |
| Endowment fund | | |
| balance | | $50,000 |
| c. Cash | 50,000 | |
| Endowment fund | | |
| balance | | 50,000 |

| | | |
|---|---|---|
| d. Cash | 50,000 | |
| Nonexpendable | | |
| endowment fund | | 50,000 |

12. Revenue from the gift shop of a hospital would normally be included in
a. Other nonoperating revenue.
b. Other operating revenue.
c. Patient service revenue.
d. Professional services revenue.

13. Which of the following normally would be included in Other Operating Revenues of a hospital?

| | Revenue from educational programs | Unrestricted gifts |
|---|---|---|
| a. | Yes | No |
| b. | Yes | Yes |
| c. | No | Yes |
| d. | No | No |

14. Revenue of a hospital from grants specified by the donor for research would normally be included in
a. Other nonoperating revenue.
b. Other operating revenue.
c. Patient service revenue.
d. Ancillary service revenue.

15. Payne Hospital received an unrestricted bequest of $100,000 in 19X6. This bequest should be recorded as
a. A memorandum entry only.
b. Other operating revenue of $100,000.
c. Nonoperating revenue of $100,000.
d. A direct credit of $100,000 to the fund balance.

16. During 19X6, Shaw Hospital purchased medicines for hospital use totaling $800,000. Included in this $800,000 was an invoice of $10,000 that was canceled in 19X6 by the vendor because the vendor wished to donate this medicine to Shaw. This donation of medicine should be recorded as
a. A $10,000 reduction of medicine expense.
b. An increase in other operating revenue of $10,000.
c. A direct $10,000 credit to the general (unrestricted) funds balance.
d. A $10,000 credit to the restricted funds balance.

17. In 19X6, Pyle Hospital received a $250,000 pure endowment fund grant. Also in 19X6, Pyle's governing board designated, for special uses, $300,000 which had originated from unrestricted gifts. What amount of these resources should be accounted for as part of general (unrestricted) funds?
a. $0
b. $250,000
c. $300,000
d. $550,000

18. Palma Hospital's patient service revenues for services provided in 19X6, at established rates, amounted to $8,000,000 on the accrual basis. For internal reporting, Palma uses the discharge method. Under this method, patient service revenues are recognized only when patients are discharged, with no recognition given to revenues accruing for services to patients not yet discharged. Patient service revenues at established rates using the discharge method amounted to $7,000,000 for 19X6. According to generally accepted accounting principles, Palma should report patient service revenues for 19X6 of
a. Either $8,000,000 or $7,000,000, at the option of the hospital.
b. $8,000,000
c. $7,500,000
d. $7,000,000

19. Cura Hospital's property, plant, and equipment, net of depreciation, amounted to $10,000,000, with related mortgage liabilities of $1,000,000. What amount should be included in the restricted fund grouping?
a. $0
b. $1,000,000
c. $9,000,000
d. $10,000,000

20. Revenue from the parking lot operated by a hospital would normally be included in
a. Patient service revenue.
b. Ancillary service revenue.
c. Other operating revenue.
d. Other nonoperating revenue.

21. On March 1, 19X8, Allan Rowe established a $100,000 endowment fund, the income from which is to be paid to Elm Hospital for general operating purposes. Elm does not control the fund's principal. Rowe appointed West National Bank as trustee of this fund. What journal entry is required by Elm to record the establishment of the endowment?

|  | Debit | Credit |
|---|---|---|
| a. Cash | $100,000 | |
| Nonexpendable endowment fund | | $100,000 |
| b. Cash | 100,000 | |
| Endowment fund balance | | 100,000 |
| c. Nonexpendable endowment fund | 100,000 | |
| Endowment fund balance | | 100,000 |
| d. Memorandum entry only | -- | -- |

22. In 19X8, Wells Hospital received an unrestricted bequest of common stock with a fair market value of $50,000 on the date of receipt of the stock. The testator had paid $20,000 for this stock in 19X6. Wells should record this bequest as
a. Nonoperating revenue of $50,000.
b. Nonoperating revenue of $30,000.
c. Nonoperating revenue of $20,000.
d. A memorandum entry only.

23. Cedar Hospital has a marketable equity securities portfolio that is appropriately included in noncurrent assets in unrestricted funds. The portfolio has an aggregate cost of $300,000. It had an aggregate fair market value of $250,000 at the end of 19X7 and $290,000 at the end of 19X6. If the portfolio was properly reported in the balance sheet at the end of 19X6, the change in the valuation allowance at the end of 19X7 should be
a. $0.
b. A decrease of $40,000.
c. An increase of $40,000.
d. An increase of $50,000.

24. Ross Hospital's accounting records disclosed the following information:

*Net resources invested
  in plant assets            $10,000,000
*Board-designated funds     2,000,000

What amount should be included as part of unrestricted funds?
a. $12,000,000
b. $10,000,000
c. $2,000,000
d. $0

25. An organization of high school seniors performs services for patients at Leer Hospital. These students are volunteers and perform services that the hospital would not otherwise provide, such as wheeling patients in the park and reading to patients. Leer has no employer-employee relationship with these volunteers, who donated 5,000 hours of service to Leer in 19X7. At the minimum wage rate, these services would amount to $18,750, while it is estimated that the fair value of these services was $25,000. In Leer's 19X7 statement of revenues and expenses, what amount should be reported as nonoperating revenue?
a. $25,000
b. $18,750
c. $6,250
d. $0

26. In June 19X8, Park Hospital purchased medicines from Jove Pharmaceutical Co. at a cost of $2,000. However, Jove notified Park that the invoice was being canceled, and that the medicines were being donated to Park. Park should record this donation of medicines as
a. A memorandum entry only.
b. Other operating revenue of $2,000.
c. A $2,000 credit to operating expenses.
d. A $2,000 credit to nonoperating expenses.

---

**Items 27 through 29** are based on the following information pertaining to Lori Hospital for the year ended May 31, 19X9:

In March 19X9, a $300,000 unrestricted bequest and a $500,000 pure endowment grant were received. In April 19X9, a bank notified Lori that the bank received $10,000 to be held in permanent trust by the

bank. Lori is to receive the income from this donation.

27. Lori should record the $300,000 unrestricted bequest as
a. Nonoperating revenue.
b. Other operating revenue.
c. A direct credit to the fund balance.
d. A credit to operating expenses.

28. The $500,000 pure endowment grant
a. May be expended by the governing board only to the extent of the principal since the income from this fund must be accumulated.
b. Should be reported as nonoperating revenue when the full amount of principal is expended.
c. Should be recorded as a memorandum entry only.
d. Should be accounted for as restricted funds upon receipt.

29. The $10,000 donation being held by the bank in permanent trust should be
a. Recorded in Lori's restricted endowment fund.
b. Recorded by Lori as nonoperating revenue.
c. Recorded by Lori as other operating revenue.
d. Disclosed in notes to Lori's financial statements.

---

**Items 30 through 33** are based on the following:

Metro General is a municipally-owned and operated hospital and a component unit of Metro City. In 19X9, the hospital received $7,000 in unrestricted gifts and $4,000 in unrestricted bequests. The hospital has $800,000 in long-term debt and $1,200,000 in fixed assets.

The hospital has transferred certain resources to a hospital guild. Substantially all of the guild's resources are held for the benefit of the hospital. The hospital controls the guild through contracts that provide it with the authority to direct the guild's activities, management, and policies. The hospital has also assigned certain of its functions to a hospital auxiliary, which operates primarily for the benefit of the hospital. The hospital does **not** have control over the auxiliary. The financial statements of the guild and the auxiliary are **not** consolidated with the hospital's financial statements. The guild and the auxiliary have total assets of $20,000 and $30,000, respectively.

Before the hospital's financial statements were combined with those of the city, the city's statements included data on one special revenue fund and one enterprise fund. The city's statements showed $100,000 in enterprise fund long-term debt, $500,000 in enterprise fund fixed assets, $1,000,000 in general long-term debt, and $6,000,000 in general fixed assets.

30. What account or accounts should be credited for the $7,000 of unrestricted gifts and the $4,000 of unrestricted bequests?

| | | |
|---|---|---|
| a. | Operating revenue | $11,000 |
| | | |
| b. | Nonoperating revenue | $11,000 |
| | | |
| c. | Operating revenue | $7,000 |
| | Nonoperating revenue | 4,000 |
| | | |
| d. | Nonoperating revenue | $7,000 |
| | Operating revenue | 4,000 |

31. The hospital's long-term debt should be reported in the city's combined balance sheet as
a. Part of $900,000 enterprise fund type long-term debt in the enterprise fund type column.
b. An $800,000 contra amount against fixed assets.
c. Part of the $1,800,000 general long-term debt account group.
d. A separate "discrete presentation" of $800,000 in the hospital column.

32. In the hospital's notes to financial statements, total assets of hospital-related organizations required to be disclosed amount to
a. $0
b. $20,000
c. $30,000
d. $50,000

33. The hospital's fixed assets should be reported in the city's combined balance sheet as
a. Hospital fixed assets of $1,200,000 in a separate "discrete presentation" hospital column.
b. Special revenue fund type fixed assets of $1,200,000 in the general fixed assets account group column.
c. Part of $1,700,000 enterprise fund type fixed assets in the enterprise fund type column.
d. Part of $7,200,000 general fixed assets in the general fixed assets account group.

34. In the loan fund of a college or university, each of the following types of loans would be found except
a. Student.
b. Staff.
c. Building.
d. Faculty.

35. What is the recommended method of accounting to be used by colleges and universities?
a. Cash.
b. Modified cash.
c. Restricted accrual.
d. Accrual.

36. Which of the following receipts is properly recorded as restricted current funds on the books of a university?
a. Tuition.
b. Student laboratory fees.
c. Housing fees.
d. Research grants.

37. Which of the following should be used in accounting for not-for-profit colleges and universities?
a. Fund accounting and accrual accounting.
b. Fund accounting but not accrual accounting.
c. Accrual accounting but not fund accounting.
d. Neither accrual accounting nor fund accounting.

38. During the years ended June 30, 19X0 and 19X1, Sonata University conducted a cancer research project financed by a $2,000,000 gift from an alumnus. This entire amount was pledged by the donor on July 10, 19X9, although he paid only $500,000 at that date. The gift was restricted to the financing of this particular research project. During the two-year research period, Sonata's related gift receipts and research expenditures were as follows:

| | Year Ended June 30 | |
|---|---|---|
| | 19X0 | 19X1 |
| Gift receipts | $1,200,000 | $ 800,000 |
| Cancer research | | |
| expenditures | 900,000 | 1,100,000 |

How much gift revenue should Sonata report in the restricted column of its statement of current funds revenues, expenditures, and other changes for the year ended June 30, 19X1?
a. $0.
b. $800,000.
c. $1,100,000.
d. $2,000,000.

39. On January 2, 19X2, John Reynolds established a $500,000 trust, the income from which is to be paid to Mansfield University for general operating purposes. The Wyndham National Bank was appointed by Reynolds as trustee of the fund. What journal entry is required on Mansfield's books?

|  | Dr. | Cr. |
|---|---|---|
| a. Memorandum entry only | | |
| b. Cash | $500,000 | |
| Endowment fund balance | | $500,000 |
| c. Nonexpendable endowment fund | $500,000 | |
| Endowment fund balance | | $500,000 |
| d. Expendable funds | $500,000 | |
| Endowment fund balance | | $500,000 |

40. For the fall semester of 19X1, Cranbrook College assessed its students $2,300,000 for tuition and fees. The net amount realized was only $2,100,000 because of the following revenue reductions:

| | |
|---|---|
| Refunds occasioned by class cancellations and student withdrawals | $ 50,000 |
| Tuition remissions granted to faculty members' families | 10,000 |
| Scholarships and fellowships | 140,000 |

How much should Cranbrook report for the period for unrestricted current funds revenues from tuition and fees?
a. $2,100,000.
b. $2,150,000.
c. $2,250,000.
d. $2,300,000.

41. Which of the following is utilized for current expenditures by a not-for-profit university?

| | Unrestricted current funds | Restricted current funds |
|---|---|---|
| a. | No | No |
| b. | No | Yes |
| c. | Yes | No |
| d. | Yes | Yes |

42. For the spring semester of 19X4, Lane University assessed its students $3,400,000 (net of refunds), covering tuition and fees for educational and general purposes. However, only $3,000,000 was expected to be realized because scholarships totaling $300,000 were granted to students, and tuition remissions of $100,000 were allowed to faculty members' children attending Lane. How much should Lane include in educational and general current funds revenues from student tuition and fees?
a. $3,400,000
b. $3,300,000
c. $3,100,000
d. $3,000,000

43. The following funds were among those of Kery University's books at April 30, 19X4:

| | |
|---|---|
| Funds to be used for acquisition of additional properties for University purposes (unexpended at 4/30/84) | $3,000,000 |
| Funds set aside for debt service charges and for retirement of indebtedness on University properties | 5,000,000 |

How much of the above-mentioned funds should be included in plant funds?
a. $0
b. $3,000,000
c. $5,000,000
d. $8,000,000

44. Which of the following should be included in the current funds revenues of a not-for-profit private university?

| | Tuition waivers | Unrestricted bequests |
|---|---|---|
| a. | Yes | No |
| b. | Yes | Yes |
| c. | No | Yes |
| d. | No | No |

45. For the summer session of 19X7, Ariba University assessed its students $1,700,000 (net of refunds), covering tuition and fees for educational and general purposes. However, only $1,500,000 was expected to be realized because scholarships totaling $150,000 were granted to students, and tuition remissions of $50,000 were allowed to faculty members' children attending Ariba. What amount should Ariba include in the unrestricted current funds as revenues from student tuition and fees?

a. $1,500,000
b. $1,550,000
c. $1,650,000
d. $1,700,000

46. Park College is sponsored by a religious group. Volunteers from this religious group regularly contribute their services to Park, and are paid nominal amounts to cover their commuting costs. During 19X6, the total amount paid to these volunteers aggregated $12,000. The gross value of services performed by them, determined by reference to lay-equivalent salaries, amounted to $300,000. What amount should Park record as expenditures in 19X6 for these volunteers' services?

a. $312,000
b. $300,000
c. $12,000
d. $0

47. Abbey University's unrestricted current funds comprised the following:

| | |
|---|---|
| Assets | $5,000,000 |
| Liabilities (including deferred revenues of $100,000) | 3,000,000 |

The fund balance of Abbey's unrestricted current funds was

a. $1,900,000
b. $2,000,000
c. $2,100,000
d. $5,000,000

48. The following receipts were among those recorded by Kery College during 19X6:

| | |
|---|---|
| Unrestricted gifts | $500,000 |
| Restricted current funds (expended for current operating purposes) | 200,000 |
| Restricted current funds (not yet expended) | 100,000 |

The amount that should be included in current funds revenues is

a. $800,000
b. $700,000
c. $600,000
d. $500,000

49. Which of the following not-for-profit organizations would use plant funds to account for land, buildings, equipment, and other capital assets?

| | Colleges and universities | Voluntary health and welfare organizations |
|---|---|---|
| a. | Yes | Yes |
| b. | Yes | No |
| c. | No | No |
| d. | No | Yes |

50. The current funds group of a not-for-profit private university includes which of the following?

| | Agency funds | Plant funds |
|---|---|---|
| a. | No | No |
| b. | No | Yes |
| c. | Yes | Yes |
| d. | Yes | No |

51. The plant funds group of a not-for-profit private university includes which of the following subgroups?

| | Investment in plant funds | Unexpended plant funds |
|---|---|---|
| a. | No | Yes |
| b. | No | No |
| c. | Yes | No |
| d. | Yes | Yes |

52. The current funds group of a not-for-profit private university includes which of the following?

| | Annuity funds | Loan funds |
|---|---|---|
| a. | Yes | Yes |
| b. | Yes | No |
| c. | No | No |
| d. | No | Yes |

53. The following information was available from Forest College's accounting records for its current funds for the year ended March 31, 19X8:

Restricted gifts received
| | |
|---|---|
| Expended | $100,000 |
| Not expended | 300,000 |

Unrestricted gifts received
| | |
|---|---|
| Expended | 600,000 |
| Not expended | 75,000 |

What amount should be included in current funds revenues for the year ended March 31, 19X8?
a. $600,000
b. $700,000
c. $775,000
d. $1,000,000

54. The following expenditures were among those incurred by Alma University during 19X7:

| | |
|---|---|
| Administrative data processing | $50,000 |
| Scholarships and fellowships | 100,000 |
| Operation and maintenance of physical plant | 200,000 |

The amount to be included in the functional classification "Institutional Support" expenditures account is
a. $50,000
b. $150,000
c. $250,000
d. $350,000

55. For the 19X7 summer session, Selva University assessed its students $300,000 for tuition and fees. However, the net amount realized was only $290,000 because of the following reductions:

| | |
|---|---|
| Tuition remissions granted to faculty members' families | $3,000 |
| Class cancellation refunds | 7,000 |

How much unrestricted current funds revenues from tuition and fees should Selva report for the period?
a. $290,000
b. $293,000
c. $297,000
d. $300,000

56. Which of the following funds are usually encountered in a not-for-profit private university?

| | Current funds | Plant funds |
|---|---|---|
| a. | No | Yes |
| b. | No | No |
| c. | Yes | No |
| d. | Yes | Yes |

57. The following information pertains to interest received by Beech University from endowment fund investments for the year ended June 30, 19X8:

| | Received | Expended for current operations |
|---|---|---|
| Unrestricted | $300,000 | $100,000 |
| Restricted | 500,000 | 75,000 |

What amount should be credited to endowment income for the year ended June 30, 19X8?
a. $800,000
b. $375,000
c. $175,000
d. $100,000

58. On July 31, 19X8, Sabio College showed the following amounts to be used for

| | |
|---|---|
| Renewal and replacement of college properties | $200,000 |
| Retirement of indebtedness on college properties | 300,000 |
| Purchase of physical properties for college purposes, but unexpended at 7/31/88 | 400,000 |

What total amount should be included in Sabio's plant funds at July 31, 19X8?
a. $900,000
b. $600,000
c. $400,000
d. $200,000

59. For the 19X7 fall semester, Brook University assessed its students $4,000,000 (net of refunds), covering tuition and fees for educational and general purposes. However, only $3,700,000 was expected to be realized because tuition remissions of $80,000 were allowed to faculty members' children attending Brook and scholarships totaling $220,000 were granted to students. What amount should Brook include in educational and general current funds revenues from student tuition and fees?

a. $4,000,000
b. $3,920,000
c. $3,780,000
d. $3,700,000

60. Which of the following should be included in a university's current funds revenue?

|   | Unrestricted gifts | Expended restricted current funds | Unexpended restricted current funds |
|---|---|---|---|
| a. | Yes | Yes | Yes |
| b. | Yes | Yes | No |
| c. | Yes | No | No |
| d. | No | No | Yes |

61. Which of the following funds of a voluntary health and welfare organization does not have a counterpart fund in governmental accounting?
a. Current unrestricted.
b. Land, building, and equipment.
c. Custodian.
d. Endowment.

62. A voluntary health and welfare organization received a pledge in 19X9 from a donor specifying that the amount pledged be used in 19X1. The donor paid the pledge in cash in 19X0. The pledge should be accounted for as
a. A deferred credit in the balance sheet at the end of 19X9, and as support in 19X0.
b. A deferred credit in the balance sheet at the end of 19X9 and 19X0, and as support in 19X1.
c. Support in 19X9.
d. Support in 19X0, and no deferred credit in the balance sheet at the end of 19X9.

63. A reason for voluntary health and welfare organization to adopt fund accounting is that
a. Restrictions have been placed on certain of its assets by donors.

b. It provides more than one type of program service.
c. Fixed assets are significant.
d. Donated services are significant.

_____

**Items 64 and 65** are based on the following data:

Community Service Center is a voluntary welfare organization funded by contributions from the general public. During 19X3, unrestricted pledges of $900,000 were received, half of which were payable in 19X3, with the other half payable in 19X4 for use in 19X4. It was estimated that 10% of these pledges would be uncollectible. In addition, Selma Zorn, a social worker on Community's permanent staff, earning $20,000 annually for a normal workload of 2,000 hours, contributed an additional 800 hours of her time to Community, at no charge.

64. How much should Community report as net contribution revenue for 19X3 with respect to the pledges?
a. $0
b. $405,000
c. $810,000
d. $900,000

65. How much should Community record in 19X3 for contributed service expense?
a. $8,000
b. $4,000
c. $800
d. $0

_____

66. Cura Foundation, a voluntary health and welfare organization supported by contributions from the general public, included the following costs in its statement of functional expenses for the year ended December 31, 19X3:

| Fund-raising | $500,000 |
|---|---|
| Administrative (including data processing) | 300,000 |
| Research | 100,000 |

Cura's functional expenses for 19X3 program services included
a. $900,000
b. $500,000
c. $300,000
d. $100,000

67. Funds which the governing board of an institution, rather than a donor or other outside agency, has determined are to be retained and invested for other than loan or plant purposes would be accounted for in the
a. Quasi-endowment fund.
b. Endowment fund.
c. Agency fund.
d. Current fund-restricted.

68. In a statement of support, revenue, and expenses and changes in fund balances of a voluntary health and welfare organization, depreciation expense should
a. Not be included.
b. Be included as an element of support.
c. Be included as an element of other changes in fund balances.
d. Be included as an element of expense.

69. Securities donated to a voluntary health and welfare organization should be recorded at the
a. Donor's recorded amount.
b. Fair market value at the date of the gift.
c. Fair market value at the date of the gift, or the donor's recorded amount, whichever is lower.
d. Fair market value at the date of the gift, or the donor's recorded amount, whichever is higher.

70. Unity Fund is a voluntary welfare organization funded by contributions from the general public. During 19X7, unrestricted pledges of $100,000 were received, half of which were payable in 19X7, with the other half payable in 19X8 for use in 19X8. It was estimated that 20% of these pledges would be uncollectible. With respect to the pledges, the amount that should be reported for 19X7 as net contributions, under public support, is
a. $100,000
b. $80,000
c. $50,000
d. $40,000

71. In April 19X7, Alice Reed donated $100,000 cash to her church, with the stipulation that the income generated from this gift is to be paid to Alice during her lifetime. The conditions of this donation are that, after Alice dies, the principal can be used by the church for any purpose voted on by the church elders. The church received interest of $8,000 on the $100,000 for the year ended March 31, 19X8, and the

interest was remitted to Alice. In the church's March 31, 19X8, financial statements
a. $8,000 should be reported under support and revenue in the activity statement.
b. $92,000 should be reported under support and revenue in the activity statement.
c. $100,000 should be reported as deferred support in the balance sheet.
d. The gift and its terms should be disclosed only in notes to the financial statements.

72. The following expenditures were among those incurred by a nonprofit botanical society during 19X7:

| | |
|---|---|
| Printing of annual report | $10,000 |
| Unsolicited merchandise sent to encourage contributions | 20,000 |

What amount should be classified as fund-raising costs in the society's activity statement?
a. $0
b. $10,000
c. $20,000
d. $30,000

73. Aviary Haven, a voluntary welfare organization funded by contributions from the general public, received unrestricted pledges of $500,000 during 19X6. It was estimated that 12% of these pledges would be uncollectible. By the end of 19X6, $400,000 of the pledges had been collected, and it was expected that $40,000 more would be collected in 19X7, with the balance of $60,000 to be written off as uncollectible. Donors did **not** specify any periods during which the donations were to be used. What amount should Aviary include under public support in 19X6 for net contributions?
a. $500,000
b. $452,000
c. $440,000
d. $400,000

Items **74** and **75** are based on the following information pertaining to the sale of equipment by Nous Foundation, a voluntary health and welfare organization:

| | |
|---|---|
| Sales price | $12,000 |
| Cost | 14,000 |
| Carrying amount | 10,000 |

Nous made the correct entry to record the $2,000 gain on this sale.

74. The additional entry that Nous should record in connection with this sale is

| | *Debit* | *Credit* |
|---|---|---|
| a. | Fund balance-- expended | Fund balance-- unexpended |
| b. | Fund balance-- unexpended | Fund balance-- expended |
| c. | Excess revenues control | Sale of equipment |
| d. | Current unrestricted funds | Fund balance-- undesignated |

75. The amount that should be debited and credited for the additional entry in connection with this sale is
a. $2,000
b. $10,000
c. $12,000
d. $14,000

---

76. Lane Foundation received a nonexpendable endowment of $500,000 in 19X6 from Gant Enterprises. The endowment assets were invested in publicly traded securities. Gant did not specify how gains and losses from dispositions of endowment assets were to be treated. No restrictions were placed on the use of dividends received and interest earned on fund resources. In 19X7, Lane realized gains of $50,000 on sales of fund investments, and received total interest and dividends of $40,000 on fund securities. The amount of these capital gains, interest, and dividends available for expenditure by Lane's unrestricted current fund is
a. $0
b. $40,000
c. $50,000
d. $90,000

77. In 19X7, the Board of Trustees of Burr Foundation designated $100,000 from its current funds for college scholarships. Also in 19X7, the foundation received a bequest of $200,000 from an estate of a benefactor who specified that the bequest was to be used for hiring teachers to tutor handicapped students. What amount should be accepted for as current restricted funds?
a. $0
b. $100,000
c. $200,000
d. $300,000

78. In 19X7, a nonprofit trade association enrolled five new member companies, each of which was obligated to pay nonrefundable initiation fees of $1,000. These fees were receivable by the association in 19X7. Three of the new members paid the initiation fees in 19X7, and the other two new members paid their initiation fees in 19X8. Annual dues (excluding initiation fees) received by the association from all of its members have always covered the organization's costs of services provided to its members. It can be reasonably expected that future dues will cover all costs of the organization's future services to members. Average membership duration is 10 years because of mergers, attrition, and economic factors. What amount of initiation fees from these five new members should the association recognize as revenue in 19X7?
a. $5,000
b. $3,000
c. $500
d. $0

79. On January 2, 19X7, a nonprofit botanical society received a gift of an exhaustible fixed asset with an estimated useful life of 10 years and no salvage value. The donor's cost of this asset was $20,000, and its fair market value at the date of the gift was $30,000. What amount of depreciation of this asset should the society recognize in its 19X7 financial statements?
a. $3,000
b. $2,500
c. $2,000
d. $0

80. Lema Fund, a voluntary welfare organization funded by contributions from the general public, received unrestricted pledges of $200,000 during 19X9. It was estimated that 10% of these pledges would be uncollectible. By the end of 19X9, $130,000 of the pledges had been collected. It was expected that $50,000 more would be collected in 19X0 and that the balance of $20,000 would be written off as uncollectible. What amount should Lema include under public support in 19X9 for net contributions?
a. $200,000
b. $180,000
c. $150,000
d. $130,000

81. Birdlovers, a community foundation, incurred $5,000 in management and general expenses during 19X9. In Birdlovers' statement of revenue, expense, and changes in fund balance for the year ended December 31, 19X9, the $5,000 should be reported as
a. A contra account offsetting revenue and support.
b. Part of program services.
c. Part of supporting services.
d. A direct reduction of fund balance.

--------

**Items 82 through 84** are based on the following:
In 19X9, Community Helpers, a voluntary health and welfare organization, received a bequest of a $100,000 certificate of deposit maturing in 19X9. The testator's only stipulations were that this certificate be held until maturity and that the interest revenue be used to finance salaries for a preschool program. Interest revenue for 19X9 was $8,000. When the certificate was redeemed, the board of trustees adopted a formal resolution designating $20,000 of the proceeds for the future purchase of equipment for the preschool program.

82. In regard to the certificate of deposit, what should be reported in the endowment fund column of the 19X9 statement of support, revenue, and expenses and changes in fund balances?
a. Legacies and bequests, $100,000.
b. Direct reduction in fund balance for transfer to current unrestricted fund, $100,000.
c. Transfer to land, building, and equipment fund, $20,000.
d. Revenues control, $100,000.

83. What should be reported in the current unrestricted funds column of the 19X9 statement of

support, revenue, and expenses and changes in fund balances?
a. Investment income, $8,000.
b. Direct reduction of fund balance for transfer to land, building, and equipment fund, $20,000.
c. Direct addition to fund balance for transfer from endowment fund, $100,000.
d. Public support, $108,000.

84. What should be reported in the 19X9 year-end current unrestricted funds balance sheet?
a. Fund balance designed for preschool program, $28,000;
Undesignated fund balance, $80,000.
b. Fund balance designated for purchase of equipment, $20,000;
Undesignated fund balance, $80,000.
c. Fund balance designated for preschool program salaries, $8,000;
Undesignated fund balance, $80,000.
d. Undesignated fund balance, $72,000.

--------

85. In a statement of support, revenue, and expenses and changes in fund balances of a voluntary health and welfare organization, depreciation expense should
a. Be included as an element of expense.
b. Be included as an element of other changes in fund balances.
c. Be included as an element of support.
d. Not be included.

86. In July 19X8, Ross donated $200,000 cash to a church with the stipulation that the revenue generated from this gift be paid to Ross during Ross' lifetime. The conditions of this donation are that, after Ross dies, the principal may be used by the church for any purpose voted on by the church elders. The church received interest of $16,000 on the $200,000 for the year ended June 30, 19X9, and the interest was remitted to Ross. In the church's June 30, 19X9, annual financial statements
a. $200,000 should be reported as deferred support in the balance sheet.
b. $184,000 should be reported under support and revenue in the activity statement.
c. $16,000 should be reported under support and revenue in the activity statement.
d. The gift and its terms should be disclosed only in notes to the financial statements.

87. Funds received by a college from donors who have stipulated that the principal is nonexpendable but that the income generated may be current operating funds would be accounted for in the
a. Endowment fund.
b. Term endowment fund.
c. Agency fund.
d. Quasi-endowment fund.

88. Dee City's community hospital, which uses enterprise fund reporting, normally includes proceeds from sale of cafeteria meals in
a. Patient service revenues.
b. Other revenues.
c. Ancillary service revenues.
d. Deductions from dietary service expenses.

89. An alumnus donates securities to Rex College and stipulates that the principal be held in perpetuity and revenues be used for faculty travel. Dividends received from the securities should be recognized as revenues in
a. Endowment funds.
b. Quasi-endowment funds.
c. Restricted current funds.
d. Unrestricted current funds.

90. A college's plant funds group includes which of the following subgroups?

I. Renewals and replacement funds.
II. Retirement of indebtedness funds.
III. Restricted current funds.

a. I and II.
b. I and III.
c. II and III.
d. I only.

91. Equipment donated for use in a hospital should be reported as
a. Other operating revenues.
b. Nonoperating revenues.
c. Additions to the unrestricted funds balance.
d. Additions to the restricted funds balance.

92. A nonprofit performing arts organization receives a donation that is restricted to its endowment and another donation that is restricted for use in acquiring a performing arts center. How should these donations be reported in the year received, assuming neither donation is expended in that year?

| | Donation for endowment | Donation for performing arts center |
|---|---|---|
| a. | Deferred capital additions | Deferred capital additions |
| b. | Deferred capital additions | Capital additions |
| c. | Capital additions | Capital additions |
| d. | Capital additions | Deferred capital additions |

93. City University made a discretionary transfer of $100,000 to its library fund. This transfer should be recorded by a debit to
a. Unrestricted current fund balance.
b. Restricted current fund balance.
c. General fund expenditures.
d. Library fund expenditures.

94. The following funds were among those held by State College at December 31, 19X1:

| | |
|---|---|
| Principal specified by the donor as nonexpendable | $500,000 |
| Principal expendable after the year 20X0 | 300,000 |
| Principal designated from current funds | 100,000 |

What amount should State College classify as regular endowment funds?
a. $100,000
b. $300,000
c. $500,000
d. $900,000

95. In the loan fund of a college, each of the following types of loans would be found except
a. Faculty.
b. Computer.
c. Staff.
d. Student.

96. A hospital should report earnings from endowment funds that are restricted to a specific operating purpose as
a. General fund revenues, when expended.
b. Endowment fund revenues, when expended.
c. General fund revenues, when received.
d. Endowment fund revenues, when received.


97. Community College had the following encumbrances at December 31, 19X1:

| | |
|---|---|
| Outstanding purchase orders | $12,000 |
| Commitments for services not received | 50,000 |

What amount of these encumbrances should be reported as liabilities in Community's balance sheet at December 31, 19X1?
a. $62,000
b. $50,000
c. $12,000
d. $0


98. During 19X1, Trent Hospital received $90,000 in third-party reimbursements for depreciation. These reimbursements were restricted as follows:

| | |
|---|---|
| For replacements of fully-depreciated equipment | $25,000 |
| For additions to property | 65,000 |

What amount of these reimbursements should Trent include in revenue for the year ended December 31, 19X1?
a. $0
b. $25,000
c. $65,000
d. $90,000


99. Environs, a community foundation, incurred $10,000 in management and general expenses during 19X1. In Environs' statement of revenue, expense, and changes in fund balance for the year ended December 31, 19X1, the $10,000 should be reported as
a. A direct reduction of fund balance.
b. Part of supporting services.
c. Part of program services.
d. A contra account to offset revenue and support.

100. In 19X1, Citizens' Health, a voluntary health and welfare organization, received a bequest of a $200,000 certificate of deposit maturing in 19X2. The testator's only stipulations were that this certificate be held until maturity and that the interest revenue b used to finance salaries for a preschool program. Interest revenue for 19X2 was $16,000. When the certificate matured and was redeemed, the board of trustees adopted a formal resolution designating $40,000 of the proceeds for the future purchase of equipment for the preschool program. What amount should Citizen report in its 19X2 year-end current funds balance sheet as fund balance designated for the preschool program?
a. $0
b. $16,000
c. $40,000
d. $56,000


101. On January 2, 19X2, a graduate of Oak College established a permanent trust fund and appointed Security Bank as the trustee. The income from the trust fund is to be paid to Oak and used only by the school of education to support student scholarships. What entry is required on Oak's books to record the receipt of cash from the interest on the trust funds?
a. Debit cash and credit restricted current funds deferred revenue.
b. Debit cash and credit restricted endowment revenue.
c. Debit cash and credit endowment fund balance.
d. Debit cash and credit unrestricted endowment revenue.


102. The following expenditures were made by Green Services, a society for the protection of the environment:

| | |
|---|---|
| Printing of the annual report | $12,000 |
| Unsolicited merchandise sent to encourage contributions | 25,000 |
| Cost of an audit performed by a CPA firm | 3,000 |

What amount should be classified as fund-raising costs in the society's activity statement?
a. $37,000
b. $28,000
c. $25,000
d. $0

103. In addition to the statement of changes in fund balance, which of the following financial statements should not-for-profit hospitals prepare?

a. Balance sheet and income statement.
b. Balance sheet, income statement, and statement of changes in financial position.
c. Balance sheet, statement of revenues and expenses, and statement of cash flows.
d. Statement of funds, statement of revenues and expenses, and statement of cash flows.

104. Land valued at $400,000 and subject to a $150,000 mortgage was donated to Beaty Hospital without restriction as to use. Which of the following entries should Beaty make to record this donation?

a.  Land                          $400,000
      Mortgage payable                         $150,000
      Endowment fund balance                     250,000

b.  Land                          400,000
      Debt fund balance                          150,000
                                                 250,000

c.  Land                          400,000
      Debt fund balance                          150,000
      Endowment fund balance                     250,000

d.  Land                          400,000
      Mortgage payable                           150,000
      Unrestricted fund balance                  250,000

105. At the end of the year, Cramer University's unrestricted current funds comprised $15,000,000 of assets and $9,000,000 of liabilities (including deferred revenues of $300,000). What is the fund balance of Cramer's unrestricted current funds?

a. $5,700,000
b. $6,000,000
c. $6,300,000
d. $15,000,000

106. In hospital accounting, restricted funds are
a. **Not** available unless the board of directors remove the restrictions.
b. Restricted as to use only for board-designated purposes.

c. **Not** available for current operating use; however, the income generated by the funds is available for current operating use.
d. Restricted as to use by the donor, grantor, or other source of the resources.

107. Super Seniors is a not-for-profit organization that provided services to senior citizens. Super employs a full-time staff of 10 people at an annual cost of $150,000. In addition, two volunteers work as part-time secretaries replacing last years' full time secretary who earned $10,000. Services performed by other volunteers for special events had an estimated value of $15,0000. These volunteers were employees of local businesses and they received small-value items for their participation. What amount should Super report for salary and wage expenses related to the above items?

a. $150,000
b. $160,000
c. $165,000
d. $175,000

108. Financial resources of a college or university that are currently expendable at the discretion of the governing board and that have **not** been restricted externally nor designated by the board for specific purposes should be reported in the balance sheet of which fund?

a. Board-designated current fund.
b. Restricted current fund.
c. Unrestricted current fund.
d. General fund.

109. For the fall semester of 19X2, Ames University assessed its students $3,000,000 for tuition and fees. The net amount realized was only $2,500,000 because scholarships of $400,000 were granted to students, and tuition remissions of $100,000 were allowed to faculty members' children attending Ames. What amount should Ames report for the period as unrestricted current fund gross revenues from tuition and fees?

a. $2,500,000
b. $2,600,000
c. $2,900,000
d. $3,000,000

110. The League, a not-for-profit organization, received the following pledges:

| | |
|---|---|
| Unrestricted | $200,000 |
| Restricted for capital additions | 150,000 |

All pledges are legally enforceable; however, the League's experience indicates that 10% of all pledges prove to be uncollectible. What amount should the League report as pledges receivable, net of any required allowance account?

a. $135,000
b. $180,000
c. $315,000
d. $350,000

111. In the balance sheet of a not-for-profit hospital, marketable equity securities should be reported at

a. The lower of aggregate cost or market in separate portfolios for unrestricted current, unrestricted noncurrent, restricted current, and restricted noncurrent assets.
b. The lower of aggregate cost or market in separate portfolios for unrestricted and restricted assets.
c. The lower of aggregate cost or market in separate portfolios for current and noncurrent assets.
d. Cost, with **no** valuation for declines in market value, and in separate portfolios for unrestricted and restricted assets.

112. In June 19X2, Reed Hospital purchased medicines from Park Pharmaceutical Co. at a cost of $1,000. However, Park notified Reed that the invoice was being canceled and that the medicines were being donated to Reed. Reed should record this donation of medicines as

a. Other operating revenue of $1,000.
b. A $1,000 credit to operating expenses.
c. A $1,000 credit to nonoperating expenses.
d. A memorandum entry only.

113. Midtown Church received a donation of marketable equity securities from a church member. The securities had appreciated in value after they were purchased by the donor, and they continued to appreciate through the end of Midtown's fiscal year. At what amount should Midtown report its investment in marketable equity securities in its year-end balance sheet?

a. Donor's cost.
b. Market value at the date of receipt.
c. Market value at the balance sheet date.
d. Market value at either the date of receipt or the balance-sheet date.

114. Maple Church has cash available for investments in several different accounting funds. Maple's policy is to maximize its financial resources. How many Maple pool its investments?

a. Maple may **not** pool its investments.
b. Maple may pool all investments, but must equitable allocate realized and unrealized gains and losses among participating funds.
c. Maple may pool only unrestricted investments, but must equitable allocate realized and unrealized gains and losses among participating funds.
d. Maple may pool only restricted investments, but must equitably allocate realized and unrealized gains and losses among participating funds.

115. Which of the following accounts would appear in the plant fund of a not-for-profit private college?

| | Fuel inventory for power plant | Equipment |
|---|---|---|
| a. | Yes | Yes |
| b. | No | Yes |
| c. | No | No |
| d. | Yes | No |

116. When a nonprofit organization combines fund-raising efforts with educational materials or program services, the total combined costs incurred are

a. Reported as program services expenses.
b. Allocated between fund-raising and program services expensed using an appropriate allocation basis.
c. Reported a fund-raising costs.
d. Reported as management and general expenses.

117. Hospital financial resources are required by a bond indenture to be used to finance construction of a new pediatrics facility. In which of the following hospital funds should these resources be reported?

a. Agency.
b. Trust.
c. General.
d. Endowment.

118. In 19X2, State University's board of trustees established a $100,000 fund to be retained and invested for scholarship grants. In 19X2, the fund earned $6,000 which had not been disbursed at December 31, 19X2. What amount should State report in a quasi-endowment fund balance at December 31, 19X2?
a. $0.
b. $6,000.
c. $100,000.
d. $106,000.

119. A not-for-profit hospital issued long-term tax-exempt bonds for the hospital's benefit. The hospital is responsible for the liability. Which fund may the hospital use to account for this liability?
a. Enterprise.
b. Specific purpose.
c. General.
d. General long-term debt account group.

120. Which fund may account for a university's internally designated fund, the income from which will be used for a specified purpose?
a. Endowment fund.
b. Term endowment fund.
c. Quasi-endowment fund.
d. Restricted current fund.

121. Valley's community hospital normally includes proceeds from sale of cafeteria meals in
a. Deductions from dietary service expenses.
b. Ancillary service revenues.
c. Patient service revenues.
d. Other revenues.

## Questions - Private Sector - Not-for-Profits (122 through 126)

122. Lea Meditators, a not-for-profit religious organization, elected early adoption of FASB Statement No. 116, *Accounting for Contributions Received and Contributions Made*. A storm broke glass windows in Lea's building. A member of Lea's congregation, a professional glazier, replaced the windows at no charge. In Lea's statement of activities, the breakage and replacement of the windows should

a. Not be reported.
b. Be reported by note disclosure only.
c. Be reported as an increase in both expenses and contributions.
d. Be reported as an increase in both net assets and contributions.

123. FASB Statement No. 117, *Financial Statements of Not-for-Profit Organizations,* focuses on
a. Basic information for the organization as a whole.
b. Standardization of funds nomenclature.
c. Inherent differences of not-for-profit organizations that impact reporting presentations.
d. Distinctions between current fund and non-current fund presentations.

124. On December 30, 19X4, Leigh Museum, a not-for-profit organization, received a $7,000,000 donation of Day Co. shares with donor stipulated requirements as follows:

• Shares valued at $5,000,000 are to be sold with the proceeds used to erect a public viewing building.
• Shares valued at $2,000,000 are to be retained with the dividends used to support current operations.

Leigh elected early adoption of FASB Statement No. 117, *Financial Statements of Not-for-Profit Organizations.* As a consequence of the receipt of the Day shares, how much should Leigh report as temporarily restricted net assets on its 19X4 statement of financial position?
a. $0
b. $2,000,000
c. $5,000,000
d. $7,000,000

125. The Jones family lost its home in a fire. On December 25, 19X4, a philanthropist sent money to the Amer Benevolent Society to purchase furniture for the Jones family. During January 19X5, Amer purchased this furniture for the Jones family. Amer, a not-for-profit organization, elected early adoption of FASB Statement No. 116, *Accounting for Contributions Received and Contributions Made.* How should Amer report the receipt of the money in its 19X4 financial statements?

a. As an unrestricted contribution.
b. As a temporarily restricted contribution.
c. As a permanently restricted contribution.
d. As a liability.


126. A large not-for-profit organization's statement of activities should report the net change for net assets that are

|  | Unrestricted | Permanently restricted |
|---|---|---|
| a. | Yes | Yes |
| b. | Yes | No |
| c. | No | No |
| d. | No | Yes |

# Chapter Twenty
# Not-for Profit Accounting
# Other Objective Answer Format Questions

## Private Sector Not-for-Profit Question

### NUMBER 1

**Number 1** consists of 6 items. Select the best answer for each item.

Alpha Hospital, a large not-for-profit organization, has adopted an accounting policy that does not imply a time restriction on gifts of long-lived assets.

**Required:**
For **Items 1 through 6,** indicate the manner in which the transaction affects Alpha's financial statements.

(A) Increase in unrestricted revenues, gains, and other support.
(B) Decrease in an expense.
(C) Increase in temporarily restricted net assets.
(D) Increase in permanently restricted net assets.
(E) No required reportable event.

1. Alpha's board designates $1,000,000 to purchase investments whose income will be used for capital improvements.

2. Income from investments in item 1 above, which was not previously accrued, is received.

3. A benefactor provided funds for building expansion.

4. The funds in item 3 above are used to purchase a building in the fiscal period following the period the funds were received.

5. An accounting firm prepared Alpha's annual financial statements without charge to Alpha.

6. Alpha received investments subject to the donor's requirement that investment income be used to pay for outpatient services.

# Chapter Twenty
# Solutions to Not-for-Profit Accounting Questions

1. (d) Other operating revenue.
Revenue from educational programs including tuition for schools of nursing, laboratory technology and x-ray technology would be included in other operating revenue.

2. (c) Gains and losses on the sale of assets in the endowment type funds are credited directly to endowment fund balance.

3. (a) $0. Property, plant and equipment are to be carried as a part of unrestricted fund.

4. (d) $130,000. The Hospital Audit Guide states that donated services or services paid at less than fair value should be reported as expense with a credit to nonoperating revenue. Donated medicines, supplies, etc. that would normally be purchased should be recorded at fair value and reported as operating revenue.

5. (d) Unrestricted noncurrent asset. Board restricted (internally) funds should not be included with restricted funds. Because such funds will not be used until FY 19X4 they should be classified as noncurrent.

6. (a) Donated medicines and other items normally purchased are recorded at fair value as other operating revenue.

7. (d) Nonoperating revenue. Gifts are not operating revenue (c), the gift is not restricted or deferred (b), and cannot be directly credited to fund balance (a).

8. (a) $6,000,000—Patient service revenue is recorded at standard rates within the revenue producing centers rendering inpatient and outpatient services.

9. (c) Other operating revenue of $1,000—Donated medicines, linen, office supplies, which would normally be purchased, should be recorded at fair value, as follows:

DR   Supplies expense
    CR   Other operating revenue

10. (d) $740,000—Board designated assets (internally restricted) should be carried in the unrestricted fund. Only funds externally restricted (by third party grantors or donors) should be carried in the specific purpose fund.

11. (a) Memorandum entry only—Since the funds are not under Waller Hospital's control or custody, no entry is appropriate for the principal.

12. (b) Other operating revenues include sales to persons other than patients per AICPA Hospital Guide.

13. (a) Revenue from educational programs—Yes, Unrestricted gifts—No
Education is not the chief function of a hospital. Similarly, parking lot or restaurant revenue, etc., would be "Other Operating Revenue". Unrestricted gifts (contributions) are "Non-Operating Revenue".

14. (b) Other operating revenue.
Includes revenue from research and other specific purpose **grants**, donated medicines, linen, office supplies, and other materials (FMV), educational programs and miscellaneous revenue from nonpatient care service to patients (rent, telephone, gift shop, parking, sale of supplies to nonpatients, cafeteria meals, vending machine sales, etc.).

15. (c) Nonoperating revenue of $100,000.
Includes **unrestricted** gifts, unrestricted income from endowments, income and gains from unrestricted funds, donated services, gains on sale of hospital properties, net rentals of facilities not used in operations and term endowment funds upon termination of restrictions.

16. (b) An increase in other operating revenue of $10,000.
Donated medicines, linen, office supplies, and other materials which normally would be purchased by a hospital should be recorded at fair market value and reported as other operating revenue.

17. (c) $300,000.
Internally restricted funds should **not** be accounted for as part of the specific purpose fund. Include such funds as part of the unrestricted fund with disclosure. The $250,000 grant would be included in the endowment fund.

18. (b) $8,000,000.
Generally accepted accounting principles would require accrual of patient service revenues. Accordingly, recognition must be given to patient service revenue on the accrual basis.

19. (a) $0.
Property, plant and equipment should be accounted for as part of unrestricted funds, since segregation in a separate fund would imply the existence of restrictions on asset use.

20. (c) Other operating revenue.
Includes revenue from sales and activities to persons other than patients. Such revenue is normal to the day-to-day operation of a hospital but should be separate from patient revenue. Other operating revenue also includes nonpatient care services to patients.

21. (d) Memorandum entry only.
Because the endowment is not under the control of the hospital, its establishment does not give rise to an accounting entry and such funds should not be included in the balance sheet of the hospital, but their existence should be disclosed (Hospital Audit Guide).

22. (a) Nonoperating revenue of $50,000.
Gifts should be recorded at FMV. Unrestricted gifts are nonoperating revenue.

23. (c) An increase of $40,000.
At the end of 19X6 the change in the "valuation allowance" would have had a balance of $10,000. As a result of the decrease in the value of the marketable equity security portfolio during 19X7, the following entry results in an increase in the valuation allowance.

|  |  |  |
|---|---|---|
| *Unrealized loss on marketable equity securities | $40,000 |  |
| Valuation allowance or marketable equity securities |  | $40,000 |

*Disclosed in nonoperating revenue section of the statement of revenues and expenses.

24. (a) $12,000,000.
According to the AICPA Industry Audit Guide for hospitals, property, plant and equipment, should be accounted for as part of unrestricted funds. Further, funds internally restricted (board designated) should be included in the unrestricted fund with disclosure as to the restrictions.

25. (d) $0. The fair value of such services should be recorded as other operating revenue. Nonoperating revenue includes only contributions, grants and investment earnings. Other operating revenue includes donated commodities among other items.

26. (b) Other operating revenue of $2,000.
Donated commodities are to be recorded at their fair value as "other operating revenue".

27. (a) Nonoperating revenue.
Contributions, grants and investment earnings are classified as nonoperating revenue.

28. (d) Should be accounted for as restricted funds upon receipt.
These funds are legally restricted for endowment purposes and therefore must be separately categorized as restricted.

29. (d) Disclosed in notes to Lori's financial statements.
Assets held in trust in the custody of third parties should not be recorded as hospital assets, but disclosed in notes to the financial statements.

30. (b) Nonoperating revenue $11,000.
Contributions, grants and investment earnings are classified as nonoperating revenue.

31. (a) Part of $900,000 enterprise fund type long-term debt in the enterprise fund type column.
As an enterprise fund, long-term debt is not part of the general long-term debt account group. Enterprise funds carry their own debt.

| | |
|---|---|
| Enterprise debt before combining hospital accounts | $100,000 |
| Hospital long-term debt | 800,000 |
| Total enterprise fund debt | $900,000 |

32. (b) $20,000.
Because the guild is controlled by the hospital, its assets must be disclosed. Auxiliary assets need not be disclosed.

33. (c) Part of $1,700,000 enterprise fund type fixed assets in the enterprise fund type column.
Enterprise funds carry their own fixed assets and are not part of the general fixed assets account group as for governmental funds.

34. (c) Loans on buildings would be carried in the Unrestricted fund.

35 (d) Colleges and universities should use the accrual method of accounting per AICPA Industry Audit Guide, Colleges and Universities.

36. (d) Because grants would be made for a particular purpose, the use of such funds would be restricted current funds for that purpose.

37. (a) Colleges and universities are recommended to use fund accounting on the accrual basis.

38. (c) $1,100,000. The Hospital Audit Guide states that "funds for specific operating purposes consist of donor-restricted resources and should be accounted for in a restricted fund or as deferred revenue in the unrestricted fund. These resources should be reported as other operating revenue in the financial statements of the period in which expenditures are made for the purpose intended—." Consequently revenue equal to the 6/30/X1 expenditures should be recognized.

39. (a) Memorandum entry only. Because the trust is not under control of the university, but is held in trust by others, it is preferable to disclose its existence in notes to the financial statements.

40. (c) $2,250,000. For comparability purposes, tuition remissions, scholarships and fellowships should be set forth as separate charges; therefore such amounts should be included in revenues from tuition and fees. Current fund revenues from tuition and fees would be $2,300,000 less $50,000 in refunds.

41. (d) Both unrestricted and restricted current funds would be used, as current expenditures would typically fall in both categories.

42. (a) $3,400,000. The accrual basis of accounting is used for colleges and universities (except that depreciation is generally not recorded) and requires that gross revenues be recorded with appropriate recognition of uncollectible accounts, scholarships and remission of tuition.

43. (d) $8,000,000—Plant Funds consist of: (a) funds to be used for acquisition of physical properties but not yet expended, (b) funds set aside for the renewal and replacement of properties, (c) funds set aside for debt service charges and debt retirement, and (d) funds expended for institutional properties.

44. (b) Tuition waivers and unrestricted bequests are included in current revenue per AICPA Colleges and Universities Audit Guide.

45. (d) $1,700,000.
The accrual basis of accounting is used for colleges and universities (except that depreciation is generally not recorded) and requires that gross revenues be recorded with appropriate recognition of uncollectible accounts, scholarships and remission of tuition.

46. (b) $300,000.
The value of contributed services should be recorded in the accounts and reported in the financial statements. The value of such services should be determined by relating them to equivalent wages of similar institutions including fringe benefits. The question states that the gross value of services performed was $300,000.

47. (b) $2,000,000.
Assets less liabilities equals fund balance by definition. Deferred revenue is properly classified as part of liabilities.

| | |
|---|---|
| Assets | $5,000,000 |
| Liabilities | 3,000,000 |
| Fund balance | $2,000,000 |

48. (b) $700,000.
This question illustrates an unusual handling of receipts which are part of restricted current funds. Revenue is recognized in the restricted current fund only to the extent of expenditures made. When receipts are received, fund balance is credited as follows:

| | | |
|---|---|---|
| Grant receipts from state | $100,000 | |
| Restricted fund balance | | $100,000 |

When expenditures are made, revenue is recognized.

49. (a) Colleges and universities, *yes;* Voluntary health and welfare organizations, *yes.*
Both of these types of entities use so-called "plant funds". Voluntary health and welfare organizations use a fund titled, "Land, building and equipment fund", which is often referred to as a plant fund.

50. (a) Agency funds, *no;* Plant funds, *no.*
For colleges and universities "current funds" include those resources available for general operating purposes, auxiliary activities and current restricted purposes. This fund is generally similar to the general fund for a governmental unit. Agency and plant funds are separate funds.

51. (d) Investment in plant funds, *yes;* Unexpended plant funds, *yes.*
The plant funds of a college or university are similar to the two account groups of a governmental unit, i.e., general fixed assets and general long-term debt. In addition, resources designated for acquisition of plant assets are included in this fund. The subdivisions include (1) unexpended plant funds, (2) funds for renewal and replacement, (3) funds for retirement of indebtedness, and (4) investment in plant. The credit side of the balance sheet includes fund balances and notes and mortgages payable.

52. (c) Annuity funds, *no;* Loan funds, *no.*
The current fund of a college and university statement does not include these funds, as they are separate funds.

53. (c) $775,000.
Revenues should include all unrestricted gifts and all restricted gifts which have been expended.

| Unrestricted gifts | $675,000 |
| Restricted gifts expended | 100,000 |
| | $775,000 |

54. (a) $50,000.
"Operation and Maintenance of Plant" and "Scholarships and Fellowships" are major separate categories of expense under "Educational and General" which also includes major categories such as Instruction, Research, Public Service, Academic Support and Student Services, and Institutional Support. Administrative data processing is a subdivision under "Institutional Support" which, in general, includes the administrative indirect costs of the institution.

55. (b) $293,000.
Tuition and fees should include all tuition and fees assessed against students, net of refunds. Tuition and fees should be recorded as revenue even though there is no intention of collection from the student.

56. (d) Current funds, *yes;* Plant funds, *yes.*
These two funds, in addition to loan, endowment, annuity and life income, and agency funds, comprise the entire list of recommended categories for a college or university.

57. (b) $375,000. In the unrestricted current fund, revenue is recorded as received, in this case $300,000. In restricted current funds, "fund balance" is credited when revenue is received. Revenue is recognized only to the extent of expenditures for fund purposes, in this case $75,000—total $375,000.

58. (a) $900,000. All of the items shown are properly included as a part of plant funds which includes: (1) amounts designated for future additions, (2) amounts designated for major repairs, etc., (3) amounts for principal and interest on debt, and (4) fixed assets and related mortgages.

59. (a) $4,000,000. Tuition remissions, scholarships and fellowships should be set forth in the financial statements as separate charges; therefore, such amounts should be included in revenues from tuition and fees. Current fund revenues should be reported net of refunds, in this case $4,000,000.

60. (b) Yes, yes, no.
Current funds revenues include (1) all unrestricted gifts and other unrestricted resources earned during the reporting period, and (2) restricted current funds to the extent that such funds were expended for current operating purposes. Current funds revenues do not include restricted current funds received but not expended.

61. (b) The governmental fund closest to "land, building and equipment" is the General Fixed Asset Group. Both record acquisitions of fixed assets; however, the similarity ends there. The voluntary health and welfare account records depreciation, related debt on fund assets and liquid assets to acquire or replace facilities. The other three choices all have governmental counterparts such as:

Current unrestricted—General Fund
Custodian—Agency
Endowment—Trust

62. (b) Where a donation received during the period is specified by the donor for use in future periods, such donation should be recorded as a deferred credit in the balance sheet of the appropriate fund and recorded as support in the year in which it may be used. In the absence of clear evidence as to a specific program period, donations and pledges should be recorded as support when received.

63. (a) In a manner similar to governmental and hospital accounting, voluntary health and welfare organizations have legal and contractual restrictions placed upon the use of their resources. For proper control and reporting, fund accounting is used.

64. (b) $405,000—If portions of the donations (including pledges) received during the period are specified by the donor for use in future periods, such portions should be recorded as a deferred credit and recorded as support in the year in which they may be used. Provision should also be made for uncollectible pledges.

| | |
|---|---|
| Total Pledge | $900,000 |
| Deferred Until 1984 | (450,000) |
| 10% Uncollectible Provision | (45,000) |
| Net Contribution Revenue | $405,000 |

65. (a) $8,000—Donated services should be recorded at fair value when there is the equivalent of an employer-employee relationship and an objective basis for valuing such services.

$$\frac{\$20,000}{2,000} = \$10 \text{ per hr.} \times 800 = \$8,000$$

66. (d) $100,000
"Expenditures for program services should be segregated from fund-raising and management and general expenditures, and the amount of each should be clearly disclosed in the financial statements." *(Industry Audit Guide for Voluntary Health and Welfare Organizations)* Fund-raising and administration are not expenses directly related to carrying out its purpose.

67. (a) Quasi-endowment fund. Such funds, under the control of the governing body, are a part of the "Unrestricted Current Fund" as endowment revenues that are unrestricted.

68. (d) Be included as an element of expense.
Depreciation expense should be recognized as a cost of rendering current services and should be included as an element of expense in the statement of support, revenue, and expenses of the fund in which the assets are recorded and in the statement of functional expenditures. *(Industry Audit Guide)*

69. (b) FMV at the date of the gift.
In general, donated assets should be recorded at fair value. The donor's recorded amount is irrelevant.

70. (d) $40,000.
Pledges should be recorded when obtained; however, where a portion of donations (cash or otherwise) are specified for use in future periods, a deferred credit should be set up. Further, provision should be made for uncollectibility.

| | |
|---|---|
| Total pledge | $100,000 |
| [1] Deferred until 19X8 | 50,000 |
| | 50,000 |
| Provision for uncollectibility | 10,000 |
| Net contribution in 19X7 | $ 40,000 |

[1] Provision required for uncollectibility of 19X8 pledge.

71. (c) $100,000 should be reported as deferred support in the balance sheet.
Where a gift has been restricted as to future use by the donor, the amount of the gift should be recognized as deferred support. The instant cast is referred to as a "life income agreement."

72. (c) Unsolicited merchandise sent to encourage contributions.
Expenditures that should be associated with "fund-raising" include costs of transmitting appeals to the public, salaries of personnel used (including regular staff) in fund-raising, cost of printed material, radio and television time, etc.

73. (c) $440,000.

| | |
|---|---|
| Unrestricted pledges | $500,000 |
| Allowance for uncollectibility | 60,000 |
| Net contribution | $440,000 |

Unrestricted pledges should be recorded as support in the year received with provision for uncollectibility.

74. (a) Fund balance—expended
           Fund balance—unexpended

Fund balances of the "Land, building and equipment" fund is **expended** to the extent of the carrying value (cost less depreciation) of fixed assets plus related debt. Conversion of fixed assets (carrying value) to cash necessitates an entry to decrease expended fund balance and increase unexpended fund balance. Unexpended fund balance represents the amount of cash, investments and receivables, etc., in the "Land, building and equipment" fund.

75. (b) $10,000.
Sequence of entries are as follows:

| | | |
|---|---|---|
| Cash | $12,000 | |
| Accumulated depreciation | 4,000 | |
| Equipment | | $14,000 |
| Unexpended fund balance (gain) | | 2,000 |
| To record sale of equipment | | |
| | | |
| Fund balance—expended | $10,000 | |
| Fund balance—unexpended | | $10,000 |
| To transfer carrying value of equipment sold to unexpended fund balance | | |

76. (b) $40,000. In a nonexpendable trust fund, gains from sale of fund assets become part of principal, and as such may not be expended. Interest and dividends are part of trust income and as such may be included in the unrestricted current fund.

77. (c) $200,000. Only the $200,000 should be included as "current restricted" because the funds are restricted for specific operating purposes by a third party. Board restricted funds (internally restricted) should be accounted for in the unrestricted current fund.

78. (a) $5,000. Not-for-profit entities should follow GAAP and as such follow the accrual basis of accounting.

79. (a) $3,000. Donor cost is not to be used in recording a donated asset by a not-for-profit entity. The asset should be recorded at fair value and depreciation recorded on that basis—$30,000 ÷ 10 = $3,000.

80. (b) $180,000.

| | |
|---|---|
| Pledges received | $130,000 |
| Expected to collect | 50,000 |
| | $180,000 |

81. (c) Part of supporting services.
Program services relate to specific activities of the entity such as education, research, training and community services. Supporting services are overhead-type activities such as management and general expense. Fundraising is also part of supporting services.

82. (b) Direct reduction in fund balance for transfer to current unrestricted fund, $100,000.
This transfer recognized that the funds were available in 1989 for unrestricted use as support.

83. (c) Direct addition to fund balance for transfer from endowment fund, $100,000.
This completes the entry for transfer of $100,000 from the endowment fund to the current unrestricted fund.

84. (b) Fund balance designated for purchase of equipment, $20,000.
Because the $8,000 interest income was restricted (designated by the donor) as to use, item (b) is the only choice that recognizes that fact.

85. (a) Be included as an element of expense.
In voluntary health and welfare organizations, depreciation should be recorded consistent with the concept of measuring the costs of the effort expended toward achieving the goals of the organization.

86. (a) $200,000 should be reported as deferred support in the balance sheet.
The $200,000 is deferred support, that is available for unrestricted use, upon the fulfillment of certain condition(s). Income derived is not recorded as support since such funds are transmitted to the donor.

87. (d) A nonexpendable trust is accounted for in the endowment fund. Only the income from the trust can be used by the college. A term endowment fund allows the college to also spend principal. A quasi-endowment fund (quasi means almost) is self-imposed by the government body of the college.

88. (b) Proceeds from sale of cafeteria are reported as other revenues. Ancillary revenues (Pharmacy, Radiology, etc.) are a subset of revenues from services to patients.

89. (c) Dividends received are income which are available for current use for the faculty to travel. They should be reported as revenues in the restricted current fund.

90. (a) A college plant funds group include subgroups for renewals, replacement and retirement of plant.

91. (c) Equipment donated to a hospital should be reported in the unrestricted fund balance. There is no restrictions placed on its use, nor it is revenue to the hospital.

92. (d) Both donation should be reported as capital additions. The endowment donation is used currently to generate spendable income. The art center is a deferred capital addition since it is not used in the current period.

93. (a) The discretionary transfer should be recorded with a debit to "unrestricted fund balance".

94. (c) $5,000 is the amount that State College should classify as a regular endowment funds, because it is the nonexpendable portion of the donated principal.

95. (b) The loan funds group consists of loans to students, faculty and staff, and of resources available to make the loans possible.

96. (a) They are reported as revenue of general funds when expenditures are incurred for the intended purpose of the donor.

97. (d) $0. Liabilities do not exist until legal title transfers, which is usually when the goods or services are received.

98. (a) $0. The amount of these reimbursements that Trent should include in revenue for the year ended December 31, 1991 is zero. They should be reported as additions in the statements of Changes in Fund Balance and not revenues.

99. (b) Part of supporting services in the statement of Revenues, Expenses, and Changes in Fund Balance.

100. (c) In 'X2 when the $200,000 CD matures, it is transferred from the endowment fund to the current fund unrestricted. Of the $200,000, $40,000 is designated, and the rest is undesignated. Amounts designated by the board should not be included in donor restricted funds. The amount designated for future purchase of equipment meets this requirement. The other $16,000 would have already been spent or would have been reported in the donor restricted fund.

101. (a) Since the income from the trust fund is donor restricted for school of education scholarships, it would be reported in the restricted current fund as a deferred revenue until the money is spent, at which time it is recognized as revenue to the extent of the expenditures.

102. (c) Fund raising expenses are incurred to induce contributions. The unsolicited merchandise sent to encourage contributions qualifies as fundraising. The printing and annual report are management and general expenses.

103. (c) The required financial statements for a nonprofit hospital are a balance sheet, a statement of revenue and expenses, a statement of cash flow, and a statement of changes in fund balance.

104. (d) The hospital would record the donation in the general fund by debiting land for the fair value of $400,000, and credit mortgage payable for $150,000. The difference of $250,000 is credited to the unrestricted fund balance, since this donation does not have any restrictions.

105. (b) The fund balance of a university's unrestricted current fund is equal to the assets less the liability. That gives us $15 million – $9 million, which equals $6 million.

106. (d) Restricted funds are restricted as to use by the donor, granter, or other sources. They are outside donor restricted.

107. (b) The value of donated services should be recorded as both contribution and an expense if the services performed are a normal part of the program, and would have been otherwise performed by salaried personnel. In this case, clearly the two volunteers who replaced the secretary would qualify under this criteria, therefore the total salary and wage expenses equals $150,000 + $10,000 = $160,000

108. (c) Unrestricted current funds are currently expendable at the discretion of the board, and are not restricted by external owners, or designated by the governing board.

109. (d) Student tuition and fees include all tuition and fees assessed against students for educational and general purposes. Tuition and fee remissions or exemptions should be assessed and reported as revenues. The following journal entry explains:

| | | |
|---|---|---|
| Cash | $2,500,000 | |
| Scholarship | $ 400,000 | |
| Tuition Remission | $ 100,000 | |
| Revenues - Tuition and Fees. | | $3,000,000 |

110. (c) The amount of all pledges should be recorded when obtained. Provisions should be made for uncollectible pledges.

$350,000 – $35,000. (10%) = $315,000

111 . (a) At the lower of aggregate cost or market.

112. (a) Donated medicine is included as other operating revenue at its fair value.

113. (d) Nonprofit organizations have traditionally carried donated investments at fair value at date of receipt. However, some organizations have been carrying their investments at market as a permissible alternative to cost. Therefore, Midtown church could report the investment at market value at either the date of receipt, or the balance sheet date.

114. (b) Nonprofit organizations such as churches may pool all investments in various funds, but must equitably allocate realized and unrealized gains and losses among participating funds.

115. (b) Fuel inventory is a current asset, and should be accounted for in a current fund. It is not a property plant and equipment asset.

116. (b) In accounting for a nonprofit organization, it is important to distinguish between costs incurred in raising funds, and costs incurred in providing services to those who are benefited by the organization. An allocation using an appropriated basis must be made between the two activities generating the costs. This is done so that those who provide resources to the organization can see in the financial statement the portion of resources that are used in program services, and the portion that are instead using for fundraising activities.

117. (c) The general fund accounts for restricted resources that are not restricted by identified purposes by donors and grantors. A bond indenture, in this case, does not meet the criteria of donors / grantors.

118. (d) Since the $6,000 earned on the funds has not been reimbursed it will be reported in the quasi-endowment fund.

119. (c) The general fund accounts for long term debts. Choice (a) is incorrect because hospitals do not use enterprise funds. Choice (b) is incorrect because this fund accounts for assets that are donor restricted for specific purposes. Choice (d) is incorrect because hospitals do not have a general long-term debt account group.

120. (c) A quasi-endowment fund board designated or created, may be restricted or unrestricted depending upon the nature of the funds the board uses to create the fund. Choice (a) is incorrect because in an endowment fund the principal must remain intact and only income may be spent according to outside donors' stipulations. Choice (b) is incorrect because principal and interest may be spent after a specific period (term) of time. Choice (d) is incorrect because restricted current funds are spent for operating purposes but restricted by donors or other outside parties.

121. (d) Cafeteria proceeds are accounted for as other revenues. Choice (a) is incorrect because the proceeds are not deductions from dietary services expenses. Choice (b) is incorrect because ancillary revenues are a subset of patient revenues from radiology, pharmacy and similar. Choice (c) is incorrect because patient service revenues are earned from service rendered when the patient checks in the hospital.

122. (c) SFAS #116 states that contributed services should be recognized if the services: 1) require specialized skills and 2) they would typically need to be purchased if not provided by donation. When recognizing donated services that entity would record the fair market value of the service as a contribution and an expense.

123. (a) FASB Statement No. 117 focuses on the entity concept and views not-for-profits as a single unit rather than prior concepts that viewed the entity as being made up of component parts (Fund accounting concepts).

124. (c) SFAS #117 states that there are three classifications of net assets - unrestricted, temporary restricted, and permanently restricted. Temporary restricted net assets are subject to a time or task requirement to use funds in a particular way. Leigh Museum received $5,000,000 of temporary restricted assets (building construction) and $2,000,000 of permanently restricted funds (amount never to be spent).

125. (b) The contribution received was for a specific purpose. It could only be spent for furniture for the Jones family. Therefore, the contribution is restricted for that purpose and no other.

126. (a) The statement of activities reports the changes in all classes of net assets (unrestricted, temporarily restricted and restricted.

# Chapter Twenty
# Not-for Profit Accounting
# Other Objective Answer Format Solutions

## NUMBER 1

1. (E)  No required reportable event.

2. (A)  Increase in unrestricted revenues, gains, and other support.

3. (C)  Increase in temporarily restricted net assets.

4. (A)  Increase in unrestricted revenues, gains, and other support.

5. (A)  Increase in unrestricted revenues, gains, and other support.

6. (D)  Increase in permanently restricted net assets.

# Notes

# Notes

# Notes

# Notes

# 2

# *Federal Income Taxes*

## (Chapters 1-10 plus Appendix)

by

Arthur Reed, MBA, MST, CPA

*Published by*

# Chapter Subjects for FEDERAL INCOME TAXES:

Introduction

Chapter One
FILING STATUS AND EXEMPTIONS, FILING REQUIREMENTS AND
PENALTIES

Chapter Two
INCOME - INCLUSIONS AND EXCLUSIONS

Chapter Three
DEDUCTIONS FOR ADJUSTED GROSS INCOME

Chapter Four
DEDUCTIONS FROM ADJUSTED GROSS INCOME

Chapter Five
ACCOUNTING METHODS AND PERIODS, AND COMPUTATION OF TAX
LIABILITY AND TAX CREDITS

Chapter Six
CAPITAL TRANSACTIONS

Chapter Seven
PARTNERSHIPS

Chapter Eight
C CORPORATIONS

Chapter Nine
CORPORATE DISTRIBUTIONS, S CORPORATIONS AND OTHER CORPORATE
MATTERS

Chapter Ten
TAXATION OF GIFTS, ESTATES AND FIDUCIARIES, AND EXEMPT
ORGANIZATIONS

Appendix
OTHER OBJECTIVE ANSWER FORMAT PROBLEMS FROM RECENT EXAMS

# Introduction
# Federal Income Taxes

The CPA Examination tests your knowledge of Federal Income Taxes during the Accounting & Reporting Examination. The guidelines established by the AICPA Board of Examiners for taxation require that the CPA candidate must be able to:

> Analyze information and identify data relevant for tax purposes
> Identify issues, elections, and alternative tax treatments
> Perform required calculations
> Formulate conclusions

You will be tested on this portion of the exam on **Thursday morning from 8:30 to 12:00**, along with managerial and governmental accounting. This textbook, which includes hundreds of selected AICPA questions and our answers, will prepare you for passing this portion of the examination.

## Exam Coverage

Under the AICPA Guidelines, the taxation portion of the CPA Examination now comprises 60% of the Accounting & Reporting Examination (ARE). The **Content Specification Outline** allocates the 60% as follows:

| | |
|---|---|
| Individuals | 20% |
| Corporations | 20% |
| Partnerships | 10% |
| Estates, gifts, trusts, exempt organizations & preparer responsibilities | 10% |

At the end of this introduction, we present the complete, detailed Content Specification Outline, along with the corresponding Lambers Chapter Reference. Use this as a quick reference to find the material you will be tested on. In addition, we have included a Summary of Coverage which recaps the past five exams. Use this as a guide to review the degree of frequency of exam questions.

## Format of Examination Questions

The questions contained in the following ten chapters are taken directly from past CPA Examinations. Where tax law has changed, we have adapted the questions from their original presentation. For example, for a married taxpayer, up to $500,000 of the gain from the sale of your principal residence may be excluded.

In terms of the style of questions, the Board of Examiners indicate that the Accounting & Reporting Examination (which includes managerial and government accounting) will include:

| | |
|---|---|
| Four-option multiple choice | 50-60% |
| Other objective answer format | 40-50% |
| Essays | None |

There are no essays or long open-ended problems. You will still be tested under a **multiple choice** format. We have included hundreds of those for your review. As far as the **Other Objective Answer Format (OOAF)** questions go, we have included them in the **Appendix**. You need to review their format and become comfortable with the presentation. **The Appendix is not optional. You must work these questions if you expect to pass.**

## Other Objective Answer Format Questions

The format of the OOAF questions and a sample question for each is presented below:

1. **Constructed (numeric) response.** Similar to a multiple choice in set-up, but the candidate must formulate an answer and write the response in preprinted spaces. These are, in essence, open-ended questions that you need to fill-in the blank. *Question*: Calculate the total compensation of the taxpayer.

2. **Matching style.** Given a list of transactions, the candidate must match the correct response from a list of choices. *Question*: Which of the following forms is interest income reported on?

3. **True/False, or Yes/No, etc.** This seems to be gaining in popularity. Usually requires no computations, but does test the underlying tax principles. In taxation, we have also seen included/excluded, taxable/non-taxable, etc. *Question*: Does the following transaction Increase, Decrease, or have No Effect on the alternative minimum tax?

## What Will I See on the Exam

While it is not possible to predict exactly what you will see on your exam, it is important to note that you must base your answers on the tax law that is in effect for the period specified in the question. Some questions specify a year, other say "during the current year." In the latter case, the year usually does not matter. On some past exams, the examiners have tested the candidates on different years during the same exam. **You must read each question carefully.**

In sitting for the May and November 2000 exams, you will see questions related to the 1999 tax year. That is what this text is based upon. Now, since the examiners consistently test on the important changes in tax law, we have provided you with a summary of some of these important topics which were the result of past tax law changes. This list should be reviewed as a list of hot topics to look at right before the exam as part of your final review. These changes have all been discussed in greater detail in their appropriate chapters.

## Additional Study Materials

In preparing our material, it was necessary to condense volumes of information into summary form. Our broad presentation of the material, with examples, is designed to give you, the candidate, a working knowledge of federal income tax law. In preparing for this portion of the exam you may want to refer to other material to reinforce or clarify issues unfamiliar to you. The AICPA Board of Examiners suggests the following publications:

> Internal Revenue Code and Income Tax Regulations
> Internal Revenue Service Circular 230
> AICPA Statements on Responsibility in Tax Practice
> Current Income Tax textbooks

In addition, many colleges require taxation of individuals but only offer the taxation of corporations, partnerships, estates and gifts as an elective, if it all. As a result, many candidates sitting for the exam have never had exposure to these areas. Accordingly, we have added more examples and illustrations in this part of our text. If you have limited exposure to this area, be sure to concentrate on Chapters Seven through Ten.

## Internal Revenue Code

Throughout the text, references will be made to the Internal Revenue Code (the Code). While the first form of federal taxation was a temporary act in 1861, it wasn't until after the ratification of the Sixteenth Amendment that Congress passed the Revenue Act of 1913. In 1939, the various acts since 1913 were "codified" into the Internal Revenue Code of 1939. In 1954 there was another major codification. The most recent codification occurred in 1986. The 1986 codification embodied most of the 1954 structure and the change was less radical than the previous. There were, however, a number of substantial acts, especially during the 1980's. These will be referred to as encountered in the text. The 1986 Code we are currently under has been amended a number of times.

## Detail of Content Specification Outline

The detail presented at the end of this introduction is a quick reference guide as to where we cover the material you will be tested on. Please note that the ten chapters we present are not equal in exam coverage. For example, Chapters 1 through 5 deal with Individuals, as does part of Chapter 6. However, only 20% of the exam deals with Individual taxation. On the other hand, 20% of the exam is on Corporations, and that is covered in only two chapters. Keep this in mind as you review the material.

## Released and Author Constructed Questions

In working through each chapter, please review the questions at the very end of each chapter. The AICPA has released 24 multiple choice questions from the non-disclosed exams and these have been included for your review. These are labeled with the letter "R" plus the appropriate year. For example, *R97* is a released question from the 1997 CPA exam. In addition, we have presented a number of Author Constructed questions which test the new provisions. These are labeled *AC*.

Federal Income Taxation is very technical, but by becoming familiar with the text material and questions from past exams, you will pass this portion of the exam.

### ACKNOWLEDGMENTS

It would be impossible to write a CPA examination book of any kind without the assistance of the American Institute of Certified Public Accountants, and their various operating divisions, in granting permission to use various materials. We respectfully acknowledge and thank those persons in the American Institute who promptly answered our inquiries.

Arthur E. Reed, CPA
Abington, Massachusetts
September 1999

# Summary of the Taxpayer Relief Act of 1997

On **August 5, 1997,** President Clinton signed the Taxpayer Relief Act of 1997. The changes are quite extensive and are somewhat difficult to plan for because of the varying effective dates of the provisions. As you read these, recognize that the examiners may create questions around the dates. For example, a taxpayer sells his house on June 30, 1997. This date is after the effective date of May 7, 1997; therefore, is subject to the new tax law.

It is likely that the examiners will only test this area heavily because of the extent of the changes. You should carefully review this material as part of your exam preparation. The following summarizes the changes on a chapter by chapter basis:

**Chapter 1**

No specific changes.

**Chapter 2**

*Effective for discharges after August 5, 1997,* there is also an exclusion for students with student loans. If the forgiveness is contingent upon the student fulfilling a work requirement in the state, the forgiveness of debt will not constitute gross income.

\*　　　\*　　　\*　　　\*　　　\*

*Effective for tax years beginning after December 31, 1997,* the foreign income exclusion is as follows:

| Tax Year | Exclusion Amount |
|---|---|
| 1998 | $72,000 |
| 1999 | 74,000 |
| 2000 | 76,000 |
| 2001 | 78,000 |
| 2002 and thereafter | 80,000 |

**Chapter 3**

*Effective for tax years beginning after December 31, 1997,* two new provisions affect the determination of the deductibility of the IRA. First, when an individual's **spouse** is an active participant in an employer-sponsored retirement plan, the IRA deduction for such an individual (the non-participant) is phased-out only for married couples with AGI between $150,000 and $160,000.

Second, for individuals who are active participants in an employer sponsored retirement plan, their increased IRA phase-out ranges are as follows for 1998:

| | **Phase-out range** |
|---|---|
| Married, filing jointly | $ 50,000 - $ 60,000 |
| Single | $ 30,000 - $ 40,000 |

\*     \*     \*     \*     \*

***Effective for tax years beginning after December 31, 1997***, a taxpayer can make a **nondeductible** IRA (Roth IRA) contribution of up to $2,000 per year. There are many interesting provisions, but generally:

- contributions may be made by individuals 70 1/2 years and older
- there are no mandatory distribution rules
- there are no restrictions due to the active participation rule

There are some limitations. For example, the phase-out range for allowing the contribution at all are as follows:

| | |
|---|---|
| Married, filing jointly | $ 150,000 - $ 160,000 |
| Single | $ 95,000 - $ 110,000 |

When distributions are made from a Roth IRA, the distributions are free of taxes and penalties assuming that the taxpayer has maintained the IRA for 5 years or more, and the distribution:

- was made on or after the taxpayer attains the age of 59 1/2.
- was paid to the beneficiary upon the death of the taxpayer
- was made on account of the taxpayer becoming disabled
- was made for first-time homebuyer expenses (up to a maximum of $10,000)

\*     \*     \*     \*     \*

***Effective for tax years beginning after December 31, 1997***, taxpayers can make nondeductible contributions of up to $500 for each beneficiary under the age of 18 to an Education IRA. The contribution limit of $500 is phased-out for individuals using the same ranges as the Roth IRAs described above. Generally, when distributions are made from an Education IRA, the distributions are free of taxes and penalties to the extent that proceeds are used for qualified education expenses (tuition, fees, room and board) of the beneficiary.

\*     \*     \*     \*     \*

***Effective for interest payments due and paid after December 31, 1997,*** a taxpayer is allowed a deduction for interest paid on qualified educational loans. Qualified educational loans include indebtedness for higher education, such as tuition, fees, room and board of the taxpayer, spouse, or dependent. The deduction is allowed only for the first 60 months that interest payments are required, to a maximum of $1,000 in 1998. This amount is increased in future years. Similar to other deductions, there is a phase-out range of deductibility as follows:

| | **Phase-out range** |
|---|---|
| Married, filing jointly | $ 60,000 - $ 75,000 |
| Single | $ 40,000 - $ 55,000 |

**Chapter 4**

Unreimbursed out-of-pocket costs for charitable purposes are allowed as deductions. This includes travel at an optional 12 cents per mile, plus parking and tolls. ***Effective for tax years beginning after December 31, 1997,*** this increases to 14 cents per mile.

**Chapter 5**

*Effective for tax years beginning after December 31, 1997,* the dependent's basic standard deduction will be increased by $250.

$$* \quad * \quad * \quad * \quad *$$

*Effective for tax years beginning after December 31, 1997,* a taxpayer engaged in the farming business may now elect to use income averaging to compute his tax. In determining income, the farmer may include the gain from the sale of farming business property.

$$* \quad * \quad * \quad * \quad *$$

*Effective for tax years beginning after December 31, 1997,* taxpayers will be able to claim a child credit of $400 for each qualifying child under the age of 17. In general, the child must be a child or direct descendant of the taxpayer and the taxpayer must be able to claim the child as his dependent. There is a threshold limitation. The credit is reduced by $50 for each $1,000 (or part thereof) of modified adjusted gross income over the following:

| | |
|---|---|
| Single | $ 75,000 |
| Married filing jointly | 110,000 |
| Married filing separately | 55,000 |

The credit has an additional feature in that if it exceeds the taxpayer's income tax for that year, the excess may be refunded if the taxpayer has three or more qualifying children, similar to the earned income credit.

$$* \quad * \quad * \quad * \quad *$$

*Effective for tax years beginning after December 31, 1997,* taxpayers may elect to take a nonrefundable HOPE Scholarship tax credit for tuition and fees paid during the first two years of postsecondary education. The credit is equal to the lessor of $1,500, or 100% of the first $1,000 paid plus 50% of the next $1,000 paid. The credit is determined per student, per year.

$$* \quad * \quad * \quad * \quad *$$

*Effective for payments made after June 30, 1998,* taxpayers may elect to take a nonrefundable Lifetime Learning tax credit for qualified tuition and related expenses for undergraduate, graduate and professional degree courses. The credit is the lessor of $1,000, or 20% of up to $5,000 in qualified tuition and fees. Unlike the HOPE Scholarship Credit, the taxpayer may claim this over an unlimited number of years. However, this credit is not based upon the number of qualifying students. The maximum credit per year is $1,000.

There are some limitations to both the Hope Scholarship Credit and the Lifetime Learning Credit. The phase-out range (credits are reduced on a pro-rata basis) for allowing the credits is as follows:

| | Phase-out range |
|---|---|
| Married, filing jointly | $ 80,000 - $ 100,000 |
| Single | $ 40,000 - $ 50,000 |

The credit is not available for married taxpayers filing separately.

$$* \quad * \quad * \quad * \quad *$$

*Effective for the tax years beginning after 1997,* an individual must make estimated payments if he expects that the underpayment after withholdings and tax credits is at least $1,000 and more than 10% of the amount of the tax shown on the return.

## Chapter 6

*Effective for assets sold after May 6, 1997,* the capital gain provisions have changed dramatically.

For long-term capital gains on assets held more than one year, the maximum rate is now 20%. If the taxpayer was in the 15% tax bracket, the maximum rate is now 10%.

For gains on the sale of real estate, the rates differ slightly. For any long-term capital gain that is attributable to the recapture of depreciation (Section 1250), the maximum rate is 25%.

The new law does not change the 28% tax rate on the sale of collectibles, nor does it impact C Corporations.

\*     \*     \*     \*     \*

*Effective for sales of a taxpayer's principal residence after May 6, 1997,* the rules have changed dramatically. Any taxpayer, regardless of age, who has owned and used their home as a principal residence for at least 2 of the last 5 years before the sale, can exclude from income up to $250,000 of the gain on the sale ($500,000 if married and filing a joint return). This exclusion is no longer available only once in the taxpayer's lifetime, but can be used repeatedly, although no more frequently than every two years.

## Chapter 7

When making partnership distributions, substantially appreciated inventory is inventory whose fair market value exceeds 120% of its adjusted basis. However, *effective for sales, exchanges and distributions after August 5, 1997*, the requirement that inventory must be "substantially appreciated" has been repealed.

If a partner receives a partnership distribution of property which had a precontribution gain within 5 years of being contributed, such gain will be recognized. For property contributed to a partnership *after June 8, 1997*, the period of time increases from 5 years to 7 years.

## Chapter 8

*Effective for tax years beginning after August 5, 1997,* the NOL carryback is reduced to 2 years and carryforward is extended to 20 years.

\*     \*     \*     \*     \*

*Effective for tax years beginning after December 31, 1997,* the corporate AMT has been repealed for small corporations (SC). A corporation with average annual gross receipts of less than $5 million for the three-year period beginning after December 31, 1994, qualifies as an SC.

## Chapter 9

No specific changes.

**Chapter 10**

***Effective for estates of decedents dying, and gifts made, after December 31, 1997***, the unified credit has been increased. For 1998, the unified credit is $202,050 for an exemption equivalent of $625,000. The phase-in of the unified credit along with the corresponding exemption amounts are presented at the end of chapter 10.

*     *     *     *     *

***Effective for gifts made after August 5, 1997***, a gift tax return is not required for a gift to a charitable organization.

*     *     *     *     *

***Effective for estates of decedents dying after December 31, 1997***, there is an exclusion from the value of a gross estate the lessor of (1) the adjusted value of the decedent's **qualified family owned business** or (2) the excess of $1,300,000 over the applicable estate tax exemption equivalent.

# FEDERAL TAXATION CONTENT SPECIFICATIONS:

| Area Tested and Percentage of Exam | Lambers Chapter |
|---|---|
| **I. Federal taxation -- individuals (20%)** | |
| A. Inclusions in gross income | Chapters 2 and 6 |
| B. Exclusions and adjustments to arrive at adjusted gross income | Chapters 2, 3 and 6 |
| C. Deductions from adjusted gross income | Chapter 4 |
| D. Filing status and exemptions | Chapter 1 |
| E. Tax accounting methods | Chapter 5 |
| F. Tax computations, credits, and penalties | Chapter 5 |
| G. Alternative minimum tax | Chapter 5 |
| H. Tax procedures | Chapter 1 |
| **II. Federal taxation -- corporations (20%)** | |
| A. Determination of taxable income or loss | Chapter 8 |
| B. Tax accounting methods | Chapter 8 |
| C. S corporations | Chapter 9 |
| D. Personal holding companies | Chapter 9 |
| E. Consolidated returns | Chapter 8 |
| F. Tax computations, credits, and penalties | Chapter 8 |
| G. Alternative minimum tax | Chapter 8 |
| H. Other | Chapter 9 |
|     1. Distributions | |
|     2. Incorporation, reorganization, liquidation, and dissolution | |
|     3. Tax procedures | |
| **III. Federal taxation -- partnerships (10%)** | |
| A. Basis of partner's interest and bases of assets contributed to the partnership. | All in Chapter 7 |
| B. Determination of partner's share of income, credits, and deductions | |
| C. Partnership and partner elections | |
| D. Partner dealing with own partnership | |
| E. Treatment of partnership liabilities | |
| F. Distribution of partnership assets | |
| G. Termination of partnership | |
| **IV. Federal taxation -- estates and trusts, exempt organizations, and preparers' responsibilities (10%)** | |
| A. Estates and trusts | Chapter 10 |
|     1. Income taxation | |
|     2. Determination of beneficiary's share of taxable income | |
|     3. Estates and gift taxation | |
| B. Exempt organizations | Chapter 10 |
|     1. Types of organizations | |
|     2. Requirements for exemption | |
|     3. Unrelated business income tax | |
| C. Preparers' responsibilities | Chapter 1 |

# Summary of Coverage

| *Accounting & Reporting – Taxation, Managerial, and Governmental and Not-for-Profit Organizations* | MULTIPLE CHOICE | | | | | OOAFs | | | | |
|---|---|---|---|---|---|---|---|---|---|---|
| | N98 | M98 | N97 | M97 | N96 | N98 | M98 | N97 | M97 | N96 |
| | 75 (60%) | 75 (60%) | 75 (60%) | 75 (60%) | 75 (60%) | 40% | 40% | 40% | 40% | 40% |
| **I. Federal Taxation – Individuals** | 0 | 25 | 7 | 25 | 0 | | | | | |
| A. Inclusions in Gross Income | 0 | 10 | 1 | 9 | 0 | 20% | 0% | 15% | 0% | 20% |
| B. Exclusions & Adjustments to Arrive at AGI | 0 | 3 | 0 | 2 | 0 | | | | | |
| C. Deductions from Adjusted Gross Income | 0 | 7 | 2 | 6 | 0 | | | | | |
| D. Filing Status and Exemptions | 0 | 0 | 1 | 0 | 0 | | | | | |
| E. Tax Accounting Methods | 0 | 1 | 1 | 0 | 0 | | | | | |
| F. Tax Computations, Credits, and Penalties | 0 | 3 | 2 | 3 | 0 | | | | | |
| G. Alternative Minimum Tax | 0 | 1 | 0 | 3 | 0 | | | | | |
| H. Tax Procedures | 0 | 0 | 0 | 2 | 0 | | | | | |
| **II. Federal Taxation -- Corporations** | 25 | 0 | 25 | 0 | 25 | 0% | 20% | 0% | 20% | 0% |
| A. Determination of Taxable Income or Loss | 8 | 0 | 10 | 0 | 8 | | | | 5% | |
| B. Tax Accounting Methods | 1 | 0 | 1 | 0 | 1 | | | | | |
| C. S Corporations | 6 | 0 | 4 | 0 | 3 | | | | 10% | |
| D. Personal Holding Companies | 0 | 0 | 0 | 0 | 0 | | | | | |
| E. Consolidated Returns | 2 | 0 | 2 | 0 | 1 | | | | | |
| F. Tax Computations, Credits, and Penalties | 1 | 0 | 2 | 0 | 3 | | | | | |
| G. Alternative Minimum Tax | 0 | 0 | 0 | 0 | 2 | | | | 5% | |
| H. Other | 7 | 0 | 6 | 0 | 7 | | | | | |
| **III. Federal Taxation -- Partnerships** | 12 | 12 | 0 | 12 | 12 | 0% | 0% | 10% | 0% | 0% |
| A. Basis of Partner's Interest and Bases of Assets Contributed to the Partnership | 3 | 3 | 0 | 3 | 3 | | | | | |
| B. Determination of Partner's Share of Income, Credits, and Deductions | 2 | 3 | 0 | 3 | 2 | | | | | |
| C. Partnership and Partner Elections | 0 | 1 | 0 | 0 | 1 | | | | | |
| D. Partner Dealing with Own Partnership | 1 | 1 | 0 | 1 | 0 | | | | | |
| E. Treatment of Partnership Liabilities | 1 | 1 | 0 | 1 | 2 | | | | | |
| F. Distribution of Partnership Assets | 3 | 3 | 0 | 3 | 2 | | | | | |
| G. Termination of Partnership | 2 | 0 | 0 | 1 | 2 | | | | | |
| **IV. Federal Taxation – Estates & Trusts, Exempt Organizations, and Preparers' Responsibilities** | 7 | 7 | 12 | 7 | 7 | 5% | 5% | 5% | 5% | 5% |
| A. Estates and Trusts | 4 | 5 | 6 | 3 | 5 | 5% | 5% | | 5% | |
| B. Exempt Organizations | 1 | 1 | 3 | 0 | 1 | | | 5% | | |
| C. Preparers' Responsibilities | 2 | 1 | 3 | 4 | 1 | | | | | 5% |

# Chapter One
# Filing Status and Exemptions, Filing Requirements and Penalties

# Chapter One
# Filing Status and Exemptions, Filing Requirements and Penalties

## OVERVIEW TO INDIVIDUAL TAXATION

The taxation of individuals starts with a very basic formula:

> Gross income
> Minus deductions
> Equals taxable income

In the first four chapters, you will examine what makes up the gross income and allowable deductions of individuals. The CPA examination will test you on various components of the income and deductions, as well as various methods of determining the tax and a host of tax credits.

This very basic formula will expand as you are introduced to various classifications of deductions. You will be exposed to limitations on certain deductions based upon thresholds or ceilings, as well as phaseouts for exemptions and special rates. To be sure, there is a lot of complexity. But in the end, it comes back to income minus deductions equals taxable income.

In broad terms, gross income includes all items of income, unless specifically excluded by the Internal Revenue Code. By contrast, nothing is deductible unless specifically allowed by the Code. As a result, you will find that Chapter 2, which deals with inclusions and exclusions of income, is relatively short in comparison to the size of Chapters 3 and 4, which deal with the various deductions.

To help you better understand Chapter 1 and what lies ahead, follow through this simple example.

---

**Example 1:** K is single, aged 63 and earned $12,000 working part-time. In addition, K earned interest income of $500 and dividend income of $400. K also received social security benefits this year of $2,000. K does not itemize her deductions.

**K's taxable income for 1999** is computed as follows:

| | |
|---|---:|
| Salary income | $ 12,000 |
| Interest income | 500 |
| Dividend income | 400 |
| Total gross income | 12,900 |
| Less: Standard deduction | (4,300) |
| Less: Personal exemption | (2,750) |
| Taxable income | $ 5,850 |

---

K's gross income, as more fully explained in Chapter 2, is comprised of salary, interest and dividend income. Social security benefits are not included in gross income unless they pass a threshold test as you will learn about later. Since K does not "itemize" her deductions, she is allowed a standard amount of deductions. You will learn more about itemized deductions in Chapter 4. For 1999, the standard deduction is $4,300 for single taxpayers. The amount of the standard deduction is based upon the filing status of the taxpayer. This is addressed in this chapter. The other deduction is the personal exemption and for 1999 it is $2,750. This, too, is discussed in this chapter.

This is the most comprehensive problem you need to understand in this chapter. Now let's look at the taxpayer's Filing Status and Exemptions in detail.

# FILING STATUS

There are five filing statuses available to individual taxpayers. A taxpayer may choose any status he qualifies for. Since filing status determines your tax rate structure (See Chapter 5 for the complete rate structure) and the amount of your standard deduction, choosing the proper filing status is important in minimizing your taxes.

**1. Single, or unmarried.** If a taxpayer is unmarried on the last day of the tax year, or is separated by a decree of divorce or separate maintenance, that taxpayer is considered single. Assuming the taxpayer does not qualify for a more favorable filing status such as head of household, or qualifying widower, the taxpayer must file as a single taxpayer.

**2. Married Filing Jointly.** To qualify for this status, the taxpayer must be married as of the last day of the year. In the event of the death of the spouse during the year, the spouse need only be alive on the first day of that year in order to qualify as being married for the entire year. Taxpayers are prohibited from filing jointly if their spouse is a non-resident alien or they have different tax year-ends from one another. Couples filing jointly may use different accounting methods in filing their joint return. A further discussion of these accounting methods can be found in Chapter 5.

**3. Married Filing Separately.** Married taxpayers may elect to file separate returns for a number of reasons. Issues of privacy, disclosure of tax returns by public officials, and possible tax planning in the shifting of deductions are some reasons as to why this status is available. In filing a separate return, both taxpayers must agree to either claiming (splitting) the standard deduction, or itemizing their deductions. One cannot itemize and the other claim the standard deduction.

**4. Head of Household.** This status is available to an unmarried taxpayer who:

1. maintains a household and provides for more than 50% of the year the cost for
2. a child, stepchild or descendent of the child, or **any other relative who is a dependent** (as is discussed under exemptions) as a member of his household.

In determining the cost of maintaining the household, you would include the cost of the food consumed in the home, as well as mortgage interest and real estate taxes (or rent), utilities and repairs. A special exception to this rule is that the taxpayer's parents are not required to live with the taxpayer. The taxpayer must maintain more than 50% of the parent's home, or more than 50% of their nursing home costs, in order to qualify. The parent must qualify as the taxpayer's dependent.

**5. Qualifying widow(er) with dependent child.** This is also referred to as surviving spouse. If your spouse dies during the taxable year, you are entitled to file married, filing jointly for that year. In the two years following the death of your spouse, the taxpayer may elect qualifying widow(er) if:

1. The taxpayer has not remarried, and
2. maintains more than 50% of the cost of the home where,
3. the dependent child resides for the entire year.

# STANDARD DEDUCTION

Once the determination of the appropriate filing status has been made, the amount of the standard deductions are as follows:

|  | 1999 |
|---|---|
| Single, or unmarried | $4,300 |
| Married, filing jointly | 7,200 |
| Married, filing separately | 3,600 |
| Head of household | 6,350 |
| Qualifying widow(er) | 7,200 |

You do not need to memorize these amounts. On past exams the candidate has been provided with these amounts as needed. You should, however, understand how amounts change in relation to one another. For example, married filing separately is exactly one-half of the married filing jointly. Qualifying widower provides a larger deduction than head of household. Understanding this helps you as a candidate select the most beneficial filing status.

# ADDITIONAL STANDARD DEDUCTION

There is an additional standard deduction available to the taxpayer who is 65 years or older, or blind. This replaced the "extra exemption" that was available before the 1986 Tax Act. The additional standard deduction is added to the regular standard deduction in the determination of taxable income. The amounts are as follows:

|  | 1999 |
|---|---|
| Single or head of household | $ 1,050 |
| Married or surviving spouse | 850 |

---

**Example 2:** K is single, 67 and blind. For 1999, she is entitled to a total standard deduction of:

| | |
|---|---|
| Regular standard deduction | $ 4,300 |
| Additional standard deductions: | |
|   65 or over | 1,050 |
|   Blind | 1,050 |
| Total standard deduction | $ 6,400 |

---

# EXEMPTIONS

The second deduction introduced in the illustrative **Example 1** was the **exemption.** For 1999, the allowable deduction for an exemption is $2,750. This has been increased from the 1998 amount of $2,700. Exemptions are divided into two types: Personal and Dependency. On the exam, you need to carefully read the each question to determine whether the examiners are asking you about total exemptions, personal exemptions, or dependency exemptions. (Later in Chapter 5, the phaseout of the personal exemption for high income taxpayers is discussed.)

## PERSONAL EXEMPTIONS

### General Rule
In general, each taxpayer is entitled to one personal exemption when filing their return. When a taxpayer files married filing jointly, they are entitled to two personal exemptions. Even when married filing separately, the taxpayer may claim two personal exemptions provided that the spouse has no gross income and is not the dependent of another taxpayer.

### Exceptions
No exemption amount is allowed for a taxpayer who is **allowed** to be claimed as a dependent of another taxpayer.

> **Example 3:** K is allowed to claim P, her ten year old son, as her dependent. When P files his return, he is not entitled to a personal exemption because K is allowed to claim P.

## DEPENDENCY EXEMPTIONS

### General Rule
When filing a return, a taxpayer is allowed a deduction for each qualifying dependent. There are five basic requirements for qualifying as a dependent.

- Support test
- Gross income test
- Relationship test
- Joint return test
- Citizenship test

**1. Support Test:** The dependent must receive more than 50% of their support from the taxpayer. Support includes, but is not limited to room and board, medical expenses, tuition payments, and purchasing of capital assets such as a car. In determining the percentage, the total support is based upon the amounts expended.

> **Example 4:** If K paid $4,000 for her son's room, board and medical costs; and her son earned and saved $1,000 from his paper route, K would have provided 100% of his support. Since his earnings were saved and not used for his support, they are not considered in determining his total support requirement.

**2. Gross Income Test:** The dependent's gross income must be less than the exemption amount. For 1998, this amount is $2,750.

**3. Relationship Test:** The dependent must have at least one of the following relationships with the taxpayer:

1. Son, daughter, or descendant (grandchild)
2. Stepson or stepdaughter
3. Brother, sister, stepbrother, or stepsister
4. Father, mother, or ancestor (grandparent)
5. Stepfather or stepmother
6. Nephew or niece
7. Uncle or aunt
8. In-laws: Son, daughter, father, mother, brother or sister
9. None of the above, but only if the individual is a member of the taxpayer's household for the entire year. On the exam this could be a good friend of the family, like an "Uncle Charlie" who is really not an uncle, but lives with you for the entire year as his principal abode.

Caution: Cousins are not considered a relationship unless they meet the ninth criteria.

**4. Joint Return Test:** The dependent does not file a joint return with his spouse (if married).

**5. Citizenship Test:** The dependent must be a citizen or resident of the United States, or resident of Canada or Mexico.

In addition, no dependency exemption deduction or dependent care credit will be allowed unless the taxpayer's identification number is included on the return.

## EXCEPTIONS TO DEPENDENCY RULES

Frequently tested exceptions to the five general dependency rules are as follows:

**Multiple Support Agreements:** In determining support, it is not unusual that one taxpayer alone does not provide more than 50% support of a dependent. Suppose several adult children support an elderly parent for part of a year, yet no one provides more than 50% of their support. When this occurs, taxpayers may enter into a multiple support agreement to allow one of the eligible taxpayers to claim them as dependent. To qualify under the multiple support agreement, the rules state:

1. Those party to the agreement must meet the other four dependency requirements.
2. To be entitled to the deduction, you must contribute more than 10% of the support.
3. No one party contributes more than 50% of the support.
4. The written consent must be filed with the return.

**Support of Divorced or Separated Parents:** In general, the custodial parent is entitled to the dependency deduction regardless of the amount of support provided. For agreements after 1984, the non-custodial parent is entitled to the dependency exemption only if written consent is given by the custodial parent. For agreements before 1985, the non-custodial parent must contribute at least $600 towards the support of the child in order to claim the exemption.

**Gross Income of Dependent Children Under Age 19:** There is no upper limit to the amount of gross income a dependent child under the age of 19 can earn.

**Gross Income of Dependent Children Under Age 24:** If a child under the age of 24 is a full-time student for at least five months of the tax year, there is no upper limit to the amount of gross income the child can earn.

**Filing of Joint Return:** If dependent is not required to file a joint return, but does so only to receive a refund of withheld taxes, then this does not disqualify the child as a dependent.

> **Example 5:** K's son P is 20 years old and attends college with his wife M. K provides 80% of P and M's support. P and M earned $2,000 working in the college bookstore and are not required to file a return. P and M file a return only to receive back the $60 withheld in federal income taxes. P does not violate the joint return test. K may claim P and M as her dependents.

## FILING REQUIREMENTS

Individuals must file a tax return if certain levels of gross income have been received by the taxpayer. Generally, that level represents the appropriate standard deduction plus the exemption amount.

> **Example 6:** A single taxpayer claiming the standard deduction would be required to file a return for 1999 if his gross income exceeded $7,050.
>
> |  | 1999 |
> | --- | --- |
> | Standard deduction | $ 4,300 |
> | Personal exemptions | 2,750 |
> | Threshold for filing | $ 7,050 |

Using the standard deduction and exemption amounts previously discussed, you can easily determine the filing requirements for taxpayers **under the age of 65\*** as follows:

|  | 1999 |
| --- | --- |
| Single | $ 7,050 |
| Married, filing jointly | 12,700 |
| Married, filing separately** | 2,750 |
| Head of household | 9,100 |
| Surviving spouse | 9,950 |

\* Note that for taxpayers **65 or older, or blind,** add the additional standard deduction ($1,050 or $850) as appropriate.

\*\* Note that for married, filing separately, the filing threshold is only the exemption amount. The low threshold is because of the rule related to both spouses using the same election as to the standard or itemized deductions. This, in essence, forces a return to be filed.

## WHEN TO FILE

Tax returns (Form 1040) are due on or before the 15th day of the fourth month following the close of the taxable year. For most taxpayers who file on a calendar year, this means April 15th. By filing Form 4868, a taxpayer may request an extension of up to four months of time to file their return. An additional two months may be requested by filing Form 2688. *A copy of both pages of Form 1040 is presented at the end of this chapter.*

# STATUTE OF LIMITATIONS

## General Rule

Once a return is filed, the government can audit the return at any time during the three year period beginning on the latest of (1) the date the return was filed, or (2) the due date of the return. This is the same time period a taxpayer has to amend a tax return as well.

> **Example 7:** K files her 1999 return on March 11, 2000. The statute of limitations expires on April 15, 2003.
>
> **Example 8:** Instead, K files her 1999 return late on November 10, 2000. The statute of limitations expires on November 10, 2003.

## Omission of Income

When there is an understatement of gross income by at least 25% of the amount reported on the return, the statute extends from three years to six years.

**Example 9:** K reported gross income of $20,000 from her salary but failed to report $6,000 she received as an award. K believed that the award was not taxable, but it really was. Since she omitted at least 25% of the amount report on her return (25% of $20,000, or $5,000), the IRS has a six year period to audit the return.

## Fraudulent Return

When a taxpayer files a fraudulent return, the statute of limitations does not begin to run. The return may be audited at any time.

## Failure to File a Return

Should a taxpayer fail to file a return, the statute does not begin to run. Once the tax return is filed, the statute runs from that date.

## Other Statute Provisions

In requesting a refund for prior taxes paid, the statute is the later of (1) the three year period, or (2) two years from the date the tax was paid. The taxpayer would file Form 1040X to amend a tax return previously filed.

If the nature of the refund is from a bad debt or worthless security, the statute is seven years rather than three years.

# PREPARER RESPONSIBILITIES

The exam routinely tests candidates on their responsibility as return preparers. The number of penalties which may be assessed on a paid preparer is staggering and would take pages to simply list, let alone describe. A summary will follow, but the thrust of the law addresses the professional due diligence which should be evident as we prepare returns. Logically, not signing returns, showing returns to unauthorized individuals, endorsing refund checks, not providing tax return copies, or willfully understating a tax liability are acts that should be penalized. Let your sound professional judgment dictate your answer on the exam if you do not remember all the issues.

## PROCEDURAL PENALTIES

$50 for failure to furnish a copy of the return to the taxpayer

$50 for failure to maintain copy, or list of returns prepared

$50 for failure to sign a return

$50 for failure to include preparer's identification number

$500 for the endorsement of refund checks payable to taxpayer

## OTHER PENALTIES

$250 for understating a taxpayer's tax liability due to an unrealistic position

$1,000 for a willful attempt to understate taxes, including reckless or intentional disregard

Besides penalties, tax preparers may be barred from practicing before the IRS if they do not comply with the provisions of **Circular 230**. Two major provisions include:

1. Tax preparer should promptly advise the taxpayer of any error or omission on a return, or lack of compliance with any federal tax law.
2. Tax preparer should exercise due diligence in the preparation of returns and in any representations to the IRS or taxpayers.

Form **1040**  Department of the Treasury—Internal Revenue Service
**U.S. Individual Income Tax Return** **1999**  (99)  IRS Use Only—Do not write or staple in this space.

For the year Jan. 1–Dec. 31, 1999, or other tax year beginning , 1999, ending , OMB No. 1545-0074

## Label
(See instructions on page 18.)

Use the IRS label. Otherwise, please print or type.

| L A B E L  H E R E | Your first name and initial | Last name | Your social security number |
| | If a joint return, spouse's first name and initial | Last name | Spouse's social security number |
| | Home address (number and street). If you have a P.O. box, see page 18. | Apt. no. | ▲ **IMPORTANT!** ▲ You **must** enter your SSN(s) above. |
| | City, town or post office, state, and ZIP code. If you have a foreign address, see page 18. | | |

**Presidential Election Campaign** (See page 18.)
▶ Do you want $3 to go to this fund? . . . . . . . . .
If a joint return, does your spouse want $3 to go to this fund? . . . . . . .

Yes  No  Note. Checking "Yes" will not change your tax or reduce your refund.

## Filing Status

Check only one box.

1 ☐ Single
2 ☐ Married filing joint return (even if only one had income)
3 ☐ Married filing separate return. Enter spouse's social security no. above and full name here. ▶ _____
4 ☐ Head of household (with qualifying person). (See page 18.) If the qualifying person is a child but not your dependent, enter this child's name here. ▶ _____
5 ☐ Qualifying widow(er) with dependent child (year spouse died ▶ 19    ). (See page 18.)

## Exemptions

If more than six dependents, see page 19.

6a ☐ **Yourself.** If your parent (or someone else) can claim you as a dependent on his or her tax return, **do not** check box 6a . . . . . . . . . . .
b ☐ **Spouse** . . . . . . . . . . . . . . . . . . . . . . .

c Dependents:

| (1) First name  Last name | (2) Dependent's social security number | (3) Dependent's relationship to you | (4) ✓ if qualifying child for child tax credit (see page 19) |
|---|---|---|---|
| | | | ☐ |
| | | | ☐ |
| | | | ☐ |
| | | | ☐ |
| | | | ☐ |
| | | | ☐ |

No. of boxes checked on 6a and 6b ____

No. of your children on 6c who:
• lived with you ____
• did not live with you due to divorce or separation (see page 19) ____

Dependents on 6c not entered above ____

Add numbers entered on lines above ▶ ☐

d Total number of exemptions claimed . . . . . . . . . . . .

## Income

Attach Copy B of your Forms W-2 and W-2G here. Also attach Form(s) 1099-R if tax was withheld.

If you did not get a W-2, see page 20.

Enclose, but do not staple, any payment. Also, please use Form 1040-V.

7 Wages, salaries, tips, etc. Attach Form(s) W-2 . . . . . . . . | 7 |
8a Taxable interest. Attach Schedule B if required . . . . . . . | 8a |
b Tax-exempt interest. DO NOT include on line 8a . . . | 8b | |
9 Ordinary dividends. Attach Schedule B if required . . . . . . | 9 |
10 Taxable refunds, credits, or offsets of state and local income taxes (see page 21) . . | 10 |
11 Alimony received . . . . . . . . . . . . . . . . . | 11 |
12 Business income or (loss). Attach Schedule C or C-EZ . . . . . | 12 |
13 Capital gain or (loss). Attach Schedule D if required. If not required, check here ▶ ☐ | 13 |
14 Other gains or (losses). Attach Form 4797 . . . . . . . . . | 14 |
15a Total IRA distributions . | 15a | b Taxable amount (see page 22) | 15b |
16a Total pensions and annuities | 16a | b Taxable amount (see page 22) | 16b |
17 Rental real estate, royalties, partnerships, S corporations, trusts, etc. Attach Schedule E | 17 |
18 Farm income or (loss). Attach Schedule F . . . . . . . . . | 18 |
19 Unemployment compensation . . . . . . . . . . . . | 19 |
20a Social security benefits . | 20a | b Taxable amount (see page 24) | 20b |
21 Other income. List type and amount (see page 24) ................... | 21 |
22 Add the amounts in the far right column for lines 7 through 21. This is your **total income** ▶ | 22 |

## Adjusted Gross Income

23 IRA deduction (see page 26) . . . . . | 23 |
24 Student loan interest deduction (see page 26) . . . . | 24 |
25 Medical savings account deduction. Attach Form 8853 . | 25 |
26 Moving expenses. Attach Form 3903 . . . | 26 |
27 One-half of self-employment tax. Attach Schedule SE . | 27 |
28 Self-employed health insurance deduction (see page 28) | 28 |
29 Keogh and self-employed SEP and SIMPLE plans . . | 29 |
30 Penalty on early withdrawal of savings . . . . . | 30 |
31a Alimony paid b Recipient's SSN ▶ | 31a |
32 Add lines 23 through 31a . . . . . . . . . . | 32 |
33 Subtract line 32 from line 22. This is your **adjusted gross income** . . . . ▶ | 33 |

For Disclosure, Privacy Act, and Paperwork Reduction Act Notice, see page 54.  Cat. No. 11320B  Form **1040** (1999)

| | | | | 34 | |
|---|---|---|---|---|---|
| **Tax and Credits** | 34 | Amount from line 33 (adjusted gross income) . . . . . . . . . | | 34 | |
| | 35a | Check if: ☐ **You** were 65 or older, ☐ Blind; ☐ **Spouse** was 65 or older, ☐ Blind. Add the number of boxes checked above and enter the total here . . . ▶ 35a | | | |
| | b | If you are married filing separately and your spouse itemizes deductions or you were a dual-status alien, see page 30 and check here . . . . . . ▶ 35b ☐ | | | |
| **Standard Deduction for Most People** | 36 | Enter your **itemized deductions** from Schedule A, line 28, **OR standard deduction** shown on the left. **But see page 30 to find your standard deduction if you checked any box on line 35a or 35b or** if someone can claim you as a dependent . . . . . . | | 36 | |
| **Single:** $4,300 | 37 | Subtract line 36 from line 34 | | 37 | |
| **Head of household:** $6,350 | 38 | If line 34 is $94,975 or less, multiply $2,750 by the total number of exemptions claimed on line 6d. If line 34 is over $94,975, see the worksheet on page 31 for the amount to enter . | | 38 | |
| **Married filing jointly or Qualifying widow(er):** $7,200 | 39 | **Taxable income.** Subtract line 38 from line 37. If line 38 is more than line 37, enter -0- | | 39 | |
| | 40 | **Tax** (see page 31). Check if any tax is from **a** ☐ Form(s) 8814 **b** ☐ Form 4972 . . ▶ | | 40 | |
| **Married filing separately:** $3,600 | 41 | Credit for child and dependent care expenses. Attach Form 2441 | 41 | | |
| | 42 | Credit for the elderly or the disabled. Attach Schedule R . . | 42 | | |
| | 43 | Child tax credit (see page 33) . . . . . . . . . | 43 | | |
| | 44 | Education credits. Attach Form 8863 . . . . . . | 44 | | |
| | 45 | Adoption credit. Attach Form 8839 . . . . . . | 45 | | |
| | 46 | Foreign tax credit. Attach Form 1116 if required . . . . | 46 | | |
| | 47 | Other. Check if from **a** ☐ Form 3800 **b** ☐ Form 8396 **c** ☐ Form 8801 **d** ☐ Form (specify)_____ | 47 | | |
| | 48 | Add lines 41 through 47. These are your **total credits** . . . . . . . . | | 48 | |
| | 49 | Subtract line 48 from line 40. If line 48 is more than line 40, enter -0- . . . . . ▶ | | 49 | |
| **Other Taxes** | 50 | Self-employment tax. Attach Schedule SE . . . . . | | 50 | |
| | 51 | Alternative minimum tax. Attach Form 6251 . . . . . . . . . | | 51 | |
| | 52 | Social security and Medicare tax on tip income not reported to employer. Attach Form 4137 | | 52 | |
| | 53 | Tax on IRAs, other retirement plans, and MSAs. Attach Form 5329 if required . . . | | 53 | |
| | 54 | Advance earned income credit payments from Form(s) W-2 . . . . . . . | | 54 | |
| | 55 | Household employment taxes. Attach Schedule H . . . . . . . . . . | | 55 | |
| | 56 | Add lines 49 through 55. This is your **total tax** . . . . . . . . . . . ▶ | | 56 | |
| **Payments** | 57 | Federal income tax withheld from Forms W-2 and 1099 . . | 57 | | |
| | 58 | 1999 estimated tax payments and amount applied from 1998 return . | 58 | | |
| | 59a | **Earned income credit.** Attach Sch. EIC if you have a qualifying child | | | |
| | b | Nontaxable earned income: amount . . ▶ ⌐_____⌐ and type ▶ --------------------- | 59a | | |
| | 60 | Additional child tax credit. Attach Form 8812 . . . . . | 60 | | |
| | 61 | Amount paid with request for extension to file (see page 48) | 61 | | |
| | 62 | Excess social security and RRTA tax withheld (see page 48) | 62 | | |
| | 63 | Other payments. Check if from **a** ☐ Form 2439 **b** ☐ Form 4136 | 63 | | |
| | 64 | Add lines 57, 58, 59a, and 60 through 63. These are your **total payments** . . . . ▶ | | 64 | |
| **Refund** Have it directly deposited! See page 48 and fill in 66b, 66c, and 66d. | 65 | If line 64 is more than line 56, subtract line 56 from line 64. This is the amount you **OVERPAID** | | 65 | |
| | 66a | Amount of line 65 you want **REFUNDED TO YOU** . . . . . . . . . ▶ | | 66a | |
| | ▶ b | Routing number | | | ▶ c Type: ☐ Checking ☐ Savings |
| | ▶ d | Account number | | | |
| | 67 | Amount of line 65 you want **APPLIED TO YOUR 2000 ESTIMATED TAX** ▶ | 67 | | |
| **Amount You Owe** | 68 | If line 56 is more than line 64, subtract line 64 from line 56. This is the **AMOUNT YOU OWE.** For details on how to pay, see page 49 . . . . . . . . . . . . ▶ | | 68 | |
| | 69 | Estimated tax penalty. Also include on line 68 . . . . | 69 | | |

**Sign Here**
Joint return? See page 18.
Keep a copy for your records.

Under penalties of perjury, I declare that I have examined this return and accompanying schedules and statements, and to the best of my knowledge and belief, they are true, correct, and complete. Declaration of preparer (other than taxpayer) is based on all information of which preparer has any knowledge.

| Your signature | | Date | Your occupation | | Daytime telephone number (optional) ( ) |
|---|---|---|---|---|---|
| ▶ | | | | | |
| Spouse's signature. If a joint return, BOTH must sign. | | Date | Spouse's occupation | | |

**Paid Preparer's Use Only**

| Preparer's signature ▶ | | Date | | Check if self-employed ☐ | Preparer's SSN or PTIN |
|---|---|---|---|---|---|
| Firm's name (or yours if self-employed) and address | ▶ | | | | EIN |
| | | | | | ZIP code |

Form **1040** (1999)

# Chapter One -- Questions
## Filing Status and Exemptions, Filing Requirements and Penalties

### Filing Status

1. John and Mary Arnold are a childless, married couple who lived apart (alone in homes maintained by each) the entire year. On December 31, 1999, they were legally separated under a decree of separate maintenance. Which of the following is the only filing status choice available to them when filing for 1999?
a. Single.
b. Head of household.
c. Married filing separate return.
d. Married filing joint return.

2. A husband and wife can file a joint return even if
a. The spouses have different tax years, provided that both spouses are alive at the end of the year.
b. The spouses have different accounting methods.
c. Either spouse was a nonresident alien at any time during the tax year, provided that at least one spouse makes the proper election.
d. They were divorced before the end of the tax year.

3. During 1999 Robert Moore, who is 50 years old and unmarried, maintained his home in which he and his widower father, age 75, resided. His father had $2,800 interest income from a savings account and also received $2,400 from social security during 1999. Robert provided 60% of his father's total support for 1999. What is Robert's filing status for 1999, and how many exemptions should he claim on his tax return?
a. Head of household and 2 exemptions.
b. Single and 2 exemptions.
c. Head of household and 1 exemption.
d. Single and 1 exemption.

4. Murray Richman, who is 60 years old and unmarried, was the sole support of his aged mother. His mother was a resident of a home for the aged for the entire year and had no income. What is Richman's filing status, and how many exemptions should he claim on his tax return?
a. Head of household and 2 exemptions.
b. Single and 2 exemptions.
c. Head of household and 1 exemption.
d. Single and 1 exemption.

5. Emil Gow's wife died in 1997. Emil did not remarry, and he continued to maintain a home for himself and his dependent infant child during 1998 and 1999, providing full support for himself and his child during these years. For 1997, Emil properly filed a joint return. For 1999, Emil's filing status is
a. Single.
b. Head of household.
c. Qualifying widower with dependent child.
d. Married filing joint return.

6. Which of the following is(are) among the requirements to enable a taxpayer to be classified as a "qualifying widow(er)" ?

I. A dependent has lived with the taxpayer for six months.
II. The taxpayer has maintained the cost of the principal residence for six months.

a. I only.
b. II only.
c. Both I and II.
d. Neither I nor II.

### Exemptions

7. Mark Erickson, age 46, filed a joint return for 1999 with his wife Helen, age 24. Their son John was born on December 16, 1999. Mark provided 60% of the support for his 72-year-old widowed mother until April 10, 1999, when she died. His mother's only income was from social security benefits totaling $2,200 during 1999. How many exemptions should the Erickson's claim on their 1999 tax return?
a. 2.
b. 3.
c. 4.
d. 5.

8. Jim and Kay Ross contributed to the support of their two children, Dale and Kim, and Jim's widowed parent, Grant. For 1999, Dale, a 19-year old full-time college student, earned $4,500 as a baby-sitter. Kim, a 23-year old bank teller, earned $12,000. Grant received $5,000 in dividend income and $4,000 in nontaxable social security benefits. Grant, Dale, and Kim are U.S. citizens and were over one-half supported by Jim and Kay. How many exemptions can Jim and Kay claim on their 1999 joint income tax return?

a. Two.
b. Three.
c. Four.
d. Five.


9. Mr. and Mrs. Brook, both age 62, filed a joint return for this taxable year. They provided all the support for their son who is 19, legally blind, and who had no income. Their daughter, age 21 and a full-time student at a university, had $4,200 of income and provided 70% of her own support. How many exemptions should Mr. and Mrs. Brook have claimed on their joint income tax return?

a. 5.
b. 4.
c. 3.
d. 2.


10. Albert and Lois Stoner, age 66 and 64, respectively, filed a joint tax return for this taxable year. They provided all of the support for their blind 19-year-old son, who has no gross income. Their 23-year-old daughter, a full-time student until her graduation on June 14, earned $2,000, which was 40% of her total support during the year. Her parents provided the remaining support. The Stoner's also provided the total support of Lois' father, who is a citizen and life-long resident of Peru. How many exemptions can the Stoner's claim on their income tax return?

a. 4.
b. 5.
c. 6.
d. 7.


11. During the year, Sam Dunn provided more than half the support for his wife, his father's brother, and his cousin. Sam's wife was the only relative who was a member of Sam's household. None of the relatives had any income, nor did any of them file an individual or a joint return. All of these relatives are U.S. citizens. Which of these relatives should be claimed as a dependent or dependents on Sam's return?

a. Only his wife.
b. Only his father's brother.
c. Only his cousin.
d. His wife, his father's brother, and his cousin.


12. Mary Dunn provided 20% of her own support; the remaining 80% was provided by her three sons as follows:

| Bill | 15% |
|------|-----|
| Jon | 25% |
| Tom | 40% |
| | 80% |

Assume that a multiple support agreement exists and that the brothers will sign multiple support declarations as required. Which of the brothers is eligible to claim the mother as a dependent?

a. None of the brothers.
b. Tom only.
c. Jon or Tom only.
d. Bill, Jon or Tom.


13. Sara Hance, who is single and lives alone in Idaho, has no income of her own and is supported in full by the following persons:

| | Amount of support | Percent of total |
|---|---|---|
| Alma (an unrelated friend) | $2,400 | 48 |
| Ben (Sara's brother) | 2,150 | 43 |
| Carl (Sara's son) | 450 | 9 |
| | $5,000 | 100 |

Under a multiple support agreement, Sara's dependency exemption can be claimed by

a. No one.
b. Alma.
c. Ben.
d. Carl.


14. Joe and Barb are married, but Barb refuses to sign a 1999 joint return. On Joe's separate 1999 return, an exemption may be claimed for Barb if

a. Barb was a full-time student for the entire 1999 school year.
b. Barb attaches a written statement to Joe's income tax return, agreeing to be claimed as an exemption by Joe for 1999.
c. Barb was under the age of 19.
d. Barb had **no** gross income and was **not** claimed as another person's dependent in 1999.

15. In 1999, Smith, a divorced person, provided over one half the support for his widowed mother, Ruth, and his son, Clay, both of whom are U.S. citizens. During 1999, Ruth did not live with Smith. She received $9,000 in social security benefits. Clay, a full-time graduate student, and his wife lived with Smith. Clay had no income but filed a joint return for 1999, owing an additional $500 in taxes on his wife's income. How many exemptions was Smith entitled to claim on his 1999 tax return?

a. 4.
b. 3.
c. 2.
d. 1.

16. Al and Mary Lew are married and filed a joint 1999 income tax return in which they validly claimed the personal exemption for their dependent 17-year old daughter, Doris. Since Doris earned $5,400 in 1999 from a part-time job at the college she attended full-time, Doris was also required to file a 1999 income tax return. What amount was Doris entitled to claim as a personal exemption in her 1999 individual income tax return?

a. $0
b. $650
c. $2,700
d. $4,250

17. For head of household filing status, which of the following costs are considered in determining whether the taxpayer has contributed more than one-half the cost of maintaining the household?

|   | Food consumed in the home | Value of services rendered in the home by the taxpayer |
|---|---|---|
| a. | Yes | Yes |
| b. | No | No |
| c. | Yes | No |
| d. | No | Yes |

18. Nell Brown's husband died in 1996. Nell did not remarry, and continued to maintain a home for herself and her dependent infant child during 1997, 1998, and 1999, providing full support for herself and her child during these three years. For 1996, Nell properly filed a joint return. For 1999, Nell's filing status is

a. Single.
b. Married filing joint return.
c. Head of household.
d. Qualifying widow with dependent child.

## Filing Requirements and Penalties

19. A calendar-year taxpayer files an individual tax return for 1996 on March 20, 1997. The taxpayer neither committed fraud nor omitted amounts in excess of 25% of gross income on the tax return. What is the latest date that the Internal Revenue Service can assess tax and assert a notice of deficiency?

a. March 20, 2000.
b. March 20, 1999.
c. April 15, 2000.
d. April 15, 1999.

20. Leo Mann, a calendar-year taxpayer, filed his 1996 individual income tax return on March 15, 1997, and attached a check for the balance of tax due as shown on the return. On June 15, 1997, Leo discovered that he had failed to include, in his itemized deductions, $1,000 interest on his home mortgage. In order for Leo to recover the tax that he would have saved by utilizing the $1,000 deduction, he must file an amended return no later than

a. December 31, 1999.
b. March 15, 2000.
c. April 15, 2000.
d. June 15, 2000.

21. On April 15, 1994, a married couple filed their joint 1993 calendar-year return showing gross income of $120,000. Their return had been prepared by a professional tax preparer who mistakenly omitted $45,000 of income, which the preparer in good faith considered to be nontaxable. No information with regard to this omitted income was disclosed on the return or attached statements. By what date must the Internal Revenue Service assert a notice of deficiency before the statute of limitations expires?

a. April 15, 2000.
b. December 31, 1999.
c. April 15, 1997.
d. December 31, 1996.

22. Richard Baker filed his 1991 individual income tax return on April 15, 1992. On December 31, 1992, he learned that 100 shares of stock that he owned had become worthless in 1991. Since he did not deduct this loss on his 1991 return, Baker intends to file a claim for refund. This refund claim must be filed no later than April 15

a. 1993.
b. 1995.
c. 1998.
d. 1999.

23. A claim for refund of erroneously paid income taxes, filed by an individual before the statute of limitations expires, must be submitted on Form
a. 1139
b. 1045
c. 1040X
d. 843

24. Harold Thompson, a self-employed individual, had income transactions for 1999 (duly reported on his return filed in April 2000) as follows:

| | |
|---|---|
| Gross receipts | $400,000 |
| Less cost of goods sold and deductions | 320,000 |
| Net business income | $ 80,000 |
| Capital gains | 36,000 |
| Gross income | $116,000 |

In March 2001 Thompson discovers that he had inadvertently omitted some income on his 1999 return and retains Mann, CPA, to determine his position under the statute of limitations. Mann should advise Thompson that the six-year statute of limitations would apply to his 1999 return only if he omitted from gross income an amount in excess of
a. $20,000
b. $29,000
c. $100,000
d. $109,000

25. If an individual paid income tax in 1999 but did **not** file a 1999 return because his income was insufficient to require the filing of a return, the deadline for filing a refund claim is
a. Two years from the date the tax was paid.
b. Two years from the date a return would have been due.
c. Three years from the date the tax was paid.
d. Three years from the date a return would have been due.

26. A married couple filed their joint 1996 calendar-year return on March 15, 1997 and attached a check for the balance of tax due as shown on the return. On June 15, 1998, the couple discovered that they had failed to include $2,000 of home mortgage interest in their itemized deductions. In order for the couple to recover the tax that they would have saved by using the $2,000 deduction, they must file an amended return no later than

a. December 31, 1999.
b. March 15, 2000.
c. April 15, 2000.
d. June 15, 2000.

27. An accuracy-related penalty applies to the portion of tax underpayment attributable to

I.   Negligence or a disregard of the tax rules or regulations.
II.  Any substantial understatement of income tax.

a. I only.
b. II only.
c. Both I and II.
d. Neither I nor II.

28. A tax return preparer is subject to a penalty for knowingly or recklessly disclosing corporate tax return information, if the disclosure is made
a. To enable a third party to solicit business from the taxpayer.
b. To enable the tax processor to electronically compute the taxpayer's liability.
c. For peer review.
d. Under an administrative order by a state agency that registers tax return preparers.

29. A tax return preparer may disclose or use tax return information without the taxpayer's consent to
a.   Facilitate a supplier's or lender's credit evaluation of the taxpayer.
b.   Accommodate the request of a financial institution that needs to determine the amount of taxpayer's debt to it, to be forgiven.
c.   Be evaluated by a quality or peer review.
d.   Solicit additional nontax business.

30. Which, if any, of the following could result in penalties against an income tax return preparer?

I.   Knowing or reckless disclosure or use of tax information obtained in preparing a return.
II.  A willful attempt to understate any client's tax liability on a return or claim for refund.

a.   Neither I nor II.
b.   I only.
c.   II only.
d.   Both I and II.

## Released and Author Constructed Questions

*R97*

31. Morgan, a sole practitioner CPA, prepares individual and corporate income tax returns. What documentation is Morgan required to retain concerning each return prepared?

a. An unrelated party compliance statement.
b. Taxpayer's name and identification number or a copy of the tax return.
c. Workpapers associated with the preparation of each tax return.
d. A power of attorney.

# Chapter One -- Answers
# Filing Status and Exemptions, Filing Requirements and Penalties

1. (a) Single. A taxpayer's filing status is determined on the last day of the taxable year. On December 31, 1999, John and Mary were legally separated under a decree of separate maintenance and therefore, not married. Since they did not have a child, they would not qualify as head of household. Single is the only status available.

2. (b) Husbands and wives cannot file a joint return if they have different tax years, if one is a non-resident alien, or they were divorced as of the end of the year. They are not, however, required to use the same accounting methods.

3. (d) Single and 1 exemption. Robert does not qualify for head of household because his father does not qualify as his dependent. His father does not qualify as his dependent because he fails the gross income test. The gross income of $2,800 from interest income exceeds the exemption amount of $2,750 for 1999. Social security is not a component of gross income at this income level.

4. (a) Murray qualifies as head of household because he is (1) unmarried; (2) maintains support for his mother at a home for the aged (parents do not have to reside in the taxpayer's home); and (3) may claim his mother as his dependent.

5. (c) Qualifying widower with dependent child. This is sometimes referred to as surviving spouse. In the year of death, Emil would have filed married, filing jointly. However, for the two years after that, Emil qualifies for this status provided he (1) has not remarried and (2) maintains a home for himself and a dependent child.

6. (d) Neither I nor II. In order to qualify as qualifying widower (or surviving spouse), your **child** must qualify as your dependent and must reside with you for the entire year. Also, you must maintain more than 50% of the cost of your household for the **entire year**.

7. (c) 4. Mark is entitled to two personal exemptions and two dependency exemptions. Their new son qualifies because he was born before the end of the year. His mother qualifies because he met the support test until she died and she did not violate the gross income test. Social security benefits are not considered gross income at this income level.

8. (b) 3. Jim and Kay may claim two personal exemptions for themselves and one dependency exemption for Dale. The children, Dale and Kim, and the father, Grant, meet the support, relationship and citizenship test. The only issue is gross income because all three earned more than the 1999 exemption amount of $2,750. Dale is not **under** 19, but under 24 and is a full-time student. He meets the exception to the gross income limitation and therefore qualifies as a dependent. Kim is also under 24, but is not a full-time student. She violates the gross income test and does not qualify. Grant, the parent, has gross income of $5,000. He does not qualify either.

9. (c) 3. The Brooks are allowed two personal exemptions and one dependency exemption for their son. Their daughter does not qualify because of the support test. There is no exception to the support test (even though she is a full-time student).

10. (a) 4. The Stoners are allowed two personal exemptions and two dependency exemptions for their children. Stoner's father does not qualify because he fails the citizenship test. Note there are no extra exemptions because the taxpayer, or dependents are 65 and over, or blind.

11. (b) Father's brother. This question specifically asks about the dependency exemption, not the personal. Sam's uncle qualifies because he satisfies the relationship test and therefore does not need to be a member of the household. Sam's cousin does not qualify as a dependent because he is not a relative and as a result must be a member of the household for the entire year, which he was not.

12. (d) Bill, Jon or Tom. Classic multiple support problem. All three sons are qualified to claim Mom as their dependent but no one person contributes more than 50%. Since each son contributed more than 10% of her support, each is eligible to claim her.

13. (c) Ben. Only Ben and Carl are initially qualified to claim Sara as a dependent. Ben and Carl contribute $2,600 of the $5,000 for a combined percentage of 52%. However, since Carl contributes less than 10%, he is not eligible to claim her as a dependent. Only Ben is eligible. Note that Alma cannot be party to this arrangement because she is not related to Sara. Sara would have to reside with Alma for the entire year in order to qualify under the relationship test.

14. (d) By definition. This would be a personal exemption on Joe's return.

15. (c) 2. Smith is entitled to one personal exemption and one dependency exemption for his mother Ruth. A mother does not have to live with the taxpayer to be considered a dependent. Clay was required to file a return (they owed additional taxes) and therefore cannot be claimed as a dependent even though the other tests were met.

16. (a) $0. Since Al and Mary were allowed to claim Doris as their dependent, Doris is not entitled to a personal exemption for herself when she files.

17. (c) In determining the cost of maintaining the household, you would include the cost of the food consumed in the home, as well as mortgage interest and real estate taxes (or rent), utilities and repairs. The value of services is not included.

18. (c) Nell qualifies as head of household because she is not married, maintains a household and provides for more than 50% of the year the cost for her child. The filing status of qualifying widow is available only for the two tax years after the year of her husband's death.

19. (c) April 15, 2000. The three-year statute runs from the date the return was filed, or April 15th, whichever is later.

20. (c) April 15, 2000. The three-year statute runs from the date the return was filed, or April 15th, whichever is later.

21. (a) April 15, 2000. Whereas the taxpayer mistakenly omitted more than 25% of the gross income reported on the return, the statute increases to six years. The six-year statute runs from the date the return was filed, or April 15th, whichever is later.

| | |
|---|---|
| Gross income reported | $ 120,000 |
| Statute percentage | 25% |
| Underreporting threshold | $ 30,000 |
| | |
| Amount not reported | $ 45,000 |

22. (d) 1999. A refund claim due to worthless stock is seven years. The seven-year statute runs from the date the return was filed, or April 15th, whichever is later.

23. (c) Form 1040X. This is the individual amended return form. Form 1139 is a claim for refund for corporations; Form 1045 is for refunds due to operating loss carrybacks; and Form 843 is for refunds due to overpayment of employment, gift and estate taxes.

24. (d)  $109,000.  The six year statute applies if the taxpayer omits more than 25% of the gross income reported on the return.  Gross income represents:

| | |
|---|---:|
| Gross receipts | $ 400,000 |
| Capital gain | 36,000 |
| Gross income | 436,000 |
| Statutory rate | 25% |
| Threshold | $ 109,000 |

25. (a)  In requesting a refund for prior taxes paid, the statute is the later of (1) the three year period, or (2) two years from the date the tax was paid.  Since no return was filed, it would two years from when the tax was paid.

26. (c)  April 15, 2000.  In requesting a refund for prior taxes paid, the statute is the later of (1) the three year period, or (2) two years from the date the tax was paid.  The statute begins running on the due date of the return or the date the return was filed, whichever is later.  In this case, even though the taxpayer filed on March 15, 1997, the statute does not begin to run until April 15, 1997.  The taxpayer would file Form 1040X to amend the tax return previously filed.

27. (c)  By definition.

28. (a)  A return preparer's responsibilities limit the disclosure or use of a client's tax return.  A preparer is allowed to disclose information for quality review, the electronic filing processor, and a governing state agency.

29. (c)  A return preparer's responsibilities limit the disclosure or use of a client's tax return.  A preparer is allowed to disclose information for quality review.

30. (d)  Both I and II.  The first violation listed carries a penalty of $250, while the second carries $1,000.

31. (b) The CPA is required to maintain a list of the taxpayer's name and identification number, or a copy of the tax return.  Failure to do so may result in a preparer penalty.  The other answers are nice to have, but are not required to be retained.

# Chapter Two
# Income—Inclusions and Exclusions

# Chapter Two
# Income – Inclusions and Exclusions

## GROSS INCOME

As a general rule, the Internal Revenue Code defines gross income as all income, from whatever source derived. Included in this broad definition of income is compensation for services, business income, property transactions, interest, dividends, rents, royalties, alimony, annuities, pensions, and discharge of indebtedness. This is not an all inclusive group, nor are all the items listed always fully included as gross income. If an item is to be excluded from gross income, there must be a specific code section excluding it. On the exam, you need to be aware of these exceptions because the examiners will concentrate on these areas.

Also, the receipt of cash is not necessarily a prerequisite to the recognition of income. Receiving property with a fair market of $100 for services rendered is just as included as receiving $100 in cash. See Chapter 5 for a full discussion of the methods of accounting for income and deductions.

## EMPLOYEE COMPENSATION

An employee receives compensation in a number of ways. Some compensation is fully taxable, some is fully excluded, and others partially excluded. Gross income that is fully included in gross income typically includes salaries and wages, bonuses, and commissions. Besides paying for compensation directly, an employee may receive other benefits which may or may not be taxable.

### Employee Fringe Benefits

**Health Insurance Premiums and Benefits:** The premiums paid by an employer for an employee's health insurance coverage are **not included** as gross income, nor are any of the benefits received from the policy. The non-taxable benefits can be for the employee, spouse, or dependent.

**Group-term Life Insurance**: An employer may provide an employee with group-term life insurance coverage of up to $50,000 as a **non-taxable** fringe benefit. The cost of coverage in excess of the $50,000 is considered income to the employee.

**Death Benefits**: The exclusion for death benefits paid to an employee's family has been repealed for tax years beginning in 1997.

**Cafeteria Plans:** Companies may offer a variety of non-taxable benefits which an employee may choose from, similar to a cafeteria. There is generally no minimum waiting period for employees to take advantage of this plan.

**Employee Discounts:** Allowed as a tax-free benefit when the discount on services is not greater than 20% and when the discount on purchases is not below the employer's cost.

**De minimis Fringe Benefits:** Refers to non-taxable benefits such as subsidized eating facilities when a plant is located in a remote location; occasional use of the company copy machine; use of company typing services, etc.

**Moving Expense Reimbursements:** These reimbursements are no longer reported as gross income to the extent that the amount represents a qualified moving expense as described in Chapter 3.

**Reimbursed Expenses:** When an employee incurs expenses on behalf of his employer, and the amount of the expenditure is reimbursed by the employer after the employee makes an accounting, that amount is not income to the employee. However, if the employee merely receives a monthly draw and is not required to provide an adequate accounting, that amount is included as gross income.

**Qualified Transportation Benefits:** Employers may provide employees with free parking of up to $170 in value per month. Employees have the choice of selecting between employer provided parking or cash, without the loss of the exclusion for parking. However, if the employee chooses cash, that will be included in gross income.

**Qualified Employer-Provided Educational Assistance:** For undergraduate studies only, the amounts paid by the employer under a qualified plan for tuition, fees, books and supplies is excluded up to an annual amount per employee of $5,250.

**Dependent Day Care:** An employee may exclude, up to $5,000 per year, the cost of child and dependent care services paid by the employer to enable the employee to work. The exclusion may not exceed the earned income of the spouse with the lesser income when the taxpayer is married.

# INTEREST INCOME

Interest earned by a taxpayer is generally included as gross income. Interest income is reported on Schedule B and typically represents interest on savings accounts, certificates of deposits, tax refunds, loans by the taxpayer, bonds and other investments. Investments include federal obligations such as U. S. Treasury Certificates and Savings Bonds. However, there are special provisions and various elections a taxpayer may make to defer or exclude from gross income the interest from certain federal obligations. Such provisions are discussed later.

Interest is recognized by cash basis taxpayer when it is credited to his account. Accrual based taxpayers recognize the income when earned. Occasionally, a taxpayer may receive a gift when opening up a savings account or certificate of deposit. The fair market value of that gift is also included as interest income.

**Municipal Bond Interest:** Interest on state and municipal obligations is excluded from gross income. Also excluded is interest on obligations of a possession of the United States, such as Puerto Rico. Tax refunds are not considered to be obligations of the state and any interest earned on the refunds are fully taxable. Also, any gain from the sale of municipal obligations is included in gross income.

**U. S. Savings Bonds:** Series E (before 1980) and Series EE (after 1979) Savings Bonds are issued at a discount, do not pay out interest, but are redeemed for fixed amounts in the future. The difference between the purchase price and the redemption price is recognized as interest income. Whereas the interest is not recognized until the bonds are redeemed, there is a deferral available to taxpayers. In addition, the Series E Bonds may be exchanged for Series HH Bonds and the interest deferred even further.

A taxpayer, however, may elect to recognize the interest income rather than waiting until redemption. Once this method is elected, it must be used for all future years unless the change is approved by the Commissioner.

**Educational Savings Bonds:** In an effort to assist parents in affording the spiraling cost of higher education, Congress passed a law stating that the interest earned on U. S. Savings Bonds is excluded from gross income if certain restrictions are met. For the exclusion to apply:

- The Series EE US Savings Bonds must be issued after December 31, 1989.
- At the time of issuance, the individual to whom the bonds are issued must be at least 24 years old.
- All the proceeds must be used for the qualified higher educational expenses (tuition and fees) of the taxpayer, his spouse or dependent.
- Qualified higher education expenses must be reduced by other scholarships or veterans' benefits received.
- At the time of redemption, the taxpayer's Modified Adjusted Gross Income (MAGI) does not exceed the specified limit described below. (MAGI is the adjusted gross income before the foreign earned income exclusion and Educational Savings Bond Interest Exclusion itself).
- This is **not** available to those electing married filing separately.

Note that these bonds **are not** being bought by the parent and held in the child's name. That is a completely different tax planning strategy. Also note that a grandparent or uncle cannot buy the bonds to have this rule apply unless the child they are buying for is their dependent.

**Limitations on the Exclusion:** In computing the limitation referred to above, there are two limitations which must be observed.

- If the total amount from the redemption (both principal and interest) exceeds the qualified higher education expenses, then there is a pro-rata reduction in the amount of interest that can be excluded.
- For married taxpayers, if their MAGI in 1999 exceeds $79,650, the exclusion from is phased-out on a pro-rata basis over the next $30,000. If the taxpayer is single, the MAGI amount is $53,100 and the range is over $15,000.

The MAGI limitation imposed by Congress severely reduces the appeal of this provision. Those who qualify without limitation, may not be able to afford to purchase the bonds. Those who are financially able to afford them will not qualify.

## Other Provisions:

Interest on Veterans Administration insurance dividends left on deposit with the Veterans Administration is also excluded from gross income.

# DIVIDENDS

Dividends represent distributions from a corporation's earning and profits, and are generally fully included as gross income. Dividends are reported on Schedule B. When a corporation makes a distribution in excess of its earnings and profits, the excess represents a return of the investor's cost or basis. See Chapter 9 for a full discussion.

Dividends received on a life insurance policy generally do not represent income, but rather represent a return of a premium. Also, the receipt of a stock dividend is generally excluded from income. However, if the taxpayer has the option to receive cash (or other property) instead of stock, the shareholder will recognize dividend income to equal to the fair market value of the distribution.

# RENTS AND ROYALTIES

Amounts received from rental property, less the related rental expenses are included as gross income. Also, royalties from books, articles, reproductions, oil and gas, etc., are included as gross income. These amounts are reported on Schedule E - Supplementary Income and Loss, along with other items of income from sources such as S Corporations, Partnerships and Trusts.

Any increase in the value of the rental property as the result of improvements made by the lessee are generally excluded from the lessor's gross income. However, if the improvements were made in lieu of rent, the fair market value of the improvements would be included as gross income.

The lessee may also provide the lessor with a **security deposit**. A security deposit does not represent gross income as a right of return exists to the lessee at the end of the lease. However, a prepayment of the last month's rent does represent gross income in the year received.

# SELF-EMPLOYED BUSINESS INCOME

Income from carrying on a trade or business on an unincorporated basis is reported on Schedule C. This is typical income from services provided (consulting, tax returns, etc.) See Chapter 3 for the various business deductions.

# ALIMONY AND SEPARATE MAINTENANCE PAYMENTS

When a married couple obtains a divorce, there is generally a requirement for one spouse to support the other. These payments are referred to as alimony (or separate maintenance payments if they are legally separated). In general, these payments are deductible by the payor spouse, and included as income by the spouse receiving them. Should the spouse also have children, there may be an element of the payment which includes child support. Child support is not a taxable to the recipient.

If the agreement further calls for the division of marital property, such as a house, investments and other property, this division, or transfer is not a taxable event. In addition, if the division of marital property includes the continuation of the mortgage payments, this amount will not be considered alimony because the mortgage payments will not terminate at the death of the former spouse. Because of the various tax consequences of these different transactions, it is important for the taxpayer as well as the IRS to be able to clearly identify what a transaction is so that both parties treat the transaction consistently.

Payments made under **written decrees and agreements after 1984** are considered to be alimony only if:

- Payments are made in cash (distinguishes it from property).
- Agreement does not state the payments are not alimony (directly or indirectly).
- The former couple are not members of the same household during the time of the payments.
- The former couple do not file a joint return.
- Payments stop after the death of the payee spouse.

> **Example 1:** B and D were married and have one child who resides with D. They are now divorced under an agreement dated 1990. They do not reside together. B is required to pay D $2,000 per month until D dies. Of the $2,000 payment, $400 is designated in the agreement as child support. Therefore, $1,600 is considered alimony and is included in D's gross income.

> **Example 2:** C and E were married and have one child who resides with E. They are now divorced under an agreement dated 1990. They do not reside together. C is required to pay E $2,000 per month until E dies. The written decree states the payment decreases to $1,600 after the child reaches age 21. Indirectly, the decree states that $400 is not alimony. Therefore, $1,600 is considered alimony and is included in E's gross income.

If payments made during the year are **less than the payments required** by the written decree or agreement, in determining the amount of alimony, payments are first allocated to the non-alimony (child support), and then the alimony. You do not pro-rate the payments.

> **Example 3:** B and D were married and have one child who resides with D. They are now divorced under an agreement dated 1990. They do not reside together. B is required to pay D $2,000 per month until D dies. Of the $2,000 payment, $400 is designated as child support. However, B only made 10 payments totaling $20,000 during 1996.
>
> | | |
> |---|---|
> | Total payments made | $ 20,000 |
> | Amount not alimony: | |
> | 12 months @ 400 | -4,800 |
> | Alimony component | $ 15,200 |

Because the alimony payments are deductible by the payor, certain taxpayers have attempted to obtain tax advantages by structuring the agreement to make large payments in the early years and smaller payments in subsequent years. Theoretically, a high income tax-bracket payor (39.6%) could make a very large payment to the payee who may be in a low bracket (15%) in the year of, or year after the divorce. A $50,000 payment could result in a significant, overall net tax savings. To prevent what is referred to as **front-loading**, agreements signed after 1986 state that if payments made in the first or second year exceed $15,000, **alimony recapture** may exist for the excess amount over an average. The computations are beyond the scope of the exam, but this concept is not. Alimony recapture effectively causes a reduction in the gross income recognized by the payee spouse and a reduction in the deduction claimed by the payor spouse. The payor's deduction for making alimony payments is addressed in Chapter 3.

Finally, alimony is considered to be **earned income** to the recipient. This is important because the earned income of the contributor determines the allowable IRA contribution. Remember this as you review the IRA deduction in Chapter 3.

# Full Inclusion -- Other Topics

**Gambling Winnings:** Amounts received from gambling winnings, lotteries, etc., are included in gross income. Gambling losses are deductible only to the extent of the earnings. See Chapter 4.

**Jury Duty Pay:** Compensation received while performing jury duty is included in gross income

**Unemployment Compensation:** Various states provide benefits to unemployed workers for a set period of time. The amounts received are included in gross income.

# Partial Exclusion or Limitations

**Social Security Benefits:** In general, these benefits are excluded from gross income. However, when a taxpayer's modified adjusted gross income (or provisional income) exceeds a base amount, they may have to include 50% to 85% of their social security benefits as gross income. The provisional income represents adjusted gross income plus tax-exempt income and one-half of the social security benefits received. However, if the taxpayer has the higher level of provisional income, 85% of the benefits will be included. For married taxpayers filing separately, there is no base amount and 85% of all benefits received will be taxed. Under OBRA '93, the base amounts for the provisional income test and benefit inclusion rate are as follows:

| Filing Status | 0% Taxed | 50% Taxed | 85% Taxed |
|---|---|---|---|
| Single or head of household | Up to $25,000 | $25,000 to $34,000 | Over $34,000 |
| Married | Up to $32,000 | $32,000 to $44,000 | Over $44,000 |

**Annuity Contracts and Pensions:** Annuities represent an investment whereby the taxpayer contributes a sum of money to an organization and receives over time a return of his investment and interest. The issue is generally the proration of the cost, or basis of the investment, over the stream of payments. The allowable methodology is a straight-line recovery of the cost. If the annuity continues after the recovery of cost, the entire payments represent income.

---

**Example 4:** Y invests $40,000 in annuity that will pay her $12,000 per year for the next 5 years. Her expected payout is $60,000. During the year, Y receives $12,000 of which $8,000 is a nontaxable return of her investment and the $4,000 is recognized as income.

| | | |
|---|---|---|
| Original investment | $ 40,000 | |
| Expected pay-out | $ 60,000 | Payout ratio 2/3 |

Current year payment of $12,000 X 2/3 = $8,000 recovery of investment

$12,000 less recovery of $8,000 = $4,000 income

---

**Tax Benefit Rule:** When a taxpayer claims a deduction in one year, and receives a refund in the subsequent year, the amount of the refund must be reported as income. However, if claiming the deduction did not result in a tax benefit, then the refund is not taxable.

> **Example 5:** In filing his 1999 tax return, J claimed $5,000 in medical deductions. Because of his threshold limitation of $4,500 (AGI of $60,000 times the medical limitation of 7.5%), J was only able to deduct $500 of the $5,000. Late in 2000, J received a $800 refund from his health insurance company due to a disputed bill he paid in 1999. Of the $800, the first $500 represents income because L received a tax benefit by being able to deduct $500 of the expenses. The balance of $300 is not included as income because J never received a tax benefit from the expense.

**Prizes and Awards:** The fair market value of prizes and awards is generally included as gross income. This includes prizes from game shows, door prizes and employer awards. However, an employee achievement award may be excluded if it is based upon length of service or safety, and does not exceed $400, or $1,600 if it is under a qualified plan. In order for other awards to be excluded from gross income, the award must meet all the following criteria:

- The award is for recognition of religious, charitable scientific, artistic, literary or civic achievement.
- The taxpayer was selected without any action on his part to enter the contest.
- There is no requirement for the taxpayer to render services in the future.
- The taxpayer contributes the award to a nonprofit organization or qualified governmental unit.

**Discharge of Indebtedness:** When a taxpayer is obligated to pay a mortgage, loan or other indebtedness, and the lender discharges the taxpayer from the obligation, the amount of the discharge generally represents ordinary income. However, if the taxpayer is insolvent or bankrupt at the time of the discharge, it will not be income. Another exception exists for individuals who are released from indebtedness related to **qualified real property business indebtedness**. Rather than recognizing income, the taxpayer may reduce the basis of the real property.

There is an exclusion for students with student loans. If the forgiveness is contingent upon the student fulfilling a work requirement in the state, the forgiveness of debt will not constitute gross income.

**Foreign Income:** When a taxpayer earns income from working in a foreign country, there is an exclusion available which is limited to the lessor of $74,000 or the foreign income less the housing cost exclusion. When the US taxpayer is not present in the foreign country for a full year, the amount is prorated on a daily basis. In general, there are two different tests to determine the exclusion:

      **Bona Fide Resident Test:** Must a be a resident for a full taxable year.
      **Physical Presence Test:** Must be physically present in the foreign country at least 330 days in a consecutive 12 month period.

The exclusion is increased as follows:

| Tax Year | Exclusion Amount |
|----------|------------------|
| 2000 | 76,000 |
| 2001 | 78,000 |
| 2002 and thereafter | 80,000 |

**Armed Services:** There are various benefits available to members of the Armed Services. In particular is the exclusion of pay from gross income when enlisted men are serving in combat areas. For officers, the exclusion is only on the first $500 of pay per month. The housing allowance for the servicemen is also excluded.

**Qualified Tuition Programs:** There is a new tax-deferred college savings vehicle. This provision allows tax-favored treatment to the various qualified state tuition programs. There are a number of limitations, similar to the rules for IRAs.

## Full Exclusion

**Inheritances and Gifts:** In general, the amount received from an estate as an inheritance, or as a gift out of detached generosity, is excluded from gross income.

**Life Insurance:** The proceeds from a life insurance policy by reason of death of the insured are excluded from gross income. If, however, the taxpayer elects to receive the payments under an installment arrangement rather than a lump sum payment, the interest component is included as gross income. See annuities for computations.

**Personal Injury:** A taxpayer receiving amounts from workers compensation, accident and health insurance claims, lawsuits for personal injuries and disability benefits are not included as gross income. However, a lawsuit settlement for lost wages would be included in gross income.

**Scholarships:** Payments made to an individual to be used for tuition and fees (such as books, supplies and fees), are excluded from gross income. The individual must be a **degree candidate** at a higher educational institution for study. Payments for room and board, or compensation for services rendered such as for a teaching or research assistant are **not excluded**. These payments are treated as earned income to the individual.

**Rental Value of Parsonage:** Amounts received by an ordained minister designated as a housing allowance is excluded to the extent of the actual costs of maintaining the parsonage.

# Chapter Two -- Questions
# Income - Inclusions and Exclusions

1. James Martin received the following compensation and fringe benefits from his employer during this year:

| | |
|---|---|
| Salary | $50,000 |
| Year-end bonus | 10,000 |
| Medical insurance premiums paid by employer | 1,000 |
| Reimbursement for moving expenses | 6,200 |

(Actual allowable moving expenses incurred were $6,200)

What amount of the preceding payments should be included in Martin's gross income?
a. $60,000.
b. $61,000.
c. $66,200.
d. $67,200.

2. Perle, a dentist, billed Wood $600 for dental services. Wood paid Perle $200 cash and built a bookcase for Perle's office in full settlement of the bill. Wood sells comparable bookcases for $350. What amount should Perle include in taxable income as a result of this transaction?
a. $0
b. $220
c. $550
d. $600

3. Benedict Atley, who is single, was out of work in the early months of this taxable year and received $2,800 of unemployment benefits from his state of residence. His adjusted gross income was $22,500 excluding the $2,800 of unemployment benefits. Assuming that Atley had no other items of income or adjustments to gross income, what amount must Atley report as adjusted gross income on his income tax return?
a. $22,500.
b. $23,750.
c. $25,150.
d. $25,300.

4. Under a "cafeteria plan" maintained by an employer,
a. Participation must be restricted to employees, and their spouses and minor children.
b. At least three years of service are required before an employee can participate in the plan.
c. Participants may select their own menu of benefits.
d. Provision may be made for deferred compensation other than 401(k) plans.

5. This year, Joan accepted and received a $10,000 award for outstanding civic achievement. Joan was selected without any action on her part, and no future services are expected of her as a condition of receiving the award. What amount is Joan required to include in her income in connection with this award?
a. $0
b. $4,000
c. $5,000
d. $10,000

6. Leon Wren, an electrician, was injured in an accident during the course of his employment. As a result of injuries sustained, he received the following payments during the year:

| | |
|---|---|
| Damages for personal injuries | $8,000 |
| Workmen's compensation | 3,000 |
| Reimbursement from his employer's accident and health plan for medical expenses paid by Wren | 1,200 |

The amount to be included in Wren's gross income should be
a. $0.
b. $1,200.
c. $3,000.
d. $12,200.

7. During the current year Hal Leff sustained a serious injury in the course of his employment. As a result of this injury, Hal received the following payments during the year:

| | |
|---|---|
| Workers' compensation | $2,400 |
| Reimbursement from his employer's accident and health plan for medical expenses paid by Hal and not deducted by him | 1,800 |
| Damages for personal injuries | 8,000 |

The amount to be included in Hal's gross income for the current year should be
a. $12,200
b. $8,000
c. $1,800
d. $0

8. The following information is available for Ann Drury for this year:

| | |
|---|---|
| Salary | $36,000 |
| Premiums paid by employer on group-term life insurance in excess of $50,000 | 500 |
| Proceeds from state lottery | 5,000 |

How much should Drury report as gross income on her tax return?
a. $36,000.
b. $36,500.
c. $41,000.
d. $41,500.

9. David Hetnar is covered by a $90,000 group-term life insurance policy of which his wife is the beneficiary. Hetnar's employer pays the entire cost of the policy, for which the uniform annual premium is $8 per $1,000 of coverage. How much of this premium is taxable to Hetnar?
a. $0.
b. $320.
c. $360.
d. $720.

10. Sam Mitchell, a calendar-year taxpayer, purchased an annuity contract for $3,600 that would pay him $120 a month beginning on January 1 of this calendar year. His expected return under the contract is $10,800. How much of this annuity is excludable from gross income for this taxable year?

a. $0.
b. $480.
c. $960.
d. $1,440.

11. Seymour Thomas named his wife Penelope the beneficiary of a $100,000 (face amount) insurance policy on his life. The policy provided that upon his death, the proceeds would be paid to Penelope with interest over her present life expectancy, which was calculated at 25 years. Seymour died on January 1 of this year and Penelope received a payment of $5,200 from the insurance company. What amount should she include in her gross income for the year?
a. $200.
b. $1,200.
c. $4,200.
d. $5,200.

12. Howard O'Brien, an employee of Ogden Corporation, died on June 30, 1999. During July Ogden made employee death payments of $10,000 to his widow, and $10,000 to his 15-year-old son. What amounts should be included in gross income by the widow and son in their respective tax returns?

| | Widow | Son |
|---|---|---|
| a. | --0-- | --0-- |
| b. | $5,000 | $5,000 |
| c. | $7,500 | $7,500 |
| d. | $10,000 | $10,000 |

13. Charles and Marcia are married cash-basis taxpayers. They had interest income this taxable year as follows:

- $500 interest on federal income tax refund.
- $600 interest on state income tax refund.
- $800 interest on federal government obligations.
- $1,000 interest on state government obligations.

What amount of interest income is taxable on Charles and Marcia's joint income tax return for this taxable year?
a. $500
b. $1,100
c. $1,900
d. $2,900

14. During 1999 Kay received interest income as follows:

On U.S. Treasury certificates $4,000
On refund of 1998 federal income tax 500

The total amount of interest subject to tax in Kay's 1999 tax return is
a. $4,500
b. $4,000
c. $500
d. $0

15. Daniel Kelly received interest income from the following sources:

New York Port Authority bonds $1,000
Puerto Rico Commonwealth bonds 1,800

What portion of such interest is tax exempt?
a. $0
b. $1,000
c. $1,800
d. $2,800

16. In 1999 Uriah Stone received the following interest payments:

- Interest of $400 on refund of federal income tax for 1997.
- Interest of $300 on award for personal injuries sustained in an automobile accident during 1995.
- Interest of $1,500 on municipal bonds.
- Interest of $1,000 on United States savings bonds (Series HH).

What amount, if any, should Stone report as interest income on his 1999 tax return?
a. $0
b. $700
c. $1,700
d. $3,200

17. During 1999, Clark received the following interest income:

On Veterans Administration
  insurance dividends left on
  deposit with the V.A. $20
On state income tax refund 30

What amount should Clark include for interest income in his 1999 return?
a. $50
b. $30
c. $20
d. $0

18. Clark bought Series EE U.S. Savings Bonds after 1989. Redemption proceeds will be used for payment of college tuition for Clark's dependent child. One of the conditions that must be met for tax exemption of accumulated interest on these bonds is that the
a. Purchaser of the bonds must be the sole owner of the bonds (or joint owner with his or her spouse).
b. Bonds must be bought by a parent (or both parents) and put in the name of the dependent child.
c. Bonds must be bought by the owner of the bonds before the owner reaches the age of 24.
d. Bonds must be transferred to the college for redemption by the college rather than by the owner of the bonds.

19. In a tax year where the taxpayer pays qualified education expenses, interest income on the redemption of qualified U.S. Series EE Bonds may be excluded from gross income. The exclusion is subject to a modified gross income limitation and a limit of aggregate bond proceeds in excess of qualified higher education expenses. Which of the following is (are) true?

I. The exclusion applies for education expenses incurred by the taxpayer, the taxpayer's spouse, or any person whom the taxpayer may claim as a dependent for the year.

II. "Otherwise qualified higher education expenses" must be reduced by qualified scholarships not included in gross income.

a. I only.
b. II only.
c. Both I and II.
d. Neither I nor II.

20. In July 1984, Dan Farley leased a building to Robert Shelter for a period of fifteen years at a monthly rental of $1,000 with no option to renew. At that time the building had a remaining estimated useful life of twenty years.

Prior to taking possession of the building, Shelter made improvements at a cost of $18,000. These improvements had an estimated useful life of twenty years at the commencement of the lease period. The lease expired on June 30, 1999 at which point the improvements had a fair market value of $2,000. The amount that Farley, the landlord, should include in his gross income for 1999 is
a.    $6,000
b.    $8,000
c.    $10,000
d.    $18,500

21. Paul Bristol, a cash basis taxpayer, owns an apartment building. The following information was available for 1999:

- An analysis of the 1999 bank deposit slips showed recurring monthly rents received totaling $50,000.
- On March 1, 1999, the tenant in apartment 2B paid Bristol $2,000 to cancel the lease expiring on December 31, 1999.
- The lease of the tenant in apartment 3A expired on December 31, 1999, and the tenant left improvements valued at $1,000. The improvements were not in lieu of any rent required to have been paid.

In computing net rental income for 1999, Bristol should report gross rents of
a.    $50,000
b.    $51,000
c.    $52,000
d.    $53,000

22. Amy Finch had the following cash receipts during 1999:

Net rent on vacant lot used by a car
  dealer (lessee pays all taxes, insurance,
  and other expenses on the lot)              6,000
Advance rent from lessee of above
  vacant lot, such advance to be applied
  against rent for the last two months
  of the 5-year lease in 2004                 1,000

How much should Amy include in her 1999 taxable income for rent?

a.    $7,000
b.    $6,800
c.    $6,200
d.    $6,000

23. Nare, an accrual-basis taxpayer, owns a building which was rented to Mott under a ten-year lease expiring August 31, 2001. On January 2, 1999, Mott paid $30,000 as consideration for canceling the lease. On November 1, 1999, Nare leased the building to Pine under a five-year lease. Pine paid Nare $10,000 rent for the two months of November and December, and an additional $5,000 for the last month's rent. What amount of rental income should Nare report in its 1999 income tax return?
a.    $10,000
b.    $15,000
c.    $40,000
d.    $45,000

24. Ace Rentals Inc., an accrual-basis taxpayer, reported rent receivable of $35,000 and $25,000 in its 1999 and 1998 balance sheets, respectively. During 1999, Ace received $50,000 in rent payments and $5,000 in nonrefundable rent deposits. In Ace's 1999 corporate income tax return, what amount should Ace include as rent revenue?
a.    $50,000
b.    $55,000
c.    $60,000
d.    $65,000

25. Hall, a divorced person and custodian of her 12-year old child, filed her 1999 federal income tax return as head of a household. She submitted the following information to the CPA who prepared her 1999 return:

- The divorce agreement, executed in 1988, provides for Hall to receive $3,000 per month, of which $600 is designated as child support. After the child reaches 18, the monthly payments are to be reduced to $2,400 and are to continue until remarriage or death. However, for the year 1999, Hall received a total of only $5,000 from her former husband. Hall paid an attorney $2,000 in 1999 in a suit to collect the alimony owed.

What amount should be reported in Hall's 1999 return as alimony income?
a.    $36,000
b.    $28,800
c.    $5,000
d.    $0

26. Ed and Ann Ross were divorced in January 1999. In accordance with the divorce decree, Ed transferred the title in their home to Ann in 1999. The home, which had a fair market value of $150,000, was subject to a $50,000 mortgage that had 20 more years to run. Monthly mortgage payments amount to $1,000. Under the terms of settlement, Ed is obligated to make the mortgage payments on the home for the full remaining 20-year term of the indebtedness, regardless of how long Ann lives. Ed made 12 mortgage payments in 1999. What amount is taxable as alimony in Ann's 1999 return?

a. $0
b. $12,000
c. $100,000
d. $112,000

27. Richard and Alice Kelley lived apart during 1999 and did not file a joint tax return for the year. Under the terms of the written separation agreement they signed on July 1, 1999, Richard was required to pay Alice $1,500 per month of which $600 was designated as child support. He made six such payments in 1999. Additionally, Richard paid Alice $1,200 per month for the first six months of 1999, no portion of which was designated as child support. Assuming that Alice has no other income, her tax return for 1999 should show gross income of

a. $0.
b. $5,400.
c. $9,000.
d. $12,600.

28. John and Mary were divorced in 1991. The divorce decree provides that John pay alimony of $10,000 per year, to be reduced by 20% on their child's 18th birthday. During 1999, John paid $7,000 directly to Mary and $3,000 to Spring College for Mary's tuition. What amount of these payments should be reported as income in Mary's 1999 income tax return?

a. $5,600.
b. $8,000.
c. $8,600.
d. $10,000.

29. With regard to the inclusion of social security benefits in gross income, for the 1999 tax year, which of the following statements is correct?

a. The social security benefits in excess of provisional income are included in gross income.

b. The social security benefits in excess of one half the provisional income are included in gross income.

c. One half of the social security benefits is the maximum amount of benefits to be included in gross income.

d. The maximum amount of social security benefits included in gross income is 85%.

30. Blake, a single individual age 67, had 1999 adjusted gross income of $60,000 exclusive of social security benefits. Blake received social security benefits of $8,400 and interest of $1,000 on tax-exempt obligations during 1999. What amount of social security benefits is included in Blake's 1999 taxable income?

a. $0
b. $4,200
c. $7,140
d. $8,400

31. In January of this year, Judy Howard was awarded a postgraduate fellowship grant of $4,800 by a tax-exempt educational organization. Ms. Howard is **not** a candidate for a degree and was awarded the grant to continue her research. The grant is for a two-year period but was paid in full on July 1 of this year. What amount should be included in her gross income for this taxable year?

a. $0.
b. $1,200.
c. $2,400.
d. $4,800.

32. Majors, a candidate for a graduate degree, received the following scholarship awards from the university in 1998:

- $10,000 for tuition, fees, books, and supplies required for courses.
- $2,000 stipend for research services required by the scholarship.

What amount of the scholarship awards should Majors include as taxable income in 1999?

a. $12,000
b. $10,000
c. $2,000
d. $0

33. Which payment(s) is(are) included in a recipient's gross income?

I. Payment to a graduate assistant for a part-time teaching assignment at a university. Teaching is not a requirement toward obtaining the degree.

II. A grant to a Ph.D. candidate for his participation in a university-sponsored research project for the benefit of the university.

a. I only.
b. II only.
c. Both I and II.
d. Neither I nor II.

34. Arthur Mends, age 19, is a full-time student at Gordon College and a candidate for a bachelor's degree. During the year he received the following payments:

| | |
|---|---|
| State scholarship for tuition for ten months | $4,200 |
| Loan from college financial aid office | 1,000 |
| Cash support from parents | 2,000 |
| Cash dividends on qualified investments | 500 |
| Cash prize awarded in contest | 300 |
| | $8,000 |

What is his adjusted gross income?
a. $700.
b. $800.
c. $5,000.
d. $8,000.

35. Clark filed form 1040EZ for the 1998 taxable year. In July 1999, Clark received a state income tax refund of $900, plus interest of $10, for overpayment of 1998 state income tax. What amount of the state tax refund and interest is taxable in Clark's 1999 federal income tax return?
a. $0
b. $10
c. $900
d. $910

## Review Questions

**Items 36 through 39** are based on the following data:
John Budd, who was 58 at the date of his death on May 1, 1999, received $1,000 interest in 1999 on municipal bonds. John's wife, Emma, age 57, received a $300 television set in 1999 as a gift for opening a long-term savings account at a bank. Upon John's death, Emma received life insurance proceeds of $60,000 under a group policy paid for by John's employer. In addition, an employee death benefit of $7,500 was paid to Emma by John's employer.

36. With regard to John's and Emma's filing status for 1999, Emma should file
a. As a single individual, and a separate return should be filed for John as unmarried head of household.
b. As a qualifying widow, and a separate return should be filed for John as married head of household.
c. As a qualifying widow, and a separate return should be filed for John as a single deceased individual.
d. A joint return including John, as married taxpayers.

37. How much taxable interest was received by John and Emma?
a. $0
b. $300
c. $1,000
d. $1,300

38. How much of the group life insurance proceeds should be excluded from taxable income?
a. $0
b. $ 5,000
c. $50,000
d. $60,000

39. How much of the employee death benefit should be excluded from taxable income?
a. $0
b. $4,500
c. $5,000
d. $7,500

_____

40. Paul is a graduate of State University in Texas. To pay for his tuition, Paul borrowed $20,000 in local government loans. As an inducement to practice his profession in Texas, the local government forgives 25% of his loan each year he practices in the state. Assuming that Paul practices in Texas for the entire year, he must recognize how much gross income?
a. $0.
b. $5,000.
c. $10,000.
d. $20,000.

**Items 41 through 44** are based on the following data: Amy Finch had the following cash receipts during 1999:

| | |
|---|---:|
| Interest on Veterans Administration insurance dividends left on deposit with the V.A. | $ 10 |
| Interest on state income tax refund | 18 |
| Net rent on vacant lot used by a car dealer (lessee pays all taxes, insurance, and other expenses on the lot) | 6,000 |
| Advance rent from lessee of above vacant lot, such advance to be applied against rent for the last two months of the 5-year lease in 2003 | 1,000 |
| Dividend from a mutual insurance company on a life insurance policy | 500 |
| Dividend on listed corporation stock; payment date by corporation was 12/30/98, but Amy received the dividend in the mail on 1/2/99 | 875 |
| Gross amount of state lottery winnings (Amy spent $900 on state lottery tickets and $700 on pari-mutuel bets during the year at the state off-track betting parlor, for which she has full documentation) | 2,400 |

41. How much should Amy include in her 1999 taxable income for interest?
a. $0
b. $10
c. $18
d. $28

42. How much should Amy include in her 1999 taxable income for rent?
a. $7,000
b. $6,800
c. $6,200
d. $6,000

43. How much should Amy report for dividend income for 1999?
a. $1,375
b. $875
c. $500
d. $0

44. How much should Amy include in taxable "Other Income" for her 1999 state lottery winnings?
a. $2,400
b. $1,700
c. $1,500
d. $800

---

## Released and Author Constructed Questions

*R97*

45. Klein, a master's degree candidate at Briar University, was awarded a $12,000 scholarship from Briar in 1996. The scholarship was used to pay Klein's 1996 university tuition and fees. Also in 1996, Klein received $5,000 for teaching two courses at a nearby college. What amount is includible in Klein's 1996 gross income?
a. $0
b. $5,000
c. $12,000
d. $17,000

*AC*

46. Ace Corporation provides free parking at the company garage to its employees as a part of its fringe benefit package. The fair value of the parking is $200 per month. Because not all of the employees take advantage of the free parking, the company offers them a cash equivalent of $200 per month. Assuming that an employee takes advantage of the cash option for the entire year, how much will he recognize in gross income for 1999.
a. $ 0
b. $ 360
c. $1,200
d. $2,400

*AC*

47. Pierre, a United States citizen, was a bonafide resident of France for all of 1999. During the year, he received a total of $80,000 in foreign earned income and housing allowances. For 1999, how much income may Pierre exclude from gross income?
a. $70,000
b. $72,000
c. $74,000
d. $80,000

# Chapter Two -- Answers
# Income - Inclusions and Exclusions

1. (a) $60,000. Only the salary and year-end bonus are included as gross income. Medical insurance premiums paid by the employer are non-taxable fringe benefits. The reimbursement of qualified moving expenses is no longer included in income.

2. (c) $550. Gross income includes the fair market value of property received, not just cash. Perle must include:

| | |
|---|---|
| Cash received | $ 200 |
| Bookcases - FMV | 350 |
| Total income | $ 550 |

3. (d) $25,300. Unemployment benefits are fully taxable. His gross income includes:

| | |
|---|---|
| Current adjusted gross income | $ 22,500 |
| Add: Unemployment benefits | 2,800 |
| New adjusted gross income | $ 25,300 |

4. (c) Cafeteria plans allow employees to choose benefits. There are no minimum service requirements as in a retirement plan.

5. (d) $10,000. Awards for outstanding civic achievement can be excluded from gross income. If the awards are made in connection with religious, charitable, scientific, educational, literary or civic nature; and the recipient must be selected without any action on her part; no future services were expected; and the award is assigned over to a charity, it would be excluded. The only thing Joan did not do was assign the award to a charity.

6. (a) $0. All items are excluded from gross income.

7. (d) $0. A taxpayer receiving amounts from workers compensation, accident and health insurance claims, lawsuits for personal injuries and disability benefits are not included as gross income. However, a lawsuit settlement for lost wages would be included in gross income.

8. (d) $41,500. Salary, premiums paid (or the IRS determined cost of) for term life insurance in excess of $50,000, and gambling winnings are all components of gross income.

| | |
|---|---|
| Salary | $ 36,000 |
| Premiums on excess insurance | 500 |
| Gambling winnings | 5,000 |
| Total | $ 41,500 |

9. (b) $320. The cost of premiums for group-term life insurance in excess of $50,000 is included as gross income. With $90,000 in total policy coverage, there is $40,000 in excess coverage. At a premium cost of $8 per thousand, the amount of income to be recognized is 40 times $8 or $320.

10. (b) $480. Under an annuity contract, the taxpayer may exclude a pro-rata share of the cost, or basis in the investment. Sam's total cost is $3,600; his expected return is $10,800; and his current year receipts are $1,440 (12 months @ $120 per month).

Current receipts x (Investment/Expect Return) = Excluded, tax-free return

$$\$ 1,440 \quad X \quad \frac{\$ \ 3,600}{\$ \ 10,800} \quad = \quad \$ 480$$

11. (b) $1,200. A lump sum distribution of life insurance is generally not included as gross income. However, when the proceeds are not being paid out immediately, but are paid over a 25 year period, there is an element of interest that must be recognized. The non-taxable recovery is determined on a straight-line basis. $100,000 divided by 25 years for a non-taxable recovery of $4,000 per year.

| | |
|---|---|
| Receipt of payment | $ 5,200 |
| Excluded portion | -4,000 |
| Taxable portion | $ 1,200 |

12. (d) Widow $10,000 - Son $10,000. The exclusion of death benefits paid to an employee's family has been repealed.

13. (c) $1,900. Only interest on the state obligation is excluded from income.

14. (a) $4,500. Interest on federal obligations is generally included in gross income as well as interest on a tax refund.

15. (d) $2,800. Interest on state and municipal obligations is excluded from gross income. Also excluded is interest on obligations of a possession of the United States, such as Puerto Rico.

16. (c) $1,700. Interest on state and municipal obligations is excluded from gross income. However, interest on the other obligations is included in gross income:

| | |
|---|---|
| Interest on tax refund | $ 400 |
| Interest on special award | 300 |
| Interest on Series HH Bond | 1,000 |
| | $ 1,700 |

17. (b) $30. Interest on Veterans Administration insurance dividends left on deposit with the Veterans Administration, are excluded from gross income. However, tax refunds are not considered to be obligations of the state and any interest earned on the refunds are fully taxable.

18. (a) In order for the interest from Series EE US Savings Bonds to be excluded from gross income, the purchaser must be the owner of the bonds and be at least 24 years old. The bonds are not held in the dependent's name nor are they transferred to the college for redemption.

19. (c) The expenses can be incurred for the taxpayer, spouse or dependent, and must be reduced by any scholarships or veteran's benefits.

20. (a) $6,000. Any increase in the value of the rental property as the result of improvements made by the lessee are generally excluded from the lessor's gross income. However, if the improvements were made in lieu of rent, the fair market value of the improvements would be included as gross income. In this instance, none of the $18,000 would be included. Farley would only recognize $6,000 (the six months of rent at $1,000 per month).

21. (c) $52,000. The rental income would include the recurring monthly rents of $50,000 plus the $2,000 for the cancellation of the lease. Any increase in the value of the rental property as the result of improvements made by the lessee are generally excluded from the lessor's gross income.

22. (a) $7,000. The gross rent would include the net rent of $6,000 on the vacant lot as well as the advance rent which is designated as rent against the last two months of the lease. The advance rent is not considered to be a security deposit.

23. (d) $45,000. The gross rent would include all three items:

| | |
|---|---:|
| Payment for canceling lease | $ 30,000 |
| Rent payment for two months | 10,000 |
| Last month's rent payment | 5,000 |
| Total rental income | $ 45,000 |

24. (d) $65,000. In this problem, you must determine how rental income Ace Rentals, Inc., (accrual based entity) earned. In addition, it initially appears that the lessee has provided Ace with a **security deposit** which would not have to be included in gross income. However, because it is a nonrefundable rent deposit, it is included in gross income. (A security deposit generally does not represent gross income as a right of return exists to the lessee at the end of the lease.) The computation of the rental income is as follows:

| | |
|---|---:|
| Rent receivable 12/31/99 | $ 35,000 |
| Rent receivable 12/31/98 | -25,000 |
| Increase in receivable | 10,000 |
| Rent collected during 1999 | 50,000 |
| Nonrefundable rent deposits | 5,000 |
| Total rental income | $ 65,000 |

25. (d) $0. If the alimony and child support payments made during the year are **less than the payments required** by the written decree or agreement, in determining the amount of alimony, payments are first allocated to the non-alimony (child support), and then the alimony. You do not pro-rate the payments. Hall's husband was required to pay her $3,000 per month. Of the $3,000 payment, $600 is designated as child support. However, Hall's husband only paid $5,000 during 1999. The $5,000 does not even cover the required child support; therefore, there is no alimony income.

| | |
|---|---:|
| Total payments made | $ 5,000 |
| Amount not alimony: | |
| 12 months @ $600 | -7,200 |
| Alimony component | $    -0- |

26. (a) $0. If the agreement further calls for the division of marital property, such as a house, investments and other property, this division, or transfer is not a taxable event. In addition, if the division of marital property includes the continuation of the mortgage payments, this amount will not be considered alimony because the mortgage payments will not terminate at the death of the former spouse.

27. (b) $5,400. The written agreement was not signed until July 1, 1999. Therefore the first six payments which were not paid pursuant to a written agreement are not considered alimony and are not included in gross income. Of the payments made after July 1, $600 was designated as being **not** alimony (child support).

| | |
|---|---:|
| Total monthly payment | $ 1,500 |
| Amount not alimony | -600 |
| Monthly alimony | $   900 |
| Months in the year | 6 |
| Total gross income | $ 5,400 |

28. (b) $8,000. The written agreement states that 20% of the payments are not alimony. Since John met his obligations during the year, $8,000 is included as gross income.

| | |
|---|---:|
| Cash payments | $ 7,000 |
| Tuition payments | 3,000 |
| Total cash payments | 10,000 |
| Percentage not alimony | 20% |
| Total gross income | $ 8,000 |

29. (d) 85% is the maximum rate. Answer (c) (50%) is the old law. Answers (a) and (b) are incorrect variations of the new law. See the section in the text for the detailed rules.

30. (c) $7,140. This could be a comprehensive problem testing the 85% maximum inclusion of social security benefits. A candidate who understands the provisional income base will quickly note that the taxpayer is far in excess of any limitation and the maximum would apply. Therefore, the quick answer is:

$$\$ 8,400 \times 85\% = \$7,140$$

The complete answer to this problem would require the candidate to compare the $7,140 to the amount computed below, and then the lessor of the two would be the amount included in gross income. Here's the full computation.

| | | |
|---|---:|---:|
| Adjusted gross income | | $ 60,000 |
| Modifications: | | |
|   Tax-exempt interest | | 1,000 |
|   50% of social security benefits | | 4,200 |
| Provisional income | | 65,200 |
| Base amount | | 34,000 |
| Excess over base | | 31,200 |
| Inclusion rate | | 85% |
| Sub-total | | 26,520 |
| Plus: Lessor of 50% SS | $4,200 | |
|          or | $4,500 | 4,200 |
| Included under this method | | $ 30,720 |

31. (d) $4,800. Judy was not a degree candidate.

32. (c) $2,000. As a degree candidate, the "scholarship" of $10,000 for tuition, fees, books and supplies is excluded from gross income. The "scholarship" of $2,000 for the stipend is compensation for services rendered and is included as earned income.

33. (c) By definition.

34. (b) $800. Only the $500 cash dividend and the $300 cash prize are included in gross income. As a degree candidate, the tuition scholarship is excluded. Loans and support from parents are not components of gross income.

35. (b) $10. Only the interest income from the state income tax refund is taxable. Under the tax benefit rule, a state income tax refund is included in gross income only if recipient derived a tax benefit from the state income tax payment. Since the taxpayer had filed a Form 1040EZ in 1998, we know that Clark did not itemize his deductions, but rather claimed the standard deduction. Therefore, Clark never received a tax benefit for any state taxes paid.

36. (d)  Joint return.  A joint return is allowed to be filed in the year of the death of a spouse.  The qualifying widow status would not be appropriate because she does not have a dependent child.

37. (b)  $300.  The fair market value of the gift for opening the savings account is treated as interest income and is included as gross income.  The interest from the municipal bonds is excluded.

38. (d)  $60,000.  The entire life insurance proceeds received as a lump sum are excluded from gross income.

39. (a)  $0.  The exclusion of death benefits paid to an employee's family has been repealed.

40. (a)  $0.  There is an exclusion for students with student loans.  If the forgiveness is contingent upon the student fulfilling a work requirement in the state, the forgiveness of debt will not constitute gross income.

41. (c)  $18.  Only the interest income from the state income tax refund is taxable.  The interest from the dividends on the insurance policy from the Veteran's Administration are not taxable.

42. (a)  $7,000.  Amy must recognize the $6,000 net rent on the vacant lot as well as the $1,000 advance rent of the last two months of the lease.  A refundable security deposit (not part of this problem) would not be included in taxable income.

43. (b)  $875.  Amy should not have recognized the 1998 corporate dividend in 1998 because even though it was paid to her in 1998, she did not have access to it until 1999.  She did not constructively receive the payment in 1998.  Therefore, Amy must recognize dividend income on the corporate stock in 1999.  Dividends from mutual life insurance policies represent a return of a premium and are generally excluded from gross income.

44. (a)  $2,400.  This full amount of her lottery winnings is included in income as "Other Income."  Any allowable losses from gambling would be treated as itemized deductions (if she itemized), and are more fully discussed in Chapter 4.  The gambling losses are not offset with the winnings to come up with a "net gambling income."

45. (b)  $5,000.  As a degree candidate, the "scholarship" of $12,000 awarded by the college to pay tuition and fees is excluded from gross income.  The $5,000 fee for teaching two courses is compensation for services rendered and is included in gross income.

46. (d)  $2,400.  While the employee fringe benefit of free parking is excluded from gross income (up to a maximum amount of $170 per month), taking the cash equivalent is fully included in gross income.  Note that the new law only provides that giving the employee the option does not cause the free parking to be included as gross income.  Thus, 12 months at $200 per month totals $2,400.

47. (c)  $74,000.  For 1999, the foreign income exclusion has been increased to $74,000.  Whereas the foreign source income exceeds that amount, the taxpayer is entitled to the full amount.

# Chapter Three
# Deductions For Adjusted Gross Income

# Chapter Three
# Deductions For Adjusted Gross Income

## CLASSIFICATION OF DEDUCTIONS

In Chapter 1, the basic definition of taxable income was introduced as gross income minus deductions equals taxable income. In this chapter, we expand that basic definition into the two broad classifications of deductions an individual taxpayer may have. A comparison showing the expansion of the statutory framework is below:

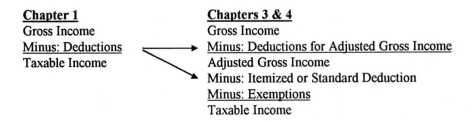

**Chapter 1**
Gross Income
Minus: Deductions
Taxable Income

**Chapters 3 & 4**
Gross Income
Minus: Deductions for Adjusted Gross Income
Adjusted Gross Income
Minus: Itemized or Standard Deduction
Minus: Exemptions
Taxable Income

The distinction between those deductions allowed in arriving at adjusted gross income and those deductions subtracted from adjusted gross income is critical for a number of reasons. First, a number of income items look to adjusted gross income as a starting point for the inclusion computation. For example, in Chapter 2 the Social Security benefits would be taxable if you exceeded a threshold base using a modified adjusted gross income amount.

Second, a number of deductions in this chapter, such as the Individual Retirement Account (IRA) or the rental loss deduction, will look to the adjusted gross income as a threshold for phasing out deductions.

Third, a number of itemized deductions covered in Chapter 4 will look to adjusted gross income as a base for computing the upper limit (ceiling) tests or threshold tests. For example, only qualified medical expenses in excess of 7.5% of adjusted gross income are allowed as an itemized deduction.

This chapter organizes the deductions for adjusted gross income by three major topics: (1) those deductions available to all taxpayers; (2) those available only to self-employed taxpayers in a trade or business; and (3) those related to passive and rental losses. Please review the first page of Form 1040 at the end of Chapter 1 to see the various deductions, or Adjustments to Income beginning on line 23.

| **General** | **Self-employed** | **Passive** |
|---|---|---|
| Individual Retirement Accounts | Trade or business expenses | Passive losses |
| Moving expenses | Hobby losses | Rental losses |
| Forfeiture penalties | Casualty losses | At risk rules |
| Alimony | Depreciation & amortization | |
| Jury duty pay | Section 179 election | |
| Student loan interest | Self-employment tax | |
| | Self-employed health insurance | |
| | Retirement accounts | |

There are also some other deductions, such as capital losses and bad debts, that are used in calculating adjusted gross income. Those will be covered in Chapter 6.

# GENERAL DEDUCTIONS

## INDIVIDUAL RETIREMENT ACCOUNT DEDUCTION

Contributions to an Individual Retirement Account (IRA) are deductible in determining adjusted gross income. The amount allowable as a deduction is the lessor of $2,000, or the taxpayer's earned income. If the taxpayer is married, each is entitled to an IRA, subject to the same earned income limitation. Alimony received by the spouse is treated as earned income for the purposes of this test. For a married couple with a non-working spouse, a spousal IRA of $2,000 is allowed for the non-working spouse provided the combined earned income of the couple exceeds the total contributors.

In order for the IRA to be deductible, it must be paid during the taxable year, or by the due date of the return. Individuals may contribute up to the age of 70.

### Active Participation in Employer Provided Plan

If the taxpayer, or the taxpayer's spouse is an active participant in an employer provided retirement plan, including a Keogh or SEP plan, then the deduction may be disallowed.

- If the taxpayer(s) adjusted gross income (AGI) does not exceed $50,000 if married or $30,000 if single, then the deduction is fully allowed.
- If the taxpayer's AGI is in excess of those limits, the IRA deduction is reduced on a pro-rata basis over the next $10,000. However, there is a $200 floor (minimim) if the AGI is not above the phaseout range.

---

**Example 1:** W is single and earned a salary of $32,000 during 1999. This is his only income. W is an active participant in his company's retirement plan. W contributes $2,000 into an IRA during 1999.

$$\$2,000 \ \times \ \frac{(32,000 - 30,000)}{\$ 10,000} \ = \ \$400 \text{ disallowed}$$

Thus, W may deduct only $1,600 of his $2,000 contribution.

**Note:** If W's AGI was $22,000, he could deduct the entire $2,000 IRA contribution because his AGI is under the $30,000. If his AGI was $42,000, none of the IRA would be deductible because he exceeded the $10,000 phase-out range.

---

Also, when an individual's **spouse** is an active participant in an employer-sponsored retirement plan, the IRA deduction for such an individual (the non-participant) is phased-out only for married couples with AGI between $150,000 and $160,000.

Effective in 1998, the 10% tax on early distributions (59 ½) will not apply to amounts withdrawn for "qualified higher education expenses" or "first time homebuyer expenses."

## ROTH IRAs

A taxpayer can make a **nondeductible** IRA (Roth IRA) contribution of up to $2,000 per year. There are many interesting provisions, but generally:

- contributions may be made by individuals who are 70 1/2 years and older
- there are no mandatory distribution rules
- there are no restrictions due to the active participation rule

There are some limitations. For example, the phase-out range for allowing the contribution is as follows:

| | |
|---|---|
| Married, filing jointly | $ 150,000 - $ 160,000 |
| Single | $ 95,000 - $ 110,000 |

When distributions are made from a Roth IRA, the distributions are free of taxes and penalties assuming that the taxpayer has maintained the IRA for 5 years or more, and the distribution:

- was made on or after the taxpayer attains the age of 59 1/2.
- was paid to the beneficiary upon the death of the taxpayer
- was made on account of the taxpayer becoming disabled
- was made for first-time homebuyer expenses (up to a maximum of $10,000)

## EDUCATION IRAs

Taxpayers can make nondeductible contributions of up to $500 for each beneficiary under the age of 18 to an Education IRA. The contribution limit of $500 is phased-out for individuals using the same ranges as the Roth IRAs described above. Generally, when distributions are made from an Education IRA, the distributions are free of taxes and penalties to the extent that proceeds are used for qualified education expenses (tuition, fees, room and board) of the beneficiary. The exclusion is not available in any year in which the Hope Credit or Lifetime Learning Credit (Chapter 5) is claimed.

## MOVING EXPENSES

A deduction is allowed for the qualified costs of moving in connection with starting work at a new place of business. This deduction is not restricted to only employees, but is available to self-employed individuals as well. In determining the allowability of the deduction there are two tests: Time and Distance.

**Time:** Basically, the taxpayer must be an employee at the new location for at least 39 weeks after the move.

**Distance:** The distance from the taxpayer's old residence to the new job must be at least 50 miles farther than the distance from the old residence to the old job. Notice that where the new residence is located is not relevant.

Qualified moving expenses include the reasonable costs of:
- Moving the household goods and personal belongings
- Traveling enroute from the old residence to the new residence. Meals are not allowed.

The Revenue Reconciliation Act of 1993 radically changed this deduction for moves after 1993. A high-level summary appears below:

| Tax issue | Before RRA 93 | After RRA 93 |
|---|---|---|
| Distance test | 35 miles | 50 miles |
| Expense classification | Deduction from AGI | Deduction for AGI |
| Direct moving costs | Allowed | Allowed |
| Meals during the move | Only 80% allowed | Not allowed |
| Indirect costs (househunting, temporary living) | Limited | Not allowed |
| Qualified moving cost reimbursement | Included as gross income | Not included |

## PENALTY ON EARLY WITHDRAWAL OF SAVINGS

When a taxpayer invests in a long-term savings account or certificate of deposit, the rate is generally higher than a conventional savings account. The long-term commitment provides the higher rate. However, should the holder withdraw the funds prematurely, the bank assesses a penalty which effectively reduces the rate of interest earned on the investment. Because the bank must report the total interest earned as gross income, the tax code allows a deduction for any penalty assessed for this early withdrawal. The net effect of the deduction is to reduce the reported interest income down to the net amount received. The penalty is deducted in the year assessed, which may not coincide with the year that the bulk of the interest is earned.

> **Example 2:** Y invests $50,000 in a one year certificate of deposit on March 31, 1999. For the year ended December 31, 1999, Y reports interest earned of $3,000. On January 10, 2000, Y withdraws the money before the maturity date and is assessed a penalty of $2,000 by the bank. Y must report the $3,000 of interest income in 1999, and deduct the penalty of $2,000 in 2000, even though the penalty effectively pertains to the 1999 interest income. You do not restate the 1999 income for the 2000 penalty.

## ALIMONY DEDUCTION

A deduction is allowed for alimony payments made under a written decree of divorce or separate maintenance. See Chapter 2 for a complete analysis of what is deductible and what is not.

## JURY DUTY PAY

If a taxpayer is called for jury duty for an extended period of time, they may receive jury duty pay. This is included as income. The amount of pay is usually very low, so employers frequently continue to pay their employees while serving on the jury, with the stipulation that any jury pay they receive be returned to the employer. The payment of the jury duty pay to the employer is a deduction allowed in arriving at adjusted gross income.

## STUDENT LOAN INTEREST

A taxpayer is allowed a deduction for interest paid on qualified educational loans. Qualified educational loans include indebtedness for higher education, such as tuition, fees, room and board of the taxpayer, spouse, or dependent. The deduction is allowed only for the first 60 months that interest payments are required, to a maximum of $1,500 in 1999. This amount is increased in future years. Similar to other deductions, there is a phase-out range of deductibility as follows:

|  | Phase-out range |
| --- | --- |
| Married, filing jointly | $ 60,000 - $ 75,000 |
| Single | $ 40,000 - $ 55,000 |

# SELF-EMPLOYED TAXPAYERS (IN A TRADE OR BUSINESS)

Gross income from a taxpayer's trade or business, minus the allowable trade or business expenses equals self-employment income. Self-employment income includes those activities where the taxpayer is conducting a trade or business. Preparing tax returns, consulting, operating a repair service, or being the director of a business are examples of carrying on a business. Being named as an executor of an estate and receiving a fee is not considered income for self-employment purposes.

According to Code Section 162, a cash basis taxpayer may deduct all **ordinary and necessary** expenses paid **in carrying on** their trade or business. On the exam, when you are told what business a taxpayer is in, think about what the ordinary and necessary expenses of that business would be. Certain expenses, however, are subject to various limitations while others are not deductible at all.

## BUSINESS MEALS & ENTERTAINMENT

The ordinary and necessary expenses paid for business meals and entertainment are deductible if they are (1) directly related or (2) associated with your trade or business. The expense may not be lavish and the taxpayer must be present at the meal. In general, you **may only deduct 50%** of your business related meals and entertainment expenses.

## BUSINESS GIFTS

A deduction is allowed for the cost of business gifts. However, the **maximum per gift is $25** per person per year. A gift to the spouse of a client is deemed to be a gift to the client if there is no business relationship with the spouse.

## CLUB DUES AND MEMBERSHIP FEES

Starting in 1994, **no deduction is allowed for dues** or membership fees in any club organized for business, pleasure, recreation, or other social purpose. Exceptions have been carved out for chamber of commerce dues, etc.

## SUBSTANTIATION

A taxpayer is required to provide substantiation for business expenses. The IRS requires substantiation for expenditures of $75 or more.

## PERSONAL EXPENSES

The payment of personal expenses through the self-employed taxpayer's business account does not make the expense deductible. Typical expenditures that you may see on the CPA exam which are not deductible by a self-employed business are:

- Estimated federal or state income tax payments.
- Salary to the owner. This is a personal draw, not a deductible expense.
- Charitable contributions. This is a personal deduction, not a business deduction.

# HOBBY LOSS RULES

In order to claim a deduction, the taxpayer must be carrying on a trade or business. There is the assumption that the taxpayer is engaged in the activity for profit. It is not unusual that business activities do not always generate a profit, especially in start-up situations, difficult market times, redeveloping periods, etc. However, when the activity has an element of pleasure in it, IRS may view the activity as if it were not engaged in for profit, and disallow any losses from that activity.

Historically, activities such as horse racing, dog breeding, stamp collecting, and log cabin sales/building, do not generate any short-term profit. IRS frequently views the loss as a lack of profit motive or intent, and disallows the losses. Section 183 of the Code has provided rules for who has to prove the profit intent. The presumptive rule states that if an activity shows a profit in at least three of the last five years, the **IRS has the burden of proof** to show the taxpayer is not in a trade or business, and that the loss is personal and non-deductible. If it shows a profit in less than the three years, the **taxpayer has the burden** to prove that he is in a trade or business and the losses are deductible. (The rule for horses is two out of seven years rather than five.)

# CASUALTY LOSS DEDUCTION

If a taxpayer in business has a loss from a casualty such as fire, storm, shipwreck, or theft, a deduction is allowed for the decrease in value, or its adjusted basis, whichever is less, minus any insurance reimbursement. As a business loss, this is **fully deductible** and not subject to the $100 floor and 10% of adjusted gross income test required for a personal casualty loss.

# COST RECOVERY AND DEPRECIATION EXPENSE

A deduction is allowed for the exhaustion, wear and tear of personal and real property. Assets placed in service after 1986 are under the Modified Accelerated Cost Recovery System (MACRS). Under MACRS, assets have class lives and no salvage value. The most popular class lives on the exam are:

| | |
|---|---|
| 5 year | Automobiles & light trucks, computers and R & D property |
| 7 year | Office furniture and equipment |
| 27.5 years | Residential rental property |
| 39 years | Non-residential (commercial) property |

Assets under the 5 and 7 year classes are recovered under the double declining balance method. Assets under the 27.5 and 39 year classes are recovered under the straight-line method.

In addition, the cost of the assets are recovered (depreciated) using three basic conventions, or methods:

| | |
|---|---|
| Half-year | For personal property, with a half year recovery in the first and last year. |
| Mid-quarter | For personal property when more than 40% of all property purchases occur in the last quarter of the year. Rates are adjusted to reflect a mid-quarter start point. |
| Mid-month | For residential and commercial real estate, recovery starts in the middle of the month the property was placed in service. |

---

**Example 3**: J purchases a computer for $10,000 on September 1, 1999. This is a five year class asset. The straight-line rate would have been 20%. Double the straight-line rate is 40%. The MACRS deduction for year 1 and 2 are

Year 1          $10,000 X 40% = $4,000 X 50% (for the half-year) = $2,000

Year 2          $10,000 - $2,000 = $8,000 X 40% = $3,200.

(Hint: The cost of $10,000 declines by the $2,000 recovery of year 1 to $8,000. The balance is recovered using the 40% rate.)

---

**Example 4:** J purchases commercial real estate, exclusive of land, for $304,200 on September 8, 1999. This is a 39 year class asset. The straight-line method is used. Under the mid-month convention, the cost recovery would be one-half of a month for September and three full months until the end of the year.

| | |
|---|---|
| Cost of the building | $ 304,200 |
| Recovery period | 39 yrs |
| Annual cost recovery | $ 7,800 |
| | |
| Monthly cost recovery | $ 650 |
| Months of cost recovery | 3.5 mths |
| 1999 cost recovery | $ 2,275 |

---

The cost recovery for **listed property** is limited to a maximum each year. For automobiles placed in service in 1999, the maximum deduction by year is:

| | |
|---|---|
| First year | $ 3,060 |
| Second year | 5,000 |
| Third year | 2,950 |
| Following years | 1,775 |

> **Example 5**: During 1999, P purchases a new automobile for business at a cost of $40,000. The automobile is used 100% for business. The automobile is five year property. The first year MACRS depreciation would be $8,000 ($40,000 X 20%), except that this is listed property. The maximum first year cost recovery is $3,160.
>
> If P used the car only 80% for business, his deduction would be 80% of $3,060, or $2,448.

## AMORTIZATION EXPENSE

Amortization is the cost of recovering intangible assets such as leasehold improvements and the new Section 197 intangibles. Effective August 10, 1993, the cost of the Section 197 intangibles may be amortized over a 15 year life on a straight-line basis. A partial listing of these assets are:

- Goodwill
- Going concern value
- Covenants not to compete
- Customer lists
- Technological know-how
- Franchise, trademark or tradename

## SECTION 179 ELECTIONS

At the election of the taxpayer, up to $19,000 for 1999 of qualifying property may be immediately expensed rather than capitalizing the asset and depreciating it over its useful life. This is an annual election and has the following limits:

- The amount expensed cannot exceed the taxable income from that trade or business
- The amount of qualifying property purchased cannot exceed $200,000 in the year. If it does, the $19,000 is reduced dollar for dollar for every dollar above $200,000.

> **Example 6:** Q purchased four computers for $12,000 and wished to make a Section 179 election. The taxable income from his service business is $4,000 before this election. Q may **elect** to expense the entire $12,000, but only $4,000 will be **allowed** as a current year deduction under Section 179. The disallowed amount of $8,000 may be carried over indefinitely until the taxpayer has taxable business income.

> **Example 7:** P purchased $207,000 of equipment during 1999 and wants to make a Section 179 election. His taxable income is $50,000. Since the amount of qualifying property purchased exceeds $200,000, P must reduce the $19,000 by the excess of $7,000. His Section 179 election is limited to $12,000.

## ONE-HALF OF THE SELF-EMPLOYMENT TAX

A deduction is allowed for one-half of the self-employment tax paid. The logic behind the allowance of one-half of the tax is that it is, in essence, the matching portion of the social security tax an employer would have to pay on its employees. The actual computation of the self-employment tax is shown in Chapter 5.

## SELF-EMPLOYED HEALTH INSURANCE DEDUCTION

A deduction is allowed for **60%** of the cost of premiums paid for medical insurance by the self-employed taxpayer. This includes insurance on the taxpayer, spouse and dependents. The balance of the health insurance premium is allowed as an itemized deduction. This deduction is not allowed if the taxpayer is eligible to participate in an employer sponsored health plan of the taxpayer or the spouse.

## SELF-EMPLOYED RETIREMENT PLANS
A deduction is allowed for contributions made to the self-employed taxpayer's qualified retirement plan.

In general, the allowable contribution into a **Keogh** plan is the lessor of (1) $30,000 or 25% of the net earnings from self-employment after being reduced by the Keogh contribution and one-half of the self-employment tax. (This is circular reasoning, therefore use 20% of the net after reduction for the 50% of the self-employment tax and you end up with 25% factor)  The actual contribution is not due until the due date of the return.

---

**Example 8:**  Y is self-employed and had self-employed income of $30,000 for the year.  His self-employment tax was $4,238 and wants to make the maximum contribution to his Keogh Plan.

| | |
|---|---:|
| Self-Employed net income | $ 30,000 |
| Less: 50% of self-employment tax | -2,119 |
| | 27,881 |
| Less: Keogh contribution (20%) | -5,576 |
| Net after contribution | $ 22,305 |

**Proof: $22,305 X 25% = $5,576**

---

Various other self-employed retirement plans, including a profit sharing Keogh plans and the Simplified Employee Pension (SEP) plan allow a contribution up to 15% of the net earnings from self-employment.

# PASSIVE ACTIVITY AND RENTAL LOSSES

## GENERAL RULE
Losses from passive activities are deductible only to the extent of passive income.  Passive losses may not be offset against active income (salaries, wages, etc.) or portfolio income (interest, dividends, etc.).  This passive loss limitation applies to individuals, personal service and closely held corporations.  A closely held corporation is defined as a corporation where more than 50% of the stock is owned, directly or indirectly, by not more than 5 individuals.  The losses are suspended until passive income is generated, or eventually deducted when the investment is disposed of.  Passive losses are reported on Form 8582.

## PASSIVE ACTIVITY DEFINED
A passive activity is defined as any trade or business, or income producing activity, where the taxpayer **does not materially participate**.  Material participation assumes that the taxpayer is involved on a regular, continuous and substantial basis.  One test issued by IRS in their 1988 regulations identified that more than 500 hours in a year qualified as in material participation.

---

**Example 9:**  P is a full-time employee and earns $70,000 as an electrical engineer for a large corporation.  P also invested $10,000 in a start-up venture to design and manufacturer cyberspace headgear.  P spends 90 hours per year (weekends and one week of his vacation time) managing this business. P's share of the current year's loss of this venture was $8,000.   This loss is considered to be from a passive activity and cannot be deducted against his ordinary income of $70,000.

---

## RENTAL ACTIVITY

The Code also defines all rental activities as passive activities, unless this is the taxpayer's business. However, an exception to the "no loss is allowed" rule exists for rental activity losses of **up to $25,000 per year**. To qualify the taxpayer must:

- **actively** participate in the activity and
- own 10% or more of the activity.

Active participation means participating in the management decisions, but is not as involved as the regular, continuous and substantial basis under the passive loss regulations.

In addition to the $25,000 limitation, there is an additional limitation as to the amount of the deductible loss when the taxpayer's adjusted gross income exceeds a threshold amount. The $25,000 maximum loss against ordinary income, is reduced by 50% of the excess of their adjusted gross income over $100,000. The loss is completely phased out at $150,000. The disallowed loss is carried over indefinitely.

---

**Example 10:** R is a full-time employee and earns $120,000 as a controller for a large corporation. R actively participates as a 30% owner of real estate located nearby. During the year, R's share of the rental loss is $30,000. R has no other rental or passive activities.

R first reduces the $30,000 rental loss to the maximum of $25,000. The excess of $5,000 is suspended. The $25,000 is then limited by the AGI test. His AGI exceeds the $100,000 by $20,000, thus the disallowed portion is determined as follows:

$$\$25,000 \text{ maximum} \times \frac{20,000}{50,000} = \$10,000 \text{ disallowed}$$

R is allowed a current deduction against ordinary income of $15,000 ($25,000 - $10,000 disallowed portion). The $15,000 disallowed portion is carried forward indefinitely. Next year, the carried forward components are added to any new losses and the same tests are applied.

---

## AT RISK LIMITATIONS

The at-risk limitations override all the previous tests of deductibility. Simply put, if a taxpayer is not at risk for the loss, then no deduction is allowed. The at-risk rules take precedent over all other rules.

---

**Example 11:** Q invests $10,000 in a business venture. Q's liability in this venture is limited to his investment of $10,000. During the year, the venture generates a loss, of which Q's share is $23,000. The most Q may claim as a loss for the current year is $10,000, because he is not at-risk for anything beyond his initial investment. Once the at-risk limitation is determined, the taxpayer would then test the $10,000 for passive loss restrictions, etc.

**Example 12:** Same facts as in Example 11 except that Q had passive income of $12,000 from another investment. Q could deduct only the $10,000 loss against the $12,000 passive income. Even though Q's total passive loss was $23,000, the at-risk limitations prevent any more than $10,000 to be offset against any income at this time.

---

# Chapter Three -- Questions
# Deductions For Adjusted Gross Income

## General Deductions

1. Sol and Julia Crane are married, and filed a joint return for 1999. Sol earned a salary of $80,000 from his job at Troy Corp., where Sol is covered by his employer's pension plan. In addition, Sol and Julia earned interest of $3,000 on their joint savings account. Julia is not employed, and the couple had no other income. On January 15, 2000, Sol contributed $2,000 to an IRA for himself, and $2,000 to an IRA for his spouse. The allowable IRA deduction in the Cranes' 1999 joint return is
a.   $0
b.   $2,000
c.   $2,250
d.   $4,000

2. For 1999, Val and Pat White filed a joint return. Val earned $35,000 in wages and was covered by his employer's qualified pension plan. Pat was unemployed and received $5,000 in alimony payments for the first 4 months of the year before remarrying. The couple had no other income. Each contributed $2,000 to an IRA account. The allowable IRA deduction on their 1999 joint tax return is
a.   $4,000
b.   $2,250
c.   $2,000
d.   $0

3. For the taxable year Fred and Wilma Todd reported the following items of income:

|  | Fred | Wilma |
|---|---|---|
| Salary | $40,000 | — |
| Interest income | 1,000 | $ 200 |
| Cash prize won on T.V. game show | — | 8,800 |
|  | $41,000 | $9,000 |

Fred is not covered by any qualified retirement plan and he and Wilma established individual retirement accounts during the year. Assuming a joint return is filed, what is the maximum amount that they can be allowed for contributions to their individual retirement accounts?
a.   $0.
b.   $2,000.
c.   $2,250.
d.   $4,000.

4. Grey, a calendar year taxpayer, was employed and resided in New York. On February 2, 1999, Grey was permanently transferred to Florida by his employer. Grey worked full-time for the entire year. In 1999, Grey incurred and paid the following unreimbursed expenses in relocating.

| | |
|---|---|
| Lodging and travel expenses while moving | $1,000 |
| Pre-move househunting costs | 1,200 |
| Costs of moving household furnishings and personal effects | 1,800 |

What amount was deductible as moving expense on Grey's 1999 tax return?
a.   $4,000
b.   $2,800
c.   $1,800
d.   $1,000

5. The unreimbursed direct moving expenses of an employee who takes a new job 100 miles away from a previous residence and place of employment are
a.   Fully deductible from gross income in arriving at adjusted gross income.
b.   Deductible only as miscellaneous itemized deductions subject to a 2% floor.
c.   Fully deductible only as itemized deductions.
d.   Not deductible.

6. In 1999, Barlow moved from Chicago to Miami to start a new job, incurring costs of $1,200 to move household goods and $2,500 in temporary living expenses. Barlow was not reimbursed for any of these expenses. What amount should Barlow deduct for moving expenses as a deduction from gross income?
a.   $1,200
b.   $2,700
c.   $3,000
d.   $3,700

7. Marc Clay was unemployed for the entire year 1998. In January 1999, Clay obtained full-time employment 60 miles away from the city where he had resided during the ten years preceding 1999. Clay kept his new job for the entire year 1999. In January 1999, Clay paid direct moving expenses of $300 in relocating to his new city of residence, but he received **no** reimbursement for these expenses. In his 1999 income tax return, Clay's direct moving expenses are

a. Not deductible.
b. Fully deductible only if Clay itemizes his deductions.
c. Fully deductible from gross income in arriving at adjusted gross income.
d. Deductible subject to a 2% threshold if Clay itemizes his deductions.

8. For the year ended December 31, 1999, Elmer Shaw earned $3,000 interest at Prestige Savings Bank, on a time savings account scheduled to mature in 2000. In January 2000, before filing his 1999 income tax return, Shaw incurred a forfeiture penalty of $1,500 for premature withdrawal of the funds from his account. Shaw should treat this $1,500 forfeiture penalty as a

a. Penalty not deductible for tax purposes.
b. Deduction from gross income in arriving at 2000 adjusted gross income.
c. Deduction from 2000 adjusted gross income, deductible only if Shaw itemizes his deductions for 1999.
d. Reduction of interest earned in 1999, so that only $1,500 of such interest is taxable on Shaw's 1999 return.

9. For the year ended December 31, 1999, Don Raff earned $1,000 interest at Ridge Savings Bank on a certificate of deposit scheduled to mature in 2000. In January 2000, before filing his 1999 income tax return, Raff incurred a forfeiture penalty of $500 for premature withdrawal of the funds. Raff should treat this $500 forfeiture penalty as a

a. Reduction of interest earned in 1999, so that only $500 of such interest is taxable on Raff's 1999 return.
b. Deduction from 2000 adjusted gross income, deductible only if Raff itemizes his deductions for 2000.
c. Penalty **not** deductible for tax purposes.
d. Deduction from gross income in arriving at 2000 adjusted gross income.

10. With regard to alimony in connection with a 1999 divorce, which of the following statements is true?
a. Alimony may be paid either in cash or in property.
b. Alimony must terminate at the death of the payee spouse.
c. The divorced couple may be members of the same household at the time alimony is paid.
d. Alimony may be deductible by the payor spouse to the extent that payment is contingent on the status of the divorced couple's child.

11. Art Hollender was divorced from his wife Diane in 1998. Under the terms of the divorce decree, he was required to make the following periodic payments each month to his former wife who retained custody of their children:

| | |
|---|---|
| Alimony | $600 |
| Child support | 400 |

For 1999 his only income was his salary of $40,000, and he paid only ten payments of $1,000 per month to his former wife under the terms of the divorce decree. What is his 1999 adjusted gross income?
a. $30,000.
b. $32,800.
c. $34,800.
d. $40,000.

12. Dale received $1,000 in 1999 for jury duty. In exchange for regular compensation from her employer during the period of jury service, Dale was required to remit the entire $1,000 to her employer in 1999. In Dale's 1999 income tax return, the $1,000 jury duty fee should be
a. Claimed in full as an itemized deduction.
b. Claimed as an itemized deduction to the extent exceeding 2% of adjusted gross income.
c. Deducted from gross income in arriving at adjusted gross income.
d. Included in taxable income without a corresponding offset against other income.

13. Which allowable deduction can be claimed in arriving at an individual's adjusted gross income.
a. Alimony payment.
b. Charitable contribution.
c. Personal casualty loss.
d. Unreimbursed business expense of an outside salesperson.

# Business Related Deductions

14. Gilda Bach is a cash basis self-employed consultant. For the year she determined that her net income from self-employment was $80,000. In reviewing her books you determine that the following items were included as business expenses in arriving at the net income of $80,000:

| | |
|---|---|
| Salary drawn by Gilda Bach | $20,000 |
| Estimated federal self-employment and income taxes paid | 6,000 |
| Malpractice insurance premiums | 4,000 |
| Cost of attending professional seminar | 1,000 |

Based upon the above information, what should Gilda Bach report as her net self-employment income?
a. $91,000.
b. $105,000.
c. $106,000.
d. $110,000.

15. Rich is a cash basis self-employed air-conditioning repairman with gross business receipts of $20,000. Rich's cash disbursements were as follows:

| | |
|---|---|
| Air conditioning parts | $2,500 |
| Yellow Pages Listing | 2,000 |
| Estimated federal income taxes on self-employment income | 1,000 |
| Business long-distance telephone calls | 400 |
| Charitable contributions | 200 |

What amount should Rich report as net self-employment income?
a. $15,100
b. $14,900
c. $14,100
d. $13,900

16. Alex Berger, a retired building contractor, earned the following income during the year:

| | |
|---|---|
| Director's fee received from Keith Realty Corp. | $600 |
| Executor's fee received from the estate of his deceased sister | 7,000 |

Berger's self-employment income is
a. $0.
b. $600.
c. $7,000.
d. $7,600.

17. During the holiday season, Barmin Corporation gave business gifts to 16 customers. The value of the gifts, which were not of an advertising nature, was as follows:

$$4 @ \$ 10$$
$$4 @ \$ 25$$
$$4 @ \$ 50$$
$$4 @ \$100$$

Barmin can deduct as a business expense a total of:
a. $0.
b. $140.
c. $340.
d. $740.

18. The self-employment tax is
a. Fully deductible as an itemized deduction.
b. Fully deductible in determining net income from self-employment.
c. One-half deductible from gross income in arriving at adjusted gross income.
d. Not deductible.

19. Davis, a sole proprietor with no employees, has a Keogh profit-sharing plan to which he may contribute 15% of his annual earned income. For this purpose, "earned income" is defined as net self-employment earnings reduced by the
a. Deductible Keogh contribution.
b. Self-employment tax.
c. Self-employment tax and one-half of the deductible Keogh contribution.
d. Deductible Keogh contribution and one-half of the self-employment tax.

20. On December 1, 1998, Michaels, a self-employed cash basis taxpayer, borrowed $100,000 to use in her business. The loan was to be repaid on November 30, 1999. Michaels paid the entire interest of $12,000 on December 1, 1998. What amount of interest was deductible on Michaels' 1999 income tax return?
a. $12,000
b. $11,000
c. $1,000
d. $0

21. Browne, a self-employed taxpayer, had 1999 business net income of $100,000 prior to any expense deduction for equipment purchases. In 1999, Browne purchased and placed into service, for business use, office machinery costing $20,000. This was Browne's only 1999 capital expenditure. Browne's business establishment was not in an economically distressed area. Browne made a proper and timely expense election to deduct the maximum amount. Browne was not a member of any pass through entity. What is Browne's deduction under the election?
a. $4,000
b. $17,000
c. $18,000
d. $19,000

22. Under the modified accelerated cost recovery system (MACRS) of depreciation for property placed in service after 1986,
a. Used tangible depreciable property is excluded from the computation.
b. Salvage value is ignored for purposes of computing the MACRS deduction.
c. No type of straight-line depreciation is allowable.
d. The recovery period for depreciable realty must be at least 27.5 years.

23. On August 1, 1999, Graham purchased and placed into service an office building costing $264,000 including $30,000 for the land. What was Graham's MACRS deduction for the office building in 1999?
a. $9,600
b. $6,000
c. $3,600
d. $2,250

24. With regard to depreciation computations made under the general MACRS method, the half-year convention provides that
a. One-half of the first year's depreciation is allowed in the year in which the property is placed in service, regardless of when the property is placed in service during the year, and a half-year's depreciation is allowed for the year in which the property is disposed of.
b. The deduction will be based on the number of months the property was in service, so that one-half month's depreciation is allowed for the month in which the property is placed in service and for the month in which it is disposed of.

c. Depreciation will be allowed in the first year of acquisition of the property only if the property is placed in service **no** later than June 30 for calendar-year corporations.
d. Depreciation will be allowed in the last year of the property's economic life only if the property is disposed of after June 30 of the year of disposition for calendar-year corporations.

25. How is the depreciation deduction of nonresidential real property, placed in service in 1999, determined for regular tax purposes using MACRS?
a. Straight-line method over 40 years.
b. 150% declining-balance method with a switch to the straight-line method over 27.5 years.
c. 150% declining-balance method with a switch to the straight-line method over 39 years.
d. Straight-line method over 39 years.

26. In 1999, Roe Corp. purchased and placed in service a machine to be used in its manufacturing operations. This machine cost $201,000. What portion of the cost may Roe elect to treat as an expense rather than as a capital expenditure?
a. $9,000
b. $17,000
c. $17,500
d. $18,000

27. Paul and Lois Lee, both age 50, are married and filed a joint return for 1999. Their 1999 adjusted gross income was $80,000, including Paul's $75,000 salary. Lois had no income of her own. Neither spouse was covered by an employer-sponsored pension plan. What amount could the Lees contribute to IRAs for 1999 to take advantage of their maximum allowable IRA deduction in their 1999 return?
a. $0
b. $2,000
c. $2,250
d. $4,000

## Rental Income & Passive Losses

28. Mort Gage, a cash basis taxpayer, is the owner of an apartment building containing 10 identical apartments. Gage resides in one apartment and rents out the remaining units. The following information is available for the current year.

| | |
|---|---|
| Gross rents | $21,600 |
| Fuel | 2,500 |
| Maintenance and repairs (rental apartments) | 1,200 |
| Advertising for vacant apartments | 300 |
| Depreciation of building | 5,000 |

What amount should Gage report as net rental income?
a. $12,600.
b. $13,350.
c. $13,500.
d. $17,600.

29. Emil Gow owns a two-family house which has two identical apartments. Gow lives in one apartment and rents out the other. In 1999, the rental apartment was fully occupied and Gow received $7,200 in rent. During the year ended December 31, 1999, Gow paid the following:

| | |
|---|---|
| Real estate taxes | $6,400 |
| Painting of rental apartment | 800 |
| Annual fire insurance premium | 600 |

In 1999, depreciation for the entire house was determined to be $5,000. What amount should Gow include in his adjusted gross income for 1999?
a. $2,900
b. $800
c. $400
d. $100

30. Cobb, an unmarried individual, had an adjusted gross income of $200,000 in 1999 before any IRA deduction, taxable social security benefits, or passive activity losses. Cobb incurred a loss of $30,000 in 1999 from rental real estate in which he actively participated. What amount of loss attributable to this rental real estate can be used in 1999 as an offset against income from nonpassive sources?
a. $0
b. $12,500
c. $25,000
d. $30,000

31. The rule limiting the allowability of passive activity losses and credits applies to
a. Partnerships.
b. S corporations.
c. Personal service corporations.
d. Widely-held C corporations.

32. If an individual taxpayer's passive losses and credits relating to rental real estate activities cannot be used in the current year, then they may be carried
a. Back three years, but they cannot be carried forward.
b. Forward up to a maximum period of 15 years, but they cannot be carried back.
c. Back three years or forward up to 15 years, at the taxpayer's election.
d. Forward indefinitely or until the property is disposed of in a taxable transaction.

33. With regard to the passive loss rules involving rental real estate activities, which one of the following statements is correct?
a. The term "passive activity" includes any rental activity without regard as to whether or not the taxpayer materially participates in the activity.
b. Gross investment income from interest and dividends **not** derived in the ordinary course of a trade or business is treated as passive activity income that can be offset by passive rental activity losses when the "active participation" requirement is **not** met.
c. Passive rental activity losses may be deducted only against passive income, but passive rental activity credits may be used against tax attributable to nonpassive activities.
d. The passive activity rules do **not** apply to taxpayers whose adjusted gross income is $300,000 or less.

34. Don Wolf became a general partner in Gata Associates on January 1, 1999 with a 5% interest in Gata's profits, losses, and capital. Gata is a distributor of auto parts. Wolf does not materially participate in the partnership business. For the year ended December 31, 1999, Gata had an operating loss of $100,000. In addition, Gata earned interest of $20,000 on a temporary investment. Gata has kept the principal temporarily invested while awaiting delivery of equipment that is presently on order. The principal will be used to pay for this equipment. Wolf's passive loss for 1999 is
a. $0
b. $4,000
c. $5,000
d. $6,000

## Released and Author Constructed Questions

*R98*

35. On December 1, 1997, Krest, a self-employed cash basis taxpayer, borrowed $200,000 to use in her business. The loan was to be repaid on November 30, 1998. Krest paid the entire interest amount of $24,000 on December 1, 1997. What amount of interest was deductible on Krest's 1997 income tax return?

a. $0
b. $2,000
c. $22,000
d. $24,000

*AC*

36. Dick and Mary are married and file a joint return for 1999. For the year, their AGI is $120,000. Dick and Mary make a $500 contribution to an Education IRA for their dependent daughter Emily. Which of the following statements is **not** true.

a. The distributed earnings from the Education IRA contribution will be excluded from gross income.
b. The exclusion is not available for any year the HOPE or Life Time Learning credit is claimed.
c. Room and board expenses constitute qualified education expenses if enrolled on at least a half-time basis.
d. The contributions are tax deductible.

*AC*

37. In order to attend college, Horace borrowed $20,000 from a local bank at an annual rate of 8% in order to pay for tuition, fees, room and board at college. The loan was not secured by his residence. During 1999, Horace paid $1,600 in interest expense to the bank. In filing his 1999 return, Horace has AGI of $40,000. Horace may claim a deduction for the interest paid of:

a. $0
b. $1,000
c. $1,500
d. $1,600

# Chapter Three -- Answers
# Deductions For Adjusted Gross Income

1. (b) $2,000. No deduction is allowed for Sol because Sol was covered by an employer plan **and** their adjusted gross income for 1999 was in excess of $60,000 (the $50,000 base plus the phase-out range of $10,000). However, Julia is entitled to a spousal IRA of $2,000.

2. (a) $4,000. Even though Val was covered by an employer plan, their combined adjusted gross income for the year did not exceed the base of $40,000 where the IRA deduction starts its phase-out. An interesting point is that the alimony received by Pat is treated as earned income for the purpose of determining the allowability of IRA contribution, but also, effective since 1997, the spousal IRA has been raised to $2,000.

3. (d) $4,000. Fred's earned income of $40,000 allows him a deductible IRA contribution of $2,000. Wilma has no earned income, but is entitled to the spousal IRA deduction of $2,000. Fred was not covered by a plan so therefore there is no concern related to their adjusted gross income.

4. (b) $2,800. Qualified moving expenses include only the direct costs of moving. The pre-move house-hunting costs are no longer deductible. Also, note that these are no longer an itemized deduction, but rather a deduction **for** adjusted gross income.

| | |
|---|---|
| Lodging & travel enroute | $ 1,000 |
| Costs of moving household | 1,800 |
| Total deduction | $ 2,800 |

5. (a) Unreimbursed direct moving expenses of an employee are fully deductible from gross income in arriving at adjusted gross income. They are no longer an itemized deduction. The distance test of 50 miles is also satisfied.

6. (a) $1,200. Qualified moving expenses include only the direct costs of moving. The temporary living expenses are no longer deductible. Also, note that these are no longer an itemized deduction, but rather a deduction **for** adjusted gross income.

7. (c) Unreimbursed direct moving expenses of an employee are fully deductible from gross income in arriving at adjusted gross income. The distance test of 50 miles and the time test of at least 39 weeks are also satisfied.

8. (b) Forfeiture penalties, or premature withdrawal penalties, are deductions for adjusted gross income. The taxpayer will be required to recognize all the interest earned on the investment in 1999 even though he will not receive it all in 2000 due to the penalty. The penalty must be reported in the year paid regardless of what period the interest was earned.

9. (d) Forfeiture penalties, or premature withdrawal penalties, are deductions from gross income in arriving at adjusted gross income. The taxpayer will be required to recognize all the interest earned on the investment in 1999 even though he will not receive it all in 2000 due to the penalty. The penalty must be reported in the year paid regardless of what period the interest was earned.

10. (b) Alimony payments must stop at the death of the payee spouse. Alimony must be paid in cash and not property, the former couple may not be members of the same household, and the payments may not be contingent (child support).

11. (c) $34,800. Only the alimony payments are allowed as a deduction for adjusted gross income. However, since Art only paid ten of his required twelve payments, the amount that is deemed to be child support for the year is determined first, then the alimony.

| | |
|---|---|
| Total payments made | $ 10,000 |
| Amount not alimony: | |
| 12 months @ $400 | -4,800 |
| Alimony component | $ 5,200 |

| | |
|---|---|
| Salary | $ 40,000 |
| Less: alimony | -5,200 |
| Adjusted gross income | $ 34,800 |

12. (c) The remittance of jury duty pay to an employer is a return of the employee's salary. This is a deduction from gross income in arriving at adjusted gross income.

13. (a) Only the alimony. Charitable contributions, personal casualty losses and unreimbursed employee expenses are all itemized deductions.

14. (c) $106,000. Not all of the items subtracted by Gilda are deductible for the determination of self-employment income. The malpractice insurance and seminar costs are both fully deductible as trade or business expenses. However, the "salary" is really a draw against her net earnings, and the estimated tax payments are personal payments and are non-deductible.

| | |
|---|---|
| Gilda's net income | $ 80,000 |
| Add back non-deductible: | |
| Salary or draw | 20,000 |
| Estimated tax payments | 6,000 |
| Self-employment income | $ 106,000 |

15. (a) $15,100. To determine the self-employment business income, Rich must subtract the expenses paid to carry on his trade or business from his business gross income. The estimated income taxes and charitable contributions are personal and not deductible. His net self-employed income is determined as follows:

| | |
|---|---|
| Gross business income | $ 20,000 |
| Less: Business expenses: | |
| Air conditioner parts | -2,500 |
| Yellow Pages Listings | -2,000 |
| Telephone expense | -400 |
| Self-employment income | $ 15,100 |

16. (b) $600. Director's fees are included as self-employed income. The executor's fee is a component of gross income, but is not considered to be income for self-employment purposes. Being an executor is not considered to be a trade or business.

17. (c) $340. The deduction for business gifts is limited to $25 per customer.

| | |
|---|---|
| 4 gifts @ $10 | $ 40 |
| 12 gifts @ $25 | 300 |
| Total deduction | $ 340 |

18. (c) One-half of the self-employment tax is allowed as a deduction from gross income in arriving at adjusted gross income.

19. (d) Earned income for the purpose of determining the Keogh profit-sharing contribution is the self-employment earnings reduced by the deductible Keogh contribution itself (circular reasoning) and one-half of the self-employment tax.

20. (b) $11,000. The amount of $12,000 paid in 1998 covered a twelve month period beginning December 1 of that year. $1,000 would have been deducted in 1998 and the prepaid balance of $11,000 deductible in 1999. The interest must be prorated.

21. (d) $19,000. In 1999, Browne may elect under Section 179 to immediately expense up to $19,000 of the cost of the equipment. He is not limited in his deduction because he has taxable income in excess of the $19,000 and he did not place in service qualifying assets in excess of $200,000.

22. (b) Salvage value is ignored. New and used property qualify, straight-line is allowable, and the general recovery periods of realty are 27.5 and 39 years.

23. (d) $2,250. Effective in 1994, the MACRS recovery period for commercial property is 39 years. Utilizing the straight-line, mid-month convention, the deduction covers one-half of August and all of September through December for a total of 4.5 months. The deduction is calculated as follows:

| | |
|---|---|
| Cost of the building & land | $ 264,000 |
| Less: cost of land | -30,000 |
| Depreciable property | 234,000 |
| Recovery period | 39 yrs |
| Annual cost recovery | $ 6,000 |
| | |
| 1999 recovery 4.5 months | $ 2,250 |

24. (a) This statement is true. Watch out for those problems where more than 40% of the property is placed in service during the last quarter of the year. In those situations, the **mid-quarter** convention is required.

25. (d) Non-residential rental property is depreciation using the straight-line method over 39 years.

26. (d) $18,000. Under the general rule of Section 179, Roe may elect to immediately expense up to $19,000 of the cost of qualified property placed in service during the year. Roe, however, is limited in how much qualifies because they placed property in service in excess of $200,000. Therefore, Roe must reduce the $19,000 on a dollar-by-dollar basis by the excess over $200,000 dollar for dollar, or in this case $1,000. Roe's portion of cost which qualifies under Section 179 is therefore $18,000. ($19,000 - 1,000).

27. (d) $4,000. Since neither Paul nor Lois was covered by an employer-sponsored plan, they are not subject to any phase-out provisions. Paul is allowed a deductible IRA contribution of $2,000. Though Lois has no earned income, she is entitled to the spousal IRA deduction of $2,000. The maximum allowable IRA deduction is $2,000 plus $2,000 or $4,000.

28. (b) $13,350. This question requires an allocation of some common operating costs of the apartment between rental and personal. The rental costs are deductible while the personal are not.

|  | Total | 90% Rental | 10% Personal |
|---|---|---|---|
| Gross rents | $ 21,600 | $ 21,600 | |
| Less: | | | |
| Fuel | 2,500 | 2,250 | 250 |
| Maintenance & repairs | 1,200 | 1,200 | 0 |
| Advertising expense | 300 | 300 | 0 |
| Depreciation | 5,000 | 4,500 | 500 |
| Total expenses | 9,500 | 8,250 | 750 |
| Net rental income | 12,600 | $ 13,350 | |

29. (c) $400. This question requires an allocation of some common operating costs of the apartment between rental and personal. The rental costs are deductible while the personal are not.

|  | Total | 50% Rental | 50% Personal |
|---|---|---|---|
| Gross rents | $ 7,200 | $ 7,200 | |
| Less: | | | |
| Real estate taxes | 6,400 | 3,200 | 3,200 |
| Painting of rental unit | 800 | 800 | 0 |
| Fire insurance cost | 600 | 300 | 300 |
| Depreciation | 5,000 | 2,500 | 2,500 |
| Total expenses | 12,800 | 6,800 | |
| Net rental income | | $ 400 | |

30. (a) $0. Rental activities are classified as passive activities. In general, passive losses are only allowed to the extent of passive income. An exception to the law allows an individual to deduct up to $25,000 per year in rental losses. In Cobb's case, his $30,000 rental loss would first be limited to $25,000, with the $5,000 balance suspended until future years. However, for those individuals with adjusted gross income in excess of $100,000, the allowable deduction is reduced by 50% of that excess. After a range of $50,000, the deduction is fully eliminated. Since Cobb's adjusted gross income is over $150,000, the loss is fully phased-out. The otherwise allowable deduction of $25,000 is not allowed in the current year and is carried over to future years.

31. (c) The passive activity rules apply to personal service corporations, as well as individuals, trusts, estate and closely held corporations. Widely held corporations are exempted from this provision. Logically, partnerships and S Corporation are not subject to these rules due to the "flow-through" nature of the separately stated items.

32. (d) There is an unlimited carryforward period. They may be used to offset future passive income, or deducted in the year the property is finally disposed of in a taxable transaction.

33. (a) By definition.

34. (c) $5,000. This problem focuses in on the determination of the passive loss and the subsequent netting that takes place with any other form of income. The company has a passive loss of $100,000 and portfolio income of $20,000. Portfolio income generally can not be used to offset passive losses. Therefore, Wolf's share of the passive loss is 5% of $100,000 or $5,000. (Note the question does not ask how much of the loss can be used as a current deduction. Assuming no other passive gains, the answer would be zero.)

35. (b) $2,000. The amount of $24,000 paid in 1997 covered a twelve month period beginning December 1 of that year. $2,000 is allowable as a deduction in 1997, and the balance is treated as a prepaid amount for 1998. The interest must be prorated.

36. (d) A taxpayer is not entitled to claim a deduction for a contribution to an Education IRA. The Education IRA does provide for tax-free accumulation of earnings. It cannot be used in conjunction with the HOPE or Lifetime Learning Credit. The phase-out does not begin until the taxpayer's AGI exceeds $150,000.

37. (c) $1,500. An above the line deduction (not an itemized) is now allowed for interest paid on debt incurred to pay for higher education costs. However, for 1999, the amount is limited to $1,500.

# Chapter Four
# Deductions From Adjusted Gross Income

# Chapter Four
# Deductions From Adjusted Gross Income

## STANDARD VS. ITEMIZED DEDUCTIONS

Rather than claiming the standard deduction, a taxpayer may elect to itemize their deductions instead. The election to itemize is made by attaching Schedule A to Form 1040 when the taxpayer files the return. Schedule A is reproduced at the end of this chapter. This decision needs to be based upon the total amount of allowable itemized deductions as compared to the standard deduction for that taxpayer. (See Chapter 1 for the various standard deductions by filing status.) The following example highlights the election process:

---

**Example 1:** T is single and has no dependents. His only source of income is a salary of $50,000. During 1999 he paid state income taxes of $3,000, qualified mortgage interest of $7,000 and made allowable contributions of $2,000. In preparing his return, T is unsure as to whether to claim the standard deduction or itemize his deductions.

**Answer:** As a single (unmarried) taxpayer who is not a head of household or qualifying widower, T is allowed a standard deduction of $4,300 in 1999. His allowable itemized deductions are:

| | |
|---|---|
| State income taxes | $ 3,000 |
| Mortgage interest | 7,000 |
| Charitable contributions | 2,000 |
| Total | $ 12,000 |

Since T's itemized deductions of $12,000 exceed the standard deduction of $4,300, he would obtain a larger deduction by electing to itemize his deductions.

---

In deciding whether or not to make the election, it is important to understand what transactions qualify as allowable itemized deductions. That is the focus of this chapter.

## MEDICAL EXPENSES

A taxpayer may deduct medical expenses paid for the diagnosis, cure, mitigation, treatment, or prevention of disease, or for the purpose of affecting any structure or function of the body. In order for the expenditures to be deductible, they must be:

- Paid for the care of the taxpayer, spouse or dependents (not just the taxpayer's child)
- The deductible portion must exceed 7.5% of adjusted gross income.

Typical qualifying expenses include, but are not limited to medical insurance payments, doctor and hospital bills, prescription drugs, dental and eye care expenses (including contact lenses). Costs of maintaining special equipment needed for the care of the dependent, such as wheelchairs, ramps, and elevators, are allowable as well.

Payments for long-term care services and insurance premiums for long-term care will be classified as medical expenses subject to the 7.5% AGI threshold. The maximum allowed for the premium deduction ranges from $200 to $2,500 based upon the age of the taxpayer.

Expenditures for the overall general health of the taxpayer, such as vitamins or health clubs, and cosmetic surgery are **not** deductible.

## Reimbursements

The deductible medical expenses must be reduced by any insurance reimbursements received during the year. If the reimbursement is received in the following year, then it must be reported in the following year as gross income, up to the extent of the tax benefit received by the taxpayer in the year of the deduction.

---

**Example 2**: T pays medical insurance premiums of $4,000 and doctors and hospital bills of $3,000 in 1999. His adjusted gross income of $40,000. He is reimbursed $1,000 in 1999 from the insurance company. His medical deduction is:

| | |
|---|---:|
| Medical insurance | $ 4,000 |
| Doctors and hospitals | 3,000 |
| Total payments | 7,000 |
| Less: reimbursements | -1,000 |
| Expenses before limitation | 6,000 |
| Less: AGI threshold limitation: | |
| 7.5% of $40,000 | -3,000 |
| Allowable deductions | $ 3,000 |

**Example 3**: If T was not reimbursed the $1,000 until 2000, his 1999 deduction would increase to $4,000 and he would have to recognize the $1,000 insurance reimbursement as gross income in 2000.

---

## Capital Expenditures

When it is necessary to make medical expenditures of a capital nature, they are deductible only to the extent that there is not a corresponding increase in the fair market value of the property. For the purpose of installing wheelchair ramps and widening hallways, etc., there is deemed to be no increase in value of the property and the expenditure is fully deductible.

---

**Example 4:** S installs an elevator for his dependent mother at a cost of $17,000 at the advice of the physician due to her ailing heart. The fair value of S's house increases by $13,000 as a result. S may deduct the excess cost over the increase in value ($4,000) as a medical expense.

---

## Nursing Home & Special Schools

Nursing home costs are deductible medical expenses when the condition of the patient requires medical or nursing attention. The deductible costs may also include the cost of staying at that facility.

In addition, expenses related to tuition, room and board, as well as the cost of medical care may be deductible if the principal reason for sending a dependent to a special school is that school's special resources for treating that specific sickness or disease.

## Transportation and Lodging

The cost of transportation for medical treatment, which includes a parent's cost if they are accompanying a child, is allowed as a deduction. In lieu of computing the out-of-pocket costs of using your own vehicle, taxpayers are allowed to deduct 10 cents per mile, plus parking and tolls. A deduction for overnight lodging is allowed provided:

- The lodging is primarily for and essential to medical care
- Medical care is provided by a doctor in a licensed hospital
- Lodging cost is not lavish or extravagant
- There is no element of personal pleasure, recreation or vacation
- The amount of the deduction cannot exceed $50 per night

## Self-Employed Health Insurance Deduction

In Chapter 3, the deduction for 60% of the health insurance for self-employed individuals was discussed. In computing the allowable itemized deduction for medical insurance, you must reduce the premium for any amount claimed as a deduction for adjusted gross income. For example, if R was self-employed and paid $6,000 in medical insurance premiums, R would allocate $3,600 (60% of the $6,000) as a deduction for adjusted gross income and $2,400 (the balance of the $6,000) as an itemized deduction.

# TAXES

A deduction is allowed for state, local and foreign taxes paid during the year. There are no itemized deductions for any federal income taxes paid except for rare situations such as the environmental tax and the allocable share of a decedent's estate tax. In order for the taxes to be deductible, they must be the taxpayer's own tax obligation. Contrast this with medical expenses where the payment of a dependent's medical expenses were deductible. The deductible taxes are:

## STATE & LOCAL INCOME TAXES

Payments for state and local income taxes made are deductible in the year paid, regardless of the tax period the tax pertains to. An individual making estimated tax payments for the 1999 calendar year would generally make four payments throughout the year. Typically three payments would be paid within the 1999 year, and the last payment in early 2000. Only the three payments made in 1999 would qualify as a 1999 deduction. The last payment made in early 2000 would be deductible in 2000, even though it was for the 1999 income tax obligation. Likewise, late payments of balances due from prior years are deductible in the year of payment. State and local taxes **withheld** from an employee's paycheck are deemed as having been paid during the year.

## REAL ESTATE TAXES

Taxes paid on the ownership of real property, wherever situated, are allowed as a deduction. This would include the tax on the taxpayer's residence(s), land, and vacation homes, both domestic and foreign. Should the real property be rental or even part rental, the real estate taxes allocable to that portion must be shown as a rental expense, not an itemized deduction.

Real estate tax payments are usually periodic, such as semi-annually or quarterly. If a taxpayer purchases or sells real property during the year, the deduction must be apportioned based upon the number of days of ownership.

> **Example 5:** On March 15th, P paid $1,800 in real estate taxes on his residence, which covered the period from January 1st until June 30th. On May 1st he sold his residence to R. Since P held the property for four months, he may only deduct two thirds (four months of the six months) of real estate taxes paid.

## PERSONAL PROPERTY TAXES

A tax on personal property is deductible if the tax is based upon the value of the property and is assessed on an annual basis. Typically, once a year a city or town will assess a personal property tax on a taxpayer's motor vehicle or boat based upon its assessed or fair market value. That is a deductible tax. A flat fee, such as a registration fee of $50 per year, is not deductible.

## FOREIGN TAXES

When a taxpayer has income from foreign sources, there is frequently a tax paid to that foreign country. Very often that tax is withheld at its source, such as on interest or dividends. In computing one's taxes, the taxpayer has an option of treating the taxes paid to that foreign country as either a credit against his US taxes, or a deduction. Since the value of a tax credit is greater than that of a deduction, the credit is more frequently elected, but a deduction is allowable. See Chapter 5 for additional information on the foreign tax credit.

# INTEREST DEDUCTION

A taxpayer is allowed an itemized deduction for payments of qualified residence interest and investment interest. Similar to state taxes, it must be on the taxpayer's indebtedness. Interest on personal indebtedness is no longer allowable as a deduction.

## QUALIFIED RESIDENCE INTEREST

Interest paid on loans for the acquisition of a qualified residence or a home equity loan generally qualify for the deduction. A **qualified residence** represents the taxpayer's principal residence plus any other one. This second residence may be a vacation home, yacht or mobile home. The taxpayer may have more than two residences, and each year select which one is his second residence for tax purposes.

**Acquisition indebtedness** includes the cost of acquiring, constructing and substantially improving the residence of the taxpayer. In computing the interest deduction, the aggregate of indebtedness for both residences cannot exceed:

$1,000,000    if married filing jointly, or single
$ 500,000    if married filing separately

To determine the allowable deduction on borrowings in excess of this amount, the interest expense must be pro-rated.

---

**Example 6:** K purchased her first personal residence for $1,500,000 and borrowed $1,200,000. During the year, she paid $90,000 in interest on the mortgage. She may deduct only $75,000 as qualified residence interest. The balance of $15,000 is non-deductible personal interest.

$$\$90,000 \quad X \quad \frac{1,000,000}{1,200,000} \quad = \quad \$75,000 \quad \text{deductible}$$

---

**Home equity indebtedness** (borrowing) is usually used for personal, or non-deductible reasons such as college tuition, vacations, etc. In order to be deductible, the borrowings against a taxpayer's residence that are not classified as acquisition indebtedness, must be:

- Limited to the fair market value of the residence less any acquisition indebtedness, **or**
- $100,000, whichever is less, and
- Be secured by the residence

**Points** paid for obtaining a loan as it relates to acquisition indebtedness are fully deductible in the year paid. Points are a percentage of the borrowing. One point on an $80,000 mortgage equals $800. Points represent an adjustment to the interest rate, and not a service charge or a finders fee. For example, a bank may charge an interest rate of 10% with no points being paid by the borrower, or offer a rate of 9.75% with the borrower paying one point.

Points paid on a **refinancing** are not immediately deductible in full. They must be capitalized and amortized on a straight-line basis over the life of the new loan.

A **penalty** for the late payment or pre-payment of a mortgage is generally deductible.

## INVESTMENT INTEREST EXPENSE

When a taxpayer borrows money to acquire investments, the interest expense is classified as investment interest expense. The general rule is that the investment interest expense is allowed only to the extent of the net investment income. Any unused investment interest expense is carried over to future years. There is no limitation on the carryforward. Investment income includes interest, dividends, and royalties, but usually not capital gains unless the taxpayer makes special elections. From investment income, you then subtract the allowable investment expenses, excluding the interest expense. These investment expenses are subject to a 2% threshold and are described later in this chapter.

> **Example 7:** Late in 1999, K borrowed $30,000 to invest in securities. During the year 1999 she paid $400 in interest expense on the loan. There was no investment income. K cannot deduct the interest expense for 1999.
>
> **Example 8:** During 2000, K earned $4,000 in dividends on her investment; paid $2,500 in interest expense on the loan; and had allowable investment expenses of $100. Her allowable interest expense is $2,900, comprised of the $400 carryforward from 1999 and the $2,500 current year interest expense. The $2,900 does not exceed the current year's net investment interest income of $3,900 ($4,000 less $100), and is fully deductible.

Note: Interest on borrowings to acquire **tax-exempt securities** are non-deductible.


# CHARITABLE CONTRIBUTIONS

A deduction is allowed for a charitable contribution or gift paid during the year to a qualified organization. Qualified organizations include churches, or other religious organizations, educational organizations, medical or research organizations, and literary organizations. Federal, state and local organizations qualify as well if the gift is made solely for public purposes. A taxpayer is considered to have paid a charitable contribution if it was charged to his credit card account during the taxable year.

In determining the allowable deduction, there are limitations based upon the taxpayer's adjusted gross income, the type of gift and carryovers.

- In general, contributions cannot exceed **50% of the taxpayer's adjusted gross income** for the year
- Contributions to organizations that are not "50% organizations", such as a fraternal order, certain private nonoperating foundations, veterans' organizations, etc., cannot exceed 30% of the taxpayer's adjusted gross income.
- Contributions of appreciated long-term capital gain property to a 50% organization at its fair market value are **limited to 30% of adjusted gross income**. If the taxpayer elects to deduct the contribution using cost instead of fair market value, the limitation rises back to 50%. Short-term capital gain property is limited to cost.
- Contributions of appreciated long-term capital gain property to a 30% organization at its fair market value are limited to 20% of adjusted gross income.
- Limitations follow a hierarchy. 50% contributions are allowed first, then the 30%.
- Unreimbursed out-of-pocket costs are allowed as deductions. This includes travel at an optional 14 cents per mile, plus parking and tolls.
- Purchases of items (at an auction, fair, etc.) in excess of their fair market value give rise to a deduction, but only for the excess paid over its fair market value. A taxpayer receiving a book for a $25 donation must reduce the contribution by the fair market value of the book received.
- Unused charitable contributions due to the 50%, 30% and 20% limitations are carried over for a maximum of 5 years. In determining the allowable deduction for the current year, you first must consider the current year contributions, then the carryovers. Carryovers may expire if the taxpayer ignores the ordering of deduction.
- For gifts of $250 or more, **written substantiation** is required on a contemporaneous basis, otherwise, no deduction is allowed.

**Example 9:** Q made a cash contribution of $5,000 to his church which was substantiated in writing and his wife contributed stock with a fair market value of $12,000 and an adjusted basis of $2,000 to her college. The contributions are to qualified 50% organizations. Their adjusted gross income for the year was $30,000.

In determining the current year's allowable contribution it is important to heed the limitations. The overall limitation is 50% of their $30,000 AGI or $15,000, but the components and carryforwards are complicated.

**Step 1.** Determine the overall 50% limitation:

| | |
|---|---|
| Adjusted gross income | $ 30,000 |
| Overall contribution limitation | 50% |
| Maximum allowed this year | $ 15,000 |

**Step 2.** Determine what is used up by qualifying 50% contributions. The residual is available for the 30% contributions:

| | |
|---|---|
| Maximum allowable | $ 15,000 |
| Less: Contributions qualifying under 50% rule | -5,000 |
| Available for 30% limitation | $ 10,000 |

**Step 3.** Determine the deductibility of the stock contribution with a $12,000 FMV. The maximum allowable on the stock is 30% of their adjusted gross income, or $9,000.

| | |
|---|---|
| Adjusted gross income | $ 30,000 |
| Contribution limitation for FMV | 30% |
| Maximum allowed this year | $ 9,000 |

Even though the stock had a fair market value of $12,000, and there was still $10,000 available in under the 50% limitation test in Step 2, we determined that the 30% limitation was the true limiting factor because only $9,000 of the property contribution was allowed. Therefore:

| **Total allowable contributions:** | |
|---|---|
| Cash contributions | $ 5,000 |
| Stock - FMV (limited) | 9,000 |
| Total | $14,000 |

The $3,000 carryover ($12,000 less the $9,000 allowed) arises from the long-term capital property and will be subject to the 30% test each year until it is utilized or expires in five years.

# CASUALTY LOSSES

A taxpayer may deduct a loss for a personal casualty loss. A casualty loss is sudden and unexpected, and may include a theft loss as well. To determine the allowable loss:

1. Determine the lessor of the decrease in the fair market value of the asset destroyed, or its adjusted basis.
2. Subtract from that event, a floor of $100.
3. Combine all personal casualties for the year together.
4. The allowable deduction is the amount that exceeds 10% of the taxpayer's adjusted gross income.

---

**Example 11:** John is single and has adjusted gross income of $30,000 for the year. Duirng the year, his boat was totally destroyed during a storm. The boat had a fair market value of $17,000 at the time of the storm. Its adjusted basis was $14,000. The insurance company reimbursed John $10,000 for the loss.

**Answer:**
The adjusted basis ($14,000) is less than the decrease in the fair market value ($17,000); therefore, that is the starting point.

| | |
|---|---:|
| Lessor of adjusted basis or decrease in FMV | $14,000 |
| Less: insurance reimbursement | (10,000) |
| | 4,000 |
| Less: statutory floor | (100) |
| | 3,900 |
| Threshhold limitation of 10% of adjusted gross income | (3,000) |
| Allowable deduction | $    900 |

---

# MISCELLANEOUS 2% DEDUCTIONS

There are a number of employee related expenses which, if unreimbursed by the employer, are allowed as itemized deductions. In addition, there are a number of deductible expenses related to investments, tax determination and trade or businesses. These expenses are grouped together as what is referred to as miscellaneous itemized deductions, and they are deductible, **only to the extent that they exceed 2% of adjusted gross income**.

A brief summary of these deductions follows:

- Tax preparation fees and other fees for the determination of tax (audit representation, appraisals, etc.). However, preparation of a will is **not** deductible.
- Job hunting expenses
- Professional dues, including union dues
- Uniforms, safety clothing, etc., not otherwise usable by the taxpayer
- Business tools
- Investment expenses such as safety deposit boxes, investment publications and fees
- IRA custodial fees
- Unreimbursed employee expenses (mileage, 50% of business meals & entertainment, etc.)
- Education costs to maintain or improve a taxpayer's existing skills, but not to prepare them for a new job

# OTHER MISCELLANEOUS DEDUCTIONS

Apart from the categories of allowable expenses already described, there are some other miscellaneous deductions allowed that are **not** subject to a threshold of 2% of adjusted gross income.

1. **Gambling losses:** Deductible up to the extent of gambling winnings. There is no carryover of any unused losses.
2. **Impairment related work expenses**
3. **Unrecovered investment in an annuity**

# LIMITATION ON DEDUCTIONS

If a taxpayer's adjusted gross income exceeds a specified threshold, there is a reduction or cutback on the amount of the allowable itemized deductions. The thresholds for 1999 are:

| | |
|---|---|
| Single or married filing jointly | $ 126,600 |
| Married, filing separately | 63,300 |

The cutback is the lessor of 3% of the excess AGI over the threshold amounts, or 80% of the itemized deductions, excluding medical costs, personal casualty losses, investment interest expense and allowable gambling losses.

---

**Example 12:** T and B are married and file a joint return. For 1999, their adjusted gross income was $626,600. Their allowable itemized deductions after the various limitations were as follows:

| | |
|---|---|
| Medical | $ 15,000 |
| Taxes | 80,000 |
| Mortgage interest | 50,000 |
| Charitable contributions | 10,000 |
| Total | $ 155,000 |

The cutback is the *lessor of*:

**3% Rule**

| | |
|---|---|
| Adjusted gross income | $ 626,600 |
| Threshold amount | -126,600 |
| Excess amount | 500,000 |
| Cutback percentage | 3% |
| Reduction amount | $ 15,000 |

**80% Rule**

| Cutback deductions: | |
|---|---|
| Taxes | $ 80,000 |
| Mortgage interest | 50,000 |
| Charitable contributions | 10,000 |
| Total | $ 140,000 |
| Cutback percentage | 80% |
| Reduction amount | $ 112,000 |

Therefore, the allowable itemized deductions on T and B's 1999 Schedule A would be:

| | |
|---|---|
| Original itemized deductions | $155,000 |
| Less: cutback amount (3% Rule) | -15,000 |
| Allowable itemized deductions | $ 140,000 |

---

# Schedule A—Itemized Deductions

(Schedule B is on back)

► **Attach to Form 1040.** ► **See Instructions for Schedules A and B (Form 1040).**

OMB No. 1545-0074

## 1999

Attachment
Sequence No. **07**

Name(s) shown on Form 1040

Your social security number

| | | | |
|---|---|---|---|
| **Medical and Dental Expenses** | | **Caution.** Do not include expenses reimbursed or paid by others. | |
| | 1 | Medical and dental expenses (see page A-1) . . . . | 1 |
| | 2 | Enter amount from Form 1040, line 34 . ⌐ 2 ⌐ | |
| | 3 | Multiply line 2 above by 7.5% (.075) . . . . . . | 3 |
| | 4 | Subtract line 3 from line 1. If line 3 is more than line 1, enter -0- . . . . . . . | 4 |
| **Taxes You Paid** (See page A-2.) | 5 | State and local income taxes . . . . . . . . | 5 |
| | 6 | Real estate taxes (see page A-2) . . . . . . . | 6 |
| | 7 | Personal property taxes . . . . . . . . . | 7 |
| | 8 | Other taxes. List type and amount ► ................ | |
| | | | 8 |
| | 9 | Add lines 5 through 8 . . . . . . . . . . . . . . | 9 |
| **Interest You Paid** (See page A-3.) | 10 | Home mortgage interest and points reported to you on Form 1098 | 10 |
| | 11 | Home mortgage interest not reported to you on Form 1098. If paid to the person from whom you bought the home, see page A-3 and show that person's name, identifying no., and address ► | |
| | | ---------------------------------------- | |
| **Note.** Personal interest is not deductible. | | ---------------------------------------- | 11 |
| | 12 | Points not reported to you on Form 1098. See page A-3 for special rules . . . | 12 |
| | 13 | Investment interest. Attach Form 4952 if required. (See page A-3.) | 13 |
| | 14 | Add lines 10 through 13 . . . . . . . . . . . . . . . | 14 |
| **Gifts to Charity** If you made a gift and got a benefit for it, see page A-4. | 15 | Gifts by cash or check. If you made any gift of $250 or more, see page A-4 . . . | 15 |
| | 16 | Other than by cash or check. If any gift of $250 or more, see page A-4. You **MUST** attach Form 8283 if over $500 | 16 |
| | 17 | Carryover from prior year . . . . . . . . | 17 |
| | 18 | Add lines 15 through 17 . . . . . . . . . . | 18 |
| **Casualty and Theft Losses** | 19 | Casualty or theft loss(es). Attach Form 4684. (See page A-5.) . . . . . . . | 19 |
| **Job Expenses and Most Other Miscellaneous Deductions** (See page A-5 for expenses to deduct here.) | 20 | Unreimbursed employee expenses—job travel, union dues, job education, etc. You **MUST** attach Form 2106 or 2106-EZ if required. (See page A-5.) ► ................ | |
| | | ---------------------------------------- | 20 |
| | 21 | Tax preparation fees . . . . . . . . . | 21 |
| | 22 | Other expenses—investment, safe deposit box, etc. List type and amount ► ................ | |
| | | | 22 |
| | 23 | Add lines 20 through 22 . . . . . . . . . | 23 |
| | 24 | Enter amount from Form 1040, line 34 ⌐ 24 ⌐ | |
| | 25 | Multiply line 24 above by 2% (.02) . . . . . . | 25 |
| | 26 | Subtract line 25 from line 23. If line 25 is more than line 23, enter -0- . . . . | 26 |
| **Other Miscellaneous Deductions** | 27 | Other—from list on page A-6. List type and amount ► .................... | |
| | | | 27 |
| **Total Itemized Deductions** | 28 | Is Form 1040, line 34, over $126,600 (over $63,300 if married filing separately)? | |
| | | ☐ **No.** Your deduction is not limited. Add the amounts in the far right column for lines 4 through 27. Also, enter this amount on Form 1040, line 36. } . ► | 28 |
| | | ☐ **Yes.** Your deduction may be limited. See page A-6 for the amount to enter. | |

For Paperwork Reduction Act Notice, see Form 1040 instructions.        Cat. No. 11330X        **Schedule A (Form 1040) 1999**

# Chapter Four -- Questions
# Deductions From Adjusted Gross Income

## Medical Deductions

1. Mr. and Mrs. Sloan incurred the following expenses on December 15, 1999, when they adopted a child:

| | |
|---|---|
| Child's medical expenses | $5,000 |
| Legal expenses | 8,000 |
| Agency fee | 2,000 |

Before consideration of any "floor" or other limitation on deductibility, what amount of the above expenses may the Sloans deduct on their 1999 joint income tax return?
a. $15,000
b. $13,000
c. $10,000
d. $5,000

2. Tom and Sally White, married and filing joint income tax returns, derive their entire income from the operation of their retail stationery shop. Their 1999 adjusted gross income was $100,000. The Whites itemized their deductions on Schedule A for 1999. The following unreimbursed cash expenditures were among those made by the Whites during 1999:

| | |
|---|---|
| Repair and maintenance of motorized wheelchair for physically handicapped dependent child | $ 600 |
| Tuition, meals, and lodging at special school for physically handicapped dependent child in an institution primarily for the availability of medical care, with meals and lodging furnished as necessary incidents to that care | 8,000 |

Without regard to the adjusted gross income percentage threshold, what amount may the Whites claim in their 1999 return as qualifying medical expenses?
a. $8,600
b. $8,000
c. $600
d. $0

3. Jim and Nancy Walton had adjusted gross income of $35,000. During the year they paid the following medical related expenses:

| | |
|---|---|
| Medicines and drugs | $ 300 |
| Doctors | 2,700 |
| Health Club membership (recommended by the family doctor for general health care) | 400 |
| Medical care insurance | 280 |

How much may the Waltons utilize as medical expenses in calculating itemized deductions?
a. $1,930.
b. $1,530.
c. $655.
d. $0.

4. In 1999 Wells paid the following expenses:

| | |
|---|---|
| Premiums on an insurance policy against loss of earnings due to sickness or accident | $3,000 |
| Physical therapy after spinal surgery | 2,000 |
| Premium on an insurance policy that covers reimbursement for the cost of prescription drugs | 500 |

In 1999 Wells recovered $1,500 of the $2,000 that she paid for physical therapy through insurance reimbursement from a group medical policy paid for by her employer. Disregarding the adjusted gross income percentage threshold, what amount could be claimed on Wells' 1999 income tax return for medical expenses?
a. $4,000
b. $3,500
c. $1,000
d. $500

5. Ruth and Mark Cline are married and will file a joint 1999 income tax return. Among their expenditures during 1999 were the following discretionary costs that they incurred for the sole purpose of improving their physical appearance and self-esteem:

Face lift for Ruth, performed by a
licensed surgeon                     $5,000
Hair transplant for Mark, performed
by a licensed surgeon                 3,600

Disregarding the adjusted gross income percentage threshold, what total amount of the aforementioned doctors' bill may be claimed by the Clines in their 1999 return as qualifying medical expenses?
a. $0
b. $3,600
c. $5,000
d. $8,600

6. Which one of the following expenditures qualifies as a deductible medical expense for tax purposes?
a. Vitamins for general health **not** prescribed by a physician.
b. Health club dues.
c. Transportation to physician's office for required medical care.
d. Mandatory employment taxes for basic coverage under Medicare A.

7. John Stenger, a cash basis taxpayer, had adjusted gross income of $35,000 in 1999. During the year he incurred and paid the following medical expenses:

Drugs and medicines prescribed
by doctors                          $ 300
Health insurance premiums            750
Doctors' fees                       2,550
Eyeglasses                            75
                                   $3,675

Stenger received $900 in 1999 as reimbursement for a portion of the doctors' fees. If Stenger were to itemize his deductions, what would be his allowable net medical expense deduction?
a. $0
b. $150
c. $1,050
d. $2,475

8. During 1999 Scott charged $4,000 on his credit card for his dependent son's medical expenses. Payment to the credit card company had not been made by the time Scott filed his income tax return in 2000. However, in 1999, Scott paid a physician $2,800 for the medical expenses of his wife, who died in 1998. Disregarding the adjusted gross income percentage threshold, what amount could Scott claim in his 1999 income tax return for medical expenses?

a. $0
b. $2,800
c. $4,000
d. $6,800

## Taxes as a Deduction

9. Seth Parker, a self-employed individual, paid the following taxes this year:

| | |
|---|---|
| Federal income tax | $5,000 |
| State income tax | 2,000 |
| Real estate taxes on land in South America | 900 |
| State sales taxes | 500 |
| Federal self-employment tax | 800 |
| State unincorporated business tax | 200 |

What amount can Parker claim as an itemized deduction for taxes paid?
a. $7,500.
b. $4,400.
c. $3,600.
d. $2,900.

10. In 1999 Lyons paid $3,000 to the tax collector of Maple Township for realty taxes on a two-family house owned by Lyons' mother. Of this amount, $1,400 covered back taxes for 1998 and $1,600 was in payment of 1999 taxes. Lyons resides on the second floor of the house, and his mother resides on the first floor. In Lyons' itemized deductions on his 1999 return, what amount may Lyons claim for realty taxes?
a. $0
b. $1,500
c. $1,600
d. $3,000

11. Mr. and Mrs. Donald Curry's real property tax year is on a calendar-year basis, with payment due annually on August 1. The realty taxes on their home amounted to $1,200 in 1999, but the Curry's did not pay any portion of that amount since they sold the house on April 1, 1999, four months before payment was due. However, realty taxes were prorated on the closing statement. Assuming that they owned no other real property during the year, how much can the Curry's deduct on Schedule A of Form 1040 for real estate taxes in 1999?
a. $0.
b. $296.
c. $697.
d. $1,200.

12. During 1999 Jack and Mary Bronson paid the following taxes:

Taxes on residence (for period
  January 1 to September 30, 1998)    $2,700
State motor vehicle tax on value of
  the car    360

The Bronsons sold their house on June 30, 1999 under an agreement in which the real estate taxes were not prorated between the buyer and sellers. What amount should the Bronsons deduct as taxes in calculating itemized deductions for 1999?
a. $1,800
b. $2,160
c. $2,700
d. $3,060

13. George Granger sold a plot of land to Albert King on July 1, 1999. Granger had not paid any realty taxes on the land since 1997. Delinquent 1998 taxes amounted to $600, and 1999 taxes amounted to $700. King paid the 1998 and 1999 taxes in full in 1999, when he bought the land. What portion of the $1,300 is deductible by King in 1999?
a. $353
b. $700
c. $953
d. $1,300

14. Sara Harding is a cash basis taxpayer who itemizes her deductions. The following information pertains to Sara's state income taxes for the taxable year 1999:

| | | |
|---|---:|---:|
| Withheld by employer in 1999 | | $2,000 |
| Payments on 1999 estimate: | | |
|    4/15/99 | $300 | |
|    6/15/99 | 300 | |
|    9/15/99 | 300 | |
|    1/15/00 | 300 | 1,200 |
| Total paid and withheld | | $3,200 |
| Actual tax, per state return | | 3,000 |
|   Overpayment | | $ 200 |

There was no balance of tax or refund due on Sara's 1998 state tax return. How much is deductible for state income taxes on Sara's 1999 federal income tax return?
a. $2,800.
b. $2,900.
c. $3,000.
d. $3,200.

15. Matthews was a cash basis taxpayer whose records showed the following:

| | |
|---|---:|
| 1999 state and local income taxes withheld | $1,500 |
| 1999 state estimated income taxes paid | |
|   December 30, 1999 | 400 |
| 1999 federal income taxes withheld | 2,500 |
| 1999 state and local income taxes paid | |
|   April 17, 2000 | 300 |

What total amount was Matthews entitled to claim for taxes on her 1999 Schedule A of Form 1040?
a. $4,700
b. $2,200
c. $1,900
d. $1,500

16. In 1999, Farb, a cash basis individual taxpayer, received an $8,000 invoice for personal property taxes. Believing the amount to be overstated by $5,000, Farb paid the invoiced amount under protest and immediately started legal action to recover the overstatement. In June, 2000, the matter was resolved in Farb's favor, and he received a $5,000 refund. Farb itemizes his deductions on his tax returns. Which of the following statements is correct regarding the deductibility of the property taxes?
a. Farb should deduct $8,000 in his 1999 income tax return and should report the $5,000 refund as income in his 2000 income tax return.
b. Farb should **not** deduct any amount in his 1999 income tax return and should deduct $3,000 in his 1999 income tax return.
c. Farb should deduct $3,000 in his 1999 income tax return.
d. Farb should **not** deduct any amount in his 1999 income tax return when originally filed, and should file an amended 1999 income tax return in 2000.

## Interest Deduction

17. For regular tax purposes, with regard to the itemized deduction for qualified residence interest, home equity indebtedness incurred this year
a. Includes acquisition indebtedness secured by a qualified residence.
b. May exceed the fair market value of the residence.
c. Must exceed the taxpayer's net equity in the residence.
d. Is limited to $100,000 on a joint income tax return.

18. The Browns borrowed $20,000, secured by their home, to pay their son's college tuition. At the time of the loan, the fair market value of their home was $400,000, and it was unencumbered by other debt. The interest on the loan qualifies as
a. Deductible personal interest.
b. Deductible qualified residence interest.
c. Nondeductible interest.
d. Investment interest expense.

19. On January 2, 1990, the Philips paid $50,000 cash and obtained a $200,000 mortgage to purchase a home. In 1999 they borrowed $15,000 secured by their home, and used the cash to add a new room to their residence. That same year they took out a $5,000 auto loan.

The following information pertains to interest paid in 1999:

| | |
|---|---|
| Mortgage interest | $17,000 |
| Interest on room construction loan | 1,500 |
| Auto loan interest | 500 |

For 1999, how much interest is deductible, prior to any itemized deduction limitations?
a. $17,000
b. $17,500
c. $18,500
d. $19,000

20. Robert and Judy Parker made the following payments during this taxable year:

| | |
|---|---|
| Interest on a life insurance policy loan (the related policy on Robert's life was purchased in 1950) | $1,200 |
| Interest on home mortgage | 3,600 |
| Penalty payment for prepayment of home mortgage on October 4, of this taxable year | 900 |

How much can the Parkers utilize as interest expense in calculating itemized deductions?
a. $5,700.
b. $4,980.
c. $4,500.
d. $3,600.

21. The 1999 deduction by an individual taxpayer for interest on investment indebtedness is
a. Limited to the investment interest paid in 1999.
b. Limited to the taxpayer's 1999 interest income.
c. Limited to the taxpayer's 1999 net investment income.
d. Not limited.

22. During the taxable year, Carmine Gross purchased the following long-term investments at par:

$5,000 general obligation bonds of Lane City (wholly tax exempt)
$5,000 debentures of Rigor Corporation on which Carmine received $500 interest income

He financed these purchases by obtaining a loan from the National Bank for $10,000. For the year he paid the following amounts as interest expense:

| | |
|---|---|
| National Bank | $ 800 |
| Interest on mortgage | 2,000 |
| Interest on installment purchases | 200 |
| | $3,000 |

What should be the amount that Gross can deduct as interest expense?
a. $2,200.
b. $2,400.
c. $2,800.
d. $3,000.

23. Phil and Joan Crawley made the following payments during 1999:

| | |
|---|---|
| Interest on bank loan (loan proceeds were used to purchase United States savings bonds Series H) | $4,000 |
| Interest on home mortgage for period April 1 to December 31, 1999 | 2,700 |
| Points paid to obtain conventional mortgage loan on April 1, 1999 | 900 |

Income of $4,500 was received on savings bonds in 1999. What is the maximum amount that the Crawleys can utilize as interest expense in calculating itemized deductions for 1999?
a. $3,600.
b. $4,900.
c. $6,700.
d. $7,600.

# Charitable Contributions

24. Judy Bishop had adjusted gross income of $35,000 and itemizes her deductions. Additional information is available as follows for this year:

| | |
|---|---|
| Cash contribution to church | $2,500 |
| Purchase of an art object at her church bazaar (with a fair market value of $500 on date of purchase) | 800 |
| Donation of used clothes to Goodwill Charities (fair value evidenced by receipt received) | 400 |

What is the maximum amount Bishop can claim as a deduction for charitable contributions?
a. $2,800.
b. $3,200.
c. $3,300.
d. $3,400.

25. Spencer, who itemizes deductions, had adjusted gross income of $60,000 in 1999. The following additional information is available for 1999:

| | |
|---|---|
| Cash contribution to church | $4,000 |
| Purchase of art object at church bazaar (with a fair market value of $800 on the date of purchase) | 1,200 |
| Donation of used clothing to Salvation Army (fair value evidenced by receipt received) | 600 |

What is the maximum amount Spencer can claim as a deduction for charitable contributions in 1999?
a. $5,400
b. $5,200
c. $5,000
d. $4,400

26. Eugene and Linda O'Brien had adjusted gross income of $30,000. Additional information is available as follows for this year:

| | |
|---|---|
| Cash contribution to church | $1,500 |
| Tuition paid to parochial school | 1,200 |
| Contribution to a qualified charity made by a bank credit card charge on December 14. The credit card obligation was paid in January of the next year | 250 |
| Cash contribution to needy family | 100 |

What is the maximum amount of the above that they can utilize in calculating itemized deductions for this year?
a. $1,500.
b. $1,750.
c. $2,700.
d. $3,050.

27. Moore, a single taxpayer, had $50,000 in adjusted gross income for 1999. During 1999 she contributed $18,000 to her church. She had a $10,000 charitable contribution carryover from her 1998 church contribution. What was the maximum amount of properly substantiated charitable contributions that Moore could claim as an itemized deduction for 1999?
a. $10,000
b. $18,000
c. $25,000
d. $28,000

28. Y's adjusted gross income this year is $30,000. He made cash contribution to the following organizations: Church $15,000; United Fund $5,000 and Salvation Army $3,000. Y's maximum contribution deduction this year is:
a. $6,000.
b. $9,000.
c. $15,000.
d. $2,000.

29. Charitable contributions subject to the 50-percent limit that are **not** fully deductible in the year made may be
a. Neither carried back nor carried forward.
b. Carried back three years or carried forward fifteen years.
c. Carried forward five years.
d. Carried forward indefinitely until fully deductible.

30. Ruth Lewis has adjusted gross income of $100,000 for this year and itemizes her deductions. On September 1, she made a contribution to her church of stock held for investment for two years which cost $10,000 and had a fair market value of $70,000. The church sold the stock for $70,000 on the same date. Assume that Lewis made no other contributions during the year and made no special election in regard to this contribution on her tax return. How much should Lewis claim as a charitable contribution deduction?
a. $50,000.
b. $30,000.
c. $20,000.
d. $10,000.

31. Stewart Samaritan had adjusted gross income of $22,000 this year. During the year he made the following contributions to recognized charitable organizations:

- $5,000 cash.
- 1,000 shares of Able Corporation common stock (acquired in 1972 at a cost of $1,600) with a fair market value of $7,000 on the date of the contribution.

What amount can Samaritan claim as a deduction for charitable contributions for the year?
a. $6,600.
b. $11,000.
c. $11,600.
d. $12,000.

32. Don and Cynthia Wallace filed a joint return in which they reported adjusted gross income of $35,000. During the year they made the following contributions to qualified organizations:

| | |
|---|---|
| Land (stated at its current fair market value) donated to church for new building site | $22,000 |
| Cash contributions to church | 300 |
| Cash contributions to the local community college | 200 |

Assuming that the Wallaces did not elect to reduce the deductible amount of the land contribution by the property's appreciation in value, how much can they claim as a deduction for charitable contributions on their tax return?
a. $10,800.
b. $11,000.
c. $17,500.
d. $22,500.

33. On December 15, 1999, Donald Calder made a contribution of $500 to a qualified charitable organization, by charging the contribution on his bank credit card. Calder paid the $500 on January 20, 2000 upon receipt of the bill from the bank. In addition, Calder issued and delivered a promissory note for $1,000 to another qualified charitable organization on November 1, 1999, which he paid upon maturity six months later. If Calder itemizes his deductions, what portion of these contributions is deductible in 1999?
a. $0
b. $500
c. $1,000
d. $1,500

## Miscellaneous 2% Deductions

34. Which of the following is **not** a miscellaneous itemized deduction?
a. An individual's tax return preparation fee.
b. Education expense to meet minimum entry level education requirements at an individual's place of employment.
c. An individual's subscription to professional journals.
d. Custodial fees for a brokerage account.

35. Which expense, both incurred and paid during the year, can be claimed as an itemized deduction subject to the two-percent-of-adjusted-gross-income floor?
a. Employee's unreimbursed business car expense.
b. One-half of the self-employment tax.
c. Employee's unreimbursed moving expense.
d. Self-employed health insurance.

36. Cathy Glover, an employee of Lawrence Inc., incurs $4,000 of unreimbursed business related meals and entertainment expenses. She also had unreimbursed auto expenses of $750 with respect to her employment this year. In addition, she incurred $600 of qualifying expenses looking for a new job. Her A.G.I. for the year is $80,000. Her allowable miscellaneous itemized deductions are:
a. $4,550.
b. $3,350.
c. $2,950.
d. $1,750.

37. Harold Brodsky is an electrician employed by a contracting firm. His adjusted gross income is $25,000. During the current year he incurred and paid the following expenses:

| | |
|---|---|
| Use of personal auto for company business (reimbursed by employer for $200) | $300 |
| Specialized work clothes | 550 |
| Union dues | 600 |
| Cost of income tax preparation | 150 |
| Preparation of will | 100 |

If Brodsky were to itemize his personal deductions, what amount should he claim as miscellaneous deductible expenses?
a. $800
b. $900
c. $1,500
d. $1,700

## Casualty Losses

38. In 1999, Joan Frazer's residence was totally destroyed by fire. The property had an adjusted basis and a fair market value of $130,000 before the fire. During 1999, Frazer received insurance reimbursement of $120,000 for the destruction of her home. Frazer's 1998 adjusted gross income was $70,000. Frazer had no casualty gains during the year. What amount of the fire loss was Frazer entitled to claim as an itemized deduction on her 1999 tax return?
a. $2,900
b. $8,500
c. $8,600
d. $10,000

------

**Items 39 and 40** are based on the following selected 1999 information pertaining to Sam and Ann Hoyt, who filed a joint federal income tax return for the calendar year 1999. The Hoyts had adjusted gross income of $34,000 and itemized their deductions for 1999. Among the Hoyt's cash expenditures during 1999 were the following:

$2,500 repairs in connection with 1999 fire damage to the Hoyt residence. This property has a basis of $50,000. Fair market value was $60,000 before the fire and $55,000 after the fire. Insurance on the property had lapsed prior to the fire for nonpayment of premium.

$800 appraisal fee to determine amount of fire loss.

39. What amount of fire loss were the Hoyts entitled to deduct as an itemized deduction on their 1999 return?
a. $5,000
b. $2,500
c. $1,600
d. $1,500

40. The appraisal fee to determine the amount of Hoyts' fire loss was
a. Deductible from gross income in arriving at adjusted gross income.
b. Subject to the 2% of adjusted gross income floor for miscellaneous itemized deductions.
c. Deductible after reducing the amount by $100.
d. Not deductible.

------

41. The following information pertains to Cole's personal residence, which sustained casualty fire damage in 1999:

| | |
|---|---|
| Adjusted basis | $150,000 |
| Fair market value immediately before the fire | 200,000 |
| Fair market value immediately after the fire | 180,000 |
| Fire damage repairs paid for by Cole in 1999 | 10,000 |

The house was uninsured. Before consideration of any "floor" or other limitation on tax deductibility, the amount of this 1998 casualty loss was
a. $30,000
b. $20,000
c. $10,000
d. $0

42. Nelson Harris had an adjusted gross income of $60,000. During the year his personal summer home was completely destroyed by a cyclone. Pertinent data with respect to the home follows:

| | |
|---|---|
| Cost basis | $39,000 |
| Value before casualty | 45,000 |
| Value after casualty | 3,000 |

Harris was partially insured for his loss and he received a $15,000 insurance settlement. What is Harris' allowable casualty loss deduction?
a. $23,900
b. $17,900
c. $26,900
d. $27,000

## Limitations

43. Which items are subject to the phase out of the amount of certain itemized deductions that may be claimed by high-income individuals?
a. Charitable contributions.
b. Medical costs.
c. Nonbusiness casualty losses.
d. Investment interest deductions.

44. For 1999, Dole's adjusted gross income exceeds $500,000. After the application of any other limitation, itemized deductions are reduced by
a. The *lesser* of 3% of the excess of adjusted gross income over the applicable amount or 80% of *certain* itemized deductions.
b. The *lesser* of 3% of the excess of adjusted gross income over the applicable amount or 80% of *all* itemized deductions.
c. The *greater* of 3% of the excess of adjusted gross income over the applicable amount or 80% of *certain* itemized deductions.
d. The *greater* of 3% of the excess of adjusted gross income over the applicable amount or 80% of *all* itemized deductions.

## Review Questions

**Items 45 through 50** are based on the following data:

Roger Efron, who is single and has no dependents, earned a salary of $50,000 in 1999, and had an adjusted gross income of $60,000. Roger has been an active participant in a qualified noncontributory pension plan since 1972. Roger itemized his deductions on his 1999 income tax return. Among Roger's 1999 cash expenditures were the following:

| | |
|---|---|
| Real estate taxes on Roger's condominium | $4,000 |
| Contribution to an individual retirement account ($200 interest was earned on this IRA in 1999) | 2,000 |
| Dental expenses | 700 |
| Premium on Roger's life insurance policy | 600 |
| Medical insurance premiums | 500 |
| Contribution to candidate for public office | 300 |
| Legal fee for preparation of Roger's will | 200 |
| Customs duties | 80 |
| City dog license fee | 10 |

In addition, Roger suffered a casualty loss of $400 in 1999 due to storm damage.

45. How much could Roger deduct for the contribution to his individual retirement account in arriving at his adjusted gross income?
a. $0.
b. $1,500.
c. $1,800.
d. $2,000.

46. How much could Roger deduct for medical and dental expenses?
a. $0.
b. $150.
c. $700.
d. $1,200.

47. How much could Roger deduct for taxes?
a. $4,000.
b. $4,010.
c. $4,080.
d. $4,090.

48. How much could Roger deduct for miscellaneous deductions?
a. $0.
b. $200.
c. $600.
d. $800.

49. How much could Roger deduct for the casualty loss?
a. $0.
b. $100.
c. $300.
d. $400.

50. How much of a credit could Roger offset against his income tax, for his contribution to a candidate for public office?
a. $0.
b. $ 50.
c. $100.
d. $150.

---

**Items 51 through 55 are based on the following:**

Alex and Myra Burg, married and filing joint income tax returns, derive their entire income from the operation of their retail candy shop. Their 1999 adjusted gross income was $50,000. The Burgs itemized their deductions on Schedule A for 1999. The following unreimbursed cash expenditures were among those made by the Burgs during 1999:

| | |
|---|---|
| Repair and maintenance of motorized wheelchair for physically handicapped dependent child | $ 300 |
| Tuition, meals, and lodging at special school for physically handicapped dependent child in the institution primarily for the availability of medical care, with meals and lodging furnished as necessary incidents to that care | 4,000 |
| State income tax | 1,200 |
| Self-employment tax | 7,650 |
| Four tickets to a theatre party sponsored by a qualified charitable organization; not considered a business expense; similar tickets would cost $25 each at the box office | 160 |
| Repair of glass vase accidentally broken in home by dog; vase cost $500 in 1989; fair value $600 before accident and $200 after accident | 90 |
| Fee for breaking lease on prior apartment residence located 20 miles from new residence | 500 |
| Security deposit placed on apartment at new location | 900 |

**51.** Without regard to the adjusted gross income percentage threshold, what amount may the Burgs claim as qualifying medical expenses?
a. $40
b. $300
c. $4,000
d. $4,300

**52.** What amount should the Burgs deduct for taxes in their itemized deductions on Schedule A?
a. $1,200
b. $3,825
c. $5,025
d. $7,650

**53.** What amount should the Burgs deduct for gifts to charity in their itemized deductions on Schedule A?
a. $160
b. $100
c. $60
d. $0

**54.** Without regard to the $100 "floor" and the adjusted gross income percentage threshold, what amount should the Burgs deduct for the casualty loss in their itemized deductions on Schedule A?
a. $0
b. $90
c. $300
d. $400

**55.** What amount should the Burgs deduct for moving expenses in their itemized deductions on Schedule A?
a. $0
b. $500
c. $900
d. $1,400

---

## Released and Author Constructed Questions

*R98*

**56.** Jackson owns two residences. The second residence, which has never been used for rental purposes, is the only residence that is subject to a mortgage. The following expenses were incurred for the second residence in 1997.

| | |
|---|---|
| Mortgage interest | $5,000 |
| Utilities | 1,200 |
| Insurance | 6,000 |

For regular income tax purposes, what is the maximum amount allowable as a deduction for Jackson's second residence in 1997?
a. $6,200 in determining adjusted gross income.
b. $11,000 in determining adjusted gross income.
c. $5,000 as an itemized deduction.
d. $12,200 as an itemized deduction.

*R97*

**57.** Jimet, an unmarried taxpayer, qualified to itemize 1996 deductions. Jimet's 1996 adjusted gross income was $30,000 and he made a $2,000 cash donation directly to a needy family. In 1996, Jimet also donated stock, valued at $3,000, to his church. Jimet had purchased the stock four months earlier for $1,500. What was the maximum amount of the charitable contribution allowable as an itemized deduction on Jimet's 1996 income tax return?
a. $0
b. $1,500
c. $2,000
d. $5,000

58. In 1996, Wood's residence had an adjusted basis of $150,000 and it was destroyed by a tornado. An appraiser valued the decline in market value at $175,000. Later that same year, Wood received $130,000 from his insurance company for the property loss and did not elect to deduct the casualty loss in an earlier year. Wood's 1996 adjusted gross income was $60,000 and he did not have any casualty gains.

What total amount can Wood deduct as a 1996 itemized deduction for the casualty loss, after the application of the threshold limitations?

a. $39,000
b. $38,900
c. $19,900
d. $13,900

59. Deet, an unmarried taxpayer, qualified to itemize 1996 deductions. Deet's 1996 adjusted gross income was $40,000 and he made a $1,500 substantiated cash donation directly to a needy family. Deet also donated art, valued at $11,000, to a local art museum. Deet had purchased the art work two years earlier for $2,000. What was the maximum amount of the charitable contribution allowable as an itemized deduction on Deet's 1996 income tax return?

a. $12,500
b. $11,000
c. $3,500
d. $2,000

60. Kristen uses her personal automobile for volunteer work for her church. During 1999, she drove 1,000 miles on behalf of her church. In addition, Kristen made a $3,000 cash contribution to the church. Assuming her AGI is $40,000, her allowable charitable contribution is:

a. $3,000
b. $3,120
c. $3,140
d. $3,315

# Chapter Four -- Answers
# Deductions From Adjusted Gross Income

1. (d) $5,000. Only the medical expenses of the adopted child qualify. Legal expenses and the agency fee are not deductible expenses. The medical expenses would be subject to a floor of 7.5% of their adjusted gross income.

2. (a) $8,600. The costs of maintenance of a wheelchair for a handicapped dependent child is fully deductible as well as the expenses related to tuition, room and board, and the cost of medical care when the principal reason for sending a dependent to a special school is that school's special resources for treating that specific sickness or disease.

3. (c) $655. The following expenses qualify as deductible medical expenses:

| | |
|---|---:|
| Medicines and drugs | $ 300 |
| Doctors | 2,700 |
| Medical insurance | 280 |
| Total expenses | $ 3,280 |
| Less: AGI limitation: | |
| $35,000 x 7.5% | -2,625 |
| Allowable deduction | $ 655 |

The health club membership is for general health and is non-deductible.

4. (c) $1,000. The qualified medical expenses include the $2,000 for physical therapy and the $500 premium for insurance on the prescription drugs, less the reimbursement. The cost of insurance for lost wages is not a deductible expense.

| | |
|---|---:|
| Physical therapy | $ 2,000 |
| Premium on insurance | 500 |
| Total before reimbursement | 2,500 |
| Less: reimbursement | -1,500 |
| Deductible expenses | $ 1,000 |

5. (a) Expenditures for the overall general health of the taxpayer, such as vitamins or health clubs, and cosmetic surgery are **not** deductible. The face lift and hair transplant would be classified as cosmetic surgery and therefore, not deductible.

6. (c) The cost of transportation for medical treatment, which includes a parent's cost if they are accompanying a child, is allowed as a deduction. Expenditures for the overall general health of the taxpayer, such as vitamins or health clubs, and cosmetic surgery are **not** deductible.

7. (b) $150. The qualified medical expenses include the medicine and drugs, health insurance premiums, doctors fees and eyeglasses, less the reimbursement on the doctors fees received during the year.

| | |
|---|---:|
| Drugs and medicine | $ 300 |
| Health insurance premiums | 750 |
| Doctors' fees | 2,550 |
| Eyeglasses | 75 |
| Total before reimbursement | 3,675 |
| Less: reimbursement | -900 |
| Expenses before limitation | $ 2,775 |
| Less: AGI limitation: | |
| $35,000 x 7.5% | -2,625 |
| Allowable deduction | $ 150 |

8. (d) $6,800. Scott can deduct the $4,000 cost of his dependent's son medical expenses which he **charged** and the $2,800 he **paid** for his spouse's medical expenses even though they were for the preceding year when she died. Charging on a credit card constitutes a payment, even though the taxpayer did not pay off the credit card until the subsequent year.

9. (d) $2,900. Parker may deduct the following taxes:

| | |
|---|---|
| State income taxes | $ 2,000 |
| Real estate taxes on land | |
| in South America | 900 |
| Total | $ 2,900 |

Sales taxes are no longer deductible, and one-half of the self-employment tax as well as the unincorporated business tax are deductions for adjusted gross income, not itemized deductions.

10. (a) $0. Lyons paid taxes on property that he does not own. There is no deduction.

11. (b) $296. When real property is sold during the year, the real estate tax must be apportioned between the buyer and seller based upon the number of days owned. Computations are as follows:

| | |
|---|---|
| Annual real estate taxes paid | $ 1,200 |
| Days in the year | 365 |
| Real estate tax per day | $ 3.28 |
| Days owned by Curry | 90 |
| Real estate tax deduction | $ 296 |

12. (b) $2,160. When real property is sold during the year, the real estate tax must be apportioned between the buyer and seller based upon the number of days owned. Computations are as follows:

| | |
|---|---|
| Annual real estate taxes paid | $ 2,700 |
| Owned for 2/3 of the period | 2/3 |
| Real estate tax deduction | $ 1,800 |
| | |
| Add: personal property tax | 360 |
| Total deductible taxes | $ 2,160 |

13. (a) $353. When real property is sold during the year, the real estate tax must be apportioned between the buyer and seller based upon the number of days owned. Computations are as follows:

| | |
|---|---|
| Annual real estate taxes paid | $ 700 |
| Days in the year | 365 |
| Real estate tax per day | $ 1.92 |
| Days owned by King | 183 |
| Real estate tax deduction | $ 353 |

14. (b) $2,900. The deductible state income taxes are those actually paid or withheld during 1999.

| | |
|---|---|
| State income taxes withheld | $ 2,000 |
| Estimated payments: | |
| 4/15/99 | 300 |
| 6/15/99 | 300 |
| 9/15/99 | 300 |
| Total deduction | $ 2,900 |

15. (c) $1,900. The deductible taxes are those state income taxes actually paid or withheld during 1999.

| | |
|---|---|
| State income taxes withheld | $ 1,500 |
| Estimated state payment | 400 |
| Total itemized deduction | $ 1,900 |

The 1999 state income taxes paid in 2000 will be deductible in 2000. Federal income taxes are not deductible.

16. (a) Farb is allowed a deduction in the year that the taxes are **paid.**

17. (d) Home equity indebtedness is limited to $100,000. It may not exceed the fair market value of the house less the acquisition indebtedness or the $100,000, whichever is less.

18. (b) Qualified residence interest includes acquisition indebtedness and home equity indebtedness. For the interest on home equity indebtedness to be deductible, the loan must be secured by the residence, and be the lesser of 100,000 or the fair market value of the house ($400,000) minus the acquisition indebtedness (none).

19. (c) $18,500. Both the mortgage and the construction loan qualify as acquisition indebtedness. The interest on those loans is fully deductible. The interest on the loan for the personal auto which was not secured by the residence is non-deductible.

| | |
|---|---|
| Mortgage interest | $ 17,000 |
| Construction loan | 1,500 |
| Total deductible interest | $ 18,500 |

20. (c) $4,500. Both the mortgage and the prepayment penalty are considered to be qualified residence interest and fully deductible. The interest on the life insurance is personal and non-deductible.

| | |
|---|---|
| Mortgage interest | $ 3,600 |
| Prepayment penalty | 900 |
| Total deductible interest | $ 4,500 |

21. (c) By definition.

22. (b) $2,400. Whereas one-half of the $800 interest expense from National Bank was related to the purchase of tax-exempt securities, one-half of the interest is clearly non-deductible. The other half ($400) is deductible only to the extent of the net investment income, which in this problem is $500, and thus fully deductible. The mortgage interest is fully deductible and the personal installment loan interest in non-deductible.

| | |
|---|---|
| National Bank 50% | $ 400 |
| Mortgage interest | 2,000 |
| Total deductible interest | $ 2,400 |

23. (d) $7,600. Interest on the loan to purchase the bonds is deductible because the net investment income of $4,500 exceeds the $4,000 investment interest expense. The interest on the home mortgage and related points are qualified residence interest.

24. (b) $3,200. The cash contributions to the church and the fair market value of clothing are allowed as deductions. Purchasing an item at a price greater than the fair market value allows the taxpayer a deduction for the excess only. The art object's purchase price of $800, less its fair market value of $500 results in a $300 contribution.

| | |
|---|---|
| Cash contribution to church | $ 2,500 |
| Excess of purchase price over fair value of art object | 300 |
| Clothing donation | 400 |
| Total deduction | $ 3,200 |

25. (c) $5,000. The cash contributions to the church and the fair market value of clothing are allowed as deductions. Purchasing an item at a price greater than the fair market value allows the taxpayer a deduction for the excess only. The art object's purchase price of $800, less its fair market value of $500 results in a $300 contribution.

| | |
|---|---|
| Cash contribution to church | $ 4,000 |
| Excess of purchase price over fair value of art object | 400 |
| Clothing donation | 600 |
| Total deduction | $ 5,000 |

26. (b) $1,750. The cash contributions to the church and qualified charity are fully deductible in this year. Payment with a credit card qualifies in the year the charge was made. Tuition to a parochial school is not deductible. A needy family is not a qualified charity and therefore, non-deductible.

27. (c) $25,000. The maximum allowed for charitable contributions in a given year is 50% of their adjusted gross income. In determining the composition of the $25,000 deduction for this year, the current year contribution is considered first and $7,000 of the carryover next.

| | |
|---|---|
| Current year contribution | $ 18,000 |
| Carryover from prior year | 10,000 |
| Contributions available | $ 28,000 |
| | |
| Taxpayer's adjusted gross income | $ 50,000 |
| Contribution limitation | 50% |
| Maximum allowed this year | $ 25,000 |

28. (c) $15,000. The maximum allowed for charitable contributions in a given year is 50% of Y's adjusted gross income. All charities listed are 50% charities.

| | |
|---|---|
| Church | $ 15,000 |
| United Fund | 5,000 |
| Salvation Army | 3,000 |
| Contributions available | $ 23,000 |
| | |
| Taxpayer's adjusted gross income | $ 30,000 |
| Contribution limitation | 50% |
| Maximum allowed this year | $ 15,000 |

The excess of $8,000 is carried over for a five year period.

29. (c) These excess contributions are only carried forward for five years.

30. (b) $30,000. When a contribution of appreciated property is made, the deduction allowed is for fair market value of the property. The deduction, however, is limited to 30% of the taxpayers adjusted gross income unless a special election is made to use the cost of the property rather than the fair market value. Whereas there was no special election, the deduction is limited to $100,000 X 30%, or $30,000. The excess of $40,000 is carried over for five years and is still subject to the 30% limitation each year.

31. (b) $11,000. Stewart's contributions include cash and the fair market value of property. In determining the current year's allowable contribution, the maximum allowable is limited to 50% of his adjusted gross income, or $11,000. However, the computations are actually more involved because of the capital gain property.

Step 1. Determine the overall 50% limitation:

| | |
|---|---:|
| Stewart's adjusted gross income | $ 22,000 |
| Overall contribution limitation | 50% |
| Maximum allowed this year | $ 11,000 |

Step 2. Determine what is used up by qualifying 50% contributions. The residual is available for the 30% contributions:

| | |
|---|---:|
| Maximum allowable | $ 11,000 |
| Less: Contributions qualifying under 50% rule | 5,000 |
| Available for 30% limitation | $ 6,000 |

Step 3. Determine the deductibility of the stock contribution with a $7,000 FMV:

| | |
|---|---:|
| Stewart's adjusted gross income | $ 22,000 |
| Contribution limitation for FMV | 30% |
| Maximum allowed this year | $ 6,600 |

The $7,000 FMV stock contribution is limited by the 30% test in Step 3 to $6,600 and by the 50% test in Step 2 to a maximum of $6,000. The excess of $1,000 ($7,000 less the $6,000 allowed) is carried over for five years, and is subject to the same percentage limitations in the carryovers. The final contribution is comprised of:

| | |
|---|---:|
| Total allowable contributions: | |
| Cash contributions | $ 5,000 |
| Stock - FMV (limited) | 6,000 |
| Total | $ 11,000 |

32. (b) $11,000. The Wallace's contributions include cash of $500 and the fair market value of property. In determining the current year's allowable contribution, the maximum allowable on the land is limited to 30% of their adjusted gross income, or $10,500.

| | |
|---|---:|
| Total allowable contributions: | |
| Cash contributions | $ 500 |
| Land - FMV (limited) | 10,500 |
| Total | $ 11,000 |

33. (b) A taxpayer is considered to have paid a charitable contribution if it was charged to his credit card account during the taxable year.

34. (b) In order to qualify as a deduction, educational costs must be paid to maintain or improve existing skills, not prepare the taxpayer for a new job.

35. (a) Only the unreimbursed employee business car expense. All others qualify, at least in part, for a deduction for adjusted gross income, not an itemized deduction.

36. (d) $1,750. Unreimbursed employee expenses are subject to a threshold of 2% of adjusted gross income. Also, business meals and entertainment are now only 50% deductible.

| | |
|---|---:|
| Business meals & entertainment | $ 2,000 |
| Automobile expenses | 750 |
| Job hunting expenses | 600 |
| Total | $ 3,350 |
| Less: 2% of AGI ($80,000) | -1,600 |
| Allowable deductions | $ 1,750 |

37. (b) $900. Unreimbursed employee expenses are subject to a threshold of 2% of adjusted gross income. The amounts paid for the preparation of the will are non-deductible.

| | |
|---|---:|
| Business use of auto, less $200 reimbursement | $ 100 |
| Specialized work clothes | 550 |
| Union dues | 600 |
| Income tax preparation | 150 |
| Total | $ 1,400 |
| Less: 2% of AGI ($25,000) | -500 |
| Allowable deductions | $ 900 |

38. (a) $2,900. The personal casualty loss deduction is determined taking the lessor of decrease in the FMV of the property or its basis; less the insurance reimbursement; subject to a $100 floor; and then subject to 10% of the taxpayer's adjusted gross income. With the FMV and basis being identical, the computations are:

| | |
|---|---:|
| Decrease in the FMV | $ 130,000 |
| Less: reimbursement | -120,000 |
| Loss by taxpayer | 10,000 |
| Less: $100 floor | -100 |
| Less: AGI limitation $70,000 X 10% | -7,000 |
| Allowable casualty loss | $ 2,900 |

39. (d) $1,500. The personal casualty loss deduction is determined taking the lessor of decrease in the FMV of the property or its basis; less the insurance reimbursement; subject to a $100 floor; and then subject to 10% of the taxpayer's adjusted gross income. The decrease in value was from $60,000 to $55,000, or $5,000. This is less than the basis of the property.

| | |
|---|---:|
| Decrease in the FMV | $ 5,000 |
| Less: reimbursement | -0 |
| Loss by taxpayer | 5,000 |
| Less: $100 floor | -100 |
| Less: AGI limitation $34,000 X 10% | -3,400 |
| Allowable casualty loss | $ 1,500 |

40. (b) The cost of the appraisal is cost used in the determination of the tax, and is allowed as a miscellaneous itemized deduction, subject to the 2% limitation.

41. (b) $20,000. The personal casualty loss deduction is determined taking the lessor of decrease in the FMV of the property or its basis; less the insurance reimbursement; subject to a $100 floor; and then subject to 10% of the taxpayer's adjusted gross income. The decrease in value of $20,000 ($200,000 less $180,000) was less than the basis of the property.

| | |
|---|---|
| Decrease in the FMV | $ 20,000 |
| Less: reimbursement | -0 |
| Loss by taxpayer | $ 20,000 |

42. (b) $17,900. The personal casualty loss deduction is determined taking the lessor of decrease in the FMV of the property or its basis; less the insurance reimbursement; subject to a $100 floor; and then subject to 10% of the taxpayer's adjusted gross income. The decrease in fair market value was $42,000 ($45,000 down to $3,000) and the cost basis was $39,000. Therefore, using the cost basis, the computations are:

| | |
|---|---|
| Cost basis of the house | $ 39,000 |
| Less: reimbursement | -15,000 |
| Loss by taxpayer | 24,000 |
| Less: $100 floor | -100 |
| Less: AGI limitation | |
| $60,000 X 10% | -6,000 |
| Allowable casualty loss | $ 17,900 |

43. (a) Charitable contributions. The cutback applies to all itemized deductions, except for medical costs, personal casualty losses, investment interest expense and allowable gambling losses.

44. (a) By definition.

45. (a) $0. A single taxpayer who is an active participant in qualified pension plan cannot deduct an IRA contribution if his adjusted gross income is in excess of $40,000.

46. (a) $0. Unreimbursed medical expenses are deductible only to the extent that they exceed 7.5% of adjusted gross income. Roger's threshold is $60,000 X 7.5% for a total of $4,500. Roger's qualifying medical expenses of $1,200 (medical insurance of $500 and dental expenses of $700) are less than the threshold, thus non-deductible.

47. (a) $4,000. Only the real estate taxes on the condominium are deductible. The customs duties and city licenses are non-deductible fees.

48. (a) $0. There are no miscellaneous deductions.

49. (a) $0. The casualty loss of $400 will not exceed the $100 floor and the 10% of adjusted gross income test.

50. (a) $0. There is no tax credit for contributions to political candidates.

51. (d) $4,300. The costs of maintenance of a wheelchair for a handicapped dependent child is fully deductible as well as the expenses related to tuition, room and board, and the cost of medical care when the principal reason for sending a dependent to a special school is that school's special resources for treating that specific sickness or disease.

52. (a) $1,200. State income taxes are allowed as an itemized deduction. One-half of the self-employment tax is allowed as a deduction for adjusted gross income, but not as an itemized deduction.

53. (c) $60. The charitable contribution is the excess of the purchase price of the ticket over its fair market value. The Burgs paid $160 for tickets that had a fair market value of $100 (four @ $25 each). The excess of $60 is the allowable deduction.

54. (a) $0. This does not meet the definition of a casualty loss.

55. (a) $0. The expenses of moving are now a deduction for adjusted gross income, not an itemized deduction. Even so, the fee for breaking the lease and security deposit are not deductible anyhow.

56. (c) $5,000. A taxpayer is entitled to deduct the acquisition indebtedness (mortgage) interest on his primary and secondary residence. Unless the other expenses listed were related to rental property, they are not allowed as a deduction. Not included in the problem was real estate taxes. These would have been allowed as an itemized deduction.

57. (b) $1,500. In determining the charitable contribution deduction, the amount paid directly to a needy family does not qualify. The amount of the allowable deduction for the stock held for only 4 months is limited to cost, or $1,500.

58. (d) $13,900. The personal casualty loss deduction is determined taking the lessor of decrease in the FMV of the property or its basis; less the insurance reimbursement; subject to a $100 floor; and then subject to 10% of the taxpayer's adjusted gross income. With the adjusted basis being lower than decrease in FMV, the computations are:

| | |
|---|---|
| Adjusted basis in the FMV | $ 150,000 |
| Less: reimbursement | -130,000 |
| Loss by taxpayer | 20,000 |
| Less: $100 floor | -100 |
| Less: AGI limitation | |
| $60,000 X 10% | -6,000 |
| Allowable casualty loss | $ 13,900 |

59. (b) $11,000. The taxpayer is entitled to deduct the fair market value of the art work since it was held for two years and qualifies as long-term. In determining the charitable contribution deduction, the amount paid directly to a needy family does not qualify.

60. (c) $3,140. Effective since 1998, the standard mileage rate has been increased from 12 to 14 cents per mile for charitable purposes. Therefore, her deduction will be based upon 1,000 miles @ $.14 or $140, plus the $3,000 for a total of $3,140.

# Chapter Five
# Accounting Methods and Periods, and Computation of Tax Liability and Tax Credits

# Chapter Five
# Accounting Methods and Periods, and Computation of Tax Liability and Tax Credits

## ACCOUNTING METHODS

### GENERAL

A taxpayer may report income and deductions under the method that he regularly keeps his books and records. However, if the IRS does not believe that the books and records accurately reflect the taxable income of the taxpayer, the IRS may change that method. There are also approved methods, subject to restrictions, that the IRS allows.

### CASH METHOD

Under the **cash method** of accounting, income is recognized income when the taxpayer actually receives the cash, or it is constructively received. Deductions are allowed when the cash is paid. This method is not limited solely to the receipt and payment of cash. The receipt, or payment, may be in the form of services or property using the fair market value.

The cash method is not available to those taxpayers where inventory is a material income producing factor. Where inventory is a factor, the accrual method must be used. It is also not available to C Corporations, unless their sales are less than $5 million per year.

Under the cash method, certain prepaid expenses may be allowed as a current year deduction if the deferral period is less than a year. Also, charging an item to the taxpayer's credit card constitutes a payment in the year charged, even though the taxpayer does not pay the credit card company until the following year. Purchases of fixed assets for cash, however, are not treated as expenses. The assets must be capitalized, and deductions are allowed through cost recovery (depreciation).

Prepaid income, or deferred revenue is usually recognized in the year of receipt even though it is not earned until next year. An exception from income treatment is the receipt of a security deposit where the amount will be returned to the tenant at the end of the lease.

### ACCRUAL METHOD

Under the **accrual method** of accounting, income is recognized when earned and expenses when incurred. The general rule addressing the concept of "recognized when earned or incurred" states that:

- All of the events fixing the taxpayer's right to receive the income, or create the liability have occurred, and
- The amount can be determined with reasonable accuracy.

The issue of reasonable accuracy allows the taxpayer to file a return even when there is some degree of uncertainty as to the actual receipt of income or the payment of expense. Under this premise, when the actual amount is determined in a later year, an amended return is not required.

When **inventory** is a material income producing factor, the taxpayer must report actual sales, and determine the cost of goods sold using inventory and accounts payable.

> **Example 1:** T has a retail store and during the year the actual sales were $400,000. T's beginning and ending inventory was $30,000 and $45,000 respectively. Cash purchases during the year totaled $310,000 and his trade payables at the beginning and end of the year were $28,000 and $31,000 respectively. T must report the following gross profit.
>
> | | |
> |---|---|
> | Sales | $ 400,000 |
> | Cost of goods sold: | |
> | Beginning inventory | 30,000 |
> | Purchases | 313,000 |
> | Goods available for sale | 343,000 |
> | Ending inventory | -45,000 |
> | Cost of goods sold | 298,000 |
> | Gross profit on sales | $ 102,000 |
>
> (Hint: Cash purchases plus ending trade payables minus beginning trade payables equals purchases under the accrual method.)

## HYBRID METHOD

The taxpayer maintaining an inventory is required to use the accrual method for reporting the gross profit on sales. However, for the other expenses such as selling and administrative, the taxpayer may use the cash method.

## CONSTRUCTIVE RECEIPT

Even though a taxpayer does not actually receive the cash, they may still have to recognize income under the constructive receipt doctrine. This doctrine states that income is to be recognized when the money or property is made available to the taxpayer and there are no real limitations to the taxpayer receiving it.

> **Example 2:** Z performed cleaning services during November 1999 and billed the client $500. The client paid Z the $500 on December 28, but Z refused to accept payment and asked to be paid in 2000 instead. Z constructively received the income in 1998 and must include it in income.

> **Example 3:** W is a shareholder of a Fortune 500 company. On December 31, 1999, the company declared and paid a dividend on their stock. The company mailed W a dividend check for $200 on that date. W received the check on January 4, 2000. W did not have access to the funds until 2000. W does not include this as 1999 income.

## INSTALLMENT SALES

When a taxpayer sells property and recognizes a gain, the taxpayer does not have to recognize the entire gain from the sale if at least one payment is received in the year after the sale. Under the "where-with-all-to-pay concept", the gain is recognized on a pro-rata basis based upon the receipt of the sale proceeds. This is not an elective provision, it is automatic. If you want to recognize all of the income in the year of the sale, you must elect out by reporting the entire gain in the year of the sale.

To determine the recognized gain for the year:

$$\frac{\text{Total gain}}{\text{Total contract price}} \quad X \quad \text{Payments received during year} = \text{Recognized gain}$$

> **Example 4:** In 1997, D sells property to B for $40,000. D's cost in the asset was $30,000, thus a $10,000 gain is to be recognized. D is to receive $20,000 in 1997, and $10,000 in 1998 and 1999. Under the installment sale provision D would recognize $5,000 in 1997, and $2,500 in each of 1998 and 1999.
>
> **1997 gain** $\qquad \dfrac{\$10,000}{\$40,000} \quad$ X $\$20,000 = \$5,000$
>
> **1998 & 1999 gain** $\qquad \dfrac{\$10,000}{\$40,000} \quad$ X $\$10,000 = \$2,500$

Should the buyer assume any indebtedness on the property being sold, then the denominator should reflect that as a reduction from the overall selling price or contract price. The installment sale provisions are not available for the ordinary gain on the sale of inventory or depreciation recapture from the sale of depreciable property. That gain is recognized immediately.

## COMPLETED CONTRACT SALES

When a taxpayer is involved in a project which extends beyond the tax year, it may be possible to defer the gain on the project until it is complete. The completed contract method usually is associated with home builders, commercial contractors, road construction, etc. Costs associated with the contract are accumulated as an asset until the project is complete. At that time, the total revenue and costs associated with that project are recognized for tax purposes. In order to qualify, the company's gross receipts must not exceed $10 million.

The alternative is the **percentage of completion** method. Here, the taxpayer recognizes income on a pro-rata basis as the job progresses.

> **Example 5:** ELK Company builds commercial projects, and during the current year expended $3,000,000 in material, labor and overhead on their only project. The total revenue at completion will be $6,000,000 and it is estimated that it will take $1,500,000 to complete the project.
>
> Under the **completed contract** method, no income or expense would be recognized in the current year because the job is not complete. Under the **percentage of completion** method, ELK would recognize $1,000,000 in income, determined as follows:
>
> $\dfrac{\text{Costs incurred to date} \quad \$3,000,000}{\text{Estimated at completion } \$4,500,000} \quad$ X Total revenue $\$6,000,000 = \$4,000,000$
>
> | | |
> |---|---|
> | Total revenue to be recognized | $4,000,000 |
> | Cost of construction | 3,000,000 |
> | Income recognized | $1,000,000 |

# ACCOUNTING PERIODS

In general, a taxpayer may select a year-end to coincide with the method used to maintain his books and records. However, most individual taxpayers use a calendar year due to the record keeping complexities. (S Corporations and partnerships have other restrictions which are addressed in Chapters 7, 8 and 9.) The length of the tax year cannot exceed 12 months. However, it is permissible for a taxpayer to use a 52 or 53 week year to coincide with the natural business cycle.

> **Example 6:** J is a grocer and is open Monday through Saturday. J elects to have his tax year end on the last Saturday in December to coincide with his business cycle. Some years this results in a 52 week year, and others a 53 week year.

Once a year-end is selected, the taxpayer must obtain written consent from the IRS in order to change. The request is filed on Form 1128 and is due on or before the 15th day of the second month following the desired year-end. This results in what is referred to as a short period. The income from the short period must be annualized to determine the appropriate tax effect.

> **Example 7:** SSC Academy has a December 31 (calendar) year-end and wishes to change to June 30th to coincide with their natural year-end. They must file the request no later than August 15th, and if approved, file a short period return covering the period from January 1 until June 30.

# COMPUTATION OF AN INDIVIDUAL'S TAX LIABILITY AND CREDITS

## GENERAL

Once the taxable income of an individual has been determined, the computation of tax is required. After the tax is computed, a reduction for payments and credits is made to determine if the individual has a refund or balance due. *See page two of Form 1040 at the back of Chapter 1 for a complete look at the taxes and credits..*

The summary of the **major** tax computations, credits and payments, is as follows:

<u>Taxable income</u>
Tax (regular)
Less:   Child and dependent care credit
          Elderly credit
          Foreign tax credit
Plus:   Self-employment tax
          Alternative minimum tax
          Penalty tax on IRAs and pensions
Less:   Withholding taxes
          Estimated tax payments
          Earned income credit
          <u>Excess Social Security tax</u>
Refund or balance due

## REGULAR COMPUTATION

In computing the amount of tax, taxpayers with taxable income of less than $100,000 may use the Tax Tables. If you are required to calculate the tax on the exam, you will use the rates, not the tax tables. Please refer to the 1999 Rate Schedules for the different filing statuses on the last page of this chapter.

The rate schedule for an unmarried taxpayer (single), shows that the tax is 15% for the first $25,750 of taxable income; 28% on the taxable income from $25,750 through $62,450, and so on. The highest marginal tax bracket for an individual is **39.6%**

---

**Example 8:** W is single and has taxable income of $35,750. His tax is computed as follows:

| | |
|---|---|
| $25,750 X 15% | $ 3,862 |
| $10,000 X 28% | 2,800 |
| Total tax | $ 6,662 |

---

The rate that the taxpayer is taxed on for the incremental amount of income is called the marginal tax bracket. W is in the 28% marginal tax bracket. W's average tax rate is 19% ($6,603/$35,350).

## DEPENDENT CHILD

In preparing the return for a dependent child, **no personal exemption** is allowed. This is because someone has already claimed the child as a dependent. Another important factor is that the dependent's standard deduction is limited to the amount of earned income, plus $250 (but not to exceed $4,300) or $700, whichever is greater.

---

**Example 9:** S is 16 and is properly claimed as a dependent on his parent's return. During 1999, S earned $5,300 working in a supermarket. He has no other income.

| | |
|---|---|
| Gross income | $ 5,300 |
| Standard deduction | -4,300 |
| Taxable income | $ 1,000 |
| | |
| Tax @ 15% | $ 150 |

---

**Example 10:** T is 16 and is properly claimed as a dependent on his parents return. During 1999, T received $5,000 from investments given to him by his grandparents. He has no other income.

| | |
|---|---|
| Gross income | $ 5,000 |
| Standard deduction | -700 |
| Taxable income | $ 4,300 |
| | |
| Tax @ 15% | $ 645 |

Since the $5,000 is not considered earned income, the standard deduction is limited to $700.

---

## CHILD UNDER THE AGE OF 14 - KIDDIE TAX

When a child under the age of 14 has net unearned income in excess of $1,400, the tax on the excess will be taxed at the parent's rate. The computations are somewhat complicated due to the use of the exemptions and standard deduction, but the thrust of the law is to counter the tax planning technique of shifting income producing property (investments) down to a child where it will be subject to a lower tax rate. At the child's level, effectively the first $700 of income is not subject to tax because of the standard deduction, the second $700 is taxed at the child's rate (15%), and the excess is taxed at the parent's rate.

**Example 11:** N, age 4, received $4,700 in interest and dividends during 1999. N had no itemized deductions. N's parents are in the 28% tax bracket.

| | |
|---|---|
| Total unearned income | $ 4,700 |
| Less: Standard deduction | -700 |
| Amount subject to tax | 4,000 |
| Less: Amount taxed at child's rate | -700 |
| Amount taxed at parent's rate | $ 3,300 |
| | |
| Tax on child's portion: | |
| $ 700 X 15% = | $ 105 |
| Tax on parental portion: | |
| $3,300 X 28% = | 924 |
| Total tax | $ 1,029 |

As an option to performing the above calculations and filing a return for their child, parents may pay an additional $105 tax plus claim the unearned income in excess of $1,400 on their return. To elect this, the gross income must be from interest and dividends only, and must be less than $5,000.

## PHASE-OUT OF EXEMPTIONS

In determining the tax for high-income taxpayers, the deduction for exemptions may be eliminated. Taxpayers with adjusted gross income in excess of a specified threshold amount must reduce their exemptions by 2% for every $2,500 or fraction thereof over the threshold. The 1999 thresholds are:

| | |
|---|---|
| Single | $ 126,600 |
| Married, filing jointly | 189,950 |
| Married, filing separately | 94,975 |
| Head of household | 158,300 |
| Qualifying widow(er) | 189,950 |

**Example 12:** P is single and has no dependents. His 1998 AGI is $136,550. Calculate how much of his $2,650 exemption is disallowed under this provision.

| | |
|---|---|
| P's adjusted gross income | $ 138,650 |
| Threshold amount | 126,600 |
| Excess over threshold | 12,050 |
| Divided by $2,500 | 4.82 |
| Round up to next whole number | 5 |
| Statutory percentage | 2% |
| Total percentage reduction | 10% |
| P's exemption | $2,750 |
| Disallowed portion of exemption | $275 |

## INCOME AVERAGING FOR FARMERS

*Effective for tax years beginning after December 31, 1997,* a taxpayer engaged in the farming business may now elect to use income averaging to compute his tax. In determining income, the farmer may include the gain from the sale of farming business property.

# ALTERNATIVE MINIMUM TAX

## GENERAL

To ensure that individuals pay their fair share of taxes, a taxpayer may be subject to an alternative minimum tax (AMT). The AMT is the **excess** of the tentative minimum tax over the regular tax. The process to determine the AMT is to first identify the various tax preferences or adjustments which were properly elected and planned for by the taxpayer, and then, effectively, disallow them.

The framework for calculating the AMT is as follows:

> Taxable income
> Plus or minus **adjustments**
> Plus the tax **preferences**
> Equals AMTI
> Less the **exemption** amount
> Equals the AMT base
> Multiplied by the AMT **tax rate**
> Equals the tentative minimum tax
> Less the regular tax
> Equals the AMT

## ADJUSTMENTS

In general, adjustments can be **positive or negative,** and are the result of timing differences in the tax treatment of certain items. For example, excess MACRS depreciation over the longer, slower AMT depreciation method of ADS (alternative depreciation system) will result in a positive adjustment that increases the alternative minimum taxable income. However, after the asset has been fully recovered under MACRS, there will still be depreciation under the AMT method, which will cause a negative adjustment and decrease AMTI.

The AMT **adjustments**, with a very brief explanation, include:

- Circulation expenditures - Must be capitalized and expensed over three years, not immediately.
- Depreciation - Excess MACRS of real property over ADS of 40 years straight-line.
- Depreciation - Excess MACRS of personal property over ADS 150% DDB.
- Differences in Recognized Gains or Losses - Because of depreciation changes, tax bases are different.
- Pollution Control Facilities Amortization - Excess of straight-line, 60 months over ADS.
- Passive Activity Losses - Uses a different taxable income level for determining losses.
- Completed Contract Method - Must use percentage of completion instead.
- Incentive Stock Options - Excess of FMV over exercise price.
- Net Operating Loss - Must be modified.

The following **itemized deductions** are also **adjustments,** and are limited in their deductibility for AMT purposes:

- Medical Expenses - Must exceed 10% of AGI instead of 7.5%.
- Taxes - State, local foreign and property - Not allowed.
- Mortgage Interest - Limited to acquisition interest, excludes home equity interest.
- Certain Investment Interest Expense - Not allowed.
- Miscellaneous 2% Deductions - Not allowed.
- Standard Deduction - Not allowed.
- Exemption Amount - Not allowed.

## TAX PREFERENCES

Tax preferences are always added to taxable income, never subtracted. The preferences are:

- Interest income on private activity bonds.
- Excess accelerated depreciation over straight-line on pre-87 real property.
- Excess accelerated depreciation over straight-line on leased pre-87 personal property.
- Excess amortization over depreciation on pre-87 certified pollution control facilities.
- Percentage depletion beyond the property's adjusted basis.
- Excess intangible drilling costs, reduced by 65% of net income from oil, gas and geothermal activity.
- 42% of the excluded gain from the sale of certain small business stock.

## EXEMPTION AMOUNT

After adding and subtracting the adjustments, and adding the tax preferences to taxable income, a taxpayer is allowed an exemption from the AMTI. The exemption amounts, by filing status, are as follows:

| | |
|---|---|
| Single | $ 33,750 |
| Married, filing jointly | 45,000 |
| Married, filing separately | 22,500 |

However, these exemptions are phased-out (at a rate of 25% over the excess) if the taxpayers AMTI before the exemption exceeds the following thresholds:

| | |
|---|---|
| Single | $ 112,500 |
| Married, filing jointly | 150,000 |
| Married, filing separately | 75,000 |

---

**Example 13:** R & S are married and file a joint return. R & S had AMTI (before the exemption amount) of $270,000. Their exemption amount would be only $15,000 ($45,000 less phase-out of $30,000):

| | |
|---|---|
| AMTI | $ 270,000 |
| Threshold for phase-out | 150,000 |
| Excess over threshold | 120,000 |
| Phase-out rate | 25% |
| Exemption phaseout | $ 30,000 |

---

## THE AMT TAX RATE

There is a two-tier tax rate for determining the tentative minimum tax.

| AMT Base Amount | AMT Rate |
|---|---|
| $ 0 up to $175,000 | 26% |
| $ 175,000 and up | 28% |

**Example 14:** During the year, K earned a significant amount of income and took advantage of many tax preferences and accelerated depreciation, and paid a large amount of real estate taxes, income taxes and home equity interest. K calculated her income tax liability under the regular method to be only $17,000. K then heard about the alternative minimum tax from a CPA candidate and after hours of calculations, she determined that her AMT base amount was $205,000.

Tentative minimum tax computation:

|  |  |  |
|---|---|---|
| First $ 175,000 @ 26% | $ 45,500 | |
| Next $30,000 @ 28% | 8,400 | |
|  | $ 53,900 | |
| K's regular income tax | 17,000 | |
| Alternative minimum tax | $ 36,900 | |

K was stunned. Remember that the alternative minimum tax is the **excess** of the tentative minimum tax over the regular tax.

# SELF-EMPLOYMENT TAX

If a taxpayer has earnings from self-employment of at least $400, a self-employment tax must be paid on earnings. The self-employment tax is equivalent to the employee's share and the employer's share of the Social Security and Medicare taxes withholding tax. The rate for Social Security tax is 6.2% and Medicare is 1.45% for a total of 7.65%. A taxpayer is subject to the Social Security tax on earnings up to $72,600 in 1999. For Medicare there is no ceiling. Since the taxpayer is employing himself, these rates must be doubled to a total rate of 15.3%.

In order to provide the self-employed taxpayer with a benefit for paying the "employer's share" of the taxes required to be paid, there are two special provisions:

- Before calculating the tax, the net earnings are reduced by 7.65%, and
- One-half of the self-employment tax is allowed as a deduction for adjusted gross income (Chapter 3).

**Example 15:** J is self-employed an has $30,000 of net earnings from self-employment. His self-employment tax is determined as follows:

|  |  |
|---|---|
| Net earnings | $ 30,000 |
| Reduction percentage | 92.35% |
| Computational base | $ 27,705 |
| Self-employment tax rate | 15.3% |
| Self-employment tax | $ 4,239 |

# COMPUTATION OF TAX CREDITS

## GENERAL

Tax credits generally reduce the amount of tax shown on the return. Most credits require special calculations to determine the amount of the credit and several are based upon the taxpayer's filing status. Most tax credits are called **non-refundable** credits because they can only reduce the tax to zero. One credit in this section (earned income credit) is a **refundable** credit. This credit provides the taxpayer with relief beyond reducing the tax liability to actually generating a refund, even if no taxes were ever paid.

> **Example 16:** Y has no taxable income this year and has no tax liability Y qualifies for an elderly credit of $60. Y cannot utilize the credit because it is a non-refundable credit and it cannot reduce his tax below zero. If Y's $60 credit was a refundable credit (such as the earned income credit), Y would receive a refund of $60, even though Y had no tax liability nor made any payments.

## EARNED INCOME CREDIT

This credit provides qualifying taxpayers with relatively low levels of income a credit against their tax liability, or a refund, if in excess of their liability. This is the only refundable credit. The nature of the credit is to encourage the taxpayer to "earn" income, rather than receive "non-earned" benefits. The credit computation excludes interest, dividends and alimony from the computation. While the credit was only for taxpayers with at least one child residing with them for over one-half of the year, it has been expanded to those without children, as is discussed later.

The credit is subject to phase-out limitations based upon the AGI and number of qualifying children of the taxpayer. Tax-exempt interest and any non-taxable pension or annuity income is added to the definition of AGI. In order to qualify, the child must be a son, daughter, stepson, stepdaughter or foster child of the taxpayer; must reside with the taxpayer as their principal place of abode; and must be under age 19, or 24 if a full-time student. For 1999, the credit schedule is as follows:

| Number of Children | Maximum Earned Income | Credit % | Phase-out Amount | Phase-out % | Phase-out Stops |
|---|---|---|---|---|---|
| One Child | $ 6,800 | 34% | $ 12,460 | 15.98% | $ 26,928 |
| Two or more | $ 9,540 | 40% | $ 12,460 | 21.06% | $ 30,580 |

> **Example 17:** L has only earned income in 1999 of $13,000 and two qualifying children. Her earned income credit is:
>
> | | | |
> |---|---|---|
> | Maximum credit | $9,540 X 40% = $3,816 | |
> | Less: phaseout: | | |
> | $13,000 – 12,460 = $540 | | |
> | $540 X 21.06% | | -114 |
> | Earned income credit | | $3,702 |
>
> If L's tax was only $200, then the credit would reduce the tax to zero and give L a refund of $3,502.

**Taxpayers,** between the ages of 25 and 64, **without children, and** who are not the dependents of another taxpayer, may qualify for the earned income credit under RRA of 1993. The credit is at the rate of 7.65% of earned income up to $4,530. (Maximum credit is $347) The credit reduces at the same rate by the excess of earned income over $5,670. The credit is fully phased-out at $10,200.

## CHILD TAX CREDIT

*Effective for tax years beginning after December 31, 1997,* taxpayers will be able to claim a child credit for each qualifying child under the age of 17. For 1999, the credit is $500 per child. In general, the child must be a child or direct descendant of the taxpayer and the taxpayer must be able to claim the child as his dependent. There is a threshold limitation. The credit is reduced by $50 for each $1,000 (or part thereof) of modified adjusted gross income over the following:

| | |
|---|---|
| Single | $ 75,000 |
| Married filing jointly | 110,000 |
| Married filing separately | 55,000 |

The credit has an additional feature in that if it exceeds the taxpayer's income tax for that year, the excess may be refunded if the taxpayer has three or more qualifying children, similar to the earned income credit.

## HOPE SCHOLARSHIP CREDIT

*Effective for tax years beginning after December 31, 1997,* taxpayers may elect to take a nonrefundable tax credit for tuition and fees paid during the first two years of postsecondary education. The credit is equal to the lessor of $1,500, or 100% of the first $1,000 paid plus 50% of the next $1,000 paid. The credit is determined per student, per year.

## LIFETIME LEARNING CREDIT

*Effective for payments made after June 30, 1998,* taxpayers may elect to take a nonrefundable tax credit for qualified tuition and related expenses for undergraduate, graduate and professional degree courses. The credit is the lessor of $1,000, or 20% of up to $5,000 in qualified tuition and fees. Unlike the HOPE Scholarship Credit, the taxpayer may claim this over an unlimited number of years. However, this credit is not based upon the number of qualifying students. The maximum credit per year is $1,000.

There are some limitations to both the Hope Scholarship Credit and the Lifetime Learning Credit. The phase-out range (credits are reduced on a pro-rata basis) for allowing the credits is as follows:

| | Phase-out range |
|---|---|
| Married, filing jointly | $ 80,000 - $ 100,000 |
| Single | $ 40,000 - $ 50,000 |

The credit is not available for married taxpayers filing separately.

## DEPENDENT CARE CREDIT

This credit applies to those taxpayers who pay for dependent or child care in order for them to work. To be eligible, the taxpayer must maintain a household for a dependent, age 12 or under, or any dependent of spouse who is physically or mentally incapacitated. The credit ranges from 30% down to 20%, based upon the AGI of the taxpayer. The credit is reduced by 1% point for each $2,000 of AGI over $10,000. The 20% credit is reached when AGI exceeds $28,000.

When computing the credit, there are two other restrictions. First, the maximum amount of qualifying expenses per child is $2,400 for one; and $4,800 for two or more. Second, the maximum amount cannot exceed the earned income of the spouse with the lower earnings. For purposes of this test, alimony counts as earned income as does a deemed amount of $200 per month per child ($2,400 per year) for full-time students.

# ELDERLY CREDIT

A credit is provided to the elderly and disabled to provide a form of relief from taxation. The credit applies to taxpayers 65 or older. It is also available to those under 65, provided they are retired with a total and permanent disability.

To determine the credit, start with an initial base amount (per Section 37) of $5,000 for a single taxpayer or $7,500 for married filing jointly. This amount needs to be reduced by

(1) any social security benefits, and
(2) one-half of the excess AGI over $7,500 if single or $10,000 if married.

This is the "qualifying income." The credit is the lessor of 15% of their qualifying income, or the amount of tax on the return.

---

**Example 18**: M is 70, single and retired. During the year he earned $3,000 from his pension and $1,000 in interest on his savings. M has no tax liability. M also received $1,500 in social security benefits.

| | |
|---|---|
| Section 37 amount | $ 5,000 |
| Less: Social Security benefits | -1,500 |
| Credit base | $ 3,500 |
| Elderly credit rate | 15% |
| Elderly credit | $   525 |

Note: This credit is only allowed to offset taxes. His taxes are zero, therefore no credit is allowed.

---

# FOREIGN TAX CREDIT

Individual taxpayers are taxed in the United States on their worldwide income. The taxpayers are entitled to a tax credit for income taxes paid to foreign countries. This prevents double taxation of the same income. The foreign tax credit cannot exceed the lessor of the amount of the foreign taxes paid or the pro-rata share of US taxes on the foreign income. The limitation is determined as follows:

$$\frac{\text{Income from foreign sources}}{\text{Worldwide income}} \times \text{US taxes paid} = \text{Foreign tax credit}$$

---

**Example 19:** K has taxable income of $50,000, of which $1,000 was dividends earned on an investment in a foreign country. K paid $300 in income taxes to that foreign country. Prior to the determination of the foreign tax credit, K's US income tax was $10,000.

$$\frac{\$1,000}{\$50,000} \times \$10,000 = \$200 \text{ maximum foreign tax credit}$$

The foreign tax credit is $200 (the lessor of $200 or the amount paid of $300). The excess of $100 may be carried back two years and then forward five years.

---

## EXCESS SOCIAL SECURITY TAXES

A taxpayer is generally subject to Social Security and Medicare taxes. For 1999, the Social Security tax of 6.2% is imposed on wages up to $72,600 per year for a maximum of $4,501, while the Medicare tax of 1.45% has no limit. Earnings above the threshold are not subject to the tax. Should an employee change jobs during the year, the new employer must withhold the Social Security and Medicare tax, subject to the same limitations again. It is possible for taxpayers to have extra Social Security taxes withheld because of this. This excess may be claimed as a credit against any taxes due.

---

**Example 20:** During 1999, G worked for ABC Company for six months and earned $40,000 in salary. Social Security taxes of $2,480 were withheld. In July, G began work for a new company and earned $50,000 for the balance of the year. Social Security taxes of $3,100 were withheld on those earnings. The maximum wages on which Social Security taxes may be withheld is $72,600. Therefore, G is entitled to a credit of $1,079 for 1999.

| | |
|---|---|
| Social Security wage base | $ 72,600 |
| Social Security rate | 6.2% |
| Ceiling on Social Security taxes | $ 4,501 |
| | |
| Actual Social Security withholdings: | |
| Job #1 | $ 2,480 |
| Job #2 | 3,100 |
| Total withholdings | 5,580 |
| Maximum social security tax | 4,501 |
| Excess withholdings | $ 1,079 |

---

# ESTIMATED INCOME TAX PAYMENTS

***Effective for the tax years beginning after 1997***, an individual must make estimated payments if he expects that the underpayment after withholdings and tax credits is at least $1,000 and more than 10% of the amount of the tax shown on the return. The tax payments are remitted with Form 1040-ES and are due in equal installments on the 15th day of the 4th, 6th, and 9th month of the tax year, and the 1st month of the filing year. In order to avoid any penalty on the underpayment of taxes, an individual must make payments equal to:

- 90% of their current year's tax.
- 100% of their prior year's tax.
- 110% of their prior year's tax if the prior year's AGI exceeds $150,000.
- 105% of their prior year's tax for tax years beginning in 1999 and 2000.
- Annualized income installment method computation.

# 1999 TAX RATE SCHEDULE

## Joint Returns and Surviving Spouses

| If taxable income is: | The tax is: |
| --- | --- |
| Not over $43,050 | 15% of taxable income |
| Over 43,050 but not over $104,050 | $6,457.50 plus 28% of the excess over $43,050 |
| Over $104,050 but not over $158,550 | $23,537.50 plus 31% of the excess over $104,050 |
| Over $158,550 but not over $283,150 | $40,432.50 plus 36% of the excess over $158,550 |
| Over $283,150 | $85,288.50 plus 39.6% of the excess over $283,150 |

## Unmarried Individuals (Single)

| If taxable income is: | The tax is: |
| --- | --- |
| Not over $25,750 | 15% of taxable income |
| Over $25,750 but not over $62,450 | $3,862.50 plus 28% of the excess over $25,750 |
| Over $62,450 but not over $130,250 | $14,138.50 plus 31% of the excess over $62,450 |
| Over $130,250 but not over $283,150 | $35,156.50 plus 36% of the excess over $130,250 |
| Over $283,150 | $90,200.50 plus 39.6% of the excess over $283,150 |

## Heads of Households

| If taxable income is: | The tax is: |
| --- | --- |
| Not over $34,550 | 15% of taxable income |
| Over $34,550 but not over $89,150 | $5,182.50 plus 28% of the excess over $34,550 |
| Over $89,150 but not over $144,400 | $20,470.50 plus 31% of the excess over $89,150 |
| Over $144,400 but not over $283,150 | $37,598 plus 36% of the excess over $144,400 |
| Over $283,150 | $87,548 plus 39.6% of the excess over $283,150 |

## Married Individuals Filing Separately

| If taxable income is: | The tax is: |
| --- | --- |
| Not over $21,525 | 15% of taxable income |
| Over $21,525 but not over $52,025 | $3,228.75 plus 28% of the excess over $21,525 |
| Over $52,025 but not over $79,275 | $11,768.75 plus 31% of the excess over $52,025 |
| Over $79,275 but not over $141,575 | $20,216.25 plus 36% of the excess over $79,275 |
| Over $141,575 | $42,644.25 plus 39.6% of the excess over $141,575 |

# Chapter Five -- Questions
## Accounting Methods and Periods, and Computation of Tax Liability and Tax Credits

## ACCOUNTING METHODS & PERIODS

1. A cash-basis taxpayer should report gross income
   a. For the year in which income is either actually or constructively received, whether in cash or in property.
   b. For the year in which income is either actually or constructively received in cash only.
   c. Only for the year in which income is actually received whether in cash or in property.
   d. Only for the year in which income is actually received in cash.

2. Alex Burg, a cash basis taxpayer, earned an annual salary of $80,000 at Ace Corp. in 1999, but elected to take only $50,000. Ace, which was financially able to pay Burg's full salary, credited the unpaid balance of $30,000 to Burg's account on the corporate books in 1999, and actually paid this $30,000 to Burg on April 30, 2000. How much of the salary is taxable to Burg in 1999?
   a. $50,000.
   b. $60,000.
   c. $65,000.
   d. $80,000.

---

Items 3 through 6 are based on the following data:
Carl Tice, an employee of Canova Corp., received a salary of $50,000 from Canova in 1999. Also in 1999, Carl bought 100 shares of Nolan Corp. common stock from Canova for $30 a share, when the market value of the Nolan stock was $50 a share. Canova had paid $20 a share for the Nolan stock in 1975. In addition, Carl owned a building which he leased to Boss Co. on January 1, 1999, for a five-year term at $500 a month. Boss paid Carl $8,000 in 1999 to cover the following:

| | |
|---|---|
| Rent for January to December 1999 | $6,000 |
| Advance rent for January 2000 | 500 |
| Security deposit, to be applied against the final three months' rent in the fifth year of the lease | 1,500 |

Carl also received the following dividends in 1999, from:

| | |
|---|---|
| Mutual Life Insurance Co., on Carl's life insurance policy | $300 |
| General Merchandise Corp., a Texas corporation, on preferred stock | 400 |
| Second National Bank, on bank's common stock | 800 |

On July 1, 1999, Carl sold for $9,500, on the open market, a $10,000 face value 10-year, noncallable, Doe Corp. bond. This bond was part of an original issue by Doe on July 1, 1996, and was purchased by Carl on that date, at a discount of $1,200, for a net price of $8,800.

3. How much should Carl report on his 1999 income tax return as compensation income received from Canova?
   a. $50,000.
   b. $51,000.
   c. $52,000.
   d. $53,000.

4. How much rent income should Carl report in his 1999 income tax return for the amounts paid to him by Boss?
   a. $6,000.
   b. $6,500.
   c. $7,500.
   d. $8,000.

5. How much dividend income should Carl report in his 1999 income tax return?
   a. $400.
   b. $1,100.
   c. $1,200.
   d. $1,500.

6. What is Carl's long-term capital gain in 1999, on the sale of the Doe bond?
   a. $0.
   b. $460.
   c. $700.
   d. $1,200.

---

7. On December 15, 1999, Donald Calder made a contribution of $500 to a qualified charitable organization by charging the contribution on his bank credit card. Calder paid the $500 on January 20, 2000, upon receipt of the bill from the bank. In addition, Calder issued and delivered a promissory note for $1,000 to another qualified charitable organization on November 1, 1999, which he paid upon maturity six months later. If Calder itemizes his deductions, what portion of these contributions is deductible in 1999?

a. $0.
b. $500.
c. $1,000.
d. $1,500.

8. In 1998, Farb, a cash basis individual taxpayer, received an $8,000 invoice for personal property taxes. Believing the amount to be overstated by $5,000, Farb paid the invoiced amount under protest and immediately started legal action to recover the overstatement. In November 1999, the matter was resolved in Farb's favor, and he received a $5,000 refund. Farb itemizes his deductions on his tax returns. Which of the following statements is correct regarding the deductibility of the property taxes?

a. Farb should deduct $8,000 in his 1998 income tax return and should report the $5,000 refund as income in his 1999 income tax return.
b. Farb should **not** deduct any amount in his 1998 income tax return and should deduct $3,000 in his 1999 income tax return.
c. Farb should deduct $3,000 in his 1998 income tax return.
d. Farb should **not** deduct any amount in his 1998 income tax return when originally filed, and should file an amended 1998 income tax return in 1999.

9. Unless the Internal Revenue Service consents to a change of method, the accrual method of tax reporting is mandatory for a sole proprietor when there are

|  | Accounts receivable for services rendered | Year-end merchandise inventories |
|---|---|---|
| a. | Yes | Yes |
| b. | Yes | No |
| c. | No | No |
| d. | No | Yes |

10. Dr. Chester is a cash basis taxpayer. His office visit charges are usually paid on the date of visit or within one month. However, services rendered outside the office are billed weekly, and are usually paid within two months as patients collect from insurance companies. Information relating to this year is as follows:

| | |
|---|---|
| Cash received at the time of office visits | $35,000 |
| Collections on accounts receivable | 130,000 |
| Accounts receivable, January 1 | 16,000 |
| Accounts receivable, December 31 | 20,000 |

Dr. Chester's gross income from his medical practice for the taxable year is

a. $165,000.
b. $169,000.
c. $181,000.
d. $185,000.

11. For a cash basis taxpayer, gain or loss on a year-end sale of listed stock arises on the

a. Trade date.
b. Settlement date.
c. Date of receipt of cash proceeds.
d. Date of delivery of stock certificate.

12. Carl Slater was the sole proprietor of a high-volume drug store which he owned for 25 years before he sold it to Statewide Drug Stores, Inc., in 1999. Besides the $800,000 selling price for the store's tangible assets and goodwill, Slater received a lump sum of $60,000 in 1999 for his agreement not to operate a competing enterprise within ten miles of the store's location, for a period of six years. How will the $60,000 be taxed to Slater?

a. As $60,000 ordinary income in 1999.
b. As $60,000 short-term capital gain in 1999.
c. As $60,000 long-term capital gain in 1999.
d. As ordinary income of $10,000 a year for six years.

## COMPUTATION OF TAX LIABILITY AND CREDITS

13. The alternative minimum tax (AMT) is computed as the

a. Excess of the regular tax over the tentative AMT.
b. Excess of the tentative AMT over the regular tax.
c. The tentative AMT plus the regular tax.
d. Lesser of the tentative AMT or the regular tax.

14. In 1999, Don Mills, a single taxpayer, had $70,000 in taxable income before personal exemptions. Mills had no tax preferences. His itemized deductions were as follows:

| | |
|---|---|
| State and local income taxes | $5,000 |
| Home mortgage interest on loan to acquire residence | 6,000 |
| Miscellaneous deductions that exceed 2% of adjusted gross income | 2,000 |

What amount did Mills report as alternative minimum taxable income before the AMT exemption?
a. $72,000
b. $75,000
c. $77,000
d. $83,000

15. Alternative minimum tax preferences include

| | *Tax exempt interest from private activity bonds issued during 1994* | *Charitable contributions of appreciated capital gain property* |
|---|---|---|
| a. | Yes | Yes |
| b. | Yes | No |
| c. | No | Yes |
| d. | No | No |

16. The credit for prior year alternative minimum tax liability may be carried
a. Forward for a maximum of 5 years.
b. Back to the 3 preceding years or carried forward for a maximum of 5 years.
c. Back to the 3 preceding years.
d. Forward indefinitely.

17. Which of the following credits is a combination of several tax credits to provide uniform rules for the current and carryback-carryover years?
a. General business credit.
b. Foreign tax credit.
c. Minimum tax credit.
d. Enhanced oil recovery credit.

18. To qualify for the child care credit on a joint return, at least one spouse must

| | *Have an adjusted gross income of $10,000 or less* | *Be gainfully employed when related expenses are incurred* |
|---|---|---|
| a. | Yes | Yes |
| b. | No | No |
| c. | Yes | No |
| d. | No | Yes |

19. Nancy and Dennis Martin are married and file a joint income tax return. Both were employed during the year and earned the following salaries:

| | |
|---|---|
| Dennis | $32,000 |
| Nancy | 14,000 |

In order to enable Nancy to work, she incurred at-home child care expenses of $6,000 for their two-year-old daughter and four-year-old son. What is the amount of the child care credit they can claim?
a. $400.
b. $960.
c. $1,200.
d. $2,800.

20. Nora Hayes, a widow, maintains a home for herself and her two dependent preschool children. Nora's earned income and adjusted gross income was $29,000. She paid work-related expenses of $3,000 for a housekeeper to care for her children. How much can Nora claim for child care credit?
a. $0.
b. $480.
c. $600.
d. $960.

21. Which of the following credits can result in a refund even if the individual had **no** income tax liability?
a. Credit for prior year minimum tax.
b. Elderly and permanently and totally disabled credit.
c. Earned income credit.
d. Child and dependent care credit.

22. Kent qualified for the earned income credit in 1999. This credit could result in a
a. Refund even if Kent had no tax withheld from wages.
b. Refund only if Kent had tax withheld from wages.
c. Carryback or carryforward for any unused portion.
d. Subtraction from adjusted gross income to arrive at taxable income.

23. Amos Kettle, a single taxpayer, age 66, filed his income tax return and reported an adjusted gross income of $6,000. He received a total of $1,200 in Social Security benefits for the year and has no other excluded pension or annuity amounts. What amount can Kettle claim as a tax credit for the elderly?
a. $180.
b. $195.
c. $570.
d. $900.

24. Melvin Crane is 66 years old, and his wife, Matilda, is 65. They filed a joint income tax return this year, reporting an adjusted gross income of $7,800, on which they paid a tax of $60. They received $1,250 from social security benefits. How much can they claim on Schedule R of Form 1040 as a credit for the elderly?
a. $0.
b. $60.
c. $938.
d. $375.

25. An employee who has had social security tax withheld in an amount greater than the maximum for a particular year, may claim
a. Such excess as either a credit or an itemized deduction, at the election of the employee, if that excess resulted from correct withholding by two or more employers.
b. Reimbursement of such excess from his employers, if that excess resulted from correct withholding by two or more employers.
c. The excess as a credit against income tax, if that excess resulted from correct withholding by two or more employers.
d. The excess as a credit against income tax, if that excess was withheld by one employer.

26. Chris Baker's adjusted gross income on her 1998 tax return was $160,000. The amount covered a 12-month period. For the 1999 tax year, Baker may avoid the penalty for the underpayment of estimated tax if the timely estimated tax payments equal the required annual amount of

I. 90% of the tax on the return for the current year, paid in four equal installments.
II. 100% of prior year's tax liability, paid in four equal installments.

a. I only.
b. II only.
c. Both I and II.
d. Neither I nor II.

## Released and Author Constructed Questions

*R98*
27. Krete, an unmarried taxpayer with income exclusively from wages, filed her initial income tax return for the 1999 calendar year. By December 31, 1999, Krete's employer had withheld $16,000 in federal income taxes and Krete had made no estimated tax payments. On April 15, 2000, Krete timely filed an extension request to file her individual tax return and paid $300 of additional taxes. Krete's 1999 income tax liability was $16,500 when she timely filed her return on April 30, 2000, and paid the remaining income tax liability balance. What amount would be subject to the penalty for the underpayment of estimated taxes?
a. $0
b. $200
c. $500
d. $16,500

*AC*
28. Jim and Mary are married and file a joint return for 1999. They have one child, Jennifer, who is 7 years old. Assuming their modified AGI for 1999 is $112,100, calculate their Child Tax Credit.
a. $250
b. $350
c. $400
d. $500

29. Bob and Carol are married and file a joint return for 1999. During 1999, they paid $5,500 in qualified adoption expenses for their new son Joshua. The amount of the adoption credit for the year is:

a. $0
b. $5,000
c. $5,500
d. $6,000

30. Bill is single and has modified AGI of $44,000 for 1999. Bill paid $4,000 in tuition for his daughter Kate to attend State University in her freshman year. Determine the amount of Bill's HOPE scholarship credit for the year.

a. $600
b. $900
c. $1,500
d. $4,000

31. Steve is single and has modified AGI of $44,000 for 1999. Steve paid $6,000 in tuition for his daughter Sue to attend State University in her senior year. Determine the amount of Steve's HOPE credit for the year.

a. $0
b. $600
c. $1,500
d. $6,000

32. Tom is 45 years old and has a dependent daughter Denise. During 1999, Tom took three premature distributions from his IRA account. The first distribution was $6,000 and was used as a down-payment on his first home. The second distribution was $10,000 and was used to pay off his credit card balances. The third distribution was $8,000 and was used to pay for tuition for his daughter Denise who is attending State University. Tom will be subject to a 10% penalty tax on the early withdrawals of:

a. $-0-
b. $1,000
c. $1,600
d. $2,400

# Chapter Five -- Answers
# Accounting Methods and Periods, and Computation of Tax Liability and Tax Credits

1. (a) Cash-basis taxpayers report income when it is constructively received. This applies to cash as well as the fair market value of property.

2. (d) $80,000. Alex constructively received the $80,000 salary in 1999. This amount was credited to him, there were no restrictions on his account, and he elected to take only $50,000 rather than the full $80,000.

3. (c) $52,000. Carl reports compensation income of his salary plus value of bargain element of the stock purchase. The difference of $20 per share between the market value ($50) and his purchase price ($30) is treated as compensation.

| Compensation: | |
|---|---|
| Salary | $ 50,000 |
| Stock purchase: | |
| 100 shares @ $20 | 2,000 |
| | $ 52,000 |

4. (d) $8,000. In general, all rent received, which includes any prepaid rent as well as the last month's rent is included as gross income. Security deposits, however, are generally not because of the right of return. In this problem, the security deposit is actually the last three months' rent and should be included as gross income.

5. (c) $1,200. Dividends on preferred and common stock are generally included as dividend income. Dividends on life insurance policies are simply a return of your premium and are nontaxable.

| Dividends - preferred stock | $ 400 |
|---|---|
| Dividends - common stock | 800 |
| Total | $ 1,200 |

6. (b) $460. To determine the gain, you must first determine the basis of the investment. The original issue discount of $1,200 ($10,000 less purchase price of $8,800) represents an adjustment to the interest rate. This discount must be recognized, pro-ratably over the life of the bond. For each year, Carl must recognize interest income of $120, which is $1,200 divided by 10 years. By recognizing interest, the taxpayer increases his basis in the investment.

| Selling price | | $9,500 |
|---|---|---|
| Original basis | $ 8,800 | |
| Increase in basis: | | |
| 2 years @ $120 | 240 | |
| Adjusted basis | | 9,040 |
| Long-term capital gain | | 460 |

7. (b) $500. In general, a cash basis taxpayer is allowed a deduction in the year paid. The charging on a credit card qualifies as being paid in 1999 even though the taxpayer does not pay the credit card company until 2000. The issuance and delivery of a promissory note does not give rise to a deduction until it is paid.

8. (a) Farb is entitled to a deduction of $8,000 in 1998 because he paid the contested liability and it remained contested until after the end of the year. Upon settling the issue, Farb must report as income, the recovery of the previously deducted excess $5,000.

9. (d) When a taxpayer maintains inventories, they must use the accrual method of accounting.

10. (a) $165,000. As a cash basis taxpayer, Dr. Chester reports the amounts actually received during the year.

| | |
|---|---:|
| Cash received - office visits | $ 35,000 |
| Cash received - receivables | 130,000 |
| Total income | $165,000 |

11. (a) Trade date. This is true for a cash or accrual based taxpayer.

12. (a) $60,000 ordinary income. Even though the covenant is for six years, it is all recognized when received. Payments for covenants not to compete are always classified as ordinary income.

13. (b) By definition

14. (c) $77,000. Adjustments to taxable income before personal exemptions for the purpose of the alternative minimum tax include an add-back for state and local taxes as well as miscellaneous deductions in excess of the 2% floor.

| | |
|---|---:|
| Taxable income, before personal exemptions | $ 70,000 |
| Adjustments: | |
| State and local taxes | 5,000 |
| Excess miscellaneous deductions | 2,000 |
| | $ 77,000 |

15. (b) The interest from private activity bonds are not included in taxable income, but are considered in the determination of the alternative minimum tax as a preference item. Charitable contributions are allowed as an itemized deduction and are not considered to be a preference item for individuals.

16. (d) The credit for prior year alternative minimum tax credit may be carried forward indefinitely.

17. (a) The general business credit incorporates the limitations for the jobs credit, research credit, disabled access credit, low income housing credit and the investment credit.

18. (d) In order to qualify for the child care credit, both spouses must be gainfully employed. The credit calculation looks to the lesser of the qualifying expenditures or earned income of the spouse with the least amount of earnings. The adjusted gross income threshold of $10,000 is used to determine the percentage of the credit. Once a taxpayer passes the $10,000 threshold, the credit percentage begins decreasing from the maximum of 30% to 20%, but does not disappear.

19. (b) $960. Assuming their adjusted gross income exceeds $28,000, the Martin's child care credit percentage is 20%. Qualifying expenditures cannot exceed $2,400 per child. With two children, a total of $4,800 times the rate of 20% will yield a credit of $960.

20. (c) $600. Nora's adjusted gross income exceeds $28,000. Therefore, her child care credit percentage is 20%. Qualifying expenditures cannot exceed $2,400 per child. Nora has two children which means her qualifying expenditures are the lesser of $4,800 or $3,000 (the amount she actually paid). Her credit $3,000 times 20% or $600.

21. (c) The earned income credit is the only refundable credit.

22. (a) The earned income credit is the only refundable credit, which means Kent could receive a refund even if he had no taxes withheld.

23. (c) $570. In computing the credit, the elderly credit considers all types of income. Starting with an initial base amount of $5,000 for a single taxpayer, this Section 37 amount needs to be reduced by social security benefits. There are no other adjustments because adjusted income is not in excess of $7,500.

| | |
|---|---|
| Section 37 amount | $ 5,000 |
| Less: Social Security | -1,200 |
| Credit base | $ 3,800 |
| Elderly credit rate | 15% |
| Elderly credit | $ 570 |

Note: This credit is only allowed to offset taxes. His taxes are not given in the problem.

24. (b) $60. The elderly credit is limited to the amount of the tax liability, which is $60. However, you must first determine if a credit is even allowable, otherwise zero may be your answer. In computing the credit, the elderly credit considers all types of income. Starting with an initial base amount of $7,500 for a married taxpayer, this Section 37 amount needs to be reduced by social security benefits. There are no other adjustments because their adjusted income is not in excess of $10,000.

| | |
|---|---|
| Section 37 amount | $ 7,500 |
| Less: Social Security | -1,250 |
| Credit base | $ 6,250 |
| Elderly credit rate | 15% |
| Elderly credit | $ 937 |

The Crane's actual tax liability is $60. Therefore, the credit is limited to $60.

25. (c) The excess social security tax withheld can be claimed as a credit against income tax only if it is the result of correct overwithholding due to having two or more employers in a taxable year.

26. (a) Only the estimated payments in Proposal I will allow Baker to avoid the penalty. The safe harbor of paying 100% of the prior year's tax is no longer available for taxpayers with adjusted gross income of more than $150,000. The new safe harbor for those individuals is 110% of the prior year's tax.

27. (a) In order to avoid any penalty on the underpayment of tax, a taxpayer must pay at least 90% of the current year's tax. Whereas the income tax liability was $16,500, the $16,000 of withholdings plus the $300 of additional taxes paid with the extension, clearly exceed the 90% threshold.

28. (b) $250. A Child Tax Credit of $500 is allowed in 1999 for those taxpayers having qualifying children under the age of 17. Therefore, Jim and Mary qualify with the 7 year old dependent. However, the credit is phased out at a rate of $50 for every $1,000, or fraction thereof, of modified AGI in excess of $110,000 for married taxpayers.

| | |
|---|---|
| Adjusted gross income | $ 112,100 |
| Threshold level | 110,000 |
| Excess over threshold | $ 2,100 |
| | |
| Rounded up to three $1,000 | 3,000 |
| | |
| Phase-out of $50 per $1,000 | 150 |

Therefore, the credit is reduced from $500 to $350.

29. (b) $5,000. The adoption credit is limited to the lessor of the amount paid for qualified adoption expenses or $5,000 per child.

30. (b) $ 900.  The HOPE scholarship credit is allowed based upon 100% of the first $1,000 paid and 50% of the next $1,000 paid in qualified higher education costs.  However, there is a phase-out for single individuals whose modified AGI is in excess of $40,000.  The phase-out is determined as:

$$\frac{\text{Modified AGI-\$40,000}}{\$10,000} \quad X \ \$1,500 = \text{Phase-out}$$

$$\frac{\$44,000 - \$40,000}{\$10,000} \quad X \ \$1,500 = \$600 \text{ phase-out}$$

Therefore, the  HOPE scholarship credit is $900  ($1,500 less the $600 phase-out amount).

31. (a) $-0-.  The HOPE scholarship credit is only available for the first two years of post-secondary education.

32. (b)  $1,000.  The 10% premature distribution tax will only be assessed on the $10,000 withdrawal used to pay off credit card balances.  Withdrawals for qualified education expenses and qualified first-time home buyers are no longer subject to the 10% premature distribution tax.

# Chapter Six
# Capital Transactions

# Chapter Six
# Capital Transactions

## GENERAL RULE

When a taxpayer sells or exchanges property, a **realized gain or loss** is determined for the difference between the amount realized and the property's adjusted basis. A realized gain or loss is usually recognized for tax purposes, unless one of the many provisions addressed within this chapter excludes it.

The **amount realized** from the sale or exchange of property usually represents its selling price. On the sale, the taxpayer often receives cash, or other property having a fair market value. Sometimes, the taxpayer may be relieved of an obligation, such as a mortgage. These are all considered part of the amount realized.

The property's **adjusted basis** is frequently its cost. If the property is real estate, it might include increases for improvements as well as decreases for depreciation allowed over the years. If the property was received as a gift or inheritance, there are special basis rules which are covered later.

---

**Example 1:** K sells her automobile to W for $10,000. K receives $4,000 in cash and a stock investment worth $6,000 from W. K had purchased the automobile last year for $8,000 and does not use it for business. K's realized gain is determined as follows:

|  |  |
|---|---|
| Amount realized: |  |
| Cash | $ 4,000 |
| FMV of securities | 6,000 |
| Total amount realized | 10,000 |
|  |  |
| Less: adjusted basis | -8,000 |
| Realized gain | $ 2,000 |

K's realized gain would also be her recognized gain, unless there is a specific tax provision that causes the gain not to be recognized.

---

## LONG-TERM vs. SHORT-TERM

Previous to the Tax Relief Act of 1997, capital transactions were classified as either long-term or short-term. The sale of property held for **more than one year** was classified as long-term. For property held for **not more than one year,** it was short-term. The holding period classification was important because long-term capital gains were taxed at a maximum of 28%, while short-term capital gains were treated as ordinary income.

*Effective for assets sold after May 6, 1997,* the capital gain provisions have changed dramatically.

For long-term capital gains on assets held more than one year, the maximum rate is now 20%. If the taxpayer was in the 15% tax bracket, the maximum rate is now 10%.

For gains on the sale of real estate, the rates differ slightly. For any long-term capital gain that is attributable to the recapture of depreciation (Section 1250), the maximum rate is 25%.

The new law does not change the 28% tax rate on the sale of collectibles, nor does it impact C Corporations.

## NETTING PROCESS

In summarizing a taxpayer's capital activity for the year, it is important to group the gains and losses correctly (mid-term gains treatment has been left out of this analysis). This is due to the various tax treatments and limitations affecting capital transactions. The hierarchy for netting capital transactions is:

- Net all the short-term transactions.
- Net all the long-term transactions.
- Net the net transactions, if possible.

If the net short-term capital gains exceed the net long-term capital losses, the result is taxed as ordinary income. If the net long-term capital gains exceed the net short-term capital losses, the result is taxed at a maximum of 28%. If the capital losses (regardless of holding period) exceed the capital gains, then up to $3,000 may be deducted from ordinary income in that year. (For taxpayers who are married filing separately, the amount allowed is $1,500.) Any loss in excess of $3,000 is carried forward indefinitely, and will retain its original (short-term or long-term) character.

---

**Example 2:** For 1999, T has a long-term capital gain of $4,000; long-term capital loss of $2,000; short-term capital gain of $2,000; and a short-term capital loss of $8,000. T also has adjusted gross income of $30,000 before this transaction.

| **Step 1**: Net the short transactions: | Capital gain | 2,000 |
| | Capital loss | -8,000 |
| | Net short-term loss | -6,000 |

| **Step 2**: Net the long-term transactions: | Capital gain | 4,000 |
| | Capital loss | -2,000 |
| | Net long-term gain | 2,000 |

| **Step 3**: Net the net transactions | Net short-term losses | -6,000 |
| | Net long-term gain | 2,000 |
| | Net short-term loss | -4,000 |

| **Step 4**: Check for any limitations | Maximum deductible | 3,000 |

| **Step 5**: Determine any carryovers | Total short-term capital loss | 4,000 |
| | Utilized in current year | -3,000 |
| | Carryover (short-term) | 1,000 |

Therefore, T's adjusted gross income will be $30,000 less the $3,000, or $27,000.

---

## RELATED PARTY TRANSACTIONS

When a taxpayer enters into a sale or exchange of property with a related party, the general rule is that **no loss is recognized**. The disallowed loss, however, is suspended until the related party disposes of the property. If the property is subsequently sold for a gain, the disallowed loss may be used to offset the gain. If, instead, the property is subsequently sold for a loss, the disallowed loss is never recognized.

The brief definition of a related party from Code Section 267 includes:

- Members of your family (brothers, sisters, spouse, ancestors and lineal descendants)
- Your corporation if you own more than 50% of the stock
- Your partnership if you have more than a 50% interest
- Your trust if you are a beneficiary or fiduciary

**Example 3:** F sells stock to his daughter D for $6,000. F had purchased the stock three years ago at a cost of $10,000. D later sells the stock for (A) $5,000, (B) $11,000 and (C) $8,000. (This example contrasts three different sales)

|  | **A** | **B** | **C** |
|---|---|---|---|
| F's initial sale | $ 6,000 | $ 6,000 | $ 6,000 |
| F's adjusted basis | -10,000 | -10,000 | -10,000 |
| F's realized & **disallowed loss** | $ -4,000 | $ -4,000 | $ -4,000 |
|  |  |  |  |
| D's sale | $ 5,000 | $ 11,000 | $ 8,000 |
| D's basis | 6,000 | 6,000 | 6,000 |
| D's realized gain or loss | $ -1,000 | $ 5,000 | $ 2,000 |
| F's disallowed loss | 0 | 4,000 | 2,000 |
| D's recognized gain or loss | $-1,000 | $ 1,000 | $ 0 |

In the first scenario, the selling price is less than D's basis, and her realized loss of $1,000 is recognized. Her father's disallowed loss is never recognized. In the second situation, the selling price is greater than D's basis, and all of her father's $4,000 disallowed loss can be used to partially offset the $5,000 gain. In the third situation, the selling price is again above D's basis, but only by $2,000. Therefore only $2,000 of her father's disallowed loss can be used to offset the gain, and the balance of his loss is never recognized.

## WASH SALES

If a taxpayer sells, and repurchases substantially identical stock within thirty days of the sale, any loss on the transaction is disallowed. This is called a **wash sale.** The situation frequently occurs when a taxpayer sells securities that have gone down in value just prior to the end of the year in order to recognize a loss for tax purposes. The taxpayer usually believes that the decrease in value is only temporary, and goes out and repurchases the same securities right after the end of the year. In essence, nothing has really happened economically. The taxpayer owns the same securities he did just a few days ago.

The wash sale rules apply only to losses and not to gains. The thirty day period runs before and after the sale. Any real loss on the sale and repurchase of the stock is added to the basis of the new stocks acquired.

## TRADE DATE/SETTLEMENT DATE

When a stock transaction takes place, there are usually two critical dates. The trade date is the day the transaction actually takes place and is the one used for tax purposes. The settlement date usually occurs a few days after the trade date, and is when the paperwork is completed, the money is transferred, etc. It is not the date to use for tax purposes.

## SECTION 1244

Most stock transactions result in a recognized capital gain or loss. A long-term capital gain provides a favorable rate, while net capital losses are limited to $3,000 per year. There is one category of stock that allows an even better capital gain treatment and gives the taxpayer a larger loss deduction. This is called Section 1244 stock. Section 1244 stock can only be issued by a small business corporation and must be the original issue. A small business corporation is one that does not have stock in excess of $1 million in the initial offering. What makes the stock attractive is that ordinary losses of up to $100,000 per year (if married filing jointly, or $50,000 if single) can be deducted as an ordinary loss. Any losses beyond that amount are treated as capital losses.

**Example 4**: F Corporation issued qualified stock under Section 1244 to T, its sole shareholder for $100,000. Three years later in 1999, T sold the stock to M for $35,000. Assume T is single and in 1998 his only other income is a salary of $75,000.

| | |
|---|---|
| Selling price | $ 35,000 |
| Adjusted basis | 100,000 |
| Recognized loss | 65,000 |
| | |
| **Character of the loss** | |
| Section 1244 loss | $ 50,000 |
| Capital loss | 15,000 |
| | $ 65,000 |

T recognizes a $65,000 loss on the transaction, of which $50,000 is ordinary and fully deducted against his salary. There is also a $15,000 capital loss, of which only $3,000 is currently deductible. The balance of $12,000 is carried forward indefinitely.

T's adjusted gross income is as follows:

| | |
|---|---|
| Salary | $ 75,000 |
| Section 1244 loss | -50,000 |
| Capital loss | -3,000 |
| Adjusted gross income | $ 22,000 |

In addition to the benefit of an ordinary loss deduction, the Revenue Reconciliation Act of 1993 now allows a non-corporate taxpayer a **50% gain exclusion** on small business stock purchased after 1992. If the stock is held for at least 5 years, only 50% of the gain is taxed at the capital gain rate.

## WORTHLESS SECURITIES

Instead of an actual sale or exchange, sometimes a security held for investment simply becomes worthless and has no value. When that occurs, the property is deemed to have been sold on the last day of the taxable year. The effect of this rule would be to possibly convert a short-term capital loss into a long-term capital loss.

**Example 5:** R purchased stock in G Corporation on September 20, 1999. On March 20, 2000, R was notified that G Corporation was insolvent and the stock was worthless. Even though R held the stock only six months before it became worthless, it is deemed sold as of December 31, 2000, and therefore the holding period for the loss is long-term (more than a year).

## BAD DEBTS

When a taxpayer extends credit to another taxpayer in the form of a loan, and then the loan becomes uncollectible, a deduction is allowed. When an accrual based taxpayer sells goods and services in exchange for a receivable, and the receivable becomes uncollectible, a deduction is allowed. The character of the deduction is based upon whether the bad debt is a business or non-business bad debt.

A **business bad debt** results from the taxpayer being in the business of lending money or the rendering goods and services in exchange for the receivable. These bad debts are treated as an **ordinary loss** in the year incurred.

A **non-business bad debt** is always treated as a **short-term capital loss**. Whereas a deduction may be allowed for the partial worthlessness of a business bad debt, no such deduction is allowed on the partial worthlessness of a non-business bad debt.

# BASIS COMPUTATIONS

## PROPERTY RECEIVED BY GIFT

In general, when a taxpayer receives property as a gift, the basis of the property is transferred from the donor to the donee. In addition, the holding period of the property "tacks over" to the donee. This general rule applies when the fair market value of the gift exceeds the adjusted basis of the property transferred.

When the fair market value of the property is less than the adjusted basis of the property, the donee's basis will be the donor's basis only for the purpose of determining a gain. For the purposes of determining a loss, the donee's basis will be the fair market value of the property. At any selling price between the fair market value and the adjusted basis the result is no gain or loss.

> **Example 6:** T gives S land with a fair market value of $40,000 and an adjusted basis of $32,000. T had purchased the land on March 15, 1990. S's basis in the land is $32,000 and his holding period begins on March 15, 1990.

> **Example 7:** V gives W land with a fair market value of $40,000 and an adjusted basis of $65,000. Determine the gain or loss if W sells the land for (A) $30,000; (B) $45,000; and (C) $75,000.
>
> |  | A | B | C |
> |---|---|---|---|
> | Selling price | $ 30,000 | $ 45,000 | $ 75,000 |
> | W's adjusted basis | 40,000 | 45,000 | 65,000 |
> | Realized gain (loss) | $ (10,000) | $ 0 | $ 10,000 |

## ADJUSTMENT TO BASIS FOR GIFT TAXES PAID

When a taxpayer makes a gift of property, that transfer may be subject to a gift tax. Chapter 10 deals with the taxation of gifts. If the donor pays a gift tax on a transfer, then the basis of the property received by the donee is increased by a prorata share of the gift tax paid.

> **Example 8:** Referring to Example 6, assume that T paid $4,000 in gift taxes on the transfer to S. The increase in the fair market value of the property was $8,000 ($40,000 - $32,000). The gift tax paid of $4,000 times the appreciation over the fair market value represents the gift tax adjustment.
>
> $$\$4,000 \ \times \ \frac{\$8,000}{\$40,000} \ = \ \$800$$
>
> | | |
> |---|---|
> | Donor's adjusted basis | $32,000 |
> | Add: Gift tax adjustment | 800 |
> | Donee's adjusted basis | $32,800 |

## PROPERTY RECEIVED BY INHERITANCE

In general, when a taxpayer receives property as an inheritance (from a decedent), the basis of the property is its fair market value as of the date of death. The holding period is automatically long-term for the purpose of determining gain or loss on the subsequent sale by the beneficiary. If the executor elects the alternate valuation date (six months after the date of death), the basis of the property will be the value on that date. However, if the alternate valuation date is elected and property is distributed prior to the six month date, then the property is valued as of the date of distribution. See Chapter 10 for more details.

> **Example 9:** T dies and bequeaths land with a fair market value of $140,000 and an adjusted basis of $40,000 to his son S. T had purchased the land on March 15, 1980. S's basis in the land will be $140,000 and his holding period is long-term. If S sells the land in three months for $150,000, the gain will be long-term even though S only held the land for three months.
>
> | | |
> |---|---|
> | Selling price | $ 150,000 |
> | S's basis | 140,000 |
> | Realized gain | $ 10,000 |

## STOCK DIVIDENDS

In general, the receipt of a stock dividend by a shareholder is **non-taxable**. If a **common stock dividend** is received on the common stock, then the basis of the stock received is determined by merely allocating the existing basis of the common stock to the new total number of common shares currently held. If a **preferred stock dividend** is received on the common stock, then the basis of the preferred stock is determined by allocating the existing basis of the common stock to the common stock and the new preferred stock based upon the relative fair market of all the stock.

Some stock dividends may be taxable. For example, if the taxpayer has the option of receiving either a stock dividend or cash dividend, that dividend will be taxable to the shareholder to the extent of the fair market value of the stock received. The income recognized will then be the basis of the stock dividend.

# NON-TAXABLE TRANSACTIONS

In general, no gain or loss is recognized on the exchange of property of a like kind. It is not unusual for a taxpayer to trade-in one vehicle for another vehicle, or exchange one machine for another. Congress believes that when there is no real change in the type of the asset being used, that no gain or loss should be recognized. However, the receipt of cash or other property as part of a like-kind exchange, could cause the recognition of gain. Exchanges which qualify for this treatment include:

- Property held for productive use or investment - referred to as like-kind exchanges
- Common stock for common stock of the same corporation, or preferred for preferred
- Common stock for assets being transferred assuming 80% control after the transfer - See Chapter 8
- Partnership interest for assets being transferred - See Chapter 7

## LIKE-KIND EXCHANGES

In order to qualify for like-kind treatment, the property being exchanged must be of a like kind. In general, real property may be exchanged for real property. Personal property may be exchanged for personal property. However, personalty cannot be exchanged for realty on a tax-free basis. Except for the tax-free exchange of common for common and preferred for preferred, the exchange of other securities do not qualify as like-kind exchanges.

When property other than of a like-kind is involved in a transfer, the receipt of this other property is considered boot and may cause the recognition of gain. The amount of the recognized gain, however, cannot exceed the amount of realized gain.

The basis of property received in a like-kind exchange is the basis of the property being transferred by the taxpayer. If any gain is recognized, the basis is increased by that amount. If the taxpayer receives boot, basis must be allocated first to the boot and then to the transferred property.

**Example 10:** F exchanges equipment used in his business that has a fair market value of $10,000 and an adjusted basis of $6,000 with T. T transfers like-kind property to F worth $10,000 and an adjusted basis of $8,000.

| | |
|---|---|
| Fair market value of property received by F | $ 10,000 |
| Adjusted basis of property transferred to T | 6,000 |
| Realized gain | $ 4,000 |
| Recognized gain | $ 0 |

No gain or loss is recognized on this like-kind exchange. F's basis in the new property is his original $6,000.

---

**Example 11:** Assume the same facts as in Example 10 except that the fair value of T's property was only $9,000. Since F is giving up an asset worth $10,000 and only receiving an asset worth $9,000, T agrees to give F $1,000 in cash. The cash is considered other property, or boot.

| | |
|---|---|
| Fair market value of property received by F | $ 9,000 |
| Cash, or boot received | 1,000 |
| Total amount realized | 10,000 |
| Adjusted basis of property transferred to T | 6,000 |
| Realized gain | $ 4,000 |
| Recognized gain | $ 1,000 |

The $1,000 in boot received causes $1,000 of the $4,000 realized gain to be recognized. The basis of the new property is $6,000, and is determined as follows:

| | |
|---|---|
| Original basis in the property | $ 6,000 |
| Plus: gain recognized | 1,000 |
| Total basis | 7,000 |
| Less: basis in cash received | -1,000 |
| Basis of equipment | $ 6,000 |

## SALE OF PRINCIPAL RESIDENCE

When a taxpayer sells his personal residence after May 6, 1997, any realized gain is excluded (up to certain limits), based upon the facts and circumstances. Any loss on the sale will never be recognized. The sale is reported on Form 2119.

As dramatically changed in the 1997 Taxpayer Relief Act, any taxpayer, regardless of age, who has owned and used their home as a principal residence for at least 2 of the last 5 years before the sale, can exclude from income up to $250,000 of the gain on the sale ($500,000 if married and filing a joint return). This exclusion is no longer available only once in the taxpayer's lifetime, but can be used repeatedly, although no more frequently than every two years.

If a taxpayer maintains his residence for less than two years, the exclusion is pro-rated if the sale is due to a change in place of employment, health or unforeseen circumstances.

> **Example 12:** J is single and has always lived in his house. J sells his residence on May 10, 1999 for $225,000 and incurs selling expenses and commission of $15,000. J originally purchased the house in 1954 for $30,000 and has paid $20,000 for capital improvements.
>
> | | | |
> |---|---:|---:|
> | Selling price | | $ 225,000 |
> | Less: | | |
> |   Original cost | $ 30,000 | |
> |   Improvements | 20,000 | |
> |   Selling expenses | 15,000 | |
> | | | 65,000 |
> | Realized gain | | 160,000 |
> | New Section 121 exclusion | | -160,000 |
> | Recognized gain | | $-0- |

## INVOLUNTARY CONVERSIONS

If a taxpayer's property is involuntarily converted (fire, flood, etc.), no gain is recognized to the extent that the insurance proceeds are reinvested in similar property within a replacement period. The replacement period is two years, after the end of the taxable year in which the event occurs. The period for real property is three years.

## RECAPTURE RULES

When a taxpayer sells property used in a trade or business, or property used for the production of income, the gain is the difference between the selling price and the adjusted basis. The adjusted basis is usually made up of the original cost less any depreciation. The depreciation claimed by the taxpayer gives rise to an ordinary deduction, not a capital deduction (loss). Therefore, logic dictates (as does Section 1245) that if a gain is recognized on the sale of the property, and some of the gain is attributable to the depreciation claimed, then that portion of the gain should be treated as ordinary income.

**Personal property** - any gain attributable to the depreciation taken is classified as ordinary income.
**Real property** - any gain attributable to excess of accelerated depreciation over straight-line depreciation is treated as ordinary income. However, if the property is held for one year or less, all the depreciation will be recaptured as ordinary income, not just the excess.

## CAPITAL ASSETS AND SECTION 1231 ASSETS

Capital assets include investment property and property held for personal use. Typical **personal** assets include investments, furniture, jewelry, and the personal residence. However, capital assets do not include:

- Inventory (stock in trade)
- Depreciable property or real estate used in the trade or business
- Accounts receivable
- Copyrights
- Covenant not to compete

If items, such as depreciable property and real estate used in a trade or business, are excluded from the definition of capital assets, then why is it that the sale of this property yields **capital** gains? The answer is Section 1231.

**Section 1231** is the Code Section that recharacterizes the gain from the sale of the depreciable property as capital even though it has been exempted from the capital asset classification. Apart from any depreciation recapture, the gain from the sale of depreciable property will result in long-term capital gain treatment (maximum of 28% tax rate) provided that the asset is **held for more than one year**. However, if the property is sold at a loss, the loss is ordinary, not capital, and is fully deductible.

**Example 13**: W operates a machine shop and sold a piece of machinery used in his trade or business for $20,000. W purchased the asset three years ago at a cost of $18,000 and claimed depreciation of $12,000 during the past three years. W will recognize a gain of $14,000 on the sale. The character of the gain is determined under Section 1245 for the depreciation recapture and Section 1231 for the capital gain treatment.

|  |  |  |
|---|---|---|
| Selling price |  | $ 20,000 |
| Adjusted basis: |  |  |
|   Original cost | $18,000 |  |
|   Acc. depreciation | -12,000 |  |
|     Adjusted basis |  | -6,000 |
| Recognized gain |  | $ 14,000 |
|  |  |  |
| **Character of the gain:** |  |  |
| **Ordinary income** recaptured |  |  |
|   under Section 1245 |  | $ 12,000 |
| **Capital gain** under |  |  |
|   Section 1231 |  | 2,000 |
| Total gain |  | $ 14,000 |

# Chapter Six -- Questions
# Capital Transactions

## CAPITAL GAINS AND LOSSES

**Items 1 and 2** are based on the following:
Conner purchased 300 shares of Zinco stock for $30,000 in 1980. On March 23, 1999, Conner sold all the stock to his daughter Alice for $20,000, its then fair market value. Conner realized no other gain or loss during 1999. On April 26, 1999, Alice sold the 300 shares of Zinco for $25,000.

1. What amount of the loss from the sale of Zinco stock can Conner deduct in 1999?
a. $0
b. $ 3,000
c. $ 5,000
d. $10,000

2. What was Alice's recognized gain or loss on her sale?
a. $0
b. $5,000 long-term gain.
c. $5,000 short-term loss.
d. $5,000 long-term loss.

---

3. Lee qualified as head of a household for 1999 tax purposes. Lee's 1999 taxable income was $100,000, exclusive of capital gains and losses. Lee had a net long-term loss of $8,000 in 1999. What amount of this capital loss can Lee offset against 1999 ordinary income?
a. $0
b. $3,000
c. $4,000
d. $8,000

4. For the 1999 year, Michael King reported salary and taxable interest income of $40,000. His capital asset transactions during the year were as follows:

| | |
|---|---|
| Long-term capital gains | $2,000 |
| Long-term capital losses | (8,000) |
| Short-term capital gains | 1,000 |

King should report adjusted gross income of
a. $35,000.
b. $37,000.
c. $39,000.
d. $40,000.

5. Paul Beyer, who is unmarried, has taxable income of $30,000 exclusive of capital gains and losses and his personal exemption. In 1999, Paul incurred a $1,000 net short-term capital loss and a $5,000 net long-term capital loss. His capital loss carryover to 2000 is
a. $5,000 long-term loss.
b. $3,000 long-term loss.
c. $6,000 short-term loss.
d. $3,000 short-term loss.

6. Among which of the following related parties are losses from sales and exchanges **not** recognized for tax purposes?
a. Father-in-law and son-in-law.
b. Brother-in-law and sister-in-law.
c. Grandfather and granddaughter.
d. Ancestors, lineal descendants, and all in-laws.

7. In 1992, Fay sold 100 shares of Gym Co. stock to her son, Martin, for $11,000. Fay had paid $15,000 for the stock in 1989. Subsequently in 1999, Martin sold the stock to an unrelated third party for $16,000. What amount of gain from the sale of the stock to the third party should Martin report on his 1999 income tax return.
a. $0
b. $1,000
c. $4,000
d. $5,000

8. Smith, an individual calendar-year taxpayer, purchased 100 shares of Core Co. common stock for $15,000 on December 15, 1998, and an additional 100 shares for $13,000 on December 30, 1998. On January 3, 1999, Smith sold the shares purchased on December 15, 1998, for $13,000. What amount of loss from the sale of Core's stock is deductible on Smith's 1998 and 1999 income tax returns:

| | _1998_ | _1999_ |
|---|---|---|
| a. | $0 | $0 |
| b. | $0 | $2,000 |
| c. | $1,000 | $1,000 |
| d. | $2,000 | $0 |

9. Fred Berk bought a plot of land with a cash payment of $40,000 and a purchase money mortgage of $50,000. In addition, Berk paid $200 for a title insurance policy. Berk's basis in this land is
a. $40,000
b. $40,200
c. $90,000
d. $90,200

10. In 1999, Joan Reed exchanged commercial real estate that she owned for other commercial real estate plus cash of $50,000. The following additional information pertains to this transaction:

**Property given up by Reed**
Fair market value          $500,000
Adjusted basis              300,000

**Property received by Reed**
Fair market value           450,000

What amount of gain should be recognized in Reed's 1999 income tax return?
a. $200,000
b. $100,000
c. $50,000
d. $0

11. Al Eng owns 55% of the outstanding stock of Rego Corp. During 1999, Rego sold a trailer to Eng for $10,000. The trailer had an adjusted tax basis of $12,000, and had been owned by Rego for three years. In its 1999 income tax return, what is the allowable loss that Rego can claim on the sale of this trailer?
a. $0.
b. $2,000 ordinary loss.
c. $2,000 Section 1231 loss.
d. $2,000 Section 1245 loss.

12. For a cash basis taxpayer, gain or loss on a year-end sale of listed stock arises on the
a. Trade date.
b. Settlement date.
c. Date of receipt of cash proceeds.
d. Date of delivery of stock certificate.

13. For assets acquired in 1999, the holding period for determining long-term capital gains and losses is more than

a. 18 months.
b. 12 months.
c. 9 months.
d. 6 months.

14. Joe Hall owns a limousine for use in his personal service business of transporting passengers to airports. The limousine's adjusted basis is $40,000. In addition, Hall owns his personal residence and furnishings, that together cost him $280,000. Hall's capital assets amount to
a. $320,000
b. $280,000
c. $40,000
d. $0

15. In March 1999, Ruth Lee sold a painting for $25,000 that she had bought for her personal use in 1991 at a cost of $10,000. In her 1999 return, Lee should treat the sale of the painting as a transaction resulting in
a. Ordinary income.
b. Long-term capital gain.
c. Section 1231 gain.
d. No taxable gain.

16. A 1999 capital loss incurred by a married couple filing a joint return
a. Will be allowed only to the extent of capital gains.
b. Will be allowed to the extent of capital gains, plus up to $3,000 of ordinary income.
c. May be carried forward up to a maximum of five years.
d. Is **not** an allowable loss.

17. For a married couple filing a joint return, the excess of net long-term capital loss over net short-term capital gain is
a. Reduced by 50% before being deducted from ordinary income.
b. Limited to a maximum deduction of $3,000 from ordinary income.
c. Allowed as a carryover against future capital gains up to a maximum period of five years.
d. Not deductible from ordinary income.

18. Which of the following is a capital asset?
a. Delivery truck.
b. Goodwill.
c. Land used as a parking lot for customers.
d. Treasury stock, at cost.

19. Olive Bell bought a house for use partially as a residence and partially for operation of a retail gift shop. In addition, Olive bought the following furniture:

| | |
|---|---|
| Kitchen sets and living room pieces for the residential portion | $ 8,000 |
| Showcases and tables for the business portion | 12,000 |

How much of this furniture comprises capital assets?
a. $0
b. $8,000
c. $12,000
d. $20,000

# GIFTS AND INHERITANCES

**Items 20 through 22** are based on the following data:
In 1992, John Cote bought 100 shares of a listed stock for $2,400. In 1999, when the fair market value was $2,200, John gave the stock to his brother, David. No gift tax was due.

20. If David sells this stock for $2,600, his basis is
a. $0.
b. $2,200.
c. $2,400.
d. $2,600.

21. If David sells this stock for $2,000, his basis is
a. $0.
b. $2,000.
c. $2,200.
d. $2,400.

22. If David sells this stock for $2,300, his reportable gain or loss is
a. $0.
b. $100 loss.
c. $100 gain.
d. $2,300 gain.

––––––––––

23. On July 1, 1999, Thomas Rich acquired certain stocks with a fair market value of $22,000 by gift from his father. The stocks had been acquired by the father on April 1, 1978, at a cost of $40,000. Thomas sold all the stocks for $28,000 on December 12, 1999. What amount should Thomas report as capital gain or loss on his tax return as a result of the above?
a. $0.
b. $2,400 gain.
c. $6,000 gain.
d. $12,000 loss.

––––––––––

**Items 24 through 26** are based on the following data:
In 1980, Iris King bought a diamond necklace for her own use, at a cost of $10,000. In 1999, when the fair market value was $12,000, Iris gave this necklace to her daughter, Ruth. No gift tax was due.

24. Ruth's holding period for this gift
a. Starts in 1999.
b. Starts in 1980.
c. Depends on whether the necklace is sold by Ruth at a gain or at a loss.
d. Is irrelevant because Ruth received the necklace for no consideration of money or money's worth.

25. This diamond necklace is a
a. Capital asset.
b. Section 1231 asset.
c. Section 1245 asset.
d. Section 1250 asset.

26. If Ruth sells this diamond necklace in 1999 for $13,000, Ruth's recognized gain would be
a. $3,000
b. $2,000
c. $1,000
d. $0

––––––––––

27. On January 10, 1970, Martin Mayne bought 3,000 shares of Hance Corporation stock for $300,000. The fair market values of this stock on the following dates were as follows:

| | |
|---|---|
| December 31, 1998 | $210,000 |
| March 31, 1999 | 240,000 |
| June 30, 1999 | 270,000 |

Martin died on December 31, 1998, bequeathing this stock to his son, Philip. The stock was distributed to Philip on March 31, 1999. The alternate valuation date was elected for Martin's estate. Philip's basis for this stock is
a. $210,000.
b. $240,000.
c. $270,000.
d. $300,000.

28. On June 1, 1999, Ben Rork sold 500 shares of Kul Corp. stock. Rork had received this stock on May 1, 1998, as a bequest from the estate of his uncle, who died on March 1, 1999. Rork's basis was determined by reference to the stock's fair market value on March 1, 1999. Rork's holding period for this stock was

a. Short-term.
b. Long-term.
c. Short-term if sold at a gain; long-term if sold at a loss.
d. Long-term if sold at a gain; short-term if sold at a loss.

29. On February 1, 1999, Hall learned that he was bequeathed 500 shares of common stock under his father's will. Hall's father had paid $2,500 for the stock in 1990. Fair market value of the stock on February 1, 1999, the date of his father's death, was $4,000 and had increased to $5,500 six months later. The executor of the estate elected the alternate valuation date for estate tax purposes. Hall sold the stock for $4,500 on June 1, 1999, the date that the executor distributed the stock to him. How much income should Hall include in his 1999 individual income tax return for the inheritance of the 500 shares of stock which he received from his father's estate?

a. $5,500
b. $4,000
c. $2,500
d. $0

_____

**Items 30 through 32** are based on the following data:

Laura's father, Albert, gave Laura a gift of 500 shares of Liba Corporation common stock in 1999. Albert's basis for the Liba stock was $4,000. At the date of this gift, the fair market value of the Liba stock was $3,000.

30. If Laura sells the 500 shares of Liba stock in 1999 for $5,000, her basis is

a. $5,000
b. $4,000
c. $3,000
d. $0

31. If Laura sells the 500 shares of Liba stock in 1999 for $2,000, her basis is

a. $4,000
b. $3,000
c. $2,000
d. $0

32. If Laura sells the 500 shares of Liba stock in 1999 for $3,500, what is the reportable gain or loss in 1999?

a. $3,500 gain.
b. $500 gain.
c. $500 loss.
d. $0.

_____

33. Fred Zorn died on January 5, 1999, bequeathing his entire $2,000,000 estate to his sister, Ida. The alternate valuation date was validly elected by the executor of Fred's estate. Fred's estate included 2,000 shares of listed stock for which Fred's basis was $380,000. This stock was distributed to Ida nine months after Fred's death. Fair market values of this stock were:

| | |
|---|---|
| At the date of Fred's death | $400,000 |
| Six months after Fred's death | 450,000 |
| Nine months after Fred's death | 480,000 |

Ida's basis for this stock is

a. $380,000
b. $400,000
c. $450,000
d. $480,000

## STOCK DIVIDENDS

34. On July 1, 1988, William Greene paid $45,000 for 450 shares of Acme Corporation common stock. Greene received a nontaxable stock dividend of 50 new common shares in December 1989. On January 15, 1999, Greene sold the 50 new shares of common stock for $5,500. In respect of this sale Greene should report on his 1999 tax return.

a. No gain or loss since the stock dividend was nontaxable.
b. $500 of long-term capital gain.
c. $1,000 of long-term capital gain.
d. $5,500 of long-term capital gain.

35. On January 5, 1989, Norman Harris purchased for $6,000, 100 shares of Campbell Corporation common stock. On July 8 of this year he received a nontaxable stock dividend of 10 shares of Campbell Corporation $100 par value preferred stock. On that date, the market values per share of the common and preferred stock were $75 and $150, respectively. Harris' tax basis for the common stock after the receipt of the stock dividend is

a. $2,000.
b. $4,500.
c. $5,000.
d. $6,000.

**Items 36 and 37** are based on the following data:
In January 1999, Joan Hill bought one share of Orban Corp. stock for $300. On March 1, 1999, Orban distributed one share of preferred stock for each share of common stock held. This distribution was nontaxable. On March 1, 1999, Joan's one share of common stock had a fair market value of $450, while the preferred stock had a fair market value of $150.

36. After the distribution of the preferred stock, Joan's bases for her Orban stocks are

|    | Common | Preferred |
|----|--------|-----------|
| a. | $300   | $0        |
| b. | $225   | $75       |
| c. | $200   | $100      |
| d. | $150   | $150      |

37. The holding period for the preferred stock starts in
a.  January 1999.
b.  March 1999.
c.  September 1999.
d.  December 1999.

---

38. On July 1, 1990, Lila Perl paid $90,000 for 450 shares of Janis Corp. common stock. Lila received a nontaxable stock dividend of 50 new common shares in August 1999. On December 20, 1999, Lila sold the 50 new shares for $11,000. How much should Lila report in her 1999 return as long-term capital gain?
a.  $0
b.  $1,000
c.  $2,000
d.  $11,000

## SALE OF RESIDENCE

**Items 39 and 40** are based on the following data:
Gary Barth, who is unmarried, owns a house which has been his principal residence for the past ten years. Gary sells this house and moves to a rental apartment on May 1, 1997. He has no intention of buying another residence at any time in the future, but wishes to avail himself of the one-time exclusion of gain on the sale of his house.

39. What is the minimum age Gary must attain in order to avail himself of the one-time exclusion of gain on sale of his house?
a.  55.
b.  65.
c.  70.
d.  72.

40. Assume that Gary has attained the required age to qualify for the one-time exclusion of gain on the sale of his house, what is the maximum amount allowable for this type of exclusion?
a.  40% of long-term gain.
b.  60% of long-term gain.
c.  $100,000.
d.  $125,000.

---

41. In January 1997, Davis purchased a new residence for $200,000. During that same month he sold his former residence for $80,000 and paid the realtor a $5,000 commission. The former residence, his first home, had cost $65,000 in 1990. David added a bathroom for $5,000 in 1991. What amount of gain is recognized from the sale of the former residence on Davis' 1997 tax return?
a.  $15,000
b.  $10,000
c.  $5,000
d.  $0

42. George Adams owned an apartment building containing 4 identical apartments. He occupied one apartment as his principal residence and rented the other three. He acquired the building in 1981 at a cost of $60,000 and has taken depreciation of $8,000 on the rented portion. On January 1, 1997, he sold the building for $80,000, incurring selling expenses of $4,000 and purchased a new residence for $45,000 in February 1997. What should Adams report as his recognized gain resulting from the sale of his principal residence?
a.  $0.
b.  $2,000.
c.  $4,000.
d.  $6,000.

43. The following information pertains to the sale of Al Oran's principal residence:

| | |
|---|---|
| Date of sale | January 1997 |
| Date of purchase | May 1979 |
| Net sales price | $260,000 |
| Adjusted basis | $ 70,000 |

In April 1997, Oran (age 70) bought a smaller residence for $90,000. Oran elected to avail himself of the exclusion of realized gain available to taxpayers age 55 and over. What amount of gain should Oran recognize on the sale of his residence?
a.  $45,000.
b.  $65,000.
c.  $70,000.
d.  $90,000.

44. Ryan, age 53, is single with no dependents. In March 1999, Ryan's principal residence was sold for the net amount of $400,000 after all selling expenses. Ryan bought the house in 1984 and occupied it until sold. On the date of sale, the house had a basis of $80,000. Ryan does not intend to buy another residence. What is the maximum exclusion of gain on sale of the residence that may be claimed in Ryan's 1999 income tax return?
a. $320,000
b. $250,000
c. $125,000
d. $0

## LIKE KIND EXCHANGES

45. In a "like-kind" exchange of an investment asset for a similar asset that will also be held as an investment, no taxable gain or loss will be recognized on the transaction if both assets consist of
a. Convertible debentures.
b. Convertible preferred stock.
c. Partnership interests.
d. Rental real estate located in different states.

46. The following information pertains to the acquisition of a six-wheel truck by Sol Barr, a self-employed contractor:

| | |
|---|---|
| Cost of original truck traded in | $20,000 |
| Book value of original truck at trade-in date | 4,000 |
| List price of new truck | 25,000 |
| Trade-in allowance for old truck | 6,000 |
| Business use of both trucks | 100% |

The new truck will be depreciated as 5-year MACRS property. The basis of the new truck is
a. $27,000.
b. $25,000.
c. $23,000.
d. $19,000.

47. On July 1 of this year, Louis Herr exchanged an office building having a fair market value of $400,000, for cash of $80,000 plus an apartment building having a fair market value of $320,000. Herr's adjusted basis for the office building was $250,000. How much gain should Herr recognize in his income tax return?
a. $0.
b. $ 80,000.
c. $150,000.
d. $330,000.

48. On July 1 of this year, Riley exchanged investment real property, with an adjusted basis of $160,000 and subject to a mortgage of $70,000, and received from Wilson $30,000 cash and other investment real property having a fair market value of $250,000. Wilson assumed the mortgage. What is Riley's recognized gain on the exchange?
a. $30,000.
b. $70,000.
c. $90,000.
d. $100,000.

49. On October 1 of this year, Donald Anderson exchanged an apartment building, having an adjusted basis of $375,000 and subject to a mortgage of $100,000, for $25,000 cash and another apartment building with a fair market value of $550,000 and subject to a mortgage of $125,000. The property transfers were made subject to the outstanding mortgages. What amount of gain should Anderson recognize on the exchange?
a. $0.
b. $25,000.
c. $125,000.
d. $175,000.

50. An office building owned by Elmer Bass was condemned by the state on January 2, 1999. Bass received the condemnation award on March 1, 1999. In order to qualify for nonrecognition of gain on this involuntary conversion, what is the last date for Bass to acquire qualified replacement property?
a. August 1, 2000.
b. January 2. 2001.
c. March 1, 2002.
d. December 31, 2002.

## SECTION 1231 ASSETS AND RECAPTURE RULES

51. Platt owns land that is operated as a parking lot. A shed was erected on the lot for the related transactions with customers. With regard to capital assets and Section 1231 assets, how should these assets be classified?

| | _Land_ | _Shed_ |
|---|---|---|
| a. | Capital | Capital |
| b. | Section 1231 | Capital |
| c. | Capital | Section 1231 |
| d. | Section 1231 | Section 1231 |

52. Mike Karp owns machinery, with an adjusted basis of $50,000, for use in his carwashing business. In addition, Karp owns his personal residence and furniture, which together cost him $100,000. The capital assets amount to
a. $0.
b. $ 50,000.
c. $100,000.
d. $150,000.

53. John Thayer purchased an apartment building on January 1, 1993, for $200,000. The building was depreciated on the straight-line method. On December 31, 1999, the building was sold for $220,000, when the asset balance net of accumulated depreciation was $170,000. On his 1999 tax return, Thayer should report
a. Section 1231 gain of $20,000 and ordinary income of $30,000.
b. Section 1231 gain of $30,000 and ordinary income of $20,000.
c. Ordinary income of $50,000.
d. Section 1231 gain of $50,000.

54. On December 31, 1999, Mark sold machinery for $48,000. The machinery which had been purchased on January 1, 1996, for $40,000 had an adjusted basis of $28,000 on the date of sale. For 1999 Mark should report
a. A section 1231 gain of $20,000.
b. Ordinary income of $20,000.
c. A section 1231 gain of $12,000 and ordinary income of $8,000.
d. A section 1231 gain of $8,000 and ordinary income of $12,000.

55. On January 2, 1997, Bates Corp. purchased and placed into service 7-year MACRS tangible property costing $100,000. On December 31, 1999, Bates sold the property for $102,000, after having taken $47,525 in MACRS depreciation deductions. What amount of the gain should Bates recapture as ordinary income?
a. $0
b. $2,000
c. $47,525
d. $49,525

## Released and Author Constructed Questions

R98

56. Leker exchanged a van that was used exclusively for business and had an adjusted tax basis of $20,000 for a new van. The new van had a fair market value of $10,000, and Leker also received $3,000 in cash. What was Leker's tax basis in the acquired van?
a. $20,000
b. $17,000
c. $13,000
d. $7,000

AC

57. On September 8, 1999, Arthur and Anne Marie sell their personal residence for $390,000. The couple purchased the residence in 1985 at a cost of $100,000. In addition, they made capital improvements of $30,000 during the years. They do not plan on replacing the residence within two years. In filing their 1999 tax return, they may exclude from gross income:
a. $-0-
b. $125,000
c. $250,000
d. $260,000

AC

58. Bill, age 58, is single and owns a residence which he purchased in 1971 for $30,000. During 1997, he married Paula, age 57. Paula had previously sold her residence in 1996, just prior to their marriage and utilized her one-time exclusion of $125,000. In 1999, when Bill and Paula file a joint return, Bill sells his residence for $300,000. In filing the return, they may exclude from gross income:
a. $-0-
b. $125,000
c. $250,000
d. $270,000

AC

59. On October 1, 1998, Ashley acquires her principal residence for $200,000. On June 1, 1999, due to a change in place of her employment, she sells the residence for $230,000. Determine the amount which can be excluded from income on the sale of the residence.
a. $-0-
b. $10,000
c. $20,000
d. $30,000

# Chapter Six -- Answers
# Capital Transactions

1. (a) $0. The selling price of $20,000 is less than Conner's adjusted basis of $30,000, resulting in a realized loss of $10,000. Because of Section 267, the realized loss is not recognized (or deducted). This is a related party transaction between a father and his daughter.

2. (a) $0. When Alice purchased the stock, her basis was $20,000. When she sells the stock for $25,000, she normally would recognize a $5,000 gain. However, since a loss deduction was denied on the original sale from Conner to his daughter, that unused loss may be used to offset any gain on a subsequent sale. Therefore, $5,000 of the $10,000 realized loss from question #1 may be used to offset the $5,000 gain, and no gain needs to be recognized by Alice.

3. (b) $3,000. When capital losses exceed capital gains, an individual taxpayer may offset up to $3,000 in ordinary income. The excess of $5,000 ($8,000 less the $3,000) may be carried forward to future periods.

4. (b) $37,000. The procedure for determining the net capital position at the end of the year is to net the long transactions, net the short transactions and net the nets.

| | | |
|---|---|---|
| Gross income before capital transactions | | $40,000 |
| Capital transactions: | | |
| Long-term capital loss | $(8,000) | |
| Long-term capital gain | 2,000 | |
| Net long-term capital loss | (6,000) | |
| Short-term capital gain | 1,000 | |
| Net long-term capital loss | (5,000) | |
| Limit on capital losses | | (3,000) |
| Adjusted gross income | | $37,000 |

5. (b) $3,000 long-term loss. Paul has a total of $6,000 in capital losses and no capital gains. The maximum capital loss allowed after netting is $3,000. In determining the loss deduction, the short-term capital losses are used first and the long-term capital losses second. Therefore, the entire $1,000 short-term capital loss is utilized and $2,000 of the long-term capital loss, leaving $3,000 of the long-term loss available for carryforward purposes.

6. (c) Grandfather and granddaughter. Section 267 defines related parties as members of a family which include a taxpayer's brothers and sisters, spouse, ancestors and lineal descendants. The grandfather and granddaughter are an ancestor and lineal descendant.

7. (b) $1,000. This problem is comprised of two transactions. First, Fay's original selling price of $11,000 to her son Martin is less than her adjusted basis of $15,000, resulting in a realized loss of $4,000. Because of Section 267, the realized loss is not recognized. Second, Martin's sale of the stock to an unrelated third party would generally result in a capital gain of $5,000 ($16,000 less his basis of $11,000). However, since a loss deduction was denied on the original sale from Fay to her son, that unused loss may be used to offset any gain on a subsequent sale. Therefore, Fay's $4,000 disallowed loss may be used to partially offset the $5,000 gain, leaving a recognized gain of only $1,000.

8. (a) $0 and $0. This is called a wash sale. It exists when an individual buys and sells substantially identical securities within a 30 day period. The disallowed loss of $2,000 is added to the basis of the shares purchased on December 15th.

9. (d) $90,200. The basis of the property is determined as follows:

| | |
|---|---|
| Cash downpayment | $ 40,000 |
| Purchase money mortgage | 50,000 |
| Title insurance policy | 200 |
| Total basis | $ 90,200 |

10. (c) $50,000. The general rule in a like-kind exchange is that no gain is recognized. However, when a taxpayer receives boot (cash or unlike property), the boot causes a gain to be recognized to lesser of the realized gain or the boot received. In this problem, the realized gain is computed as follows:

| | |
|---|---|
| Fair market value of new real estate | $450,000 |
| Cash received (boot) | 50,000 |
| Amount realized | 500,000 |
| Less adjusted basis of old apartment | (300,000) |
| Realized gain | $200,000 |
| | |
| Recognized gain (limited to lesser of the cash received) | $ 50,000 |

11. (a) $0. The realized loss of $2,000 on the transaction is not recognized because Eng is a related party. When a shareholder owns more than 50% of a corporation's stock, he is considered to be a related party under Section 267, and the losses are disallowed.

12. (a) For purposes of determining the gain or loss for tax purposes, the trade date is used.

13. (b) 12 months. By definition, the holding period for determining whether a capital transaction qualifies for long-term is **more than 12 months**.

14. (b) $280,000. Hall's personal residence and furnishings are capital assets. Equipment used in a trade or business is not a capital asset.

15. (b) The painting is for personal use and is considered to be a capital asset. Her holding period is more than one year. Therefore, the gain of $15,000 on the sale will be classified as a long-term capital gain.

16. (b) Capital losses are used first to offset capital gains. Once the capital gains are offset, the net capital loss is then used to reduce ordinary income up to $3,000. The excess over $3,000 may be carried over indefinitely.

17. (b) Capital losses are used first to offset capital gains. Once the capital gains are offset, the net capital loss is then used to reduce ordinary income up to $3,000. The excess over $3,000 may be carried over indefinitely.

18. (b) Goodwill. The delivery truck and land used as a parking lot are excluded from capital assets. A company's treasury stock is a reduction of stockholder's equity, not a capital asset.

19. (b) $8,000. Capital assets include property held for personal use, such as the kitchen sets and living room pieces. However, the showcases and tables used in a trade or business are excluded from the definition of capital assets.

20. through 22. When a gift of property is made, the general rule is that the basis and holding period of the donor tacks over to the donee. However, when the fair market value of the gift is less than the adjusted basis of the property, the rules change. If the property is sold for a gain, the cost basis is used. If the property is sold for a loss (as compared with the donor's basis), the basis is the lessor of the fair market value or the "gain" basis. If the selling price is between the fair market value and adjusted basis, no gain or loss is recognized.

| | #20 | #21 | #22 |
|---|---|---|---|
| Selling price | $ 2,600 | $ 2,000 | $2,300 |
| "Adjusted basis" | 2,400 | 2,200 | 2,300 |
| Gain (loss) | 200 | ( 200) | -0- |
| Answer | (c) | (c) | (a) |

23. (a) $0. When a gift of property is made, the general rule is that the basis and holding period of the donor tacks over to the donee. However, when the fair market value of the gift is less than the adjusted basis of the property, the rules change. If the property is sold for a gain, the cost basis is used. If the property is sold for a loss (as compared with the donor's basis), the basis is the lessor of the fair market value or the "gain" basis. If the selling price is between the fair market value and adjusted basis, no gain or loss is recognized.

24. (b) Starts in 1980. When a gift of property is made, the general rule is that the basis and holding period of the donor tacks over to the donee. Ruth's basis would be $10,000.

25. (a) Capital asset. By definition

26. (a) $3,000. Using the carryover basis as described in question #24:

| | |
|---|---|
| Selling price | $13,000 |
| Basis | 10,000 |
| Recognized gain | $ 3,000 |

27. (b) $240,000. Assuming that a proper alternative valuation date was elected (overall value of the estate decreases and the estate tax liability decreases) then the date of the distribution, not the alternative valuation date, determines the valuation of the asset.

28. (b) Long-term. Even though the holding period appears to be only one month, the holding period for property received from a decedent is automatically long-term.

29. (d) $0. Hall's basis in the stock received from his father's estate will be the fair market value as of the distribution date because the executor elected the alternative valuation date. Hall's selling price of the $4,500 is identical to the adjusted basis of $4,500, and therefore no income or gain is included.

30 - 32. These three questions ask about basis, and gain or loss. The answers below show more computations than are required in the problem. When a gift of property is made, the general rule is that the basis and holding period of the donor tacks over to the donee. However, when the fair market value of the gift is less than the adjusted basis of the property, the rules change. If the property is sold for a gain, the cost basis is used. If the property is sold for a loss (as compared with the donor's basis), the basis is the lessor of the fair market value or the "gain" basis. If the selling price is between the fair market value and adjusted basis, no gain or loss is recognized.

| | #30 | #31 | #32 |
|---|---|---|---|
| Selling price | $ 5,000 | $ 2,000 | $3,500 |
| "Adjusted basis" | 4,000 | 3,000 | 3,500 |
| Gain (loss) | 1,000 | ( 1,000) | -0- |
| Answer | (b) | (b) | (d) |

33. (c) $450,000. Ida's basis in the stock received from his brother's estate will be the fair market value as of the alternate valuation date because the executor elected the alternate valuation date. The rule for electing the alternate valuation date requires that the overall taxable estate be reduced from the valuation at the date of death. We can assume that if the executor made a valid election, then the overall estate decreased, even though the value of this specific item increased.

34. (c) $1,000 of long-term capital gain. Whereas Greene received a nontaxable stock dividend of the same stock, the original basis of his 450 shares of Acme must be allocated to all the shares he now possesses. In addition, the holding period tacks to the original purchase of July 1, 1988, thus making this transaction long-term.

| | | |
|---|---|---|
| Original basis | $ 45,000 | |
| Number of shares: | | |
|    Original | 450 | |
|    Dividends | 50 | |
|    Total | | 500 Shares |
| Basis per share | $ 90 | |
| | | |
| Selling price | $ 5,500 | |
| Basis of shares sold: | | |
|    50 shares @ $90 | 4,500 | |
| Long-term capital gain | $ 1,000 | |

35. (c) $5,000. Whereas Harris received a nontaxable stock dividend of different stock (preferred stock, not common), the original basis of $6,000 from his 100 shares of common stock must be allocated to all the shares he now owns using the fair market value as of the date of distribution.

| | | Total | Ratio | Basis |
|---|---|---|---|---|
| Fair market value - common | 100 shares @ $ 75 | $ 7,500 | 5/6 | $5,000 |
| Fair market value - preferred | 10 shares @ $150 | 1,500 | 1/6 | 1,000 |
| | | $ 9,000 | | $6,000 |

36. (b) $225 and $75. Whereas Hill received a nontaxable stock dividend of different stock (preferred stock, not common), the original basis of $300 from her 1 share of common stock must be allocated to the preferred share she now owns using the fair market value as of the date of distribution.

| | | Total | Ratio | Basis |
|---|---|---|---|---|
| Fair market value - common | 1 share @ $ 450 | $ 450 | 3/4 | $ 225 |
| Fair market value - preferred | 1 share @ $ 150 | 150 | 1/4 | 75 |
| | | $ 600 | | $ 300 |

37. (a) January 1999. Hill's holding period for the preferred stock begins on the date she acquired the common stock.

38. (c) $2,000 of long-term capital gain. Whereas Lila received a nontaxable stock dividend of the same stock, the original basis of her 450 shares of Janis must be allocated to all the shares she now possesses. In addition, the holding period tacks to the original purchase of July 1, 1990, thus making this transaction long-term.

| | | |
|---|---|---|
| Original basis | $ 90,000 | |
| Number of shares: | | |
|    Original | 450 | |
|    Dividend | 50 | |
|    Total | | 500 Shares |
| Basis per share | $ 180 | |
| | | |
| Selling price | $ 11,000 | |
| Basis of shares sold: | | |
|    50 shares @ $180 | 9,000 | |
| Long-term capital gain | $ 2,000 | |

39. (a) 55. By definition. Sale was prior to the enactment date of May 6, 1997.

40. (d) $125,000. By definition.

41. (d) $0. To determine the recognized gain on the sale of a personal residence, first determine the realized gain.

| | |
|---|---|
| Selling price of old residence | $80,000 |
| Less: selling expenses | ( 5,000) |
| Adjusted selling price | $75,000 |
| | |
| Less: Adjusted basis | |
| Original cost of residence | $65,000 |
| Add: Bathroom addition | 5,000 |
| Basis of residence sold | $70,000 |
| | |
| Realized gain | $ 5,000 |

The realized gain is recognized only to the extent that the adjusted selling price of the old residence ($75,000) exceeds the purchase price of the new residence ($200,00). Therefore, no gain is recognized. The unrecognized gain of $5,000 reduces the basis on the new residence from $200,000 to $195,000. This is under prior law.

42. (a) $0. The realized gain is recognized only to the extent that the adjusted selling price of the old residence ($19,000) exceeds the purchase price of the new principal residence ($45,000). Therefore, no gain is recognized. Because this apartment building was used 25% for personal use and 75% for rental use, an allocation of selling price and costs is needed. Note that there is no reduction in the basis of the property which is used as his principal residence. Depreciation only pertains to the rental portion.

| | Total | 25% Personal |
|---|---|---|
| Selling price | $80,000 | $20,000 |
| Selling expenses | (4,000) | (1,000) |
| Adjusted selling price | 76,000 | 19,000 |
| Adjusted basis | 60,000 | 15,000 |
| Realized gain | | $ 4,000 |
| | | |
| Recognized gain | | $ -0- |

43. (a) $45,000. There are two factors to consider in this problem. The first is the determination of the realized gain of $190,000 (net sales price of $260,000 less the adjusted basis of $70,000). The realized gain of $190,000 is recognized only to the extent that the adjusted selling price of the old residence ($260,000) exceeds the purchase price of the new principal residence ($90,000). This means a gain of $170,000 is recognized. The second factor is the exclusion of $125,000 available to taxpayers age 55 and over. The $170,000 gain, less the $125,000 exclusion, results in a reportable gain of $45,000. This is under prior law.

44. (b) $250,000. Under the new law, a single taxpayer excludes up to a maximum of $250,000. His realized gain was $320,000.

45. (d) Rental real estate. Property held for productive use in a business or for investment qualifies for like-kind exchanges which are nontaxable. The convertible bonds, preferred stock and partnership interests do not qualify.

46. (c) $23,000. This is a like-kind exchange and no gain or loss is recognized. The basis of the new property represents the adjusted basis of the property transferred plus any cash paid.

| | | |
|---|---|---|
| Adjusted basis of old truck | | $ 4,000 |
| Plus cash paid at trade-in: | | |
| List price | $25,000 | |
| Less trade-in | (6,000) | 19,000 |
| Basis of new truck | | $23,000 |

47. (b) $80,000. The general rule in a like-kind exchange is that no gain is recognized. However, when a taxpayer receives boot (cash or unlike property), the boot causes a gain to be recognized to lesser of the realized gain or the boot received. In this problem, the realized gain is computed as follows:

| | |
|---|---|
| Fair market value of new apartment | $320,000 |
| Cash received (boot) | 80,000 |
| Amount realized | 400,000 |
| Less adjusted basis of old apartment | (250,000) |
| Realized gain | $150,000 |
| | |
| Recognized gain (limited to lesser of the cash received) | $ 80,000 |

48. (d) $100,000. The general rule in a like-kind exchange is that no gain is recognized. However, when a taxpayer receives boot (cash or unlike property such as the release of a mortgage), the boot causes a gain to be recognized to lesser of the realized gain or the boot received. In this problem, the realized gain is computed as follows:

| | |
|---|---|
| Fair market value of new investment | $250,000 |
| Cash received (boot) | 30,000 |
| Release of mortgage | 70,000 |
| Amount realized | 350,000 |
| Less adjusted basis of old apartment | (160,000) |
| Realized gain | $190,000 |
| | |
| Recognized gain (limited to lesser of the boot received) | |
| Cash | $ 30,000 |
| Release of mortgage | 70,000 |
| Total recognized gain | $100,000 |

49. (b) $25,000. The general rule in a like-kind exchange is that no gain is recognized. However, when a taxpayer receives boot(cash or unlike property such as the release of a mortgage), the boot causes a gain to be recognized to lesser of the realized gain or the boot received. Because the taxpayer assumed a larger mortgage than he was relieved of, the release of the mortgage is not considered boot. The boot in this transaction is limited to cash received. In this problem, the realized gain is computed as follows:

| | | |
|---|---|---|
| Fair market value of new apartment | $550,000 | |
| Less mortgage assumed | (125,000) | $425,000 |
| Cash received (boot) | | 25,000 |
| Release of mortgage | | 100,000 |
| Amount realized | | 550,000 |
| Less adjusted basis of old apartment | | (375,000) |
| Realized gain | | $175,000 |
| | | |
| Recognized gain (limited to lesser of the boot received) | | $ 25,000 |

50. (d)  The replacement period is three years after the close of the taxable year in which the gain is realized (which was 1998).  The gain would therefore be realized in the year 2001.

51. (d)  By definition. Land and depreciable property used in a trade or business are not, by definition, capital assets.  However, Section 1231 gives them capital treatment.

52. (c)  $100,000.  Depreciable property used in a trade or business is not, by definition, capital assets.  Only Karp's personal residence is a capital asset.

53. (d)  Section 1231 gain of $50,000.  The building is a Section 1231 asset.  None of the gain is ordinary because the depreciation, or cost recovery, was under the straight-line method.  (There was no excess over straight-line.)

| | |
|---|---|
| Selling price of building | $220,000 |
| Adjusted basis of building | 170,000 |
| Realized Section 1231 gain | $ 50,000 |

54. (d)  Section 1231 gain of $8,000 and ordinary income of $12,000.   Section 1245 requires that a taxpayer must recapture as ordinary income that portion of the gain to the extent of depreciation taken.  The problem does not specifically tell the candidate that $12,000 was taken in depreciation.  By starting with the original cost of the machinery ($40,000) and comparing it to its adjusted basis of $28,000, it can be assumed that the difference of $12,000 in the depreciation taken,

| | |
|---|---|
| Selling price of machinery | $48,000 |
| Adjusted basis of machinery | 28,000 |
| Realized gain | $20,000 |

Character of gain:
| | | |
|---|---|---|
| Ordinary | (Up to depreciation taken) | $12,000 |
| Section 1231 | (Excess gain over cost) | 8,000 |
| | | $20,000 |

55. (c)  $47,525.  Section 1245 requires that a taxpayer must recapture as ordinary income, that portion of the gain to the extent of any depreciation taken.  The basis of the property at the time of the sale must be determined first, then the total gain, then the character of the gain, as presented below:

| | |
|---|---|
| Original cost | $ 100,000 |
| Less: depreciation allowed | 47,525 |
| Adjusted basis | $ 52,475 |

| | |
|---|---|
| Selling price of equipment | $ 102,000 |
| Adjusted basis of the equipment | 52,475 |
| Realized gain | $ 49,525 |

Character of the gain:
| | |
|---|---|
| Ordinary (up to the depreciation taken) | $ 47,525 |
| Capital | 2,000 |
| | $ 49,525 |

56. (b) $17,000. The general rule in a like-kind exchange is that no gain or loss is recognized. However, if the taxpayer receives boot (cash), the boot can cause the recognition of a realized gain, but not a loss. Therefore, the receipt of cash impacts the problem by reducing the basis.

| | |
|---|---|
| Fair market value | |
| of new van | $ 10,000 |
| Cash | 3,000 |
| Amount realized | 13,000 |
| | |
| Less adjusted basis of old van | (20,000) |
| Realized loss | $ 7,000 |

Therefore, the tax basis of the old van ($20,000) is allocated to the cash ($3,000) and the new van ($17,000).

57. (d) $260,000. For married taxpayers who sell their principal residence after May 6, 1997, they may exclude up to $500,000 of the income from that sale. For this taxpayer, the amount of the income is $260,000.

| | | |
|---|---|---|
| Gross selling price | | $ 390,000 |
| | | |
| Cost | $ 100,000 | |
| Improvements | 30,000 | |
| Total basis | | 130,000 |
| Amount realized on sale | | $ 260,000 |

58. (c) $250,000. Under prior law, when a taxpayer married another taxpayer who had previously elected the one-time exclusion it was uncertain as to whether that would taint the one-time election for the new married couple. Current law allows each taxpayer in a married, filing jointly return $250,000 amount. Thus, Bill is allowed to exclude up to $250,000 of his total realized gain of $270,000.

59. (b) $10,000. Even though Ashley did not own the residence for the entire two years, she is entitled to a pro-rata exclusion for the amount of time she owned the house. Her exclusion is based upon:

| | |
|---|---|
| Selling price | $ 230,000 |
| Cost | -200,000 |
| Amount realized | $ 30,000 |

Realized gain times the months owned over 24 months

$30,000 X 8/24 = $10,000

# Chapter Seven
# Partnerships

# Chapter Seven
# Partnerships

## NATURE AND CHARACTERISTICS

### GENERAL
The Internal Revenue Code defines a partnership as an association of two or more persons carrying on a trade or business, financial operation or venture. The partnership includes a syndicate, group, pool, joint venture, or other unincorporated organization. A partnership must not be a corporation, trust, or estate.

A partnership is not a taxpaying entity, but rather a conduit, which flows items of income, gain, loss, deduction and credit through down to the partners. The allocation of these items is usually based upon a written partnership agreement. However, in absence of an agreement, the items would be allocated under a pro-rata basis according to the capital interests.

### AGGREGATE VS. ENTITY THEORY
A partnership is a group of taxpayers, joined together with one another, yet each partner treats their proportionate share of income, deduction, gain, loss, and credit as if it were their own. This is called the aggregate, or conduit theory. However, filing a partnership return as a single entity, and making certain elections at the partnership level, such as depreciation methods, inventory methods, installment gain and Section 179 elections, indicate that the partnership is also an entity and not just a collection of individual partners.

### ORGANIZATION COSTS AND SYNDICATION FEES
Costs incurred related to the creation of the partnership, such as accounting and legal fees, are not deductible, but are instead capitalized. If the partnership files a proper election by the due date of the return, including extensions, this amount may be amortized over a period of not less than 60 months. Syndication fees, however, are neither deductible or amortizable. These fees are usually the marketing, registration and underwriting fees associated with selling partnership interests in an offering.

### ALLOWABLE TAX YEARS
A partner must report income and deductions in the tax year that includes the last day of the partnership year. Because a partnership may easily defer income from one year to another merely by adopting a fiscal year end different from that of its partners, Congress and IRS have established a series of rules limiting the availability of certain year ends.

Briefly the hierarchy for year-end selection is as follows:
1. The year-end of the majority of the partners.
2. The year-end of the principal partners.
3. The year-end resulting in the "least aggregate deferral" of income.

If the selection of the fiscal year-end using the rules above is not acceptable, the partnership may select a year-end under one of these three alternatives:
1. Establish that a business purpose exists, usually supported by cyclical income.
2. Establish a natural business tax year following the IRS procedures where gross receipts of 25% or more were recognized in a two month period for three consecutive years.
3. Select a tax year where no more than three months of partnership income is deferred from the required tax year.

### FILING REQUIREMENTS
A partnership is required to file Form 1065 each year. The return is due by the 15th day of the 4th month following the end of the taxable year. For a calendar year partnership, this means April 15th. Failure to file a timely return results in a penalty of $50 per month, per partner. The maximum number of months over which the penalty may be applied is five. A partnership may request a three month extension by timely filing Form 8736. *On the following page is a copy of Form 1065.*

Form **1065**

Department of the Treasury
Internal Revenue Service

## U.S. Partnership Return of Income

For calendar year 1999, or tax year beginning .......... , 1999, and ending .......... , ..... .
▶ See separate instructions.

OMB No. 1545-0099

**1999**

| A Principal business activity | Use the IRS label. Otherwise, please print or type. | Name of partnership | D Employer identification number |
|---|---|---|---|
| B Principal product or service | | Number, street, and room or suite no. If a P.O. box, see page 12 of the instructions. | E Date business started |
| C Business code number | | City or town, state, and ZIP code | F Total assets (see page 12 of the instructions) $ |

G  Check applicable boxes: **(1)** ☐ Initial return   **(2)** ☐ Final return   **(3)** ☐ Change in address   **(4)** ☐ Amended return

H  Check accounting method: **(1)** ☐ Cash   **(2)** ☐ Accrual   **(3)** ☐ Other (specify) ▶.........................................

I  Number of Schedules K-1. Attach one for each person who was a partner at any time during the tax year ▶ ...........................

**Caution:** *Include **only** trade or business income and expenses on lines 1a through 22 below. See the instructions for more information.*

### Income

| | | | |
|---|---|---|---|
| 1a | Gross receipts or sales | 1a | |
| b | Less returns and allowances | 1b | 1c |
| 2 | Cost of goods sold (Schedule A, line 8) | | 2 |
| 3 | Gross profit. Subtract line 2 from line 1c | | 3 |
| 4 | Ordinary income (loss) from other partnerships, estates, and trusts *(attach schedule)* | | 4 |
| 5 | Net farm profit (loss) *(attach Schedule F (Form 1040))* | | 5 |
| 6 | Net gain (loss) from Form 4797, Part II, line 18 | | 6 |
| 7 | Other income (loss) *(attach schedule)* | | 7 |
| 8 | **Total income (loss).** Combine lines 3 through 7 | | 8 |

### Deductions (see page 14 of the instructions for limitations)

| | | | |
|---|---|---|---|
| 9 | Salaries and wages (other than to partners) (less employment credits) | | 9 |
| 10 | Guaranteed payments to partners | | 10 |
| 11 | Repairs and maintenance | | 11 |
| 12 | Bad debts | | 12 |
| 13 | Rent | | 13 |
| 14 | Taxes and licenses | | 14 |
| 15 | Interest | | 15 |
| 16a | Depreciation (if required, attach Form 4562) | 16a | |
| b | Less depreciation reported on Schedule A and elsewhere on return | 16b | 16c |
| 17 | Depletion **(Do not deduct oil and gas depletion.)** | | 17 |
| 18 | Retirement plans, etc. | | 18 |
| 19 | Employee benefit programs | | 19 |
| 20 | Other deductions *(attach schedule)* | | 20 |
| 21 | **Total deductions.** Add the amounts shown in the far right column for lines 9 through 20 | | 21 |

| 22 | Ordinary income (loss) from trade or business activities. Subtract line 21 from line 8 | | 22 |

### Please Sign Here

Under penalties of perjury, I declare that I have examined this return, including accompanying schedules and statements, and to the best of my knowledge and belief, it is true, correct, and complete. Declaration of preparer (other than general partner or limited liability company member) is based on all information of which preparer has any knowledge.

▶ _____   ▶ _____
Signature of general partner or limited liability company member        Date

### Paid Preparer's Use Only

| Preparer's signature ▶ | Date | Check if self-employed ▶ ☐ | Preparer's SSN or PTIN |
|---|---|---|---|
| Firm's name (or yours if self-employed) and address ▶ | | EIN ▶ | |
| | | ZIP code ▶ | |

For Paperwork Reduction Act Notice, see separate instructions.        Cat. No. 11390Z        Form **1065** (1999)

# FORMATION - CONTRIBUTIONS OF PROPERTY

### GENERAL RULE FOR CONTRIBUTIONS OF PROPERTY

When a partner transfers property to a partnership in exchange for a partnership interest, the general rule is that no gain or loss is recognized. There is a carryover of basis to the partnership of the property transferred by the partner as well as a carryover of basis to the partner's new interest in the partnership. The carryover also pertains to the holding period of the property contributed. The logic behind this non-taxable transfer is that only the form of ownership of the property transferred has changed.

> **Example 1:** On January 1, 1999, K contributes land with a fair market value of $40,000 and an adjusted basis of $15,000 to KL partnership, in exchange for a 50% interest worth $40,000. K purchased the land in 1980 for the $15,000. L contributes cash of $40,000 on the same day. No gain or loss is recognized by either the partnership, or to the partners on the exchange. K's tax basis in the partnership is $15,000. The partnership's basis in the land is $15,000 even though the fair market value is $40,000. K's holding period for her partnership interest is long-term (since 1980) and the partnership's holding period for the land is also long-term. L's tax basis is $40,000. His holding period begins January 1, 1999.

### CONTRIBUTIONS OF PROPERTY WHEN LIABILITIES ARE ASSUMED BY THE PARTNERSHIP

When a partner transfers property to a partnership that is subject to liabilities which the partnership assumes, the general rule is that no gain or loss is recognized. The amount of liabilities assumed by the other partners as a result of the transfer, reduce the tax basis of the contributing partner. However, if the assumption of the liabilities of the other partners is greater than the contributing partner's basis in the property, this would result in a gain.

> **Example 2:** Assume in Example 1 that the land contributed by K was subject to a mortgage of $20,000, and that the partnership assumed the mortgage. No gain or loss is recognized by either the partnership or K. Her tax basis in the partnership is now $5,000. That is comprised of her basis in the land of $15,000 less the 50% share of the $20,000 mortgage assumed by L as a partner. L's basis is now $50,000, which is comprised of $40,000 from his cash contribution plus $10,000 from the assumption of debt. The basis of the land in the partnership is still $15,000.
>
> | | |
> |---|---|
> | Basis of property transferred | $ 15,000 |
> | Less: liabilities assumed by other partners | (10,000) |
> | Basis of K's partnership interest | $ 5,000 |

> **Example 3:** Assume the same facts as in Example 2, except that the mortgage being assumed by the partnership is $40,000. K must recognize a gain of $5,000 and her tax basis in the partnership is now zero. Her basis in the land was $15,000, however, the other partner assumed $20,000 of the mortgage. This would result in a negative basis of $5,000 to K. Since a negative basis is not allowed, K recognizes a $5,000 gain and restores her basis in the partnership to zero. L's basis is now $60,000 ($40,000 plus $20,000 assumption of debt).

### SERVICES RENDERED IN EXCHANGE FOR A PARTNERSHIP INTEREST

When a partner performs services in exchange for a partnership interest, the partner must recognize ordinary income to the extent of the fair market value of the interest received. The partner's basis in the partnership will be equal to the amount of income recognized.

# OPERATIONS OF THE PARTNERSHIP AND BASIS COMPUTATIONS

## GENERAL RULE

Each year when the partnership files the Form 1065, it reports each partner's allocable share of income, deductions, gains, losses and credits on Schedule K-1. In preparing the return, it is necessary to group items into separately stated and non-separately stated items.

## SEPARATELY AND NON-SEPARATELY STATED ITEMS

Separately stated items are those items which when treated at the partner's level, could have a special tax treatment or limitation. Grouping them together could circumvent the tax laws. For example, since an individual taxpayer can only deduct charitable contributions up to 50% of his adjusted gross income, any charitable contributions made by the partnership must be reported separately to the partner in order that these be grouped with other contributions the partner may have made individually. Only then can the 50% test truly tested. Likewise, on an individual basis, net capital losses can only be deducted to a maximum of $3,000 per year, and all Section 179 elections cannot exceed the maximum allowed per taxpayer ($19,000 in 1999 and $20,000 in 2000). Other separately stated items include, but are not limited to:

- Portfolio income, such as interest, dividends and royalties
- Investment interest expense
- Personal expenses such as medical insurance
- AMT preference and adjustment items
- Passive activities, including rental activities
- Intangible drilling costs
- Taxes paid to foreign countries
- Tax-exempt income

All other items of income and expense that are not separately stated are netted together at the partnership level to determine ordinary income. Refer back to the Form 1065 on page 2. Notice that line 22 is the amount of ordinary income.

After the determination of ordinary income (or loss) and of each separately stated item, the amounts flows through proportionately to each partner on a K-1 based upon the partner's percentage interest in the capital, profits and losses. It is also possible to allocate certain items in a different percentage so long as the allocation has *substantial economic effect*. A partial first page of Form K-1 is presented on the following page.

| SCHEDULE K-1 (Form 1065) Department of the Treasury Internal Revenue Service | Partner's Share of Income, Credits, Deductions, etc. ► See separate instructions. | OMB No. 1545-0099 1999 |
|---|---|---|

For calendar year 1999 or tax year beginning , 1999, and ending ,

**Partner's identifying number ►**      **Partnership's identifying number ►**

| | (a) Distributive share item | | (b) Amount | (c) 1040 filers enter the amount in column (b) on: |
|---|---|---|---|---|
| **Income (Loss)** | 1 Ordinary income (loss) from trade or business activities . . . | 1 | | See page 6 of Partner's Instructions for Schedule K-1 (Form 1065). |
| | 2 Net income (loss) from rental real estate activities . . . . . | 2 | | |
| | 3 Net income (loss) from other rental activities . . . . . . . | 3 | | |
| | 4 Portfolio income (loss): | | | |
| | a Interest . . . . . . . . . . . . . . | 4a | | Sch. B, Part I, line 1 |
| | b Ordinary dividends . . . . . . . . . . | 4b | | Sch. B, Part II, line 5 |
| | c Royalties . . . . . . . . . . . . . | 4c | | Sch. E, Part I, line 4 |
| | d Net short-term capital gain (loss) . . . . . . | 4d | | Sch. D, line 5, col. (f) |
| | e Net long-term capital gain (loss): | | | |
| |   (1) 28% rate gain (loss) . . . . . . . . . | e(1) | | Sch. D, line 12, col. (g) |
| |   (2) Total for year . . . . . . . . . . . | e(2) | | Sch. D, line 12, col. (f) |
| | f Other portfolio income (loss) *(attach schedule)* . . . . . | 4f | | Enter on applicable line of your return. |
| | 5 Guaranteed payments to partner . . . . . . . . | 5 | | See page 6 of Partner's Instructions for Schedule K-1 (Form 1065). |
| | 6 Net section 1231 gain (loss) (other than due to casualty or theft) . | 6 | | |
| | 7 Other income (loss) *(attach schedule)* . . . . . . . . | 7 | | Enter on applicable line of your return. |
| **Deductions** | 8 Charitable contributions (see instructions) *(attach schedule)* . . | 8 | | Sch. A, line 15 or 16 |
| | 9 Section 179 expense deduction . . . . . . . . . . . | 9 | | See pages 7 and 8 of Partner's Instructions for Schedule K-1 (Form 1065). |
| | 10 Deductions related to portfolio income *(attach schedule)* . . . | 10 | | |
| | 11 Other deductions *(attach schedule)* . . . . . . . . . . | 11 | | |
| **Credits** | 12a Low-income housing credit: | | | |
| |   (1) From section 42(j)(5) partnerships for property placed in service before 1990 . . . . . . . | a(1) | | Form 8586, line 5 |
| |   (2) Other than on line 12a(1) for property placed in service before 1990 | a(2) | | |
| |   (3) From section 42(j)(5) partnerships for property placed in service after 1989 . . . . . . . | a(3) | | |
| |   (4) Other than on line 12a(3) for property placed in service after 1989 | a(4) | | |
| | b Qualified rehabilitation expenditures related to rental real estate activities . . . . . . . . . . . . . . . | 12b | | See page 8 of Partner's Instructions for Schedule K-1 (Form 1065). |
| | c Credits (other than credits shown on lines 12a and 12b) related to rental real estate activities. . . . . . . . . . . | 12c | | |
| | d Credits related to other rental activities . . . . . . . | 12d | | |
| | 13 Other credits . . . . . . . . . . . . . . . . | 13 | | |

For Paperwork Reduction Act Notice, see Instructions for Form 1065.     Cat. No. 11394R     Schedule K-1 (Form 1065) 1999

## ALLOCATION OF INCOME ITEMS AND THE RELATED BASIS COMPUTATION

The items of income cause an increase in the basis of the partner's interest, while the deductions and losses cause reductions. In no case may the basis of a partner's interest be less than zero. In allocating the items, income items are allocated first.

> **Example 4:** For 1999, KL partnership had ordinary income of $20,000, a long-term capital gain of $10,000 and tax-exempt interest of $4,000. K and L are still equal partners, and K's basis at the beginning of the year was $3,000. K's basis will increase by $17,000 (50% of the $20,000, $10,000 and $4,000) to $20,000. K will recognize $10,000 as ordinary income and $5,000 as a long-term capital gain. Her $2,000 share of the tax-exempt interest is not taxable, but does increase her tax basis.

## ALLOCATION OF LOSSES AND DEDUCTIONS AND THE RELATED BASIS COMPUTATION

Items of losses and deductions cause a decrease in the partner's basis. Non-deductible items decrease a partner's basis as well. Since a partner's basis cannot be reduced below zero, it may be necessary to pro-rate items of losses and deductions until sufficient basis exists. Note that in addition to basis limitations, a partner may be subject to at risk and passive loss limitations at the partner level. See Chapter 5 for a fuller discussion.

---

**Example 5:** Assume in Example 4 that K's share of the ordinary income was only $7,000 and there was no capital gain or exempt income. Assume her beginning basis was still $3,000 and that there was a charitable contribution of $9,000 and a Section 179 election of $6,000. Her basis is first increased by the ordinary income of $7,000 to $10,000. The most she can now reduce her basis by is $10,000. K must prorate the deductions and suspend the excess to future periods until she has sufficient basis. K's basis cannot be negative.

|  | Deductions | Ratio | Basis | Allowed | Deductions Suspended |
|---|---|---|---|---|---|
| Charitable contribution | 9,000 | 3/5 | $10,000 | $ 6,000 | $3,000 |
| Section 179 election | 6,000 | 2/5 | $10,000 | 4,000 | 2,000 |
|  | $15,000 |  |  | $ 10,000 | $5,000 |

---

## GUARANTEED PAYMENTS

Payments made between a partnership and a partner oftentimes represent withdrawals of the partner's capital. However, some payments represent a payment for services rendered by that partner (similar to salary expense), or for the use of that partner's capital (similar to interest expense). These payments are called guaranteed payments and represent a pre-distribution of partnership ordinary income.

---

**Example 6:** K and L have agreed to split the income and loss of the partnership in half. However, K works at the business each day, while L resides in Florida and does not work. The partnership has agreed to pay K $40,000 per year as a guaranteed payment for her work. During 1999, the partnership has gross income of $300,000 and business expenses of $210,000 before this guaranteed payment to K. This resulted in a profit of $90,000. There were no other items of income or deduction. In computing the allocation of income, the first $40,000 is allocated to K as a guaranteed payment. The balance of $50,000 is allocated based upon the profit and loss sharing ratio of 50%. Therefore, K reports $65,000 of ordinary income and L $25,000 of ordinary income.

| | |
|---|---|
| Ordinary income before guaranteed payment | $90,000 |
| Less: Guaranteed payment to K | 40,000 |
| Ordinary income to be allocated | $50,000 |
| K's share | $25,000 |
| | |
| Summary: | |
| K's share (40,000 + 25,000) | $65,000 |
| L's share | 25,000 |
| | $90,000 |

---

Should the partnership adopt a fiscal year-end, only those payments made for the fiscal year ended in the partner's tax year are included as ordinary income.

## LIABILITIES

When a partnership incurs liabilities, the individual partners share in the responsibility to pay these liabilities. Because the partners are at-risk, the tax code allows an increase in the basis of a partner's interest for their proportionate share of the debt. Should the liability be non-recourse, (which means the holder of the debt has no recourse against the partner), this generally does not increase their basis.

---

**Example 7:** During 1999, the CDE partnership is formed and each partner contributes $5,000. On December 31, 1999, the partnership borrows $12,000 for working capital purposes. The basis of the three equal partners, C, D and E, would be increased by their share ($4,000) of the recourse debt. Their ending basis, assuming no other transactions, would be $9,000 each.

**Example 8:** If in Example 7, the borrowing was to purchase land and the debt was non-recourse, there would be no increase in the basis of the partners.

---

### PARTNER WITHDRAWALS

During the course of the year, partners typically withdraw capital in anticipation of their earnings. Generally, these withdrawals do not represent income to the partner. A partner is taxed on his share of the partnership income, not on what is withdrawn. The withdrawals do, however, reduce the basis of the partner's interest. When computing the balance in a partner's account, withdrawals are subtracted out before losses and deductions are.

Should a partner withdraw more than the balance in the capital account, the excess will be treated as a capital gain.

## DEALINGS BETWEEN THE PARTNERS AND PARTNERSHIP

In general, transactions between a partner and the partnership are treated as if they were not related parties, and were conducted at an arm's length basis. However, when a partner owns, directly or indirectly, more than 50% of a partnership's capital, losses even at an arm's length are disallowed.

If a partner owns more than 50% of a partnership's capital, any gain from the sale of property between the partnership and partner must be recognized as ordinary income, unless the property is a capital asset to both the partnership and partner. Then the gain is capital.

## SALE OR EXCHANGE OF A PARTNERSHIP INTEREST

When a partner sells their partnership interest, the difference between the amount realized and the adjusted basis of the interest represents the gain or loss. The amount realized typically involves the receipt of cash and the release of any partnership liabilities that partner had assumed by being a partner. The adjusted basis involves updating the activity to the date of sale for all the items of income, deductions, withdrawals, liabilities, etc.

After the recognized gain is determined, the character of the gain must be determined. In general, the gain or loss from the sale of a partnership interest is capital, but if the underlying assets in the partnership are those assets which if sold produce ordinary income, then the gain from the sale of that part of the partner's interest must be classified as ordinary. These assets are referred to as "hot assets" or Section 751 assets. Briefly, the hot assets include unrealized receivables, inventory and depreciation recapture. Congress enacted this provision to insure that partners would not escape ordinary income taxation merely by selling off their interests in the partnership rather than the assets.

**Example 9:** The EFG Partnership has three equal partners and the following balance sheet on June 30, 1999.

|  | Basis | FMV |
|---|---|---|
| Cash | 10,000 | 10,000 |
| Accounts receivable | -0- | 6,000 |
| Inventory | 6,000 | 9,000 |
| Land | 5,000 | 14,000 |
|  | 21,000 | 39,000 |
|  |  |  |
| Liabilities | 3,000 | 3,000 |
| Capital: |  |  |
| Partner E | 8,000 | 12,000 |
| Partner F | 4,000 | 12,000 |
| Partner G | 6,000 | 12,000 |
|  | 21,000 | 39,000 |

Partner G sells his interest to H for $12,000 cash, plus H assumes G's share of the partnership liabilities.

**1. First determine the gain recognized by G.**

| | |
|---|---|
| Amount realized by G: | |
|     Cash received | $12,000 |
|     Release of debt  (1/3 of $3,000) | 1,000 |
| | 13,000 |
| Adjusted basis of G: | |
|     Capital tax basis | 6,000 |
|     Share of liabilities at 6/30/99 | 1,000 |
| | 7,000 |
| Recognized gain | $ 6,000 |

**2. Then determine the character of the gain:**

|  | Basis | FMV | Gain | G's 1/3 share | Character |
|---|---|---|---|---|---|
| Cash | 10,000 | 10,000 | -0- | -0- |  |
| Accounts receivable | -0- | 6,000 | 6,000 | 2,000 | Ordinary |
| Inventory | 6,000 | 9,000 | 3,000 | 1,000 | Ordinary |
| Land | 5,000 | 14,000 | 9,000 | 3,000 | Capital |
|  | 21,000 | 39,000 | 18,000 | 6,000 |  |

# DISTRIBUTIONS TO PARTNERS

## NON-LIQUIDATING DISTRIBUTIONS

As discussed under withdrawals, the general rule is that no gain is recognized on a cash withdrawal by a partner, unless the cash exceeds the adjusted basis of the partner's interest. A similar rule applies to distributions of property other than cash. When a partnership makes an "in-kind" distribution (property) to a partner, no gain or loss is recognized. However, if the partner receives a partnership distribution of property which had a precontribution gain within 5 years of being contributed, such gain will be recognized. For property contributed to a partnership *after June 8, 1997*, the period of time increases from 5 years to 7 years.

If the adjusted basis of the property (being distributed) in the hands of the partnership is **less than or equal to** the adjusted basis of the partner prior to the distribution, then the property retains its partnership basis and the partner's interest in the partnership is correspondingly reduced.

If the adjusted basis of the property (being distributed) in the hands of the partnership is **greater than** the adjusted basis of the partner prior to the distribution, then the property receives that partner's basis and the partners interest in the partnership is reduced to zero.

Remember to update the partner's basis to the time just prior to the distribution. This includes reducing it for any cash distributions made first.

---

**Example 10:** K has a basis of $16,000 in the KL partnership at the time a non-liquidating distribution is made to her. The property being distributed is $1,000 in cash and land with a basis of $12,000 and fair market value of $30,000. K's basis is first reduced by the $1,000 cash received, leaving her a basis of $15,000. Since she has sufficient basis remaining, the land retains the partnership basis of $12,000 and her basis in the partnership is reduced to $3,000.

| | |
|---|---|
| K's basis | $16,000 |
| Less: cash received | (1,000) |
| Basis available | 15,000 |
| Land's basis | 12,000 |
| Remaining basis | $ 3,000 |

---

**Example 11:** Same facts as in Example 10 except that K's basis is now $10,000. K's basis is first reduced by the $1,000 cash received, leaving her a basis of $9,000. Since she does not have sufficient basis remaining to absorb the partnership's basis in the land of $12,000, the land picks up her remaining basis of $9,000. The excess basis of $3,000 stays with the partnership which may make certain elections well beyond the scope of the CPA exam.

| | |
|---|---|
| K's basis | $10,000 |
| Less: cash received | (1,000) |
| Basis available | 9,000 |
| Land's basis limited | 9,000 |
| Remaining basis | $ 0 |

---

Note: There are also special rules pertaining to disproportionate (or non-pro-rata) distributions and the distribution of hot assets. These too, are generally beyond the scope of the exam.

## LIQUIDATING DISTRIBUTIONS

In a liquidating distribution, the partner's interest is being terminated. When the distribution is cash only, gain or loss will be recognized. The character of the gain or loss will be capital unless there are Section 751 assets.

If cash and property is distributed in a liquidating distribution, cash reduces the partner's basis first, then the property distributed takes a substituted basis equal to that partner's remaining basis. Assuming there is basis remaining after the reduction for the cash distribution, no gain or loss is recognized.

Should the property being allocated include Section 751 assets, the partner's basis should be allocated to those assets next. If the partner does not have sufficient basis remaining to allocate to the Section 751 assets, a capital loss is recognized for the shortfall. Any non-Section 751 assets would get no basis. However, if there is any remaining partner basis after Section 751 allocation, the remaining basis is allocated to the non-Section 751 assets and no gain or loss is recognized.

---

**Example 12:** On December 31, 1999, K, a 50% partner has an adjusted basis in the KL partnership of $10,000. The KL partnership's only assets are cash of $12,000 and land with a basis of $9,000 and fair market value of $12,000 and land. There are no partnership liabilities. K receives a liquidating cash distribution from the partnership of $12,000. K will recognize a capital gain of $2,000.

| | |
|---|---|
| Cash distribution | $12,000 |
| K's basis | 10,000 |
| Capital gain | $ 2,000 |

---

**Example 13:** Same facts as Example 12 except that K receives the land instead of the cash. No gain is recognized at the partnership level even though the fair value of the land is $12,000 and the basis is only $9,000. No gain is recognized by K even though she is receiving an asset worth $12,000 when her basis is only $10,000. The basis of the land in the hands of K is now a substituted $10,000.

---

**Example 14:** If the land in Example 13 was inventory (a Section 751 asset) instead, a capital loss of $1,000 is recognized by the partner for the difference between the adjusted basis of the inventory in the partnership and the remaining adjusted basis of the partner.

---

# TERMINATION OF A PARTNERSHIP

There are two events that signal the end of a partnership.

1. No part of any business, financial operation, or venture of the partnership continues to be carried on by any of its partners in a partnership,   OR
2. Within a 12-month period there is a sale or exchange of 50% or more of the total interest in partnership capital and profits.

At that time, the taxable year closes and a final return must be filed for that period.

# Chapter Seven -- Questions
# Partnerships

## FORMATION OF THE PARTNERSHIP

1. Eng contributed the following assets to a partnership in exchange for a 50% interest in the partnership's capital and profits:

| | |
|---|---|
| Cash | $50,000 |
| Equipment: | |
| Fair market value | 35,000 |
| Carrying amount (adjusted basis) | 25,000 |

The basis for Eng's interest in the partnership is
a. $37,500
b. $42,500
c. $75,000
d. $85,000

2. The following information pertains to property contributed by Gray on July 1, 1999, for a 40% interest in the capital and profits of Kag & Gray, a partnership:

As of June 30, 1999

| *Adjusted basis* | *Fair market value* |
|---|---|
| $24,000 | $30,000 |

After Gray's contribution, Kag & Gray's capital totaled $150,000. What amount of gain was reportable in Gray's 1999 return on the contribution of property to the partnership?
a. $0
b. $6,000
c. $30,000
d. $36,000

3. Lee inherited a partnership interest from Dale. The adjusted basis of Dale's partnership interest was $50,000, and its fair market value on the date of Dale's death (the estate valuation date) was $70,000. What was Lee's original basis for the partnership interest?
a. $70,000
b. $50,000
c. $20,000
d. $0

4. The holding period of a partnership interest acquired in exchange for a contributed capital asset begins on the date
a. The partner is admitted to the partnership.
b. The partner transfers the asset to the partnership.
c. The partner's holding period of the capital asset began.
d. The partner is first credited with the proportionate share of the partnership capital.

5. On January 2, 1999, Black acquired a 50% interest in New Partnership by contributing property with an adjusted basis of $7,000 and a fair market value of $9,000, subject to a mortgage of $3,000. What was Black's basis in New at January 2, 1999?
a. $3,500
b. $4,000
c. $5,500
d. $7,500

6. Strom acquired a 25 percent interest in Ace Partnership by contributing land having an adjusted basis of $16,000 and a fair market value of $50,000. The land was subject to a $24,000 mortgage, which was assumed by Ace. No other liabilities existed at the time of the contribution. What was Strom's basis in Ace?
a. $0.
b. $16,000.
c. $26,000.
d. $32,000.

7. On June 1, 1999, Kelly received a 10% interest in Rock Co., a partnership, for services contributed to the partnership. Rock's net assets at that date had a basis of $70,000 and a fair market value of $100,000. In Kelly's 1999 income tax return, what amount must Kelly include as income from transfer of partnership interest?
a. $7,000 ordinary income.
b. $7,000 capital gain.
c. $10,000 ordinary income.
d. $10,000 capital gain.

8. Barker acquired a 50% interest in Kode Partnership by contributing $20,000 cash and a building with an adjusted basis of $26,000 and a fair market value of $42,000. The building was subject to a $10,000 mortgage which was assumed by Kode. The other partners contributed cash only. The basis of Barker's interest in Kode is
a. $36,000
b. $41,000
c. $52,000
d. $62,000

9. At partnership inception, Black acquires a 50% interest in Decorators Partnership by contributing property with an adjusted basis of $250,000. Black recognizes a gain if

I. The fair market value of the contributed property exceeds its adjusted basis.

II. The property is encumbered by a mortgage with a balance of $100,000.

a. I only.
b. II only.
c. Both I and II.
d. Neither I nor II.

10. On January 4, 1999, Smith and White contributed $4,000 and $6,000 in cash, respectively, and formed the Macro General Partnership. The partnership agreement allocated profits and losses 40% to Smith and 60% to White. In 1999, Macro purchased property from an unrelated seller for $10,000 cash and a $40,000 mortgage note that was the general liability of the partnership. Macro's liability
a. Increases Smith's partnership basis by $16,000.
b. Increases Smith's partnership basis by $20,000.
c. Increases Smith's partnership basis by $24,000.
d. Has **no** effect on Smith's partnership basis.

11. Hart's adjusted basis in Best Partnership was $9,000 at the time he received the following nonliquidating distributions of partnership property:

| | |
|---|---|
| Cash | $ 5,000 |
| Land | |
|   Adjusted basis | 7,000 |
|   Fair market value | 10,000 |

What was the amount of Hart's basis in the land?
a. $0
b. $4,000
c. $7,000
d. $10,000

12. Ola Associates is a limited partnership engaged in real estate development. Hoff, a civil engineer, billed Ola $40,000 in 1999 for consulting services rendered. In full settlement of this invoice, Hoff accepted a $15,000 cash payment plus the following:

| | Fair market value | Carrying amount on Ola's books |
|---|---|---|
| 3% limited partnership interest in Ola | $10,000 | N/A |
| Surveying equipment | 7,000 | $3,000 |

What amount should Hoff, a cash-basis taxpayer, report in his 1999 return as income for the services rendered to Ola?
a. $15,000
b. $28,000
c. $32,000
d. $40,000

13. The holding period of property acquired by a partnership as a contribution to the contributing partner's capital account
a. Begins with the date of contribution to the partnership.
b. Includes the period during which the property was held by the contributing partner.
c. Is equal to the contributing partner's holding period prior to contribution to the partnership.
d. Depends on the character of the property transferred.

14. In 1999, Dave Burr acquired a 20% interest in a partnership by contributing a parcel of land. At the time of Burr's contribution, the land had a fair market value of $35,000, an adjusted basis to Burr of $8,000, and was subject to a mortgage of $12,000. Payment of the mortgage was assumed by the partnership. Burr's basis for his interest in the partnership is
a. $0
b. $5,600
c. $8,000
d. $23,000

15. When a partner's share of partnership liabilities increases, that partner's basis in the partnership
a. Increases by the partner's share of the increase.
b. Decreases by the partner's share of the increase.
c. Decreases, but **not** to less than zero.
d. Is **not** affected.

16. Alt Partnership, a cash basis calendar year entity, began business on October 1, 1999. Alt incurred and paid the following in 1999:

Legal fees to prepare the partnership
  agreement                               $12,000
Accounting fees to prepare the representations in offering materials      15,000

Alt elected to amortize costs. What was the maximum amount that Alt could deduct on the 1999 partnership return?
a. $0.
b. $600.
c. $3,000.
d. $6,750.

17. The method used to depreciate partnership property is an election made by
a. The partnership and must be the same method used by the "principal partner."
b. The partnership and may be any method approved by the IRS.
c. The "principal partner."
d. Each individual partner.

18. Under Section 444 of the Internal Revenue Code, certain partnerships can elect to use a tax year different from their required tax year. One of the conditions for eligibility to make a Section 444 election is that the partnership must
a. Be a limited partnership.
b. Be a member of a tiered structure.
c. Choose a tax year where the deferral period is **not** longer than three months.
d. Have less than 35 partners.

19. Which one of the following statements regarding a partnership's tax year is correct?
a. A partnership formed on July 1 is required to adopt a tax year ending on June 30.
b. A partnership may elect to have a tax year other than the generally required tax year if the deferral period for the tax year elected does **not** exceed three months.
c. A "valid business purpose" can **no** longer be claimed as a reason for adoption of a tax year other than the generally required tax year.
d. Within 30 days after a partnership has established a tax year, a form must be filed with the IRS as notification of the tax year adopted.

20. Without obtaining prior approval from the IRS, a newly formed partnership may adopt
a. A taxable year which is the same as that used by one or more of its partners owning an aggregate interest of more than 50% in profits and capital.
b. A calendar year, only if it comprises a 12-month period.
c. A January 31 year end if it is a retail enterprise, and all of its principal partners are on a calendar year.
d. Any taxable year that it deems advisable to select.

## DETERMINATION OF PARTNERSHIP INCOME AND PARTNER'S DISTRIBUTIVE SHARE

21. Dale's distributive share of income from the calendar-year partnership of Dale & Eck was $50,000 in 1999. On December 15, 1999, Dale, who is a cash-basis taxpayer, received a $27,000 distribution of the partnership's 1999 income, with the $23,000 balance paid to Dale in May 2000. In addition, Dale received a $10,000 interest-free loan from the partnership in 1999. This $10,000 is to be offset against Dale's share of 2000 partnership income. What total amount of partnership income is taxable to Dale in 1999?
a. $27,000
b. $37,000
c. $50,000
d. $60,000

22. The partnership of Felix and Oscar had the following items of income during the taxable year:

Income from operations               $156,000
Tax-exempt interest income           8,000
Dividends from foreign corporations    6,000
Net rental income                 12,000

What is the total ordinary income of the partnership?
a. $156,000.
b. $162,000.
c. $174,000.
d. $168,000.

23. On January 2, 1999, Arch and Bean contribute cash equally to form the JK Partnership. Arch and Bean share profits and losses in a ratio of 75% to 25%, respectively. For 1999, the partnership's ordinary income was $40,000. A distribution of $5,000 was made to Arch during 1999. What is Arch's share of taxable income for 1999?

a. $5,000
b. $10,000
c. $20,000
d. $30,000

24. In computing the ordinary income of a partnership, a deduction is allowed for

a. Contributions to recognized charities.
b. The first $100 of dividends received from qualifying domestic corporations.
c. Short-term capital losses.
d. Guaranteed payments to partners.

## BASIS OF PARTNER'S INTEREST AND SHARE OF LOSS

25. Gray is a 50% partner in Fabco Partnership. Gray's tax basis in Fabco on January 1, 1999, was $5,000. Fabco made no distributions to the partners during 1999, and recorded the following:

| | |
|---|---|
| Ordinary income | $20,000 |
| Tax exempt income | 8,000 |
| Portfolio income | 4,000 |

What is Gray's tax basis in Fabco on December 31, 1999?

a. $21,000
b. $16,000
c. $12,000
d. $10,000

26. The partnership of Martin & Clark sustained an ordinary loss of $84,000 in 1999. The partnership, as well as the two partners, are on a calendar-year basis. The partners share profits and losses equally. At December 31, 1999, Clark had an adjusted basis of $36,000 for his partnership interest, before consideration of the 1999 loss. On his individual income tax return for 1999, Clark should deduct an

a. Ordinary loss of $36,000.
b. Ordinary loss of $42,000.
c. Ordinary loss of $36,000 and a capital loss of $6,000.
d. Capital loss of $42,000.

27. A contributed $23,000 and B contributed $5,000 on January 1st of this current year, to form a partnership. Profits and losses are to be shared equally. Each withdrew $3,000 during the year. The partnership's operating loss this year is $7,000. B's share of the loss allowable to him this year is:

a. $500.
b. $7,000.
c. $2,000.
d. $3,500.

28. Beck and Nilo are equal partners in B&N Associates, a general partnership. B&N borrowed $10,000 from a bank on an unsecured note, thereby increasing each partner's share of partnership liabilities. As a result of this loan, the basis of each partner's interest in B&N was

a. Increased.
b. Decreased.
c. Unaffected.
d. Dependent on each partner's ability to meet the obligation if called upon to do so.

29. At the beginning of 1999, Paul owned a 25% interest in Associates partnership. During the year, a new partner was admitted and Paul's interest was reduced to 20%. The partnership liabilities at January 1, 1999, were $150,000, but decreased to $100,000 at December 31, 1999. Paul's and the other partners' capital accounts are in proportion to their respective interests. Disregarding any income, loss or drawings for the year, the basis of Paul's partnership interest at December 31, 1999, compared to the basis of his interest at January 1, 1999 was

a. Decreased by $37,500.
b. Increased by $20,000.
c. Decreased by $17,500.
d. Decreased by $5,000.

30. On January 1, 1999, John Pierce acquired a 10% interest in the Saratoga and Company partnership for a cash investment of $20,000. In 1999 the partnership reported an ordinary loss of $40,000 of which Pierce's distributive share was $4,000. On January 1, 1999, the partnership had no liabilities; however, during 1999 the partnership had the following transactions:

- A $50,000 loan from the Second National Bank due June 30, 2000.
- A $100,000 nonrecourse loan (secured by inventory) from the Union Finance Company due December 31, 2000.

Before allocation of the operating loss, what should be the tax basis of Pierce's partnership interest at December 31, 1999, for determining the amount of loss he can share in?

a. $16,000.
b. $25,000.
c. $21,000.
d. $31,000.

31. Lewis & Clark, partners, have a P & L ratio of 2:1. For the year the partnership return showed a net S.T.C.L. of $3,000 and a net L.T.C.G. of $15,000. Lewis also had a personal net S.T.C.L. of $2,000. What is the net capital gain that should be included in Lewis' taxable income on his return?

a. $3,000.
b. $3,500.
c. $6,000.
d. $10,000.

32. Clark and Lewis are partners who share profits and losses 60% and 40% respectively. The tax basis of each partner's interest in the partnership as of December 31, 1998, was as follows:

| | |
|---|---|
| Clark | $24,000 |
| Lewis | $18,000 |

During 1999 the partnership had ordinary income of $50,000 and a long-term capital loss of $10,000 from the sale of securities. There were no distributions to the partners during 1999. What is the amount of Lewis' tax basis as of December 31, 1999?

a. $33,000.
b. $34,000.
c. $38,000.
d. $42,000.

33. Which of the following limitations will apply in determining a partner's deduction for that partner's share of partnership losses?

| | At-risk | Passive loss |
|---|---|---|
| a. | Yes | No |
| b. | No | Yes |
| c. | Yes | Yes |
| d. | No | No |

## GUARANTEED PAYMENTS TO PARTNERS

34. White has a one-third interest in the profits and losses of Rapid Partnership. Rapid's ordinary income for the 1999 calendar year is $30,000, after a $3,000 deduction for a guaranteed payment made to White for services rendered. None of the $30,000 ordinary income was distributed to the partners. What is the total amount that White must include from Rapid as taxable income in his 1999 tax return?

a. $3,000.
b. $10,000.
c. $11,000.
d. $13,000.

35. Under the Internal Revenue Code sections pertaining to partnerships, guaranteed payments are payments to partners for

a. Payments of principal on secured notes honored at maturity.
b. Timely payments of periodic interest on bona fide loans that are **not** treated as partners' capital.
c. Services or the use of capital without regard to partnership income.
d. Sales of partners' assets to the partnership at guaranteed amounts regardless of market values.

36. Guaranteed payments made by a partnership to partners for services rendered to the partnership, that are deductible business expenses under the Internal Revenue Code, are

I. Deductible expenses on the U.S. Partnership Return of Income, Form 1065, in order to arrive at partnership income (loss).
II. Included on Schedules K-1 to be taxed as ordinary income to the partners.

a. I only.
b. II only.
c. Both I and II.
d. Neither I nor II.

37. A partnership owned by Joe Meeker and Taylor Corporation has a fiscal year ending March 31. Meeker files his tax return on a calendar-year basis. The partnership paid Meeker a guaranteed salary of $500 per month during the calendar year 1998 and $750 a month during the calendar year 1999. After deducting this salary, the partnership realized ordinary income of $40,000 for the year ended March 31, 1999, and $60,000 for the year ended March 31, 2000. Meeker's share of the profits is the salary paid to him plus 30% of the partnership profits after deducting this salary. For 1999 Meeker should report taxable income of:

a. $18,750.
b. $20,250.
c. $21,000.
d. $22,500.

38. Nash and Ford are partners in a calendar year partnership and share profits and losses equally. For the current year, the partnership had book income of $80,000 which included the following deductions:

Guaranteed salaries to partners:
| | |
|---|---|
| Nash | $35,000 |
| Ford | 25,000 |
| Contributions | 5,000 |

What amount should be reported as ordinary income on the partnership return?

a. $80,000.
b. $85,000.
c. $140,000.
d. $145,000.

39. A guaranteed payment by a partnership to a partner for services rendered, may include an agreement to pay

I. A salary of $5,000 monthly without regard to partnership income.
II. A 25 percent interest in partnership profits.

a. I only.
b. II only.
c. Both I and II.
d. Neither I nor II.

40. Evan, a 25% partner in Vista Partnership, received a $20,000 guaranteed payment in 1999 for deductible services rendered to the partnership. Guaranteed payments were not made to any other partner. Vista's 1999 partnership income consisted of:

| | |
|---|---|
| Net business income before guaranteed payments | $80,000 |
| Net long-term capital gains | 10,000 |

What amount of income should Evan report from Vista Partnership on her 1999 tax return?

a. $37,500
b. $27,500
c. $22,500
d. $20,000

41. Dunn and Shaw are partners who share profits and losses equally. In the computation of the partnership's 1999 book income of $100,000, guaranteed payments to partners totaling $60,000 and charitable contributions totaling $1,000 were treated as expenses. What amount should be reported as ordinary income on the partnership's 1999 return?

a. $100,000
b. $101,000
c. $160,000
d. $161,000

# PARTNER DEALING WITH OWN PARTNERSHIP

42. Debra Wallace and Joan Pedersen are equal partners in the capital and profits of Wallace & Pedersen, but are otherwise unrelated. On August 1 of this taxable year, Wallace sold 100 shares of Kiandra Mining Corporation stock to the partnership for its fair market value of $7,000. Wallace had bought the stock in 1975 at a cost of $10,000. What is Wallace's recognized loss on the sale of this stock?

a. $0.
b. $1,500 long-term capital loss.
c. $3,000 long-term capital loss.
d. $3,000 ordinary loss.

43. On December 1, 1999, Alan Younger, a member of a three-man equal partnership, bought securities from the partnership for $27,000, their market value. The securities were acquired by the partnership for $15,000 on July 1, 1999. By what amount will this transaction increase Younger's taxable income for 1999?

a. $0.
b. $1,600.
c. $4,000.
d. $12,000.

44. Edward owns a 70% interest in the capital and profits of the partnership of Edward and Moore. During 1999 Edward purchased a piece of surplus machinery from the partnership for $5,000. On the date of sale the machinery had an adjusted basis to the partnership of $8,000. For the year ended December 31, 1999, the partnership's net income was $50,000 after recording the loss on sale of machinery. Assuming that there were no other partnership items to be specially reported, what is Edward's distributive share of the partnership's ordinary income for 1999?
a. $35,000
b. $35,630
c. $36,470
d. $37,100

45. In March 1999, Lou Cole bought 100 shares of a listed stock for $10,000. In May 1999, Cole sold this stock for its fair market value of $16,000 to the partnership of Rook, Cole & Clive. Cole owned a one-third interest in this partnership. In Cole's 1999 tax return, what amount should be reported as short-term capital gain as a result of this transaction?
a. $6,000
b. $4,000
c. $2,000
d. $0

## SALE OF PARTNERSHIP INTEREST

46. Which of the following should be used in computing the basis of a partner's interest acquired from another partner?

| | Cash paid by transferee to transferor | Transferee's share of partnership liabilities |
|---|---|---|
| a. | No | Yes |
| b. | Yes | No |
| c. | No | No |
| d. | Yes | Yes |

47. On November 30, 1999, Diamond's adjusted basis for his one-third interest in the capital and profits of Peterson and Company was $95,000 ($80,000 capital account plus $15,000 share of partnership liabilities). On that date Diamond sold his partnership interest to Girard for $120,000 cash and the assumption of Diamond's share of the partnership liabilities. What amount and type of gain should Diamond recognize in 1999 from the sale of his partnership interest?

| | Amount | Type of gain |
|---|---|---|
| a. | $25,000 | Ordinary income |
| b. | $25,000 | Capital gain |
| c. | $40,000 | Ordinary income |
| d. | $40,000 | Capital gain |

**Items 48 and 49** are based on the following:

The personal service partnership of Allen, Baker & Carr had the following cash basis balance sheet at December 31, 1999:

Assets

| | Adjusted basis per books | Market value |
|---|---|---|
| Cash | $102,000 | $102,000 |
| Unrealized accounts receivable | -- | 420,000 |
| Totals | $102,000 | $522,000 |

Liability and Capital

| | | |
|---|---|---|
| Note payable | $ 60,000 | $ 60,000 |
| Capital accounts: | | |
| Allen | 14,000 | 154,000 |
| Baker | 14,000 | 154,000 |
| Carr | 14,000 | 154,000 |
| Totals | $102,000 | $522,000 |

Carr, an equal partner, sold his partnership interest to Dole, an outsider, for $154,000 cash on January 1, 2000. In addition, Dole assumed Carr's share of the partnership's liability.

48. What was the total amount realized by Carr on the sale of his partnership interest?
a. $174,000
b. $154,000
c. $140,000
d. $134,000

49. What amount of ordinary income should Carr report in his 2000 income tax return on the sale of his partnership interest?
a. $0
b. $20,000
c. $34,000
d. $140,000

50. On December 31, 1999, after receipt of his share of partnership income, Clark sold his interest in a limited partnership for $30,000 cash and relief of all liabilities. On that date, the adjusted basis of Clark's partnership interest was $40,000, consisting of his capital account of $15,000 and his share of the partnership liabilities of $25,000. The partnership has no unrealized receivables or inventory. What is Clark's gain or loss on the sale of his partnership interest?

a. Ordinary loss of $10,000.
b. Ordinary gain of $15,000.
c. Capital loss of $10,000.
d. Capital gain of $15,000.

# DISTRIBUTION OF PARTNERSHIP ASSETS

## NON-LIQUIDATING DISTRIBUTIONS

51. Day's adjusted basis in LMN Partnership interest is $50,000. During the year Day received a non-liquidating distribution of $25,000 cash plus land with an adjusted basis of $15,000 to LMN, and a fair market value of $20,000. How much is Day's basis in the land?

a. $10,000
b. $15,000
c. $20,000
d. $25,000

52. Fred Elk's adjusted basis of his partnership interest in Arias & Nido was $30,000. Elk received a current nonliquidating distribution of $12,000 cash, plus property with a fair market value of $26,000 and an adjusted basis to the partnership of $14,000. How much is Elk's basis for the distributed property?

a. $18,000.
b. $14,000.
c. $26,000.
d. $30,000.

53. Hart's adjusted basis of his interest in a partnership was $30,000. He received a nonliquidating distribution of $24,000 cash plus a parcel of land with a fair market value and partnership basis of $9,000. Hart's basis for the land is

a. $9,000
b. $6,000
c. $3,000
d. $0

54. Dean is a 25 percent partner in Target Partnership. Dean's tax basis in Target on January 1, 1999, was $20,000. At the end of 1999, Dean received a nonliquidating cash distribution of $8,000 from Target. Target's 1999 accounts recorded the following items:

| Municipal bond interest income | $12,000 |
| Ordinary income | 40,000 |

What was Dean's tax basis in Target on December 31, 1999?

a. $15,000.
b. $23,000.
c. $25,000.
d. $30,000.

55. Curry's adjusted basis in Vantage Partnership was $5,000 at the time he received a nonliquidating distribution of land. The land had an adjusted basis of $6,000 and a fair market value of $9,000 to Vantage. What was the amount of Curry's basis in the land?

a. $9,000.
b. $6,000.
c. $5,000.
d. $1,000.

56. Stone's basis in Ace Partnership was $70,000 at the time he received a nonliquidating distribution of partnership capital assets. These capital assets had an adjusted basis of $65,000 to Ace, and a fair market value of $83,000. Ace had no unrealized receivable, appreciated inventory, or properties which had been contributed by its partners. What was Stone's recognized gain or loss on the distribution?

a. $18,000 ordinary income.
b. $13,000 capital gain.
c. $5,000 capital loss.
d. $0.

Items 57 and 58 are based on the following:

The adjusted basis of Jody's partnership interest was $50,000 immediately before Jody received a current distribution of $20,000 cash and property with an adjusted basis to the partnership of $40,000 and a fair market value of $35,000.

57. What amount of taxable gain must Jody report as a result of this distribution?

a. $0.
b. $5,000.
c. $10,000.
d. $20,000.

58. What is Jody's basis in the distributed property?
a. $0.
b. $30,000.
c. $35,000.
d. $40,000.

_____

## LIQUIDATING DISTRIBUTIONS

59. The basis to a partner of property distributed "in kind" in complete liquidation of the partner's interest is the
a. Adjusted basis of the partner's interest increased by any cash distributed to the partner in the same transaction.
b. Adjusted basis of the partner's interest reduced by any cash distributed to the partner in the same transaction.
c. Adjusted basis of the property to the partnership.
d. Fair market value of the property.

60. In 1985, Lisa Bara acquired a one-third interest in Dee Associates, a partnership. In 1999, when Lisa's entire interest in the partnership was liquidated, Dee's assets consisted of the following: cash, $20,000; tangible property with a basis of $46,000 and a fair market value of $40,000. Dee had no liabilities. Lisa's adjusted basis for her one-third interest was $22,000. Lisa received cash of $20,000 in liquidation of her entire interest. What was Lisa's recognized loss in 1999 on the liquidation of her interest in Dee?
a. $0.
b. $2,000 short-term capital loss.
c. $2,000 long-term capital loss.
d. $2,000 ordinary loss.

61. At December 31, 1999, Max Curcio's adjusted basis in the partnership of Madura & Motta was $36,000. On December 31, 1999, Madura & Motta distributed cash of $6,000 and a parcel of land to Curcio in liquidation of Curcio's entire interest in the partnership. The land had an adjusted basis of $18,000 to the partnership and a fair market value of $42,000 at December 31, 1999. How much is Curcio's basis in the land?
a. $0
b. $12,000
c. $30,000
d. $36,000

62. The Choate, Hamm and Sloan partnership's balance sheet on a cash basis at Sept. 30 of the current year was as follows:

| Assets | Basis | F.M.V. |
|---|---|---|
| Cash | $12,000 | $ 12,000 |
| Accounts receivable | -0- | 48,000 |
| Land | 63,000 | 90,000 |
| | $75,000 | $150,000 |

| Equities | | |
|---|---|---|
| Notes payable | $30,000 | $ 30,000 |
| Choate, capital | 15,000 | 40,000 |
| Hamm, capital | 15,000 | 40,000 |
| Sloan, capital | 15,000 | 40,000 |
| | $75,000 | $150,000 |

If Choate withdraws under an agreement whereby he takes one-third of each of the three assets and assumes $10,000 of the notes payable, he should report:
a. $9,000 capital gain.
b. $9,000 ordinary gain.
c. $16,000 ordinary gain and $9,000 capital gain.
d. No gain or loss.

_____

**Items 63 and 64** are based on the following data:

Mike Reed, a partner in Post Co., received the following distribution from Post:

| | Post's basis | Fair market value |
|---|---|---|
| Cash | $11,000 | $11,000 |
| Land | 5,000 | 12,500 |

Before this distribution, Reed's basis in Post was $25,000.

63. If this distribution were nonliquidating, Reed's recognized gain or loss on the distribution would be
a. $11,000 gain.
b. $9,000 loss.
c. $1,500 loss.
d. $0.

64. If this distribution were in complete liquidation of Reed's interest in Post, Reed's basis for the land would be
a. $14,000
b. $12,500
c. $5,000
d. $1,500

_____

65. For tax purposes, a retiring partner who receives retirement payments ceases to be regarded as a partner
a. On the last day of the taxable year in which the partner retires.
b. On the last day of the particular month in which the partner retires.
c. The day on which the partner retires.
d. Only after the partner's entire interest in the partnership is liquidated.

66. On June 30, 1999, Berk retired from his partnership. At that time, his capital account was $50,000 and his share of the partnership's liabilities was $30,000. Berk's retirement payments consisted of being relieved of his share of the partnership liabilities and receipt of cash payments of $5,000 per month for 18 months, commencing July 1, 1999. Assuming Berk makes **no** election with regard to the recognition of gain from the retirement payments, he should report income therefrom of

|    | _1999_ | _2000_ |
|----|--------|--------|
| a. | $13,333 | $26,667 |
| b. | 20,000 | 20,000 |
| c. | 40,000 | -- |
| d. | -- | 40,000 |

## TERMINATION OF PARTNERSHIP

67. A partnership is terminated for tax purposes
a. Only when it has terminated under applicable local partnership law.
b. When at least 50% of the total interest in partnership capital and profits changes hands by sale or exchange within 12 consecutive months.
c. When the sale of partnership assets is made only to an outsider, and not to an existing partner.
d. When the partnership return of income (Form 1065) ceases to be filed by the partnership.

68. Cobb, Danver, and Evans each owned a one-third interest in the capital and profits of their calendar-year partnership. On September 18, 1999, Cobb and Danver sold their partnership interests to Frank, and immediately withdrew from all participation in the partnership. On March 15, 2000, Cobb and Danver received full payment from Frank for the sale of their partnership interests. For tax purposes, the partnership
a. Terminated on September 18, 1999.
b. Terminated on December 31, 1999.
c. Terminated on March 15, 2000.
d. Did **not** terminate.

69. David Beck and Walter Crocker were equal partners in the calendar-year partnership of Beck & Crocker. On July 1, 1999, Beck died. Beck's estate became the successor in interest and continued to share in Beck & Crocker's profits until Beck's entire partnership interest was liquidated on April 30, 2000. At what date was the partnership considered terminated for tax purposes?
a. April 30, 2000.
b. December 31, 1999.
c. July 31, 1999.
d. July 1, 1999.

70. On November 1, 1999, Kerry and Payne, each of whom was a 20% partner in the calendar-year partnership of Roe Co., sold their partnership interests to Reed who was a 60% partner. For tax purposes, the Roe Co. partnership
a. Was terminated as of November 1, 1999.
b. Was terminated as of December 31, 1999.
c. Continues in effect until a formal partnership dissolution notice is filed with the IRS.
d. Continues in effect until a formal partnership dissolution resolution is filed in the office of the county clerk where Roe Co. had been doing business.

71. On January 3, 1999, the partners' interests in the capital, profits, and losses of Able Partnership were:

|      | % of capital, profits and losses |
|------|----------------------------------|
| Dean | 25% |
| Poe  | 30% |
| Ritt | 45% |

On February 4, 1999, Poe sold her entire interest to an unrelated party. Dean sold his 25% interest in Able to another unrelated party on December 20, 1999. No other transactions took place in 1999. For tax purposes, which of the following statements is correct with respect to Able?
a. Able terminated as of February 4, 1999.
b. Able terminated as of December 20, 1999.
c. Able terminated as of December 31, 1999.
d. Able did **not** terminate.

72. Curry's sale of her partnership interest causes a partnership termination. The partnership's business and financial operations are continued by the other members. What is(are) the effect(s) of the termination?

I. There is a deemed distribution of assets to the remaining partners and the purchaser.

II. There is a hypothetical recontribution of assets to a new partnership.

a. I only.
b. II only.
c. Both I and II.
d. Neither I nor II.

## Released and Author Constructed Questions

*R96*

**Questions 73 and 74** are based on the following:

Jones and Curry formed Major Partnership as equal partners by contributing the assets below:

|  | Asset | Adjusted basis | Fair market value |
|---|---|---|---|
| Jones | Cash | $45,000 | $45,000 |
| Curry | Land | 30,000 | 57,000 |

The land was held by Curry as a capital asset, subject to a $12,000 mortgage, that was assumed by Major.

73. What was Curry's initial basis in the partnership interest?
a. $45,000
b. $30,000
c. $24,000
d. $18,000

74. What was Jones' initial basis in the partnership interest?
a. $51,000
b. $45,000
c. $39,000
d. $33,000

—————————

*R96*

75. Basic Partnership, a cash-basis calendar year entity, began business on February 1, 1999. Basic incurred and paid the following in 1999:

| | |
|---|---|
| Filing fees incident to the creation of the partnership | $3,600 |
| Accounting fees to prepare the representations in offering materials | 12,000 |

Basic elected to amortize costs. What was the maximum amount that Basic could deduct on the 1999 partnership return?
a. $11,000
b. $3,300
c. $2,860
d. $660

*R98*

76. On January 1, 1999, Kane was a 25% equal partner in Maze General Partnership, which had partnership liabilities of $300,000. On January 2, 1999, a new partner was admitted and Kane's interest was reduced to 20%. On April 1, 1999, Maze repaid a $100,000 general partnership loan. Ignoring any income, loss, or distributions for 1999, what was the **net** effect of the two transactions on Kane's tax basis in Maze partnership interest?
a. Has **no** effect.
b. Decrease of $20,000.
c. Increase of $15,000.
d. Decrease of $75,000.

*R97*

77. Under which of the following circumstances is a partnership that is **not** an electing large partnership considered terminated for income tax purposes?

I. Fifty-five percent of the total interest in partnership capital and profits is sold within a 12-month period.
II. The partnership's business and financial operations are discontinued.

a. I only.
b. II only.
c. Both I and II.
d. Neither I nor II.

# Chapter Seven -- Answers
# Partnerships

1. (c) $75,000. There is a carryover basis from the contributed property (cash of $50,000 and the adjusted basis of the equipment of $25,000). In general, no gain or loss is recognized in the case of a contribution of property in exchange for a partnership interest. Even though there is a realized gain of $10,000 on the equipment, no gain is recognized, and therefore, there is no additional increase in basis.

2. (a) $0. In general, no gain or loss is recognized in the case of a contribution of property in exchange for a partnership interest. Even though Gray is receiving an interest equal to $60,000 (40% of the $150,000), no gain is recognized.

3. (a) $70,000. The basis of property in the hands of a person acquiring it from a decedent is the fair market value of the property at the decedent's death, unless an alternative valuation date is elected.

4. (c) The holding period of the partner's interest in the partnership is the same as the holding period of the property contributed to the partnership. There is a carryover of both the basis and holding period.

5. (c) $5,500. A partner's basis of an interest in the partnership is the basis of the property transferred, less any liabilities assumed by the other partners. The basis of the property transferred by Black into the partnership was $7,000, less the liability of $1,500 (50% of the $3,000) assumed by the other partners. You may also compute it as:

| | |
|---|---|
| Basis of property transferred | 7,000 |
| Less: total liabilities assumed by partnership | (3,000) |
| | 4,000 |
| Plus: liability assumed by Black as 50% partner | 1,500 |
| Basis of partnership interest | 5,500 |

6. (a) $0. The basis of an interest in the partnership is the basis of the property transferred, less any liabilities assumed by the other partners. The basis of the land transferred by Strom into the partnership was $16,000, less the liability of $18,000 (75% of the $24,000) assumed by the other partners. This, however, would result in a negative basis of $2,000. Since a partner's basis cannot be negative, a $2,000 gain must be recognized by Strom, thus increasing his basis to zero.

7. (c) $10,000 ordinary income. When a partner renders services in exchange for a partnership interest, the partner must recognize ordinary income equal to the fair market value of the partnership interest received. This is computed as 10% of the $100,000.

8. (b) $41,000. A partner's basis of an interest in the partnership is the basis of the property transferred, less any liabilities assumed by the other partners. The basis of the property transferred by Barker into the partnership was $20,000 for the cash, $26,000 for the building, less the liability of $5,000 (50% of the $10,000) assumed by the other partners. You may also compute it as:

| | |
|---|---|
| Basis of property transferred: | |
| Cash | $ 20,000 |
| Building | 26,000 |
| | 46,000 |
| Less: Liabilities assumed by partnership | -10,000 |
| | 36,000 |
| Plus: Liability assumed by Barker (50%) | 5,000 |
| | $ 41,000 |

9. (d) In general, no gain or loss is recognized in the case of a contribution of property in exchange for a partnership interest. When the partnership assumes the liability on property contributed by a partner, no gain results when the liability is less than the adjusted basis of the property.

10. (a) $16,000. An increase in general liabilities to a partnership will increase each partner's basis by their share of the partnership account. Since Smith is a 40% partner, Smith's basis will be increased by 40% of $40,000, or $16,000.

11. (b) $4,000. In a non-liquidating distribution to a partner, any cash received is first used to reduce that partner's basis. Then, any in-kind property distributed by the partnership to the partner decreases that partner's basis by the adjusted basis of that property, but only to the extent of the partner's remaining basis. Hart's basis prior to the distribution was $9,000. After the $5,000 cash distribution, Hart's partnership basis was only $4,000. Even though the fair market value of the land in the partnership was $10,000 and the basis was $7,000, Hart's basis in the land will be limited to his remaining basis in the partnership, or $4,000. No gain or loss is recognized on this transaction. Hart's eventual sale of the property in the future will trigger the gain due to the low basis allocated at this time.

12. (c) $32,000. Hoff must recognize cash plus the fair market value of the other property received in this transaction. Whereas Hoff is a cash basis taxpayer, the difference between the invoice rendered of $40,000 and the $32,000, is not recognized as a bad debt since the $40,000 of income was never recognized originally.

13. (b) When a partner transfers in property to a partnership, the holding period of that property in the hands of the contributing partner transfers over to the partnership.

14. (a) $0. A partner's basis of an interest in the partnership is the basis of the property transferred, less any liabilities assumed by the other partners. Burr is a 20% partner, and as a result the other partners will be liable for $9,600 (80% of the $12,000 mortgage) of the debt being assumed. Since the $9,600 exceeds the basis of $8,000 in the property, Burr must recognize a $1,600 gain on this transfer. His basis in the partnership is as follows:

| | |
|---|---|
| Basis of land transferred | $ 8,000 |
| Plus: Gain recognized | 1,600 |
| | 9,600 |
| Less: Liabilities assumed by other partners | -9,600 |
| Ending basis | $     0 |

15. (a) Whereas partners are individually liable on their share of the partnership debt, an increase in the partnership liabilities results in a proportionate increase in their partnership basis.

16. (b) $600. Organization costs can be amortized over a period of not less than sixty months assuming a proper and timely election has been made. The organization costs of $12,000 divided by 60 months would provide for $200 per month of amortization. The amount for 1996 would be three months, or $600. The $15,000 for accounting fees would be charged to capital, and not amortized.

17. (b) This election is made by the partnership. There is no requirement to adopt the depreciation method used by the principal partner. See discussion on Aggregate vs. Entity Theory.

18. (c) Section 444 allows a deferral period for certain partnerships of up to three months.

19. (b) Because a partnership may easily defer income from one year to another merely by adopting a fiscal year end different from that of its partners, Congress and IRS have established a series of rules limiting the availability of certain year ends. Briefly the hierarchy for year-end selection is as follows:
1. The year-end of the majority of the partners.
2. The year-end of the principal partners.
3. The year-end resulting in the "least aggregate deferral" of income.

If the selection of the fiscal year-end using the rules above is not acceptable, the partnership may select a year-end under one of these three alternatives:
1. Establish that a business purpose exists, usually supported by cyclical income.
2. Establish a natural business tax year following the IRS procedures where gross receipts of 25% or more were recognized in a two month period for three consecutive years.
3. Select a tax year where **no more than three months** of partnership income is deferred from the required tax year.

In this problem, the only correct answer is the last alternative listed, selecting a tax year where no more than three months of partnership income is deferred.

20. (a) See answer #19 above for a full discussion regarding the selection of year-ends. This question is answered by the first criteria that states the partnership must choose the same year-end as the majority of the partners.

21. (c) $50,000. Dale must report his distributive share of income, regardless of whether the amount is distributed or not. The distributions generally serve to reduce the partner's basis and not cause the recognition of income, unless a cash distribution in excess of the partner's basis is made.

22. (a) $156,000. Partnership ordinary income from its business activity is determined by subtracting the non-separately stated business deductions from its non-separately stated income. In this problem, tax-exempt interest, dividends from foreign corporations and net rental income are all separately stated and not netted against ordinary income. Each of these three items are separately stated since they have a special effect on the partner on his individual return.

23. (d) $30,000. Arch's share of the ordinary income is 75% of the $40,000 partnership ordinary income. The distributions generally serve to reduce the partner's basis and not cause the recognition of income. The $5,000 cash distribution is not in excess of Arch's capital account.

24. (d) In determining the amount of ordinary income to allocate to the partners, guaranteed payments must first be subtracted and allocated to that partner. The other three items listed in the question represent items which must be separately stated.

25. (a) $21,000. Gray's tax basis starts with his beginning basis and includes his proportionate share of the following items of income. Note that a partner's tax basis is affected by items which are non-taxable as well as taxable.

| | | |
|---|---|---|
| Gray's opening tax basis | | $5,000 |
| Fabco Partnership 1999 income: | | |
|     Ordinary income | $20,000 | |
|     Tax exempt income | 8,000 | |
|     Portfolio income | 4,000 | |
|       Total partnership income | 32,000 | |
| Gray's 50% share of the partnership income | | 16,000 |
| | | |
| Gray's tax basis on December 31, 1999 | | $21,000 |

26. (a) $36,000 ordinary loss. A partner can deduct losses only to the extent of his basis in his partnership interest at the end of the year. Any additional losses (in this case $6,000) are suspended at the partner level until there is sufficient basis, oftentimes obtained through additional capital contributions, loans, or partnership income.

27. (c) $2,000. A partner can deduct losses only to the extent of his basis in his partnership interest at the end of the year. The partner's basis is first reduced by any withdrawals during the year before the determination of any losses. Any additional losses (in this case $1,500) are suspended until the partner has sufficient basis.

28. (a) Increased. A partner's basis in his partnership interest is increased by his share of the partnership liabilities.

29. (c) $17,500 decrease. A partner's basis in his partnership interest is increased or decreased by his share of the partnership liabilities at the end of the year. By analyzing the change in liabilities and the partner's percentage of interest from the beginning to the end of the year, the decrease in basis of $17,500 can be seen below.

|  | Jan 1, 1999 | Dec. 31, 1999 |
|---|---|---|
| Partnership liabilities | $150,000 | $100,000 |
| Paul's partnership interest | 25% | 20% |
| Paul's interest through liabilities | $ 37,500 | $ 20,000 |

30. (b) $25,000. A partner can deduct losses only to the extent of his basis in his partnership interest at the end of the year. A partner's basis in his partnership interest is increased by his share of the partnership liabilities at the end of the year. In computing Pierce's basis through liabilities, non-recourse debt is not included. Therefore, his basis is equal to his initial basis of $20,000, plus his 10% proportionate share of the liability of $50,000, or another $5,000.

31. (c) $6,000. This problem integrates the flow-through nature of partnership activity with that of the individual partner. The partner's 2/3 share of the net STCL of $3,000 and the 2/3 share of the net LTCG of $15,000 are combined with Lewis' personal net STCL of $2,000.

|  |  | Lewis' |
|---|---|---|
| Partnership level: | Total | 2/3 share |
| STCL | $ 3,000 | $(2,000) |
| LTCG | 15,000 | 10,000 |
|  |  |  |
| Individual level: |  |  |
| STCL 100% |  | (2,000) |
|  |  |  |
| Lewis' net capital gain reported as taxable income |  | $6,000 |

32. (b) $34,000. The partner's ending basis is the beginning basis, plus his proportionate share of the ordinary income less his share of the capital loss. In computing Lewis' basis, there is no $3,000 limitation on capital losses.

| Lewis' opening tax basis | $18,000 |
|---|---|
| Add: 40% share of partnership ordinary income | 20,000 |
| Less: 40% share of partnership capital loss | ( 4,000) |
| Lewis' tax basis on December 31, 1999 | $34,000 |

33. (c) In determining the deductibility of a partners losses, there is a limitation to the amount of the loss to which the partner is a risk for. In addition, the partner is also subject to the passive loss restrictions. These limitations are determined at the partner level and not the partnership level.

34. (d) $13,000. In determining the amount of ordinary income to allocate to the partners, guaranteed payments must first be subtracted and allocated to that partner. The balance is then allocated according to the agreement. Any distributions or withdrawals generally have no impact on the amount of taxable income recognized by the partner.

| | |
|---|---|
| Ordinary income before guaranteed payment | $33,000 |
| Less: Guaranteed payment to White | (3,000) |
| Ordinary income to be allocated | 30,000 |
| White's share (1/3) | $10,000 |

| Total recognized by White: | |
|---|---|
| Guaranteed payment | $ 3,000 |
| Share of ordinary income | 10,000 |
| Total taxable income | $13,000 |

35. (c) By definition.

36. (c) By definition. There is a separate line on page one of the partnership's Form 1065 for this deduction. Guaranteed payments must be reported as ordinary income on the partner's Form K-1. Note the examiner's questioning as to the form that an item is reported on.

37. (a) $18,750. Partners report their share of the partnership income in the year that the partnership ends its fiscal year. For 1999, Meeker would report his share of the ordinary income for the fiscal year ended March 31, 1999. In addition, Meeker would report only the guaranteed payments for the fiscal year ended March 31, 1999, even though he received some in 1998. Meeker would not report any of the guaranteed payments for the fiscal 1999 year even though nine payments were actually received in 1999.

| | |
|---|---|
| Partnership income, March 31, 1999 | |
| $40,000 @ 30% (Meeker's share) | $12,000 |
| Guaranteed payments: | |
| 4/1/98 through 12/31/98 | |
| 9 months @ $500 | 4,500 |
| 1/1/99 through 3/31/99 | |
| 3 months @ $750 | 2,250 |
| Total share of taxable income | 18,750 |

38. (b) $85,000. Book income should include the deductions for guaranteed payments and contributions. However, for the computation of ordinary income, only guaranteed payments are allowed. The contributions represent a separately stated item and are not deductible in computing ordinary income.

| | |
|---|---|
| Income per books | $ 80,000 |
| Add back contributions | 5,000 |
| Ordinary income | 85,000 |

39. (a) A payment for service rendered by a partner without regard to their interest in partnership profits is treated as a guaranteed payment.

40. (a) $37,500. In determining the amount of ordinary income to allocate to the partners, guaranteed payments must first be subtracted and allocated to that partner. The balance is then allocated according to the agreement. Any distributions or withdrawals generally have no impact on the amount of taxable income recognized by the partner.

| | |
|---|---|
| Ordinary income before guaranteed payment | $80,000 |
| Less: Guaranteed payment to Evan | (20,000) |
| Ordinary income to be allocated | 60,000 |
| Evan's 25% of ordinary income | $15,000 |

| Total recognized by Evan: | |
|---|---|
| Guaranteed payment | $20,000 |
| Share of ordinary income (above) | 15,000 |
| Share of long-term capital gain (25%) | 2,500 |
| Total taxable income | $37,500 |

41. (b) $101,000. In determining the amount of ordinary income to allocate to the partners, guaranteed payments must first be subtracted and allocated to that partner. The balance is then allocated according to the agreement. In this problem, the guaranteed payments and charitable contributions have already been subtracted out in coming up with the $100,000. The charitable contributions of $1,000 are not allowed as a deduction in determining the ordinary income, and accordingly, must be added back. Therefore, the answer is:

| | |
|---|---|
| Partnership book income | $ 100,000 |
| Add: Charitable contributions | 1,000 |
| Ordinary income | $ 101,000 |

42. (c) $3,000 long-term capital loss. Since the stock was sold at its fair market value and the partner's ownership interest was not in excess of 50%, the transaction is treated as if it were with an unrelated party. Therefore, the $3,000 loss (Selling price of $7,000 less the cost of $10,000) is recognized.

43. (c) $4,000. The gain of $12,000 on the sale of securities (selling price of $27,000 less the cost basis of $15,000) must be recognized by the partnership. Younger must recognize his proportionate share of the gain, which is one third of the $12,000 or $4,000.

44. (d) $37,100. When a partner owns a partnership interest of more than 50%, any losses are disallowed. Since the loss of $3,000 was deducted in coming up with the partnerships "net income", it must be added back before determining Edward's 70% share of the income.

| | |
|---|---|
| "Net income" after the loss | $50,000 |
| Add back disallowed loss | 3,000 |
| Ordinary income to allocate | 53,000 |
| Edward's percentage share | 70% |
| Edward's share of ordinary income | $37,100 |

45. (a) $6,000. In general, transactions between a partner and the partnership are treated as if they were not related parties, and were conducted at an arm's length basis. However, when a partner owns, directly or indirectly, more than 50% of a partnership's capital, losses even at an arm's length are disallowed. In this transaction, Cole has a **gain** which is fully recognized because it is a **sale**, not a transfer. Cole's holding period for the stock is short-term. The gain is determined as follows:

| | |
|---|---|
| Selling price of stock to partnership | $ 16,000 |
| Cole's adjusted basis | 10,000 |
| Short-term capital gain | $ 6,000 |

46. (d) In acquiring a partner's interest, both the amount paid by the new partner and any liabilities assumed by the new partner are to be used in the determination of that partner's basis. In addition, the amounts received by the selling partner, and the release of any liabilities are used in the determination of the overall selling price by that partner.

47. (d) $40,000 capital gain. The sale of a partnership interest results in capital gain unless there are any "hot assets" (assets that cause the recognition of ordinary income such as unrealized receivables, inventory or depreciation recapture). There is no mention of these in the problem. Determination of the amount realized and the adjusted basis does include the assumption of liabilities as illustrated below.

| | |
|---|---:|
| Selling price: | |
| Cash | $ 120,000 |
| Liabilities assumed | 15,000 |
| Amount realized | 135,000 |
| | |
| Partner's adjusted basis | |
| Capital interest | 80,000 |
| Share of liabilities | 15,000 |
| Adjusted basis | 95,000 |
| Capital gain | $ 40,000 |

48. (a) $174,000. The amount realized from the sale equals the amount of cash received ($154,000) plus Carr's share of the liabilities (1/3 of $60,000) assumed by Dole.

49. (d) $140,000. The sale of a partnership interest results in capital gain unless there are any "hot assets" (assets that cause the recognition of ordinary income such as unrealized receivables, inventory or depreciation recapture). In this problem, there are unrealized receivables (tax basis zero, but fair market value of $420,000). Carr has no basis in the unrealized receivables. These Section 751 assets will cause Carr to recognize ordinary income to the extent of his proportionate interest in the receivables. In allocating the gain between ordinary and capital, the sales proceeds are first allocated to the Section 751 assets.

| | | Allocation of Gain | |
|---|---:|---:|---:|
| | _Total_ | _Ordinary_ | _Capital_ |
| Amount realized (from above) | $174,000 | $140,000 | $34,000 |
| Carr's adjusted basis | 34,000 | -0- | 34,000 |
| Gain to be recognized | $140,000 | $140,000 | $ -0- |

50. (d) Capital gain of $15,000. The sale of a partnership interest results in capital gain unless there are any "hot assets." The problem states that the partnership has no unrealized receivables or inventory. Determination of the amount realized and the adjusted basis does include the assumption of liabilities as illustrated.

| | |
|---|---:|
| Selling price: | |
| Cash | $ 30,000 |
| Liabilities assumed | 25,000 |
| Amount realized | 55,000 |
| | |
| Partner's adjusted basis | |
| Capital interest | 15,000 |
| Share of liabilities | 25,000 |
| Adjusted basis | 40,000 |
| Capital gain | $ 15,000 |

51. (b) $15,000. In a non-liquidating distribution to a partner, any cash received is first used to reduce that partner's basis. Then, any in-kind property distributed by the partnership to the partner decreases that partner's basis by the adjusted basis of that property, but only to the extent of the partner's remaining basis. Prior to the distribution, Day's basis was $50,000. After the $25,000 cash distribution, Day still had a $25,000 basis in his partnership interest. The land received by Day would have the same basis of $15,000 that it had in the partnership because Day had sufficient basis to allocate to the land.

52. (b) $14,000. In a non-liquidating distribution to a partner, any cash received is first used to reduce that partner's basis. Then, any in-kind property distributed by the partnership to the partner decreases that partner's basis by the adjusted basis of that property, but only to the extent of the partner's remaining basis. Elk's basis prior to the distribution was $30,000. After the $12,000 cash distribution, Elk still had an $18,000 basis in his partnership interest. The property received by Elk would have the same basis of $14,000 that it had in the partnership because Elk had sufficient basis in the partnership to allocate to the property.

53. (b) $6,000. In a non-liquidating distribution to a partner, any cash received is first used to reduce that partner's basis. Then, any in-kind property distributed by the partnership to the partner decreases that partner's basis by the adjusted basis of that property, but only to the extent of the partner's remaining basis. Hart's basis prior to the distribution was $30,000. After the $24,000 cash distribution, Hart's partnership basis was only $6,000. Even though the basis and fair market value of the land in the partnership was $9,000, Hart's basis in the land will be limited to his remaining basis in the partnership, or $6,000. No gain or loss is recognized on this transaction. Hart's eventual sale of the property in the future will trigger the gain due to the low basis allocated at this time.

54. (c) $25,000. First, Dean's tax basis must be updated for activity incurred during 1999. His basis begins at $20,000 and is increased by $13,000 for his 25% share of the interest and ordinary income. Then, Dean's basis is reduced by the non-liquidating cash distribution, leaving a December 31, 1999 basis of $25,000.

| | | |
|---|---|---|
| Dean's tax basis, January 1, 1999 | | $ 20,000 |
| Partnership activity: | | |
|   Municipal bond interest | $12,000 | |
|   Ordinary income | 40,000 | |
| | 52,000 | |
| Dean's 25% share of $52,000 | | 13,000 |
| Tax basis before non-liquidating distribution | | 33,000 |
| Non-liquidating cash distribution | | ( 8,000) |
| Dean's tax basis, December 31, 1999 | | 25,000 |

55. (c) $5,000. In a non-liquidating distribution to a partner involving only in-kind property, the adjusted basis of the property distributed by the partnership to the partner decreases that partner's basis by the adjusted basis of that property, but only to the extent of the partner's remaining basis. Curry's basis prior to the distribution was $5,000. Even though the adjusted basis of the land was $6,000 and the fair market value of the land was $9,000, Curry's basis in the land will be limited to his remaining basis in the partnership, or $5,000. No gain or loss is recognized on this transaction.

56. (d) $0. The general rule is that no gain or loss is recognized on a **non-liquidating** distribution, unless cash is being distributed in excess of basis. In a non-liquidating distribution to a partner, any cash received is first used to reduce that partner's basis. Then, any in-kind property distributed by the partnership to the partner decreases that partner's basis by the adjusted basis of that property, but only to the extent of the partner's remaining basis. Prior to the distribution, Stone's basis was $70,000. There was no cash distributed. The capital assets received by Stone would have the same basis of $65,000 that they had in the partnership because Stone had sufficient basis ($70,000) to allocate to the capital assets. No gain or loss is recognized.

57. (a) $0. The general rule is that no gain or loss is recognized on a **non-liquidating** distribution, unless cash is being distributed in excess of basis. In this problem, Jody's basis was $50,000 immediately before the distribution. Whereas the cash distributed of $20,000 was less than her basis, no gain is recognized.

58. (b) $30,000. In a non-liquidating distribution to a partner, any cash received is first used to reduce that partner's basis. Then, any in-kind property distributed by the partnership to the partner decreases that partner's basis by the adjusted basis of that property, but only to the extent of the partner's remaining basis. Jody's basis prior to the distribution was $50,000 as just described. After the $20,000 cash distribution, Jody's partnership basis was $30,000. Even though the basis and fair market value of the property in the partnership was $40,000 and $35,000 respectively, Jody's basis in the property will be limited to her remaining basis in the partnership of $30,000. No gain or loss is recognized on this transaction. Jody's eventual sale of the property in the future will trigger the gain due to the low basis allocated at this time.

59. (b) In a complete liquidation of a partner's interest, the remaining adjusted basis of a partner's interest after a reduction for any cash received, is the adjusted basis of the in-kind property received.

60. (c) $2,000 long-term capital loss. Lisa received a liquidating cash distribution of $20,000 in exchange for her partnership interest. At the time of the distribution, Lisa's adjusted basis of her 1/3 interest was $22,000. Since she held her interest longer that one year, she recognizes a $2,000 long-term capital loss.

61. (c) $30,000. In a complete liquidation of a partner's interest, the remaining adjusted basis of a partner's interest after a reduction for any cash received, is the adjusted basis of the in-kind property received. Curcio's basis before the liquidating distribution was $36,000. The cash distribution reduces his remaining basis to $30,000 which is allocated to the land.

62. (d) No gain or loss. In a complete liquidation, no gain is recognized by the partner unless the partner receives cash in excess of his basis (1/3 of the cash is $4,000 which is less than his basis), or there is a disproportionate distribution of Section 751 property (Choate took 1/3, or a pro-rata share of each of the three assets).

63. (d) $0. The general rule is that no gain or loss is recognized on a **non-liquidating** distribution, unless cash is being distributed in excess of basis. In this problem, Reed's basis was $25,000 immediately before the distribution. Whereas the cash distributed of $11,000 was less than his basis, no gain is recognized on that part of the transaction. Then, any in-kind property distributed by the partnership to the partner decreases that partner's basis by the adjusted basis of that property, but only to the extent of the partner's remaining basis. Reed's basis after the $11,000 cash distribution was $14,000. The land would receive the same basis as it was in the partnership ($5,000). No gain or loss is recognized on this entire transaction.

64. (a) $14,000. In a **complete liquidation**, no gain is recognized by the partner unless the partner receives cash in excess of his basis or there is a disproportionate distribution of Section 751 property. For the purpose of determining basis, the hierarchy is first, his basis is reduced by any cash received, then any Section 751 assets. His remaining basis is allocated to the other property received.

| | |
|---|---|
| Reed's basis | $ 25,000 |
| Less: cash received | -11,000 |
| Remaining basis allocated to land | $ 14,000 |

65. (d) A retiring partner ceases to be a partner only after his entire interest in the partnership has been liquidated.

66. (d) 2000 - $40,000. Berk has two different transactions which need to be addressed in the determination of the income. He receives $30,000 in retirement payments in 1999 and $60,000 in 2000. In addition he is relieved of partnership debt of $30,000. In total, Berk receives $120,000 between the cash payments and release of debt. At the time of the agreement, Berk's basis is $80,000, which is comprised of his capital account and his share of the liabilities. The question is when is the $40,000 ($120,000 amount realized less adjusted basis of $80,000) recognized. The release of debt in 1999 reduces his basis from $80,000 to $50,000. The next six payments of $5,000 each received in 1999 reduce Berk's basis to $20,000. In 2000, Berk receives $60,000 in payments when his basis is only $20,000. The excess payments of $40,000 over his basis represent the income to be reported in 2000.

67. (b) By definition.

68. (a)  On September 18, 1999, at least 50% of the total interest in the partnership's capital and profits changed. This terminates the partnership.  In addition, Frank is no longer conducting the business as a partnership.

69. (a)  April 30, 2000.  Even though Beck owned at least 50% of the partnership, the death of a partner generally does not terminate the partnership.  Since the estate of Beck became the successor partner, the partnership exists until the deceased partner's interest is liquidated.

70. (a)  November 1, 1999.  On this date, Reed owned the entire interest in the entity, and it was no longer a partnership.

71. (b)  December 20, 1999. On December 20, 1999, at least 50% of the total interest in the partnership's capital and profits changed.  This terminates the partnership.

72. (c)  When a termination occurs, there is a deemed distribution of assets to the remaining partners and the purchaser as well as a hypothetical recontribution of assets to a new partnership.

73. (c)  $24,000. A partner's basis of an interest in the partnership is the basis of the property transferred, less any liabilities assumed by the other partners.  The basis is determined as follows:

| | |
|---|---|
| Basis of property transferred | $ 30,000 |
| Less: total liabilities assumed | -12,000 |
| | 18,000 |
| Plus: liabilities assumed | 6,000 |
| Basis of partnership interest | $ 24,000 |

74. (a) $51,000. A partner's basis of an interest in the partnership is the basis of the property transferred, plus any liabilities assumed.  As a 50% partner, Jones assumes 50% of the mortgage transferred by Jones. The basis is determined as follows:

| | |
|---|---|
| Basis of property transferred | $ 45,000 |
| Plus: liabilities assumed | 6,000 |
| Basis of partnership interest | $ 51,000 |

75. (d) $660.  Organization costs can be amortized over a period of not less than sixty months assuming a proper and timely election has been made.  In this problem, the organization costs of $3,600 divided by 60 months would provide a deduction of $60 per month.  Since there were 11 months remaining until the end of the year, the maximum expense would be $660.  The accounting fees for the offering materials are charged to the capital account and are neither deductible or amortizable.

76. (b)  Decrease of $20,000. Kanes's basis is determined by reference to his percentage interest in the partnership liabilities.  During the year, there was a decrease in the liabilities of $100,000.  Since Kane's interest in the partnership was reduced to 20%, his basis decreased by 20% of the $100,000 decrease, or $20,000.

77. (c)  By definition, either of these events could terminate a partnership.

# Chapter Eight
# C Corporations

# Chapter Eight
# C Corporations

## NATURE AND CHARACTERISTICS

### GENERAL

A corporation is a separate taxpaying entity. Shareholders contribute assets or services in exchange for stock which represents the ownership of the corporation. A corporation has its own rate structure, files its own return, and makes its own elections apart from its shareholders.

An organization is treated as a corporation if it possess more characteristics of a corporation than a partnership. Regardless of how the entity is registered or incorporated by the state, if the organization acts more like a corporation than a partnership, the IRS will treat it like a corporation. The six characteristics to consider which are cited in the regulations are:

- Associates
- To carry on a trade or business and divide the profits
- Continuity of life
- Centralization of management
- Limited liability
- Free transferability of interests

For example, in contrasting a partnership with a corporation, a partnership generally has associates, carries on a trade or business and has centralized management. But a corporation usually has continuity of life, limited liability and free transferability of interest as well.

### ORGANIZATION COSTS AND STOCK ISSUANCE COSTS
Costs incurred related to the creation of the corporation, such as accounting and legal fees, are not deductible, but are instead capitalized. If the corporation files a proper election by the due date of the return, including extensions, this amount may be amortized on a straight-line basis over a period of not less than 60 months. Cost associated with the issuance of stock and securities are neither deductible or amortizable. These fees are usually the marketing, registration and underwriting fees associated with selling corporation stock.

### ALLOWABLE TAX YEARS
A corporation generally has no restrictions on the selection of a year end. There are special rules for Personal Service Corporations and S Corporations, and those are addressed in the next chapter.

### FILING REQUIREMENTS
A corporation is required to file Form 1120 each year. The return is due by the 15th day of the 3rd month following the end of the taxable year. For a calendar year corporation the due date is March 15th. A corporation may request a six month extension by timely filing Form 7004. An S Corporation, covered later in Chapter 9, is required to file Form 1120S. *Pages 1 and 4 of Form 1120 appear at the end of this chapter.*

# FORMATION - CONTRIBUTIONS OF PROPERTY

## GENERAL RULE FOR CONTRIBUTIONS OF PROPERTY

When a taxpayer transfers property to a corporation solely in exchange for stock, the general rule under Section 351 is that no gain or loss is recognized, provided that the shareholder(s) is in control after the transfer. Control is defined as owning at least 80% of the corporation. There is a carryover of basis to the corporation of the property transferred by the shareholder as well as a carryover of basis to the shareholder's stock in the corporation. The carryover also pertains to the holding period of the property contributed. The logic behind this non-taxable transfer is that only the form of ownership of the property transferred has changed.

> **Example 1:** On January 1, 1999, K contributes land with a fair market value of $40,000 and an adjusted basis of $15,000 to KL Corporation, in exchange for 50% of the stock worth $40,000. K purchased the land in 1980 for the $15,000. L contributes cash of $40,000 on the same day. No gain or loss is recognized by either the corporation, or to the shareholders on the exchange. K's tax basis in the corporation is $15,000. The corporation's basis in the land is $15,000 even though the fair market value is $40,000. K's holding period for her stock is long-term (since 1980) and the corporation's holding period for the land is also long-term. L's tax basis is $40,000. Her holding period begins January 1, 1999.

## CONTRIBUTIONS OF PROPERTY WHEN BOOT IS RECEIVED

When a shareholder transfers property to a corporation in exchange for stock and other property, the other property constitutes boot and may cause the recognition of gain.

> **Example 2:** Assume that in Example 1 the land contributed by K had a fair market value of $45,000, and that the corporation paid K $5,000 in order that her net contribution was worth $40,000. The $5,000 cash is considered to be boot and will cause the recognition of income.
>
> | Amount realized: | |
> |---|---:|
> | FMV of stock received | $ 40,000 |
> | Cash (boot) | 5,000 |
> | Total amount realized | 45,000 |
> | Less: Adjusted basis | -15,000 |
> | Realized gain | $ 30,000 |
> | Recognized gain | $ 5,000 |
>
> K's basis is still the $15,000, which is her initial basis in the land of $15,000, plus the gain recognized of $5,000 for a total of $20,000. The cash received gets a basis of $5,000, leaving $15,000 as her interest in the corporation.

## CONTRIBUTIONS OF PROPERTY WHEN LIABILITIES ARE ASSUMED BY THE CORPORATION

When a shareholder transfers property to a corporation that is subject to liabilities which the corporation assumes, the general rule is that no gain or loss is recognized. The amount of liabilities assumed by the corporation as a result of the transfer reduces the tax basis of the contributing shareholder. However, if the assumption of the liabilities is greater than the contributing shareholder's basis in the property, then the excess over the basis is considered boot and will result in a gain to the shareholder.

> **Example 3:** Assume that in Example 1 the land contributed by K was subject to a mortgage of $10,000, and that the corporation assumed the mortgage. Since the mortgage is less than the adjusted basis of the land, it is not treated as boot. No gain or loss is recognized by either the corporation or K on the transfer. Her tax basis in the corporation is now $5,000. That is comprised of her basis in the land of $15,000 less the $10,000 mortgage assumed by the corporation. The basis of the land in the corporation is still $15,000.
>
> **Example 4:** Assume the same facts as in Example 3, except that the mortgage being assumed by the corporation is $20,000. K must recognize a gain of $5,000 because the liability assumed is greater than the adjusted basis in the land. K's tax basis in the corporation is now zero and is determined as follows. Her basis in the land was $15,000, it is increased by the gain recognized of $5,000 and then decreased by the mortgage assumed by the corporation.

### SERVICES RENDERED IN EXCHANGE FOR A CORPORATION'S STOCK
When a shareholder performs services in exchange for stock, the shareholder must recognize ordinary income to the extent of the fair market value of the stock received. The shareholder's basis in the corporation will be equal to the amount of income recognized.


# TAXATION OF A CORPORATION
The taxation of a corporation follows the same basic framework of that of an individual. Income minus deductions equals taxable income. (See Chapter 5 for the actual tax calculations of an individual.) Unlike an individual, a corporation is not allowed a standard deduction or any personal exemptions. However, there are some special deductions and limitations a corporation must be aware of. Five major corporate differences include:

- Charitable contributions
- Net operating losses
- Capital losses
- Dividends received deduction
- Keyman life insurance

### CHARITABLE CONTRIBUTIONS
A corporation is allowed a deduction for charitable contributions. However, the timing and the limitation of deduction is different from that of the individual. With regards to **timing**, the general rule is that in order to be deductible, the contribution must be paid during the taxable year. However, an accrual based taxpayer is allowed a deduction for contributions paid on or before the 15th day of the third month following the close of the taxable year if the Board of Directors authorizes the contribution prior to the end of the year.

As to the **limitation**, contributions are limited to 10% of a corporation's adjusted taxable income. The adjusted taxable income is taxable income without regard to:

- The charitable contribution itself
- Any net operating loss carryback
- Any capital loss carryback
- Any dividends received deduction

Any excess charitable contribution is carried forward for five years. In determining the allowable contribution for any given year, the current contribution is considered first, then any carryforward.

### NET OPERATING LOSSES
When a corporation's allowable deductions exceed its gross income, a net operating loss (NOL) exists. An NOL must be carried back 3 years, then forward 15 years. A corporation, however, may elect to waive the carryback requirement by filing such election with a timely filed return. However, *effective for tax years beginning after August 5, 1997,* the NOL carryback is reduced to 2 years and carryforward is extended to 20 years.

## CAPITAL GAINS & LOSSES

Corporate taxpayers, unlike individual taxpayers, receive **no special tax rate** for capital gains. Net capital gains are treated as ordinary income. In addition, corporate taxpayers, unlike individuals who can deduct up to $3,000 in net capital losses, **may not deduct** any net capital losses. Capital losses may only be used to offset capital gains. Excess net capital losses, regardless of whether they are long or short-term, are carried back and forward as **short-term capital losses.** The carryback period is 3 years and carryforward period is 5 years.

## DIVIDENDS RECEIVED DEDUCTION

When a corporation makes a distribution with regards to its stock, the distribution (or dividend) comes from the corporation's after-tax income. The dividend distribution is generally taxed to the shareholder at ordinary income rates. This is referred to as **double taxation**. If the shareholder is another corporation, then that corporation would pay taxes on the dividend received and then with its after-tax income, distributes a dividend to its shareholders. This would result in **triple taxation**. To prevent this from occurring, Congress enacted the dividends received deduction (DRD). The DRD is classified as a special deduction and is based upon the percentage of stock ownership in the corporation. The deduction percentages to memorize for the exam are:

- 70% of the dividend received from less than 20% companies
- 80% of the dividend received from at least 20% and less than 80% owned companies
- 100% of the dividend received from at least 80% owned companies

The deduction, however, is limited to the same percentage of taxable income without regard to the dividend received deduction. This limitation is overridden if the DRD creates or increase the corporation's net operating loss. However, there is no limitation on the 100% DRD. Another limitation to the DRD is that no DRD is allowed if the stock is held for 45 days or less.

---

**Example 5:** Given the following independent situations, determine the dividend received deduction when the corporations own 50% of the stock of the dividend paying corporation.

|  | A Corp | B Corp | C Corp |
|---|---|---|---|
| Sales | $ 400,000 | $ 400,000 | $ 400,000 |
| Cost of sales | -250,000 | -250,000 | -250,000 |
| Gross margin | 150,000 | 150,000 | 150,000 |
| Dividends | 100,000 | 100,000 | 30,000 |
| Total income | 250,000 | 250,000 | 180,000 |
| Operating expenses | -100,000 | -170,000 | -200,000 |
| Income before DRD | 150,000 | 80,000 | -20,000 |
| **DRD** | -80,000 | -64,000 | -24,000 |
| Taxable income (loss) | $ 70,000 | $ 16,000 | $ -44,000 |

*Solutions:*

**A Corporation:** The general rule applies. 80% of the dividend received is allowed as a deduction.

**B Corporation:** The exception applies. 80% of the taxable income before the DRD ($64,000) is less than 80% of the dividend received ($80,000), therefore the $64,000 is used. Using the $80,000 does not generate a NOL.

**C Corporation:** The corporation has a net operating loss before the determination of the DRD. The DRD of $24,000 will increase the net operating loss, and therefore overrides the exception.

---

## KEYMAN LIFE INSURANCE

When the corporation is the beneficiary of a life insurance policy on an officer or keyman, no deduction is allowed for premiums paid on that policy. However, upon the death of an officer, the amount of the life insurance proceeds received by the corporation is not considered taxable income.

## BAD DEBTS

A corporation is only allowed to deduct bad debts written off during the year. No longer is the allowance method of recognizing debt expense allowable.

## DEALINGS BETWEEN THE SHAREHOLDERS AND CORPORATION

In general, transactions between a shareholder and the corporation are treated as if they were not related parties, and were conducted at an arm's length basis. However, when a shareholder owns, directly or indirectly, more than 50% of a corporation's capital, all losses, even at an arm's length basis, are disallowed.

In addition, if a shareholder owns 50% or more of a corporation's capital, any gain from the sale of property between the corporation and shareholder must be recognized as ordinary income. If the property is a capital asset to both the corporation and shareholder, then the gain is capital.

## BOOK TO TAX RECONCILIATION

Because a corporation is allowed special deductions and frequently follows financial accounting principles which differ from tax provisions, it is necessary to reconcile a corporation's book income to its taxable income. This is required of corporations and is submitted on Schedule M-1, located on page 4 of Form 1120. In performing a book to tax reconciliation, you must identify those items of income and deduction which differ from book to tax. It is important to note that Schedule M-1 reconciles book income to taxable income **before** the special deductions (dividends received deduction and net operating loss deduction).

A typical exam fact pattern provides either book income or taxable income as a starting point, and requires the candidate to determine the other. Going from book income to taxable income, the adjustments might look as follows:

> **Net income per books**
> **Add:**
> > Federal income taxes
> > Excess capital loss (carried forward)
> > Excess charitable contributions (carried forward)
> > Keyman life insurance premiums
> > Disallowed municipal interest expense
> > Disallowed entertainment expenses
> **Subtract:**
> > Municipal interest income
> > Keyman life insurance proceeds
> > Allowable capital loss carryforward from prior years
> > Allowable contribution carryforward from prior years
> **Taxable income**

## ANALYSIS OF UNAPPROPRIATED RETAINED EARNINGS

Similar to the reconciliation of book to tax income, it is also necessary to analyze the activity in unappropriated retained earnings. This appears on Schedule M-2. The major increases in retained earnings would be net income plus any refund of prior year's tax. Typical decreases include dividends paid and reserves for contingencies and other appropriations.

# CONSOLIDATED RETURNS

An affiliated group of corporations is allowed to file a consolidated return rather than each corporation filing a separate return. An affiliated group includes one or more chains of corporations where the parent corporation owns directly at least 80% of one of the corporations and at least 80% of each corporation in the group is owned directly by one or more of the other corporations in the group. Once the election is made to file on a consolidated basis, it is binding for future returns. The advantages of filing a consolidated return include:

- The ability to offset losses of one company against another's profits
- The deferral of income on intercompany transactions
- The elimination of intercompany dividends

The major disadvantage of filing on a consolidated basis is the deferral of any intercompany losses until the property is sold to an outside party.

# CONTROLLED GROUPS

## GENERAL

Because corporations are provided various tax incentives, creative individuals attempt to take an unfair advantage of these incentives by forming multiple corporations. If the multiple corporations have common ownership, they are identified as controlled groups. The two controlled groups are parent-subsidiary and brother-sister. If a group of corporations (two or more) are classified as a controlled group, they are limited to:

- One surtax exemption (for example, the first $50,000 of income which is taxed at 15%) must be allocated to the related corporations.
- One accumulated earnings credit ($250,000 or $150,000) must be allocated to the related corporations.
- One $40,000 alternative minimum tax credit must be allocated to the related corporations.

## PARENT-SUBSIDIARY CONTROLLED GROUP

When one or more corporations are connected through the stock ownership with a common parent corporation, a parent-subsidiary controlled group may exist. The rule is that if at least 80% of the total voting power or value of all classes of stock in a chain is owned by one or more of the other corporations, and the common parent owns at least 80% of the stock of at least one of the other corporations in the controlled group, then a parent-subsidiary control group exists.

> **Example 6:** Red Corporation owns 80% of White Corporation and 20% of Blue Corporation. White Corporation owns 60% Blue Corporation. Red, White and Blue are members of a parent-subsidiary group. Red is deemed to own 80% of Blue (20% directly and 60% through White). There is no reduction in the percentage of ownership in Blue because Red only owns 80% of White. (You do not multiply 80% times 60% and include only 48%).

## BROTHER-SISTER CORPORATIONS

If two or more corporations are owned by the same parents (individuals, trusts or estates), they may be classified as brother-sister corporations. A brother-sister relationship exists if the shareholder group of five or fewer persons meets an 80% and 50% ownership test.

- The 80% test is met if the shareholder group owns at least 80% of the total ownership of the corporation.
- The 50% test is met if there is more than 50% common ownership by the shareholder group in each corporation.

**Example 7:** Bill owns 25% of Blue Corporation and 65% of Gold Corporation. Dave owns 60% of Blue Corporation and 35% of Gold Corporation. Blue and Gold are brother-sister corporations. Bill and Dave own at least 80% of Blue and Gold, and have common ownership of 60%.

| Shareholder | Blue | Gold | Common |
|---|---|---|---|
| Bill | 25% | 65% | 25% |
| Dave | 60% | 35% | 35% |
| Total | 85% | 100% | 60% |

**Example 8:** Fran owns 55% of Blue Corporation and 100% of Grey Corporation. Steve owns 45% of Blue Corporation. Blue and Grey are not brother-sister corporations. Even though it appears that they own at least 80% of Blue and Grey, they are not part of a shareholder group because Steve does not own any stock in Grey. Fran does meet the common ownership test in Blue and Grey, but alone does not meet the 80% test.

| Shareholder | Blue | Grey | Common |
|---|---|---|---|
| Fran | 55% | 100% | 55% |
| Steve | 45% | 0% | 0% |
| Total | 100% | 100% | 55% |

## COMPUTATION OF CORPORATE TAX LIABILITY AND CREDITS

### GENERAL

Once taxable income has been determined for the corporation, the computation of tax is required. After the tax is computed, a reduction for payments and credits is made to determine if the corporation has a refund or balance due.

The summary of the flow of the basic tax computations, credits and payments, is as follows:

> Taxable income
> Tax (regular)
> Less: Credits foreign taxes or business credits
> Plus: Alternative minimum tax
> Personal holding tax (Chapter 9)
> Environmental tax
> Less: Estimated tax payments
> Refund or balance due

# REGULAR COMPUTATION

A corporation is taxed on its taxable income based upon three basic rates: 15%, 25% and 34%. The rates are increased by what are referred to surcharges or surtaxes, to make corporations give back the benefit of receiving a lower rate at the lower levels of income. Because of the 1% surtax on income over $10,000,000, the highest tax bracket for corporations is 35%. The full corporate rate structure is presented below:

| | |
|---|---|
| On the first $50,000 | 15% |
| From $50,000, but not over $75,000 | 25% |
| From $75,000, but not over $100,000 | 34% |
| From $100,000, but not over $335,000 | 39% |
| From $335,000 but not over $10,000,000 | 34% |
| From $10,000,000, but not over $15,000,000 | 35% |
| From $15,000,000, but not over $18,333,333 | 38% |
| Over $18,333,333 | 35% |

---

**Example 9:** W Corporation has taxable income of $60,000. Their tax is computed as follows:

| | |
|---|---|
| $50,000 X 15% | $ 7,500 |
| $10,000 X 25% | 2,500 |
| Total tax | $10,000 |

---

# ALTERNATIVE MINIMUM TAX

To ensure that corporation taxpayers pay their fair share of taxes, there is a corporate alternative minimum tax (AMT). It is similar to the individual AMT in concept discussed in Chapter 5. The process to determine this AMT is, identify the various tax preferences or adjustments (all available in the tax code) which were properly elected and planned for, and effectively disallow them. However, *effective for tax years beginning after December 31, 1997,* the corporate AMT has been repealed for small corporations (SC). A corporation with average annual gross receipts of less than $5 million for the three-year period beginning after December 31, 1994, qualifies as an SC. Major rates and/or differences from the individual computations include:

| AMT issue | Corporate | Individual |
|---|---|---|
| Tax rate | 20% | 26 - 28% |
| Exemption amount | $40,000 | $45,000 |
| Phaseout begins | $150,000 | $150,000 |
| Preferences | Contributions | Not a preference |
| Adjustments | No adjustment | Itemized deductions |
| Adjustments | ACE | No ACE |

The framework for calculating the AMT, assuming no operating losses is as follows:

Taxable income
Plus or minus the AMTI adjustments
Plus the tax preferences
Equals pre-adjustment AMTI **before** ACE adjustment
Plus or minus 75% of difference between ACE and AMTI
Equals AMTI **after** the ACE adjustment
Less the exemption amount
Equals the AMT base
Multiplied by the 20% tax rate
Equals the tentative minimum tax
Less the regular tax
Equals the AMT

## ADJUSTMENTS

The adjustments to taxable income are similar to the ones discussed in Chapter 5. In general, adjustments can be **positive or negative,** and are the result of timing differences in the tax treatment of certain items. For example, excess MACRS depreciation over the longer, slower AMT depreciation method of ADS (alternative depreciation system) will result in a positive adjustment that increases the alternative minimum taxable income. However, after the asset has been fully recovered under MACRS, there will still be depreciation under the AMT method, which will cause a negative adjustment and decrease AMTI.

The AMT **adjustments**, with a very brief explanation, include:

- Circulation expenditures - Must be capitalized and expensed over three years, not immediately.
- Depreciation - Excess MACRS of real property over ADS of 40 years straight-line.
- Depreciation - Excess MACRS of personal property over ADS 150% DDB.
- Differences in Recognized Gains or Losses - Because of depreciation changes, tax bases are different.
- Pollution Control Facilities Amortization - Excess of straight-line, 60 months over ADS.
- Passive Activity Losses - Uses a different taxable income level for determining losses.
- Completed Contract Method - Must use percentage of completion instead.
- Incentive Stock Options - Excess of FMV over exercise price.
- Net Operating Loss - Must be modified.

In addition, corporations are subject to the adjusted current earnings adjustment (ACE), which is discussed separately further on. Note that since a corporation does not have itemized deductions there are no adjustments needed for **itemized deductions.**

## TAX PREFERENCES

Tax preferences are always added to taxable income, never subtracted. The preferences are:

- Interest income on private activity bonds
- Excess accelerated depreciation over straight-line on pre-87 real property
- Excess accelerated depreciation over straight-line on leased pre-87 personal property
- Excess amortization over depreciation on pre-87 certified pollution control facilities
- Percentage depletion beyond the property's adjusted basis.
- Excess intangible drilling costs, reduced by 65% of net income from oil, gas and geothermal activity

## THE ACE ADJUSTMENT

For post-89 years, a positive adjustment equal to 75% of the Adjusted Current Earnings (ACE) over the AMTI before the ACE adjustment is required. ACE is similar to earnings and profits which is discussed in Chapter 8. The ACE adjustments are designed to bring the corporation's income closer to economic reality. The comprehensive, but not exclusive list of ACE adjustments include:

- Interest income on other tax-free bonds than private activity
- Life insurance proceeds
- LIFO inventory adjustment
- Depreciation - straight-line over a longer year
- The 70% dividends received deduction, but not the 80% and 100%
- The amortization expense of organization costs

The ACE adjustments can be both positive and negative. However, the negative adjustment can only be to the extent of the positive adjustments. Any unused negative ACE adjustments cannot be carried forward.

**Example 10:** L Corporation started operations in 1997. They computed their Adjusted Current Earnings (ACE) and alternative minimum taxable income before the ACE (pre-AMTI) for the following three years. Determine the ACE adjustment for the three years.

|  | 1997 | 1998 | 1999 |
|---|---|---|---|
| Adjusted Current Earnings | 3,000 | 4,000 | 5,000 |
| Pre-adjustment AMTI | 2,000 | 6,000 | 2,000 |
| Excess ACE over pre-AMTI | 1,000 | -2,000 | 3,000 |
| 75% of the excess | 750 | -1,500 | 2,250 |
| ACE adjustment | 750 | -750 | 2,250 |

**1997** - In L's first year of operations, the excess ACE yields a 750 positive adjustment.
**1998** - In year 2, there is a negative adjustment of 1,500. However, since the positive adjustments through 1997 were only 750, L can only reduce its AMTI by 750. There is no carryforward of the unused negative adjustment.
**1999** - In 1999, there is a positive adjustment of 2,250. (If this was a negative adjustment, none would be allowed because there are no positive adjustments remaining.)

## EXEMPTION AMOUNT

After adding and subtracting the adjustments, adding the tax preferences to taxable income and adding the ACE adjustment, the corporation is allowed an exemption from the AMTI. The exemption amount for the corporation is $40,000. However, this exemption is phased-out (at a rate of 25% over the excess) if the corporation's AMTI before the exemption exceeds $150,000.

**Example 11:** For 1999, J Corporation's regular tax on its taxable income was $19,500. J Corporation also had AMTI (before the exemption amount) of $170,000. Calculate the alternative minimum tax.

1. J Corporation's exemption amount for 1999 would be only $35,000 ($40,000 less phase-out of $5,000):

| | |
|---|---|
| AMTI | $ 170,000 |
| Threshold for phase-out | 150,000 |
| Excess over threshold | 20,000 |
| Phase-out rate | 25% |
| Exemption phaseout | $ 5,000 |

2. Calculation of the tax:

| | |
|---|---|
| AMTI | $ 170,000 |
| Exemption | 35,000 |
| Tax base | 135,000 |
| AMT tax rate | 20% |
| Tentative minimum tax | 27,000 |
| Regular tax | 19,500 |
| Alternative minimum tax | $ 7,500 |

# ENVIRONMENTAL TAX

The environmental tax is .12% of the excess of the corporate modified alternative minimum taxable income over $2,000,000.

# COMPUTATION OF TAX CREDITS

## FOREIGN TAX CREDIT

Corporate taxpayers are taxed in the United States on their worldwide income. The taxpayers are entitled to a tax credit for income taxes paid to foreign countries. This prevents double taxation of the same income. The foreign tax credit cannot exceed the lessor of the amount of the foreign taxes paid or the pro-rata share of US taxes on the foreign income. The limitation is determined as follows:

$$\frac{\text{Income from foreign sources}}{\text{Worldwide income}} \ \text{X US taxes paid} = \text{Foreign tax}$$

## GENERAL BUSINESS CREDITS

The credits described below are limited in total to 25% of the regular tax liability that exceeds $25,000, or the tentative minimum tax, whichever is greater. Any excess is available for a 3 year carryback and a 15 year carryforward.

## JOBS CREDIT

This credit is designed to encourage employment of targeted groups. Some of these groups include:

- **Economically disadvantage youths, convicts and Vietnam veterans**
- **Vocational rehabilitation referrals**
- **Qualified summer youth employees**

The credit is 40% of the first $6,000 or wages paid during the first twelve months of employment. For the summer youth employees, the maximum wages is not $6,000, but rather $3,000 for a maximum credit of $1,200.

## RESEARCH CREDITS

This credit is designed to encourage research in the United States. There are two credits. The incremental credit is based upon 20% of the excess amount of qualified research over a base amount. The basic research credit, also a 20% credit, is available for qualified corporations making payments to qualified organizations over a base amount.

## DISABLED ACCESS

This credit is available to small business, and is 50% of the eligible disable access expenditures that exceed $250. The maximum credit is $5,000.

# ESTIMATED INCOME TAX PAYMENTS

A corporation must make installment payments if it expects the estimated tax, after credits, to be at least $500. The tax payments are due on the 15th day of the 4th, 6th, 9th and 12th month of the year.

In order to avoid any penalty on the underpayment of taxes, the corporation must make payments equal to:

- 100% of its current year's tax
- 100% of its prior year's tax
- Annualized income installment method computation

However, in order to rely on paying 100% of the prior year tax, the taxpayer must have a prior year tax. For example, a corporation with no tax liability in 1999 due to a NOL, must pay 100% of the current year's tax to avoid the penalty. Paying zero, which was 1999's tax, does not qualify per Revenue Ruling 92-54.

Form **1120**

Department of the Treasury
Internal Revenue Service

# U.S. Corporation Income Tax Return

For calendar year 1999 or tax year beginning ........., 1999, ending ........., ...
► Instructions are separate. See page 1 for Paperwork Reduction Act Notice.

OMB No. 1545-0123

**1999**

| A Check if a: | Use IRS label. Otherwise, print or type. | Name | B Employer identification number |
|---|---|---|---|
| 1 Consolidated return (attach Form 851) ☐ | | | |
| 2 Personal holding co. (attach Sch. PH) ☐ | | Number, street, and room or suite no. (If a P.O. box, see page 5 of instructions.) | C Date incorporated |
| 3 Personal service corp. (as defined in Temporary Regs. sec. 1.441-4T— see instructions) ☐ | | City or town, state, and ZIP code | D Total assets (see page 6 of instructions) |

E Check applicable boxes: (1) ☐ Initial return  (2) ☐ Final return  (3) ☐ Change of address    $

| | | | | |
|---|---|---|---|---|
| **Income** | 1a | Gross receipts or sales [____] b Less returns and allowances [____] c Bal ► | 1c | |
| | 2 | Cost of goods sold (Schedule A, line 8) | 2 | |
| | 3 | Gross profit. Subtract line 2 from line 1c | 3 | |
| | 4 | Dividends (Schedule C, line 19) | 4 | |
| | 5 | Interest | 5 | |
| | 6 | Gross rents | 6 | |
| | 7 | Gross royalties | 7 | |
| | 8 | Capital gain net income (attach Schedule D (Form 1120)) | 8 | |
| | 9 | Net gain or (loss) from Form 4797, Part II, line 18 (attach Form 4797) | 9 | |
| | 10 | Other income (see page 7 of instructions—attach schedule) | 10 | |
| | 11 | **Total income.** Add lines 3 through 10 ► | 11 | |
| **Deductions (See instructions for limitations on deductions.)** | 12 | Compensation of officers (Schedule E, line 4) | 12 | |
| | 13 | Salaries and wages (less employment credits) | 13 | |
| | 14 | Repairs and maintenance | 14 | |
| | 15 | Bad debts | 15 | |
| | 16 | Rents | 16 | |
| | 17 | Taxes and licenses | 17 | |
| | 18 | Interest | 18 | |
| | 19 | Charitable contributions (see page 9 of instructions for 10% limitation) | 19 | |
| | 20 | Depreciation (attach Form 4562) ... 20 [____] | | |
| | 21 | Less depreciation claimed on Schedule A and elsewhere on return . . 21a [____] | 21b | |
| | 22 | Depletion | 22 | |
| | 23 | Advertising | 23 | |
| | 24 | Pension, profit-sharing, etc., plans | 24 | |
| | 25 | Employee benefit programs | 25 | |
| | 26 | Other deductions (attach schedule) | 26 | |
| | 27 | **Total deductions.** Add lines 12 through 26 ► | 27 | |
| | 28 | Taxable income before net operating loss deduction and special deductions. Subtract line 27 from line 11 | 28 | |
| | 29 | **Less:** a Net operating loss (NOL) deduction (see page 11 of instructions) 29a [____] | | |
| | | b Special deductions (Schedule C, line 20) 29b [____] | 29c | |
| **Tax and Payments** | 30 | **Taxable income.** Subtract line 29c from line 28 | 30 | |
| | 31 | **Total tax** (Schedule J, line 12) | 31 | |
| | 32 | **Payments:** a 1998 overpayment credited to 1999  32a [____] | | |
| | b | 1999 estimated tax payments  32b [____] | | |
| | c | Less 1999 refund applied for on Form 4466  32c ([____]) d Bal ► 32d [____] | | |
| | e | Tax deposited with Form 7004  32e [____] | | |
| | f | Credit for tax paid on undistributed capital gains (attach Form 2439)  32f [____] | | |
| | g | Credit for Federal tax on fuels (attach Form 4136). See instructions  32g [____] | 32h | |
| | 33 | Estimated tax penalty (see page 12 of instructions). Check if Form 2220 is attached ► ☐ | 33 | |
| | 34 | **Tax due.** If line 32h is smaller than the total of lines 31 and 33, enter amount owed | 34 | |
| | 35 | **Overpayment.** If line 32h is larger than the total of lines 31 and 33, enter amount overpaid | 35 | |
| | 36 | Enter amount of line 35 you want: **Credited to 2000 estimated tax** ►          **Refunded** ► | 36 | |

**Sign Here**

Under penalties of perjury, I declare that I have examined this return, including accompanying schedules and statements, and to the best of my knowledge and belief, it is true, correct, and complete. Declaration of preparer (other than taxpayer) is based on all information of which preparer has any knowledge.

| ► | | ► | |
|---|---|---|---|
| Signature of officer | Date | Title | |

**Paid Preparer's Use Only**

| Preparer's signature ► | Date | Check if self-employed ☐ | Preparer's SSN or PTIN |
|---|---|---|---|
| Firm's name (or yours if self-employed) and address ► | | EIN ► | |
| | | ZIP code ► | |

Cat. No. 11450Q

Form **1120** (1999)

| **Schedule L** | **Balance Sheets per Books** | Beginning of tax year | | End of tax year | |
|---|---|---|---|---|---|
| | **Assets** | **(a)** | **(b)** | **(c)** | **(d)** |
| 1 | Cash | | | | |
| 2a | Trade notes and accounts receivable | | | | |
| b | Less allowance for bad debts | ( ) | | ( ) | |
| 3 | Inventories | | | | |
| 4 | U.S. government obligations | | | | |
| 5 | Tax-exempt securities (see instructions) | | | | |
| 6 | Other current assets (attach schedule) | | | | |
| 7 | Loans to shareholders | | | | |
| 8 | Mortgage and real estate loans | | | | |
| 9 | Other investments (attach schedule) | | | | |
| 10a | Buildings and other depreciable assets | | | | |
| b | Less accumulated depreciation | ( ) | | ( ) | |
| 11a | Depletable assets | | | | |
| b | Less accumulated depletion | ( ) | | ( ) | |
| 12 | Land (net of any amortization) | | | | |
| 13a | Intangible assets (amortizable only) | | | | |
| b | Less accumulated amortization | ( ) | | ( ) | |
| 14 | Other assets (attach schedule) | | | | |
| 15 | Total assets | | | | |
| | **Liabilities and Shareholders' Equity** | | | | |
| 16 | Accounts payable | | | | |
| 17 | Mortgages, notes, bonds payable in less than 1 year | | | | |
| 18 | Other current liabilities (attach schedule) | | | | |
| 19 | Loans from shareholders | | | | |
| 20 | Mortgages, notes, bonds payable in 1 year or more | | | | |
| 21 | Other liabilities (attach schedule) | | | | |
| 22 | Capital stock:  a Preferred stock | | | | |
| | b Common stock | | | | |
| 23 | Additional paid-in capital | | | | |
| 24 | Retained earnings—Appropriated (attach schedule) | | | | |
| 25 | Retained earnings—Unappropriated | | | | |
| 26 | Adjustments to shareholders' equity (attach schedule) | | | | |
| 27 | Less cost of treasury stock | | ( ) | | ( ) |
| 28 | Total liabilities and shareholders' equity | | | | |

**Note:** *The corporation is not required to complete Schedules M-1 and M-2 if the total assets on line 15, col. (d) of Schedule L are less than $25,000.*

| **Schedule M-1** | **Reconciliation of Income (Loss) per Books With Income per Return (See page 18 of instructions.)** |
|---|---|

| 1 | Net income (loss) per books | | 7 | Income recorded on books this year not included on this return (itemize): | |
|---|---|---|---|---|---|
| 2 | Federal income tax | | | Tax-exempt interest $ .................... | |
| 3 | Excess of capital losses over capital gains | | | ........................................ | |
| 4 | Income subject to tax not recorded on books this year (itemize): ................ | | 8 | Deductions on this return not charged against book income this year (itemize): | |
| | ........................................ | | a | Depreciation . . . . $............ | |
| 5 | Expenses recorded on books this year not deducted on this return (itemize): | | b | Contributions carryover  $ ........... | |
| a | Depreciation . . . . $.............. | | | ........................................ | |
| b | Contributions carryover  $ ............. | | | ........................................ | |
| c | Travel and entertainment  $ .............. | | | ........................................ | |
| | ........................................ | | 9 | Add lines 7 and 8 . . . . . . . . | |
| 6 | Add lines 1 through 5 . . . . . . . | | 10 | Income (line 28, page 1)—line 6 less line 9 | |

| **Schedule M-2** | **Analysis of Unappropriated Retained Earnings per Books (Line 25, Schedule L)** |
|---|---|

| 1 | Balance at beginning of year | | 5 | Distributions:  a Cash | |
|---|---|---|---|---|---|
| 2 | Net income (loss) per books | | | b Stock | |
| 3 | Other increases (itemize): .................. | | | c Property | |
| | ........................................ | | 6 | Other decreases (itemize): ............ | |
| | ........................................ | | 7 | Add lines 5 and 6 | |
| 4 | Add lines 1, 2, and 3 . . . . . . . | | 8 | Balance at end of year (line 4 less line 7) | |

Form **1120** (1999)

# Chapter Eight -- Questions
# C Corporations

## FORMATION OF CORPORATION

1. To qualify for tax-free incorporation, a sole proprietor must be in control of the transferee corporation immediately after the exchange of the proprietorship's assets for the corporation's stock. "Control" for this purpose means ownership of stock amounting to at least
a. 50.00%.
b. 51.00%.
c. 66.67%.
d. 80.00%.

2. Stone, a cash basis taxpayer, incorporated her CPA practice this year. No liabilities were transferred. The following assets were transferred to the corporation:

| | |
|---|---|
| Cash (checking account) | $ 500 |
| Computer equipment | |
| Adjusted basis | 30,000 |
| Fair market value | 34,000 |
| Cost | 40,000 |

Immediately after the transfer, Stone owned 100% of the corporation's stock. The corporation's total basis for the transferred assets is
a. $30,000
b. $30,500
c. $34,500
d. $40,500

3. Adams, Beck, and Carr organized Flexo Corp. with authorized voting common stock of $100,000. Adams received 10% of the capital stock in payment for the organizational services that he rendered for the benefit of the newly formed corporation. Adams did not contribute property to Flexo and was under no obligation to be paid by Beck or Carr. Beck and Carr transferred property in exchange for stock as follows:

| | Adjusted basis | Fair market value | Percentage of Flexo stock acquired |
|---|---|---|---|
| Beck | 5,000 | 20,000 | 20% |
| Carr | 60,000 | 70,000 | 70% |

What amount of gain did Carr recognize from this transaction?
a. $40,000
b. $15,000
c. $10,000
d. $0

4. Mr. Breck and Mr. Witt decide to form a corporation on January 2. Mr. Breck contributes a building, in which he has an adjusted basis of $10,000, worth $25,000 on the market. Mr. Witt contributes $25,000 in cash to the corporation. In exchange for these properties the corporation issues its entire capital stock equally to Mr. Breck and Mr. Witt. What is the basis of the building to the corporation?
a. $10,000.
b. $15,000.
c. $25,000.
d. $35,000.

5. Jenkins transferred land to his controlled corporation for stock of the corporation worth $20,000 and cash of $20,000. The basis of the property to him was $15,000 and it was subject to a $10,000 mortgage which the corporation assumed. Jenkins must report a gain of
a. $10,000.
b. $20,000.
c. $30,000.
d. $35,000.

6. Roberta Warner and Sally Rogers formed the Acme Corporation on October 1 of this year. On the same date Warner paid $75,000 cash to Acme for 750 shares of its common stock. Simultaneously, Rogers received 100 shares of Acme's common stock for services rendered. How much should Rogers include as taxable income for this taxable year, and what will be the basis of her stock?

| | Taxable income | Basis of stock |
|---|---|---|
| a. | --0-- | --0-- |
| b. | --0-- | $10,000 |
| c. | $10,000 | --0-- |
| d. | $10,000 | $10,000 |

7. Clark and Hunt organized Jet Corp. with authorized voting common stock of $400,000. Clark contributed $60,000 cash. Both Clark and Hunt transferred other property in exchange for Jet stock as follows:

|  | *Other property* | | |
| --- | --- | --- | --- |
|  | *Adjusted basis* | *Fair market value* | *Percentage of Jet stock acquired* |
| Clark | $ 50,000 | $100,000 | 40% |
| Hunt | 120,000 | 240,000 | 60% |

What was Clark's basis in Jet stock?
a. $0
b. $100,000
c. $110,000
d. $160,000

8. Jones incorporated a sole proprietorship by exchanging all the proprietorship's assets for the stock of Nu Co., a new corporation. To qualify for tax-free incorporation, Jones must be in control of Nu immediately after the exchange. What percentage of Nu's stock must Jones own to qualify as "control" for this purpose?
a. 50.00%
b. 51.00%
c. 66.67%
d. 80.00%

9. Feld, the sole stockholder of Maki Corp., paid $50,000 for Maki's stock in 1991. In 1999, Feld contributed a parcel of land to Maki but was not given any additional stock for this contribution. Feld's basis for the land was $10,000, and its fair market value was $18,000 on the date of the transfer of title. What is Feld's adjusted basis for the Maki stock?
a. $50,000
b. $52,000
c. $60,000
d. $68,000

10. The costs of organizing a corporation
a. May be deducted in full in the year in which these costs are incurred even if paid in later years.
b. May be deducted only in the year in which these costs are paid.
c. May be amortized over a period of not less than 60 months even if these costs are capitalized on the company's books.
d. Are nondeductible capital expenditures.

11. Brown Corp., a calendar-year taxpayer, was organized and actively began operations on July 1, 1999, and incurred the following costs:

| Legal fees to obtain corporate charter | $40,000 |
| --- | --- |
| Commission paid to underwriter | 25,000 |
| Other stock issue costs | 10,000 |

Brown wishes to amortize its organizational costs over the shortest period allowed for tax purposes. In 1999, what amount should Brown deduct for the amortization of organizational expenses?
a. $8,000
b. $7,500
c. $5,000
d. $4,000

12. Which of the following costs are amortizable organizational expenditures?
a. Professional fees to issue the corporate stock.
b. Printing costs to issue the corporate stock.
c. Legal fees for drafting the corporate charter.
d. Commissions paid by the corporation to an underwriter.

13. Filo, Inc. began business on July 1, 1999, and elected to file its income tax returns on a calendar-year basis. The following expenditures were incurred in organizing the corporation:

| August 1, 1999 | $300 |
| --- | --- |
| September 3, 1999 | $600 |

The maximum allowable deduction for amortization of organization expense in 1999 is
a. $60
b. $65
c. $81
d. $90

## CAPITAL TRANSACTIONS

14. This year, Mud Corporation sold 1,000 shares of its $10 par value common stock for $20,000. The stock had originally been issued in 1980 for $12 a share and was reacquired by Mud in 1983 for $15 a share. For the tax year, Mud Corporation should report a long-term capital gain of
a. $0.
b. $5,000.
c. $8,000.
d. $10,000.

15. The following information pertains to treasury stock sold by Lee Corp. to an unrelated broker in 1999:

| | |
|---|---|
| Proceeds received | $50,000 |
| Cost | 30,000 |
| Par value | 9,000 |

What amount of capital gain should Lee recognize in 1998 on the sale of this treasury stock?
a. $0
b. $8,000
c. $20,000
d. $30,500

16. During 1999, Ral Corp. exchanged 5,000 shares of its own $10 par common stock for land with a fair market value of $75,000. As a result of this exchange, Ral should report in its 1999 tax return
a. $25,000 Section 1245 gain.
b. $25,000 Section 1231 gain.
c. $25,000 ordinary income.
d. No gain.

17. Gilbert Manufacturing Company, in need of additional factory space, exchanged 10,000 shares of its common stock with a par value of $100,000 for a building with a fair market value of $120,000. On the date of the exchange the stock had a market value of $130,000. How much and what type of gain or loss should Gilbert report on this transaction?
a. No gain or loss.
b. $10,000 capital loss.
c. $20,000 capital gain.
d. $20,000 section 1231 gain.

18. A corporation's capital losses are
a. Deductible only to the extent of the corporation's capital gains.
b. Deductible from the corporation's ordinary income to the extent of $3,000.
c. Carried back three years and forward 15 years.
d. Forfeited if the corporation had **no** capital gains in the year in which the capital losses were incurred.

19. When a corporation has an unused net capital loss that is carried back or carried forward to another tax year,
a. It retains its original identity as short-term or long-term.
b. It is treated as a short-term capital loss whether or not it was short-term when sustained.
c. It is treated as a long-term capital loss whether or not it was long-term when sustained.
d. It can be used to offset ordinary income up to the amount of the carryback or carryover.

**Items 20 and 21 are based on the following data:**

In its first year of operation, 1999, Bell Corporation had net short-term capital gains of $3,000 and net long-term capital losses of $8,000.

20. What is Bell's net capital-loss deduction and what is the capital-loss carryover to 2000 respectively?
a. $0 and $5,000.
b. $1,000 and $3,000.
c. $1,000 and $4,000.
d. $2,500 and $2,500.

21. How will the 1999 capital-loss carryover be treated in Bell's 2000 income tax return?
a. Ordinary loss.
b. Section 1231 loss.
c. Long-term capital loss.
d. Short-term capital loss.

22. A C corporation's net capital losses are
a. Carried forward indefinitely until fully utilized.
b. Carried back 3 years and forward 5 years.
d. Deductible in full from the corporation's ordinary income.
d. Deductible from the corporation's ordinary income only to the extent of $3,000.

23. Capital assets include
a. A corporation's accounts receivable from the sale of its inventory.
b. Seven-year MACRS property used in a corporation's trade or business.
c. A manufacturing company's investment in U.S. Treasury bonds.
d. A corporate real estate developer's unimproved land that is to be subdivided to build homes, which will be sold to customers.

24. Baker Corp., a calendar year C corporation, realized taxable income of $36,000 from its regular business operations for calendar year 1999. In addition, Baker had the following capital gains and losses during 1999:

| | |
|---|---|
| Short-term capital gain | $8,500 |
| Short-term capital loss | (4,000) |
| Long-term capital gain | 1,500 |
| Long-term capital loss | (3,500) |

Baker did not realize any other capital gains or losses since it began operations. What is Baker's total taxable income for 1999?
a. $46,000
b. $42,000
c. $40,500
d. $38,500

25. Bruce Williams owns 55% of the outstanding stock of Flextool Corporation. Flextool sold a machine to Williams for $40,000. The machine had an adjusted tax basis of $46,000, and had been owned by Flextool for three years. What is the allowable loss that Flextool can claim in its income tax return?
a. $0.
b. $6,000 ordinary loss.
c. $6,000 Section 1231 loss.
d. $6,000 Section 1245 loss.

## TAXATION OF A CORPORATION

26. In the case of a corporation that is **not** a financial institution, which of the following statements is correct with regard to the deduction for bad debts?
a. Either the reserve method or the direct charge-off method may be used, if the election is made in the corporation's first taxable year.
b. On approval from the IRS, a corporation may change its method from direct charge-off to reserve.
c. If the reserve method was consistently used in prior years, the corporation may take a deduction for a reasonable addition to the reserve for bad debts.
d. A corporation is required to use the direct charge-off method rather than the reserve method.

27. For the year ended December 31, 1999, Kelly Corp. had net income per books of $300,000 before the provision for Federal income taxes. Included in the net income were the following items:

| | |
|---|---|
| Dividend income from an unaffiliated domestic taxable corporation (taxable income limitation does not apply and there is no portfolio indebtedness) | $50,000 |
| Bad debt expense (represents the increase in the allowance for doubtful accounts) | 80,000 |

Assuming no bad debt was written off, what is Kelly's taxable income for the year ended December 31, 1999?
a. $250,000
b. $330,000
c. $345,000
d. $380,000

28. Micro Corp., a calendar year, accrual basis corporation, purchased a 5-year, 8%, $100,000 taxable corporate bond for $108,530, on July 1, 1999, the date the bond was issued. The bond paid interest semiannually. Micro elected to amortize the bond premium. For Micro's 1999 tax return, the bond premium amortization for 1999 should be

I. Computed under the constant yield to maturity method.
II. Treated as an offset to the interest income on the bond.

a. I only.
b. II only.
c. Both I and II.
d. Neither I nor II.

29. Banks Corp., a calendar year corporation, reimburses employees for properly substantiated qualifying business meal expenses. The employees are present at the meals, which are neither lavish nor extravagant, and the reimbursement is not treated as wages subject to withholdings. For 1999, what percentage of the meal expense may Banks deduct?
a. 0%
b. 50%
c. 80%
d. 100%

30. Axis Corp. is an accrual basis calendar year corporation. On December 13, 1999, the Board of Directors declared a two percent of profits bonus to all employees for services rendered during 1999 and notified them in writing. None of the employees own stock in Axis. The amount represents reasonable compensation for services rendered and was paid on March 13, 2000. Axis' bonus expense may

a. Not be deducted on Axis' 1999 tax return because the per share employee amount **cannot** be determined with reasonable accuracy at the time of the declaration of the bonus.
b. Be deducted on Axis' 1999 tax return.
c. Be deducted on Axis' 2000 tax return.
d. Not be deducted on Axis' tax return because payment is a disguised dividend.

31. Tapper Corp., an accrual basis calendar year corporation, was organized on January 2, 1999. During 1999, revenue was exclusively from sales proceeds and interest income. The following information pertains to Tapper:

Taxable income before charitable
contributions for the year ended
December 31, 1999                                    $500,000

Tapper's matching contribution to
employee-designated qualified
universities made during 1999                         10,000

Board of Directors' authorized
contribution to a qualified charity
(authorized December 1, 1999,
made February 1, 2000)                                30,000

What is the maximum allowable deduction that Tapper may take as a charitable contribution on its tax return for the year ended December 31, 1999?
a. $0
b. $10,000
c. $30,000
d. $40,000

32. Dowell Corporation had operating income of $100,000, after deducting $6,000 for contributions, but not including dividends of $10,000 received from nonaffiliated domestic taxable corporations. How much is the base amount to which the percentage limitation should be applied in computing the maximum allowable deduction for contributions?
a. $106,000.
b. $107,500.
c. $110,000.
d. $116,000.

33. In 1999, Garland Corp. contributed $40,000 to a qualified charitable organization. Garland's 1999 taxable income before the deduction for charitable contributions was $410,000. Included in that amount is a $20,000 dividends-received deduction. Garland also had carryover contributions of $5,000 from the prior year. In 1999, what amount can Garland deduct as charitable contributions?
a. $40,000
b. $41,000
c. $43,000
d. $45,000

34. In 1999, Cable Corp., a calendar year C corporation, contributed $80,000 to a qualified charitable organization. Cable's 1999 taxable income before the deduction for charitable contributions was $820,000 after a $40,000 dividends-received deduction. Cable also had carryover contributions of $10,000 from the prior year. In 1999, what amount can Cable deduct as charitable contribution?
a. $90,000
b. $86,000
c. $82,000
d. $80,000

35. If a corporation's charitable contributions exceed the limitation for deductibility in a particular year, the excess
a. Is **not** deductible in any future or prior year.
b. May be carried back or forward for one year at the corporation's election.
c. May be carried forward to a maximum of five succeeding years.
d. May be carried back to the third preceding year.

36. In 1999, Stewart Corp. properly accrued $5,000 for an income item on the basis of a reasonable estimate. In 2000, after filing its 1999 federal income tax return, Stewart determined that the exact amount was $6,000. Which of the following statements is correct?
a. No further inclusion of income is required as the difference is less than 25% of the original amount reported and the estimate had been made in good faith.
b. The $1,000 difference is includable in Stewart's 2000 income tax return.
c. Stewart is required to notify the IRS within 30 days of the determination of the exact amount of the item.
d. Stewart is required to file an amended return to report the additional $1,000 of income.

37. The uniform capitalization method must be used by

I. Manufacturers of tangible personal property.

II. Retailers of personal property with $2 million dollars in average annual gross receipts for the 3 preceding years.

a. I only.
b. II only.
c. Both I and II.
d. Neither I nor II.

38. Lyle Corp. is a distributor of pharmaceuticals and sells only to retail drug stores. During 1999, Lyle received unsolicited samples of nonprescription drugs from a manufacturer. Lyle donated these drugs in 1999 to a qualified exempt organization and deducted their fair market value as a charitable contribution. What should be included as gross income in Lyle's 1999 return for receipt of these samples?
a. Fair market value.
b. Net discounted wholesale price.
c. $25 nominal value assigned to gifts.
d. $0.

39. Gero Corp. had operating income of $160,000, after deducting $10,000 for contributions to State University, but not including dividends of $2,000 received from nonaffiliated taxable domestic corporations.

In computing the maximum allowable deduction for contributions, Gero should apply the percentage limitation to a base amount of

a. $172,000
b. $170,400
c. $170,000
d. $162,000

40. If a corporation's charitable contributions exceed the limitation for deductibility in a particular year, the excess
a. May be carried back to the third preceding year.
b. May be carried forward to a maximum of five succeeding years.
c. May be carried back or forward for one year at the corporation's election.
d. Is **not** deductible in any future or prior year.

41. Acorn, Inc. had the following items of income and expense this taxable year:

| | |
|---|---|
| Sales | $500,000 |
| Cost of sales | 250,000 |
| Dividends received | 25,000 |

The dividends were received from a corporation of which Acorn owns 30%. In Acorn's corporate income tax return, what amount should be reported as income before special deductions?
a. $525,000
b. $505,000
c. $275,000
d. $250,000

42. The corporate dividends-received deduction
a. Must exceed the applicable percentage of the recipient shareholder's taxable income.
b. Is affected by a requirement that the investor corporation must own the investee's stock for a specified minimum holding period.
c. Is unaffected by the percentage of the investee's stock owned by the investor corporation.
d. May be claimed by S corporations.

43. This taxable year, Trapp, Inc., had $400,000 of gross profit from operations and $160,000 of dividends from Von Corporation in which Trapp had a 25% ownership interest. Trapp's operating expenses totaled $410,000. What is Trapp's dividends received deduction?
a. $80,000.
b. $128,000.
c. $136,000.
d. $120,000.

44. In 1999, Best Corp., an accrual-basis calendar year C corporation, received $100,000 in dividend income from the common stock that it held in an unrelated domestic corporation. The stock was not debt-financed, and was held for over a year. Best recorded the following information for 1999:

| | |
|---|---|
| Loss from Best's operations | ($ 10,000) |
| Dividends received | 100,000 |
| Taxable income (before divi-dends-received deduction) | $ 90,000 |

Best's dividends-received deduction on its 1999 tax return was
a. $100,000
b. $80,000
c. $70,000
d. $63,000

45. During 1999, Nale Corp. received dividends of $1,000 from a 10%-owned taxable domestic corporation. When Nale computes the maximum allowable deduction for contributions in its 1999 return, the amount of dividends to be included in the computation of taxable income is
a. $0
b. $200
c. $300
d. $1,000

46. In 1999, Ryan Corp. had the following income:

| | |
|---|---|
| Income from operations | $300,000 |
| Dividends from unrelated taxable domestic corporations less than 20% owned | 2,000 |

Ryan had no portfolio indebtedness. In Ryan's 1999 taxable income, what amount should be included for the dividends received?
a. $400
b. $600
c. $1,400
d. $1,600

47. In 1999, Daly Corp. had the following income:

| | |
|---|---|
| Profit from operations | $100,000 |
| Dividends from 20%-owned taxable domestic corporation | 1,000 |

In Daly's 1999 taxable income, how much should be included for the dividends received?
a. $0
b. $200
c. $800
d. $1,000

48. For the year ended December 31, 1999, Atkinson, Inc. had gross business income of $160,000 and dividend income of $100,000 from unaffiliated domestic corporations that are at least 20%-owned. Business deductions for 1999 amounted to $170,000. What is Atkinson's dividends received deduction for 1999?
a. $0
b. $72,000
c. $80,000
d. $90,000

49. In its first year of operation, Commerce Corporation had a gross profit from operations of $360,000 and deductions of $500,000 excluding any special deductions. Commerce also received dividends of $100,000 from a 30% owned unaffiliated domestic corporation. What is the net operating loss for that year?
a. $34,000.
b. $40,000.
c. $55,000.
d. $120,000.

50. Kisco Corp.'s taxable income for 1999 before taking the dividends received deduction was $70,000. This includes $10,000 in dividends from an unrelated taxable domestic corporation. Given the following tax rates, what would Kisco's income tax be before any credits?

| Partial rate table | Tax rate |
|---|---|
| Up to $50,000 | 15% |
| Over $50,000 but not over $75,000 | 25% |

a. $10,000
b. $10,750
c. $12,500
d. $15,750

51. For the year ended December 31, 1999, Taylor Corp. had a net operating loss of $200,000. Taxable income for the earlier years of corporate existence, computed without reference to the net operating loss, was as follows:

| Taxable income | |
|---|---|
| 1994 | $ 5,000 |
| 1995 | $10,000 |
| 1996 | $20,000 |
| 1997 | $30,000 |
| 1998 | $40,000 |

If Taylor makes **no** special election to waive the net operating loss carryback, what amount of net operating loss will be available to Taylor for the year ended December 31, 2000?
a. $200,000
b. $130,000
c. $110,000
d. $90,000

52. When a corporation has an unused net capital loss that is carried back or carried forward to another tax year,
a. It retains its original identity as short-term or long-term.
b. It is treated as a short-term capital loss whether or not it was short-term when sustained.
c. It is treated as a long-term capital loss whether or not it was long-term when sustained.
d. It can be used to offset ordinary income up to the amount of the carryback or carryover.

53. Would the following expense items be reported on Schedule M-1 of the corporation income tax return showing the reconciliation of income per books with income per return?

| | Interest incurred on loan to carry U.S. obligations | Provision for state corporation income tax |
|---|---|---|
| a. | Yes | Yes |
| b. | No | No |
| c. | Yes | No |
| d. | No | Yes |

54. Dale Corporation's book income before federal income taxes was $520,000 for the year ended December 31, 1999. Dale was organized three years earlier. Organization costs of $260,000 are being written off over a ten-year period for financial statement purposes. For tax purposes these costs are being written off over the minimum allowable period. For the year ended December 31, 1999, Dale's taxable income was
a. $468,000.
b. $494,000.
c. $520,000.
d. $546,000.

55. For the taxable year, Apollo Corporation had net income per books of $1,200,000. Included in the determination of net income were the following items:

| | |
|---|---|
| Interest income on municipal bonds | $ 40,000 |
| Gain on settlement of life insurance policy (death of officer) | 200,000 |
| Interest paid on loan to purchase municipal bonds | 8,000 |
| Provision for federal income tax | 524,000 |

What should Apollo report as its taxable income?
a. $1,492,000.
b. $1,524,000.
c. $1,684,000.
d. $1,692,000.

56. In 1999, Cape Co. reported book income of $140,000. Included in that amount was $50,000 for meals and entertainment expense and $40,000 for federal income tax expense. In Cape's Schedule M-1 of Form 1120, which reconciles book income and taxable income, what amount should be reported as taxable income?
a. $190,000
b. $180,000
c. $205,000
d. $140,000

57. For the year ended December 31, 1999, Maple Corp.'s book income, before federal income tax, was $100,000. Included in this $100,000 were the following:

| | |
|---|---|
| Provision for state income tax | $1,000 |
| Interest earned on U.S. Treasury Bonds | 6,000 |
| Interest expense on bank loan to purchase U.S. Treasury Bonds | 2,000 |

Maple's taxable income for 1999 was
a. $96,000
b. $97,000
c. $100,000
d. $101,000

58. For the year ended December 31, 1999, Bard Corp.'s income per accounting records, before federal income taxes, was $450,000 and included the following:

| | |
|---|---|
| State corporate income tax refunds | $4,000 |
| Life insurance proceeds on officer's death | 15,000 |
| Net loss on sale of securities bought for investment in 1993 | 20,000 |

Bard's 1999 taxable income was
a. $435,000
b. $451,000
c. $455,000
d. $470,000

59. Norwood Corporation is an accrual-basis taxpayer. For the year ended December 31, 1999, it had book income before tax of $500,000 after deducting a charitable contribution of $100,000. The contribution was authorized by the Board of Directors in December 1999 but was not actually paid until March 1, 2000. How should Norwood treat this charitable contribution for tax purposes to minimize its 1999 taxable income?
a. It cannot claim a deduction in 1999, but must apply the payment against 2000 income.
b. Make an election claiming a deduction for 1999 of $25,000 and carry the remainder over a maximum of five succeeding tax years.
c. Make an election claiming a deduction for 1999 of $60,000 and carry the remainder over a maximum of five succeeding tax years.
d. Make an election claiming a 1999 deduction of $100,000.

60. Lake Corp., an accrual-basis calendar year corporation, had the following 1999 receipts:

| | |
|---|---|
| 2000 advanced rental payments where the lease ends in 2000 | $125,000 |
| Lease cancellation payment from a 5-year lease tenant | 50,000 |

Lake had no restrictions on the use of the advance rental payments and renders no services. What amount of income should Lake report on its 1999 tax return?
a. $0
b. $50,000
c. $125,000
d. $175,000

61. Ram Corp.'s operating income for the year ended December 31, 1999 amounted to $100,000. Also in 1999, a machine owned by Ram was completely destroyed in an accident. This machine's adjusted basis immediately before the casualty was $15,000. The machine was not insured and had no salvage value.

In Ram's 1999 tax return, what amount should be deducted for the casualty loss?
a. $5,000
b. $5,400
c. $14,900
d. $15,000

62. For the first taxable year in which a corporation has qualifying research and experimental expenditures, the corporation
a. Has a choice of either deducting such expenditures as current business expenses, or capitalizing these expenditures.
b. Has to treat such expenditures in the same manner as they are accounted for in the corporation's financial statements.
c. Is required to deduct such expenditures currently as business expenses or lose the deductions.
d. Is required to capitalize such expenditures and amortize them ratably over a period of not less than 60 months.

## SCHEDULE M-2

63. Olex Corporation's books disclosed the following data for the calendar year:

| | |
|---|---|
| Retained earnings at beginning of year | $50,000 |
| Net income for year | 70,000 |
| Contingency reserve established at end of year | 10,000 |
| Cash dividends paid during year | 8,000 |

What amount should appear on the last line of reconciliation Schedule M-2 of Form 1120?
a. $102,000.
b. $120,000.
c. $128,000.
d. $138,000.

64. Barbaro Corporation's retained earnings at January 1, 1999, were $600,000. During 1999 Barbaro paid cash dividends of $150,000 and received a federal income tax refund of $26,000 as a result of an IRS audit of Barbaro's 1996 tax return. Barbaro's net income per books for the year ended December 31, 1999, was $274,900 after deducting federal income tax of $183,300. How much should be shown in the reconciliation schedule M-2 of Form 1120, as Barbaro's retained earnings at December 31, 1999?
a. $443,600.
b. $600,900.
c. $626,900.
d. $750,900.

## CONSOLIDATED RETURNS

65. With regard to consolidated tax returns, which of the following statements is correct?
a. Operating losses of one group member may be used to offset operating profits of the other members included in the consolidated return.
b. Only corporations that issue their audited financial statements on a consolidated basis may file consolidated returns.
c. Of all intercompany dividends paid by the subsidiaries to the parent, 70% are excluded from taxable income on the consolidated return.
d. The common parent must directly own 51% or more of the total voting power of all corporations included in the consolidated return.

66. In the filing of a consolidated tax return for a corporation and its wholly owned subsidiaries, intercompany dividends between the parent and subsidiary corporations are
a. Not taxable.
b. Included in taxable income to the extent of 20%.
c. Included in taxable income to the extent of 80%.
d. Fully taxable.

67. The minimum total voting power that a parent corporation must have in a subsidiary's stock in order to be eligible for the filing of a consolidated return is
a. 20%
b. 50%
c. 51%
d. 80%

68. In 1999, Portal Corp. received $100,000 in dividends from Sal Corp., its 80%-owned subsidiary. What net amount of dividend income should Portal include in its 1999 consolidated tax return?
a. $100,000
b. $80,000
c. $70,000
d. $0

69. When a consolidated return is filed by an affiliated group of includable corporations connected from inception through the requisite stock ownership with a common parent,
a. Intercompany dividends are excluded to the extent of 80%.
b. Operating losses of one member of the group offset operating profits of other members of the group.
c. The parent's basis in the stock of its subsidiaries is unaffected by the earnings and profits of its subsidiaries.
d. Each of the subsidiaries is entitled to an accumulated earnings tax credit.

70. Potter Corp. and Sly Corp. filed consolidated tax returns. In January 1998, Potter sold land, with a basis of $60,000 and a fair value of $75,000, to Sly for $100,000. Sly sold the land in December 1999 for $125,000. In its 1999 and 1998 tax returns, what amount of gain should be reported for these transactions in the consolidated return?

|    | *1999* | *1998* |
|----|--------|--------|
| a. | $25,000 | $40,000 |
| b. | $50,000 | $0 |
| c. | $50,000 | $25,000 |
| d. | $65,000 | $0 |

71. Able Corporation and Baker Corporation file a consolidated return on a calendar-year basis. In 1992, Able sold land to Baker for its fair market value of $50,000. At the date of sale, Able had an adjusted basis in the land of $35,000 and had held the land for several years as an investment. Baker held the land primarily for sale to its customers in the ordinary course of its business and sold it to a customer in early 1999 for $60,000. As a result of the sale of the land in 1999, the corporations should report on their consolidated return
a. $10,000 ordinary gain.
b. $25,000 ordinary gain.
c. $25,000 long-term capital gain.
d. $15,000 long-term capital gain and $10,000 ordinary gain.

72. Bank Corp. owns 80% of Shore Corp.'s outstanding capital stock. Shore's capital stock consists of 50,000 shares of common stock issued and outstanding. Shore's 1999 net income was $140,000. During 1999, Shore declared and paid dividends of $60,000. In conformity with generally accepted accounting principles, Bank recorded the following entries in 1999:

|  | Debit | Credit |
|--|-------|--------|
| Investment in Shore Corp. common stock | $112,000 | |
| Equity in earnings of subsidiary | | $112,000 |
| Cash | 48,000 | |
| Investment in Shore Corp. common stock | | 48,000 |

In its 1999 consolidated tax return, Bank should report dividend revenue of
a. $48,000
b. $14,400
c. $9,600
d. $0

73. Page Corp. owns 80% of Saga Corp.'s outstanding capital stock. Saga's capital stock consists of 50,000 shares of common stock issued and outstanding. Saga's 1999 net income was $70,000. During 1998 Saga declared and paid dividends of $30,000. In conformity with generally accepted accounting principles, Page recorded the following entries in 1998:

|  | Debit | Credit |
|--|-------|--------|
| Investment in Saga Corp. common stock | $56,000 | |
| Equity in earnings of subsidiary | | $56,000 |
| Cash | 24,000 | |
| Investment in Saga Corp. common stock | | 24,000 |

In its 1999 consolidated tax return, Page should report dividend revenue of
a. $0
b. $4,800
c. $7,200
d. $24,000

74. Dana Corp. owns stock in Seco Corp. For Dana and Seco to qualify for the filing of consolidated returns, at least what percentage of Seco's total voting power and total value of stock must be directly owned by Dana?

|    | *Total voting power* | *Total value of stock* |
|----|---------------------|------------------------|
| a. | 51% | 51% |
| b. | 51% | 80% |
| c. | 80% | 51% |
| d. | 80% | 80% |

# ALTERNATIVE MINIMUM TAX

Items 75 through 84 refer to a corporation's need to determine if it will be subject to the alternative minimum tax. Determine whether the statement is true (T) or False (F).

75. The method of depreciation for commercial real property to arrive at alternative minimum taxable income before the adjusted current earnings (ACE) adjustment, is the straight-line method.

76. The corporate exemption amount reduces the alternative minimum taxable income.

77. The ACE adjustment can be a positive or negative amount.

78. Depreciation on personal property to arrive at alternative minimum taxable income before the ACE adjustment is straight-line over the MACRS recovery period.

79. The alternative minimum tax is the excess of the tentative minimum tax over the regular tax liability.

80. Municipal bond interest, other than from private activity bonds, is includable as income in arriving at alternative minimum taxable income before the ACE adjustment.

81. The maximum corporate exemption amount for minimum tax purposes is $150,000.

82. The 70% dividends received deduction is available to determine ACE.

83. Municipal bond interest is includable income to determine ACE.

84. The method of depreciation for personal property placed in service after 1989 for determining ACE is the sum-of-the-years'-digits method.

---

85. Rona Corp.'s 1999 alternative minimum taxable income was $200,000. The exempt portion of Rona's 1999 alternative minimum taxable income was
a. $0
b. $12,500
c. $27,500
d. $52,500

86. The credit for prior year alternative minimum tax liability may be carried
a. Forward for a maximum of 5 years.
b. Back to the 3 preceding years or carried forward for a maximum of 5 years.
c. Back to the 3 preceding years.
d. Forward indefinitely.

87. If a corporation's tentative minimum tax exceeds the regular tax, the excess amount is
a. Carried back to the first preceding taxable year.
b. Carried back to the third preceding taxable year.
c. Payable in addition to the regular tax.
d. Subtracted from the regular tax.

88. Eastern Corp., a calendar year corporation, was formed January 3, 1999, and on that date placed five-year property in service. The property was depreciated under the general MACRS system. Eastern did not elect to use the straight-line method. The following information pertains to Eastern:

| | |
|---|---|
| Eastern's 1999 taxable income | $300,000 |
| Adjustment for the accelerated depreciation taken on 1999 five-year property | 1,000 |
| 1999 tax-exempt interest from specified private activity bonds issued after August 7, 1986 | 5,000 |

What was Eastern's 1999 alternative minimum taxable income before the adjusted current earnings (ACE) adjustment?
a. $306,000
b. $305,000
c. $304,000
d. $301,000

89. A corporation's tax preference items that must be taken into account for 1999 alternative minimum tax purposes include
a. Use of the percentage-of-completion method of accounting for long-term contracts.
b. Casualty losses.
c. Accelerated depreciation on pre-1987 real property to the extent of the excess over straight-line depreciation.
d. Capital gains.

90. In computing its 1999 alternative minimum tax, a corporation must include as a tax preference
a. The dividends received deduction.
b. ACRS excess deduction on 18-year real property.
c. Charitable contributions.
d. Interest expense on investment property.

## COMPUTATION OF TAX CREDITS

91. A corporation may reduce its income tax by taking a tax credit for
a. Foreign taxes.
b. Political contributions.
c. State taxes.
d. Excess charitable contributions.

92. Which of the following tax credits **cannot** be claimed by a corporation?
a. Foreign tax credit.
b. Earned income credit.
c. Alternative fuel production credit.
d. General business credit.

93. Foreign income taxes paid by a corporation
a. May be claimed either as a deduction or as a credit, at the option of the corporation.
b. May be claimed only as a deduction.
c. May be claimed only as a credit.
d. Do **not** qualify either as a deduction or as a credit.

94. This year, Bell Corporation had worldwide taxable income of $675,000 and a tentative United States income tax of $270,000. Bell's taxable income from business operations in Country A was $300,000, and foreign income taxes imposed were $135,000 stated in United States dollars.

How much should Bell claim as a credit for foreign income taxes on its United States income tax return?
a. $0.
b. $75,000.
c. $120,000.
d. $135,000.

95. A corporation may reduce its regular income tax by taking a tax credit for
a. Dividends-received exclusion.
b. Foreign income taxes.
c. State income taxes.
d. Accelerated depreciation.

## MISCELLANEOUS

96. Blink Corp., an accrual basis calendar year corporation, carried back a net operating loss for the tax year ended December 31, 1999. Blink's gross revenues have been under $500,000 since inception. Blink expects to have profits for the tax year ending December 31, 2000. Which method(s) of estimated tax payment can Blink use for its quarterly payments during the 2000 tax year to avoid underpayment of federal estimated taxes?

I.   100% of the preceding tax year method
II.  Annualized income method

a. I only.
b. Both I and II.
c. II only.
d. Neither I nor II.

97. Jackson Corp., a calendar year corporation, mailed its 1999 tax return to the Internal Revenue Service by certified mail on Friday, March 11, 2000. The return, postmarked March 11, 2000, was delivered to the Internal Revenue Service on March 18, 2000. The statute of limitations on Jackson's corporate tax return begins on
a. December 31, 1999.
b. March 11, 2000.
c. March 16, 2000.
d. March 18, 2000.

98. A corporation's penalty for underpaying federal estimated taxes is
a. Not deductible.
b. Fully deductible in the year paid.
c. Fully deductible if reasonable cause can be established for the underpayment.
d. Partially deductible.

99. In 1999, Brun Corp. properly accrued $10,000 for an income item on the basis of a reasonable estimate. In 2000, Brun determined that the exact amount was $12,000. Which of the following statements is correct?

a. Brun is required to file an amended return to report the additional $2,000 of income.
b. Brun is required to notify the IRS within 30 days of the determination of the exact amount of the item.
c. The $2,000 difference is includable in Brun's 2000 income tax return.
d. No further inclusion of income is required as the difference is less than 25% of the original amount reported and the estimate had been made in good faith.

100. A civil fraud penalty can be imposed on a corporation that underpays tax by

a. Omitting income as a result of inadequate recordkeeping.
b. Failing to report income it erroneously considered **not** to be part of corporate profits.
c. Filing an incomplete return with an appended statement, making clear that the return is incomplete.
d. Maintaining false records and reporting fictitious transactions to minimize corporate tax liability.

101. Bass Corp., a calendar year C corporation, made qualifying 1999 estimated tax deposits based on its actual 1998 tax liability. On March 15, 2000, Bass filed a timely automatic extension request for its 1999 corporate income tax return. Estimated tax deposits and the extension payment totaled $7,600. This amount was 95% of the total tax shown on Bass' final 1999 corporate income tax return. Bass paid $400 additional tax on the final 1999 corporate income tax return filed before the extended due date. For the 1999 calendar year, Bass was subject to pay

I. Interest on the $400 tax payment made in 2000.

II. A tax delinquency penalty.

a. I only.
b. II only.
c. Both I and II.
d. Neither I nor II.

102. Edge Corp., a calendar year C corporation, had a net operating loss and zero tax liability for its 1999 tax year. To avoid the penalty for underpayment of estimated taxes, Edge could compute its first quarter 2000 income tax payment using the

| | Annualized income method | Preceding year method |
|---|---|---|
| a. | Yes | Yes |
| b. | Yes | No |
| c. | No | Yes |
| d. | No | No |

103. A corporation's tax year can be reopened after all statutes of limitations have expired if

I. The tax return has a 50% nonfraudulent omission from gross income.

II. The corporation prevails in a determination allowing a deduction in an open tax year that was taken erroneously in a closed tax year.

a. I only.
b. II only.
c. Both I and II.
d. Neither I nor II.

104. A penalty for understated corporate tax liability can be imposed on a tax preparer who fails to
a. Audit the corporate records.
b. Examine business operations.
c. Copy all underlying documents.
d. Make reasonable inquiries when taxpayer information appears incorrect.

105. When computing a corporation's income tax expense for estimated income tax purposes, which of the following should be taken into account?

| | Corporate tax credits | Alternative minimum tax |
|---|---|---|
| a. | No | No |
| b. | No | Yes |
| c. | Yes | No |
| d. | Yes | Yes |

## Released and Author Constructed Questions

*R97*

106. How are a C Corporation's net capital losses used?
a. Deducted from the corporation's ordinary income only to the extent of $3,000.
b. Carried back three years and forward five years.
c. Deductible in full from the corporation's ordinary income.
d. Carried forward 15 years.

*R96*

107. On January 2, 1995, Tek Corp., an accrual-basis calendar-year C Corporation, purchased all the assets of a sole proprietorship, including $60,000 in goodwill. Tek's 1995 reported book income before federal income taxes was $400,000. A $1,500 deduction for annual amortization of goodwill was taken based on a 40-year amortization period. What should be the amount of Tek's 1995 taxable income, as reconciled on Tek's Schedule M-1 of Form 1120, U.S. Corporation Income Tax Return?
a. $389,500
b. $397,500
c. $400,000
d. $401,500

———————

*R96*

**Questions 108 through 110 are based on the following:**

Lind and Post organized Ace Corp., which issued voting common stock with a fair market value of $120,000. They each transferred property in exchange for stock as follows:

|  | Property | Adjusted basis | Fair market value | Percentage of Ace stock acquired |
|---|---|---|---|---|
| Lind | Building | $40,000 | $82,000 | 60% |
| Post | Land | $5,000 | $48,000 | 40% |

108. The building was subject to a $10,000 mortgage that was assumed by Ace. What amount of gain did Lind recognize on the exchange?
a. $0
b. $10,000
c. $42,000
d. $52,000

109. What was Ace's basis in the building?
a. $30,000
b. $40,000
c. $72,000
d. $82,000

110. What was Lind's basis in Acc stock?
a. $82,000
b. $40,000
c. $30,000
d. $0

———————

# Chapter Eight -- Answers
# C Corporations

1. (d) 80%. By definition.

2. (b) $30,500. The corporation receives a transfer basis of property contributed in a tax-free exchange for stock. The basis is determined as follows:

| | |
|---|---:|
| Cash | $ 500 |
| Computer - adjusted basis | 30,000 |
| Total | $ 30,500 |

3. (d) $0. This transaction meets the criteria that when shareholders transfer property to a corporation solely in exchange for stock, no gain or loss is recognized. The transferors of property (Beck and Carr) are in control (90% ownership) immediately after the transfer. The fact that Adams did not transfer in property does not taint the transaction for Beck and Carr because their ownership was at least 80%. If the question was how much income Adams must recognize, it would be $10,000 of ordinary income.

4. (a) $10,000. The corporation receives a transfer basis of property contributed in a tax-free exchange for stock. Mr. Breck and Mr. Witt have 100% control after the transfer. There is a carryover of both the basis and holding period.

5. (b) $20,000. Jenkins received stock, cash and the release of debt from the transfer. When boot accompanies the transfer, it causes the recognition of any realized gain. Since the liability is not in excess of the basis of the property, it does not cause any additional gain to be recognized.

| | |
|---|---:|
| **Amount realized:** | |
| Cash received | $ 20,000 |
| FMV of stock | 20,000 |
| Release of debt | 10,000 |
| Total amount realized | 50,000 |
| Less: adjusted basis of land | -15,000 |
| Realized gain | $ 35,000 |
| Recognized to the extent of | |
| boot (cash) received | $ 20,000 |

6. (d) $10,000. When a shareholder performs services in exchange for corporation stock, the shareholder must recognize ordinary income to the extent of the fair market value of the stock received. This will also be the basis of Rogers' stock.

7. (c) $110,000. This transaction meets the criteria that when shareholders transfer property to a corporation solely in exchange for stock (at least 80% control), no gain or loss is recognized. Clark's basis is comprised of the cash as well as the basis of the property transferred.

| | |
|---|---:|
| Cash transferred | $ 60,000 |
| Basis of property transferred | 50,000 |
| Total basis | $ 110,000 |

8. (d) 80%. When a taxpayer transfers property to a corporation solely in exchange for stock, the general rule under Section 351 is that no gain or loss is recognized, provided that the shareholder(s) is in control after the transfer. Control is defined as owning **at least 80%** of the corporation.

9. (c) $60,000. When a taxpayer transfers property to a corporation solely in exchange for stock, the general rule under Section 351 is that no gain or loss is recognized, provided that the shareholder(s) is in control after the transfer. Control is defined as owning **at least 80%** of the corporation. Whereas Feld owns 100% he meets the control test. There is also a carryover of basis to the corporation of the property transferred by the shareholder. Therefore, his basis is as follows:

| | |
|---|---|
| Feld's original basis | $ 50,000 |
| Additional basis from transfer | 10,000 |
| Total adjusted basis of stock | $ 60,000 |

10. (c) Costs incurred related to the creation of the corporation, such as accounting and legal fees, are not deductible, but are instead capitalized. If the corporation files a proper election by the due date of the return, including extensions, this amount may be amortized over a period of not less than 60 months. Costs associated with a stock offering, however, are neither deductible nor amortizable. These fees are usually the marketing, registration and underwriting fees associated with selling of the shares.

11. (d) $4,000. Organization costs can be amortized over a period of not less than sixty months assuming a proper and timely election has been made. The organization costs of $40,000 divided by 60 months would provide for $667 per month of amortization. The amount for 1998 would be six months, or $4,000. The $35,000 for underwriter fees and other stock issue costs would be charged to capital, and not amortized.

12. (c) The fees paid for underwriter fees and other stock issue costs would be charged to capital, and not amortized.

13. (d) $90. Organization costs can be amortized over a period of not less than sixty months assuming a proper and timely election has been made. The organization costs of $900 divided by 60 months would provide for $15 per month of amortization. The period begins with when the corporation begins business, not the month paid. The amount for 1998 would be six months, or $90.

14. (a) $0. No gain or loss is recognized by a corporation on the sale or exchange of its own stock.

15. (a) $0. No gain or loss is recognized by a corporation on the sale or exchange of its own stock.

16. (d) No gain. No gain or loss is recognized by a corporation on the sale or exchange of its own stock.

17. (a) $0. No gain or loss is recognized by a corporation on the sale or exchange of its own stock .

18. (a) Capital losses can only be offset against capital gains. The $3,000 loss pertains to individuals and the carry forward is five years, not fifteen.

19. (b) By definition.

20. (a) $0 and $5,000. The net long-term capital loss is first netted against the net short-term capital gain, resulting in a net capital loss of $5,000. This amount is available as a five year carryforward. No carryback exists because it is the first year of operations.

21. (d) Short-term capital loss. All capital loss carryovers and carrybacks are treated as short-term.

22. (b) Capital losses may only be used to offset capital gains. Excess net capital losses, regardless of whether they are long or short-term, are carried back and forward as **short-term capital losses.** The carryback period is 3 years and carryforward period is 5 years.

23. (c) Capital assets do not include accounts receivable, property used in a taxpayer's trade or business or land which is to be subdivided and sold (inventory).

24. (d) $38,500. The net capital gains of $2,500 are added to taxable income from operations of $36,000 to determine total taxable income of $38,500. There is no difference in the tax rates for capital gains, unlike an individual. Baker Corporation must first net its capital transactions together as follows:

| | |
|---|---:|
| Short-term capital gain | $ 8,500 |
| Short-term capital loss | -4,000 |
| Net short-term capital gain | 4,500 |
| | |
| Long-term capital gain | 1,500 |
| Long-term capital loss | -3,500 |
| Net long-term capital loss | -2,000 |
| | |
| Net short-term capital gain | $ 2,500 |

25. (a) $0. This sale has a realized loss of $6,000. However, because this is a related party transaction, no loss is recognized. The shareholder owns more than 50% of the stock.

26. (d) The reserve method of providing for bad debts is no longer allowed for tax purposes. The direct write-off method is now required.

27. (c) $345,000. The dividends received deduction is 70% of the dividend for a total of $35,000. The reserve method is no longer allowed for recording of the bad debt expense. Therefore, Kelly Corporations taxable income should be:

| | |
|---|---:|
| Unadjusted taxable income | $ 300,000 |
| Add: Disallowed bad debts | 80,000 |
| Less: Dividends received deduction | -35,000 |
| Taxable income | $ 345,000 |

28. (c) Both I and II. This is the acceptable method to recognize interest income on a bond.

29. (b) 50%. By definition. This percentage was 80% in prior years.

30. (b) An accrual of bonuses will be allowed as a deduction provided that the employees are not shareholders and it is paid within two and one-half months of the tax year-end. The amount of 2% does not appear to be unreasonable.

31. (d) $40,000. The two contributions are both fully deductible. Since Tapper was an accrual based taxpayer, the authorization of the Board was by December 31 and the payment before March 15th. The $40,000 is under the limitation of 10% of the taxable income of $500,000.

32. (d) $116,000. The base amount to determine the contribution limit is taxable income, without regard to the charitable contribution itself and the dividends received deduction. In this problem the DRD has not yet been computed and does not need to be. However, the dividends of $10,000 are not included in the operating income, and must be added in.

| | |
|---|---:|
| Operating income | $ 100,000 |
| Add: Dividend income | 10,000 |
| Add: Contributions | 6,000 |
| Base amount | $ 116,000 |

33. (c) $43,000. The contributions available for use in 1999 total $45,000. This is comprised of the current year contribution of $40,000 plus the carryover of $5,000. To determine the allowable portion, the base amount must be determined. The base is taxable income, without regard to the charitable contribution itself and the dividends received deduction (DRD).

|                            |           |
|----------------------------|-----------|
| Unadjusted taxable income  | $ 410,000 |
| Add back the DRD           | 20,000    |
| Base amount                | 430,000   |
| Contribution limitation %  | 10%       |
| Maximum deduction          | $ 43,000  |

(The excess of $2,000 ($45,000 less the current year deduction of $43,000) is from the $5,000 carryover portion, and may be carried forward no longer than four more years.)

34. (b) $86,000. The contributions available for use in 1999 total $90,000. This is comprised of the current year contribution of $80,000 plus the carryover of $10,000. To determine the allowable portion, the base amount must be determined. The base is taxable income, without regard to the charitable contribution itself and the dividends received deduction (DRD).

|                            |           |
|----------------------------|-----------|
| Unadjusted taxable income  | $ 820,000 |
| Add back the DRD           | 40,000    |
| Base amount                | 860,000   |
| Contribution limitation %  | 10%       |
| Maximum deduction          | $ 86,000  |

(The excess of $4,000 ($90,000 less the current year deduction of $86,000) is from the $10,000 carryover portion, and may be carried forward no longer than four more years.)

35. (c) Any excess charitable contribution is carried forward for five years. In determining the allowable contribution for any given year, the current contribution is considered first, and then any carryforward.

36. (b) In determining its taxable income, a taxpayer may use a reasonable estimate to accrue items when the exact amount is not known. Since Stewart properly accrued the $5,000 of income for 1999, and did not discover the exact amount until 2000, the additional $1,000 of income is recognized in 2000.

37. (a) The uniform capitalization method generally pertains to those companies engaged in manufacturing or constructing real or personal property. The uniform capitalization rules do not apply to small retailers whose average annual gross receipts do not exceed $10,000,000 for the 3 preceding years.

38. (a) Lyle must include, as gross income, the fair market value of the unsolicited samples of the nonprescription drugs (inventory) they received from the manufacturer because they later donated the items as a charitable contribution. Correspondingly, they are allowed a charitable deduction equal to the fair market value of the inventory contributed.

39. (a) $172,000. The base amount to determine the contribution limit is taxable income, without regard to the charitable contribution itself and the dividends received deduction. In this problem the DRD has not yet been computed and does not need to be. However, the dividends of $2,000 are not included in the operating income, and must be added in.

|                        |           |
|------------------------|-----------|
| Operating income       | $ 160,000 |
| Add: Dividend income   | 2,000     |
| Add: Contributions     | 10,000    |
| Base amount            | $ 172,000 |

40. (b) Any excess charitable contribution is carried forward for five years. In determining the allowable contribution for any given year, the current contribution is considered first, and then any carryforward.

41. (c) $275,000. This is a deceiving question. Since the dividends received deduction is classified as a special deduction, the income **before special deductions** is merely the income less the expenses.

| | |
|---|---|
| Sales | $ 500,000 |
| Cost of sales | 250,000 |
| Gross profit | 250,000 |
| Dividends | 25,000 |
| Total income | $ 275,000 |

42. (b) In order to qualify for the dividends received deduction, a corporation must own the stock for more than 45 days.

43. (d) $120,000. To determine the dividends received deduction:

| | |
|---|---|
| Gross profit | $ 400,000 |
| Dividends | 160,000 |
| Total income | 560,000 |
| Operating expenses | -410,000 |
| Taxable income before DRD | $ 150,000 |

Limitation tests:
(1) 80% of 160,000 = $128,000
(2) 80% of 150,000 = $120,000

The lesser of 80% of the (1) dividends received or (2) taxable income is used. Therefore the $120,000 is the DRD for this year. (Note: Using the $128,000 will not cause a net operating loss.)

44. (d) $63,000. As an unrelated corporation, we assume that the ownership is less than 20%, thus resulting in a 70% dividends received deduction. To determine the dividends received deduction, the limitations must be tested as follows:

| | |
|---|---|
| Operating loss | $ -10,000 |
| Dividend income | 100,000 |
| Taxable income before DRD | $ 90,000 |

Limitation tests:
(1) 70% of 100,000 = $70,000
(2) 70% of  90,000 = $63,000

The lesser of 70% of the (1) dividends received or (2) taxable income is used. Therefore the $63,000 is the DRD for this year. (Note: Using the $70,000 will not cause a net operating loss.)

45. (d) $1,000. The base amount to determine the contribution limit is taxable income, **without** regard to the charitable contribution itself and the dividends received deduction.

46. (b) $600. As an unrelated corporation (less than 20%) the investment qualifies for a 70% dividends received deduction. To determine the dividends received deduction, the limitations must be tested as follows:

| | |
|---|---|
| Operating income | $ 300,000 |
| Dividend income | 2,000 |
| Taxable income before DRD | $ 302,000 |

Limitation tests:
(1) 70% of     2,000 = $   1,400
(2) 70% of  302,000 = $211,400

The lesser of 70% of the (1) dividends received or (2) taxable income is used. Therefore the $1,400 is the DRD for this year. Therefore, the net amount of the dividends to be included in the computation of taxable income is:

| | |
|---|---|
| Dividend income | $ 2,000 |
| Dividend received deduction | -1,400 |
| Amount included in taxable income | $    600 |

47. (b) $600. When the dividend income is from a 20% owned company, the investment qualifies for a 80% dividends received deduction. To determine the dividends received deduction, the limitations must be tested as follows:

|                          |           |
|--------------------------|-----------|
| Operating income         | $ 100,000 |
| Dividend income          | 1,000     |
| Taxable income before DRD | $ 101,000 |

Limitation tests:     (1) 80% of    1,000 = $    800
                      (2) 80% of  101,000 = $ 80,800

The lesser of 80% of the (1) dividends received or (2) taxable income is used. Therefore the $ 800 is the DRD for this year. Therefore, the net amount of the dividends to be included in the computation of taxable income is:

|                          |          |
|--------------------------|----------|
| Dividend income          | $ 1,000  |
| Dividend received deduction | -800  |
| Amount included in taxable income | $   200 |

48. (b) $72,000. To determine the dividends received deduction:

|                          |           |
|--------------------------|-----------|
| Gross business income    | $ 160,000 |
| Dividends                | 100,000   |
| Total income             | 260,000   |
| Operating expenses       | -170,000  |
| Taxable income before DRD | $  90,000 |

Limitation tests:     (1) 80% of 100,000 = $80,000
                      (2) 80% of  90,000 = $72,000

The lesser of 80% of the (1) dividends received or (2) taxable income is used. Therefore the $72,000 is the DRD for this year. (Note: Using the $80,000 will not cause a net operating loss.)

49. (d) $120,000. The DRD based upon the dividend received **will increase** the NOL in this problem, this overriding the 80% test on the taxable income limitation.

|                          |           |
|--------------------------|-----------|
| Gross profit             | $ 360,000 |
| Dividends                | 100,000   |
| Total income             | 460,000   |
| Operating expenses       | -500,000  |
| NOL before DRD           | -40,000   |
| DRD (80% of 100,000)     | 80,000    |
| Net operating loss       | $-120,000 |

50. (b) $10,750. The unadjusted taxable income must be reduced by the 70% dividends received deduction. The rates are then applied per the rate schedule.

|                          |          |
|--------------------------|----------|
| Unadjusted taxable income | $ 70,000 |
| Less: 70% DRD            | -7,000   |
| Taxable income           | $ 63,000 |

|                          |          |
|--------------------------|----------|
| Tax computation:         |          |
| First 50,000  @ 15%      | $  7,500 |
| Next $13,000 @ 25%       | 3,250    |
| Total tax                | $ 10,750 |

51. (b) $130,000. Net operating losses may be carried back 2 years, then forward 20 years, unless the corporation makes a special election waiving the carryback. Carrying back the $200,000 two years utilizes $70,000 of the loss, leaving $130,000 to be carried forward.

52. (b) Capital losses may only be used to offset capital gains. Excess net capital losses, regardless of whether they are long or short-term, are carried back and forward as **short-term capital losses.** The carryback period is 3 years and carryforward period is 5 years.

53. (b) Both of these items are allowable deductions in computing taxable income, therefore no items would appear on Schedule M-1 which reconciles book and tax income.

54. (b) $494,000. Organizational costs may be written-off on a straight-line basis over a 60 month period. That would result in an annual deductible expense of $52,000. ($260,000 divided by 5 years). The restated taxable income is as follows:

| | |
|---|---|
| Book income | $ 520,000 |
| Add: Book amortization | 26,000 |
| Less: Tax amortization | -52,000 |
| Taxable income | $ 494,000 |

55. (a) $1,492,000. The items listed in the problem are not included in gross income nor deductible, as appropriate. The following steps are necessary to reconcile book income to tax income:

| | |
|---|---|
| Book income | $ 1,200,000 |
| Add: Non-deductible interest expense | 8,000 |
| Non-deductible federal income taxes | 524,000 |
| | 1,732,000 |
| Less: Non-taxable interest income | -40,000 |
| Non-taxable life insurance proceeds | -200,000 |
| Taxable income | $ 1,492,000 |

56. (c) $205,000. Schedule M-1 would show the following:

| | |
|---|---|
| Book income | $ 140,000 |
| Add: Non-deductible meals (50%) | 25,000 |
| Non-deductible federal income taxes | 40,000 |
| Taxable income | $ 205,000 |

57. (c) $100,000. The book income is actually equal to Maple Corporation's taxable income. The state income tax provision is an allowable deduction; the interest earned on U.S. Treasury Bonds is fully included as gross income; and the interest expense on the bank loan to purchase the U.S. Treasury Bonds is fully deductible.

58. (c) $455,000. To reconcile the reported book income to taxable income, there are certain adjustments which need to be made:

| | |
|---|---|
| Book income | $ 450,000 |
| Add: Non-deductible loss on sale | |
| of investments | 20,000 |
| | 470,000 |
| Less: Non-taxable life insurance proceeds | -15,000 |
| Taxable income | $ 455,000 |

The state income tax refunds are properly recorded in both book and taxable income.

59. (c) $60,000. The charitable contribution is deductible in the 1999 year since it was voted by the Board by December 31, 1999 and paid by March 15th. The base to perform the 10% test for the current year deductibility is **before the charitable contribution.**

| | |
|---|---|
| Book income | $ 500,000 |
| Add: Charitable contributions | 100,000 |
| Contribution base | $ 600,000 |
| Contribution limit percentage | 10% |
| Contribution allowed in current year | $ 60,000 |

60. (d) $175,000. Regardless of whether the taxpayer uses the cash or accrual method of accounting, advance rental payments (not security deposits) must be included in gross income. Likewise, a lease cancellation payment is also included in gross income.

61. (d) $15,000. If a taxpayer in business has a loss from a casualty such as fire, storm, shipwreck, or theft, a deduction is allowed for the decrease in value, or its adjusted basis, whichever is less, minus any insurance reimbursement. As a business loss, this is **fully deductible** and not subject to the $100 floor and 10% of adjusted gross income test required for a personal casualty loss.

62. (a) The corporation may **elect** to either deduct these expenditures as a current business expense or capitalize them and amortize them over a period of not less than 60 months.

63. (a) $102,000. An analysis of retained earnings per the tax return is similar to that for financial accounting.

| | |
|---|---|
| Beginning retained earnings | $ 50,000 |
| Add: Net income for the year | 70,000 |
| Less: Dividends paid | -8,000 |
| Less: Contingency reserve | -10,000 |
| Ending retained earnings | $ 102,000 |

Note that the contingency reserve is not a deduction, but rather an allocation of retained earnings.

64. (d) $750,900. An analysis of retained earnings per the tax return is similar to that for financial accounting.

| | |
|---|---|
| Beginning retained earnings | $ 600,000 |
| Add: Net income for the year | 274,900 |
| Add: Federal income tax refund | 26,000 |
| Less: Dividends paid | -150,000 |
| Ending retained earnings | $ 750,900 |

Note: The refund of federal income taxes paid is an add back to retained earnings because in prior years only the book income (which is net of taxes) is added to retained earnings. This is an adjustment to the retained earnings of the company.

65. (a) A major advantage of filing a consolidated return is the ability to offset operating losses of one group member with operating profits of other members. Intercompany dividends are fully eliminated on a consolidated income tax return.

66. (a) Not taxable. Intercompany dividends are fully eliminated on a consolidated income tax return.

67. (d) 80%. By definition. The 80% test is applied either on a direct basis with the subsidiary, or in a chain of related companies.

68. (d) $0. Intercompany dividends are fully eliminated on a consolidated income tax return.

69. (b)  A major advantage of filing a consolidated return is the ability to offset operating losses of one group member with operating profits of other members.  Intercompany dividends are fully eliminated on a consolidated income tax return.  Only one accumulated earnings credit is available to the parent and subsidiaries.

70. (d)  $65,000 and $0.  In the filing of consolidated returns, any gains or losses realized on sales within the consolidated group are deferred until the eventual sale to an outside party.  The basis and holding period is transferred to the acquiring company.  Therefore, the $40,000 realized gain from the 1998 sale is not recognized until 1999.  The computations for determining the gains are:

| Transaction | 1998 | 1999 |
|---|---|---|
| Selling price | $ 100,000 | $ 125,000 |
| Adjusted basis | 60,000 | 100,000 |
| Realized gain | $  40,000 | 25,000 |
| Deferred gain recognized | | 40,000 |
| Total recognized gain | | $  65,000 |

71. (d)  $15,000 long-term capital gain and $10,000 ordinary gain.  In the filing of consolidated returns, any gains or losses realized on sales within the consolidate group are deferred until the eventual sale to an outside party.  The basis and holding period are transferred to the acquiring company.  Therefore, the $15,000 realized gain from the 1992 sale is not recognized until 1999.  One important issue in this problem is that the character of the 1992 is capital because it was held for investment.  Baker, however, held the land as inventory.  Baker's share of the gain will result in ordinary income while Able's gain will be capital. The computations for determining the gains are:

| Transaction | 1992 | 1999 | |
|---|---|---|---|
| Selling price | $ 50,000 | $ 65,000 | |
| Adjusted basis | 35,000 | 50,000 | |
| Realized gain | $ 15,000 | 10,000 | Ordinary |
| Deferred gain recognized | | 15,000 | Capital |
| Total recognized gain | | $ 25,000 | |

72. (d)  $0.  In a consolidated return, any dividends received from a member of an affiliated group (at least 80%) are eliminated as part of the consolidation and therefore no income is reported.

73. (a)  $0.  In a consolidated return, any dividends received from a member of an affiliated group (at least 80%) are eliminated as part of the consolidation and, therefore, no income is reported.

74. (d)  80% and 80%.  An affiliated group of corporations is allowed to file a consolidated return rather than each corporation filing a separate return.  An affiliated group includes one or more chains of corporations where the parent corporation owns directly at least 80% of the voting stock or total value of the stock of one of the corporations and at least 80% of each corporation in the group is owned directly by one or more of the other corporations in the group.

75. True.  By definition.

76. True.  It is the last reduction before the actual tax calculation and the amount is $40,000.

77. True.  However, the amount of negative adjustments cannot exceed the amount of previous positive adjustments.

78. False.  The length of the period is over the ADR (Asset Depreciation Range) system, not MACRS.

79. True.  By definition.  Very common exam question.

80. False.  Municipal bond interest excluded from taxable income, which is the starting point for determining the alternative minimum taxable income.

81. False.  The amount of the corporate exemption is $40,000.  The $150,000 pertains to the base of the phase-out on the exemption.

82. False.  If available means deductible, then the answer is false.  The 70% dividends received deduction increases pre-adjusted AMTI in arriving at ACE.  The 80% and 100% DRDs do not.

83. True.  While it does not directly increase AMTI through taxable income, it does increase ACE, which may be added back as a positive adjustment.

84. False.  The method used is the alternative depreciation system, which is the straight-line rate.

85. (c)  $27,500.  The corporate exemption amount is $40,000, less 25% of the amount by which the AMTI exceeds $150,000.

| | |
|---|---:|
| AMTI before exemption | $200,000 |
| Base amount before phase-out | 150,000 |
| Excess over base | 50,000 |
| Phase-out percentage | 25% |
| Phaseout amount | $ 12,500 |
| | |
| Exemption | $ 40,000 |
| Less: phaseout | ( 12,500) |
| Allowable exemption | $ 27,500 |

86. (d)  Forward indefinitely.  There are no carryback provisions or limits on the carryforward.  For individuals, the credit is computed only on those items which arise due to timing issues, not exclusions.  For corporations, it is computed for both.

87. (c)  This is the alternative minimum tax.  It is the additional amount over the regular tax.

88. (a)  306,000.  The alternative minimum taxable income before the ACE adjustment starts with taxable income and adds back certain tax preferences and adjustments.  For Eastern Corporation, it is determined as follows:

| | |
|---|---:|
| Taxable income | $ 300,000 |
| Add: Tax preference: | |
|     Tax-exempt interest | 5,000 |
| Add: Adjustment: | |
|     Excess depreciation | 1,000 |
| AMTI before ACE adjustment | $ 306,000 |

89. (c)  Accelerated depreciation on pre-87 real property to the extent of the excess over straight-line depreciation is a tax preference.

90. (b)  Accelerated depreciation on pre-87 (ACRS) real property to the extent of the excess over straight-line depreciation is a tax preference.

91. (a)  The foreign tax credit reduces a corporation's tax.  State taxes are deductions, and the political contributions and excess contributions are non-deductible.

92. (b)  The earned income credit is only available to individuals.

93. (a)  This is an election made by the corporation.

94. (c) $120,000. Corporate taxpayers are taxed in the US on their worldwide income. The taxpayers are entitled to a tax credit for income taxes paid to foreign countries. This prevents double taxation of the same income. The foreign tax credit cannot exceed the lessor of the amount of the foreign taxes paid ($135,000), or the pro-rata share of US taxes on the foreign income. The limitation is determined as follows:

$$\frac{\text{Income from foreign sources}}{\text{Worldwide income}} \quad \frac{\$300,000}{\$675,000} \times \$270,000 = \$120,000$$

95. (b) Corporate taxpayers are taxed in the US on their worldwide income. The taxpayers are entitled to a tax credit for income taxes paid to foreign countries. The other items do not qualify for credits, but rather deductions.

96. (c) Blink can only use the annualized method. In order to rely on the prior year's tax, there must be a tax liability for that prior year (Revenue Ruling 92-54). Since the company had a net operating loss in 1999, it can be assumed that there was no tax in that year.

97. (c) March 16, 2000. The statute begins the day after the due date of the return or the date the return was filed, whichever is later. The mailing date is considered the date filed.

98. (a) Not deductible. A penalty for violation of the law is not deductible.

99. (c) When Brun Corporation accrued the $10,000 of income, that amount was based upon a reasonable estimate. Since the estimate was fixed and reasonably determinable, the difference of $2,000 will be recorded as income in 2000 when received. There is no requirement to file an amended 1998 return.

100. (d) A civil fraud penalty may be imposed on a corporation for maintaining false records and reporting fictitious transactions to minimize corporate tax liability. A penalty of up to 75% of the portion of the underpayment attributable to fraud may be assessed.

101. (a) A corporation must make installment payments if it expects the estimated tax, after credits, to be at least $500. The tax payments are due on the 15th day of the 4th, 6th, 9th and 12th month of the year. In order to avoid any penalty on the underpayment of taxes, the corporation must make payments equal to:

- 100% of its current year's tax
- 100% of its prior year's tax
- Annualized income installment method computation

Whereas Bass made estimates based upon 100% of its prior year's tax, no penalties will be assessed, and only interest on the $400 underpayment will be assessed.

102. (b) A corporation must make installment payments if it expects the estimated tax, after credits, to be at least $500. The tax payments are due on the 15th day of the 4th, 6th, 9th and 12th month of the year. In order to avoid any penalty on the underpayment of taxes, the corporation must make payments equal to:

- 100% of its current year's tax
- 100% of its prior year's tax
- Annualized income installment method computation

However, in order to rely on paying 100% of the prior year's tax, the taxpayer must have a prior year's tax. For example, a corporation with no tax liability in 1999 due to a NOL, must pay 100% of the current year's tax to avoid the penalty. Paying "zero," which was 1999's tax, does not qualify per Revenue Ruling 92-54.

103. (b) In the unusual situation that a corporation prevails in a determination allowing a deduction in an open tax year that was taken erroneously in a closed year, a corporation's tax year can be reopened after all the statutes of limitations have expired. A 50% nonfraudulent omission of income only extends the statute from 3 years to 6 years.

104. (d)  A tax preparer is not required to audit the corporate records, examine business operations, or copy all underlying documents.  However, a penalty may be assessed if the preparer fails to make reasonable inquiries when the taxpayer's information appears incorrect.

105. (d)  A corporation must make installment payments if it expects the estimated tax, after credits, to be at least $500.  The estimated tax includes all taxes, including the alternative minimum tax.

106. (b) Capital losses may only be used to offset capital gains.  Any excess capital losses, may be carried back three years and forward five.

107. (b) $397,500.  This is a difficult question because it requires the understanding of both book versus tax differences, and the rules for amortizing intangible assets.  In Chapter 3, we discuss that intangible assets are amortized over a fifteen year period for tax purposes.  This is different than for book purposes which is frequently a forty year period.  Since the book amortization is less than tax amortization, a Schedule M-1 adjustment is necessary.  Here's the result:

| | | |
|---|---|---|
| Net income per books | | $ 400,000 |
| Tax amortization: | | |
| $ 60,000 / 15 years = | $ 4,000 | |
| Book amortization: | | |
| $ 60,000 / 40 years = | 1,500 | |
| Difference | | - 2,500 |
| Taxable income | | $ 397,500 |

108. (a) $ -0-  When a taxpayer transfers property to a corporation solely in exchange for stock, the general rule under Section 351, is that no gain or loss is recognized provided that the shareholders are in control after the transfer.  Control is defined as at least 80% of the corporation.  Whereas the amount of liabilities assumed by the corporation do not exceed the basis of the property transferred, no gain is recognized on the assumption of the debt.

109. (b) $40,000. When a shareholder transfers property to a corporation in exchange for stock under Section 351, there is a carryover of basis to the corporation.  The basis would be increased by any gain recognized by the shareholder, which in this case is zero.

110. (c) $30,000. Referring to the answers above, Lind's basis in Ace's stock is determined by the basis of the property transferred, less any liabilities assumed.

| | |
|---|---|
| Basis of the building transferred | $ 40,000 |
| Less: mortgage assumed by Ace Corp | -10,000 |
| Lind's basis | $ 30,000 |

# Chapter Nine
# Corporate Distributions, S Corporations and Other Corporate Matters

# Chapter Nine
# Distributions, S Corporations and Other Corporate Matters

## NON-LIQUIDATING DISTRIBUTIONS TO SHAREHOLDERS

### GENERAL RULE
The general rule is that a distribution made to a shareholder with regard to his stock is considered dividend income. For purposes of measuring the income, the fair market value of the property, not its adjusted basis is used. Distributions are taxable to the extent of the earnings and profits (E & P) available in the corporation. A corporation's E & P is similar in concept to its retained earnings. E & P represents the corporation's ability to pay dividends. When a distribution exceeds the available E & P, the excess represents a return of the shareholder's basis in their stock. If that amount exceeds the basis, the excess is treated as capital gain. Thus, distributions are treated as follows:

- Dividend income (to the extent of E & P)
- Return of basis
- Capital gain

### IMPACT ON THE SHAREHOLDER
Earnings and profits are divided into two parts: accumulated E & P (old E & P) and current E & P. When a distribution is made during the year, the corporation determines the amount of the available earnings and profits as of the time of the distribution. The rules for applying accumulated and current E & P to the distributions is as follows:

- If the current E & P is positive and the accumulated E & P is negative, the distribution is treated as coming from the current E & P.
- If the current E & P is negative and the accumulated E & P is positive, the corporation nets the two as of the date of the distribution. If there is positive E & P at that time, the distribution is treated as a dividend to that extent. If there is negative E & P at that time, the distribution is treated as a return of capital, or basis.
- If there are distributions made throughout the year, the current E & P is allocated on a prorata basis. However, accumulated E & P is allocated to the distributions in a chronological order.

---

**Example 1**: D Corporation has accumulated E & P of $2,000 and current E & P of $5,000. D Corporation distributes $15,000 to its sole shareholder. The shareholder's basis in her stock is $3,000. Determine the tax implications of the distribution.

| | |
|---|---|
| Accumulated E & P | $ 2,000 |
| Current E & P | 5,000 |
| Total available E & P | $ 7,000 |
| | |
| Distribution to shareholder | $ 15,000 |
| Dividend income | -7,000 |
| Return of capital | 8,000 |
| Basis in stock | -3,000 |
| Capital gain | $ 5,000 |

Both the accumulated and current E & P are positive and they are added together. The first $7,000 of the $15,000 is dividend income (to the extent of E & P). The excess of $8,000 is then applied to the $3,000 stock basis, which leaves $5,000 as a capital gain. There is no basis remaining in the shareholder's stock after the distribution.

---

## IMPACT ON THE CORPORATION

When a corporation makes a distribution of cash to its shareholders, no gain or loss is recognized by the corporation. The amount of the distribution then reduces the E & P. However, when the corporation distributes appreciated property, the excess of the fair market value over its basis is treated as gain. The income recognized causes an increase in the corporation's current E & P. The fair market value of the distribution then reduces the E & P. Remember, E & P must be brought up to date before the determination of how the distribution is taxable is made.

---

**Example 2**: T Corporation has accumulated E & P of $50,000, and currently has no current E & P. T Corporation distributes land with a fair market value of $40,000 and an adjusted basis of $30,000 to its sole shareholder.

| | |
|---|---|
| Fair market value | $ 40,000 |
| Adjusted basis | -30,000 |
| Gain recognized | $ 10,000 |
| | |
| Accumulated E & P | $ 50,000 |
| Current E & P (gain) | 10,000 |
| Available E & P at the | |
| time of distribution | 60,000 |
| Less: Distributions - FMV | -40,000 |
| Ending E & P | $ 20,000 |

T Corporation recognizes $10,000 of income from the distribution which correspondingly increases E & P. The E & P is then reduced by the fair market value of the distribution.

---

# LIQUIDATING DISTRIBUTIONS TO SHAREHOLDERS

## GENERAL

In a liquidating distribution, the shareholder's stock is being returned to the corporation in exchange for assets. This is similar to the transaction that began the corporation, but varies significantly in the tax treatment. Rather than the general rule that no gain or loss is recognized, the general rule under Section 331 states that a gain or loss is recognized. In addition to gain recognition at the shareholder level, the liquidating corporation also recognizes a gain or loss. The tax treatment to the corporation is as if the property was sold at its fair market value. The character of the gain (ordinary versus capital) must also be determined in order to properly compute any taxes due.

In determining the gain or loss at the shareholder level, the fair market value of the property received by the shareholder, less any liabilities assumed represents the amount realized. On the exam this usual represents cash, accounts receivable, inventory and land.

## EXCEPTIONS

When the shareholder is another corporation which is at least 80% owned by the parent, no gain or loss is recognized on the liquidation. Instead, the basis of the assets being transferred become the basis to the parent as well as any tax attributes such as excess charitable contributions, loss carryforwards, etc.

**Example 3:** On December 31, 1999, K, the sole shareholder has an adjusted basis in the KL corporation of $10,000. The KL Corporation's only assets are cash of $12,000 and land with a basis of $9,000 and fair market value of $12,000. There are no corporate liabilities. K receives a liquidating cash distribution of $12,000 plus the land.

**Impact to the Corporation:** KL Corporation will recognize a gain of $3,000 from the distribution of the land to K (FMV of $12,000 less its adjusted basis of $9,000).

**Impact to the Shareholder:** Assuming KL Corporation distributes the entire $12,000 in cash and the land at the fair market value of $12,000. The result is a $14,000 recognized gain to K.

| | |
|---|---:|
| Cash distributed | $ 12,000 |
| FMV of land | 12,000 |
| Amount realized | 24,000 |
| Less: K's adjusted basis | -10,000 |
| Recognized gain | $ 14,000 |

## REORGANIZATIONS

When stock or securities of one corporation are exchanged for stock, securities and/or assets of another corporation, the transaction may qualify as a tax-free exchange if they are "party to a reorganization." Benefits of a qualified reorganization include the carryover of unused tax attributes such as net operating losses. Under the Internal Revenue Code, the various types of reorganization include:

**Type A**     A statutory merger or consolidation. For example, in a merger a corporation would transfer some of its stock for all the assets and liabilities of a (T) target corporation, and then the target corporation would distribute that stock to its shareholders and liquidate.

**Type B**     One corporation (P) acquires at least 80% of the stock of another corporation (T), solely in exchange for stock. In essence, stock for stock. The voting stock of P goes to T's shareholders and T remains as a sub of P.

**Type C**     This is a stock for asset transaction. Only "substantially all" (not all) of the assets of T need to be acquired in this transaction for P's voting stock. T then transfers the voting stock it received from P and its remaining assets to its shareholders in a complete liquidation.

**Type D**     Typically a divisive reorganization where a transfer of part of the transferor corporation's assets to a controlled corporation, and then distributed to the shareholders. Usually called spin-offs, split-offs or split-ups.

**Type E**     A recapitalization or change to the capital structure.

**Type F**     A mere change in the identity, form or place of the organization.

**Type G**     Assets are transferred to another corporation in a bankruptcy situation.

## PERSONAL SERVICE CORPORATIONS

A corporation will be classified as a personal service corporation (PSC) when (1) its principal activity is the performance of personal services (accountants, actuaries, attorneys, architects, etc.) and (2) its owners-employees own more than 10% of the stock. A PSC generally must use calendar year-end, but may request a fiscal year similar to an S Corporation or partnership, if it can establish a business purpose or does not result in a deferral period of more than three months. A PSC is also limited in certain deductions for its owner-employee, and is taxed at the highest corporate marginal tax bracket.

# PERSONAL HOLDING COMPANIES

## GENERAL

When an individual shareholder receives a dividend from an investment, the individual pays a tax on the dividend distributions. If the shareholder is a corporation, however, it may deduct anywhere from 70% to 100% of the dividend as a dividends received deduction. In addition, because a corporation is initially subject to low marginal tax rates, it is possible for an individual in a high income tax bracket to shift other investments to their corporation to shelter that income from taxation. To prevent any possible abuses, Congress enacted a **personal holding company** status to certain corporations that are very closely held and receive significant amounts of unearned income.

A **personal holding company** is assessed a tax at the **rate of 39.6%** (an individual's highest marginal tax bracket) on its undistributed personal holding company income (UPHCI). This tax is **in addition** to the regular income tax. A company that meets the following two tests is classified as a personal holding company:

- **Five or fewer** shareholders own **more than 50%** of the value of the outstanding stock at any time during the last half of the taxable year, and
- **60% or more** of the corporation's adjusted ordinary gross income (AOGI) is unearned income, such as interest, dividends, rents, royalties or personal service income.

If there are nine or fewer shareholders, the company automatically meets the shareholder test. For purposes of the test, the constructive ownership rules are very broad. Family attribution includes the taxpayer's spouse, brothers, sisters, ancestors and decedents. Stock owned by a corporation, partnership, estate or trust are deemed to be owned proportionately by the shareholders, partners, or beneficiaries.

In performing the unearned income test, rental income may be excluded if (1) it represents 50% or more of the company's AOGI and (2) the company pays out dividends equal to at least the amount that the nonrent personal holding company income exceeds 10% of the ordinary gross income.

In calculating the UPHCI, no deduction is allowed for the dividends **received** deduction. However, a deduction is allowed for federal income taxes, excess charitable contributions and dividends paid. For the purpose of this deduction, the definition of dividends paid is greatly expanded to include:

- Dividends paid during the year,
- Dividends paid within 2 1/2 months of the end of the year,
- Consent dividends, and
- Deficiency dividends

The deduction for dividends paid **within 2 1/2 months** of the end of the year **cannot exceed 20%** of the dividends actually paid during the year. **Consent dividends** represent hypothetical distributions to shareholders. No distribution is actually made. The shareholder recognizes the income and a corresponding increase in the shareholder's basis is recognized. The consent must be filed with the return, and is treated as if it occurred on the last day of the year. **Deficiency dividends** are delayed distributions, usually paid within 90 days of a court determination of PHC deficiency.

Unlike the accumulated earnings tax, the PHC tax is a self-assessed tax. Also, a company may qualify as a PHC in one year and not another. Therefore, each year a company must go through the two tests to determine if they are a PHC.

# ACCUMULATED EARNINGS TAX

## GENERAL

A corporation is first taxed on its earnings at the corporate level, and then the shareholder is then taxed again when the income is distributed as a dividend. To avoid this double taxation, corporations often accumulate rather than distribute earnings. To encourage corporations to distribute and not accumulate earnings, Section 531 imposes a penalty tax on unreasonable accumulations of earnings.

**Penalty tax rate** - The accumulated earnings tax is 39.6% of the accumulated taxable income, or ATI. This is in addition to the regular income tax. The penalty rate of 39.6% is easy to remember because it is the highest marginal tax rate.

The term **accumulated taxable income** (ATI) is a misnomer, because it refers to the current year's addition to the accumulated earnings, not the total accumulated earnings as the name suggests. Briefly, **accumulated taxable income** is determined by:

> Taxable income
> Plus: Dividend received deduction
> Net operating loss
> Capital loss carryover or carrybacks
> Less: Charitable contributions over 10% limit
> Capital loss adjustment
> Federal income taxes
> Dividend paid deduction
> Accumulated earnings credit

The **dividends paid deduction** includes those dividends paid during the year plus those paid two and one-half months after the close of the year. In addition, shareholders may consent to a dividend by filing a statement. No cash is actually distributed, but the shareholder recognizes income and a corresponding contribution to capital is recorded. The consent dividend increases the dividends paid deduction and usually is used to prevent IRS from assessing the penalty. This is not a self-imposed tax.

The **accumulated earnings credit** is the greater of :
> 1. the reasonable needs of the business less the accumulated earnings and profits of prior years,
>    or
> 2. $250,000 less the accumulated earnings and profits of prior years.

For certain service businesses such as consulting, accounting and architecture, the minimum credit is $150,000 rather than $250,000.

Reasonable needs of the business are defined as the business's reasonably anticipated needs and must be specific, definite and feasible. Typical needs include:

- Working capital
- Capital improvements or replacement
- Loans to suppliers
- Reserve for a lawsuit
- Debt retirement

The accumulated earnings tax cannot be imposed on a Personal Holding Company. Nor is there any minimum shareholder requirement.

**Example 4:** Falcon Corporation manufactures trophies. For the year ended December 31, 1998, the company had accumulated earnings and profits of $232,000. Its 1999 taxable income was $40,000 and its federal income taxes were $6,000. In addition the company paid $5,000 in dividends during 1999 and paid $1,000 on March 6, 2000. An analysis of the reasonable needs of the business showed a requirement of $240,000. How much is their accumulated earnings tax exposure for 1999?

*Solution*:

| | |
|---|---:|
| Taxable income | $ 40,000 |
| Less: Federal income tax | ( 6,000) |
| Dividends paid deduction | ( 6,000) |
| Accumulated earnings credit | ( 18,000) |
| | 10,000 |
| Penalty tax rate | 39.6% |
| Accumulated earnings tax | $ 3,960 |

---

# S CORPORATIONS

The shareholders of corporations may consent to be treated under Subchapter S of the Internal Revenue Code. These are referred to as S Corporations, or sometimes Subchapter S Corporations. The corporate structure itself does not change. In fact, most of the language addressing what is referred to as the C Corporations remains intact. What is now changed is how the entity is taxed. While much is written about the distinctions between the taxation of a partnership and an S Corporation, the flow-through nature of the items of income, deductions, credits and losses is quite similar to that of a partnership.

## ELIGIBILITY

In order to be a qualified S Corporation, there are strict limitations which must be adhered to. Failure to maintain compliance with these provisions generally means the termination of S Corporation status.

## SHAREHOLDER REQUIREMENTS

The maximum number of shareholders is 75. For purposes of this test, a husband and wife are considered one shareholder. **Eligible** shareholders include:

- Individuals
- Estates of a decedent and bankruptcy estates
- Grantor trusts, voting trusts, qualified Subchapter S trusts, and "electing small business trusts"

**Ineligible** shareholders include:

- Partnerships (could circumvent the number of shareholder rules)
- Corporations
- Certain trusts
- Non-resident aliens

## CLASSES OF STOCK

An S Corporation is only allowed one class of stock. This means an S Corporation cannot have common and preferred stock. However, it is possible to have voting and non-voting common stock as long as the rights as to shareholder distributions and liquidations are identical.

## DEBT INSTRUMENTS

In general, debt instruments (amounts payable to the shareholders whether they are straight debt or deferred compensation) are not considered a second class of stock. A safe harbor exists for unwritten loans from the corporation to the shareholder if the amount is under $10,000.

## PASSIVE INVESTMENT INCOME LIMITATION

If, prior to becoming an S Corporation, a corporation has accumulated earnings and profits, the Code imposes a passive investment income limitation. If that corporation has passive investment income in excess of 25% of gross receipts for three consecutive taxable years, the S Corporation election is terminated as of the beginning of the next year. Included in the definition of passive investment income is interest, dividends, capital gains and rents (unless significant duties are performed by the corporation as landlord).

## ELECTION PROCEDURES

In order to make a valid S Corporation election, **all the shareholders** must consent in writing. Form 2553 must be filed by the 15th day of the third month of the year in which the election is to be valid, or anytime during the preceding year. For a new corporation, that date begins the first day (1) the corporation has shareholders, (2) acquires assets or (3) starts business. The election is **not** made every year.

---

**Example 5**: K Corporation has been in existence since 1980. On March 12, 1999, R, the corporation's sole shareholder consents to be taxed as an S Corporation. R must file Form 2553 with the Internal Revenue Service by March 15, 1999 in order to be treated as an S Corporation for the 1999 calendar year.

---

## LOSS OF THE S CORPORATION ELECTION

In general, the S Corporation election remains in effect until it is revoked. The revocation may be voluntary or involuntary. A voluntary revocation may be made when the shareholders of the majority of the shares simply consent to the termination. To be valid for that year, the revocation must be filed by the 15th day of the third month of the taxable year.

An involuntary termination occurs when the S Corporation no longer qualifies due to one of the following factors:

- The number of shareholders exceed 75
- An additional class of stock is issued
- The corporation fails the passive investment income limitation
- A nonresident shareholder becomes a shareholder

After the election has been terminated, the general rule is that the shareholders must wait five years before a new election can be made. However, the IRS is allowed to make exception to this rule under the following conditions:

- There is an ownership change of more than 50% of the stock after the first year of the termination.
- The event causing the termination was not reasonably in the control of the majority of the shareholders or the S Corporation.

# OPERATIONS OF THE S CORPORATION AND BASIS COMPUTATIONS

## GENERAL RULE
Each year when the corporation files Form 1120S, it reports each shareholder's allocable share of income, deductions, gains, losses and credits on Schedule K-1. In preparing the return, it is necessary to group items into separately stated and non-separately stated items.

## SEPARATELY AND NON-SEPARATELY STATED ITEMS
Separately stated items are those items which when treated at the shareholder's level, could have a special tax treatment or limitation. Grouping them together as ordinary income could circumvent the tax laws. For example, since an individual taxpayer can only deduct charitable contributions up to 50% of his adjusted gross income, any charitable contributions made by the corporation must be reported separately to the shareholder in order that these be grouped with other contributions the shareholder may have made individually. Only then can the 50% test truly be tested. Likewise, on an individual basis, net capital losses can only be deducted to a maximum of $3,000 per year, and all Section 179 elections cannot exceed $19,000 in 1999. Other separately stated items include, but are not limited to:

- Portfolio income, such as stock, dividends and royalties
- Investment stock expense
- Personal expenses such as medical insurance
- AMT preference and adjustment items
- Passive activities, including rental activities
- Intangible drilling costs
- Taxes paid to foreign countries
- Tax-exempt income

All other items of income and expense that are not separately stated are netted together at the corporation level to determine ordinary income. Refer to the Form 1120S and K-1 at the end of the chapter. Notice that line 21 is the amount of ordinary income.

After the determination of ordinary income (or loss) and of each separately stated item, the amounts flows through proportionately to each shareholder on a K-1 based upon the shareholder's percentage stock in the corporation. If stock is sold during the year, the ordinary income (or loss) and separately stated items are allocated to the shareholder based upon the length of time owning the stock. Notice the similarities to the Form K-1 for partnerships in Chapter 7.

## ALLOCATION OF INCOME ITEMS AND THE RELATED BASIS COMPUTATION
The items of income cause an increase in the basis of the shareholder's stock, while the deductions and losses cause reductions. In no case may the basis of a shareholder's stock be less than zero. In allocating the items, income items are allocated first.

> **Example 6:** For 1999, KL Corporation had ordinary income of $20,000, a long-term capital gain of $10,000 and tax-exempt interest of $4,000. K and L are still equal shareholders, and K's basis at the beginning of the year was $3,000. K's basis will increase by $17,000 (50% of the $20,000, $10,000 and $4,000) to $20,000. K will recognize $10,000 as ordinary income and $5,000 as a long-term capital gain. Her $2,000 share of the tax-exempt interest is not taxable, but does increase her tax basis.

## ALLOCATION OF LOSSES AND DEDUCTIONS AND THE RELATED BASIS COMPUTATION
Items of losses and deductions cause a decrease in the shareholder's basis. Non-deductible items decrease a shareholder's basis as well. Since a shareholder's basis cannot be reduced below zero, it may be necessary to pro-rate items of losses and deductions until sufficient basis exists.

**Example 7:** Assume that in Example 6, K's share of the ordinary income was only $7,000 and there was no capital gain or exempt income. Assume her beginning basis was still $3,000 and that her share of separately stated items included a charitable contribution of $9,000 and a Section 179 election of $6,000. Her basis is first increased by the ordinary income of $7,000 to $10,000. The most she can now reduce her basis by is $10,000. K must prorate the deductions and suspend the excess to future periods until she has sufficient basis. K's basis cannot be negative.

| | Deductions | Ratio | Basis | Allowed | Deductions Suspended |
|---|---|---|---|---|---|
| Charitable contribution | 9,000 | 3/5 | $10,000 | $ 6,000 | $3,000 |
| Section 179 election | 6,000 | 2/5 | $10,000 | 4,000 | 2,000 |
| | $15,000 | | | $ 10,000 | $5,000 |

## SHAREHOLDER COMPENSATION

Unlike partnerships, S Corporations may claim a deduction for compensation paid to the shareholders. Payments must be made by the last day of the taxable year in order to be deducted in that year.

## LIABILITIES

When a corporation incurs liabilities, the individual shareholders do not necessarily share in the responsibility to pay these liabilities. One characteristic of a corporation is limited liability. However, even if a shareholder was personally responsible for a debt (the shareholder guaranteed a bank loan), the shareholder's basis is not increased for the liability. This is a major difference from the rules related to partnerships. If, however, the shareholder lends money to the corporation, the shareholder's basis is increased by that amount. Contrawise, a repayment of a shareholder's loan reduces that shareholder's tax basis.

**Example 8:** During 1999, the DEF Corporation is formed and each shareholder contributes $5,000. On December 31, 1999, the corporation borrows $12,000 for working capital purposes. Each of the shareholders personally guarantees the loan at the bank. The basis of the three equal shareholders, D, E and F, will **not** be increased by their share ($4,000) of the recourse debt. Their ending basis would be $5,000 each.

**Example 9:** If in Example 8, shareholder D personally loaned the $12,000 to the corporation instead, D's tax basis would increase by the $12,000 to $17,000. There would be no increase in the basis of the other shareholders.

## SHAREHOLDER DISTRIBUTIONS

During the course of the year, shareholders typically withdraw capital in anticipation of their earnings to pay income taxes and for other reasons. Generally, these withdrawals do not represent income to the shareholder. A shareholder is taxed on his share of the corporation income, not on what is withdrawn. The withdrawals do, however, reduce the basis of the shareholders stock. When computing the balance in a shareholders account, withdrawals are subtracted out before losses and deductions are.

Should a shareholder withdraw more than the balance in the capital account, the excess will be treated as a capital gain. It is also important to note that these withdrawals are viewed as dividends. Therefore, shareholders should only withdraw (receive distributions) equal to their proportionate share of stock.

**Example 10:** H and J are 50% shareholders of HJ Corporation (an S Corporation). During 1998, H received distributions of $10,000 while J received only $4,000. The IRS may try to terminate the S Corporation status on the grounds that there are two classes of stock. One class provides the shareholder with a larger "dividend" than the other.

## BUILT-IN GAINS TAX

An S Corporation that was previously a C Corporation, may be subject to a built-in gains tax for the appreciation in assets not yet realized, up until the point of the conversion from C to S. The character of the gain recognized will be the basis of the underlying assets when the assets are sold.

---

**Example 11:** The EFG Corporation, a C Corporation, has the following assets on June 30, 1998, the date of the S Corporation election.

|                     | Basis  | FMV    |
|---------------------|--------|--------|
| Cash                | 10,000 | 10,000 |
| Accounts receivable | -0-    | 6,000  |
| Inventory           | 6,000  | 9,000  |
| Land                | 5,000  | 14,000 |
|                     | 21,000 | 39,000 |

On the date of the election, there is a built-in gain to the old C Corporation equal to $18,000. This represents the gain that would be recognized if the assets were sold on that date for $39,000 as compared to their adjusted basis of $21,000. The character of the gain would be $6,000 ordinary from the "collection" of accounts receivable; $3,000 ordinary from the "sale" of inventory; and $9,000 capital from the "sale" of land. The gain would be recognized at the highest corporate rate when the assets are actually sold or exchanged.

---

Form **1120S**

Department of the Treasury
Internal Revenue Service

# U.S. Income Tax Return for an S Corporation

▶ Do not file this form unless the corporation has timely filed
Form 2553 to elect to be an S corporation.
▶ See separate instructions.

OMB No. 1545-0130

**1999**

For calendar year 1999, or tax year beginning _____ , 1999, and ending _____

| A Effective date of election as an S corporation | Use IRS label. Otherwise, please print or type. | Name | C Employer identification number |
|---|---|---|---|
| B Business code no. (see pages 26-28) | | Number, street, and room or suite no. (If a P.O. box, see page 10 of the instructions.) | D Date incorporated |
| | | City or town, state, and ZIP code | E Total assets (see page 10) $ |

F Check applicable boxes: (1) ☐ Initial return   (2) ☐ Final return   (3) ☐ Change in address   (4) ☐ Amended return
G Enter number of shareholders in the corporation at end of the tax year . . . . . . . . . . . . . ▶

**Caution:** *Include only trade or business income and expenses on lines 1a through 21. See page 10 of the instructions for more information.*

**Income**

| | | | |
|---|---|---|---|
| 1a | Gross receipts or sales |_____| b Less returns and allowances |_____| c Bal ▶ | **1c** | |
| 2 | Cost of goods sold (Schedule A, line 8) . . . . . . . . . | **2** | |
| 3 | Gross profit. Subtract line 2 from line 1c . . . . . . . . | **3** | |
| 4 | Net gain (loss) from Form 4797, Part II, line 18 (attach Form 4797) | **4** | |
| 5 | Other income (loss) (attach schedule) . . . . . . . . . | **5** | |
| 6 | **Total income (loss).** Combine lines 3 through 5 . . . . . . ▶ | **6** | |

**Deductions** (see page 11 of the instructions for limitations)

| | | | |
|---|---|---|---|
| 7 | Compensation of officers . . . . . . . . . . . | **7** | |
| 8 | Salaries and wages (less employment credits) . . . . . . | **8** | |
| 9 | Repairs and maintenance. . . . . . . . . . . | **9** | |
| 10 | Bad debts . . . . . . . . . . . . . . | **10** | |
| 11 | Rents . . . . . . . . . . . . . . . | **11** | |
| 12 | Taxes and licenses. . . . . . . . . . . . | **12** | |
| 13 | Interest . . . . . . . . . . . . . . . | **13** | |
| 14a | Depreciation (if required, attach Form 4562) . . . . . . | **14a** | |
| b | Depreciation claimed on Schedule A and elsewhere on return . . | **14b** | |
| c | Subtract line 14b from line 14a . . . . . . . . . | **14c** | |
| 15 | Depletion (**Do not deduct oil and gas depletion.**) . . . . | **15** | |
| 16 | Advertising . . . . . . . . . . . . . . | **16** | |
| 17 | Pension, profit-sharing, etc., plans . . . . . . . . | **17** | |
| 18 | Employee benefit programs . . . . . . . . . . | **18** | |
| 19 | Other deductions (attach schedule) . . . . . . . . | **19** | |
| 20 | **Total deductions.** Add the amounts shown in the far right column for lines 7 through 19 ▶ | **20** | |
| 21 | Ordinary income (loss) from trade or business activities. Subtract line 20 from line 6 . . . . | **21** | |

**Tax and Payments**

| | | | |
|---|---|---|---|
| 22 | **Tax: a** Excess net passive income tax (attach schedule). . . | **22a** | |
| | **b** Tax from Schedule D (Form 1120S) | **22b** | |
| | **c** Add lines 22a and 22b (see page 14 of the instructions for additional taxes) . . . . | **22c** | |
| 23 | **Payments: a** 1999 estimated tax payments and amount applied from 1998 return | **23a** | |
| | **b** Tax deposited with Form 7004 . . . . . . . . . | **23b** | |
| | **c** Credit for Federal tax paid on fuels (attach Form 4136) . . . | **23c** | |
| | **d** Add lines 23a through 23c | **23d** | |
| 24 | Estimated tax penalty. Check if Form 2220 is attached . . . . . . . . ▶☐ | **24** | |
| 25 | **Tax due.** If the total of lines 22c and 24 is larger than line 23d, enter amount owed. See page 4 of the instructions for depository method of payment . . . . . . . . . | **25** | |
| 26 | **Overpayment.** If line 23d is larger than the total of lines 22c and 24, enter amount overpaid ▶ | **26** | |
| 27 | Enter amount of line 26 you want: **Credited to 2000 estimated tax** ▶ _____ Refunded ▶ | **27** | |

**Please Sign Here**

Under penalties of perjury, I declare that I have examined this return, including accompanying schedules and statements, and to the best of my knowledge and belief, it is true, correct, and complete. Declaration of preparer (other than taxpayer) is based on all information of which preparer has any knowledge.

▶ _____
Signature of officer

Date _____

▶ _____
Title

**Paid Preparer's Use Only**

| Preparer's signature ▶ | Date | Check if self-employed ▶ ☐ | Preparer's SSN or PTIN |
|---|---|---|---|
| Firm's name (or yours if self-employed) and address ▶ | | EIN ▶ | |
| | | ZIP code ▶ | |

For Paperwork Reduction Act Notice, see the separate instructions.       Cat. No. 11510H       Form **1120S** (1999)

| SCHEDULE K-1 (Form 1120S) | Shareholder's Share of Income, Credits, Deductions, etc. | OMB No. 1545-0130 |
|---|---|---|
| Department of the Treasury Internal Revenue Service | ► See separate instructions. For calendar year 1999 or tax year beginning , 1999, and ending , | **1999** |

**Shareholder's identifying number ►** | **Corporation's identifying number ►**

Shareholder's name, address, and ZIP code | Corporation's name, address, and ZIP code

**A** Shareholder's percentage of stock ownership for tax year (see instructions for Schedule K-1) . . . . . . . ► .............. %
**B** Internal Revenue Service Center where corporation filed its return ► ........................................................
**C** Tax shelter registration number (see instructions for Schedule K-1) . . . . . . ► ..............................
**D** Check applicable boxes: **(1)** ☐ Final K-1 **(2)** ☐ Amended K-1

| | (a) Pro rata share items | | (b) Amount | (c) Form 1040 filers enter the amount in column (b) on: |
|---|---|---|---|---|
| **Income (Loss)** | **1** Ordinary income (loss) from trade or business activities . . . | 1 | | See pages 4 and 5 of the Shareholder's Instructions for Schedule K-1 (Form 1120S). |
| | **2** Net income (loss) from rental real estate activities . . . . . | 2 | | |
| | **3** Net income (loss) from other rental activities . . . . . . . | 3 | | |
| | **4** Portfolio income (loss): | | | |
| | **a** Interest . . . . . . . . . | 4a | | Sch. B, Part I, line 1 |
| | **b** Ordinary dividends . . . . . . . . . | 4b | | Sch. B, Part II, line 5 |
| | **c** Royalties . . . . . . . . . | 4c | | Sch. E, Part I, line 4 |
| | **d** Net short-term capital gain (loss). . . . . . . . . | 4d | | Sch. D, line 5, col. (f) |
| | **e** Net long-term capital gain (loss): | | | |
| | **(1)** 28% rate gain (loss) . . . . . . . | e(1) | | Sch. D, line 12, col. (g) |
| | **(2)** Total for year . . . . . . . | e(2) | | Sch. D, line 12, col. (f) |
| | **f** Other portfolio income (loss) *(attach schedule)* . . . | 4f | | (Enter on applicable line of your return.) |
| | **5** Net section 1231 gain (loss) (other than due to casualty or theft) | 5 | | See Shareholder's Instructions for Schedule K-1 (Form 1120S). |
| | **6** Other income (loss) *(attach schedule)* . . . . . . . . | 6 | | (Enter on applicable line of your return.) |
| **Deductions** | **7** Charitable contributions *(attach schedule)* . . . . . . . | 7 | | Sch. A, line 15 or 16 |
| | **8** Section 179 expense deduction . . . . . . . . . | 8 | | See page 6 of the Shareholder's Instructions for Schedule K-1 (Form 1120S). |
| | **9** Deductions related to portfolio income (loss) *(attach schedule)* . | 9 | | |
| | **10** Other deductions *(attach schedule)* . . . . . . . . . | 10 | | |
| **Investment Interest** | **11a** Interest expense on investment debts . . . . . . . . | 11a | | Form 4952, line 1 |
| | **b (1)** Investment income included on lines 4a, 4b, 4c, and 4f above | b(1) | | See Shareholder's Instructions for Schedule K-1 (Form 1120S). |
| | **(2)** Investment expenses included on line 9 above . . . . . | b(2) | | |
| **Credits** | **12a** Credit for alcohol used as fuel . . . . . . . . . | 12a | | Form 6478, line 10 |
| | **b** Low-income housing credit: | | | |
| | **(1)** From section 42(j)(5) partnerships for property placed in service before 1990. | b(1) | | |
| | **(2)** Other than on line 12b(1) for property placed in service before 1990 | b(2) | | Form 8586, line 5 |
| | **(3)** From section 42(j)(5) partnerships for property placed in service after 1989 | b(3) | | |
| | **(4)** Other than on line 12b(3) for property placed in service after 1989 | b(4) | | |
| | **c** Qualified rehabilitation expenditures related to rental real estate activities | 12c | | |
| | **d** Credits (other than credits shown on lines 12b and 12c) related to rental real estate activities . . . . . . . . . . | 12d | | See page 7 of the Shareholder's Instructions for Schedule K-1 (Form 1120S). |
| | **e** Credits related to other rental activities. . . . . . . . | 12e | | |
| | **13** Other credits . . . . . . . . . | 13 | | |

For Paperwork Reduction Act Notice, see the Instructions for Form 1120S. | Cat. No. 11520D | **Schedule K-1 (Form 1120S) 1999**

# Chapter Nine -- Questions
## Distributions, S Corporations and Other Corporate Matters

## DISTRIBUTIONS

1. Kent Corp. is a calendar year, accrual basis C corporation. In 1999, Kent made a nonliquidating distribution of property with an adjusted basis of $150,000 and a fair market value of $200,000 to Reed, its sole shareholder. The following information pertains to Kent:

| | |
|---|---|
| Reed's basis in Kent stock at January 1, 1999 | $500,000 |
| Accumulated earnings and profits at January 1, 1999 | 125,000 |
| Current earnings and profits for 1999 | 60,000 |

What was taxable as dividend income to Reed for 1999?
a. $60,000
b. $150,000
c. $185,000
d. $200,000

2. The following information pertains to Lamb Corp.:

| | |
|---|---|
| Accumulated earnings and profits at January 1, 1999 | $ 60,000 |
| Earnings and profits for the year ended December 31, 1999 | 80,000 |
| Cash distributions to individual stockholders during 1999 | 180,000 |

What is the total amount of distributions taxable as dividend income to Lamb's stockholders in 1999?
a. $180,000
b. $140,000
c. $ 80,000
d. $0

3. On January 1, 1999, Kee Corp., a C corporation, had a $50,000 deficit in earnings and profits. For 1999 Kee had current earnings and profits of $10,000 and made a $30,000 cash distribution to its stockholders. What amount of the distribution is taxable as dividend income to Kee's stockholders?
a. $30,000
b. $20,000
c. $10,000
d. $0

4. Nyle Corp. owned 100 shares of Beta Corp. stock that it bought in 1991 for $9 per share. In 1999, when the fair market value of the Beta stock was $20 per share, Nyle distributed this stock to a noncorporate shareholder. Nyle's recognized gain on this distribution was
a. $2,000
b. $1,100
c. $900
d. $0

_____

**Items 5 through 7 are based on the following:**

A Corporation distributes to its sole stockholder property having a basis to the corporation of $10,000 and a FMV of $25,000. Assume that the basis of the shareholder's stock is $22,000. Assume also that accumulated earnings and profits after recognizing the gain on distribution was $20,000.

5. What amount is taxable to the shareholder as an ordinary dividend?
a. None.
b. $10,000.
c. $20,000.
d. $25,000.

6. What amount is taxable to the shareholder as capital gain?
a. None.
b. $3,000.
c. $5,000.
d. $15,000.

7. What is the basis of the stock to the shareholder after the distribution?
a. None.
b. $17,000.
c. $19,000.
d. $22,000.

_____

8. The following information pertains to Dahl Corp.:

| | |
|---|---|
| Accumulated earnings and profits at January 1, 1999 | $120,000 |
| Earnings and profits for the year ended December 31, 1999 | 160,000 |
| Cash distributions to individual stockholders during 1999 | 360,000 |

What is the total amount of distributions taxable as dividend income to Dahl's stockholders in 1999?
a. $0
b. $160,000
c. $280,000
d. $360,000

9. Dahl Corp. was organized and commenced operations in 1990. At December 31, 1999, Dahl had accumulated earnings and profits of $9,000 before dividend declaration and distribution. On December 31, 1999, Dahl distributed cash of $9,000 and a vacant parcel of land to Green, Dahl's only stockholder. At the date of distribution, the land had a basis of $5,000 and a fair market value of $40,000. What was Green's taxable dividend income in 1999 from these distributions?
a. $9,000
b. $14,000
c. $44,000
d. $49,000

10. On June 30, 1999, Ral Corporation had retained earnings of $100,000. On that date, it sold a plot of land to a noncorporate stockholder for $50,000. Ral had paid $40,000 for the land in 1987, and it had a fair market value of $80,000 when the stockholder bought it. The amount of dividend income taxable to the stockholder in 1999 is
a. $0
b. $10,000
c. $20,000
d. $30,000

11. On December 1, 1999, Gelt Corporation declared a dividend and distributed to its sole shareholder, as a dividend in kind, a parcel of land that was not an inventory asset. On the date of the distribution, the following data were available:

| | |
|---|---|
| Adjusted basis of land | $ 6,500 |
| Fair market value of land | 14,000 |
| Mortgage on land | 5,000 |

For the year ended December 31, 1999, Gelt had earnings and profits of $30,000 without regard to the dividend distribution. By how much should the dividend distribution reduce the earnings and profits for 1999?
a. $1,500
b. $6,500
c. $9,000
d. $14,000

12. Tank Corp., which had earnings and profits of $500,000, made a nonliquidating distribution of property to its shareholders in 1999 as a dividend in kind. This property, which had an adjusted basis of $20,000 and a fair market value of $30,000 at the date of distribution, did not constitute assets used in the active conduct of Tank's business. How much gain did Tank recognize on this distribution?
a. $30,000
b. $20,000
c. $10,000
d. $0

## LIQUIDATIONS

13. A corporation was completely liquidated and dissolved during the year. The filing fees, professional fees, and other expenditures incurred in connection with the liquidation and dissolution are
a. Deductible in full by the dissolved corporation.
b. Deductible by the shareholders and **not** by the corporation.
c. Treated as capital losses by the corporation.
d. Not deductible either by the corporation or shareholders.

14. What is the usual result to the shareholders of a distribution in complete liquidation of a corporation?
a. No taxable effect.
b. Ordinary gain to the extent of cash received.
c. Ordinary gain or loss.
d. Capital gain or loss.

15. Krol Corp. distributed marketable securities in redemption of its stock in a complete liquidation. On the date of distribution, these securities had a basis of $100,000 and a fair market value of $150,000. What gain does Krol have as a result of the distribution?
a. $0
b. $50,000 capital gain.
c. $50,000 Section 1231 gain.
d. $50,000 ordinary gain.

16. Edgewood Corporation was liquidated in 1999 by Roberts, its sole shareholder. Pursuant to the liquidation, Roberts' stock in Edgewood was canceled and he received the following assets on July 15, 1999:

| | Basis to Edgewood | Fair market value |
|---|---|---|
| Cash | $ 40,000 | $ 40,000 |
| Accounts receivable | 20,000 | 20,000 |
| Inventory | 30,000 | 45,000 |
| Land | 50,000 | 75,000 |
| | $140,000 | $180,000 |

How much gain should be recognized by Edgewood Corporation on the liquidation?
a. $0.
b. $15,000.
c. $25,000.
d. $40,000.

17. Lark Corp. and its wholly-owned subsidiary, Day Corp., both operated on a calendar year. In January of this taxable year, Day adopted a plan of complete liquidation. Two months later, Day paid all of its liabilities and distributed its remaining assets to Lark. These assets consisted of the following:

| | |
|---|---|
| Cash | $50,000 |
| Land (at cost) | 10,000 |

Fair market value of the land was $30,000. Upon distribution of Day's assets to Lark, all of Day's capital stock was canceled. Lark's basis for the Day stock was $7,000. Lark's recognized gain on receipt of Day's assets in liquidation was
a. $0.
b. $50,000.
c. $53,000.
d. $73,000.

18. At January 1, 1999, Pearl Corp. owned 90% of the outstanding stock of Seso Corp. Both companies were domestic corporations. Pursuant to a plan of liquidation adopted by Seso in March 1999, Seso distributed all of its property in September, 1999, in complete redemption of all its stock, when Seso's accumulated earnings equaled $18,000. Seso had never been insolvent. Pursuant to the liquidation, Seso transferred to Pearl a parcel of land with a basis of $10,000 and a fair market value of $40,000. How much gain must Seso recognize in 1999 on the transfer of this land to Pearl?
a. $0.
b. $18,000.
c. $27,000.
d. $30,000.

19. Ridge Corp., a calendar year C corporation, made a nonliquidating cash distribution to its shareholders of $1,000,000 with respect to its stock. At that time, Ridge's current and accumulated earnings and profits totaled $750,000 and its total paid-in capital for tax purposes was $10,000,000. Ridge had no corporate shareholders. Ridge's cash distribution

I. Was taxable as $750,000 in ordinary income to its shareholders.

II. Reduced its shareholders' adjusted bases in Ridge stock by $250,000.

a. I only.
b. II only.
c. Both I and II.
d. Neither I nor II.

20. When a parent corporation completely liquidates its 80%-owned subsidiary, the parent (as stockholder) will ordinarily
a. Be subject to capital gains tax on 80% of the long-term gain.
b. Be subject to capital gains tax on 100% of the long-term gain.
c. Have to report any gain on liquidation as ordinary income.
d. Not recognize gain or loss on the liquidating distributions.

21. Carmela Corporation had the following assets on January 2, 1999, the date on which it adopted a plan of complete liquidation:

| | Adjusted basis | Fair-market value |
|---|---|---|
| Land | $ 75,000 | $150,000 |
| Inventory | 43,500 | 66,000 |
| Totals | $118,500 | $216,000 |

The land was sold on June 30, 1999 to an unrelated party at a gain of $75,000. The inventory was sold to various customers during 1999 at an aggregate gain of $22,500. On December 10, 1999, the remaining asset (cash) was distributed to Carmela's stockholders, and the corporation was liquidated. What is Carmela's recognized gain in 1999?
a. $0
b. $22,500
c. $75,000
d. $97,500

# REORGANIZATIONS

22. Par Corp. acquired the assets of its wholly owned subsidiary, Sub Corp., under a plan that qualified as a tax-free complete liquidation of Sub. Which of the following of Sub's unused carryovers may be transferred to Par?

| | Excess charitable contributions | Net operating loss |
|---|---|---|
| a. | No | Yes |
| b. | Yes | No |
| c. | No | No |
| d. | Yes | Yes |

23. Corporations A and B combine in a qualifying reorganization, and form Corporation C, the only surviving corporation. This reorganization is tax-free to the

| | Shareholders | Corporation |
|---|---|---|
| a. | Yes | Yes |
| b. | Yes | No |
| c. | No | No |
| d. | No | Yes |

24. Pursuant to a plan of reorganization adopted this year, Daly Corporation exchanged property with an adjusted basis of $100,000 for 1,000 shares of the common stock of Galen Corporation. The 1,000 shares of Galen common stock had a fair market value of $110,000 on the date of the exchange. As a result of this exchange, what is Daly's recognized gain and what is its basis in the Galen common stock, respectively?
a. $0 and $100,000.
b. $0 and $110,000.
c. $10,000 and $100,000.
d. $10,000 and $110,000.

25. Jaxson Corp. has 200,000 shares of voting common stock issued and outstanding. King Corp. has decided to acquire 90 percent of Jaxson's voting common stock solely in exchange for 50 percent of its voting common stock and retain Jaxson as a subsidiary after the transaction. Which of the following statements is true?
a. King must acquire 100 percent of Jaxson stock for the transaction to be a tax-free reorganization.
b. The transaction will qualify as a tax-free reorganization.
c. King must issue at least 60 percent of its voting common stock for the transaction to qualify as a tax-free reorganization.
d. Jaxson must surrender assets for the transaction to qualify as a tax-free reorganization.

26. In a type B reorganization, as defined by the Internal Revenue Code, the

I. Stock of the target corporation is acquired solely for the voting stock of either the acquiring corporation or its parent.
II. Acquiring corporation must have control of the target corporation immediately after the acquisition.

a. I only.
b. II only.
c. Both I and II.
d. Neither I nor II.

27. Pursuant to a plan of corporate reorganization adopted in July 1999, Gow exchanged 500 shares of Lad Corp. common stock that he had bought in January 1991 at a cost of $5,000 for 100 shares of Rook Corp. common stock having a fair market value of $6,000. Gow's recognized gain on this exchange was
a. $1,000 long-term capital gain.
b. $1,000 short-term capital gain.
c. $1,000 ordinary income.
d. $0.

28. Ace Corp. and Bate Corp. combine in a qualifying reorganization and form Carr Corp., the only surviving corporation. This reorganization is tax-free to the

| | Shareholders | Corporation |
|---|---|---|
| a. | Yes | Yes |
| b. | Yes | No |
| c. | No | Yes |
| d. | No | No |

29. Which one of the following is a corporate reorganization as defined in the Internal Revenue Code?
a. Mere change in place of organization of one corporation.
b. Stock redemption.
c. Change in depreciation method from accelerated to straight-line.
d. Change in inventory costing method from FIFO to LIFO.

30. With regard to corporate reorganizations, which one of the following statements is correct?
a. A mere change in identity, form, or place of organization of one corporation does **not** qualify as a reorganization.
b. The reorganization provisions can **not** be used to provide tax-free treatment for corporate transactions.
c. Securities in corporations **not** parties to a reorganization are always "boot."
d. A "party to the reorganization" does **not** include the consolidated company.

31. Which one of the following is **not** a corporate reorganization as defined in the Internal Revenue Code?
a. Stock redemption.
b. Recapitalization.
c. Mere change in identity.
d. Statutory merger.

# PERSONAL HOLDING COMPANY TAX

32. The personal holding company tax
a. Is imposed on corporations having 50 or more equal stockholders.
b. Applies regardless of the extent of dividend distributions.
c. Should be self-assessed by filing a separate schedule along with the regular tax return.
d. May apply if at least 20% of the corporation's gross receipts constitute passive investment income.

33. Where passive investment income is involved, the personal holding company tax may be imposed
a. On both partnerships and corporations.
b. On companies whose gross income arises solely from rentals, if the lessors render no services to the lessees.
c. If more than 50% of the company is owned by five or fewer individuals.
d. On small business investment companies licensed by the Small Business Administration.

34. Acme Corp. has two common stockholders. Acme derives all of its income from investments in stocks and securities, and it regularly distributes 51% of its taxable income as dividends to its stockholders. Acme is a
a. Corporation subject to tax only on income **not** distributed to stockholders.
b. Corporation subject to the accumulated earnings tax.
c. Regulated investment company.
d. Personal holding company.

35. Edge Corp. met the stock ownership requirements of a personal holding company. What sources of income must Edge consider to determine if the income requirements for a personal holding company have been met?

I. Interest earned on tax-exempt obligations.
II. Dividends received from an unrelated domestic corporation.

a. I only.
b. II only.
c. Both I and II.
d. Neither I nor II.

36. Zero Corp. is an investment company authorized to issue only common stock. During the last half of 1999, Edwards owned 450 of the 1,000 outstanding shares of stock in Zero. Another 350 shares of stock outstanding were owned, 10 shares each, by 35 shareholders who are neither related to each other nor to Edwards. Zero could be a personal holding company if the remaining 200 shares of common stock were owned by
a. An estate where Edwards is the beneficiary.
b. Edwards' brother-in-law.
c. A partnership where Edwards is **not** a partner.
d. Edwards' cousin.

37. Cromwell Investors, Inc., has ten unrelated equal stockholders. For the year, Cromwell's adjusted gross income comprised the following:

| | |
|---|---|
| Dividends from domestic taxable corporations | $10,000 |
| Dividends from savings and loan associations on passbook savings accounts | 1,000 |
| Interest earned on notes receivable | 5,000 |
| Net rental income | 3,000 |

The corporation paid no dividends during the taxable year. Deductible expenses totaled $4,000 for the year. Cromwell's liability for personal holding company tax for the year will be based on undistributed personal holding company income of
a. $0.
b. $3,500.
c. $6,500.
d. $15,000.

38. Kane Corp. is a calendar year domestic personal holding company. Which deduction(s) must Kane make from its taxable income to determine undistributed personal holding company income prior to the dividend-paid deduction?

|  | Federal income taxes | Net long-term capital gain less related federal income taxes |
|---|---|---|
| a. | Yes | Yes |
| b. | Yes | No |
| c. | No | Yes |
| d. | No | No |

39. Benson, a singer, owns 100% of the outstanding capital stock of Lund Corp. Lund contracted with Benson, specifying that Benson was to perform personal services for Magda Productions, Inc., in consideration of which Benson was to receive $50,000 a year from Lund. Lund contracted with Magda, specifying that Benson was to perform personal services for Magda, in consideration of which Magda was to pay Lund $1,000,000 a year. Personal holding company income will be attributable to
a. Benson only.
b. Lund only.
c. Magda only.
d. All three contracting parties.

40. The personal holding company tax
a. Qualifies as a tax credit that may be used by partners or stockholders to reduce their individual income taxes.
b. May be imposed ·on both corporations and partnerships.
c. Should be self-assessed by filing a separate schedule with the regular tax return.
d. May be imposed regardless of the number of equal stockholders in a corporation.

41. The personal holding company tax may be imposed
a. As an alternative tax in place of the corporation's regularly computed tax.
b. If more than 50% of the corporation's stock is owned, directly or indirectly, by more than ten stockholders.
c. If at least 60% of the corporation's adjusted ordinary gross income for the taxable year is personal holding company income, and the stock ownership test is satisfied.
d. In conjunction with the accumulated earnings tax.

42. Kee Holding Corp. has 80 unrelated equal stockholders. For the year ended December 31, 1999, Kee's income comprised the following:

| | |
|---|---|
| Net rental income | $ 1,000 |
| Commissions earned on sales of franchises | 3,000 |
| Dividends from taxable domestic corporations | 90,000 |

Deductible expenses for 1999 totaled $10,000. Kee paid no dividends for the past three years. Kee's liability for personal holding company tax for 1999 will be based on
a. $12,000
b. $11,000
c. $9,000
d. $0

## ACCUMULATED EARNINGS TAX

43. The accumulated earnings tax can be imposed
a. Regardless of the number of stockholders of a corporation.
b. On personal holding companies.
c. On companies that make distributions in excess of accumulated earnings.
d. On both partnerships and corporations.

44. In determining accumulated taxable income for the purpose of the accumulated earnings tax, which one of the following is allowed as a deduction?
a. Capital loss carryover from prior year.
b. Dividends-received deduction.
c. Net operating loss deduction.
d. Net capital loss for current year.

45. The accumulated earnings tax
a. Depends on a stock ownership test based on the number of stockholders.
b. Can be avoided by sufficient dividend distributions.
c. Is computed by the filing of a separate schedule along with the corporation's regular tax return.
d. Is imposed when the entity is classified as a personal holding company.

46. The minimum accumulated earnings credit is
a. $150,000 for all corporations.
b. $150,000 for nonservice corporations only.
c. $250,000 for all corporations.
d. $250,000 for nonservice corporations only.

47. Kari Corp., a manufacturing company, was organized on January 2, 1999. Its 1999 federal taxable income was $400,000 and its federal income tax was $100,000. What is the maximum amount of accumulated taxable income that may be subject to the accumulated earnings tax for 1999 if Kari takes only the minimum accumulated earnings credit?
a. $300,000
b. $150,000
c. $ 50,000
d. $0

48. Daystar Corp., which is not a mere holding or investment company, derives its income from consulting services. Daystar had accumulated earnings and profits of $45,000 at December 31, 1998. For the year ended December 31, 1999, it had earnings and profits of $215,000 and a dividends-paid deduction of $15,000. It has been determined that $20,000 of the accumulated earnings and profits for 1999 is required for the reasonable needs of the business. How much is the available accumulated earnings credit at December 31, 1999?
a. $105,000.
b. $205,000.
c. $150,000.
d. $250,000.

49. Dart Corp., a calendar year domestic C corporation, is not a personal holding company. For purposes of the accumulated earnings tax, Dart has accumulated taxable income for 1999. Which step(s) can Dart take to eliminate or reduce any 1999 accumulated earnings tax?

I. Demonstrate that the "reasonable needs" of its business require the retention of all or part of the 1999 accumulated taxable income.

II. Pay dividends by March 15, 2000.

a. I only.
b. II only.
c. Both I and II.
d. Neither I nor II.

50. The accumulated earnings tax can be imposed
a. On both partnerships and corporations.
b. On companies that make distributions in excess of accumulated earnings.
c. On personal holding companies.
d. Regardless of the number of stockholders in a corporation.

51. The accumulated earnings tax does **not** apply to
a. Corporations that have more than 100 stockholders.
b. Personal holding companies.
c. Corporations filing consolidated returns.
d. Corporations that have more than one class of stock.

52. The accumulated earnings tax
a. Should be self-assessed by filing a separate schedule along with the regular tax return.
b. Applies only to closely held corporations.
c. Can be imposed on S corporations that do not regularly distribute their earnings.
d. Can **not** be imposed on a corporation that has undistributed earnings and profits of less than $150,000.

# S CORPORATIONS

53. Which one of the following will render a corporation ineligible for S corporation status?
a. One of the stockholders is a decedent's estate.
b. One of the stockholders is a bankruptcy estate.
c. The corporation has both voting and nonvoting common stock issued and outstanding.
d. The corporation has 80 stockholders.

54. Which of the following conditions will prevent a corporation from qualifying as an S Corporation?
a. The corporation has both common and preferred stock.
b. The corporation has one class of stock with different voting rights.
c. One shareholder is an estate.
d. One shareholder is a grantor trust.

55. Village Corp., a calendar year corporation, began business in 1990. Village made a valid S Corporation election on December 5, 1999, with the unanimous consent of its shareholders. The eligibility requirements for S status continued to be met throughout 2000. On what date did Village's S status become effective?
a. January 1, 1999.
b. January 1, 2000.
c. December 5, 1999.
d. December 5, 2000.

56. On February 10, 1999, Ace Corp., a calendar year corporation, elected S corporation status and all shareholders consented to the election. There was no change in shareholders in 1999. Ace met all eligibility requirements for S status during the preelection portion of the year. What is the earliest date on which Ace can be recognized as an S corporation?
a. February 10, 2000.
b. February 10, 1999.
c. January 1, 2000.
d. January 1, 1999.

57. Bristol Corp. was formed as a C corporation on January 1, 1980, and elected S corporation status on January 1, 1986. At the time of the election, Bristol had accumulated C corporation earnings and profits which have not been distributed. Bristol has had the same 25 shareholders throughout its existence. In 1999 Bristol's S election will terminate if it
a. Increases the number of shareholders to 75.
b. Adds a decedent's estate as a shareholder to the existing shareholders.
c. Takes a charitable contribution deduction.
d. Has passive investment income exceeding 90% of gross receipts in each of the three consecutive years ending December 31, 1998.

58. An S corporation has 30,000 shares of voting common stock and 20,000 shares of non-voting common stock issued and outstanding. The S election can be revoked voluntarily with the consent of the shareholders holding, on the day of the revocation,

|   | Shares of voting stock | Shares of nonvoting stock |
|---|---|---|
| a. | 0 | 20,000 |
| b. | 7,500 | 5,000 |
| c. | 10,000 | 16,000 |
| d. | 20,000 | 0 |

59. After a corporation's status as an S corporation is revoked or terminated, how many years is the corporation generally required to wait before making a new S election, in the absence of IRS consent to an earlier election?
a. 1
b. 3
c. 5
d. 10

60. Tau Corp. which has been operating since 1980, has an October 31 year end, which coincides with its natural business year. On May 15, 1999, Tau filed the required form to elect S corporation status. All of Tau's stockholders consented to the election, and all other requirements were met. The earliest date that Tau can be recognized as an S corporation is
a. November 1, 1998.
b. May 15, 1999.
c. November 1, 1999.
d. November 1, 2000.

61. Which of the following is **not** a requirement for a corporation to elect S corporation status?
a. Must be a member of a controlled group.
b. Must confine stockholders to individuals, estates, and certain qualifying trusts.
c. Must be a domestic corporation.
d. Must have only one class of stock.

62. If a calendar-year S corporation does not request an automatic six-month extension of time to file its income tax return, the return is due by
a. January 31
b. March 15
c. April 15
d. June 30

63. A corporation that has been an S corporation from its inception may

|   | Have both passive and nonpassive income | Be owned by a bankruptcy estate |
|---|---|---|
| a. | No | Yes |
| b. | Yes | No |
| c. | No | No |
| d. | Yes | Yes |

64. For the taxable year ended December 31, Elk Inc., an S corporation, had net income per books of $54,000, which included $45,000 from operations and a $9,000 net long-term capital gain. During the year, $22,500 was distributed to Elk's three equal stockholders, all of whom are on a calendar-year basis. On what amounts should Elk compute its income and capital gain taxes?

|   | Ordinary income | Long-term capital gain |
|---|---|---|
| a. | $31,500 | $ 0 |
| b. | $22,500 | $ 0 |
| c. | $ 0 | $9,000 |
| d. | $ 0 | $ 0 |

65. If an S corporation has **no** accumulated earnings and profits, the amount distributed to a shareholder
a. Must be returned to the S corporation.
b. Increases the shareholder's basis for the stock.
c. Decreases the shareholder's basis for the stock.
d. Has **no** effect on the shareholder's basis for the stock.

66. The Haas Corp., a calendar year S corporation, has two equal shareholders. For the year ended December 31, 1999, Haas had taxable income and current earnings and profits of $60,000, which included $50,000 from operations and $10,000 from investment interest income. There were no other transactions that year. Each shareholder's basis in the stock of Haas will increase by
a. $50,000
b. $30,000
c. $25,000
d. $0

67. Bern Corp., an S corporation, had an ordinary loss of $36,500 for the year ended December 31, 1998. At January 1, 1999, Meyer owned 50% of Bern's stock. Meyer held the stock for 40 days in 1999 before selling the entire 50% interest to an unrelated third party. Meyer's basis for the stock was $10,000. Meyer was a full-time employee of Bern until the stock was sold. Meyer's share of Bern's 1999 loss was
a. $0
b. $2,000
c. $10,000
d. $18,250

68. An S corporation is **not** permitted to take a deduction for
a. Compensation of officers.
b. Interest paid to individuals who are not stockholders of the S corporation.
c. Charitable contributions.
d. Employee benefit programs established for individuals who are not stockholders of the S corporation.

69. An S corporation may deduct
a. Charitable contributions within the percentage of income limitation applicable to corporations.
b. Net operating loss carryovers.
c. Foreign income taxes.
d. Compensation of officers.

70. Zinco Corp. was a calendar year S corporation. Zinco's S status terminated on April 1, 1999, when Case Corp. became a shareholder. During 1999 (365-day calendar year), Zinco had nonseparately computed income of $310,250. If no election was made by Zinco, what amount of the income, if any, was allocated to the S short year for 1999?
a. $233,750
b. $155,125
c. $76,500
d. $0

71. As of January 1, 1999, Kane owned all the 100 issued shares of Manning Corp., a calendar year S corporation. On the 41st day of 1999, Kane sold 25 of the Manning shares to Rodgers. For the year ended December 31, 1999 (a 365-day calendar year), Manning had $73,000 in nonseparately stated income and made no distributions to its shareholders. What amount of nonseparately stated income from Manning should be reported on Kane's 1999 tax return?
a. $56,750
b. $54,750
c. $16,250
d. $0

72. With regard to S corporations and their stockholders, the "at risk" rules applicable to losses
a. Depend on the type of income reported by the S corporation.
b. Are subject to the elections made by the S corporation's stockholders.
c. Take into consideration the S corporation's ratio of debt to equity.
d. Apply at the shareholder level rather than at the corporate level.

73. An S corporation's accumulated adjustments account, which measures the amount of earnings that may be distributed tax-free,
a. Must be adjusted downward for the full amount of federal income taxes attributable to any taxable year in which the corporation was a C corporation.
b. Must be adjusted upward for the full amount of federal income taxes attributable to any taxable year in which the corporation was a C corporation.
c. Must be adjusted upward or downward for only the federal income taxes affected by capital gains or losses, respectively, for any taxable year in which the corporation was a C corporation.
d. Is **not** adjusted for federal income taxes attributable to a taxable year in which the corporation was a C corporation.

74. An S corporation may
a. Have both common and preferred stock.
b. Have a corporation as a shareholder.
c. Be a member of an affiliated group.
d. Have as many as 75 shareholders.

75. Brooke, Inc., an S corporation, was organized on January 2, 1999, with two equal stockholders who materially participate in the S corporation's business. Each stockholder invested $5,000 in Brooke's capital stock, and each loaned $15,000 to the corporation. Brooke then borrowed $60,000 from a bank for working capital. Brooke sustained an operating loss of $90,000 for the year ended December 31, 1999. How much of this loss can each stockholder claim on his 1999 income tax return?
a. $5,000
b. $20,000
c. $45,000
d. $50,000

76. A shareholder's basis in the stock of an S corporation is increased by the shareholder's pro rata share of income from

|  | Tax-exempt interest | Taxable interest |
|---|---|---|
| a. | No | No |
| b. | No | Yes |
| c. | Yes | No |
| d. | Yes | Yes |

## Released and Author Constructed Questions

77. Mintee Corp., an accrual-basis calendar-year C corporation, had no corporate shareholders when it liquidated in 1996. In cancellation of all their Mintee stock, each Mintee shareholder received in 1996, a liquidating distribution of $2,000 cash and land with a tax basis of $5,000 and a fair market value of $10,500. Before the distribution, each shareholder's tax basis in Mintee stock was $6,500. What amount of gain should each Mintee shareholder recognize on the liquidating distribution?
a. $0
b. $500
c. $4,000
d. $6,000

78. Elm Corp. is an accrual-basis calendar-year C corporation with 100,000 shares of voting common stock issued and outstanding as of December 28, 1995. On Friday, December 29, 1995, Hall surrendered 2,000 shares of Elm stock to Elm in exchange for $33,000 cash. Hall had no direct or indirect interest in Elm after the stock surrender. Additional information follows:

Hall's adjusted basis in 2,000 shares of
Elm on December 29, 1995 ($8 per share)  $16,000

Elm's accumulated earnings and profits at
January 1, 1995                                              25,000

Elm's 1995 net operating loss                        (7,000)

What amount of income did Hall recognize from the stock surrender?
a. $33,000 dividend.
b. $25,000 dividend.
c. $18,000 capital gain.
d. $17,000 capital gain.

# Chapter Nine -- Answers
## Corporate Distributions, S Corporations and Other Corporate Matters

1. (c) $185,000. In a non-liquidating distribution, dividend income is recognized only to the extent of the earnings and profits of the corporation. Any excess of the distribution over the E & P represents a return of the taxpayer's basis in his stock. Reed must recognize dividend income of $185,000.

| | |
|---|---|
| Beginning E & P | $ 125,000 |
| Current E & P | 60,000 |
| Available E & P | $ 185,000 |
| | |
| Shareholder distribution | $ 200,000 |
| Dividend income - (E & P) | -185,000 |
| Return of basis | $ 15,000 |

2. (b) $140,000. In a non-liquidating distribution, dividend income is recognized only to the extent of the earnings and profits of the corporation. Any excess of the distribution over the E & P represents a return of the taxpayer's basis in his stock. Lamb must recognize dividend income of $140,000.

| | |
|---|---|
| Beginning E & P | $ 60,000 |
| Current E & P | 80,000 |
| Available E & P | $ 140,000 |
| | |
| Shareholder distribution | $ 180,000 |
| Dividend income - (E & P) | -140,000 |
| Return of basis | $ 40,000 |

3. (c) $10,000. When there is an accumulated deficit and positive current earnings, the distribution is deemed to come out of the current earnings first. (There is no netting of the accumulated deficit and current E & P). Kee must recognize $10,000 of dividend income. The balance is a return of the taxpayer's basis in his stock.

| | |
|---|---|
| Shareholder distribution | $ 30,000 |
| Dividend income - (E & P) | -10,000 |
| Return of basis | $ 20,000 |

4. (b) $1,100. When a corporation makes a distribution of property other than cash to a shareholder, any excess of the fair market value over the adjusted basis, or cost, will be recognized as a gain.

| | |
|---|---|
| Fair market value of distribution | |
| 100 shares @ $20 | $ 2,000 |
| Adjusted basis of property | |
| 100 shares @ $9 | 900 |
| Gain on distribution | $ 1,100 |

5. (c) $20,000. In a non-liquidating distribution, dividend income is recognized only to the extent of the earnings and profits of the corporation. Any excess of the distribution over the E & P represents a return of the taxpayer's basis in his stock. In this comprehensive problem, the shareholder recognizes $20,000 in dividend income; receives a $5,000 tax-free return of his basis (investment) and his new basis is $17,000.

| | |
|---|---|
| Available E & P | $ 20,000 |

| | |
|---|---|
| Shareholder distribution | $ 25,000 |
| Dividend income - (E & P) | -20,000 |
| Return of basis | $ 5,000 |

| | |
|---|---|
| Original shareholder basis | $ 22,000 |
| Return of capital | -5,000 |
| Ending basis after distribution | $ 17,000 |

6. (a) None. See #5.

7. (b) $17,000. See #5.

8. (c) $280,000. In a non-liquidating distribution, dividend income is recognized only to the extent of the earnings and profits of the corporation. Any excess of the distribution over the E & P represents a return of the taxpayer's basis in his stock. Lamb must recognize dividend income of $280,000. The excess of $80,000 is a return of capital.

| | |
|---|---|
| Beginning E & P | $ 120,000 |
| Current E & P | 160,000 |
| Available E & P | $ 280,000 |

| | |
|---|---|
| Shareholder distribution | $ 360,000 |
| Dividend income - (E & P) | -280,000 |
| Return of basis | $ 80,000 |

9. (c) $44,000. In a non-liquidating distribution, dividend income is recognized **only** to the extent of the earnings and profits of the corporation. However, when a corporation distributes property to a shareholder, the corporation must recognize any gain to the extent of the excess of the fair market value of the property over its adjusted basis. In this problem, the fair market of $40,000 exceeds the adjusted basis of $5,000 by $35,000. This gain increases the company's E & P.

| | |
|---|---|
| Cash distribution | $ 9,000 |
| Fair market value of land | 40,000 |
| Total distribution | $ 49,000 |

| | |
|---|---|
| Beginning E & P | $ 9,000 |
| Amount recognized on land distribution | 35,000 |
| Available E & P | $ 44,000 |

10. (d) $30,000. When a corporation has dealings with its own shareholders, transactions must be conducted on an arm's length basis. By selling the property to the shareholder for less than the fair market value, the shareholder has received a disguised dividend to the extent the difference. Since there is sufficient E & P, the calculations are as follows:

| | |
|---|---|
| Fair market value of property | $ 80,000 |
| Amount paid for by shareholder | -50,000 |
| Constructive dividend | $ 30,000 |

11. (a) $1,500. When a corporation makes a distribution of property other than cash to a shareholder, any excess of the fair market value of the distribution over the adjusted basis will be recognized as a gain. However, the impact to the corporation's earnings and profits require an increase based upon any gain recognized; a increase for the release of any indebtedness; and a decrease for the fair market value of the property being distributed.

| | |
|---|---|
| Fair market value of property | $ 14,000 |
| Adjusted basis | -6,500 |
| Recognized gain | $ 7,500 |

Impact on E & P:

| | |
|---|---|
| Recognized gain | $ 7,500 |
| Release of debt | 5,000 |
| Less: FMV of distribution | -14,000 |
| Overall decrease in E & P | $ 1,500 |

12. (c) $10,000. When a corporation makes a distribution of property other than cash to a shareholder, any excess of the fair market value over the adjusted basis will be recognized as a gain.

| | |
|---|---|
| Fair market value of property | $ 30,000 |
| Adjusted basis | -20,000 |
| Recognized gain | $ 10,000 |

13. (a) The fees and expenditures incurred in connection with the liquidation are deducted in full as a corporate expense.

14. (d) This is the general rule. The shareholder is exchanging stock for the assets of the corporation. The amount realized by the shareholder usually includes cash and the fair market value of any property. The shareholder's basis in the stock is then subtracted from the amount realized to determine the capital gain or loss.

15. (b) $50,000 capital gain. A corporation recognizes a gain on the distribution of appreciated property in excess of its adjusted basis.

16. (d) $40,000. A corporation recognizes a gain on the distribution of appreciated property in excess of its adjusted basis.

| | |
|---|---|
| Fair market value | $ 180,000 |
| Adjusted basis | -140,000 |
| Recognized gain | $ 40,000 |

17. (a) $0. Even though the fair market value of the assets distributed ($80,000) exceeded the basis of Day's stock held by Lark, no gain or loss is recognized. The liquidation of a subsidiary into its parent is non-taxable.

18. (a) $0. No gain or loss is recognized on the liquidation of a subsidiary into its parent.

19. (c) Both I and II. In a non-liquidating distribution, dividend income is recognized only to the extent of the earnings and profits of the corporation. Any excess of the distribution over the E & P represents a return of the taxpayer's basis in his stock.

20. (d) No gain or loss is recognized on the liquidation of a subsidiary into its parent.

21. (d) $97,500. When a corporation adopts a plan of liquidation, the difference between the selling price of the assets and their adjusted basis is recognized as a gain, even if the corporation then distributes the remaining cash to the shareholders. The total gain is determined as:

| | |
|---|---|
| Gain on the sale of land | $ 75,000 |
| Gain on the sale of inventory | 22,500 |
| Total recognized gain | $ 97,500 |

22. (d) Under a qualified plan of tax-free liquidation, the tax attributes of the acquired corporation transfer over to the acquiring corporation. This allows the parent to utilize the excess charitable contributions and net operating losses.

23. (a) This is a statutory merger and qualifies as a tax-free reorganization. It is tax-free to both the shareholders and the corporation.

24. (a) $0 and $100,000. No gain or loss is recognized when a corporation exchanges property pursuant to a plan of reorganization solely in exchange for stock in another corporation. Daly's basis in the Galen Corporation stock is the basis of the transferred property, or $100,000.

25. (b) This is Type B reorganization. King acquired control (at least 80%) of Jaxson's stock in exchange for part of its own stock.

26. (c) By definition. The control test means at least 80%.

27. (d) $0. No gain or loss is recognized by an individual, if pursuant to a plan of corporate reorganization, the taxpayer exchanges stock of one corporation for another.

28. (a) Yes and Yes. This qualifies as a Type A reorganization and is non-taxable to both the shareholders and corporation.

29. (a) A mere change in the place of organization of one corporation qualifies as a Type F reorganization. The other answers listed are not reorganizations, but rather changes in accounting methods.

30. (c) In general, when securities in corporations which are **not** party to the reorganization are exchanged, they are treated as boot.

31. (a) A stock redemption is **not** considered to be a corporate reorganization. A recapitalization (Type E); mere change in identity (Type F); and statutory merger (Type A) are reorganizations.

32. (c) The personal holding company status is self-assessed. It is imposed on corporations with a limited number of shareholders; dividend distributions are critical in determining the tax; and investment income must be at least 60%.

33. (c) The rule is that 5 or fewer shareholders cannot own more than 50% of the corporation's stock.

34. (d) Acme Corporation meets the shareholder test (5 or fewer shareholders cannot own more than 50% of the corporation's stock) and the passive investment income test (60% or more of its AOGI is PHCI). The investment income is 100%. The fact that it distributes dividends does not change its classification.

35. (b) Dividends are considered personal holding company income, but tax-exempt interest is excluded.

36. (a) Through the attribution rules, Edwards is deemed to own the shares of stock held by the estate naming him as the beneficiary. This gives Edwards 650 shares of stock. With this ownership, Zero Corporation meets the shareholder test.

$$650 > 50\% \text{ of } 1000$$

37. (a) $0. The corporation is not a PHC because it fails the shareholder test. More than 50% of the value of the stock is **not** owned by five or fewer shareholders.

38. (a) In calculating the UPHCI, no deduction is allowed for the dividends **received** deduction. However, a deduction is allowed for federal income taxes, excess charitable contributions and dividends paid. In addition, a deduction is allowed for the net long-term capital gain, which is not included as personal holding company income.

39. (b) Personal holding company income includes unearned income, such as interest, dividends, rents, royalties or **personal service income.** Since Benson owns 25% or more of the corporation, and he has the right to assign the income, the amount is considered to be Lund's PHCI.

40. (c) A **personal holding company** is assessed a tax at the **rate of 39.6%** (an individual's highest marginal tax bracket) on its undistributed personal holding company income (UPHCI). A separate schedule is attached to the return.

41. (c) A company that meets the following two tests is classified as a personal holding company:

- **Five or fewer** shareholders own **more than 50%** of the value of the outstanding stock at any time during the last half of the taxable year, and
- **60% or more** of the corporation's adjusted ordinary gross income (AOGI) is unearned income, such as interest, dividends, rents, royalties or personal service income.

42. (d) $0. Kee Holding does not meet the shareholder test because it has 80 unrelated equal shareholders. To be classified as a PHC, there must be **five or fewer** shareholders who own **more than 50%** of the value of the outstanding stock at any time during the last half of the taxable year. Therefore, it is not a personal holding company.

43. (a) Unlike the personal holding company tax, there is **no minimum number of shareholders** requirement.

44. (d) In determining a current year's ATI, the net capital loss which is not allowed in determining taxable income is allowed to determine a company's dividend paying ability.

45. (b) The thrust of the accumulated earnings tax is to require companies to pay out dividends and not retain them. By making sufficient dividend distributions of current earnings, a company can avoid the penalty tax.

46. (d) $250,000. This is the amount for nonservice corporations. For service corporations the amount is $150,000.

47. (c) $50,000. In order to determine the corporation's accumulated taxable income, several adjustments are needed. One is the reduction for federal income taxes paid. The other is the amount of the accumulated earnings credit. Whereas the company is in its first year of operations, the full $250,000 for nonservice corporations is available.

| | |
|---|---:|
| Taxable income | $ 400,000 |
| Less: Federal income taxes | -100,000 |
| Minimum AE credit | -250,000 |
| Accumulated taxable income | $  50,000 |

48. (a) $105,000. A service business is allowed a minimum accumulated earnings credit of $150,000. As of the start of 1997, the corporation had used $45,000 of the $150,000 against its 1998 earnings. This would leave a balance of $105,000. The amount of earnings needed by the corporation was only $20,000, and this is far less than the minimum.

49. (c) Both I and II. Dart can eliminate or reduce the accumulated earnings tax through the **dividends paid deduction,** which includes those dividends paid during the year plus those paid two and one-half months after the close of the year. It may also be eliminated or reduced by the **accumulated earnings credit, which** is the greater of:

1. the reasonable needs of the business less the accumulated earnings and profits of prior years,
   or
2. $250,000 less the accumulated earnings and profits of prior years.

50. (d) Unlike the personal holding company tax, there is **no minimum number of shareholders** requirement.

51. (b) The accumulated earnings tax cannot be assessed on personal holding companies.

52. (d) A service business is allowed a minimum accumulated earnings credit of $150,000, while a manufacturing company is allowed up to $250,000.

53. (d) The maximum number of shareholders allowed in an S Corporation is 75.

54. (a) An S Corporation is allowed only one class of stock. That stock may, however, have different voting rights.

55. (b) Since the shareholders of Village Corporation did not make the consent by March 15, 1999, the election takes effect on January 1, 2000 (the next year).

56. (d) Since the shareholders of Ace Corporation made the consent by March 15, 1999, the election takes effect on January 1, 1999 (the current year).

57. (d) An S Corporation may have 75 shareholders. It may also have a decedent's estate as a shareholder. However, if it has accumulated C Corporation earnings and profits, then violating the passive income rules for three consecutive years will cause the termination of the S Corporation status.

58. (c) 10,000 and 16,000. What is needed is a majority of the voting and nonvoting shares to revoke the election. In this problem the total number of shares is 50,000, therefore more than 25,000 is needed. Only answer (c) with 26,000 shares qualifies.

59. (c) 5 years. Once an S Corporation is revoked or terminated, the corporation generally may not re-elect for five years without IRS consent to an earlier election.

60. (c) November 1, 1999. In order to make a valid S Corporation election, **all the shareholders** must consent in writing. Form 2553 must be filed by the 15th day of the third month of the year in which the election is to be valid, or anytime during the preceding year. Since the election was not made by January 15, 1999, the election is effective for the following tax year beginning November 1, 1999.

61. (a) An S Corporation has restrictions on its shareholders, must be a domestic corporation and have only one class of stock. However, it does not need to be a member of a controlled group.

62. (b) March 15. This is same as for a regular C Corporation. The 15th day of the third month following the close of the taxable year.

63. (d) Yes and Yes. Since the corporation was always an S Corporation (and therefore cannot have any accumulated C Corporation earnings) the passive income is not an issue. A shareholder may be a bankruptcy estate.

64. (d) $0 and $0. An S Corporation is a pass-through entity. The ordinary income and long-term capital gains flow-through to its shareholders.

65. (c) Distributions to a shareholder decrease the shareholder's basis.

66. (b) $30,000. A shareholder in an S Corporation must recognize his proportionate share of income, deductions, credits and losses. In addition, the amounts of income reported by Haas Corporation will cause each shareholder's basis to increase by their share of the income (50% of $60,000, or $30,000). Recognize that the total income of $60,000 is passed through to the shareholders in their separate components of ordinary income and interest income. Also note that any tax-exempt income, while not present in this problem, also increases a shareholder's basis.

67. (b) $2,000. Meyer's share of the $36,500 loss is based upon two factors: (1) his share of the corporate stock and (2) the length of time holding the stock. As a 50% shareholder for 40 days, Meyer's loss is determined as follows:

$36,500 ÷ 365 days = $100 per day per shareholder

$100 × 40 days = $4,000 loss for 40 days

$4,000 loss × 50% ownership = $2,000.

68. (c) Charitable contributions are separately stated items which are not allowed as deductions in the determination of ordinary income. Separately stated items are passed through to the individual shareholders to be used on their own returns. In this case, if the shareholder was an individual, the charitable contribution would be claimed as an itemized deduction on Schedule A. Unlike a partnership compensating its partners, the compensation of a corporation's officers is allowable as a deduction.

69. (d) An S Corporation may deduct the compensation paid to its officers in determining its ordinary income. The charitable contributions, net operating losses and foreign income taxes represent flow-through items which are required to be separately stately on the shareholders' K-1.

70. (c) $76,500. Zinco must allocate a prorata share of the income to the S Corporation's short year. The allocation is based upon the 90 days Zinco was an S Corporation.

$310,250 ÷ 365 days = $850 per day

$850 × 90 days = $76,500

71. (a) $56,750. Kane's share of the $73,000 income is based upon two factors: (1) his share of the corporate stock and (2) the length of time holding the stock. As a 100% shareholder for 40 days, and then as a 75% shareholder for 325 days, Kane's share of the income is determined as follows:

**Step 1** $73,000 ÷ 365 days = $200 per day

$200 × 40 days = $8,000 (as **sole shareholder**)

**Step 2** $73,000 ÷ 365 days = $200 per day

$200 × 325 days = $65,000 total income

$65,000 × 75% ownership = $48,750

**Step 3**

| | |
|---|---|
| Share of income as 100% shareholder | $ 8,000 |
| Share of income as 75% shareholder | 48,750 |
| Total reported income by Kane | $ 56,750 |

72. (d) Similar to the rules for a partnership, the "at risk" rules are determined at the shareholder level rather than at the corporate level.

73. (d) The payment of federal income taxes which are attributable to when the corporation was a C Corporation, would be reflected in the Accumulated Earnings and Profits account, not the Accumulated Adjustments Account. The AAA account measures the undistributed earnings of the S Corporation.

74. (d) A S Corporation may have up to 75 shareholders. However, it may **not** have both common and preferred stock; have a corporation as a shareholder; or be a member of an affiliated group (at least 80%).

75. (b) $20,000. When a corporation incurs liabilities, the individual shareholders do not necessarily share in the responsibility to pay these liabilities. One characteristic of a corporation is limited liability. However, even if a shareholder was personally responsible for a debt (the shareholder guaranteed a bank loan), the shareholder's basis is not increased for the liability. This is a major difference from the rules related to partnerships. If, however, the shareholder lends money to the corporation, the shareholder's basis is increased by that amount. The basis of each shareholder determines the amount of the loss they can claim. Their basis is determined as follows:

| | |
|---|---|
| Initial investment | $ 5,000 |
| Personal loan | 15,000 |
| Total basis | $ 20,000 |

76. (d) A shareholder's basis is increased by the interest from **both** taxable and tax-exempt interest.

77. (d) $6,000. Since this is a liquidating distribution, the total amount realized less the shareholder's basis represents the recognized capital gain.

| | |
|---|---|
| Amount realized: | |
| Cash | $ 2,000 |
| Land - FMV | 10,500 |
| Total amount realized | 12,500 |
| Less: Shareholder's basis | -6,500 |
| Recognized capital gain | $ 6,000 |

78. (d) $17,000 capital gain. This is a complete redemption of a shareholder's stock and qualifies as a liquidating distribution. Since it is a liquidating distribution, the amount realized less the shareholder's basis represents the recognized capital gain. The accumulated and current earnings and profits is irrelevant in this problem.

| | |
|---|---|
| Amount realized (cash) | $ 33,000 |
| Less: Shareholder's basis | -16,000 |
| Recognized capital gain | $ 17,000 |

# Chapter Ten
# Taxation of Gifts, Estates and Fiduciaries, and Exempt Organizations

# Chapter Ten
# Taxation of Gifts, Estates and Fiduciaries, and Exempt Organizations

## THE TRANSFER OF WEALTH
The federal tax laws impose a tax of the accumulation and transfer of wealth. This is separate from the taxation of income which has been the subject of the past nine chapters. If a taxpayer maintains or controls assets in excess of a base amount on the date of death, a federal estate tax is levied on the estate. To avoid being assessed an estate tax, taxpayers frequently attempt to distribute their assets prior to their death. The transfer of these assets during their lifetime may be subject to the gift tax as well.

## THE TAX REFORM ACT OF 1976
Perhaps the most sweeping change in the area of estate and gift taxation occurred in 1976 when Congress voted to combine the gifting of assets and the estate laws together. Viewed as a life-long plan to redistribute wealth, Congress unified the laws pertaining to the accumulation and distribution of wealth. Put simply, a taxpayer would be assessed a progressive tax on a taxable estate and cumulative gifts. To provide relief to the relatively small estates, the law provides a **unified credit** to be used to offset any tax. For 1999, the unified credit is $211,300 for an exemption equivalent of $650,000.

The unified transfer rates (for estates and gifts) are included at the end of the chapter. Similar to individual and corporate taxes, the rates are progressive. For taxable estates up to $10,000 the rate is only 18%, yet on estates in excess of $3,000,000, the marginal rate is 55%. The cumulative and progressive nature of the unified transfer tax and the unified credit is illustrated below:

---

**Example 1:** B died on December 6, 1999. On the date of death, B's taxable estate was $700,000. In addition, since 1980, B made taxable gifts totaling $70,000. Calculate B's estate tax:

| | |
|---|---|
| Taxable estate | $ 700,000 |
| Taxable gifts | 70,000 |
| Tentative tax base | $ 770,000 |
| | |
| Tax on the first $750,000 | $ 248,300 |
| Tax on the next $ 20,000 | |
| $20,000 @ 39% | 7,800 |
| Estate tax | 256,100 |
| Less: Unified credit | -211,300 |
| Estate tax payable | $ 44,800 |

Note that the cumulative taxable gifts made during B's lifetime are included in the overall estate tax calculation. Notice also the progressive nature of the tax from the table and the use of the unified credit in reducing the tax payable.

---

# GIFT TAXATION

Gifting is a common event amongst taxpayers. A parent may give a child money for the downpayment of a house as a wedding present. A boyfriend may give an engagement ring to his fiancee. A grandparent may pay for a grandchild's education. A wife may give investments to her husband. All these are transfers, and may be subject to taxation under the gift tax laws.

- A gift is made out of **detached generosity**. Nothing is expected in return. This is not the payment for services or any future benefits.
- A taxpayer may exclude from gift taxation, **up to $10,000** per year, per donee. This is referred to as a non-taxable gift.
- Husbands and wives may elect to **split their gifts** to take advantage of the $10,000 exclusion.
- Gifts between a husband and wife are fully excluded because of the **unlimited marital deduction**.

> **Example 2:** G, a widower, gives his single daughter $15,000 as a downpayment on her first house. The first $10,000 is excluded and represents a non-taxable gift. The balance of $5,000 is a taxable gift.

> **Example 3:** J, a widower, gives his daughter and her husband $15,000 as a downpayment on their first house. The $15,000 gift represents a $15,000 non-taxable gift. J could have given non-taxable gifts of up to $20,000 to his daughter and husband ($10,000 each).

> **Example 4:** L and M are married and file a joint return. L has no assets, but M has investments worth $750,000. M gives her daughter a $25,000 gift. The $25,000 gift represents a $10,000 non-taxable gift and a $15,000 taxable gift from M. However, L and M may **elect** to split the gift. The result would be a $20,000 non-taxable gift and a $5,000 taxable gift even though L did not actually make a gift.

> **Example 5:** N and O are married and file a joint return. N has an investment portfolio worth $2,000,000 while O has, effectively, no assets. N gives his spouse $500,000. This gift qualifies for the unlimited marital deduction and is fully non-taxable.

## VALUATION OF THE GIFT

In determining the amount of the gift for **gift tax** purposes, the taxpayer uses the fair market value, not the adjusted basis of the gift. However, for **income tax** purposes the general rule is that the adjusted basis of the gifted property and the related holding period transfers over from the donor to the donee. (See Chapter 6 for the rules related to basis).

Payments of medical expenses made **directly** to a medical facility are not considered to be taxable gifts, nor are tuition payments made **directly** to an educational institution. Gifts to charity are also excluded and are treated as a deduction for income tax purposes.

In order to qualify for the $10,000 exclusion, the gift must be for a present interest in property, not a future interest. An exception exists for a gift made to a child under the age of 21 where the child does not have access to the funds (both the principal and interest) until they reach age 21.

> **Example 6:** R leaves a future interest in an investment trust to his brother M who is 40 years old. M will receive the principal and interest from the trust upon R's death. The present value of the $2,000,00 investment trust using the IRS tables is $625,000. There is no $10,000 gift tax exclusion because this is a future interest.

## THE PROGRESSIVE AND CUMULATIVE NATURE OF THE TAX

The unified transfer tax (gift tax) is progressive and cumulative. As the taxable gifts are made over the years, they are accumulated and a new cumulative tax is determined at a progressively higher tax rate. (Please refer again to the rates at the end of the chapter for this next example).

---

**Example 7:** K first began making gifts to her son in 1998 after she won the lottery. During 1998, K made a gift to her son of $50,000. During 1999, K made another gift of $50,000. Exclusive of the unified credit, determine the gift tax.

| | |
|---|---:|
| **1998 gift** | $ 50,000 |
| Less: Annual exclusion | -10,000 |
| 1998 taxable gift | $ 40,000 |
| | |
| Tax on $40,000 per rate schedule | $ 8,200 |
| | |
| **1999 gift** | $ 50,000 |
| Less: Annual exclusion | -10,000 |
| 1999 taxable gift | $ 40,000 |
| Prior year's taxable gift | 40,000 |
| Cumulative taxable gifts | $ 80,000 |
| | |
| Tax on $80,000 per rate schedule | $ 18,200 |
| Less: Previous gift taxes | -8,200 |
| Tax on 1999 gift | $ 10,000 |

Notice that her gift tax on the first gift is $8,200, yet the tax jumps to $10,000 on the second identical gift due to the cumulative and progressive nature of the tax.

---

## FILING REQUIREMENTS

Gift tax returns (Form 709) are required to be filed on an annual basis if a taxable gift is made during the taxable year. The Form 709 is due on April 15th. If a gift is made for less than the $10,000 exclusion, or it qualifies for the marital deduction, then no return is required. Also, a gift tax return is not required for a gift to a charitable organization.

## ESTATE TAXATION

The gross estate of a decedent, who is a citizen or resident of the United States, includes the fair market value of their property and their right to control property, wherever situated, as of the date of death. Deductions are allowed for various expenses and debts of the estate. As previously mentioned, any taxable gifts made after 1976 are added to the estate in order to determine the unified transfer tax. This is then reduced by any gift taxes paid and the unified credit. The flow of this is as follows:

> Gross estate
> Less: Allowable deductions
> Taxable estate
> Plus: Post-76 taxable gifts
> Tentative tax base
>
> Tentative Unified Transfer Tax
> Less: Gift taxes paid
> Less: Unified Credit and other credits
> Estate tax liability

## GROSS ESTATE

Included in the gross estate is the property which the taxpayer has an interest in. Items typically included are:

- Cash
- Investments
- Real estate
- Personal property
- Life insurance proceeds

The proceeds of a life insurance policy are included in the gross estate if:

- the decedent possessed an incident of ownership at death, and
- they are received by the estate or, by another for the benefit of the estate.

If a taxpayer owns property jointly, only the portion of the property related to the taxpayer's **own** contribution is included. However, if the taxpayer is married, 50% of the property is included.

*Effective for estates of decedents dying after December 31, 1997*, there is an exclusion from the value of a gross estate the lessor of (1) the adjusted value of the decedent's **qualified family owned business** or (2) the excess of $1,300,000 over the applicable estate tax exemption equivalent.

The executor may also elect to value the estate at an alternate date, rather than at the date of death. This **alternate valuation date is 6 months** after the date of death, and must result in a lowering of the gross estate and the estate tax liability. If the alternate valuation date is elected, and any property is distributed prior to that date, that property is valued as of the distribution date.

There is, however, a **special rule** relating to certain transfers. When a decedent acquires appreciated property as a gift within one year of their death, and the property then passes back to that donor or that donor's spouse upon death, then the basis stays at the basis as it was in the hands of the decedent. There is no step-up in basis.

## ALLOWABLE DEDUCTIONS

Various deductions are allowed the estate in determining its taxable amount. These deductions include:

- Administrative expenses - ordinary and necessary, commissions, etc.
- Funeral expenses
- Debts of the estate, including medical bills
- Other claims against the estate
- Charitable contributions - only if provided in the will and it is a qualified charity.
- The unlimited marital deduction, if married - only for property passing to the spouse.

The executor may waive the right to claim certain expenses on the estate return if favor of claiming them as a deduction on the fiduciary return which may be required for income activity after the date of death.

## UNIFIED CREDIT AND OTHER CREDITS

The unified credit of $211,300 is the equivalent to the tax on the first $650,000 of a taxable estate for 1999. This unified credit is allowed to all decedents. There is also a state tax credit. Rather than a deduction for **state estate** taxes paid, a credit is allowed. The state tax credit is allowed based upon a schedule that looks to the actual amount of the state estate taxes being paid and the value of the estate. Many states adopt a "sponge tax" equal to the amount of the credit because the payment to the state for an estate tax does not increase the overall tax of the decedent.

Due to the recent tax law change, the unified credit will be indexed up over the next years as follows:

| Tax Year | Unified Credit | Exemption Equivalent |
|----------|----------------|----------------------|
| 1999 | 211,300 | 650,000 |
| 2000 and 2001 | 220,550 | 675,000 |
| 2002 and 2003 | 229,800 | 700,000 |
| 2004 | 287,300 | 850,000 |
| 2005 | 326,300 | 950,000 |
| 2006 and thereafter | 345,800 | 1,000,000 |

## FILING REQUIREMENTS

An estate return (Form 706) is required to be filed within **9 months** after the date of death. A return is not required to be filed unless the value of the gross estate exceeds $650,000, less any taxable gifts made during their lifetime.

# INCOME TAXATION OF FIDUCIARIES

Separate from the unified transfer tax previously discussed, the estate may also be subject to an income tax on the earnings after the date of death. For example, once the taxpayer dies, any income producing property is frequently held for the benefit of the beneficiaries. Until it is distributed, an income tax must be paid on the income.

Apart from an income tax on an estate, a trust may also be subject to tax. A trust is a legal entity that holds title to property for its beneficiaries. In general, trusts are either simple or complex. A **simple** trust is required to distribute all its income to its beneficiaries each year. A simple trust should not have any taxable income and is not allowed a deduction for charitable contributions. A **complex trust** is any other trust. It is allowed a deduction for charitable contributions and may also distribute principal.

In determining the taxable income for an estate or a trust (the fiduciary), the basic definition is income minus deductions equals taxable income.

- Any income distributed to the beneficiary is allowed as a deduction to prevent double taxation. The beneficiary recognizes the income (which is reported on a K-1 similar to that of a partnership), and the fiduciary receives the corresponding deduction. See DNI discussion below for limitations.
- A personal exemption is allowed as well. The amounts are:

| | |
|--|--|
| Simple Trust | $ 300 |
| Complex Trust | $ 100 |
| Estate | $ 600 |

## DISTRIBUTABLE NET INCOME

The amount of income that is taxable to the beneficiary is limited to the amount of distributable net income (DNI). This is regardless of the amount that is actually distributed to the beneficiary. In determining the DNI, no deduction is allowed for the personal exemption. In general, capital gains and losses are also excluded from the computation. Tax-exempt interest is included on a limited basis.

# TAX RATES

The income tax rates for estates and trusts for the 1999 year are:

## ESTATES AND TRUSTS

| If taxable income is: | | The tax is: | |
|---|---|---|---|
| Over --- | but not over --- | | of the amount over --- |
| $ 0 | $ 1,750 | 15% | $ 0 |
| 1,750 | 4,050 | $ 262.50 + 28% | 1,750 |
| 4,050 | 6,200 | $ 906.50 + 31% | 4,050 |
| 6,200 | 8,450 | $1,573.00 + 36% | 6,200 |
| 8,450 | ---- | $2,383.00 +39.6% | 8,450 |

# FILING REQUIREMENTS

A fiduciary is required to file Form 1041 on the 15th day of the fourth month following the close of the taxable year. An estate may adopt a calendar year, or may choose a fiscal year. However, trusts are required to file on a calendar year basis. The gross income filing requirements for an estate and trust is $600 or more. If a trust has less than $600 of gross income, but has taxable income, it must also file.

# TAXATION OF EXEMPT ORGANIZATIONS

The Internal Revenue Code exempts certain types of organizations from taxation. These organizations must:

- Provide for the common good
- Be a not-for-profit entity
- Its net earnings do not benefit its members
- It does not exert political influence

The Internal Revenue Code classifies these organization under Section 501. For example, an educational institution is a 501(c)(3) organization, while a social club is under 501(c)(7). Being classified as an exempt organization generally allows the organization to be a qualified organization so that donors may deduct any charitable contributions. Exemption organizations also receive a discount on postal rates and may be exempt from state and local taxes. Also, tax exempt organizations and Indian Tribes may maintain 401(k) plans.

Exempt organizations include, but are not limited to:

- Churches
- US Government organizations
- Chambers of commerce, business leagues, labor organizations, etc.
- Social clubs, recreation clubs if supported by membership dues, fees, etc.
- Private foundations
- Educational, research, medical, scientific and charitable organizations
- Condominium associations

In order to obtain an exempt status classification, the organization must request a determination from the Internal Revenue Service. The organization applying may be a corporation or a trust. Churches are not required to file a written request. Once qualified, they must maintain their status and not engage in prohibited transactions. For example, lobbying to exert political influence may cause the loss of exempt status of an otherwise qualified organization, if the lobbying is deemed to be substantial.

Certain organizations **cannot** qualify as exempt organizations. They include:

- An organization created to influence legislation
- A feeder organization organized primarily for profit
- An organization that provides athletic facilities and equipment, to foster national and international sports competition

## UNRELATED BUSINESS INCOME

Simply because an exempt organization conducts a trade or business, it does not negate its not-for-profit status. For example, an exempt organization may conduct the following activities:

- The activity utilizes volunteers conducting substantially all the work
- The activity sells merchandise received as contributions (Goodwill thrift shops)
- The activity is for the convenience of the employees, students, members, etc. (Bookstore)
- The activity is for employee unions, selling trade materials, work clothes, etc.

However, an organization may have what is referred to as unrelated business income (UBI) if it **regularly conducts** the activity which is **not related** to the exempt purpose and the activity produces income. Selling products to the general public and providing non-exempt services are possible examples.

There are **exceptions** to the UBI classification. The distribution of low cost items of $5 or less such as pens, stickers, etc., for purposes of solicitation is not an unrelated activity. Exchanging or the renting of membership lists is not an unrelated activity. A popular exam question pertains to **bingo games**. A qualified bingo game is not an unrelated business if:

- The game is legal under state and local law, and
- Commercial bingo games are generally not allowed in the area.

## TAX ON UNRELATED BUSINESS INCOME

When it is determined that there is UBI, the entity is taxed on its UBI only if the UBI **exceeds $1,000**. The rate of tax on UBI is the corporate rate if the organization is a corporation, and the trust rate if the entity is a trust. The organization must make estimated tax payments as required by that entity (i.e., quarterly).

## PRIVATE FOUNDATIONS

An organization may be classified as a private foundation. Private foundations are governed by a written charter and are generally required to distribute their net earnings during the year, or be subject to an excise tax on it. A foreign corporation may be a private foundation. The definition of a private organization is more of a default provision. The Code states that an organization described in Section 501(c)(3) which is **not** one of the following is a private foundation:

- Churches, their integrated auxiliaries, and conventions or associations
- Organizations with less than $5,000 in receipts
- An educational organization or medical research
- Organizations operated exclusively for testing public safety
- Organizations which are **broadly supported** by the general public or government units.

By broadly supported, the organization must receive more than one-third of its support from **external sources** (the general public, government units, churches, educational institutions, etc.) and less than one-third from **internal support** (investment income and unrelated business income).

## FILING REQUIREMENTS

An exempt organization (with the exception of churches, federal agencies, and organizations with receipts which do not exceed $25,000) is required to file Form 990 by the 15th day of the fifth month after the close of their year. A penalty of $10 per day is assessed for late filing. An extension of three months is available by filing Form 2758. If the organization has UBI of at least $1,000, it is required to file Form 990-T as well. A private foundation must file Form 990-PF.

# UNIFIED TRANSFER TAX RATES

For Transfers Made in 1983 and later years:

| If the Amount with Respect to Which the Tentative Tax to Be Computed Is: | The Tentative Tax Is: |
| --- | --- |
| Not over $10,000 | 18% of such amount |
| Over $10,000 but not over $20,000 | $1,800 plus 20% of the excess over $10,000 |
| Over $20,000 but not over $40,000 | $3,800 plus 22% of the excess over $20,000 |
| Over $40,000 but not over $60,000 | $8,200 plus 24% of the excess over $40,000 |
| Over $60,000 but not over $80,000 | $13,000 plus 26% of the excess over $60,000 |
| Over $80,000 but not over $100,000 | $18,200 plus 28% of the excess over $80,000 |
| Over $100,000 but not over $150,000 | $23,800 plus 30% of the excess over $100,000 |
| Over $150,000 but not over $250,000 | $38,800 plus 32% of the excess over $150,000 |
| Over $250,000 but not over $500,000 | $70,800 plus 34% of the excess over $250,000 |
| Over $500,000 but not over $750,000 | $155,800 plus 37% of the excess over $500,000 |
| Over $750,000 but not over $1,000,000 | $248,300 plus 39% of the excess over $750,000 |
| Over $1,000,000 but not over $1,250,000 | $345,800 plus 41% of the excess over $1,000,000 |
| Over $1,250,000 but not over $1,500,000 | $448,300 plus 43% of the excess over $1,250,000 |
| Over $1,500,000 but not over $2,000,000 | $555,800 plus 45% of the excess over $1,500,000 |
| Over $2,000,000 but not over $2,500,000 | $780,800 plus 49% of the excess over $2,000,000 |
| Over $2,500,000 but not over $3,000,000 | $1,025,800 plus 53% of the excess over $2,500,000 |
| Over $3,000,000* | $1,290,800 plus 55% of the excess over $3,000,000 |

*For transfers made after 1992:  An additional tax is imposed in the amount of 5% of tax bases in excess of $10,000,000, but not in excess of $18,340,000.

# Chapter Ten -- Questions
# Taxation of Gifts, Estates and Fiduciaries, and Exempt Organizations

## GIFT AND ESTATE TAXATION

1. Under the unified rate schedule,
a. Lifetime taxable gifts are taxed on a non-cumulative basis.
b. Transfers at death are taxed on a non-cumulative basis.
c. Lifetime taxable gifts and transfers at death are taxed on a cumulative basis.
d. The gift tax rates are 5% higher than the estate tax rates.

2. What amount of a decedent's taxable estate is effectively tax-free if the maximum unified estate and gift credit is taken for 1999?
a. $192,800
b. $600,000
c. $625,000
d. $650,000

3. On July 1, 1999, Vega made a transfer by gift in an amount sufficient to require the filing of a gift tax return. Vega was still alive in 2000. If Vega did **not** request an extension of time for filing the 1999 gift tax return, the due date for filing was
a. March 15, 2000.
b. April 15, 2000.
c. June 15, 2000.
d. June 30, 2000.

4. In 1999, Sayers, who is single, gave an outright gift of $50,000 to a friend, Johnson, who needed the money to pay medical expenses. In filing the 1999 gift tax return, Sayers was entitled to a maximum exclusion of
a. $0
b. $3,000
c. $10,000
d. $50,000

5. When Jim and Nina became engaged in April, Jim gave Nina a ring that had a fair market value of $50,000. After their wedding in July, Jim gave Nina $75,000 in cash so that Nina could have her own bank account. Both Jim and Nina are U.S. citizens.

What was the amount of Jim's marital deduction?
a. $0
b. $75,000
c. $115,000
d. $125,000

6. Blake transferred a corporate bond this year with a face amount and fair market value of $20,000 to a trust for the benefit of her 16-year-old child. Annual interest on this bond is $2,000, which is to be accumulated in the trust and distributed to the child on reaching the age of 21. The bond is then to be distributed to the donor or her successor-in-interest in liquidation of the trust. Present value of the total interest to be received by the child is $8,710. The amount of the gift that is excluded from taxable gifts is
a. $20,000
b. $10,000
c. $8,710
d. $0

7. Steve and Kay Briar, U.S. citizens, were married for the entire calendar year. During the year, Steve gave a $30,000 cash gift to his sister. The Briars made no other gifts. They each signed a timely election to treat the $30,000 gift as made one-half by each spouse. Disregarding the unified credit and estate tax consequences, what amount of the gift is taxable to the Briars?
a. $30,000
b. $20,000
c. $10,000
d. $0

8. Which of the following requires filing a gift tax return, if the transfer exceeds the available annual gift tax exclusion?
a. Medical expenses paid directly to a physician on behalf of an individual unrelated to the donor.
b. Tuition paid directly to an accredited university on behalf of an individual unrelated to the donor.
c. Payments for college books, supplies, and dormitory fees on behalf of an individual unrelated to the donor.
d. Campaign expenses paid to a political organization.

9. Jan, an unmarried individual, gave the following outright gifts during the year:

| Donee | Amount | Use by donee |
|-------|--------|--------------|
| Jones | $15,000 | Down payment on house |
| Craig | 12,000 | College tuition |
| Kande | 5,000 | Vacation trip |

Jan's exclusions for gift tax purposes should total
a. $27,000
b. $25,000
c. $20,000
d. $9,000

**Items 10 through 12** are based on the following data:
Alan Curtis, a U.S. citizen, died on March 1 of this year, leaving a gross estate with a fair market value of $1,400,000 at the date of death. Under the terms of Alan's will, $375,000 was bequeathed outright to his widow, free of all estate and inheritance taxes. The remainder of Alan's estate was left to his mother. Alan made no taxable gifts during his lifetime.

10. Disregarding extensions of time for filing, within how many months after the date of Alan's death is the federal estate tax return due?
a. 2½
b. 3½
c. 9
d. 12

11. In computing the taxable estate, the executor of Alan's estate should claim a marital deduction of
a. $250,000
b. $375,000
c. $700,000
d. $1,025,000

12. If the executor of a decedent's estate elects the alternate valuation date and none of the property included in the gross estate has been sold or distributed, the estate assets must be valued as of how many months after the decedent's death?
a. 12
b. 9
c. 6
d. 3

13. Eng and Lew, both U.S. citizens, died this year. Eng made taxable lifetime gifts of $100,000. Lew made no lifetime gifts. At the dates of death, Eng's gross estate was $300,000, and Lew's gross estate was $400,000. A federal estate tax return must be filed for

| | Eng | Lew |
|---|-----|-----|
| a. | No | No |
| b. | No | Yes |
| c. | Yes | No |
| d. | Yes | Yes |

14. Which of the following credits may be offset against the gross estate tax to determine the net estate tax of a U.S. citizen?

| | Unified credit | Credit for gift taxes paid on gifts made after 1976 |
|---|------|------|
| a. | Yes | Yes |
| b. | No | No |
| c. | No | Yes |
| d. | Yes | No |

15. The following are the fair market values of Wald's assets at the date of death:

| | |
|---|---|
| Personal effects and jewelry | $150,000 |
| Land bought by Wald with Wald's funds five years prior to death and held with Wald's sister as joint tenants with right of survivorship | 800,000 |

The executor of Wald's estate did not elect the alternate valuation date. The amount included as Wald's gross estate in the federal estate tax return is
a. $150,000
b. $550,000
c. $800,000
d. $950,000

16. Fred and Amy Kehl, both U.S. citizens, are married. All of their real and personal property is owned by them as tenants by the entirety or as joint tenants with right of survivorship. The gross estate of the first spouse to die
a. Includes 50% of the value of all property owned by the couple, regardless of which spouse furnished the original consideration.
b. Includes only the property that had been acquired with the funds of the deceased spouse.
c. Is governed by the federal statutory provisions relating to jointly held property, rather than by the decedent's interest in community property vested by state law, if the Kehls reside in a community property state.
d. Includes one-third of the value of all real estate owned by the Kehls, as the dower right in the case of the wife or curtesy right in the case of the husband.

17. In connection with a "buy-sell" agreement funded by a cross-purchase insurance arrangement, business associate Adam bought a policy on Burr's life to finance the purchase of Burr's interest. Adam, the beneficiary, paid the premiums and retained all incidents of ownership. On the death of Burr, the insurance proceeds will be

a. Included in Burr's gross estate, if Burr owns 50% or more of the stock of the corporation.
b. Included in Burr's gross estate only if Burr had purchased a similar policy on Adam's life at the same time and for the same purpose.
c. Included in Burr's gross estate, if Adam has the right to veto Burr's power to borrow on the policy that Burr owns on Adam's life.
d. Excluded from Burr's gross estate.

18. Which of the following is (are) deductible from a decedent's gross estate?

I. Expenses of administering and settling the estate.
II. State inheritance or estate tax.

a. I only.
b. II only.
c. Both I and II.
d. Neither I nor II.

19. Bell, a cash basis calendar year taxpayer, died on June 1, 1999. In 1999, prior to her death, Bell incurred $2,000 in medical expenses. The executor of the estate paid the medical expenses, which were a claim against the estate, on July 1, 1999. If the executor files the appropriate waiver, the medical expenses are deductible on

a. The estate tax return.
b. Bell's final income tax return.
c. The estate income tax return.
d. The executor's income tax return.

20. With regard to the federal estate tax, the alternate valuation date

a. Is required to be used if the fair market value of the estate's assets has increased since the decedent's date of death.
b. If elected on the first return filed for the estate, may be revoked in an amended return provided that the first return was filed on time.
c. Must be used for valuation of the estate's liabilities if such date is used for valuation of the estate's assets.
d. Can be elected only if its use decreases both the value of the gross estate and the estate tax liability.

21. Proceeds of a life insurance policy payable to the estate's executor, as the estate's representative, are

a. Included in the decedent's gross estate only if the premiums had been paid by the insured.
b. Included in the decedent's gross estate only if the policy was taken out within three years of the insured's death under the "contemplation of death" rule.
c. Always included in the decedent's gross estate.
d. Never included in the decedent's gross estate.

22. In 1991, Edwin Ryan bought 100 shares of a listed stock for $5,000. In June 1999, when the stock's fair market value was $7,000, Edwin gave this stock to his sister, Lynn. No gift tax was paid. Lynn died in October 1999, bequeathing this stock to Edwin, when the stock's fair market value was $9,000. Lynn's executor did not elect the alternate valuation. What is Edwin's basis for this stock after he inherits it from Lynn's estate?

a. $0
b. $5,000
c. $7,000
d. $9,000

## TAXATION OF FIDUCIARIES

23. Ordinary and necessary administration expenses paid by the fiduciary of an estate are deductible

a. Only on the fiduciary income tax return (Form 1041) and never on the federal estate tax return (Form 706).
b. Only on the federal estate tax return and never on the fiduciary income tax return.
c. On the fiduciary income tax return only if the estate tax deduction is waived for these expenses.
d. On both the fiduciary income tax return and on the estate tax return by adding a tax computed on the proportionate rates attributable to both returns.

24. Ross, a calendar-year, cash basis taxpayer who died in June 1999, was entitled to receive a $10,000 accounting fee that had not been collected before the date of death. The executor of Ross' estate collected the full $10,000 in July 1999. This $10,000 should appear in

a. Only the decedent's final individual income tax return.
b. Only the estate's fiduciary income tax return.
c. Only the estate tax return.
d. Both the fiduciary income tax return and the estate tax return.

25. With regard to estimated income tax, estates
a. Must make quarterly estimated tax payments starting no later than the second quarter following the one in which the estate was established.
b. Are exempt from paying estimated tax during the estate's first two taxable years.
c. Must make quarterly estimated tax payments only if the estate's income is required to be distributed currently.
d. Are **not** required to make payments of estimated tax.

26. An executor of a decedent's estate that has only U.S. citizens as beneficiaries is required to file a fiduciary income tax return, if the estate's gross income for the year is at least
a. $400
b. $500
c. $600
d. $1,000

27. The charitable contribution deduction on an estate's fiduciary income tax return is allowable
a. If the decedent died intestate.
b. To the extent of the same adjusted gross income limitation as that on an individual income tax return.
c. Only if the decedent's will specifically provides for the contribution.
d. Subject to the 2% threshold on miscellaneous itemized deductions.

28. Raff died in 1999 leaving her entire estate to her only child. Raff's will gave full discretion to the estate's executor with regard to distributions of income. For 1999 the estate's distributable net income was $15,000, of which $9,000 was paid to the beneficiary. None of the income was tax exempt. What amount can be claimed on the estate's 1998 fiduciary income tax return for the distributions deduction?
a. $0
b. $6,000
c. $9,000
d. $15,000

---

**Items 29 and 30** are based on the following:

Lyon, a cash basis taxpayer, died on January 15, 1999. In 1999, the estate executor made the required periodic distribution of $9,000 from estate income to Lyon's sole heir. The following pertains to the estate's income and disbursements in 1999:

*1999 Estate Income*

| | |
|---|---|
| $20,000 | Taxable interest |
| 10,000 | Net long-term capital gains allocable to corpus |

*1999 Estate Disbursements*

| | |
|---|---|
| $5,000 | Administrative expenses attributable to taxable income |

29. For the 1999 calendar year, what was the estate's distributable net income (DNI)?
a. $15,000.
b. $20,000.
c. $25,000.
d. $30,000.

30. Lyon's executor does not intend to file an extension request for the estate fiduciary income tax return. By what date must the executor file the Form 1041, U.S. Fiduciary Income Tax Return, for the estate's 1999 calendar year?
a. March 15, 2000.
b. April 15, 2000.
c. June 15, 2000.
d. September 15, 2000.

---

31. A distribution from estate income, that was *currently* required, was made to the estate's sole beneficiary during its calendar year. The maximum amount of the distribution to be included in the beneficiary's gross income is limited to the estate's
a. Capital gain income.
b. Ordinary gross income.
c. Distributable net income.
d. Net investment income.

32. A distribution to an estate's sole beneficiary for the 1999 calendar year equaled $15,000, the amount currently required to be distributed by the will. The estate's 1999 records were as follows:

*Estate income*

| | |
|---|---|
| $40,000 | Taxable interest |

*Estate disbursements*

| | |
|---|---|
| $34,000 | Expenses attributable to taxable interest |

What amount of the distribution was taxable to the beneficiary?
a.  $40,000
b.  $15,000
c.  $6,000
d.  $0

33. The 1999 standard deduction for a trust or an estate in the fiduciary income tax return is
a.  $0
b.  $650
c.  $750
d.  $800

34. Which of the following fiduciary entities are required to use the calendar year as their taxable period for income tax purposes?

|  | Estates | Trusts (except those that are tax exempt) |
|---|---|---|
| a. | Yes | Yes |
| b. | No | No |
| c. | Yes | No |
| d. | No | Yes |

## EXEMPT ORGANIZATIONS

35. To qualify as an exempt organization other than a church or an employees' qualified pension or profit-sharing trust, the applicant
a.  Cannot operate under the "lodge system" under which payments are made to its members for sick benefits.
b.  Need **not** be specifically identified as one of the classes on which exemption is conferred by the Internal Revenue Code, provided that the organization's purposes and activities are of a nonprofit nature.
c.  Is barred from incorporating and issuing capital stock.
d.  Must file a written application with the Internal Revenue Service.

36. To qualify as an exempt organization, the applicant
a.  May be organized and operated for the primary purpose of carrying on a business for profit, provided that all of the organization's net earnings are turned over to one or more tax exempt organizations.
b.  Need **not** be specifically identified as one of the classes upon which exemption is conferred by the Internal Revenue Code, provided that the organization's purposes and activities are of a nonprofit nature.
c.  Must **not** be classified as a social club.
d.  Must **not** be a private foundation organized and operated exclusively to influence legislation pertaining to protection of the environment.

37. Carita Fund, organized and operated exclusively for charitable purposes, provides insurance coverage, at amounts substantially below cost, to exempt organizations involved in the prevention of cruelty to children. Carita's insurance activities are
a.  Exempt from tax.
b.  Treated as unrelated business income.
c.  Subject to the same tax provisions as those applicable to insurance companies.
d.  Considered "commercial-type" as defined by the Internal Revenue Code.

38. Which of the following exempt organizations must file annual information returns?
a.  Churches.
b.  Internally supported auxiliaries of churches.
c.  Private foundations.
d.  Those with gross receipts of less than $5,000 in each taxable year.

39. The private foundation status of an exempt organization will terminate if it
a.  Becomes a public charity.
b.  Is a foreign corporation.
c.  Does **not** distribute all of its net assets to one or more public charities.
d.  Is governed by a charter that limits the organization's exempt purposes.

40. Which of the following statements is correct regarding the unrelated business income of exempt organizations?
a.  If an exempt organization has any unrelated business income, it may result in the loss of the organization's exempt status.
b.  Unrelated business income relates to the performance of services, but **not** to the sale of goods.
c.  An unrelated business does **not** include any activity where all the work is performed for the organization by unpaid volunteers.
d.  Unrelated business income tax will **not** be imposed if profits from the unrelated business are used to support the exempt organization's charitable activities.

41. Which of the following activities regularly carried out by an exempt organization will **not** result in unrelated business income?
a. The sale of laundry services by an exempt hospital to other hospitals.
b. The sale of heavy duty appliances to senior citizens by an exempt senior citizen's center.
c. Accounting and tax services performed by a local chapter of a labor union for its members.
d. The sale by a trade association of publications used as course materials for the association's seminars which are oriented towards its members.

42. If an exempt organization is a corporation, the tax on unrelated business taxable income is
a. Computed at corporate income tax rates.
b. Computed at rates applicable to trusts.
c. Credited against the tax on recognized capital gains.
d. Abated.

43. The filing of a return covering unrelated business income
a. Is required of all exempt organizations having at least $1,000 of unrelated business taxable income for the year.
b. Relieves the organization of having to file a separate annual information return.
c. Is **not** necessary if all of the organization's income is used exclusively for charitable purposes.
d. Must be accompanied by a minimum payment of 50% of the tax due as shown on the return, with the balance of tax payable six months later.

44. During 1999, Help, Inc., an exempt organization, derived income of $15,000 from conducting bingo games. Conducting bingo games is legal in Help's locality and is confined to exempt organizations in Help's state. Which of the following statements is true regarding this income?
a. The entire $15,000 is subject to tax at a lower rate than the corporate income tax rate.
b. The entire $15,000 is exempt from tax on unrelated business income.
c. Only the first $5,000 is exempt from tax on unrelated business income.
d. Since Help has unrelated business income, Help automatically forfeits its exempt status for 1999.

45. An incorporated exempt organization subject to tax on its unrelated business income
a. Must make estimated tax payments if its tax can reasonably be expected to be $100 or more.
b. Must comply with the Code provisions regarding installment payments of estimated income tax by corporations.
c. Must pay at least 70% of the tax due as shown on the return when filed, with the balance of tax payable in the following quarter.
d. May defer payment of the tax for up to nine months following the due date of the return.

46. An organization that operates for the prevention of cruelty to animals will fail to meet the operational test to qualify as an exempt organization if

|   | The organization engages in insubstantial nonexempt activities | The organization directly participates in any political campaign |
|---|---|---|
| a. | Yes | Yes |
| b. | Yes | No |
| c. | No | Yes |
| d. | No | No |

47. Which one of the following statements is correct with regard to unrelated business income of an exempt organization?
a. An exempt organization that earns any unrelated business income in excess of $100,000 during a particular year will lose its exempt status for that particular year.
b. An exempt organization is not taxed on unrelated business income of less than $1,000.
c. The tax on unrelated business income can be imposed even if the unrelated business activity is intermittent and is carried on once a year.
d. An unrelated trade or business activity that results in a loss is excluded from the definition of unrelated business.

48. The organizational test to qualify a public service charitable entity as tax exempt requires the articles of organization to

I. Limit the purpose of the entity to the charitable purpose.

II. State that an information return should be filed annually with the Internal Revenue Service.

a. I only.
b. II only.
c. Both I and II.
d. Neither I nor II.

49. Which of the following activities regularly conducted by a tax exempt organization will result in unrelated business income?

I. Selling articles made by handicapped persons as part of their rehabilitation, when the organization is involved exclusively in their rehabilitation.

II. Operating a grocery store almost fully staffed by emotionally handicapped persons as part of a therapeutic program.

a. I only.
b. II only.
c. Both I and II.
d. Neither I nor II.

## Released and Author Constructed Questions

R98

50. Gem Trust, a simple trust, reported the following items of income and expenses during 1997:

| | |
|---|---|
| Interest income from corporate bonds | $4,000 |
| Taxable dividend income | 2,000 |
| Trustee fees allocable to income | 1,500 |

What is Gem's 1997 distributable net income (DNI)?
a. $6,000
b. $4,500
c. $2,500
d. $500

R97

51. Under the provisions of a decedent's will, the following cash disbursements were made by the estate's executor:

I. A charitable bequest to the American Red Cross.
II. Payment of the decedent's funeral expenses.

What deduction(s) is(are) allowable in determining the decedent's taxable estate?
a. I only.
b. II only.
c. Both I and II.
d. Neither I nor II.

R97

52. Maple Avenue Assembly, a tax-exempt religious organization, operates an outreach program for the poor in its community. A candidate for the local city council has endorsed Maple's anti-poverty program. Which of the following activities is(are) consistent with Maple's tax-exempt status?

I. Endorsing the candidate to members.
II. Collecting contributions from members for the candidate.

a. I only.
b. II only.
c. Both I and II.
d. Neither I nor II.

# Chapter Ten -- Answers
# Taxation of Gifts, Estates and Fiduciaries, and Exempt Organizations

1. (c) Taxable gifts made over a lifetime are taxed on a cumulative basis at progressive rates. The lifetime gifts are added to the transfers at death, and taxed at progressive rates.

2. (d) $650,000. The unified estate and gift tax credit is $211,300. The credit is equivalent to the tax on a $650,000 taxable estate. For 1998, the amount was $625,000.

3. (b) April 15, 2000. The gift tax return (Form 709) must be filed by April 15, 1999 unless an extension is granted.

4. (c) $10,000. The maximum gift exclusion is $10,000 per year, per donee. An exception does exist for the payment of medical expenses, but only if the payment is made **directly to** the medical provider. If that were the case, the entire $50,000 would have been excluded.

5. (b) $75,000. The marital deduction only applies to transfers between a husband and wife. Only the $75,000 in cash was transferred while they were married. While not required for the problem, the gift of the ring results in a $40,000 taxable gift to Nina.

| | |
|---|---|
| Fair market value of ring | $ 50,000 |
| Annual exclusion | -10,000 |
| Taxable gift | $ 40,000 |

6. (d) $0. Even though the child is receiving a **future interest** in the trust and this appears to meet the exception, no gift tax exclusion exists because only the interest is being turned over to the child upon reaching age 21. The principal reverts back to the donor.

7. (c) The Briar's election to treat the $30,000 as a split gift means that each is treated as if they a $15,000 gift. Since each would be eligible for the $10,000 exclusion, there would be two taxable gifts of $5,000 each ($15,000 less the $10,000 exclusion).

8. (c) In order for the transfer to be excluded from the gift tax rules, the payment must be for tuition, not college books, supplies and dormitory fees.

9. (b) This problem states the gifts were paid outright to the individual. Therefore, each gift is subject to the gift tax rules.

| Donee | Amount | Exclusion |
|---|---|---|
| Jones | $ 15,000 | $ 10,000 |
| Craig | 12,000 | 10,000 |
| Kande | 5,000 | 5,000 |
| | | $ 25,000 |

Note that if the college tuition was paid directly to the college, all $12,000 could have been excluded.

10. (c) 9 months. The estate tax return (Form 706) must be filed 9 months after the date of death, unless an extension is granted.

11. (b) $375,000. Only the value of the property bequeathed outright to his wife qualifies for the marital deduction.

12. (c) 6. An executor may elect to value the estate on the alternate valuation date which is 6 months after the date of death. Any property distributed before this date is valued as of the date of distribution. The property remaining in the estate is valued as of this alternate valuation date.

13. (a) The requirement to file an estate return is a gross estate plus cumulative taxable gifts of $650,000. Neither Eng or Lew exceed $650,000.

|  | Eng | Lew |
|---|---|---|
| Cumulative taxable gifts | $ 100,000 | $ 0 |
| Gross estate | 300,000 | 400,000 |
| Total | $ 400,000 | $ 400,000 |

14. (d) The unified credit is allowed, but it is the amount of the gift taxes **paid** on the post-1976 gifts, not the gift tax credit.

15. (d) $950,000. The amount included in the gross estate is all the property owned by Wald at his death. This includes his personal effects as well as the land. Even though the land is jointly held with his sister (not his spouse), it will be totally included in his estate because Wald paid for the land with his own funds. To exclude the land, or part of it, Wald's sister would have to prove she contributed to the purchase of the property.

16. (a) The gross estate of a married couple includes 50% of the value of all jointly held property. Who furnished the consideration is only an issue when the property is held jointly with a non-spouse.

17. (d) Life insurance is included in your estate when you retain an incident of ownership. Adam purchased the policy, retained ownership and paid the premiums. Burr had no ownership interest, and accordingly it is excluded from his estate.

18. (a) The expenses of administering and settling the estate are deductible expenses. However, the state taxes paid qualify as a credit, not a deduction.

19. (b) Bell's final income tax return. The medical expense will be allowed as a deduction from income rather than be an estate deduction. Based upon the taxpayer's marginal tax bracket, this may result in a tax savings.

20. (d) The executor may elect to value the estate at an alternate date, rather than at the date of death. This **alternate valuation date is 6 months** after the date of death, and **must** result in a lowering of the gross estate and the estate tax liability.

21. (c) The proceeds of a life insurance policy are included in the gross estate if the decedent possessed an incident of ownership at death, and they are received by the estate or, by another for the benefit of the estate.

22. (b) When a decedent acquires appreciated property as a gift within one year of their death, and the property then upon death passes back to that donor or that donor's spouse, then the basis stays at the basis as it was in the hands of the decedent. There is no step-up in basis.

23. (c) The ordinary and necessary administrative expenses of an estate may be deducted on the estate return or the fiduciary return, but not both. The estate tax deduction is waived by attaching a statement to the fiduciary return indicating the expense has not already been claimed as a deduction on the estate return.

24. (d) This must be reported on both. As a cash basis taxpayer, Ross would recognized income up until his date of death. Cash received after that date is taxed to his estate "as income in respect of the decedent." Ross's estate must file a fiduciary return showing the $10,000 income. The $10,000 will also be reported as an asset in Ross's estate tax return, not as income but as an asset. (Note: If Ross had received this on the day he died, he would have included this on his final return and it would still be an asset of his estate.)

25. (b) Estates are not required to make estimated tax payments until two years after the date of death.

26. (c) $600. The threshold for filing of a fiduciary return of an estate is the amount of the estate personal exemption of $600. $100 is the exemption of a simple trust and $300 is the exemption for the complex trust. The $650 is the standard deduction which is not available to a fiduciary.

27. (c) In order for the charitable contribution to be deductible on the estate's fiduciary return, the decedent's will must specifically state it. The limitations in answers (b) and (d) do not exist for an estate.

28. (c) $9,000. The amount distributed to the beneficiary by the estate is allowed as a deduction from income provided it does not exceed the distributable net income. The $9,000 distribution is less than the $15,000 DNI.

29. (a) $15,000. The distributable net income (DNI) is equal to:

| | |
|---|---|
| Taxable interest | $ 20,000 |
| Allowable deductions | -5,000 |
| Distributable net income | $ 15,000 |

30. (b) April 15, 2000. The return is due by the 15th day of the fourth month after the close of the taxable year. The fiduciary has a calendar year-end of December 31.

31. (c) By definition.

32. (c) The amount of income that is taxable to the beneficiary is limited to the amount of distributable net income (DNI). This is regardless of the amount that is actually distributed to the beneficiary. In this problem, the estate income of $40,000 less the expenses of $34,000 results in distributable net income of $6,000.

33. (a) There is no standard deduction for a trust or an estate in the fiduciary return. There are, however, personal exemptions of $100 for a complex trust; $300 for a simple trust; and $600 for an estate.

34. (d) An estate is not **required** to use a calendar year-end end, but may adopt one. However, all trusts are generally required to use the calendar year-end.

35. (d) In order to qualify the organization must file a written application with the Internal Revenue Service. Churches and pension/profit sharing trusts are not required to file the request.

36. (d) An exempt organization cannot be a private foundation organized and operated exclusively to influence legislation. Operating at a profit and turning it over to non-profits is clearly incorrect. Exempt organizations must be identified (i.e., 501(c)(7)) and they can be social clubs.

37. (a) Because this entity was organized exclusively to provide below cost services to exempt organizations it is not deemed to be engaged in an unrelated business activity. The entity has a charitable function and is exempt from tax.

38. (c) Private foundations are required to file a return regardless of the amount of their receipts.

39. (a) By definition, a private foundation is a non-profit organization under 501(c)(3) that is not a public charity. A private foundation may be a foreign corporation. It may be assessed an excise tax for not distributing its net assets, but it will not be terminated. The foundation must be governed by a charter.

40. (c) Activity specifically exempted from unrelated business income is the business where all the work is performed for the organization by volunteers.

41. (d) The sale of publications of course material for seminars to members of a trade association appears to be substantially related to the organization's exempt purposes, and will not result in unrelated business income.

42. (a)  As a corporation, it will be taxed at the corporate rates.

43. (a)  The unrelated business income is reported on Form 990-T and is due on the 15th day of the 5th month following the end of the tax year, along with the annual Form 990.

44. (b)  The amount is exempt because a business is not considered to be substantially related with respect to income from conducting games of chance in a locality where such activity is legal for exempt organizations only.

45. (b)  As a corporation, the exempt organization follows the corporate quarterly estimated tax rules.

46. (c)  Any organization created to influence legislation is not able to qualify as an exempt organization. However, a non-substantial part of an organization's activities may be in non-exempt activity without a loss of exempt status.

47. (b)  There is no tax on unrelated business income of less than $1,000.  Unrelated business income generates a tax, not a loss in exempt status, plus the business must be conducted on a regular basis.

48. (a)  While an information is generally required when gross receipts are in excess of $25,000, it is not required that the articles of organization state that the return by filed annually with the IRS.

49. (d)  By definition, neither of these activities will result in unrelated business income.


50. (b) $4,500.  The distributable net income (DNI) is equal to:

| | |
|---|---|
| Taxable interest income | $ 4,000 |
| Taxable dividend income | 2,000 |
| | 6,000 |
| Less: allowable deductions | -1,500 |
| Distributable net income | $ 4,500 |

51. (c) Various deductions are allowed the estate in determining its taxable amount.  Charitable contributions are allowed, but only if provided in the will and it is to a qualified charity.  Also, funeral expenses are allowed.

52. (d) Neither of these activities are consistent (allowable) with Maple's tax-exempt status.

# Appendix

## WHAT IS IN THE APPENDIX?

This Appendix contains eleven problems updated to reflect current tax law. Problems 1 through 6 deal with individuals, Problems 7 through 10 deal with corporations and Problem 11 deals with partnerships. Ten of these problems represent the Other Objective Answer Format questions that have been asked on recent exams. It is important that you work through these problems to become comfortable with the new format. You do not want to spend time during the exam trying to figure out the format on how to answer the questions.

## ANSWER SHEET

During the actual examination, you will be placing your answers on a separate sheet of paper. This sheet will be a scanable sheet, where you write in numbers and blacken circles for your responses. In presenting the Appendix Problems, we have provided you with a space within the problem to write in the answer to help speed up your exam review. **Your exam will not have these spaces**. You will have a separate answer sheet.

## TIMING

Many of these problems include an estimate as to the amount of time needed to answer the problem. In practice, you should be finished well within the recommended time frame because of the repetitive nature of your review. During the exam these estimates are good indicators. Look for these estimates and make sure you **jot down your start time** for a section, as well as the anticipated stopping time so that you don't spend too much or too little time on an area.

## HIGH LEVEL SUMMARY OF APPENDIX PROBLEMS

### Individuals

**Problem 1** is a matching problem where you select the proper tax treatment for a listing of twenty-five transactions. Notice that the tax treatment sometimes includes which tax form an item may be reported on.

**Problem 2** has 31 parts and has you answering questions on individual filing status, exemptions, gross income inclusion and deductions using various letters as well as true/false answers. Note that there are very few numerical calculations or responses in this problem.

**Problem 3** has 29 parts and requires both numerical responses and true/false answers, similar to Problem 2.

**Problem 4** is a released problem and is comprised of three distinct parts. The first nine questions ask the appropriate tax treatment on a variety of transactions. The next ten questions require a numerical response, but the response is limited to 13 different possibilities. This is like a 13 part multiple choice answer. The third component solely tests the exemption provisions.

**Problem 5** is comprised of twenty other objective style questions. The first five review what is included in an individual's gross estate, while the last five question what is deductible.

**Problem 6** contains nine questions, looking at the tax preparer's role and the Internal Revenue Service.

## Corporations

**Problem 7** requires that the candidate determine if a transaction increases, decreases or has no effect on the corporation's taxable income and once determined, what that amount is. The emphasis on the first four questions is on Schedule M items.

**Problem 8** has 28 parts and has very few numerical responses. The candidate responds to questions such as to whether an item is fully deductible, partially deductible, or not deductible at all; whether a statement is true or false; etc. There are also five questions on the corporate alternative minimum tax.

**Problem 9** is a relatively short S Corporation problem. Its emphasis is on the flow through nature of the items of income and deductions, as well as S Corporation eligibility.

**Problem 10** is under the old problem format but represents a good comprehensive corporate tax problem. When you attack this problem, envision ways the examiners could ask you the same questions under the Other Objective Answer Format approach. For example, how much is the dividends received deduction, or what is the bad debt expense deduction?

## Partnerships

**Problem 11** is a part of Problem 2 from the November 94 exam. The problem deals with partnerships and requires an unusual three part multiple choice format answer as well as true/false responses. Notice the emphasis on partnership distributions. Do not ignore these questions.

# Appendix Problems

## PROBLEM 1 (Estimated time 40 to 50 minutes)

**Problem Number 1** consists of 25 items. Select the **best** answer for each item. **Answer all items.** Your grade will be based on the total number of correct answers.

Green is self-employed as a human resources consultant and reports on the cash basis for income tax purposes. Listed on the following page are Green's 1999 business and nonbusiness transactions, as well as possible tax treatments.

**Required:**
For each of Green's transactions (Items 1-25), select the appropriate tax treatment. A tax treatment may be selected once, more than once, or not at all.

___1. Retainer fees received from clients.

___2. Oil royalties received.

___3. Interest income on general obligation state and local government bonds.

___4. Interest on refund of federal taxes.

___5. Death benefits from term life insurance policy on parent.

___6. Interest income on US Treasury bonds.

___7. Share of ordinary income from an investment in a limited partnership reported in Form 1065, Schedule K-1.

___8. Taxable income from rental of a townhouse owned by Green.

___9. Prize won as a contestant on a TV quiz show.

___10. Payment received for jury service.

___11. Dividends received from mutual funds that invest in tax-free government obligations.

___12. Qualifying medical expenses not reimbursed by insurance.

___13. Personal life insurance premiums paid by Green.

___14. Expenses for business-related meals where clients were present.

___15. Depreciation on personal computer purchased in 1996 used for business.

___16. Business lodging expenses, while out of town.

___17. Subscriptions to professional journals used for business.

___18. Self-employment taxes paid.

___19. Qualifying contributions to a simplified employee pension plan.

___20. Election to expense business equipment purchased in 1999.

___21. Qualifying alimony payments made by Green.

___22. Subscriptions for investment-related publications.

___23. Interest expense on a home-equity line of credit for an amount borrowed to finance Green's business.

___24. Interest expense on a loan for an auto used 75% for business.

___25. Loss on sale of residence.

a. Taxable as other income on Form 1040.

b. Reported in Schedule B—Interest and Dividend Income.

c. Reported in Schedule C as trade or business income.

d. Reported in Schedule E—Supplemental Income and Loss.

e. Not taxable.

f. Fully deductible on Form 1040 to arrive at adjusted gross income.

g. Fifty percent deductible on Form 1040 to arrive at adjusted gross income.

h. Reported in Schedule A—Itemized Deductions (deductibility subject to threshold of 7.5% of adjusted gross income).

i. Reported in Schedule A—Itemized Deductions (deductibility subject to threshold of 2% of adjusted gross income)

j. Reported in Form 4562—Depreciation and Amortization and deductible in Schedule A—Itemized Deductions (deductibility subject to threshold of 2% of adjusted gross income).

k. Reported in Form 4562—Depreciation and Amortization, and deductible in Schedule C—Profit or Loss from Business.

l. Fully deductible in Schedule C—Profit or Loss from Business.

m. Partially deductible in Schedule C—Profit or Loss from Business.

n. Reported in Form 2119—Sale of Your Home, and deductible in Schedule D—Capital Gains and Losses.

o. Not deductible.

## PROBLEM 2 (Estimated time—25 to 40 minutes)

**Problem Number 2** consists of 31 items. Select the best answer for each item. Answer all items. Your grade will be based on the total number of correct answers.

Mrs. Vick, a 40-year-old cash basis taxpayer, earned $45,000 as a teacher and $5,000 as a part-time real estate agent in 1999. Mr. Vick, who died on July 1, 1999, had been permanently disabled on his job and collected state disability benefits until his death. For all of 1999 and 2000, the Vick's residence was the principal home of both their 11-year old daughter Joan and Mrs. Vick's unmarried cousin, Fran Phillips, who had no income in either year. During 1999, Joan received $200 a month in survivor social security benefits that began on August 1, 1998, and will continue at least until her 18th birthday. In 1999 and 2000, Mrs. Vick provided over one-half the support for Joan and Fran, both of whom were US citizens. Mrs. Vick did not remarry. Mr. and Mrs. Vick received the following in 1999:

| | |
|---|---|
| Earned income | $50,000 |
| State disability benefits | 1,500 |
| Interest on: | |
|     Refund from amended tax return | 50 |
|     Savings account & certificates of deposit | 350 |
|     Municipal bonds | 100 |
| Gift | 3,000 |
| Pension benefits | 900 |
| Jury duty pay | 200 |
| Gambling winnings | 450 |
| Life insurance proceeds | 5,000 |

*Additional information:*

- Mrs. Vick received the $3,000 cash gift from her uncle.

- Mrs. Vick received the pension distributions from a qualified pension plan, paid for exclusively by her husband's employer.

- Mrs. Vick had $100 in gambling losses in 1999.

- Mrs. Vick was the beneficiary of the life insurance policy on her husband's life. She received a lump-sum distribution. The Vicks had paid $500 in premiums.

- Mrs. Vick received Mr. Vick's accrued vacation pay of $500 in 2000.

For **items 1 and 2**, determine and select from the choices below, **BOTH** the filing status and the number of exemptions for each item.

**Filing Status**
S   Single
M   Married filing joint
H   Head of household
Q   Qualifying widow with dependent child

**Exemptions**
1
2
3
4

1. Determine the filing status and the number of exemptions that Mrs. Vick can claim on the 1999 federal income tax return, to get the most favorable tax results.

        Filing Status?_____           Exemptions?_____

2. Determine the filing status and the number of exemptions that Mrs. Vick can claim on the 2000 federal income tax return to get the most favorable tax results, if she solely maintains the costs of her home.

        Filing Status?_____           Exemptions?_____

For **items 3 through 9**, determine the amount, if any, that is taxable and should be included in Adjusted Gross Income (AGI) on the 1999 federal income tax return filed by Mrs. Vick.

**Numeric responses**

3. State disability benefits    ____ ____ ____ ____

4. Interest income    ____ ____ ____ ____

5. Pension benefits    ____ ____ ____ ____

6. Gift    ____ ____ ____ ____

7. Life insurance proceeds    ____ ____ ____ ____

8. Jury duty pay    ____ ____ ____ ____

9. Gambling winnings    ____ ____ ____ ____

During 1999 the following payments were made or losses were incurred. For items 10 through 23, select the appropriate tax treatment. A tax treatment may be selected once, more than once, or not at all.

**Payments and Losses**

___10. Premiums on Mr. Vick's personal life insurance policy.

___11. Penalty on Mrs. Vick's early withdrawal of funds from a certificate of deposit.

___12. Mrs. Vick's substantiated cash donation to the American Red Cross.

___13. Payment of estimated state income taxes.

___14. Payment of real estate taxes on the Vick home.

___15. Loss on the sale of the family car.

___16. Cost in excess of the increase in value of residence, for the installation of a stairlift in January 1998, related directly to the medical care of Mr. Vick.

___17. The Vick's health insurance premiums for hospitalization coverage.

___18. CPA fees to prepare the 1998 tax return.

___19. Amortization over the life of the loan of points paid to refinance the mortgage at a lower rate on the Vick home.

___20. One-half the self-employment tax paid by Mrs. Vick.

___21. Mrs. Vick's $100 in gambling losses.

___22. Mrs. Vick's union dues.

___23. 1998 federal income tax paid with the Vick's tax return on April 15, 1999.

**Tax Treatment**

A. Not deductible.

B. Deductible in Schedule A-Itemized Deductions, subject to threshold of 7.5% of adjusted gross income.

C. Deductible in Schedule A-Itemized Deductions, subject to threshold of 2% of adjusted gross income.

D. Deductible on page 1 of Form 1040 to arrive at adjusted gross income.

E. Deductible in full in Schedule A-Itemized Deductions.

F. Deductible in Schedule A-Itemized Deductions, subject to threshold of 50% of adjusted gross income.

**For items 24 through 31**, determine whether the statement is true (T) or false (F) regarding the Vick's' 1999 income tax return.

___24.  The funeral expenses paid by Mr. Vick's estate is a 1999 itemized deduction.

___25.  Any federal estate tax on the income in respect of decedent, to be distributed to Mrs. Vick, may be taken as a miscellaneous itemized deduction not subject to the 2% of adjusted gross income floor.

___26.  A casualty loss deduction on property used in Mrs. Vick's part-time real estate business is reported as an itemized deduction.

___27.  The Vicks' income tax liability will be reduced by the credit for the elderly or disabled.

___28.  The CPA preparer is required to furnish a completed copy of the 1999 income tax return to Mrs. Vick.

___29.  Since Mr. Vick died during the year, the income limitation for the earned income credit does not apply.

___30.  Mr. Vick's accrued vacation pay, at the time of his death, is to be distributed to Mrs. Vick in 2000. This income should be included in the 1999 Federal income tax return.

___31.  The Vicks paid alternative minimum tax in 1998. The amount of alternative minimum tax that is attributable to "deferral adjustments and preferences" can be used to offset the alternative minimum tax in the following years.

# PROBLEM 3 (Estimated time—25 to 40 minutes)

**Problem Number 3** consists of 29 items. Select the **best** answer for each item. Answer all items.

Tom and Joan Moore, both CPAs, filed a joint 1999 federal income tax return showing $70,000 in taxable income. During 1999, Tom's daughter Laura, age 16, resided with Tom's former spouse. Laura had no income of her own and was not Tom's dependent.

**Required:**
**a.** For **Items 1 through 10,** determine the amount of income or loss, if any, that should be included on page one of the Moore's 1999 Form 1040.

1.  The Moores had no capital loss carryovers from prior years. During 1999 the Moores had the following stock transactions which resulted in a net capital loss:

|  | Date acquired | Date sold | Sales price | Cost |
|---|---|---|---|---|
| Revco | 2-1-97 | 3-17-99 | $15,000 | $25,000 |
| Abbco | 2-18-98 | 4-1-99 | $8,000 | 4,000 |

Numeric ___ ___ ___ ___ ___

2. In 1994, Joan received an acre of land as an inter-vivos gift from her grandfather. At the time of the gift, the land had a fair market value of $50,000. The grandfather's adjusted basis was $60,000. Joan sold the land in 1999 to an unrelated third party for $56,000.

   Numeric  __ __ __ __ __

3. The Moores received a $500 security deposit on their rental property in 1999. They are required to return the amount to the tenant.

   Numeric  __ __ __ __ __

4. Tom's 1999 wages were $53,000. In addition, Tom's employer provided group-term life insurance on Tom's life in excess of $50,000. The value of such excess coverage was $2,000.

   Numeric  __ __ __ __ __

5. During 1999, the Moores received a $2,500 federal tax refund and a $1,250 state tax refund for 1998 overpayments. In 1998, the Moores were not subject to the alternative minimum tax and were not entitled to any credit against income tax. The Moores' 1998 adjusted gross income was $80,000 and itemized deductions were $1,450 in excess of the standard deduction. The state tax deduction for 1998 was $2,000.

   Numeric  __ __ __ __ __

6. In 1999, Joan received $1,300 in unemployment compensation benefits. Her employer made a $100 contribution to the unemployment insurance fund on her behalf.

   Numeric  __ __ __ __ __

7. The Moores received $8,400 in gross receipts from their rental property during 1999. The expenses for the residential rental property were:

   | | |
   |---|---|
   | Bank mortgage interest | $1,200 |
   | Real estate taxes | 700 |
   | Insurance | 500 |
   | MACRS depreciation | 3,500 |

   Numeric  __ __ __ __ __

8. The Moores received a stock dividend in 1999 from Ace Corp. They had the option to receive either cash or Ace stock with a fair market value of $900 as of the date of distribution. The par value of the stock was $500.

   Numeric  __ __ __ __ __

9. In 1999, Joan received $3,500 as beneficiary of the death benefit which was provided by her brother's employer. Joan's brother did not have a nonforfeitable right to receive the money while living.

   Numeric  __ __ __ __ __

10. Tom received $10,000, consisting of $5,000 each of principal and interest, when he redeemed a Series EE savings bond in 1999. The bond was issued in his name in 1987 and the proceeds were used to pay for Laura's college tuition. Tom had not elected to report the yearly increases in the value of the bond.

    Numeric  __ __ __ __ __

**Required:**

**b.** For **Item 11,** determine the amount of the adjustment, if any, to arrive at adjusted gross income.

11. As required by a 1990 divorce agreement, Tom paid an annual amount of $8,000 in alimony and $10,000 in child support during 1999.

Numeric ___ ___ ___ ___ ___

**Required:**

**c.** During 1999, the following events took place. For **Items 12 to 23,** select the appropriate tax treatment from the Tax Treatment List. A tax treatment may be selected once, more than once, or not all.

*Tax Treatments:*

(A)    Not deductible on Form 1040.

(B)    Deductible in full in Schedule A-Itemized Deductions.

(C)    Deductible in Schedule A-Itemized Deductions, subject to a threshold of 7.5% of adjusted gross income.

(D)    Deductible in Schedule A-Itemized Deductions, subject to a limitation of 50% of adjusted gross income.

(E)    Deductible in Schedule A-Itemized Deductions, subject to a $100 floor and a threshold of 10% of adjusted gross income.

(F)    Deductible in Schedule A-Itemized Deductions, subject to a threshold of 2% of adjusted gross income.

*Events:*

___12. On March 23, 1999, Tom sold 50 shares of Zip stock at a $1,200 loss. He repurchased 50 shares of Zip on April 15, 1999.

___13. Payment of a personal property tax based on the value of the Moores' car.

___14. Used clothes were donated to church organizations.

___15. Premiums were paid covering insurance against Tom's loss of earnings.

___16. Tom paid for subscriptions to accounting journals.

___17. Interest was paid on a $10,000 home-equity line of credit secured by the Moores' residence. The fair market value of the home exceeded the mortgage by $50,000. Tom used the proceeds to purchase a sailboat.

___18. Amounts were paid in excess of insurance reimbursement for prescription drugs.

___19. Funeral expenses were paid by the Moores for Joan's brother.

___20. Theft loss was incurred on Joan's jewelry in excess of insurance reimbursement. There were no 1998 personal casualty gains.

___21. Loss on the sale of the family's sailboat.

___22. Interest was paid on the $300,000 acquisition mortgage on the Moores' home. The mortgage is secured by their home.

___23. Joan performed free accounting services for the Red Cross. The estimated value of the services was $500.

**Required:**
**d.** For **Items 24 to 29,** indicate if the statement is True (T) or False (F) regarding the Moores' 1999 tax return.

___24. For 1999, the Moores were subject to the phaseout of half their personal exemptions for regular tax because their adjusted gross income was $75,000.

___25. The Moores' unreimbursed medical expenses for AMT had to exceed 10% of adjusted gross income.

___26. The Moores' personal exemption amount for regular tax was not permitted for determining 1999 AMT.

___27. The Moores paid $1,200 in additional 1999 taxes when they filed their return on Friday, April 14, 2000. Their 1999 federal tax withholdings equaled 100% of 1998 tax liability. Therefore, they were not subject to the underpayment of tax penalty.

___28. The Moores, both being under age 50, were subject to an early withdrawal penalty on their IRA withdrawals used for medical expenses.

___29. The Moores were allowed an earned income credit against their 1999 tax liability equal to a percentage of their wages.

# PROBLEM 4
*R97*

**Problem Number 4** consists of 3 parts. **Part A** consists of 9 items, **Part B** consists of 10 items, and **Part C** consists of 1 item. Select the **best** answer for each item.

**a.** The Internal Revenue Service is auditing Oate's 1999 Form 1040 – Individual Income Tax Return. During 1999, Oate, an unmarried custodial parent, had one dependent three-year-old child and worked in a CPA firm. For 1999, Oate, who had adjusted gross income of $40,000, qualified to itemize deductions and was subject to federal income tax liability.

**Required:**
For **Items 1 through 9,** select from the following list of tax treatments the appropriate tax treatment. A tax treatment may be selected once, more than once, or not at all.

*Tax Treatments:*
**A.** Not deductible on Form 1040.

**B.** Deductible in full on Schedule A – Itemized Deductions.

**C.** Deductible in Schedule A – Itemized Deductions subject to a limitation of 50% of adjusted gross income.

**D.** Deductible in Schedule A – Itemized Deductions as miscellaneous deduction subject to a threshold of 2% of adjusted gross income.

**E.** Deductible in Schedule A – Itemized Deductions as miscellaneous deduction NOT subject to a threshold of 2% of adjusted gross income.

**F.** Deductible on Schedule E – Supplemental Income and Loss.

**G.** A credit is allowable.

___1.   In 1999, Oate paid $900 toward continuing education courses and was not reimbursed by her employer.

___2.   For 1999, Oate had a $30,000 cash charitable contribution carryover from her 1999 cash donation to the American Red Cross. Oate made no additional charitable contributions in 1999.

___3.   During 1999, Oate had investment interest expense that did not exceed her net investment income.

___4.   Oate's 1999 lottery ticket losses were $450. She had no gambling winnings.

___5.   During 1999, Oate paid $2,500 in real property taxes on her vacation home, which she used exclusively for personal use.

___6.   In 1999, Oate paid a $500 premium for a homeowner's insurance policy on her principal residence.

___7.   For 1999, Oate paid $1,500 to an unrelated babysitter to care for her child while she worked.

___8.   In 1999, Oate paid $4,000 interest on the $60,000 acquisition mortgage of her principal residence. The mortgage is secured by Oate's home.

___9.   During 1999, Oate paid $3,600 real property taxes on residential rental property in which she actively participates. There was no personal use of the rental property.

b.  Frank and Dale Cumack are married and filing a joint 1999 income tax return. During 1999, Frank, 65, was retired from government service and Dale, 55, was employed as a university instructor. In 1999, the Cumacks contributed all of the support to Dale's father, Jacques, an unmarried French citizen and French resident who had no gross income.

**Required:**
For **Items 10 through 19**, select the correct amount of income, loss, or adjustment to income that should be recognized on page 1 of the Cumacks' 1999 Form 1040 – Individual Income Tax Return to arrive at the adjusted gross income for each separate transaction. A response may be selected once, more than once, or not at all.

Any information contained in an item is unique to that item and is not to be incorporated in your calculations when answering other items.

_**Amounts:**_
A.   $0

B.   $1,000

C.   $2,000

D.   $2,250

E.   $3,000

F.   $4,000

G.   $5,000

H.   $9,000

I.   $10,000

J.   $25,000

K.   $30,000

L.   $125,000

M.   $150,000

___10. During 1999, Dale received a $30,000 cash gift from her aunt.

___11. Dale contributed $2,000 to her Individual Retirement Account (IRA) on January 15, 2000. In 1999, she earned $60,000 as a university instructor. During 1999, the Cumacks were not active participants in an employer's qualified pension or annuity plan.

___12. In 1999, the Cumacks received a $1,000 federal income tax refund.

___13. During 1999, Frank, a 50% partner in Diske General Partnership, received a $4,000 guaranteed payment from Diske for services that he rendered to the partnership that year.

___14. In 1999, Frank received $10,000 as beneficiary of his deceased brother's life insurance policy.

___15. Dale's employer pays 100% of the cost of all employees' group term life insurance under a qualified plan. Policy cost is $5 per $1,000 of coverage. Dale's group term life insurance coverage equals $450,000.

___16. In 1999, Frank won $5,000 at a casino and had $2,000 in gambling losses.

___17. During 1999, the Cumacks received $1,000 interest income associated with a refund of their prior years' federal income tax.

___18. In 1999, the Cumacks sold their first and only residence for $200,000. They purchased their home in 1985 for $50,000 and have lived there since then. There were no other capital gains, losses, or capital loss carryovers. The Cumacks do not intend to buy another residence and they have properly elected the lifetime exclusion.

___19. In 1999, Zeno Corp. declared a stock dividend and Dale received one additional share of Zeno common stock for three shares of Zeno common stock that she held. The stock that Dale received had a fair market value of $9,000. There was no provision to receive cash instead of stock.


c. Frank and Dale Cumack are married and filing a joint 1999 income tax return. During 1999, Frank, 65, was retired from government service and Dale, 55, was employed as a university instructor. In 1999, the Cumacks contributed all of the support to Dale's father, Jacques, an unmarried French citizen and French resident who had no gross income.


**Required:**
For **Item 20,** determine whether the Cumacks overstated, understated, or correctly determined the number of both personal and dependency exemptions.

*Selections:*
**O.** Overstated the number of both personal and dependency exemptions.

**U.** Understated the number of both personal and dependency exemptions.

**C.** Correctly determined the number of both personal and dependency exemptions.


___20. The Cumacks claimed 3 exemptions on their 1999 joint income tax return.

# PROBLEM 5

**Problem Number 5** consists of 2 parts concerning federal estate and gift taxation. **Part A** consists of 5 items and **Part B** consists of 5 items. Select the best answer for each item. **Answer all items.**

**Items 1 through 5** are based on the following fact pattern:

Before his death, Remsen, a U.S. citizen, made cash gifts of $7,000 each to his four sisters. In 1999, Remsen also paid $2,000 in tuition directly to his grandchild's university on the grandchild's behalf. Remsen made no other lifetime transfers. Remsen died on January 19, 1999, and was survived by his wife and only child, both of whom were U.S. citizens. The Remsens did not live in a community property state.

At his death, Remsen owned:

| | |
|---|---|
| Cash | $650,000 |
| Marketable securities | |
|   (Fair market value) | 900,000 |
| Live insurance policy with Remsen's wife | |
|   named as the beneficiary (fair market value) | 500,000 |

Under the provisions of Remsen's will, the net cash, after payment of executor's fees and medical and funeral expenses, was bequeathed to Remsen's son. The marketable securities were bequeathed to Remsen's spouse. During 1999, Remsen's estate paid:

| | |
|---|---|
| Executor's fees to distribute the decedent's property | |
|   (deducted on the fiduciary tax return) | $ 15,000 |
| Decedent's funeral expenses | 25,000 |

The estate's executor extended the time to file the estate tax return.

On January 3, 2000, the estate's executor paid the decedent's outstanding $10,000 1999 medical expense and filed the extended estate tax return.

**Required:**
a. For **Items 1 through 5,** identify the federal tax treatment for each item. An answer may be selected once, more than once, or not at all.

*Estate Tax Treatments:*
**F.**    Fully includible in Remsen's gross estate.

**P.**    Partially includible in Remsen's gross estate.

**N.**    Not includible in Remsen's gross estate.

____1.    What is the estate tax treatment of the $7,000 cash gift to each sister?

____2.    What is the estate tax treatment of the life insurance proceeds?

____3.    What is the estate tax treatment of the marketable securities?

____4.    What is the estate tax treatment of the $2,000 tuition payment?

____5.    What is the estate tax treatment of the $650,000 cash?

**Required:**

**b.** For **Items 6 through 10,** identify the federal estate tax treatment for each item. An answer may be selected once, more than once, or not at all.

*Estate Tax Treatments:*

**G.**     Deductible from Remsen's gross estate to arrive at Remsen's taxable estate.

**I.**     Deductible on Remsen's 1999 individual income tax return.

**E.**     Deductible on either Remsen's estate tax return or Remsen's 1999 individual income tax return.

**N.**     Not deductible on either Remsen's estate tax return or Remsen's 1999 individual income tax return.

\_\_\_6.     What is the estate tax treatment of the executor's fees?

\_\_\_7.     What is the estate tax treatment of the cash bequest to Remsen's son?

\_\_\_8.     What is the estate tax treatment of the life insurance proceeds paid to Remsen's spouse?

\_\_\_9.     What is the estate tax treatment of the funeral expenses?

\_\_\_10.     What is the estate tax treatment of the $10,000 1999 medical expense incurred before the decedent's death and paid by the executor on January 3, 2000?

# PROBLEM 6                                                        *R97*

**Problem Number 6** consists of 9 items. Select the best answer for each item. Answer all items. Your grade will be based on the total number of correct answers.

A CPA sole practitioner has tax preparers' responsibilities when preparing tax returns for clients.

**Required:**

**Items 1 through 9** each represent an independent factual situation in which a CPA sole practitioner has prepared and signed the taxpayer's income tax return. For each item, select from the following list the correct response regarding the tax preparer's responsibilities. A response may be selected once, more than once, or not at all.

*Answer List:*

**P.**     The tax preparer's action constitutes an act of tax preparer misconduct subject to the Internal Revenue Code penalty.

**E.**     The Internal Revenue Service will examine the facts and circumstances to determine whether the reasonable cause exception applies; the good faith exception applies; or both exceptions apply.

**N.**     The tax preparer's action does **not** constitute an act of tax preparer misconduct.

___1. The tax preparer disclosed taxpayer income tax return information under an order from a state court, without the taxpayer's consent.

___2. The tax preparer relied on the advice of an advisory preparer to calculate the taxpayer's tax liability. The tax preparer believed that the advisory preparer was competent and that the advice was reasonable. Based on the advice, the taxpayer had understated income tax liability.

___3. The tax preparer did **not** charge a separate fee for the tax return preparation and paid the taxpayer the refund shown on the tax return less a discount. The tax preparer negotiated the actual refund check for the tax preparer's own account after receiving power of attorney from the taxpayer.

___4. The tax preparer relied on information provided by the taxpayer regarding deductible travel expenses. The tax preparer believed that the taxpayer's information was correct but inquired about the existence of the travel expense records. The tax preparer was satisfied by the taxpayer's representations that the taxpayer had adequate records for the deduction. Based on this information, the income tax liability was understated.

___5. The taxpayer provided the tax preparer with a detailed check register to compute business expenses. The tax preparer knowingly overstated the expenses on the income tax return.

___6. The tax preparer disclosed taxpayer income tax return information during a quality review conducted by CPAs. The tax preparer maintained a record of the review.

___7. The tax preparer relied on incorrect instructions on an IRS tax form that were contrary to the regulations. The tax preparer was **not** aware of the regulations nor the IRS announcement pointing out the error. The understatement was immaterial as a result of the isolated error.

___8. The tax preparer used income tax return information without the taxpayer's consent to solicit additional business.

___9. The tax preparer knowingly deducted the expenses of the taxpayer's personal domestic help as wages paid in the taxpayer's business on the taxpayer's income tax return.

# PROBLEM 7

*R97*

**Problem Number 7** consists of 11 items about C Corporations. Select the **best** answer for each item. Answer all items. Your grade will be based on the total number of correct answers.

Capital Corp., an accrual-basis calendar-year C corporation, began operations on January 2, 1998. Capital timely filed its 1999 federal income tax return on Monday, March 17, 2000.

**Required:**
**Items 1 through 4** each require **two** responses:

a. For each item below, determine the amount of Capital's 1999 Schedule M-1 adjustment necessary to reconcile book income to taxable income. In answering this part, the zeroes on the thousands have been omitted. For example, if your answer is $5,000, you write it as 005.

b. In addition, determine if the Schedule M-1 adjustment necessary to reconcile book income to taxable income increases, decreases, or has no effect on Capital's 1999 taxable income. An answer may be selected once, more than once, or not at all.

I.      Increases Capital's 1999 taxable income.

D.      Decreases Capital's 1999 taxable income.

N.      Has no effect on Capital's 1999 taxable income.

___1.   At its corporate inception in 1998, Capital incurred and paid $40,000 in organizational costs for legal fees to draft the corporate charter. In 1998, Capital correctly elected, for book purposes, to amortize the organizational expenditures over 40 years and for the minimum required period on its federal income tax return. For 1999, Capital amortized $1,000 of the organizational costs on its books.

        Numeric   _ _ _

___2.   Capital's 1999 disbursements included $10,000 for reimbursed employees' expenses for business meals and entertainment. The reimbursed expenses met the conditions of deductibility and were properly substantiated under an accountable plan. The reimbursement was not treated as employee compensation.

        Numeric   _ _ _

___3.   Capital's 1999 disbursements included $15,000 for life insurance premium expense paid for its executives as part of their taxable compensation. Capital is neither the direct nor the indirect beneficiary of the policy, and the amount of the compensation is reasonable.

        Numeric   _ _ _

___4.   In 1999, Capital increased its allowance for uncollectible accounts by $10,000. No bad debt was written off in 1999.

        Numeric   _ _ _

————————————————

Sunco Corp., an accrual-basis calendar-year C corporation, timely filed its 1999 federal income tax return on Monday, March 17, 2000.

**Required:**
c. For **Items 5 and 6**, determine if the following items are fully taxable, partially taxable, or nontaxable for regular income tax purposes on Sunco's 1999 federal income tax return. An answer may be selected once, more than once, or not at all.

*Selections:*
F.      Fully taxable for regular income tax purposes on Sunco's 1999 federal income tax return.

P.      Partially taxable for regular income tax purposes on Sunco's 1999 federal income tax return.

N.      Nontaxable for regular income tax purposes on Sunco's 1999 federal income tax return.

___5.   In 1999, Sunco received dividend income from a 35%-owned domestic corporation. The dividends were not from debt-financed portfolio stock, and the taxable income limitations did not apply.

___6.   In 1999, Sunco received a $2,800 lease cancellation payment from a three-year lease tenant.

Quest Corp., an accrual-basis calendar-year C corporation, timely filed its 1999 federal income tax return on Monday, March 17, 2000.

**Required:**

d. For **Items 7 and 8,** determine if the following items are fully deductible, partially deductible, or nondeductible for regular income tax purposes on Quest's 1999 federal income tax return. An answer may be selected once, more than once, or not at all.

*Selections:*

**F.** Fully deductible for regular income tax purposes on Quest's 1999 federal income tax return.

**P.** Partially deductible for regular income tax purposes on Quest's 1999 federal income tax return.

**N.** Nondeductible for regular income tax purposes on Quest's 1999 federal income tax return.

___7. Quest's 1999 taxable income before charitable contributions and dividends-received deduction was $200,000. Quest's Board of Directors authorized a $38,000 contribution to a qualified charity on December 1, 1999. The payment was made on February 1, 2000. All charitable contributions were properly substantiated.

___8. During 1999, Quest was assessed and paid a $300 uncontested penalty for failure to pay its 1998 federal income taxes on time.

**Required:**

e. For **Items 9 through 11,** determine if each item, taken separately, contributes to overstating, understating, or correctly stating Gelco's 1999 alternative minimum taxable income (AMTI) prior to the adjusted current earnings adjustment (ACE). An answer may be selected once, more than once, or not at all.

*Selections:*

**O.** Overstating Gelco's 1999 AMTI prior to the ACE.

**U.** Understating Gelco's 1999 AMTI prior to the ACE.

**C.** Correctly stating Gelco's 1999 AMTI prior to the ACE.

___9. For regular tax purposes, Gelco deducted the maximum MACRS depreciation on seven-year personal property placed in service on January 1, 1999. Gelco made no Internal Revenue Code Section 179 election to expense the property in 1999.

___10. For regular income tax purposes, Gelco depreciated nonresidential real property placed in service on January 1, 1999, under the general MACRS depreciation system for a 39-year depreciable life.

___11. Gelco excluded state highway construction general obligation bond interest income earned in 1999 for regular income tax and alternative minimum tax (AMT) purposes.

**PROBLEM 8** (Estimated time—45 to 55 minutes)

**Problem Number 8** consists of 28 items. Select the best answer for each item. Answer all items. Your grade will be based on the total number of correct answers.

Reliant Corp., an accrual basis calendar-year C corporation, filed its 1999 federal income tax return on March 15, 2000.

**Required:**
The following **two** responses are required for each of the **Items 1 through 6.**

**a.** Determine the amount of Reliant's 1999 Schedule M-1 adjustment.
**b.** Indicate if the adjustment (I) increases, (D) decreases, or (N) has no effect, on Reliant's 1999 taxable income.

1. Reliant's disbursements included reimbursed employees' expenses in 1999 for travel of $100,000, and business meals of $30,000. The reimbursed expenses met the conditions of deductibility and were properly substantiated under an accountable plan. The reimbursement was not treated as employee compensation.

    Numeric _ _ _ _ _          Letter _ _ _ _ _

2. Reliant's books expensed $7,000 in 1999 for the term life insurance premiums on the corporate officers. Reliant was the policy owner and beneficiary.

    Numeric _ _ _ _ _          Letter _ _ _ _ _

3. Reliant's books indicated an $18,000 state franchise tax expense for 1999. Estimated state tax payments for 1999 were $15,000.

    Numeric _ _ _ _ _          Letter _ _ _ _ _

4. Book depreciation on computers for 1999 was $10,000. These computers, which cost $50,000, were placed in service on January 2, 1998. Tax depreciation used MACRS with the half-year convention. No election was made to expense part of the computer cost or to use a straight-line method or the alternative depreciation system.

    Numeric _ _ _ _ _          Letter _ _ _ _ _

5. For 1999, Reliant's books showed a $4,000 short-term capital gain distribution from a mutual fund corporation and a $5,000 loss on the sale of Retro stock that was purchased in 1994. The stock was an investment in an unrelated corporation. There were no other 1999 gains or losses and no loss carryovers from prior years.

    Numeric _ _ _ _ _          Letter _ _ _ _ _

6. Reliant's 1999 taxable income before the charitable contribution and the dividends received deductions was $500,000. Reliant's books expensed $15,000 in board-of-director authorized charitable contributions that were paid on January 5, 2000. Charitable contributions paid and expensed during 1999 were $35,000. All charitable contributions were properly substantiated. There were no net operating losses or charitable contributions that were carried forward.

    Numeric _ _ _ _ _          Letter _ _ _ _ _

**Required:**
**c.** For **Items 7 through 11,** indicate if the expenses are (F) fully deductible, (P) partially deductible, or (N) nondeductible for regular tax purposes on Reliant's 1999 federal income tax return. All transactions occurred during 1999.

___7. Reliant purchased theater tickets for its out of town clients. The performance took place after Reliant's substantial and bona fide business negotiations with its clients.

___8. Reliant accrued advertising expenses to promote a new product line. Ten percent of the new product line remained in ending inventory.

___9. Reliant incurred interest expense on a loan to purchase municipal bonds.

___10. Reliant paid a penalty for the underpayment of 1998 estimated taxes.

___11. On December 9, 1999, Reliant's board of directors voted to pay a $500 bonus to each non-stockholder employee for 1999. The bonuses were paid on February 3, 2000.

**Required:**
**d.** For **Items 12 through 16,** indicate if the following items are (F) fully taxable, (P) partially taxable, or (N) nontaxable for regular tax purposes on Reliant's 1999 federal income tax return. All transactions occurred during 1999.

**Items 12 and 13** are based on the following:
Reliant filed an amended federal income tax return for 1997 and received a refund that included both the overpayment of the federal taxes and interest.

___12. The portion of Reliant's refund that represented the overpayment of the 1997 federal taxes.

___13. The portion of Reliant's refund that is attributable to the interest on the overpayment of federal taxes.

___14. Reliant received dividend income from a mutual fund that solely invests in municipal bonds.

___15. Reliant, the lessor, benefited from the capital improvements made to its property by the lessee in 1998. The lease agreement is for one year ending December 31, 1999, and provided for a reduction in rental payments by the lessee in exchange for the improvements.

___16. Reliant collected the proceeds on the term life insurance policy on the life of a debtor who was not a shareholder. The policy was assigned to Reliant as collateral security for the debt. The proceeds exceeded the amount of the debt.

**Required:**
**e.** For **Items 17 through 21,** indicate if the following (I) increase, (D) decrease, or (N) have no effect on Reliant's 1999 alternative minimum taxable income (AMTI) *prior to* the adjusted current earnings adjustment (ACE).

___17. Reliant used the 70% dividends-received deduction for regular tax purposes.

___18. Reliant received interest from a state's general obligation bonds.

___19. Reliant used MACRS depreciation on seven-year personal property placed into service January 3, 1999, for regular tax purposes. No expense or depreciation election was made.

___20. Depreciation on nonresidential real property placed into service on January 3, 1999, was under the general MACRS depreciation system for regular tax purposes.

___21. Reliant had only cash charitable contributions for 1999.

**Required:**

f. For **Items 22 through 28,** indicate if the statement is true (T) or false (F) regarding Reliant's compliance with tax procedures, tax credits and the alternative minimum tax.

____22. Reliant's exemption for alternative minimum tax is reduced by 20% of the excess of the alternative minimum taxable income over $150,000.

____23. The statute of limitations on Reliant's fraudulent 1994 federal income tax return expires six years after the filing date of the return.

____24. The statute of limitations on Reliant's 1995 federal income tax return, which omitted 30% of gross receipts, expires 2 years after the filing date of the return.

____25. The targeted job tax credit may be combined with other business credits to form part of Reliant's general business credit.

____26. Reliant incurred qualifying expenditures to remove existing access barriers at the place of employment in 1999. As a small business, Reliant qualifies for the disabled access credit.

____27. Reliant's tax preparer, a CPA firm, may use the 1999 corporate tax return information to prepare corporate officers' tax returns without the consent of the corporation.

____28. Reliant must file an amended return for 1999 within 1 year of the filing date.

# PROBLEM 9 (Estimated time—5 to 10 minutes)

**Problem Number 9** consists of 6 items. Select the best answer for each item. Answer all items.

Lan Corp., an accrual-basis calendar year repair-service corporation, began business on Monday, January 3, 1999. Lan's valid S corporation election took effect retroactively on January 3, 1999.

**Required:**

a. For **Items 1 through 4,** determine the amount, if any, using the fact pattern for each item.

1. Assume the following facts:

Lan's 1999 books recorded the following items:

| | |
|---|---|
| Gross receipts | $7,260 |
| Interest income on investments | 50 |
| Charitable contributions | 1,000 |
| Supplies | 1,120 |

What amount of net business income should Lan report on its 1999 Form 1120S, U.S. Income Tax Return for an S Corporation, Schedule K?

Numeric  __ __ __ __ __

2. Assume the following facts:

As of January 3, 1999, Taylor and Barr each owned 100 shares of the 200 issued shares of Lan stock. On January 31, 1999, Taylor and Barr each sold 20 shares to Pike. No election was made to terminate the tax year. Lan had net business income of $14,520 for the year ended December 31, 1999, and made no distributions to its shareholders. Lan's 1999 calendar year had 363 days.

What amount of net business income should have been reported on Pike's 1999 Schedule K-1 from Lan? (1999 is a 363-day tax year.) Round the answer to the nearest hundred.

        Numeric  __ __ __ __ __


3. Assume the following facts:

Pike purchased 40 Lan shares on January 31, 1999, for $4,000. Lan made no distributions to shareholders, and Pike's 1999 Schedule K-1 from Lan reported:

| | |
|---|---|
| Ordinary business loss | ($1,000) |
| Municipal bond interest income | 150 |

What was Pike's basis in his Lan stock at December 31, 1999?

        Numeric  __ __ __ __ __


4. Assume the following facts:

On January 3, 1999, Taylor and Barr each owned 100 shares of the 200 issued shares of Lan stock. Taylor's basis in Lan shares on that date was $10,000. Taylor sold all of his Lan shares to Pike on January 31, 1999, and Lan made a valid election to terminate its tax year. Taylor's share of ordinary income from Lan prior to the sale was $2,000. Lan made a cash distribution of $3,000 to Taylor on January 30, 1999.

What was Taylor's basis in Lan shares for determining gain or loss from the sale to Pike?

        Numeric  __ __ __ __ __


**Required:**
**b.** For **Items 5 and 6,** indicate if the item is True (T) or False (F) regarding Lan's S corporation status.

___5.    Lan issues shares of both preferred and common stock to shareholders at inception on January 3, 1999. This will **not** affect Lan's S corporation eligibility.

___6.    Lan, an S corporation since inception, has passive investment income for 3 consecutive years following the year a valid S corporation election takes effect. Lan's S corporation election is terminated as of the first day of the fourth year.

# PROBLEM 10 (Estimated time—40 to 50 minutes)

Following is Ral Corp.'s condensed income statement, before federal income tax, for the year ended December 31, 1999:

| | | |
|---|---:|---:|
| Sales | | $1,000,000 |
| Cost of sales | | 700,000 |
| Gross profit | | 300,000 |
| Operating expenses | | 220,000 |
| Operating income | | 80,000 |
| Other income (loss): | | |
| Interest | $ 5,200 | |
| Dividends | 19,200 | |
| Net long-term capital loss | (6,400) | 18,000 |
| Income before federal income tax | | $ 98,000 |

*Additional information:*

Interest arose from the following sources:

| | | |
|---|---:|---:|
| U.S. Treasury notes | | $ 3,000 |
| Municipal arbitrage bonds | | 2,000 |
| Other municipal bonds | | 200 |
| Total interest | | $ 5,200 |

Dividends arose from the following sources:

| Taxable domestic corporation | Date stock acquired | Percent owned by Ral | |
|---|:---:|:---:|---:|
| Clove Corp. | 7-1-87 | 30.0 | $ 7,000 |
| Ramo Corp. | 9-1-89 | 10.0 | 6,000 |
| Sol Corp. (stock sold 1/10/99) | 12-1-98 | 5.0 | 1,000 |
| Real Estate Investment Trust | 6-1-94 | 1.0 | 2,700 |
| Mutual Fund Corp. (capital gains dividends only) | 4-1-92 | 0.1 | 400 |
| Money Market Fund (invests only in interest-paying securities) | 3-1-91 | 0.1 | 2,100 |
| Total dividends | | | $ 19,200 |

Operating expenses include the following:

- Bonus of $5,000 paid to Ral's sales manager on January 31, 2000. This bonus was based on a percentage of Ral's 1999 sales and was computed on January 25, 2000, under a formula in effect in 1999.
- Estimate of $10,000 for bad debts. Actual bad debts for the year amounted to $8,000. No pre-1987 bad debt reserve remained on Ral's books since January 1, 1987.
- Keyman life insurance premiums of $4,000. Ral is the beneficiary of the policies.
- State income taxes of $12,000.

During 1999, Ral made estimated federal income tax payments of $35,000. These payments were debited to prepaid tax expense on Ral's books.

Ral does **not** exercise significant influence over Clove and accordingly did **not** use the equity method of accounting for this investment.

Ral declared and paid dividends of $11,000 during 1999.

Corporate income tax rates are as follows:

| Taxable income | | Pay | + | % on excess | Of the amount over— |
|---|---|---|---|---|---|
| over | but not over | | | | |
| $    0—$  50,000 | | $    0 | | 15 | $    0 |
| 50,000—   75,000 | | 7,500 | | 25 | 50,000 |
| 75,000—  100,000 | | 13,750 | | 34 | 75,000 |
| 100,000—  335,000 | | 22,250 | | 39 | 100,000 |
| 335,000—  ............... | | 113,900 | | 34 | 335,000 |

Ral was not subject to the alternative minimum tax in 1999.

**Required:**
a. Prepare a schedule of Ral's 1999 taxable income.
b. Compute Ral's 1999 federal income tax and the amount of tax overpaid or payable.
c. Prepare a reconciliation of Ral's income per books with income per return.

# PROBLEM 11 (Estimated time—5 to 10 minutes)

This problem consists of 8 items. Select the best answer for each item. Answer all items. Your grade will be based on the total number of correct answers.

During 1990, Adams, a general contractor, Brinks, an architect, and Carson, an interior decorator, formed the Dex Home Improvement General Partnership by contributing the assets below.

| | Asset | Adjusted basis | Fair market value | % of partner share in capital, profits & losses |
|---|---|---|---|---|
| Adams | Cash | $40,000 | $40,000 | 50% |
| Brinks | Land | $12,000 | $21,000 | 20% |
| Carson | Inventory | $24,000 | $24,000 | 30% |

The land was a capital asset to Brinks, subject to a $5,000 mortgage, which was assumed by the partnership.

**For items 1 and 2**, determine and select the initial basis of the partner's interest in Dex.

1. Brinks' initial basis in Dex is
A. $21,000
B. $12,000
C. $ 8,000

2. Carson's initial basis in Dex is
A. $25,500
B. $24,000
C. $19,000

During 1999, the Dex partnership breaks even but decides to make distributions to each partner.

**For items 3 through 8**, determine whether the statement is true (T) or false (F).

___3. A nonliquidating cash distribution may reduce the recipient partner's basis in his partnership interest below zero.

___4. A nonliquidating distribution of unappreciated inventory reduces the recipient partner's basis in his partnership interest.

___5. In a liquidating distribution of property other than money, where the partnership's basis of the distributed property exceeds the basis of the partner's interest, the partner's basis in the distributed property is limited to his pre-distribution basis in the partnership interest.

___6. Gain is recognized by the partner who receives a nonliquidating distribution of property, where the adjusted basis of the property exceeds his basis in the partnership interest before the distribution.

___7. In a nonliquidating distribution of inventory, where the partnership has no unrealized receivables or appreciated inventory, the basis of inventory that is distributed to a partner cannot exceed the inventory's adjusted basis to the partnership.

___8. The partnership's nonliquidating distribution of encumbered property to a partner who assumes the mortgage, does not affect the other partners' bases in their partnership interests.

# Appendix Answers

## ANSWER 1

1. (c) Retainer fees are reported on Schedule C which is where trade or business income is presented. Retainer fees, even though they may not be "earned", still represent gross income to a cash basis taxpayer.

2. (d) Oil royalties are reported along with income from rents, trusts, estates, partnerships and S Corporations on Schedule E, which is called Supplemental Income and Loss.

3. (e) Interest income on general obligations of the state and local obligations is **not** included in gross income.

4. (b) Interest earned on refunds of federal income taxes (as well as state income taxes) is included in gross income.

5. (e) This is a pure exclusion and is not taxable.

6. (b) Interest income on US Treasury bonds is included in gross income.

7. (d) A partner's share of partnership **ordinary income** is reported on Schedule E. Watch out for other components of income, such as interest, which must be reported on Schedule B.

8. (d) Rental income is reported on Schedule E.

9. (a) Prizes, as well as awards, are included in gross income. Prizes are reported "other income" on page one of Form 1040.

10. (a) Jury duty pay is included as gross income. The pay is reported on page one of Form 1040 as "other income."

11. (e) Dividends received from mutual funds that invest **solely** in tax-free government obligations are not taxable to the recipient.

12. (h) Unreimbursed medical expenses are reported on Schedule A--Itemized Deductions, subject to a threshold of 7.5% of adjusted gross income.

13. (o) Personal life insurance premiums are personal and non-deductible.

14. (m) This is a business deduction reported on Schedule C--Profit or Loss From Business. Only 50% of the expenditure is allowed as a deduction. Remember, Green is self-employed and not an employee.

15. (k) Depreciation on personal computers used in a trade or business is allowed as a deduction against business income as reported on Schedule C. Depreciation expense is reported on Form 4562 - Depreciation and Amortization. Note that this is also listed property and limitations might exist (but not in this problem).

16. (l) These travel expenses (expenses incurred while out of town) are fully deductible business expenses and are reported on Schedule C.

17. (l) These business expenses are fully deductible and reported on Schedule C.

18. (g) 50% of the self-employment taxes paid are allowed as a deduction for adjusted gross income.

19. (f) Qualifying contributions to a simplified employee pension plan are fully deductible on Form 1040 in arriving at adjusted gross income. They are not business expenses reported on a Schedule C. Also the word qualifying assumes that the % limitation has been met in calculating the qualifying amount.

20. (k) Section 179 states that a taxpayer may elect to expense up to $19,000 of qualifying tangible personal property. This is reported on Form 4562 - Depreciation and Amortization.

21. (f) Qualifying alimony payments are fully deductible by Green on Form 1040 in arriving at adjusted gross income. Qualifying assumes no front loading, etc.

22. (i) Subscriptions for investment related publications are allowable as investment expenses. They are reported on Schedule A--Itemized deductions and are subject to a threshold of 2% of adjusted gross income.

23. (l) The interest on the home equity loan would be reported as a deduction on Schedule C because the loan was used for Green's trade or business.

24. (m) Because the automobile is used 75% for business, only 75% of the interest would be deductible on Schedule C. The balance of 25% is non-deductible because it is personal interest.

25. (o) Since the residence is neither a business or investment asset, the loss is not deductible.

## ANSWER 2

1. M and 4. When a taxpayer's spouse dies during the year, the taxpayer retains the married filing jointly status for the year. The number of exemptions include two personal exemptions and two dependency exemptions. A personal exemption is allowed for Mr. Vick even though he died during the year. The two dependency exemptions include Joan and Fran. The survivor benefits received by her daughter Joan do not disqualify her. Fran qualifies as a dependent even though he does not meet the relationship test. Fran is a resident in the taxpayer's home for the whole year, has income less than the exemption amount, is a US citizen and the taxpayer provides more than 50% of his support.

2. Q and 3. In 2000, Mrs. Vick can no longer file a joint return because she is not married for this tax year. She does qualify, however, for Qualifying Widow with dependent child. Also, since her husband was not alive during 2000, there is no exemption for him. There are no changes in the dependents.

**Note:** The answers to items 3 through 9 are presented in the four digit numeric response format.

3. 0,000. These are not taxable.

4. 0,400. Interest income on federal and state income tax returns is included as gross income as well as interest on savings accounts and certificates of deposit. Interest from municipal bonds is not included.

| | |
|---|---:|
| Refund from amended tax return | $ 50 |
| Savings accounts & CD's | 350 |
| Total | $ 400 |

5. 0,900. These are fully included.

6. 0,000. Gifts are not included as gross income.

7. 0,000. Lump sum distributions from life insurance policies are not included as gross income.

8. 0,200. Fully included.

9. 0,450. Fully included. Watch for any gambling losses to be used as itemized deductions (not as direct offsets to gross income).

10. (A) There is no deduction for premium payments on personal life insurance.

11. (D) Penalties for premature withdrawals on certificates of deposit are deductions **for** adjusted gross income.

12. (F) Charitable contributions are itemized deductions and reported on Schedule A. They are generally subject to a ceiling (not threshold) of not more than 50% of adjusted gross income.

13. (E) A deduction is allowed for state income tax payments made during the year. They are reported as an itemized deduction with no limitation.

14. (E) A deduction is allowed for real estate tax payments made during the year. They are reported as an itemized deduction with no limitation.

15. (A) A personal loss, other than a casualty loss, in not deductible.

16. (B) Qualified medical expenses, such as chairlift, are allowed as an itemized deduction to the extent that they exceed the threshold of 7.5% of adjusted gross income. Note that it is only the excess of cost over the increase in the fair market value that is the qualified medical expense.

17. (B) Qualified medical expenses, such as health insurance premiums, are allowed as an itemized deduction to the extent that they exceed the threshold of 7.5% of adjusted gross income.

18. (C) Clearly one of our more favorite deductions. Fees for the determination of a tax are allowed as an itemized deduction, subject to a threshold of 2% of adjusted gross income. These are grouped in with "Miscellaneous Deductions".

19. (E) Points paid under a refinancing are not immediately deductible, but must be amortized over the life of the loan. The amortized portion is fully deductible and is reported on Schedule A.

20. (D) A taxpayer may deduct 50% of the self-employment taxes paid as a deduction in arriving at adjusted gross income.

21. (E) Gambling losses are allowed as an itemized deduction to the extent of the gambling income. Since the losses were only $100 and the gambling income was $450, the entire loss is allowed. These are not subject to the 2% test.

22. (C) Union dues are treated as "Miscellaneous Deductions" on Schedule A, and are subject to a threshold of 2% of adjusted gross income.

23. (A) There is no deduction allowed for federal income taxes paid.

24. (F) This is a deduction on Mr. Vick's estate return.

25. (T) This is an election which can be made.

26. (F) A business casualty loss is a deduction for adjusted gross income, not an itemized deduction.

27. (F) Even though Mr. Vick was disabled, they clearly exceed the income threshold level and would not qualify.

28. (T) This is one of the preparer's responsibilities.

29. (F) There is no exception for the income limitation.

30. (F) The vacation pay paid in the following year should be recognized by Mr. Vick's estate as income in respect of a decedent. Mr. Vick had earned it and the estate had an enforceable right to receive it.

31. (F) Deferral adjustments can be both positive and negative. The adjustment itself may carry over to future periods in terms of reversal and offset future adjustments, thus reducing the alternative minimum taxable income. However, any adjustments due to these timing differences (as opposed to exclusions) result in alternative minimum tax credits which may be carried forward indefinitely to **offset future regular tax**, not the alternative minimum tax.

# ANSWER 3

**Note:** The answers to Items 1 through 11 are presented in the five digit numeric response format as is required on the exam.

1. 03,000. The Moore's stock transactions result in an overall net capital loss of $6,000, of which a maximum of $3,000 is currently deductible. The stock transactions are as follows:

| Revco | Long-term loss | $ -10,000 |
|-------|----------------|-----------|
| Abbco | Short-term gain | 4,000 |
|       | Net capital loss | $ -6,000 |

2. 00,000. When the fair market value of the property is less than the adjusted basis of the property, the donee's basis will be the donor's basis only for the purpose of determining a gain. For the purposes of determining a loss, the donee's basis will be the fair market value of the property. At any selling price between the fair market value and the adjusted basis the result is no gain or loss.

3. 00,000. The receipt of a security deposit is not considered to be gross income. The receipt of the last month's rent, however, would be classified as gross income.

4. 55,000. Gross income includes Tom's wages and the value of the group term life insurance in excess of $50,000.

| Tom's salary | $ 53,000 |
|--------------|----------|
| Value of excess coverage | 2,000 |
| Total income | $ 55,000 |

5. 01,250. When a taxpayer claims a deduction for state income taxes paid in one year, and receives a refund of those taxes in a subsequent year, the taxpayer must recognize that amount as income if there was a tax benefit received. Since Tom's itemized deductions exceeded the standard deduction by $1,450, and the state tax deduction of $2,000 was part of that excess, the receipt of $1,250 (being less than the excess of $1,450) must be included as income. A federal income tax refund is not included because there is no corresponding deduction allowed for federal income taxes.

6. 01,300. Unemployment compensation benefits are included in gross income.

7.  02,500. The amount of income from rental activities is determined as follows:

| | |
|---|---|
| Rental income | $ 8,400 |
| Less: | |
| Bank mortgage interest | 1,200 |
| Real estate taxes | 700 |
| Insurance | 500 |
| MACRS depreciation 3,500 | |
| Total deductions | 5,900 |
| Rental income | $ 2,500 |

8.  00,900. Since the taxpayer had the option to receive either cash or stock, the Moore's must recognize dividend income equal to the fair market value of the stock received, or $900.

9.  03,500. The receipt of employee death benefits are no longer excluded from gross income.

10. 05,000. In general, the interest on redeemed Series EE U.S. savings bonds used to pay for college education can be excluded from gross income. However, the proceeds must be used for the qualified higher educational expenses (tuition and fees) of the taxpayer, **his spouse or dependent**. Laura is not Tom's dependent.

11. 08,000. The payment of alimony is a deduction in determining adjusted gross income.

12. (A) If a taxpayer sells, and repurchases substantially identical stock within thirty days of the sale, any loss on the transaction is disallowed. This is called a **wash sale.**

13. (B) A tax on personal property is deductible (as an itemized deduction on Schedule A) if the tax is based upon the value of the property and is assessed on an annual basis.

14. (D) An itemized deduction, subject to a limitation of 50% of adjusted gross income, is allowed for charitable contributions. The amount allowed would be the fair market value of the clothing.

15. (A) Payment of premiums for insurance covering lost earnings does not qualify as an itemized deduction.

16. (F) A deduction is allowed, subject to a threshold of 2%, for business related publications. Tom is a CPA and the accounting journals would be related to his trade or business as an employee.

17. (B) Interest paid on loans for the acquisition of a qualified residence or a home equity loan generally qualifies as an itemized deduction. The home equity loan of $10,000 (which is under the $100,000 limitation) is also less than the excess of the fair market value over the original mortgage. The use of the proceeds to buy a sailboat does not disqualify the transaction.

18. (C) The unreimbursed portion of the prescription drugs qualifies as an itemized deduction, subject to a threshold of 7.5% of adjusted gross income.

19. (A) Funeral expenses are nondeductible personal expenses.

20. (E) A theft loss on Joan's jewelry would be classified as a personal loss and qualify as an itemized deduction, subject to a $100 floor and a threshold of 10% of adjusted gross income.

21. (A) A loss on the **sale** of a personal item, such as a sailboat, is a nondeductible personal expense.

22. (B) Interest paid on loans for the acquisition of a qualified residence or a home equity loan generally qualifies as an itemized deduction. Whereas the amount of the acquisition indebtedness ($300,000) is less the $1,000,000 limitation and is secured by the real estate, the deduction is fully allowed.

23. (A) There is no deduction allowed for the value of accounting services (or any other service) provided for a charitable organization.

24. (F) The phaseout of personal exemptions occurs at a much higher income level and uses a different methodology. In determining the tax for high-income taxpayers, the deduction for exemptions may be eliminated. Taxpayers with adjusted gross income in excess of a specified threshold amount must reduce their exemptions by 2% for every $2,500 or fraction thereof over the threshold. The 1999 threshold for a married couple filing jointly is $189,950.

25. (T) In determining the Moore's taxable income, the threshold for medical expenses was 7.5%. However, for the purposes of determining the alternative minimum tax (AMT), the threshold rises to 10%.

26. (T) In determining the Moore's taxable income, a deduction is allowed for the personal exemption. However, for the purposes of determining the alternative minimum tax (AMT), no deduction is allowed.

27. (T) In order to avoid any penalty on the underpayment of taxes, an individual must make payments equal to:

   - 90% of their current year's tax
   - **100% of their prior year's tax.**
   - 110% of their prior year's tax if the prior year's AGI exceeds $150,000.
   - Annualized income installment method computation

28. (T) When taxpayers withdraw amounts from their IRA's prior to age 59 1/2, they are subject to a 10% early withdrawal penalty. There is no provision to exempt withdrawals for medical purposes from this penalty unless the taxpayer is unemployed (subject to strict guidelines).

29. (F) This credit provides qualifying taxpayers with relatively low levels of income a credit against their tax liability, or a refund, if in excess of their liability. The Moore's income of $75,000 as stated in question #24, is far beyond the phase-out range.

## ANSWER 4

1. (D) This qualifies as a deductible employee expense, subject to a threshold limitation of 2% of AGI.

2. (C) Charitable contribution carryovers are subject to the same 50% AGI limitation.

3. (B) Investment interest expense is allowed as an itemized to the extent of the net investment income. Any excess is allowed as a carryforward.

4. (A) Gambling losses are only allowed to the extent of gambling winnings. Therefore, no deduction allowed this year. There are no carryforwards.

5. (B) Real estate taxes are fully allowed as an itemized deduction. There is no limitation for a second home, etc., as there is for mortgage interest.

6. (A) This is a personal expense. No deduction allowed.

7. (G) This qualifies for the dependent care credit.

8. (B) As acquisition indebtedness (mortgage) interest, this qualifies as an itemized deduction.

9. (F) Because this property is used for rental purposes, the real estate taxes paid are offset against the rental income from the property, and reported on Schedule E.

10. (A) $ -0-. Receipt of a bonafide gift does not constitute gross income.

11. (C) $ 2,000. When a taxpayer is not an active participant in an employer-sponsored plan, there are no threshold limitations. In addition, the limitations for non-covered spouse have changed subsequent to the inclusion of this Released problem.

12. (A) $ -0-. Since there was never a tax deduction obtained for the federal income taxes paid, there is consequently, no income to be recognized.

13. (F) $ 4,000. Guaranteed payments are includible in gross income because they represent a pre-distribution of a partners earnings for the year. There is the assumption that the partnership is a calendar year partnership. See Chapter 7's discussion of guaranteed payments.

14. (A) $ -0-. The receipt of life insurance proceeds is generally non-taxable.

15. (C) $ 2,000. A company can provide up to $50,000 of group term life insurance to its employees on a tax-free basis. For any coverage beyond the $50,000, the employee must recognize the cost of providing the coverage as additional income.

| | |
|---|---|
| Total insurance coverage | $ 450,000 |
| Less: $50,000 exclusion | -50,000 |
| Excess over the base | $ 400,000 |
| | |
| Cost per $1,000 of coverage | $ 5 |
| | |
| Total gross income | $ 2,000 |

16. (G) $5,000. This is an easy question, but a difficult answer. Even though gambling losses may be deducted to the extent of gambling winnings, this question asks for income and deductions up through adjusted gross income. Since the loss deduction is an itemized deduction, only the $5,000 income is considered in this answer.

17. (B) $ 1,000. Interest income is gross income, even if associated with a federal income tax refund.

18. (J) $ 25,000. Under the law in existence at the time of this problem, of the realized gain of $150,000 ($200,000 less the basis of $50,000), the Cumacks would have been able to exclude up to $125,000 of the $150,000 gain under the one-time exclusion provision.

19. (A) Since there was no provision to receive either stock or cash, then the stock dividend is tax-free.

20. (O) Frank and Dale are entitled to two personal exemptions on their return. No deduction is allowed for Jacques, Dales's father, because he is a French citizen and a French resident.

## ANSWER 5

1.  (N) These gifts of $7,000 fall under the $10,000 exclusion and are not includible in the gross estate.

2.  (F) Proceeds of a life insurance policy are includible in the gross estate if the decedent possessed an incident of ownership at death.

3.  (F) Since Remsen owned the marketable securities at death, they are includible in his estate.

4.  (N) This may be excluded from his estate since the payment was made directly to the institution.

5.  (F) Since Remsen owned the cash at death, they are includible in his estate.

6.  (N) The executor fees cannot be deducted on the estate return because they are already being deducted on the fiduciary return.

7.  (N) There is no deduction on the estate return for payments to a beneficiary, unless it qualifies as a marital deduction. Since this is his son, it obviously does not apply.

8.  (G) This qualifies for the unlimited marital deduction.

9.  (G) Funeral expenses are allowable deductions in determining the taxable estate.

10. (E) The executor made elect to treat this as either an estate tax deduction or a federal income tax deduction.


## ANSWER 6

1.  (N) Disclosing taxpayer information under a court order is allowed.

2.  (E) This appears to be a realistic position to take by the preparer.

3.  (P) This is clearly an act subject to penalty.

4.  (N) The preparer is taking a realistic position and appears to have applied due diligence.

5.  (P) When a preparer knowingly understates a taxpayer's liability, they are subject to the penalty.

6.  (N) Disclosing taxpayer information during a quality review is allowed.

7.  (E) Because the preparer relied on information presented by the IRS, and was not aware of information to the contrary, the exception applies.

8.  (P) This is clearly an act subject to penalty.

9.  (P) This appears to be a willful attempt to understate taxes, therefore subject to a penalty.

# ANSWER 7

1. (D) 007. Organization cost, when properly elected, are amortized over a period of not less than five years (or 60 months). Therefore, there is a book to tax difference of:

| | |
|---|---|
| Tax amortization: | |
| $ 40,000 / 5 years = | $ 8,000 |
| Book amortization | |
| $ 40,000 / 40 years = | 1,000 |
| Excess of tax over book | $ 7,000 |

2. (I) 005. Employee expenses for business meals and entertainment are allowable only to the extent of 50% of the expenditure. Therefore, the reimbursements of $10,000, which are fully deductible for book purposes are only deductible to the extent of $5,000 for tax purposes, thus increasing taxable income by $5,000.

3. (N) 000. When a corporation is the beneficiary of a life insurance policy on an officer or key employee, no deduction is allowed for the premiums paid. Since Capital is not the beneficiary, the deduction is allowable. No book to tax difference.

4. (I) 010. For tax purposes, only the direct write-off of bad debts is allowed in determining taxable income. Therefore, the increase in the allowance of $10,000 is not allowed for tax purposes and must be added back to net income.

5. (P) Since Sunco owns 35% of the stock of a domestic corporation, Sunco is entitled to an 80% dividends received deduction. Without doing the computations and testing for limits, Sunco would only be taxable on approximately 20% of the dividend.

6. (F) This is simply treated as income in the year received.

7. (P) The general rule is that the contribution must be authorized by the Board of Directors by the end of the end, and paid by the 15th day of the third month following the end of the year. Having met that provision, the current year's limitation on the $38,000 contribution is 10% of the corporation's adjusted taxable income ($200,000), or $20,000.

8. (N) No deduction is allowed for penalties.

9. (U) For AMTI purposes, seven-year personal property must be depreciated over a longer period of time, resulting in a smaller amount of annual depreciation. A proper adjustment will cause AMTI to be higher. Since these three questions assume that if no adjustment/preference is identified, how will this impact AMTI, the proper answer is Understated.

10. (U) For AMTI purposes, 39-year non-residential property must be depreciated over a longer period of time, resulting in a smaller amount of annual depreciation. A proper adjustment will cause AMTI to be higher. Since these three questions assume that if no adjustment/preference is identified, how will this impact AMTI, the proper answer is Understated.

11. (C) Only interest income on private activity bonds would be treated as a tax preference and require an adjustment. However, the excluded interest would be an ACE adjustment, but your question asks for the AMTI **prior to ACE.**

# ANSWER 8

**Note:** The answers to Items 1 through 6 have dual answers. They are presented in the five digit numeric response format and followed by the appropriate letter response.

1. 15,000 / (I)  Only 50% of business meals are deductible. The travel expenses are fully deductible. The disallowed expense of $15,000 increases taxable income.

2. 07,000 / (I)  Premiums paid for the life insurance of corporate officers are not deductible when the beneficiary is the corporation. (Likewise, the receipt of the insurance proceeds upon the death of an officer would not be taxable as income.) The disallowed expense causes an increase in taxable income.

3. 00,000 / (N)  A state franchise tax expense is a fully deductible item. The estimated tax payments of only $15,000 assumes an accrual of $3,000 which is proper in coming up with the full $18,000. No adjustment is needed.

4. 06,000 / (D)  The MACRS depreciation for 1999 would be $16,000, resulting in an additional deduction of $6,000. This decreases the taxable income. The computer is five year property and the straight-line rate is 20%. MACRS uses double the straight-line rate, or 40% of the declining balance. (Alternatively, the second year MACRS rate is 32% of the original cost of $50,000.)

| | |
|---|---|
| Original cost | $ 50,000 |
| First year MACRS: | |
| $50,000 X 40% X 50% | -10,000 |
| Remaining balance | $ 40,000 |
| | |
| Second year MACRS: | |
| $40,000 X 40% | $16,000 |

5. 01,000 / (I)  There is a net capital loss of $1,000 from these two transactions. A corporation cannot deduct a net capital loss. It can, however, carry the loss back three years and forward five. The disallowed loss increases taxable income this year.

6. 00,000 / (N)  Charitable contributions authorized by the Board by December 31 and paid by March 15 are allowed as current deductions by accrual corporations. The total contributions of $50,000 do not exceed the ceiling which is exactly 10% of $500,000 (taxable income without regard to the charitable contributions and dividends received deduction). No adjustment is needed.

7. (P)  Only 50% of entertainment expenses are deductible.

8. (F)  The expense relates to products which are predominantly sold. No proration required.

9. (N)  No deduction is allowed for interest expense incurred to purchase tax-free bonds.

10. (N)  Penalties for violating laws are not deductible business expenses.

11. (F)  Bonuses for non-shareholder employees, properly accrued are deductible if paid within two and one-half months after the year-end.

12. (N)  The federal income taxes paid are not deductions, nor is the refund of them taxable.

13. (F)  Interest income on the federal refund is fully taxable.

14. (N)  Interest from a municipal bond is tax-free. The "dividends" are derived **solely** from the municipal bond interest.

15. (F) The reduction in the lease agreement due to capital improvements causes the recognition of income.

16. (P) The portion of the life insurance which equaled the debt is a tax-free return of basis. The excess is treated as income to the corporation.

17. (N) The 70% dividends-received deduction is not an adjustment, but does represent an ACE adjustment.

18. (N) Only private activity bonds are preference items. The state's general obligation bond interest in an ACE adjustment.

19. (I) The acceptable method uses 150% declining balance over a longer ADR life, where MACRS uses 200% declining balance.

20. (I) Commercial real property is depreciated using a straight-line rate over a longer period than MACRS.

21. (N) Cash contributions have no alternative minimum tax impact, only the contributions of appreciated property.

22. (F) The reduction is 25% of the amount over $150,000.

23. (F) There is no statute on fraudulent returns.

24. (F) The statute for an omission of more than 25% is six years from the date the return was filed or the due date of the return, whichever is later.

25. (T) This is one of the general business credits.

26. (T) This is a credit allowed to small businesses.

27. (T) The CPA may use them for certain restricted uses.

28. (F) Reliant may file an amended return up to three years after the filing of the return.


## ANSWER 9

1.  06,140. The amount of net business income, or ordinary income as is more appropriate, represents:

| | |
|---|---|
| Gross receipts | $ 7,260 |
| Less: Supplies expense | -1,120 |
| Ordinary income | $ 6,140 |

In the computation of ordinary income, you must exclude any separately stated items which possess special characteristics. In this problem. interest income is separately stated because it is portfolio income; and charitable contributions are excluded because of the percentage limitation of the shareholder's adjusted gross income.

2.  02,700.  Whereas there was no election to terminate the tax year, the income of an S Corporation is allocated on a per-share, per-day approach.  Because the S Corporation was formed on January 3 the problem states that there are 363 days.  Therefore, the computation is as follows:

| | |
|---|---:|
| Ordinary income | $ 14,520 |
| Divided by # of days | 363 |
| Per day ordinary income | 40 |
| Number of shares | 200 |
| Ordinary income per-day, per share | $   .20 |

Because Pike purchased his 40 shares on January 31, he has held the shares for 334 days.  His share of the ordinary income is therefore:

40 shares x 334 days x $.20 = $2,672.

As required in the problem, this answer rounded up to the nearest $100 is now $2,700.

3.  03,150.  An S Corporation's shareholder's basis needs to take into consideration any pass-through items and distributions occurring during the year.  The items of income are allocated first (even the tax-exempt income from the municipal bonds increase basis), and the items of deductions next.  Pike has sufficient basis to absorb the loss.  Pike's basis is determined as follows:

| | |
|---|---:|
| Beginning basis | $ 4,000 |
| Pike's share of interest income | 150 |
| Pike's share of the ordinary loss | -1,000 |
| Ending basis | $ 3,150 |

4.  09,000.  An S Corporation's shareholder's basis needs to take into consideration any pass-through items and distributions occurring during the year.  The items of income are allocated first and the items of deductions next.  A shareholder's basis is then reduced by any distributions, but not below zero.  Taylor's basis is determined as follows:

| | |
|---|---:|
| Beginning basis | $ 10,000 |
| Taylor's share of ordinary income | 2,000 |
| Taylor's cash distribution | -3,000 |
| Ending basis | $ 9,000 |

5.  (F)  The eligibility requirements restrict an S Corporation to only one class of stock.  Having both common and preferred stock violates that provision.

6.  (F)  There is a provision that if an S Corporation  has passive investment income for 3 consecutive years following the year a valid S Corporation takes effect, the S Corporation election will terminate.  However, that is only if there are C Corporation accumulated earnings and profits.  Whereas Lan has been an S Corporation since inception, it could not have an C Corporation earnings and profits; this provision does not apply.

# ANSWER 10

The following answers are the AICPA's Unofficial Answers to the problem. The format in response "a" is slightly different from the way we present the material in the text and the way a tax return is prepared. An illustration of this is their "net approach" of reporting the dividend income. For example, Clove Corporation's dividends qualify for the 80% dividends received deduction, thus only 20% is included. At Lambers CPA Review Course we feel that this may be confusing and ultimately lead to wrong answers if limitations are exceeded, etc. Dividend income should be reported at the gross amount and then the dividends received deduction should be calculated and deducted later on as a special deduction. Regardless, follow the flow of their answer in part "a" because the examiners may revert to a similar format on future exams and this will help prepare you for them. Parts "b" and "c" are presented in a format consistent with our text.

**a.**

*Ral Corp.*
**SCHEDULE OF TAXABLE INCOME**
*For the Year Ended December 31, 1999*

| | | | |
|---|---|---|---|
| Sales | | | $1,000,000 |
| Cost of sales | | | 700,000 |
| Gross profit | | | 300,000 |
| Expenses: | | | |
| Per books | | $220,000 | |
| Excess of estimated over actual bad debts | $2,000 | | |
| Keyman life insurance premiums | 4,000 | 6,000 | 214,000 |
| Balance before other income | | | 86,000 |
| Dividend income: | | | |
| Clove Corp. ($7,000 × 20%) | $1,400 | | |
| Ramo Corp. ($6,000 × 30%) | 1,800 | | |
| Sol Corp. ($1,000 × 100%) | 1,000 | | |
| Real Estate Investment Trust (fully taxable) | 2,700 | | |
| Money Market Fund (fully taxable) | 2,100 | $ 9,000 | |
| Interest income | | 5,000 | 14,000 |
| Taxable income | | | $ 100,000 |

(Hint: (1) The $400 capital gain distribution is netted against the $6,400 in capital losses, resulting in a net capital loss of $6,000 which is not allowed as a deduction. See part c for this reconciling item. (2) Since the stock in Sol Corporation was not held for at least 45 days, the dividends received deduction is not available.)

**b.**

*Ral Corp.*
**COMPUTATION OF FEDERAL INCOME TAX**
*For the Year Ended December 31, 1999*

| | |
|---|---|
| Taxable income | $100,000 |
| Income tax | |
| [$13,750 + (34% × $25,000)] | $ 22,250 |
| Estimated tax paid | 35,000 |
| Overpayment | $ 12,750 |

**c.**

*Ral Corp.*
**RECONCILIATION OF INCOME PER BOOKS WITH INCOME PER RETURN**
*For the Year Ended December 31, 1999*

| | | |
|---|---:|---:|
| Income per books | | $ 98,000 |
| Excess of capital losses over capital gains | | 6,000 |
| Expenses recorded on books not deducted on return: | | |
|     Bad debts | $2,000 | |
|     Life insurance premiums | 4,000 | 6,000 |
| Subtotal | | $110,000 |
| | | |
| Income recorded on books not included on return: | | |
|     Dividends | | $ 9,800 |
|     Interest | | 200 |
| Subtotal | | 10,000 |
| Taxable income ($110,000 less $10,000) | | $100,000 |

# ANSWER 11

1. **(C) $8,000.** In 1990 when the partnership was formed, Brink's basis would have been his transferred basis in the land, adjusted for any change in the liabilities. Brink was relieved of the $5,000 mortgage on the land, but as partner became liable for his share (20%) of the partnership debt ($5,000).

| | |
|---|---:|
| Original basis in land | $ 12,000 |
| Less: debt transferred | -5,000 |
| Plus: debt assumed | +1,000 |
| Initial basis | $ 8,000 |

2. **(A) $25,500.** In 1990 when the partnership was formed, Carson's basis would have been his transferred basis in the inventory, adjusted for any change in the liabilities. As a partner, Carson assumed 30% of the partnership debt ($5,000).

| | |
|---|---:|
| Original basis in inventory | $ 24,000 |
| Plus: liabilities assumed (30%) | 1,500 |
| Initial basis | $ 25,500 |

3. **(F)** A partner's basis cannot be reduced below zero. Cash distributions in excess of basis will cause the recognition of gain.

4. **(T)** The nonliquidating distribution reduces the partner's basis dollar for dollar, but not below zero.

5. **(T)** Basis must be allocated to the non-cash property received when the basis of the partnership property exceeds the partner's basis prior to the distribution. No gain is recognized.

6. **(F)** See item 5 above.

7. **(T)** See item 4 above.

8. **(F)** When a partner is no longer liable for partnership debt, there is a reduction in that partner's basis. (This is just the opposite of when a partner's basis is increased by their share of the partnership debt.)

# Notes

# Notes

# Notes

# Notes